M000251968

THE LAW AND BUSINESS OF
INTERNATIONAL PROJECT FINANCE

THIRD EDITION

This extensively updated third edition continues to be the most comprehensive and authoritative guide to the business, practice, law, and practical use of project finance. It covers the complete project finance structure, from conception to negotiation to debt closing, and from project difficulties to successful restructuring. The book continues to be accessible to those with little experience in project finance, while maintaining the insight and detail of previous editions that has made it a valuable reference for the experienced lawyer, manager, banker, contractor, and government official. This new edition focuses on a real-world, practical approach to project finance, without the overuse of case studies and economic theory. Yet, the contract forms, detailed glossary, index, and project finance bibliography ensure its continuing place as the most complete text available.

Scott L. Hoffman is an internationally recognized legal authority in project finance. His active involvement in the project finance industry in the past 22-plus years includes representation of Fortune 500 countries, utilities, and banks and testimony before the U.S. Congress on energy policy making. As a partner at Evans, Evans & Hoffman LLP, he practices energy and environmental project finance, international banking, and commercial law and represents energy development companies in the development, acquisition, and financing of energy projects throughout the world. He received his Juris Doctor degree from Syracuse University College of Law; while at the College of Law, he was on the Managing Editorial Board of the *Syracuse Law Review* and served as Editor of its *Annual Survey of New York Law*. Mr. Hoffman has published numerous editions of his books, as well as many international project finance articles for professional and trade journals. He is a member of the U.S. Supreme Court, New York State, District of Columbia, and Ohio bars.

The Law and Business of International Project Finance

THIRD EDITION

Scott L. Hoffman

Partner, Evans, Evans & Hoffman LLP, Attorneys

CAMBRIDGE
UNIVERSITY PRESS

CAMBRIDGE UNIVERSITY PRESS
Cambridge, New York, Melbourne, Madrid, Cape Town, Singapore, São Paulo, Delhi

Cambridge University Press
32 Avenue of the Americas, New York, NY 10013-2473, USA

www.cambridge.org
Information on this title: www.cambridge.org/9780521708784

First published 2008
Reprinted 2008, 2009

A catalog record for this publication is available from the British Library.

Library of Congress Cataloging in Publication Data

Hoffman, Scott L., 1957–
The law and business of international project finance / Scott L. Hoffman. – 3rd ed.
    p.   cm.
Includes bibliographical references and index.
ISBN-13: 978-0-521-88220-0 (hardback)
ISBN-13: 978-0-521-70878-4 (pbk.)
1. Construction contracts.   2. Construction industry – Finance – Law and legislation.
3. Loans – Law and legislation.   4. Construction industry – Finance.   I. Title.
K891.B8H64   2008
624.068'1–dc22   2007013563

ISBN 978-0-521-88220-0 hardback
ISBN 978-0-521-70878-4 paperback

For Margo, Kelsey Elizabeth,

and Evan Andrew Thomas

CONTENTS

PART FOUR. TECHNICAL, POLITICAL, AND ECONOMIC FEASIBILITY

PART FIVE. PROJECT FINANCE DOCUMENTATION

PART SIX. CREDIT ENHANCEMENT

CHAPTER TWENTY. PROJECT FINANCE CREDIT ENHANCEMENT 245

PART SEVEN. DEBT AND EQUITY FINANCING

PREFACE TO THE THIRD EDITION

The project finance industry has undergone many changes and challenges since the first edition of this book was written in 1997. During this time, there has been an amazing growth in project finance among multilateral and bilateral agencies, governments, financial institutions, rating agencies, and development companies. The financing of infrastructure projects in developing countries was in its infancy in 1997 and since then has experienced many great successes and a few failures.

Project finance is now a recognized course offering at business and law schools throughout the world. As seen in the Select Bibliography to this edition, the scholarly research is expanding, as are general books about project finance.

This third edition is a complete update of the first and second editions, including all of the major developments in project finance over the past decade. It is my hope that this book will continue to be useful as a college course book for students sufficiently curious to wonder what project finance is about, a training tool for those thrown into the world of project finance, a research tool for those needing a project finance treatise, and a structuring and drafting tool for those involved in transactions, including project finance counsel, lenders, government agencies, project sponsors, and equity investors.

The basic organizational structure of the earlier editions is retained. This book is organized into ten parts:

Part I, a comprehensive introduction to the financing concept called "project finance";

Part II, risk identification, allocation, and mitigation, including transnational and commercial risks;

Part III, project finance structures;

Part IV, technical, political, and economic feasibility of a project;

Part V, project finance documentation;

Part VI, credit enhancement;

Part VII, sources of, and techniques for, debt and equity financing;

Part VIII, collateral security;

Part IX, project sponsor and investor agreements; and

Part X, special topics in project finance.

The book concludes with a glossary, a select bibliography, and a checklist of issues to consider in negotiating project contracts.

Project finance continues to be a complex area. In addition to knowledge of international law, project finance requires competence in promotion and protection of investments, property law, security interests, intellectual property, governmental contracts, private contracts, tax law, accounting rules and practice, environmental laws, consumer protection, insolvency law, anticorruption, and securities laws. Although this book cannot provide a complete discussion of these areas, I have nonetheless introduced the subjects and provided some of the important issues that may require additional thought and research.

I am indebted to a great many people in connection with this work. First, to John Berger of Cambridge University Press, my gratitude for believing in the concept for this book and for patiently guiding it through three editions. Also, my thanks to Katie Greczylo of Aptara, Inc. and Andre Barnett for their excellent editing skills and keeping me on schedule.

I wish to thank my colleagues in the project finance community who reviewed or otherwise helped with this work and, in particular, to my clients and friends with whom I have been involved in transactions; you have each taught me a great deal.

I thank most of all my wife, Margo, who encouraged me in writing this third edition.

S.L.H.
Marion, Ohio
2007

PREFACE TO THE SECOND EDITION

Since the publication of the first edition of this book much has happened in international project finance. The financial volatility of crises in emerging markets has had far-reaching implications on project development, finance, and operations. Bilateral and multilateral agencies have introduced more flexible policies to aid this type of financing. And, emerging countries have become more comfortable with long-term contracts designed to support project finance.

This edition incorporates these developments and adds significantly to the first edition. New information has been added on such topics as merchant facilities; multilateral prohibitions on anti-competitive activity; the new OPIC bond financing program designed to enhance emerging market bond issuances; changes in bilateral and multilateral programs; lessons learned from the Dabhol project; mini-perm and amortizing mini-perm financing structures; securitization for project financings; the OECD project finance consensus; and amendments to the U.S. Foreign Corrupt Practices Act.

I am indebted to a many people in connection with the revision of this work. First, to John Berger of Transnational Publishers, my gratitude for continuing to support this book into a new edition. And finally, thank you to the many project financiers who sent me comments, suggestions, and kind words on the book.

Most of all, thank you to my family, who patiently waited for the last word to be typed.

S.L.H.
Marion, Ohio
Labor Day, 2000

PREFACE TO THE FIRST EDITION

In 1989, I published in the American Bar Association's journal, *The Business Lawyer*, a paper on project finance, which at the time was the first widely circulated primer on project finance techniques. I was overwhelmed by the kind reception of "A Practical Guide to Transactional Project Finance: Basic Concepts, Risk Identification, and Contractual Considerations," and I was overwhelmed by how quickly it became outdated and how much more information existed than could be conveyed in a brief article.

Since its publication, much has changed in the financing method called "project finance." In this work, I have undertaken the sometimes daunting task of assembling in one volume the wealth of experience, resources, and scholarship that have appeared in the last seven years concerning project finance. I have also undertaken to broaden the usefulness of this work beyond the legal community while recognizing nevertheless that it is a financing technique based on contracts. It is my hope that this book will be useful both as a training tool for those new to the world of project finance, a research tool for those needing a heretofore absent project finance treatise, and a structuring and drafting tool for those involved in transactions.

The topic of this book is the considerations for project finance counsel, lenders, government agencies, project sponsors, equity investors, and other project finance participants, when structuring a nonrecourse or limited recourse project financing, and drafting, negotiating, or reviewing documents for use in the financing.

This book is organized into ten parts:

Part I, a comprehensive introduction to the financing concept called "project finance";

Part II, risk identification, allocation, and mitigation, including transnational and commercial risks;

Part III, project finance structures;

Part IV, technical and economic feasibility of a project;

Part V, project finance documentation;

Part VI, credit enhancement;

Part VII, sources of, and techniques for, debt and equity financing;

Part VIII, collateral security;

Part IX, project sponsor and investor agreements; and

Part X, special topics in project finance.

The book concludes with a glossary, a selected bibliography, and a checklist of issues to consider in negotiating project contracts.

I am indebted to a great many people in connection with this work. First, to John Berger of Kluwer Law International, my gratitude for believing in the concept for this book and for patiently guiding it and me through the process. Also, my thanks to Lisa Cordaro of Kluwer and to Jean Campbell, who read the manuscript and provided excellent guidance.

I wish to thank my colleagues in the project finance community who reviewed or otherwise helped with this work, and in particular, to my clients and friends with whom I have been involved in transactions; you have each taught me a great deal. In particular, I thank my former partners and colleagues at Nixon, Hargrave, Devans & Doyle LLP (especially, Bill Andrews, Phil Cronin, Bob Daileader, Mona Ehlenberger [now at Skadden, Arps], George Middleton, Bob Pender [now at Hogan & Hartson], Dan Rowley [now with General Electric Company], Rodger Tighe [now with

Dewey Ballantine], and Gary Valby), where I was fortunate to practice in and, for a brief time chair, the Global Project Finance Group. And last, but not least, I thank my partners, Robert E. Evans, Jr., and Jeffrey L. Evans, who gave me the time and support to finish this book. None of them, of course, are responsible for the content.

I thank most of all my wife, Margo, who encouraged me to finish this book, which would have otherwise remained one-tenth its current scope and would have languished on computer disks in my library. And last, to my four-year-old daughter, Kelsey, who sat in my library patiently thumbing the pages of *Goodnight Moon*[1] until I finished "just one more sentence."

S.L.H.
Marion, Ohio
All Saint's Day, 1997

[1] Margaret Wise Brown, Goodnight Moon (1947, 1975).

PART ONE

AN INTRODUCTION TO PROJECT FINANCE

CHAPTER ONE

AN INTRODUCTION TO PROJECT FINANCE

§ 1.01 DEFINITION OF PROJECT FINANCE

The term *project finance* is generally used to refer to a nonrecourse or limited recourse financing structure in which debt, equity, and credit enhancement are combined for the construction and operation, or the refinancing, of a particular facility in a capital-intensive industry, in which lenders base credit appraisals on the projected revenues from the operation of the facility, rather than the general assets or the credit of the sponsor of the facility, and rely on the assets of the facility, including any revenue-producing contracts and other cash flow generated by the facility, as collateral for the debt.[1]

In a project financing, therefore, the debt terms are not based on the sponsor's credit support or on the value of the physical assets of the project. Rather, project performance, both technical and economic, is the nucleus of project finance.

§ 1.02 CONFUSION OF TERMS

The term *project finance* is often misused, owing to a general misunderstanding of the term.[2] In some circles, it refers to raising funds to pay the costs of a project – *any* project. In others, the term is used to describe a hopeless financial situation remediable only with extreme financing options. The emerging meaning for the term is the definition above.[3]

The term project finance does not necessarily imply that the underlying debt is nonrecourse to the project sponsor. As the definition indicates, project finance debt can be nonrecourse or limited recourse. Project finance transactions can be placed on a continuum, with recourse to project sponsors ranging from nonrecourse to almost complete recourse, as is increasingly common in structured project finance. Complete recourse is a different financing technique, usually called direct lending.

§ 1.03 NONRECOURSE PROJECT FINANCE

As indicated above, a common form of project finance is nonrecourse[4] financing, predicated completely on the merits of a project rather than the credit of the project sponsor. The credit appraisal of the nonrecourse project finance lender is therefore based on the underlying cash flow from the revenue – producing project contracts, independent of the non-project assets of the project sponsor. Because the debt is nonrecourse, the project sponsor has no direct legal

---

[1] Scott L. Hoffman, *A Practical Guide to Transactional Project Finance: Basic Concepts, Risk Identification, and Contractual Considerations*, 45 Bus. Law. 181 n.1 (1989).

Other definitions have been suggested. *See, e.g.*, Clifford Chance, Project Finance 1 (1991) ("The term 'project finance' is used to refer to a wide range of financing structures. However, these structures have one feature in common – the financing is not primarily dependent on the credit support of the sponsors or the value of the physical assets involved. In project financing, those providing the senior debt place a substantial degree of reliance on the performance of the project itself."); Peter K. Nevitt, Project Financing 3 (1983) ("A financing of a particular economic unit in which a lender is satisfied to look initially to the cash flows and earnings of that economic unit as the source of funds from which a loan will be repaid and to the assets of the economic unit as collateral for the loan.").

See generally Jeffrey Delmon, Project Finance, BOT Projects and Risk (2005); Graham D. Vinter & Gareth Price, Practical Project Finance (3rd ed. 2005); Hossein Razavi, Financing Energy Projects in Emerging Economies (1996); Clifford Chance, Project Finance (1991); Peter K. Nevitt, Project Financing (7th ed. 2000); John G. Manuel, *Common Contractual Risk Allocations in International Power Projects*, 1996 Colum. Bus. L. Rev. 37 (1996); Harold F. Moore and Evelyn D. Giaccio, *International Project Finance (A Practitioner's Guide to International Banking and Trade Finance)*, 11 N.C.J. Int'l L. & Com. Reg. 597 (1986); Stewart E. Rauner, *Project Finance: A Risk Spreading Approach to the Commercial Financing of Economic Development*, 24 Harv. Int'l L.J. 145 (1983); Larry Wynant, *Essential Elements of Project Financing*, Harv. Bus. Rev., May–June 1980, at 165.

[2] One commentator has ventured to provide a short history of project finance, beginning in Roman times. Reinhard Zimmermann, *Non-Recourse – The Most Condemnable of Loan Transactions*, Project Finance International, July 3, 1996, at 62; *see also* Esteban C. Buljevich & Yoon S. Park, Project Financing and the International Financial Markets 87 n.1 (1999); Stewart E. Rauner, *Project Finance: A Risk Spreading Approach to the Commercial Financing of Economic Development*, 24 Harv. Int'l L.J. 146 (1983).

[3] "When *I* use a word," Humpty Dumpty said in rather a scornful tone, "it means just what I choose it to mean – neither more nor less." Lewis Carroll, *Through the Looking-Glass*, ch. 6 (1872).

[4] *See* Hauser v. Western Group Nurseries, Inc., 767 F. Supp. 475, 483 n.11 (S.D.N.Y. 1991).

obligation to repay the project debt or make interest payments if the project cash flows prove inadequate to service debt.

Because the ability of the project sponsor to produce revenue from project operation is the foundation of a project financing, the contracts form the framework for project viability and control the allocation of risks. Contracts that represent the obligation to make a payment to the project company on the delivery of some product or service are very important because these contracts govern cash flow.[5]

Each contract necessary to construct and operate a project, such as the output sales contract, feedstock contract, site lease, and construction contract, must not interfere unduly with the expectation for debt repayment from project revenues. If risks are allocated in an unacceptable way from the project lender's perspective, credit enhancement from a creditworthy third party is needed in such forms as letters of credit, capital contribution commitments, guarantees, and insurance. Also, the project finance contracts must be enforceable and have value to the lender as collateral security.

A project financing is also based on predictable regulatory and political environments and stable markets, which combine to produce dependable cash flow. To the extent this predictability is unavailable or the risks of dependability are allocated unacceptably, credit enhancement is necessary to protect the lender from external uncertainties, such as fuel supply, product market instability, and changes in law. Commonly, however, the project exists in an uncertain environment that subjects the project lender to some unallocated risks.

The project finance documents should be designed to anticipate regulatory problems unique to the project and the environment in which the project will exist. Many projects receive benefits from statutory and regulatory structures, which can be forfeited if the requirements are not fulfilled throughout the life of the project. Examples include conditions in government licenses and implementation agreements, statutory requirements for the efficient use of natural resources, and regulatory air pollution standards.[6] In these situations, the project documents should allocate responsibility for the risk that such standards are not complied with because of the fault of a project participant.

§ 1.04 LIMITED RECOURSE PROJECT FINANCE

The classic nonrecourse project financing would result in no potential liability to the project sponsor for the debts or liabilities of an individual project. It would be *nonrecourse*. This is rarely the case. In most project financings, there are limited obligations and responsibilities of the project sponsor; that is, the financing is *limited recourse*.

How much recourse necessary to support a financing is determined by the unique risks presented in a project and the appetite of the credit markets to accept the risks. For example, if the lenders perceive that a substantial risk exists during the construction phase of a project, they could require that the project sponsor agree to infuse additional equity if the risk actually materializes. The lender would have recourse to the project sponsor's assets until the risk subsides or construction is complete. Thereafter, the loan would be nonrecourse.

§ 1.05 STRUCTURED PROJECT FINANCE – TOWARD GREATER ECONOMIC EFFICIENCY?

An economic argument can be made that classic nonrecourse project finance is an inefficient, expensive financing technique. As discussed above, in a nonrecourse project financing, project finance lenders base credit appraisals on the projected revenues from the operation of the facility, rather than the general assets or the credit of the sponsor of the facility, and rely on the assets of the facility, including the revenue-producing contracts and cash flow, as collateral for the debt.

---

[5] *See generally* NEVITT, *supra* note 1, at 183–95; Joseph Ryan & Lorin M. Fife, *Take-or-Pay Contracts: Alive and Well in California*, 19 URB. LAW. 233 (1987); Robert B. Nolan, Jr., *Take-or-Pay Contracts: Are They Necessary for Municipal Project Financing?*, 4 MUN. FIN. J.111 (1983).

[6] Host-country concessions and implementation agreements are discussed in Chapter 14.

Any component of the project that could result in less revenue or greater expense than anticipated by the lender can result in project failure; that is, unexpected events are an anathema to project finance.

In answer to this risk, project financings are designed to avoid uncertainty. This is particularly true with the underlying contracts, and it is with the contracts that the economist makes the inefficiency argument.

For example, the construction contract in a project financing must serve to provide the project company with a finished facility that satisfies certain agreed-upon performance criteria for a fixed or reasonably predictable price on a definite date. The tension between the project company and contractor in a project financing is based on the turnkey nature of the construction contract: the contractor must deliver the project at a fixed or predictable price, on a date certain, warranted to perform at agreed levels. The contractor is, of course, concerned with the difficulty of predicting events that could result in delivery of a delayed project, at an increased price, that does not perform as expected. Thus, unless the contract price is extremely attractive (that is, the risk premium sufficiently high), the three main objectives of the contractor in contract negotiation are to limit risks of any change in the cost of the project, to ensure there is sufficient contractual excuse for late delivery, and to provide sufficient time to satisfy performance guarantees.

For the project company and lender, the risk that construction costs will exceed the funds available from the construction loan, other debt sources, and equity is a significant risk in a project financing. Increased construction costs may result in increased debt service costs during construction, unavailability of sufficient funds to complete construction, and even if funded, in the inability of the project company to pay increased interest and principal that result from the additional debt required to complete construction.

To convince the contractor to shoulder these risks, the project company must pay the contractor a premium for the risks taken. A customary reward for the contractor in return for assuming the risk of completion on a date certain for a fixed price is through both the contract

price and a bonus payment, which is paid by the project company to the contractor if the project is completed ahead of the scheduled completion date. In return, the project company achieves predictability of construction costs. However, the cost paid for the risks allocated to the contractor is not inexpensive. In addition, the extra amount paid arguably adds minimal value to the project assets; that is, the additional money is attributable to risk assumed by the contractor, not equipment value or improved performance.

In situations in which the project company can access additional debt or equity needed to pay for construction cost overruns, it can decide to assume some construction cost overrun or delay risks. In such a situation, the price paid to the contractor is reduced because the risk premium, otherwise payable to the contractor, is not necessary.

This technique is called a *structured* project financing. In a structured project financing, the project sponsor assumes some uncertainty in the project in return for a reduction in the risk premium otherwise payable to various contracting parties. The financing is not without recourse to the project sponsor, however, because the lender will require that the risks not allocated to the various project contracting parties, such as the contractor or fuel supplier, be retained by the project sponsor. To be meaningful to the lender, however, the structured project finance technique requires that the project sponsor has the assets to infuse additional capital or debt into the project company if necessary.

For example, the project company and the project contractor could enter into a construction contract that requires the contractor to finish the project within a set period, well within the contractor's abilities. Feasibility consultants could agree that the contractor has a long period to complete the project and will likely finish construction well before the date required in the contract.

A delay in project completion may result in an increase in project construction costs and a concomitant increase in debt service costs. The delay may also affect the scheduled flow of project revenues necessary to cover debt service and operations and maintenance expenses. In addition, a delay in project completion may result in damage payments payable under, or termination of, project contracts, such as fuel supply and output contracts.

Nonetheless, because of the unlikelihood of this, as verified by project consultants and the project sponsor's own expertise and experience, the project sponsor agrees to accept this risk. The project lender will require that the project sponsor enter into agreements to provide additional equity to the project company to the extent the risk materializes. The project sponsor, of course, must have the financial ability to complete such an obligation. In return, the project sponsor can reduce the construction price by avoiding the risk premium to the contractor. In effect, the project financing is recourse to the project sponsor, at least in part, during the construction phase of the project. Once the project is completed at the time required under the project loan documents, the financing is structured to transform into a non-recourse financing.

§ 1.06 CONTRAST WITH OTHER FINANCING TYPES

[1] Balance Sheet Finance

A project financing is in contrast with balance sheet finance. With this approach, a company uses retained earnings or short-term debt to finance the development and construction of the facility. Upon completion, when the project requires permanent financing, long-term debt, equity sales, or other corporate finance techniques are used to obtain the needed funds.

Where debt is used, the lending decision is based on the overall corporate balance sheet, as opposed to a specific stand-alone project. The cash flow and assets of the company are relied upon by the lender as the basis for servicing the additional debt necessary to develop, construct, and operate the project and to collateralize the loan. The entire company is thus the focus of the credit decision, including the effect of the new project on the company's continued viability.

The decision to use corporate financing is primarily determined by corporate philosophy. The relevant criteria a project must satisfy to qualify for balance sheet financing include whether the corporation has access to the needed capital at a reasonable cost, whether the project feasibility study projects a return on investment acceptable to the project sponsor's internal investment criteria, whether the project risks are satisfactory, and whether other types of financing provide greater advantages to the project sponsor.

[2] Asset-Based Finance

The project financing and asset-based financing methods are very different. An asset-based financing is founded on the value of the assets financed. A project financing, however, is based on the ability of the project to generate sufficient revenue to service the debt. Indeed, in a project financing, the hard assets probably would not produce sufficient cash in a foreclosure sale to justify the value of an asset-based loan.

§ 1.07 USES OF PROJECT FINANCE

Project finance is an emerging solution for financing infrastructure needs in many parts of the globe. In emerging markets, where the demand for infrastructure far outstrips the economic resources, it provides a financing scheme for important development. In countries moving from centralized to market-based economies, it provides needed upgrades or replacement of existing infrastructure assets that have not been maintained adequately. The needs for enormous debt and capital, coupled with the risks involved in large project development, often make a project financing one of the few available financing alternatives in the energy, transportation, and other infrastructure industries.[7]

Projects financed using this model tend to be large and require large financing packages for two reasons. First, economies of scale can be enjoyed in both development and operation. Second, the needs that are the genesis for the projects necessitate that larger projects be developed to provide

---

[7] *See* Daniel Hurstel & Mary Ann Carpenter-Pecquet, *Privatization and the Public Interest*, 13 INT'L FIN. L. REV. 34 (1994). For an excellent summary of the recent efforts with privatization and foreign investment in developing countries, *see* Christopher J. Sozzi, Comment, *Project Finance and Facilitating Telecommunications Infrastructure Development in Newly-Industrialized Countries*, 12 COMPUTER & HIGH TECH. L.J. 435 (1996).

as much needed infrastructure as is possible, as soon as possible.[8]

§ 1.08 BASIC COMPONENTS OF PROJECT FINANCE

All project financings have nearly identical fundamental elements: debt, from banks or institutional and governmental lenders, or subordinated notes from the project sponsor or other project participants is, of course, the most common element. Collateral security is similarly present, in the form of assignments of contract rights and project revenues, to support the underlying debt obligations. Also, various types of credit enhancement from the project sponsor or third parties are included to support the risk allocation. Finally, equity, whether active or passive in management of the project, is needed. The precise structure selected is dependent upon a range of variables, influenced in large part by project viability and the goals of the project sponsor. Project finance structures are discussed in Chapter 6.

§ 1.09 ADVANTAGES OF PROJECT FINANCE

Project financing is used by companies that desire any or all of several objectives. Established, well-capitalized corporations often select a project finance structure to assist in undertaking large debt commitments with a minimum of risk. Entrepreneurial developers rely on project financing to permit development of several projects in different geographic areas, each based on the merits of the project, independent of the financial obligations of the other projects, and with minimal equity requirements. These objectives, which are discussed in more detail below, include: (i) elimination of, or limitation on, the recourse nature of the financing of a project; (ii) off-balance-sheet treatment of debt financing (where still available); (iii) leverage of debt to avoid dilution of existing equity;

(iv) avoidance of restrictive covenants in other debt or equity arrangements that would otherwise preclude project development; (v) arrangement of attractive debt financing and credit enhancement, available to the project itself but unavailable to the project sponsor as a direct loan; (vi) internal capital commitment policies; (vii) diversification of the project sponsor's investments to eliminate political risk; (viii) risk sharing; (ix) limiting collateral to the project assets; (x) more incentive for the lender to cooperate in a workout of a troubled loan; (xi) matching specific assets with specific liabilities; and (xii) expanded credit opportunities. The advantages that result from a project financing differ based on the unique nature of each project, with different risks, capital needs, capital access, and motives.

[1] Nonrecourse Debt Financing – It Ain't Necessarily So

Classic nonrecourse project financing provides a structure that does not impose on the project sponsor any obligation to guarantee the repayment of the project debt if the project revenues are insufficient to cover principal and interest payments. The nonrecourse nature of a project financing provides financial independence to each other project owned and provides protection of the sponsor's general assets from most difficulties in any particular project. A typical nonrecourse project finance loan provision provides that no recourse is available against the sponsor or any affiliate for liability to the lender in connection with any breach or default, except to reach project collateral.[9] Thus, the lender relies solely on the project collateral in enforcing rights and obligations in connection with the project finance loan.

The nonrecourse nature of the debt in a project financing need not extend throughout the term of the financing. A project financing may be structured to provide recourse liability to the project sponsor during a limited period of the project

---

[8] *See generally* David Baughman & Matthew Buresch, *Mobilizing Private Capital for the Power Sector: Experience in Asia and Latin America*, Joint World Bank-USAID Discussion Paper (1994).

[9] The terms *nonrecourse* and *limited recourse* are sometimes used interchangeably. Regardless of nomenclature, unless otherwise agreed, a project financing is recourse to the project sponsor only to the limited extent of liability for fraudulent representations made in connection with the financing. *See generally* 12 S. Williston, A Treatise on the Law of Contracts §§ 1486–1509 (1970).

development. For example, under that structure, if a project uses a new, unproven technology that causes the lender to conclude that additional project risks are present, the project sponsor's full recourse liability for the debt could be limited to the construction period. Thereafter, if the technology satisfies minimum performance tests, the lender could release the project sponsor from recourse liability and shift the risk from the assets of the project sponsor to the project assets.

An example of a nonrecourse loan provision for use in a project finance loan agreement is reproduced below.

The [*Project Sponsor*] shall not be personally liable for payment of the amounts evidenced by the Note executed by the [*Project Company*]. Nothing contained herein, however, shall (i) preclude the [*Lender*] or any holder of the Notes from exercising any right or enforcing any remedy under this Agreement, or the Note, whether upon an Event of Default or otherwise, under this Agreement, the Note, or any other Collateral hereunder or furnished as security for any of the indebtedness evidenced by the Note, or (ii) limit the [*Project Sponsor's*] liability hereunder in respect of any damages suffered by the Lender as a result of any inaccuracy of any representation in this Agreement or as a result of any fraudulent conduct on the part of the [*Project Sponsor*].

The nonrecourse provision is also a part of project finance documents other than loan documents. An example follows.

Any claim against the Sponsor [*actual project owner*] that may arise under this Agreement shall be made only against, and shall be limited to the assets of, the [*Project Company*], and no judgment, order, or execution entered in any suit, action, or proceeding thereon shall be obtained or enforced against any partner of the [*Project Company*] or the assets of such partner or any incorporator, shareholder, officer, or director of the [*Project Company*] or such partner or against any direct or indirect parent corporation or affiliate or any incorporator, shareholder, officer, or director of any thereof for any purpose of obtaining satisfaction of any payment of any amount arising or owing under this Agreement.

A conceptual difficulty sometimes arises in project financings when one of the project sponsors agrees to act as the operator, fuel supplier, or as some other participant of the project financed. In those circumstances, although the underlying project finance loan is typically nonrecourse to the project sponsor in concept, liability may nonetheless arise from contractual undertakings, guarantees, or other obligations undertaken in the related project agreement.

[2] Off-Balance-Sheet Debt Treatment

A second objective of some project financings is the potential for using off-balance-sheet accounting techniques for project commitments.[10] From the perspective of the project sponsor, accounting rules in the United States generally require the consolidation of financial statements of a company and certain of its subsidiaries and other entities over which it can exercise control. A subsidiary controlled more than 50 percent by the parent company is consolidated on a line by line basis with the parent. Otherwise, the equity method of accounting is used whereby the investment in the subsidiary is shown as a one line entry. Debt in such circumstances is not reported on the parent company's financial statements.[11]

---

[10] For a general discussion of off-balance-sheet financing, *see* David L. Landsittel & John E. Stewart, *Off-Balance-Sheet Financing; Commitments and Contingencies*, in HANDBOOK OF MODERN ACCOUNTING 26–2 TO 26–23 (Sidney Davidson & Roman L. Weil eds., 4th ed., 1980).

[11] United States accounting rules are summarized in Accounting Research Bulletin No. 51 (consolidations); Accounting Principles Board Opinion No. 18 (nonconsolidated entities; equity method and joint ventures); American Institute of Certified Public Accountants Interpretation of APB Opinion No. 18 (application of Opinion No. 18 to partnerships and undivided interests). For a summary of U.S. accounting rules related to issues unique to project financings, *see* H. Ronald Weissman, *General Guidelines Under Present Accounting Rules, in* Project Financing, 23 PLI REAL EST. L. & PRACTICE COURSE HANDBOOK SERIES No. 252 (1984).

The Financial Accounting Standards Board (FASB) in the United States Statement No. 94, Consolidation of All Majority Owned Subsidiaries, requires a company to consolidate financial information on all majority-owned subsidiaries in its own financial statements, even if those subsidiaries have operations that are different ("nonhomogenous") from the parent, have a large minority ownership interest, or are subject to substantial foreign restrictions. The statement requires consolidation of financial

In the United Kingdom, the advantage of off-balance-sheet debt treatment has declined.[12] Previously, legal structures were created that did not require consolidation of the project company with the project sponsor. These structures no longer accomplish that result, however, unless the project company is established as a joint venture.

The importance of off-balance-sheet debt treatment as an advantage for project financings in the United States and the United Kingdom is diminishing, if not completely eliminated in most situations. The risk of debt repayment to a company's potential lenders and investors is not diminished simply because it is not reported on a balance sheet. These entities, along with credit-rating agencies, are particularly adept at analyzing financial information, whether reported in a footnote or otherwise.

[3] Leveraged Debt

A third objective of project finance sponsors is the ability to finance a project using highly leveraged debt, without a dilution of existing equity. This advantage is available to a small entrepreneurial developer with limited resources and to large, well-capitalized corporations that have competing demands for capital investment.

That is not to say, however, that lenders do not look for a high level of equity investment in project financings. They do. The leverage acceptable to a lender varies from project to project. Often the leverage percentage is between 75 and 80 percent, but transactions are sometimes structured with ratios between 90 and 100 percent.[13] In general, equity requirements for projects in developing countries are in the 20 to 25 percent range, and often higher.

The amount of the equity contribution required depends upon the risk perceived by the lender. The exact percentage is influenced by many factors, including the country; the project economics and how much debt can be serviced by the project; whether any other project participants, such as the contractor or equipment supplier, invest equity in the project; and the competitiveness among project finance lenders to finance the transaction.

Also, a lender's view that a high level of equity will translate into a high commitment by the project sponsor, may influence how much equity the lender requires. This view holds that there is a direct correlation between the percentage of equity invested in a project and the project sponsor's dedication to the project success. The more equity contributed by the project sponsor, the greater the commitment.

This is particularly true in project financings of facilities in developing countries. A large equity investment, coupled with a reasonably high rate of return, will help ensure the involvement of the project sponsors when the project suffers from unanticipated risks.

The view that equity investment increases project sponsor support of a facility is similarly embraced by many output purchasers. In some developing countries, for example, minimum equity contribution requirements are imposed on project companies to help assure that a long-term supply of the contracted for good or service is available.

Subordinated debt can serve as an equity substitute in project financings. There are sometimes

statements unless control of the subsidiary is temporary or the majority owner does not have control of the subsidiary (i.e., where the subsidiary is in legal reorganization or bankruptcy). Also, the statement requires that summarized information about the assets, liabilities, and results of operations (or separate statements) of previously unconsolidated majority-owned subsidiaries continue to be provided after those subsidiaries are consolidated. Statement No. 94, Consolidation of All Majority Owned Subsidiaries, Financial Accounting Standards Board (Oct. 30, 1987).

[12] *See* Companies Act, 1995, ch. 6, §§ 258 *et seq.* (Eng.); Standard No. 5, Reporting the Substance of Transactions, Accounting Standards Board's Financial Reporting Standards (April 1994).

Section 258 of the English Companies Act may require a project sponsor to consolidate its own accounts with partnership accounts if it has a "participating interest" and if it exercises a "dominant influence" over the partnership. Companies Act, 1995, ch. 6, § 258 (Eng.). *Participating interest* is defined as "an interest held by an undertaking in the shares of another undertaking which it holds on a long-term basis for the purpose of securing a contribution to its activities by the exercise of control or influence arising from or related to that interest." *Id.* § 260(1). Twenty percent is presumed to be a participating interest unless facts to the contrary are shown. *Id.* § 260(2).

[13] Wynant, *supra* note 1, at 170. For a discussion of equity investments in international project finance, *see* Matthew Barrett, *Putting Your Equity on the Line*, EUROMONEY, October 1987, at 119.

advantages to a project sponsor that lends money on a subordinated basis, such as tax deductibility of interest payments. However, lenders will want the subordinated debt to be truly junior, in payment priority and lien priority, to the senior loans.

[4] Avoidance of Restrictive Covenants in Other Transactions

A fourth reason for selecting a project financing is that the structure permits a project sponsor to avoid restrictive covenants, such as debt coverage ratios and provisions that cross-default for a failure to pay debt, in existing loan agreements and indentures at the project sponsor level. Because the project financed is separate and distinct from other operations and projects of the sponsor, existing restrictive covenants do not typically reach to the project financing. Similarly, the distinct nature of the project financed permits the sponsor to leverage debt to an extent that may be prohibited under existing agreements. However, parent-level financing arrangements must be reviewed to make certain that covenants and defaults at the project level do not create noncompliance or default at the parent level.

[5] Favorable Financing Terms

A project financing is selected in many circumstances because more attractive interest rates and credit enhancement are available to the project than are otherwise available to the project sponsor. A credit appraisal of an individual project is sometimes more favorable than a credit appraisal of the project sponsor. Thus, a more attractive risk profile can result in more favorable interest rates and lower credit enhancement costs.

[6] Internal Capital Commitment Policies

The rate of return goals of the project sponsor for new capital investments can also make project finance attractive. Companies that typically establish goals for rates of return generated from a proposed capital investment often determine that the return on a project investment is improved with a project financing, which permits highly leveraged debt financing with a minimum of equity commitment.

[7] Political Risk Diversification

Establishment of project-specific entities that finance projects on a nonrecourse basis also serves to diversify the project sponsor's global investments and to eliminate the effects of political risk beyond any independent projects undertaken in a specific country. Thus, the economic effects of a political risk that exists in one country will not affect other projects in other countries.

[8] Risk Sharing

The risk allocation process in structuring a project financing permits the project sponsor to spread risks over all the project participants, including the lender. This risk diversification, or sharing, can improve the possibility of project success because each project participant accepts risks and is interested economically in the project success. Although there is an economic cost associated with allocating risks to other project participants, the project sponsor will accept the cost, if reasonable, as a necessary element of a nonrecourse or limited recourse project financing.

[9] Collateral Limited to Project Assets

Nonrecourse project finance loans are generally based on the premise that the only collateral that the project company must pledge to the lenders as security for the loans is the project assets. No other assets of the project sponsor are necessary as collateral. Although this is generally the structure, as is discussed in this chapter, limited recourse to the assets of the project sponsor is sometimes required.

[10] Lenders Are More Likely to Participate in a Workout Than Foreclose

The nonrecourse or limited recourse nature of project finance leaves few remedies available to project lenders in the event a project experiences financial problems. Also, because the project assets have value only with the project contracts, and because the project contracts have value only if the facility operates, the only practical way a lender can have its debt repaid is for the project to operate, not foreclose and sell the equipment. For example, it is of little use to the project lender to foreclose on a toll road project financing if less than expected use is the sole reason the project is in trouble.

[11] Matching Specific Assets With Liabilities
Project finance allows a business to match specific assets with specific liabilities. By segregating the assets of each individual project from other assets of the project sponsor, and matching these assets to the debt undertaken to finance them, the business, its lenders, and its investors are better able to judge individual project profitability.

[12] Expanded Credit Opportunities
Because a project finance transaction is usually founded on the credit support provided by long-term revenue contracts, the project sponsor benefits from any higher credit rating earned by the output purchaser under those contracts. This benefit is achieved through a lower cost of borrowing, based on the higher credit rating of the output purchaser. This is only true, however, when the output purchaser enjoys a higher rating than the project sponsor does.

§ 1.10 DISADVANTAGES OF PROJECT FINANCE

[1] Complexity of Risk Allocation
At the core of a project financing is the identification and allocation of project risks. If a project is to be successful, risks must be allocated in an economically efficient manner among the project participants. These risks are discussed in Chapters 3 and 4. Project financings are complex transactions involving many participants with diverse interests. Risk allocation tensions exist between the lender and project sponsor regarding the degree of recourse for the loan, between the contractor and project sponsor concerning the nature of guarantees, and so on, resulting in protracted negotiations and increased costs to compensate third parties for accepting risks.

The complexity of this risk allocation process has slowed the success of project financing as a financing mechanism in developing countries. With countless demands upon a developing country's credit support capabilities, these countries do not often have unlimited ability to accept an allocation of a risk and back it up with credible assets or payment promises. This inability has necessitated involvement by

bilateral and multilateral institutions, such as the International Finance Corporation and export-import banks, which are institutionally designed to accept some of the risks in a way to make projects financeable.

[2] Increased Lender Risk
In addition to third-party project participants, the degree of risk for the lender in a project financing is not insignificant. Although, by definition, and by law in some countries, a bank is not an equity risk taker, many project financing risks cannot be effectively allocated or the resultant credit risk enhanced. This high-risk scenario results in higher fees charged by lenders than are charged in other types of transactions and results in an expensive process of due diligence conducted by the lender's lawyer, the independent engineer, and other consultants.

[3] Higher Interest Rates and Fees
Similarly, interest rates charged in project financings may be higher than on direct loans made to the project sponsor. This is not universally true, however, because interest rates vary with market conditions. Also, the documentation is complex and lengthy. The complexity results in higher transaction costs than is typical of traditional asset-based lending.

[4] Lender Supervision
Another disadvantage of a project financing is the greater level of supervision a lender will impose on the management and operation of the project. The lender will nonetheless want to avoid any liability associated with too much control of the borrower.[14] This obligation is incorporated into the project loan agreements, which require the project company to agree not to amend project contracts without lender approval, and to submit annual operating budgets to the lender for review.

The degree of lender supervision during construction, start-up, and operations results in higher costs that are typically borne by the project

---

[14] *See generally* K. Thor Lundgren, *Liability of a Creditor In a Control Relationship With Its Debtor*, 67 MARQUETTE L. REV. 523 (1984) (instrumentality theory); RESTATEMENT (SECOND) OF AGENCY § 14 (1957) (agency theory).

company. For example, site visits by the lender's engineers and consultants, engineering reviews, and similar consultant services to monitor construction progress and technical performance may be required.

Also, because of the limited recourse to a project sponsor that is inherent in a project financing, the practical remedies available to project lenders in a default setting are very limited. In general, because the hard assets financed have value only in combination with the project contracts, and because the project contracts have value only if the facility operates, the only way a lender can probably have its debt repaid is for the project to operate. The lack of meaningful remedies results in a high level of due diligence by lenders, coupled with strong, restrictive borrower covenants and restrictions on distributions, among other protections.

[5] Lender Reporting Requirements

The requirements of the project company to provide information to the lender is significantly increased in a project financing. Reporting requirements include financial reporting; project operating information; reports on force majeure events and corrections undertaken; and notices delivered pursuant to project contracts, such as notices of default.

[6] Increased Insurance Coverage

The nonrecourse nature of project finance results in a risk adverse loan and investment environment for the lenders and equity investors. Consequently, to the extent risks can be covered by insurance available at commercially acceptable rates, it is employed in the project finance structure. The insurance program may be very expensive in comparison to insurance programs required in other financing structures. In transnational projects, political risk insurance may also be required.

[7] Encourages Potentially Unacceptable Risk Taking

Project finance is, in the final analysis, risk allocation. Risk allocation is required by the nonrecourse (or limited recourse) characteristics of project finance. Consequently, it might be argued

that a project sponsor, having no recourse liability, is more likely to aggressively accept risks.[15]

§ 1.11 INTERNATIONAL PROJECT FINANCE

Whether termed *international project finance*, *global project finance*, or *transnational project finance*, the financing technique of bringing together development, construction, operation, financing, and investment capabilities from throughout the world to develop a project in a particular country is very successful. The technique is being used throughout the world in emerging and industrialized societies.

§ 1.12 EXAMPLES OF FACILITIES DEVELOPED WITH PROJECT FINANCE

[1] Energy Generation

Project finance is used repeatedly as a financing technique for construction of new energy infrastructure.[16] It is used in industrialized countries, such as the United States, in emerging countries, such as in Eastern Europe and the Pacific Rim, and in countries with tremendous new infrastructure demands, such as in Latin America.

In emerging countries, project finance presents an alternative to non-market-based development of electricity resources. Traditionally, in these countries, electrical resources were owned by vertically integrated public monopolies that generated, transmitted, and distributed electrical power, financed by the utility or official borrowing, and subsidized by the local government or cross-subsidized by various customer groups (industrial versus residential, for

---

[15] It has been argued that such risk taking is particularly unacceptable in infrastructure facilities, which were traditionally provided by the public sector. Jonathan R. Macey, *The Limited Liability Company: Lessons for Corporate Law*, 73 Wash. U. L.Q. 433, 448 (1995).

[16] Ada K. Izaguirre, *Private Participation in Energy*, Public Policy for the Private Sector, World Bank Note No. 208 (May 2000). *See* Michael J. Schewel, *Jurassic Sparks! Project Finance Revives Extinct Deals*, 12-APR Prob. & Prop. 26 (1998); Nagla Nassar, *Project Finance, Public Utilities, and Public Concerns: A Practitioner's Perspective*, 23 Fordham Int'l L.J. 60 (2000).

example). Project finance permits the traditional structure to move from these monopolies to private generation of electricity.[17] The traditional monopoly is being broken down through various models, including privatizing existing assets, encouraging private development of new electrical production, and establishing the government-owned utility as a purchaser of power for transmission and distribution over existing facilities, or a combination of these. Project finance is possible when a firm, creditworthy purchaser of power enters into a long-term contract to purchase the electricity generated by the facility.

Private power projects financed on a project finance basis are developed by a special-purpose company formed for the specific purpose of developing, owning, and operating the facility. It has no other assets or previous operations. Lenders rely on the cash flow of the project for debt repayment and collateralize the loan with all of the project's assets. A power sales agreement, a type of off-take contract, is the linchpin of the project. This contract creates a long-term obligation by the power purchaser to purchase the energy produced at the project for a set price. To the extent the project is unable to produce sufficient revenues to service the debt, the project's lenders have recourse to the project assets.

[2] Pipelines, Storage Facilities, and Refineries

Development of new pipelines and refineries are also successful uses of project finance. Large natural gas pipelines and oil refineries have been financed with this model. Before the use of project finance as a financing technique, these facilities were financed either by the internal cash generation of oil companies or by governments.

[3] Mining

Project finance is also used as a financing technique for development of copper, iron ore, and bauxite mining operations in countries as diverse as Chile, Peru, and Australia.[18]

[4] Toll Roads

Development of new roads is sometimes financed with the project finance model.[19] The capital-intensive nature of these projects, in a time of intense competition for limited governmental resources, make project finance based on toll revenues particularly attractive.

[5] Waste Disposal

Similarly, project finance is an attractive financing vehicle for household, industrial, and hazardous waste disposal facilities. The revenue generated by so-called tipping fees (the term has its genesis in the physical act of a garbage truck tipping its contents at a landfill) can be the revenue flow necessary to support a project financing.

[6] Water

The water industry (impounding and treating raw water, distributing water, collecting sewage, and treating sewage) is the last utility business to open up to privatization and project finance. The industry is generally monopolistic (water is important to society; water systems are typically local in nature; multiple wastewater treatment vendors usually do not coexist in a service area). As such, while marketplace risk is greatly reduced, government regulation is often assured.[20] Apart from the risks inherent in ongoing governmental rate regulation, weak local government credit, competition between agricultural irrigation and urban city needs, small facility size, and high transaction costs can combine to make project financing a challenging solution. Further, because water is highly subsidized in many emerging economy countries, successful commercial pricing may be prevented unless meaningful tariff reform is implemented successfully. Yet, each of these issues must be addressed

---

[17] See generally RAZAVI, supra note 1, at 3–5 (1996).

[18] See generally Ian R. Coles, The Julietta Gold Mining Project: Lessons for Project Finance in the Emerging Markets, 24 FORDHAM INT'L L.J. 1052 (2001).

[19] See generally Peter V. Darrow et al., Financing Infrastructure Projects in the International Capital Markets: The Tribasa Toll Road Trust, THE FINANCIER, Aug. 1994, at 9.

[20] David Haarmeyer & Ashoko Mody, Financing Water and Sanitation Projects –The Unique Risks, PUBLIC POLICY FOR THE PRIVATE SECTOR, WORLD BANK NOTE NO. 151(Sept. 1998); David Haarmeyer & Ashoko Mody, Pooling Water Projects to Move Beyond Project Finance, PUBLIC POLICY FOR THE PRIVATE SECTOR, WORLD BANK NOTE NO. 152 (Sept. 1998); Penelope J. Brook Cowen, The Private Sector in Water and Sanitation – How to Get Started, PUBLIC POLICY FOR THE PRIVATE SECTOR, WORLD BANK NOTE NO. 126 (Sept. 1997).

by emerging countries in some manner. The private sector has sometimes found that increased operational efficiencies possible in many water systems can produce reasonable equity returns and justify privatization and project financing.

[7] Telecommunications

The information revolution is creating enormous demand for telecommunications infrastructure in developed and developing countries. In developing countries, expansion and modernization are important needs. Project finance provides a financing vehicle that can be used for this infrastructure development.[21]

[8] Uses by Industrial Companies for Growth and Restructuring

In addition, project financing can be used by industrial companies for expansions, new project development, financing joint venture assets, and financial restructuring. Also, industrial companies apply project financing structures in connection with unbundling capital intensive, non-core assets, such as energy production facilities.

[9] Leisure and Sports Stadium Projects

Leisure projects – sports stadia, amusement centers, exhibition and concert halls – are sometimes financed using the project finance model. In these projects, long-term assurances of revenue under binding contracts to support the entire debt are generally not possible. With a leisure facility, revenues are dependent on discretionary spending by consumers, unlike an infrastructure project that provides a necessary service. Lenders and project sponsors patch together a collection of revenue assurances and credit support to support the project debt repayment.

In a sports stadium project, for example, the project cash flows are conservatively estimated and rely, in part, on long-term stadium naming contracts, agreements with a sports team to use the stadium over a specified period, and premium

seat and luxury box licenses. Another long-term source of revenues is a concessionaire contract, which provides a company with the right to operate all concessions within the facility. Forward sale agreements with concert booking agencies, albeit short term, are sometimes also added to the revenue projections. Credit support can include guarantees from local and state governments, which can also provide the land at a reduced rental or the infrastructure (roads and utilities) free of charge (in anticipation of higher tax revenues generated from the facility's operation).

Leisure facility financings can be structured with several tranches of debt. One tranche can be based on, and collateralized by, a long-term contract with a creditworthy party, such as a contract with a company in which it is agreed that the facility will bear the name of this entity in return for payments over time. Another tranche, paying a higher interest rate, can be based on, and collateralized by, a specific type of revenue, such as that earned from concerts. That tranche can be strengthened somewhat with concert bookings for the first few years of the facility's operation.

At least one leisure project financing is based solely on expected use. The 135-meter Millennium Wheel Ferris wheel project financing in London is based on conservative forecasts of use.

[10] Ethanol Production

In the past twenty years, global demand for fuel has increased about 40 percent. Much of this increase is from China and India. For example, in the past five years, the G-7 countries accounted for only 15 percent of the growth in global demand; demand in China was 30 percent of the growth. The rise of the per-barrel price of oil in 2006 was, in part, a reflection of this emerging trend in supply and demand.

Ethanol, an environment-friendly, octane-enhancing additive to gasoline, is viewed as one solution to the increasing vehicle fuel needs of the planet, and the goal of some countries, such as the United States, toward energy independence. Ethanol is produced by converting such agricultural crops as corn or sugarcane into alcohol.

Environmental demands to reduce CO_2 emissions are also being satisfied with hope in ethanol.

---

[21] *See generally* Ada Karina Izaquirre, *Private Participation in Telecommunications – Recent Trends*, PUBLIC POLICY FOR THE PRIVATE SECTOR, WORLD BANK NOTE NO. 204 (Dec. 1999); Christopher J. Sozzi, Comment, *Project Finance and Facilitating Telecommunications Infrastructure Development in Newly-Industrialized Countries*, 12 COMPUTER & HIGH TECH. L.J. 435 (1996).

The addition of ethanol to gasoline increases the oxygen content of the fuel and reduces emissions from internal combustion engines. Several U.S. states require ethanol-blended fuel, including Hawaii, Minnesota, Montana, and Washington. Environmental law changes may result in ethanol production facilities emerging as a leading energy infrastructure need in the United States.

Brazil is the pioneer in ethanol production. In the mid-1980s, Brazil succeeded in mass-producing ethanol derived from its bountiful supply of sugarcane. Today, ethanol accounts for 40 percent of all automobile fuel in Brazil. The emergence of major ethanol plants beyond the United States and Brazil is dependent on the supply of carbohydrates, such as corn and sugarcane, which can be economically produced into petrol.

The development of ethanol projects in the United States is supported by national tax policy. The United States has often used tax policy to provide incentives to businesses for the development of energy projects. However, each of these tax advantages is set to expire in 2008, unless extended by the U.S. Congress. Because U.S. ethanol projects are dependent on these tax benefits for success, it is likely Congress will extend, and perhaps increase, these benefits.

Financing of ethanol projects using the project finance model is problematic. Although the technology risk is minimal, and construction risks are manageable, fuel and market risks require credit enhancement and other risk mitigation.

Although corn and other food fuels are plentiful in the United States, crop success each year is not without risk. Long-term, fixed-price, and creditworthy fuel supply agreements are typically unavailable. Also, ethanol facilities must be located very near the crop production, to minimize the cost and risk of fuel transportation.

Long-term, fixed-price off-take contracts from a single, creditworthy purchaser, are not often available in the ethanol industry. This results in a project tied more closely to the whims of the marketplace, than is typical of current project finance.

Project lenders typically require that the project use a fuel marketer to assist in ethanol sale at the local, regional, and national levels. The use of a marketer can result in more predictable prices. Also, the lender may require a long-term, forward sales contract be signed so that at least some of the market risk is significantly reduced. The project sponsors may resist this requirement because the price will sometimes be lower than the spot market could provide.

The future of ethanol demand is uncertain. U.S. energy policy, like that of most other G-7 nations, does not yet require significant reduction in use of gasoline as a fuel. Also, car manufacturers do not yet see significant demand for ethanol-powered cars.

Regional competition for corn, transportation of corn, and proximity to locations where demand for ethanol is high, all combine to make project success less than predictable. Project due diligence must consider these factors, as well as the effects of additional projects in close proximity to a planned project, or to a planned project's market.

These project risks combine to result in debt-equity ratios of 50 to 60 percent for ethanol projects. That is, senior project lenders are unwilling to lend more than about one-half of project costs, resulting in very high equity contribution requirements. This results, of course, in lower rates of return on equity. It may be possible to increase the return on equity, however, with carefully structured subordinated debt.

[11] Other Projects

The use of project financing is limited only by the necessity of a predictable revenue stream and the creativity of financiers and lawyers. Other uses include pulp and paper projects, chemical facilities, manufacturing, retirement care facilities, airports,[22] and oceangoing vessels.

[12] Contrasting Risks

Each of these categories of projects have their own unique risk profile. For example, in an extractive project (such as mining, oil exploration and recovery, and salt evaporation), risks include geological uncertainties, depleting reserves, and the likely requirement of export sales. In an infrastructure project (such as a toll road), the technology is well-known, the assets are not depletable,

---

[22] Gisele F. Silva, *Private Participation in the Airport Sector – Recent Trends*, PUBLIC POLICY FOR THE PRIVATE SECTOR, WORLD BANK NOTE NO. 202 (Nov. 1999).

and rather than an export economy, the market is strictly local. In a leisure facility, the market is local and dependent on the discretionary spending habits of consumers. It is important, therefore, to carefully consider the risks in relation to the specific industry involved and to develop a project finance structure that addresses those risks.

§ 1.13 CHICKEN OR THE EGG: THE EFFECT OF A PROJECT'S FINANCING STRUCTURE ON ITS COMMERCIAL STRUCTURE

Which comes first: a project's commercial structure or its financing structure? In a very real sense, the type of financing structure selected for a project defines the commercial structure. It also determines the speed of project implementation, the technology, and other components.

For example, if a balance-sheet financing is selected for a project, off-take contracts are not required, new technologies can be used, and the project construction can proceed immediately. By contrast, a project financing will require off-take contracts, proven technologies, and a lengthy financial closing process involving a myriad of parties.

So, which comes first? The answer to that question follows in the rest of the book. The answer is somewhat circular: The financing structure determines the commercial structure; the commercial structure is developed in contemplation of the financing structure.

§ 1.14 MERCHANT FACILITIES: PROJECTS FINANCED WITHOUT REVENUE CONTRACTS

Long-term contracts in which a creditworthy purchaser agrees to purchase the output of a facility are not always necessary for a nonrecourse or limited recourse project financing.[23] In lieu of this arrangement, the project company and the project lenders rely on the general

market for the credit support. This type of structure works effectively where the need for the project is well established and the price for the project output will remain generally stable throughout the term of the project debt. Nonetheless, the project company and project lender assume risks related to output price fluctuations, obsolescence, competition, and other market risks. It is an approach not recommended for the risk-adverse lender or project sponsor. The financing of merchant facilities is discussed in Chapter 33.

§ 1.15 PROJECT FINANCE IN DEVELOPING COUNTRIES

Until the early 1970s, much of the financing of infrastructure development in emerging countries came from government sources, such as the host-country government, multilateral institutions, and export financing agencies. More recently, however, constraints on public funding have emerged. These constraints include reductions in developing country financial aid funding. Also, host-country governments lack the financial creditworthiness to support financially, through direct funding or credit support, the volume of infrastructure projects required to develop their economies.

At the same time, a global sea change took place in the view of many governments, multilateral institutions, and public entities in infrastructure development. In this new world order, more reliance is placed on the private sector, in both developing and industrialized countries, as governments accept that the private sector is often better able to develop, construct, and operate large-scale infrastructure projects.[24] A

---

[23] *See generally* Keith W. Kriebel & Michael D. Hornstein, *United States: Financing Merchant Power Plants*, 1999 INT'L FIN. L. REV. 3034; Peter N. Rigby, *Merchant Power: Assessing Project Finance Risks*, 2 J. PROJECT FIN. 33 (1996).

[24] *See generally* Clive Harris et al., *Infrastructure Projects – A Review of Canceled Private Projects*, PUBLIC POLICY FOR THE PRIVATE SECTOR, WORLD BANK NOTE NO. 252 (Jan. 2003) (48 infrastructure projects were cancelled in 1990–2001, while 2,500 reached financial closure); Neil Roger, *Recent Trends in Private Participation Infrastructure*, PUBLIC POLICY FOR THE PRIVATE SECTOR, WORLD BANK NOTE NO. 196 (Sept. 1999) ("In 1990–98, 154 developing countries had some private activity in one infrastructure area, and 14 had private activity in three or four sectors. Middle-income countries have attracted most private activity; among low-income countries, only China and India have attracted

deterioration of financial conditions in developing countries, a move toward privatization of
infrastructure in both developing and industrialized countries,[25] and increased demand for financial aid from former Soviet-block countries[26]
and countries in Central Asia,[27] are combining
to make private-sector involvement very important.[28]

These changes, coupled with the lack of capital in developing countries, result in a need
for foreign investment to satisfy growing infrastructure needs. This need is based on the
tenet that infrastructure projects are the corner-
stone for economic development. The private
sector is emerging as an important financing
source for infrastructure development in these
countries.[29]

The stability and predictability favored in
project financings make structuring project
finance transactions difficult and expensive in
the developing countries of the world because
of the complexity of risk allocation among multiple parties (including lenders, political risk insurers, multilaterals, and bilaterals) and the higher
returns required to compensate parties for the
risks involved.[30] Investors and project lenders,

preferring predictability to uncertainty, must be
assured that the economic assumptions underlying a project, including revenues, taxes, repatriation, and other economic factors, will not be disrupted by host-country action. These countries,
of course, are by nature developing economic,
labor, legislative, regulatory, and political frameworks for growth and prosperity, not yet as settled
(or at least as predictable) as the developed world.
Although project finance risk allocation is important in all countries, it is of particular importance
in the developing world.

The business environment in a developing
country is different in at least four major respects
from the developed world: legislative and regulatory systems, political security, economic security, and centralized infrastructure systems.

Legislative and regulatory systems are usually not as defined as in the developed countries. Environmental laws and policies, for example, have not yet been aggressively pursued
in developing countries. Also, these countries
might not have in place detailed systems for
dealing with foreign lenders and foreign equity
investors, on such matters as ownership of infrastructure projects, taxation, and repatriation of
profits.

Political security is another area of uncertainty
for project financings in developing countries.
This uncertainty typically results in higher costs
necessitated by the need for complex insurance
programs and higher equity and debt rates. Political risks, including expropriation, civil unrest,
war, expatriation of profits, inconvertibility of
currency, and breach of contractual or other
undertakings by the host government, are discussed in Chapter 3.

Economic insecurity arises in a project financing from the inability of the potential project user
to support the project through use or purchases,
either in demand or in ability to pay. Infrastructure projects might provide a needed service, but
at a price that cannot be afforded by the great
majority of the population. Even if delivered, collections practices may be poor.

Either because of political theory, a lack of private capital, multilateral investments, or nationalization programs, most infrastructure is owned
by the government in developing countries. This
public-sector ownership structure eliminates the

substantial private investment."); Martin Stewart-Smith,
*Private Financing and Infrastructure Provision in Emerg-
ing Markets*, 26 Law & Pol'y Int'l Bus. 987 (1995).

[25] *See, e.g.*, Mark R. Yzaguirre, *Project Finance and Privatization: The Bolivian Example*, 20 Hous. J. Int'l L. 597
(1998); Mario Andrade & Mario A. de Castro, *The Privatization and Project Finance Adventure: Acquiring a Colom-
bian Public Utility Company*, 19 N.W. J. Int'l L. & Bus. 425
(1999).

[26] Richard C. Schneider, Jr., *Property and Small-Scale Privati-
zation in Russia*, 24 St. Mary's L.J. 507 (1993); Zbignew M.
Czarny, *Privatization of State Industries in Poland*, 20 Int'l
Bus. Law. 151 (1992); Olympiad S. Ioffe, *Privatization in the
U.S.S.R. and Commonwealth*, 8 Conn. J. Int'l L. 19 (1992).

[27] Laura A. Malinasky, *Rebuilding With Broken Tools: Build-
Operate-Transfer Law in Vietnam*, 14 Berk. J. Int'l L. 438
(1996).

[28] Philippe Benoit, Project Finance at the World Bank 3–5
(1996).

[29] *See* Yves Alhouy & Reda Bousha, *The Impact of IPPs in Developing Countries – Out of the Crisis and into the Future*, Public Policy for the Private Sector, World Bank Note No.
162 (Dec. 1998).

[30] John D. Crothers, *Emerging Markets in Central and Eastern Europe: Project Finance in Central and Eastern Europe
from a Lender's Perspective: Lessons Learned in Poland and
Romania*, 41 McGill L. J. 285, 290–293 (1995) (comparing
project finance in Poland and Romania, and structuring
foreign investments in projects to reduce risk).

effects of competition and increases the likelihood of inefficiencies.

Consequently, developers of proposed infrastructure projects must consider the effect of this public-sector structure on the proposed private-sector project. Possible effects include whether the private project will compete with the existing public-sector projects, which are arguably more likely to reduce charges for output or use in exchange for short-term political gains; whether there will be a privatization of all government-owned infrastructure projects, and the effect of that on the private-sector project; and ongoing rigidity inherent in working with government bureaucrats responsible for existing facilities.

Each of these four differences (legislative and regulatory systems, political security, economic security, and centralized infrastructure systems) results in a risk portfolio for the private-sector project that potentially includes higher construction and operating costs (such as inflation, unavailability of efficient foreign exchange markets, no long-term currency swap market, delays, cost overruns); great demand for project output or use; inability of population to afford the project output or to use the project (existing output prices are low; collections are poor); and transferability of profits is difficult (a mismatch between host-government revenues from local customers and foreign debt; questionable safety of investment from nationalization). Therefore, nonrecourse and limited recourse project financings are considered extremely difficult to accomplish in the developing world and require intensive attention to risk mitigation.

The easiest solution is to use government guarantees covering payment, convertibility, and other risks. However, this approach is neither a long-term solution nor in favor with host governments and multilateral institutions. There is a financial limit to the amount of contingent guarantees that a government can and should enter into. Other alternatives can be explored.

Project-based financing is emerging as a hybrid financing technique that mixes project finance and corporate finance techniques. Although project sponsors desire to achieve many of the goals of nonrecourse project financings, the risk involved in developing countries often requires that some sort of recourse to the project

sponsors be in place. Consequently, rather than full recourse corporate finance, project-based financing in developing countries probably will require project sponsors to accept some form of limited-recourse obligation. The extent of recourse will vary project-by-project and country-by-country.

§ 1.16 OTHER FINANCING ALTERNATIVES

In addition to project finance, other financing structures are available for infrastructure and other projects. These include (i) government funding, through grants, loans, and guarantees; (ii) government investment; (iii) third-party project participant financing, such as from equipment suppliers, off-take purchasers, and construction financing from contractors; (iv) non-project finance structures from multi- and bilateral agencies and from banks and other lenders, in reliance on the assets of a creditworthy project sponsor or creditworthy host government; (v) capital market financing, in reliance on the assets of a creditworthy project sponsor or creditworthy host government (domestic bond offerings, Eurobond offerings, private placements); and (vi) securitization[31] of project revenue flows (toll revenues, take-or-pay contracts).

§ 1.17 BANKABILITY, FINANCEABILITY, AND OTHER ASSAULTS ON LANGUAGE

An interesting phenomenon of small groups of people is that words are often invented to describe shared experiences that are unique to that group. The project finance community is no exception. The words *bankable* and *financeable* and their various forms are used frequently, although locating consistent acceptance in dictionaries has not been successful.

Whether the King's English or not, the terms are used to signify the acceptability, for financing purposes, of the structure or any element of a

---

[31] J. Paul Forrester et al., *Securitization of Project Finance Loans and Other Private Sector Infrastructure Loans*, THE FINANCIER, Feb. 1994.

project. If the concept were capable of a more helpful definition, this book would be greatly reduced in size. Rather, it is a complicated concept, which changes over time, and from deal-to-deal, based on the demands and concerns, rational or not, of the debt providers.

§ 1.18 THE LAW OF PROJECT FINANCE – SOURCES OF PROJECT FINANCE LAW AND STANDARDS

There is an international dimension to almost every business transaction. In project finance, the international dimension is also present in the laws that apply. From the viewpoint of a United States project finance lawyer, for example, four bodies of law need to be considered in any transnational project: (i) U.S. laws that regulate international transactions or disputes, which apply to conduct inside the United States and extraterritorially; (ii) laws of foreign countries; (iii) public international law; and (iv) conflict of law rules[32] that determine which laws courts or arbitral tribunals will apply to a dispute. In addition are procedures of various arbitration organizations, such as the International Chamber of Commerce, which may need to be consulted if incorporated into commercial agreements used in the project. Lawyers in every country involved in a project finance transaction must consider comparable laws in their countries. The legal and structural framework for project finance has developed over time. There are three general sources: project finance legislation and regulations, developed by the *host government*; standard contractual and financing requirements developed by the *private sector*; and project finance standards established by *multilateral institutions*, such as the United Nations Commission on International Trade Law.[33]

Host countries differ in their approach to laws and regulations specifically designed for project

finance transactions. In some countries, such as Finland, no general or industry-specific laws designed for project finance exist, and the general body of commercial law is applicable. In other countries, such as China, Italy, and Turkey, the legal framework or risk climate has required that general laws be enacted to attract private investment.[34] In still other countries, such as Russia, industry-specific laws have been enacted to promote and encourage private investment in project financings. Finally, other countries, such as the United Kingdom, have developed standardized contracts to encourage private investment.[35]

At the *private-sector* level, financial institutions, law firms with project finance specialties, and industry groups have developed contracts and procedures that form part of the basis of the project finance structure. A project finance loan agreement produced by one major law firm is often identical in important provisions to an agreement generated by another firm. Similarly, financial institution credit risk allocation and risk enhancement requirements vary little from institution to institution. Finally, trade organizations, such as the Edison Electric Institute, have developed and published "model" contracts. These private-sector standards help to produce a consistent framework for financings, and reduce transaction costs.

Multilateral agencies can assist in reducing legal and political risks and thereby generate standards for financings. One such multilateral agency, the United Nations Commission on International Trade Law (UNCITRAL), was chartered by the United Nations to remove barriers to trade among countries with diverse legal systems. In 2000, UNCITRAL published the *Legislative Guide on Privately Financed Infrastructure Projects*.[36] This document is designed to provide

---

[32] *See generally* SKADDEN, ARPS, SLATE, MEAGHER & FLOM, PROJECT FINANCE: SELECTED ISSUES IN CHOICE OF LAW (1996).

[33] *See generally* Catherine Pedamon, *Essay: How Is Convergence Best Achieved in International Project Finance?*, 24 FORDHAM INT'L L.J. 1272, 1277–1287 (2001).

[34] *See generally id.* at 1280–1286.

[35] *See generally id.* at 1278–1280.

[36] UNCITRAL, Legislative Guide on Privately Financed Infrastructure Projects, 33rd Sess. (2000), General Assembly, Official Records, 55th Sess., Supplement No. 17 (A/55/17). *See generally* Pedamon, *supra* note 33, at 1300–1317; Don Wallace, Jr., *Host Country Legislation: A Necessary Condition?*, 24 FORDHAM INT'L L.J. 1396 (2001); Don Wallace, Jr., *UNCITRAL Draft Legislation Guide on Privately Financed Infrastructure Projects: Achievements and Prospects*, 8 TUL. J. INT'L & COMP. L. 283 (2000).

a set of recommended legislative recommendations to assist in the establishment of a legislative framework favorable to privately financed infrastructure projects. It attempts to achieve a balance between the desire to facilitate and encourage private participation in infrastructure projects, on the one hand, and various public interest concerns of the host country, on the other.

The guide contains 71 recommendations, ranging from concessions to dispute resolution. Although these recommendations, reproduced in an appendix to this book, are general and imprecise, a review of these is a useful exercise in any project financing. To the extent one of the recommendations is not followed in a host country, then it is important to consider whether the project is at risk.

§ 1.19 ECONOMIC STUDIES OF PROJECT FINANCE

The study of project finance by the economists has developed significantly over the past decade, particularly through the work of Harvard Professor Benjamin C. Esty. Many economic implications of project finance, such as the economic cost of risk shifting discussed in Section 1.05, are largely untested. Only a few studies have been undertaken, with a handful published.[37]

---

[37] Benjamin C. Esty & William L. Megginson, *Creditor Rights, Enforcement, and Debt Ownership Structure: Evidence From the Global Syndicated Loan Market*, 38 J. FIN. QUANTITATIVE ANALYSIS, No. 1, 37–59 (2003); Benjamin C. Esty, *Returns on Project-Financed Investments: Evolution and Managerial Implications*, 15 J. APPLIED CORPORATE FIN., No. 1, 71–86 (Spring 2002); Benjamin C. Esty, *Improved Techniques for Valuing Large-Scale Projects*, 5 J. PROJECT FIN. 9 (Spring 1999).

See also Teresa A. John & Kose John, *Optimality of Project Financing: Theory and Empirical Implications in Finance and Accounting*, 1 REV. QUANTITATIVE FIN. & ACCT. 51 (Jan. 1991); John Kensinger & John Martin, *Project Financing: Raising Money the Old-Fashioned Way*, 3 J. APPLIED CORP. FIN. 69 (Fall 1988); Salman Shah & Anjan V. Thakor, *Optimal Capital Structure and Project Financing*, 42 J. ECON. THEORY 209 (June 1987); Wynant, *supra* note 1. See also JOHN D. FINNERTY, PROJECT FINANCING – ASSET-BASED FINANCIAL ENGINEERING 14 (1996) (citing Thomas J. Chemmanur & Kose John, Optimal Incorporation, Structure of Debt Contracts, and Limited-Recourse Project Financing (1992) (New York University Working Paper FD-92–60); and

§ 1.20 THE LESSONS OF A FINANCIAL CRISIS – WHAT THE EAST ASIAN FINANCIAL CRISIS TEACHES ABOUT PROJECT FINANCE

The 1997 East Asian financial crisis is particularly instructive about the effects of such a crisis on project financings.[38] The four most severely affected economies – Indonesia, Malaysia, the Phillippines, and Thailand – all have private power projects financed under the project finance model. Although the full effects of the financial crisis will be unknown for years, this much is certain: The private power projects experienced an increased cost of power, attempts to renegotiate power contracts surfaced, and the region experienced a decrease in market demand for private power.[39]

[1] Increased Cost of Power

The currency depreciation that East Asian countries experienced caused an increase in the costs of goods and services, and an increase in the cost of power. While the magnitude of the increase varied by country, all experienced pressure to increase power rates. At the same time, the cost of capital and interest rates, increased sharply as a result of new financial risks – real and perceived – associated with the crisis. These effects were magnified by a general underlying decline in the credit quality of the governmentally owned utilities that purchased project power. These utilities, with high levels of foreign debt, experienced associated foreign exchange losses in servicing that debt.

Andrew H. Chen et al., Project Financing as a Means of Preserving Financial Flexibility (1989) (University of Texas Working Paper)).

[38] Nan Zhang, *Moving Towards a Competitive Electricity Market? The Dilemma of Project Finance in the Wake of the Asian Financial Crisis*, 9 MINN. J. GLOBAL TRADE 715 (2000).

[39] For an excellent analysis, *see* R. David Gray & John Schuster, *The East Asian Financial Crisis – Fallout for Private Power Projects*, PUBLIC POLICY FOR THE PRIVATE SECTOR, WORLD BANK NOTE NO. 146 (Aug. 1998). *See also* Richard Walsh, *Pacific Rim Collateral Security Laws: What Happens When the Project Goes Wrong*, 4 STAN. J. L. BUS. & FIN. 115 (1999); Yves Alhouy & Reda Bousha, *The Impact of IPPs in Developing Countries – Out of the Crisis and into the Future*, PUBLIC POLICY FOR THE PRIVATE SECTOR, WORLD BANK NOTE NO. 162 (Dec. 1998).

Also, the cost of fuel supply for some of the projects was severely increased, particularly in countries where fuel is imported for power projects.[40] Typically, fuel costs are a pass-through for power purchasers in emerging country project finance. Thus, the cost of wholesale power must increase to offset the increased fuel costs.

The selection of currency for power purchases from private power projects also caused an increase in some countries. Where the wholesale power price was tied to a hard currency, the power cost increase was severe. In other countries, where the wholesale power price was tied to local currency, the effect was less severe.[41]

Similarly, the currency for project debt affected the degree of power cost increase. Those projects with high levels of host-country debt experienced less exchange rate volatility, whereas those with high levels of hard currency debt were more exposed to a mismatch between wholesale power prices tied to local currency and borrowing tied to hard currency.[42]

Finally, the extent of progress in power tariff reform had a direct effect on the purchasing utilities. The ideal, post-reform average wholesale price for power is generally thought to be two-thirds of the retail price charged end-users. The other one-third is the amount available to the purchasing utility for costs of transmission, distribution, and administration. Those countries with advanced tariff reform have sufficient price spreads between wholesale and retail prices to allow some absorption of higher power costs without a challenge to the financial health of the purchasing utility. Where this was not the case, these utilities needed additional capital or government subsidies to ensure financial stability.

[2] Power Purchase Contract Renegotiation

Demands for renegotiation of power purchase contracts are a tempting host-country solution to an underlying financial crisis.[43] A contract renegotiation, threatened or actual, can cause negative long-term uncertainty about a host-government's commitment to contract performance and sector reform. This effect is perhaps most pronounced on lenders and investors. Nonetheless, some form of contract renegotiation may be in the long-term best interests of a private power project located in a country with a severe financial crisis. Although a great deal of effort is employed in the risk allocation and mitigation process, it is in no one's interest to have a failed project.

Renegotiation may be less likely in a project financing where the host government and purchasing utility analyze, in advance, the potential financial implications of the power contracts and limit governmental credit support. However, in some countries, such as the Philippines, governmental guarantees and other support were determined to be necessary to attract development and financing of early private power projects.

The East Asian financial crisis reveals the implications of government risk sharing in a project. Where the host government accepts certain financial risks, such as through governmental guarantees of purchasing utility obligations, the implications of that risk absorption can be particularly severe in a financial crisis.[44]

Also, the financial crisis suggests that renegotiation will take place less frequently for projects that are selected for development in a competitive bidding process, rather than through direct negotiation with a developer. Competitive bidding should produce lower wholesale power

---

[40] For example, most private power projects in the Philippines and Thailand import fuel.

[41] Thailand's national utility makes payments to most private power generators in the local currency.

[42] Malaysia and Thailand had higher levels of local country borrowing than the negligible levels in Indonesia and the Philippines.

[43] See generally J. Luis Guasch, Granting and Renegotiating Infrastructures Concessions – Getting It Right (World Bank Development Studies, 2004); Jeswald W. Selacuse, Renegotiating International Project Agreements, 24 Fordham Int'l L.J. 1319 (2001).

[44] For example, the governments of Malaysia and Thailand, although assuming some project risks, have offered no guarantees. The Philippines, however, provided sovereign guarantees to some projects in the early stages of power sector reform. See generally R. Doak Bishop et al., Strategic Options Available When Catastrophe Strikes the Major International Energy Project, 36 Tex. Int'l L. J. 635 (2001); Note, International Arbitration and Project Finance in Developing Countries: Blurring the Public/Private Distinction, 26 B.C. Int'l & Comp. L. Rev. 355 (2003).

costs, thereby improving a project's chance for success in a financial crisis.[45]

[3] Decrease in Market Demand for Private Power

Finally, the crisis caused an immediate reduction in demand for private power in the region, as the economies slowed. The decline made clear that market projections for power are, in the end, a function of economic health of a host country and the region and the financial assumptions made about that health.

[4] Conclusions

Obviously, the East Asian financial crisis will result in greater scrutiny of projects by lenders and investors. More importantly, it reveals that contractual risk allocation among the host country, its state-owned utilities, and the project company have financial implications that can be experienced in the real world. Its ultimate lesson may be that domestic financing, local currency purchases of output, competitive bidding, tariff reform, and reduced levels of governmental credit support will be important components of future project development discussions. Perhaps its greatest lesson is that sovereign guarantees and other forms of host-country credit support do not necessarily remove risk in a financial crisis.

§ 1.21 POLITICAL RISK: THE DABHOL PROJECT

In addition to host-country financial risk, political risk is significant in international project finance. An example of political risk in an international project financing is the Dabhol power project in India, located in Maharashtra state. This project was completed in 1995. There were three project sponsors: the multinational, privately held Bechtel Corporation; the now defunct and much maligned Enron Corporation; and General Electric Capital Corporation, the financing arm of the respected multinational corporation, General Electric Company.[46] These corporations created a project development company, Dabhol Power Company, to develop, construct, own, and operate the power project.

Dabhol Power Company borrowed funds for the construction of the project from local lenders, multinational lending agencies, and a syndicate of investment banks. The security for the debt consisted of the project assets, including the project contracts, and the cash flow generated by the project operation. The project was structured to achieve the benefits for the project sponsors of nonrecourse project finance, discussed above.

In addition, the host country, India, was able to stimulate economic and social development through this financing model. The lives of millions of people would be affected by the project, with minimal government support and without accessing public funds.

However, as discussed in Chapter 3, project finance presents risks to both project sponsors and lenders. These include currency risks, legal risks, and political risks.

Of these, political risks materialized as the most significant. At financing of the project, Maharashtra was controlled by the Congress Party, which encouraged private investment in India's infrastructure. Soon after the financing was completed, however, the political control changed to the Bharatiya Janata Party (BJP). Importantly, it gained political control, in part, because of its opposition to the Dabhol project.

Soon after it gained power, the BJP announced that it would cease construction on the project and abandon the portions already under construction. The party justified its actions for several reasons, including the high cost of the power, environmental concerns, and the lack of competitive bids to select the project. Ultimately, the project company was forced to renegotiate the project power sales agreement.

What went wrong in Dabhol has been heavily debated. Irrespective of the exact nature of

---

[45] Malaysia and Thailand used competitive bidding for private power solicitations; most projects in Indonesia and the Philippines did not.

[46] *See generally* Jeswald W. Selacuse, *Renegotiating International Project Agreements*, 24 FORDHAM INT'L L.J. 1319 (2001); *Dabhol Financing*, INT'L CORP. L., Apr. 1995.

the problems, the public importance of infrastructure projects invite political opposition and contract changes in times of economic instability. The remainder of this book discusses how best to address this risk and others when structuring an international project financing.

§ 1.22 PROJECT CANCELLATIONS

Despite several well-publicized project cancellations and renegotiations, infrastructure projects in developing countries have been very successful in getting to financial closure and operation. A World Bank study[47] noted that in developing countries, 2,500 projects reached financial closure from 1990 to 2001, representing investment commitments of US$750 billion. During the same period, only forty-eight projects were formally cancelled, some before and some after financial closure. The projects were cancelled for various reasons. For toll road projects, a lack of consumer demand was the culprit. For water, sewer, and power projects, consumer price sensitivity (either because of macroeconomic shocks, as in Indonesia, or because the cost of service was higher than when provided by the public sector) and bill collection were common problems. Still other projects were cancelled because of problems that began during the competitive bidding stage. Interestingly, one-half of the cancelled projects involved allegations of corruption and impropriety and were not competitively tendered.

---

[47] Clive Harris et al., *Infrastructure Projects – A Review of Canceled Private Projects*, PUBLIC POLICY FOR THE PRIVATE SECTOR, WORLD BANK NOTE NO. 252 (Jan. 2003).

PART TWO

RISK IDENTIFICATION, ALLOCATION, AND MITIGATION

CHAPTER TWO

PROJECT FINANCE RISKS

OVERVIEW

§ 2.01 RISK

What is risk? It has been defined as "uncertainty in regard to cost, loss, or damage."[1] Uncertainty is the important aspect of the definition. Project finance abhors it.[2]

An important part of the successful closing of a project financing is the risk structuring process.[3] It is during this process that risks are identified, analyzed, quantified, mitigated, and allocated so that no individual risk threatens the development, construction, or operation of the project in such a way that the project is unable to generate sufficient revenues to repay the project debt, pay operating expenses, and provide an attractive equity return to investors.[4] This is done primarily through the contracting-out process – allocating risks among parties in contract form.[5] In the following chapters, which make up Part 2 of this book, the risk structuring process will be examined.

Risks in a transnational project financing may be classified into two general categories: transnational and commercial. Subclassification is made for each risk in these two categories in the chapters dedicated to them. Beyond this classification system, risks can be examined at the participant level, identifying the risks most important to each.

By itself, risk identification is only a starting point. The processes of risk analysis and

---

[1] C. HARDY, RISK AND RISK-BEARING 1 (1923).
[2] For a comprehensive overview of risk theory, see JEFFREY DELMON, PROJECT FINANCE, BOT PROJECTS AND RISK 1–53 (2005). See also David Blumenthal, Sources of Funds

and Risk Management for International Energy Projects, 16 BERKLEY J. INT'L L. 267 (1998).
[3] For an interesting history of risk and probability analysis, see PETER L. BERNSTEIN, AGAINST THE GODS – THE REMARKABLE STORY OF RISK (1996).
[4] See Thomas W. Waelde & George Ndi, Stabilizing International Investment Commitments: International Law Versus Contract Interpretation, 31 TEX. INT'L L.J. 216, 220 (1996) ("Life is inherently uncertain.... Nevertheless, it is the time-honored tradition of lawyers to try to regulate the behavior of the parties to a deal in extreme detail and for a very long period. There may sometimes be excessive zeal on the part of lawyers wishing to "play God" with contract drafting under the illusion that the draftsman can draft away all the vagaries of the future.").
[5] See C. HARDY, RISK AND RISK-BEARING 60–61 (1923).

management are important next steps in structuring a successful project. The methods available to manage these risks (transfer to another participant by contract; mitigating the risk by sharing equity ownership with an entity that can reduce the risk; risk minimization and loss prevention; and credit enhancement), singularly or in combination, are discussed in the following chapters.

The project sponsor does not make its investment without risk. Rather, the unallocated, residual risk is the sponsor's economic risk for the economic return expected from the project operation. To the extent that return is inadequate in comparison to the expected return on investment, the project should be abandoned.

§ 2.02 THE RISK MATRIX

Because of the importance of risk allocation in the project finance structure, a convenient, organized format for identifying the risk, and understanding the allocation and mitigation techniques used, is helpful. A risk matrix is the tool typically used by project finance participants.

On the following pages, sample risk matrixes for the construction period and the operating period of an electric generation facility are reproduced as Tables 2-1 and 2-2, respectively.

§ 2.03 PROJECT FINANCE PARTICIPANTS AND PERSPECTIVES

Because a project financing is either nonrecourse, or of limited recourse, to the project sponsor, financial responsibility for the various risks in a project financing must be allocated to parties that will assume recourse liability and that possess adequate credit to accept the risk allocated. The allocation of risks varies from transaction to transaction and is largely dependent on the bargaining position of the participants and the ability of the project to cover risk contingencies with the underlying cash flow and reserve accounts.

In general, risks should be allocated to the party that is best able to control the risk or influence its outcome. In return for the risk allocated to it, a party will demand compensation that is consistent with the magnitude of the risk assumed.

There are four general risk periods in the typical project financing: development risks, design engineering and construction risks, start-up risks, and operating risks.

[1] Development Risks

Development risks are primarily risks to the project sponsors and the development loan lenders. Risks during this stage include failure to obtain permits or other governmental approvals; public opposition to the project; and weaknesses in the business framework of the deal (in the vernacular, "the deal doesn't make sense"). Risks are very high during the developmental stage of the process. However, potential rewards are high, and funds at risk are relatively small, although they increase with each day of development.

[2] Design Engineering and Construction Risks

Design engineering and construction risks are risks that are inherent during project design and construction phases. As construction moves forward, new risks arise and others subside. Design development and construction risks are primarily risks to the project sponsors and the construction loan lenders, although each project participant is concerned with whether the project will be constructed on time for the price upon which project financial projections are based.

The classic construction risk is the necessity of a change in the work that is not contemplated in the construction price, such as a change necessitated by technical design refinements. Other project construction risks include price changes caused by currency fluctuation or inflation, construction delays, material shortages, design changes required by law, and strikes. Losses during this stage can be significant, particularly for the construction lender.

If a project is unsuccessful during the construction phase, the project assets will not likely be of sufficient value to repay the construction loan. Thus, the risk structuring process attempts to create a managed risk profile during this stage of project development, through turnkey construction contracts with guaranteed completion dates, prices, and performance levels. In addition, in some projects, construction lenders will require project sponsors to guarantee the availability of funds for project completion, thereby requiring limited recourse to the project sponsors for the construction loan.

[3] Start-up Risks

Start-up of a project is the most important risk-shifting phase of a project financing because achievement of the performance guarantees through performance tests signals the end of the contractor risk period and the beginning of the risk period for the operator and the project company. Until this time, the contractor is responsible for almost all construction risks, pursuant to the turnkey construction contract. At start-up, permanent lenders and equity investors, including the sponsor, require the contractor to prove that the project can operate at a level of performance necessary to service debt and pay operating costs.

[4] Operating Risks

Operating risks are those risks that arise after the project is accepted or is in preliminary operation. Each operating risk affects whether the project will perform at projected levels, thereby producing sufficient funds to cover debt service and operating costs and provide a return on equity invested. Operating risks are exemplified by a decrease in the availability of raw materials or fuel or a decrease in demand for the output of the project. Other operating risks include technical problems, inflation, foreign exchange rates and convertibility, strikes and other production risks, supply risks, regulatory changes, political changes, uninsured losses, and management inefficiencies. Operating risks are primarily risks to the project company and the permanent loan lenders, although other project participants, such as the off-take purchaser, are concerned with whether the project operates.

The magnitude of losses during this stage is dependent upon the operating year in which the problem develops. If a project is unsuccessful during the early years of project operation, the project assets will not likely be of sufficient value to repay the project loans, and the project sponsors will not have received the equity

return for which they hoped. With the passage of time, however, the potential loss decreases as project debt is amortized and investment returns are achieved. Thus, the risk structuring process attempts to create a managed risk profile during the operations phase that recognizes the decreasing needs for expensive risk mitigation techniques as the project matures. In the early years of operation, however, risk mitigation and allocation techniques, such as take-and-pay off-take contracts, fixed price fuel and raw material supply contracts, and political risk insurance, are important.

§ 2.04 OBJECTIVES OF PROJECT FINANCE PARTICIPANTS

An analysis of a project financing by each participant, and the negotiation approach for the project documents significant to that participant, begins typically with a compilation of risks and a determination of the party best capable of bearing each identified risk through various methods of credit support. The allocation of risks is generally determined on the basis of control over the risk, reward associated with that control, the role in the project, and creditworthiness. As an oversimplification, it is generally true that the participant that can best exercise control over a risk or that will realize the greatest reward if the risk does not materialize, considering the role of the participant in the project, typically is allocated the risk.

For example, a risk identified in a project may be that a key contract will terminate if project completion is not achieved by a definite date. Although no party can control the occurrence of all risks associated with construction, all parties in the project will benefit if the project is completed. The participant ultimately selected to bear the completion risk is typically the contractor. If the contractor lacks the financial resources to address this risk, other participants must examine the risk, determine the likelihood of the risk and the value of participation in the project, and establish the terms upon which allocation of the risk is acceptable. The allocation accepted often results in the transfer of some project reward to the participant accepting the

Table 2-1. *Sample construction period risk matrix for electric generation facility*

RISK	PARTY ALLOCATED RISK	MITIGATION	EFFECT ON LENDER	EFFECT ON DEVELOPER
cost overrun that is within contractor's control	contractor	construction contract is for a fixed price	creditworthiness of contractor to finish project	construction price reflects risk assumed by contractor
cost overrun not within contractor's control – insured event	insurance company	insurance proceeds	none if proceeds are sufficient	none if proceeds are sufficient
cost overrun not within contractor's control – uninsured force majeure event	developer	stand-by equity commitment is drawn upon	none	equity returns deferred until completion occurs
cost overrun not within contractor's control – change of law	developer/power purchaser	stand-by finance facility drawn until tariff adjustment is made	stand-by debt facility reduced and unavailable for other contingencies	increased financing costs offset by increased tariff, but timing of adjustment may reduce equity returns
cost overrun not within contractor's control – subsurface site conditions	developer	stand-by finance facility drawn	stand-by debt facility reduced and unavailable for other contingencies	increased financing costs; equity returns reduced
completion delay that is within contractor's control	contractor	fixed completion date in construction contract; daily liquidated damages to cover debt service, fixed operating costs and fuel supply contract late delivery payments	creditworthiness of contractor to finish project	construction price reflects risk assumed by contractor
completion delay that is not within contractor's control – insured event	insurance company	insurance proceeds	none if proceeds are sufficient	none if proceeds are sufficient

Risk	Responsible party	Mechanism	Consequence	Effect on returns
completion delay not within contractor's control – uninsured force majeure event	power purchaser and central government	if cost is less than $5MM, stand-by finance facility drawn until tariff adjustment is made; if more than $5MM, government pays developer fee, retires debt and assumes project	stand-by debt facility reduced and unavailable for other contingencies; government credit risk	increased financing costs offset by increased tariff, but timing of adjustment may reduce equity returns; if over $5MM, equity returns lost
completion delay not within contractor's control – change of law	power purchaser and central government	if cost is less than $5MM, stand-by finance facility drawn until tariff adjustment is made; if more than $5MM, government pays developer fee, retires debt and assumes project	stand-by debt facility reduced and unavailable for other contingencies; government credit risk	increased financing costs offset by increased tariff, but timing of adjustment may reduce equity returns
cost overrun not within contractor's control – subsurface site conditions	developer	stand-by finance facility drawn	stand-by debt facility reduced and unavailable for other contingencies	increased financing costs; equity returns reduced
failure of contractor to satisfy performance guarantees at completion due to contractor fault	contractor	performance guarantees in construction contract; liquidated damages for reduced performance payable by contractor	creditworthiness of contractor to pay	creditworthiness of contractor to pay may affect equity returns
increased interest during construction period	power purchaser	stand-by finance facility drawn until tariff adjustment is made	stand-by debt facility reduced and unavailable for other contingencies	increased financing costs offset by increased tariff, but timing of adjustment may reduce equity returns
unfavorable exchange rates during construction period	power purchaser	stand-by finance facility drawn until tariff adjustment is made	stand-by debt facility reduced and unavailable for other contingencies	increased financing costs offset by increased tariff, but timing of adjustment may reduce equity returns
country risk – expropriation, nationalization, interference	central government	government pays debt and guaranteed equity return to developer	government creditworthiness	government creditworthiness

Table 2-2. *Sample operating period risk matrix*

RISK	PARTY ALLOCATED RISK	MITIGATION	EFFECT ON LENDER	EFFECT ON DEVELOPER
operating cost overrun – government fault	power purchaser	tariff adjustment	increased operating costs until tariff adjusted	increased operating costs until tariff adjusted
operating cost overrun – operator failure to satisfy operating guarantees	operator	performance guarantees in operating agreement; liquidated damages for reduced performance payable by operator	creditworthiness of operator	creditworthiness of operator
increased interest, unfavorable exchange rates, inflation during operation period	power purchaser	tariff adjustment	debt coverage could be affected	increased financing costs offset by increased tariff
unavailability/unconvertibility of foreign exchange	central government	government pays debt and guaranteed equity return to developer	government creditworthiness	government creditworthiness
country risk – expropriation, nationalization, interference	central government	government pays debt and guaranteed equity return to developer	government creditworthiness	government creditworthiness
equipment destruction	insurance company	insurance proceeds	none if proceeds are sufficient	none if proceeds are sufficient
operator default	operator	penalties and termination payments	operator creditworthiness and coverage ratios affected	operator creditworthiness; and reduced equity return
power purchaser default	central government	developer option to terminate; if terminated, government pays debt and guaranteed equity return to developer	government creditworthiness	government creditworthiness

risk, through a higher contract price or an addition of a role, such as from the role of contractor only to the dual roles of contractor and equity participant.

§ 2.05 RISK IDENTIFICATION BY PARTICIPANTS

Each project finance participant has a different perspective on risk allocation. Only by understanding the risk perspectives of a participant can its appetite for risk acceptance be understood.

Risk is subjective in application. The significance of any particular risk is determined by the party considering taking that risk. Thus, an event or condition unacceptable to one entity may be considered manageable and routine by another.

The identification of risks is essential in an analysis of a project financing because of the nonrecourse nature of the project debt and contractual undertakings of the project company. For an international project financing, these risks can be divided into three categories: international, commercial, and legal, which are discussed in later chapters.

[1] Sponsor

The project sponsor is the entity that coordinates the development of the project. There may be more than one project sponsor, such as a development group or joint venture of companies. The project sponsor is in contrast to the project company, the special-purpose entity established by the sponsors to enter into the project contracts and own the project assets.

The project sponsor's objectives are based in the very reasons a project finance model is the selected financing scheme. These objectives, more fully discussed in Chapter 1, include limiting the exposure of the sponsor's other assets to a project failure by using nonrecourse or limited recourse financing; off-balance-sheet accounting treatment, where available; use of a highly leveraged financing structure; flexibility with loan covenants in existing and future transactions; favorable financing terms; internal capital commitment policies; political risk diversification; risk sharing; collateral limited to project assets; greater willingness of lenders to participate in a workout than foreclose; matching specific assets with specific liabilities; and expanded credit opportunities. Simultaneously, the project sponsor seeks efficient use of tax benefits, flexibility in both future financings of other projects and in the permanent financing and refinancing of the specific project, and an acceptable degree of autonomy in the construction, start-up, operation, and maintenance of the project.

The financial closing process for a project financing is lengthy, complicated, and expensive. Yet, the project sponsor may have spent many months, and even years, developing the project and incurring development expenses. Thus, the sponsor is immediately interested in several objectives: limiting further development costs, minimizing transaction costs, recovering development stage expenses, and earning construction management or similar fees to fund overhead costs.

Further, looking at the long-term, the sponsor is motivated with the potential to receive a cash return on operation of the project. The sooner the project financing is closed and construction begins on the project, the sooner the sponsor can begin to receive the financial benefits of its investment.

[2] Construction Lender

The construction lender in a project financing is concerned with the design engineering and construction risks, because the completion of the project is a condition precedent to the payment of the construction loan with the proceeds of the permanent financing, or if the construction and permanent loans are a part of one debt facility, to the repayment of the debt from operating revenues.[6] Thus, it is concerned primarily with the construction contract, including provisions relating to timely completion and performance at expected levels. If the project is not completed on time, at the agreed-upon price and performance levels, then credit enhancement devices must be in place that will increase the likelihood

[6] *See generally* Mei Han & Jerry Shi Zhiyong, *How to Assess the Profitability of a Project Finance Deal – From the Lender's Perspective* 3 J. PROJECT FIN. 21 (1997).

of repayment of the construction loan. These are often in the form of completion guarantees and performance and payment bonds.

Of primary importance to the construction lender is to ensure that the contractor's obligations are of a "turnkey" nature, because sufficient funds must be available to complete construction of the project on time, at agreed-upon performance levels. This obligation has various components, each of which relate to the cost of construction and the ability of the project to produce cash flows at a predictable rate. These components include a firm price, a firm time of completion, performance standards relating to the output of the project, and the compliance of the project with applicable laws.

In addition, the construction lender is concerned with the implications of late completion of project construction on other agreements, especially where the late completion excuses the obligations of the permanent lender to finance the project. Other potential concerns include contractual obligations of the sponsor to deliver products or take deliveries of supplies on a date certain. The failure to make or take deliveries by the date specified may require the project company to pay damages or allow the other contracting party to terminate the contract. Thus, any adverse change in the condition of the project during construction, including adverse changes in financial condition of any of the participants, changes in law, and changes in the technical feasibility of the project, may affect the construction lender's ability to have the construction debt paid, whether from the permanent lender or from operating revenues.

[3] Permanent Lender

The permanent lender has several requirements in a project financing. These include the arrangement of sufficient debt to finance the total construction cost of the project, the absence of any other lender in a more senior collateral or control position, and satisfactory intercreditor agreements if more than one lender is involved in the financing.[7]

As discussed earlier, the permanent lender also wants a project that is risk-free when the perma-

nent loan is made available on the completion date. Project finance permanent lenders, however, recognize the imperfect world of project finance and are willing to make long-term loans even where the project is not yet operating in a risk-free environment. For example, the permanent lender may commit permanent loan financing to the project even if the guaranteed level of performance is not achieved, provided that the requisite performance is attainable in a reasonable time at a reasonable price, nothing financially adverse has occurred to the contractor, and the project can pay debt service and expenses at the level of performance already achieved. Similarly, the permanent lender could decide to make available permanent loan financing even with a material adverse change to the economic condition of a project participant, provided the change is temporary or the operation of the project will substantially improve or correct the economic condition.

For the permanent lender, project finance risk allocation issues center on the project contracts that are the credit support for the financing. The permanent lender is generally concerned with the economic value of the contracts, the legal adequacy of the contracts, and the viability of the contracts in a loan workout environment. In addition, similar to the desire of the construction lender that the construction contract has a firm price, a firm time for performance, and certain performance standards, the permanent lender wants similar commitments from the operator, the suppliers, and the output purchasers.

The permanent lender also wants each of the project finance contracts to be assignable. First, it will want the contracts to be assignable to it as collateral for the project finance loan. Further, the lender will want to ensure that if there is a foreclosure the contracts are assignable to and assumable by it and by a subsequent project owner. This concept is discussed in detail in Chapter 26.

Overall, the lender attempts to structure a financing that provides that (i) all costs before construction completion are without recourse to the lender for additional funds; (ii) the contractor satisfies performance guarantees, as evidenced by performance tests; (iii) there is recourse to other creditworthy project participants for delay

---

[7] *See generally id.*

and completion costs, if the project is abandoned and if minimum performance levels are not achieved; (iv) there are predictable revenue streams that can be applied to service debt, in the currency of the debt (or easily convertible at an adequate exchange rate); (v) the revenue streams are long-term, from a creditworthy source, and in an amount that covers operating costs and debt service; and (vi) the incentives under the operating agreement ensure that the project will be operated at levels necessary to maximize revenue while minimizing costs, comply with environmental laws, and maintain long-term facility integrity.

[4] Contractor

The tension between the sponsor and contractor in a project financing is based on the turnkey nature of the construction contract: The contractor must deliver the project at a fixed or predictable price, on a date certain, warranted to perform at agreed levels. The contractor is, of course, concerned with the difficulty of predicting events that could result in delivery of a delayed project, at an increased price, that does not perform as expected. Thus, unless the contract price is extremely attractive to the contractor, the main objective of the contractor in a project financing is to limit risks of any change in the cost of the project, to provide excuses for late delivery, and to provide sufficient time to satisfy performance guarantees.

There are two customary rewards for the contractor in return for assuming the risk of completion on a date certain for a fixed price. The first is through the increase in the construction price to include a risk premium. The second is through a bonus payment, which the project company pays to the contractor if the project is completed ahead of the scheduled completion date. In a project financing, the bonus concept must relate to the other project contracts so that if the facility is completed earlier than the scheduled date, the other contracts permit an earlier commencement of operation.

The contractor is also concerned with the underlying financing documents, including whether the sponsor has arranged financing to pay the contractor for the work performed. In addition, the contractor is interested in provisions assuring that the financing documents require the lender to make payments directly to the contractor and limit the conditions to advancing construction draws to a default by the project company (except disputes under the construction contract). However, the contractor is not always successful in obtaining these rights.

[5] Operator

The tension between the project sponsor and operator is analogous to the tension that exists between the project sponsor and contractor: the need for predictability of price and performance of the project. While the other project participants will want to ensure that the operating costs are sufficiently fixed or predictable so that feasibility can be analyzed, the operator, in contrast, wants to limit price risk.

It is common for the operator to address this risk by agreeing to operate the project pursuant to a budget prepared by the operator and approved by the project company. In addition, the operator agrees to operate the project within the parameters of the agreed-upon performance levels and according to laws and industry practice.

[6] Technology Owner

The technology owner is typically not a direct participant in the project financing. Rather, the project company or contractor has a license agreement with the technology owner for use of the technology. Sometimes, the technology owner gives performance guarantees with respect to the technology provided. These guarantees are similar to performance guarantees provided by the contractor and allocate technology risk to a third party.

The technology owner may be required to enter into agreements with the project company that ensure the continued availability of the technology to the project if the licensed contractor is terminated by the project company, or if the licensed contractor defaults under the license agreement or otherwise loses the right to the technology during the expected life of the project. These agreements, called technology supply or license agreements, often provide that the technology owner is not obligated to disclose any confidential information to a competitor that agrees to complete construction or operate the project.

Also, the technology owner will limit the approved use of the technology and confidential information to only the extent required for project construction and operation.

[7] Supplier

The fuel or raw material supplier to the project is concerned with the objective of delivery to the project of necessary fuel or raw material in exchange for the market price, with acceptable excuses for nondelivery. The project participants, however, seek predictable price, quality, and delivery commitments, with a minimum of uncertainty in the price, terms, and obligations for supply. Sometimes, dedicated reserves or supply sources are required to be committed to the exclusive use of the project.

[8] Output Purchaser

In many respects, the output purchaser is in the same position as the project company when the project company purchases fuel or raw materials. The output purchaser desires firm price and quality, with a minimum of uncertainty. The project company, in contrast, wants to increase prices as the market will permit, and to be excused from performance without penalties for limited periods.

[9] Host Government

The host government can benefit on a short-term and long-term basis from the success of the project. Short-term, the government can use the project for political benefits and for attracting other developers to a country. Long-term, the successful project should improve economic prosperity and, perhaps, political stability by providing the needed infrastructure. Other benefits include the importation to the host country of new technologies and the associated intellectual property, training of its citizens in that new technology, job creation, and increased tax revenues.

Allocating some risks to the host country is therefore justifiable. This is particularly important for large, high-profile projects that are significant in the economic development plans of the host-country government. For example, implementation agreements, negotiated and executed with the host government, can provide a variety of government assurances with respect to the project risks. These agreements are discussed in Chapter 14.

The host government might be involved in a project in one or several ways. These include as equity contributor, debt provider, guarantee provider (particularly political risks), supplier of raw materials and other resources, output purchaser, and provider of fiscal support (reduced import fees, tax holidays, and other incentives).

The host government also has an ongoing role. It can regulate the project in the future by ensuring permit compliance and through regulatory structures.

[10] Other Governments – Export and Transit Countries

A project might require the cooperation of other countries, besides the host country, for project success. For example, the fuel supply could be insufficient in the host country, requiring a supply from another country. The perspective of the export country – a country from which equipment, raw materials, fuel, or another project input will be supplied to the project – will vary based on political and financial goals. The export country, for example, might not be willing to approve a long-term fuel supply arrangement where its natural resources are exploited to benefit another country. Alternatively, use of its natural resources might be permissible if sufficient export taxes are earned and political or economic cooperation exists between the two countries.

A transit country – a country through which the output of the project must pass to ensure project success – might have a similar perspective, depending on the method by which the project input or output must pass through the country.

[11] Equity Investor

Equity investors bring investment capital to projects, supplementing equity invested by project owners. The equity can take various forms, including (i) limited or general partnership interests in a limited or general partnership, formed to be the project company; (ii) lessor equity in a single-investor lease transaction; (iii) lessee equity in a sale-leaseback transaction; (iv) stock ownership of the project company organized as a corporation; (v) convertible debt instruments; and (vi) deeply subordinated debt.

Equity investors have three general goals in a project financing. These are nonrecourse liability for the project company in which they invest and for the special-purpose entity formed to invest in the project company; maximization of debt-to-equity leverage; and off-balance-sheet accounting treatment for the underlying project debt.

The equity return goal of the equity investor is one factor that determines the timing of the equity investment. There are four equity investment points: development stage; construction stage; upon completion; and operation stage. Risks taken by equity vary at each stage. Generally, the earlier the investment, the greater the risk to the equity investor. Similarly, the earlier the equity investment is made, the greater the return that the investor expects.

Equity investors have differing appetites for management control over a project. Passive investors want very little management control and prefer to receive limited liability in return for losing that control. Other investors are more active, expecting to provide greater management control and supervision.

Equity investors make a risk analysis similar to lenders. The types of project risks that can affect the debt will also likely affect the equity. The structuring goals are quite different, however.

Project lenders hold a first priority security interest on all project assets; want sufficient project revenues generated to pay debt service and operating costs and fund debt service, maintenance, and other reserve accounts; restrict when distributions of profits can be made to the project owners; and want an acceptable return to equity investors. Equity investors, however, while sharing these goals (but with differing levels of concern), attempt to receive distributions frequently, to keep reserve account balances to a minimum and to preserve potential residual value in the project that exists after the debt is paid or substantially reduced.

[12] Multilateral and Bilateral Agencies

Multilateral and bilateral agencies have similar perspectives. Political and government funding constraints drive each somewhat. Each has separate charters and goals, however, which define precisely the perspectives each has in a project. Multilateral and bilateral agencies are discussed in Chapter 21.

§ 2.06 DEVELOPMENT STAGE RISKS

The development phase of a project is sometimes overlooked by project finance participants as an area of risk analysis. More attention is focused on risks that occur during construction and operation of a project, when project debt is outstanding. Yet, significant risks exist for the project sponsors during the developmental period. Also, for participants that are relying on the project for long-term needs, such as off-take purchasers, risks during the developmental phase may have significant implications for them. If a financeable project is not structured, long-term benefits for the off-take purchaser may evaporate.

Project development is expensive. Estimates of the cost of developing a transnational project range from $2 million to $20 million. Funds for project development come from one or all of three sources: governmental grants, developmental loans, and equity. The sources are discussed in later chapters.

During project development, any of several risks could render the development efforts worthless. These include the following: loss of the right to develop the project in a competitive bidding process; inability to negotiate financeable agreements or concessions with the host country; unavailability of permits, licenses, and concessions from the host government; political opposition; citizen opposition; lack of creditworthy, long-term off-take purchasers; development of competing projects; unavailability of needed inputs on financeable terms, such as raw materials, fuel, and water; effects of the project on the environment and indigenous peoples; changes in foreign exchange controls and in the availability and convertibility of currency; availability of political risk and commercial risk insurance; changes in the availability of private, bilateral and multilateral financing and credit support based on such things as market perceptions, regional currency problems, and political changes; changes in law; and outright rejection of the project after months, or years, of development, based on political grounds.

§ 2.07 THE JOINT VENTURE AS A RISK MITIGATION DEVICE

A joint venture is a form of risk sharing used in project financings. In a joint venture, sometimes called a joint development company, two or more parties join to develop a project or series of projects. Joint venturers might include a company particularly skilled in construction, another skilled in project development, and a third in the political and developmental climate of the host country. Together, each brings different, useful skills to project development, while allowing for a risk sharing that may be more attractive to them than if one of the entities developed the project singly. Also, joint ventures provide the framework for accelerating the negotiation process with governments and financial institutions. Further, the increased creditworthiness and experience of individual companies combined into a joint venture allow the joint venture to be competitive, though the individual members, acting alone, would not have the resources necessary to compete with larger and more experienced companies.

§ 2.08 A CAVEAT ABOUT RISK ALLOCATION

A project financing invites risk taking. All risks in a project financing must be allocated so a nonrecourse or limited recourse financing is possible. This invitation to risk taking is sometimes accepted with an aggressiveness toward a risk that is unsupported by the probabilities of the risk materializing. The project participant may find that the acceptance of the invitation came attached with a high price. Even if the price is not high, the project sponsors should not declare victory. Rather, where the risk-reward equation is out of balance, the situation is created where the participant shortchanged is a prime candidate to trigger a project disaster.

CHAPTER THREE

PROJECT FINANCE CROSS-BORDER RISKS

§ 3.01 GENERALLY

In any project financing, whether domestic or transnational, the project is subject to governmental jurisdiction and action. This can result in risks to the project that, if realized, affect the success of the project, cash flows, and operating costs. There are limits on the control a project sponsor can have over the political stability surrounding a project. Nonetheless, mitigation techniques do exist.

The degree of political risk[1] the project faces is sometimes determined by the nature of the project. Projects of particular importance to a host government's social welfare strategies might be less susceptible to many political risks described in this chapter. In contrast, projects significant to the country's security or basic infrastructure might be more susceptible to certain political risks, such as expropriation.

More subtle, informal factors also influence the seriousness of political risk. For example, the involvement of the World Bank or regional development banks in a project might convince a host government to consider more fully the implications of any political action against a project, and use it less frequently. In addition, involvement by host-country lenders and investors, or

lenders and investors in other countries with material stakes in the project's success, might have a similar effect. The possibility of jeopardizing these relationships can be sufficient to protect the lenders and the project sponsors from many risks discussed below.

Allocation of political risks and mitigation of those risks are possible in several ways, as further discussed in this chapter.[2] These include project sponsor support, through guarantees and other credit enhancement; host-government guarantees or undertakings; political risk insurance; reserve funds; formation of joint ventures to spread the risks among several project owners; participation by bilateral and multilateral institutions in the project; participation by local banks in the financing; and contractual protections (choice of law, international arbitration, offshore accounts, stabilization clauses, and implementation agreements). Also, companies can manage political risks by portfolio diversification, limiting the exposure taken in particularly high-risk countries.

§ 3.02 CURRENCY-RELATED RISKS

[1] Generally

Exposure to foreign currency is a risk present in almost every transnational transaction. It is a particularly significant risk in project financings because the long-term nature of the underlying contracts increases the likelihood that a currency-related risk will materialize over time. The labyrinth of contracts in a project financing, with the twists and turns of contract interrelationships, makes the risks even more acute.

The foreign exchange risk arises in a project financing most often because of the differences in the revenue currency, on the one hand, and the debt and expense currency, on the other hand. In a project, the revenue paid under an off-take sales contract will most likely be paid in the host country's local currency. However, the project company will incur debt and contractual obligations in another currency.

In general terms, there are three areas of foreign exchange risk: unavailability of foreign exchange;

---

[1] *See generally* Thomas W. Waelde & George Ndi, *Stabilizing International Investment Commitments: International Law Versus Contract Interpretation*, 31 Tex. Int'l L. J. 216, 231–235 (1996); Gerald T. West, *Managing Project Political Risk: The Role of Investment Insurance*, 2 J. of Project Finance 5 (1996).

[2] *See generally* Waelde & Ndi, *supra* note 1, at pp. 233–34.

transfer of exchange out of the host country; and depreciation in the value of the host-country currency. These are discussed in the following sections.

Several structures and credit enhancement alternatives are available and should be considered in any attempt to manage currency risks. As discussed below, these include controls on the payment of project revenues; frequent conversions of local currency to hard currency; establishment of special deposit accounts; minimizing local currency requirements; establishing offshore accounts in which project revenues are deposited; negotiating exchange agreements with the host government; obtaining monetary board or central bank approvals; maintaining cash flow flexibility and reserves to cover currency fluctuations; establishing currency reserve accounts; entering into currency hedge transactions; project sponsor guarantees or support agreements; and matching currencies in which revenue is paid to currencies in which operating costs and debt service are paid.

[2] Nonconvertibility of Currency (Unavailability of Foreign Exchange)

The nonconvertibility risk concerns the ability to convert currency into foreign exchange, as a predecessor to moving money out of a country. A foreign exchange shortage in the host country (insufficient foreign exchange reserves to convert local currency) may result in the risk that the project entity will be unable to convert local currency into the foreign currency in which loan or other payments must be made.

To determine the seriousness of this risk, the project's lenders and other project participants should examine the foreign exchange position of the host country. As part of that analysis, the government's priorities for foreign currency use must be understood. Often, the highest priorities are for loans from multilateral development banks, payments for imports essential to the economy, and interest payments due financial institutions on public sector loans. If an excess is available, the project can compete with other entities for the scarce remaining foreign currency.

Most developing countries have a shortage of foreign exchange, experience negative trade balances, or have foreign debt that is excessive in amount. These result in nonconvertibility risks.

Mitigation of this risk is possible in several ways. For example, the revenue-producing project contracts could require payment in a hard currency. If the government or a government-owned entity is making the payment under the revenue-producing contract, this should provide the convertibility assurances needed for the project.

Also, in an infrastructure project financing, the project business could be tied to a local export business that generates foreign exchange. This structure is often called a *countertrade*. The project revenues are countertraded for a local company's products that can generate hard currency. The sale of the local company's products thereby produces a steady stream of foreign exchange that can be used to reduce convertibility risk. There are limitations to the efficacy of this structure, however, in a widely fluctuating currency.

If possible, in the host country, agreements can be negotiated with the host-country government for priority access to foreign exchange or a guarantee of availability. These agreements can be part of a sovereign guarantee of currency convertibility, or part of existing regulations and government approval processes.

In addition, currency swaps on a commercial basis could be entered into to help ensure convertibility. However, these arrangements might be prohibitively expensive, or completely unavailable, in some countries.

Finally, political risk insurance covering currency nonconvertibility can be obtained from organizations such as the Overseas Private Investment Corporation (OPIC), a U.S. agency, and the Multilateral Investment Guarantee Agency (MIGA), an affiliate of the World Bank. Potential sources of this type of coverage are discussed in Chapter 20.

[3] Currency Transfer (Inability to Transfer Foreign Exchange Abroad)

Generally. The currency transfer risk arises in situations in which currency (local or foreign) is not allowed to be transferred out of the country. An exchange control is like an ancient fortress wall around a country, with gates through which currencies may pass. The government holds the keys to the gates. It keeps capital needed for domestic purposes in the country and unwanted capital out.

For example, this risk could manifest itself in the situation in which the central bank of the host country notionally converts the local currency into foreign exchange on its books, acknowledges the obligation but refuses to make the transfer out of the country. This type of activity sometimes precedes a rescheduling of foreign exchange obligations.

Most developing countries have exchange controls. Exchange risks are most often manifested in situations in which a limited supply of the specified currency is available. It can also occur where the host government imposes burdensome approvals for, or requires conversion fees to complete, a conversion transaction. If these occur, the international investor or lender will not receive the required currency and will need either to accept a shortfall or accept another currency.

Foreign currency can sometimes be retained in the form received. Host governments may permit foreign currency to be retained if it is received as loan proceeds, from equity investors or off-take sales, and if it is needed by the project for project-related expenditures, such as payment of debt service, equity payments, equipment costs, and fees to service providers.

Mitigation of this risk is possible in the same ways discussed above for the convertibility risk. Thus, for example, the revenue-producing project contracts could require payment in a hard currency. In an infrastructure project financing, the project business could be tied to a local export business that generates foreign exchange, a so-called countertrade. As discussed above, in such an arrangement, the sale of the local company's products produces a steady stream of foreign exchange that can be used to reduce convertibility risk.

If possible in the host country, agreements can be negotiated with the host-country government for priority access to foreign exchange or a guarantee of availability. These agreements can be part of a sovereign guaranty of currency convertibility, or as part of existing regulations and government approval processes.

Also, currency swaps on a commercial basis could be entered into to help ensure convertibility. However, these arrangements might be prohibitively expensive, or completely unavailable, in some countries.

Finally, political risk insurance covering currency nonconvertibility can be obtained from organizations such as the MIGA, an affiliate of the World Bank. Potential sources of this type of coverage are discussed in Chapter 20.

Types and Characteristics of Exchange Controls. It is extremely difficult to provide a survey of the exchange control laws of the world; they change frequently. Some generalizations can be made, however, which will give project participants a framework for understanding these controls.

Examples of exchange controls include the following: requirements to surrender foreign exchange and convert it to local currency; control over which exchange rate applies; ownership of foreign bank accounts is prohibited, as are local accounts denominated in foreign exchange; no borrowing in foreign currency; no borrowing from nonresidents; prohibition on nonresidents borrowing locally; prohibition on purchase or sale of foreign currency; and prohibition on making payments to a nonresident. Any of these examples show why an international project finance transaction is practically impossible in a country with exchange controls. Consequently, specific government permission is needed.

REQUIREMENT TO SURRENDER AND CONVERT. The requirement to surrender all foreign currency and convert it to local currency is particularly troublesome in export projects. Under this type of exchange control, foreign currency typically must be converted at the official exchange rate, through the central bank or a commercial bank delegated this authority by the government.

CONTROL OVER WHICH EXCHANGE RATE IS APPLICABLE. The local government might have several exchange rates. The project company needs to determine which will apply to each transaction.

PROHIBITION ON FOREIGN BANK ACCOUNTS. No bank accounts can be maintained in a foreign country under this type of control. The restriction includes a prohibition of maintenance of bank accounts in the local country denominated in a foreign currency.

Typical exceptions include accounts maintained by diplomats or international organizations; blocked accounts, such as accounts payable to nonresidents awaiting foreign exchange conversion or transfer permission; and accounts held by nonresidents, with deposits only allowed from foreign sources.

PROHIBITION ON FOREIGN BORROWING. No borrowing in foreign currency is permitted.

PROHIBITION ON BORROWING FROM NONRESIDENTS. Residents are prohibited from borrowing in any currency, local or foreign, if the lender is a nonresident.

PROHIBITION ON NONRESIDENT BORROWING. A prohibition may block nonresidents from borrowing from local sources, regardless of whether the funds borrowed are domestic or foreign.

PROHIBITION ON PURCHASE OR SALE OF FOREIGN CURRENCY. There may be a prohibition of the purchase, sale, trade, or exchange of foreign currency, except through authorized procedures.

PROHIBITION ON PAYMENTS TO NONRESIDENTS. There may be a restriction on making payments to, or for the credit of, a nonresident.

Violation of Exchange Laws. Violation of an exchange law is treated severely in most countries. In some countries, a contract entered into in violation of an exchange law may be void and unenforceable.

Enforcement of Transactions That Violate a Country's Exchange Controls

ENFORCEMENT IN THE HOST COUNTRY. If one of the project transactions is entered into in violation of a country's exchange control laws, without the necessary permission, it is unlikely that the contract is enforceable in the host country. Although the local law of the host country should be researched on the topic, in general, courts do not enforce contracts that cannot be performed lawfully.

ENFORCEMENT OUTSIDE OF THE HOST COUNTRY. The outcome may be different if a foreign court, rather than a court in the host country, is asked to enforce a contract entered into in violation of a country's exchange control laws. The outcome is based, in part, on whether the foreign court is in a country party to the Articles of Agreement of the International Monetary Fund (IMF Articles).[3]

Under the IMF Articles, exchange contracts that involve the currency of any member country of the IMF that are contrary to that country's exchange controls are unenforceable in any member country.[4] Specifically, Article VIII 2(b) of the IMF Articles provides that "[e]xchange contracts which involve the currency of any member and which are contrary to the exchange control regulations of that member maintained or imposed consistently with this Agreement shall be unenforceable in the territories of any member country."[5] This simple sentence has been the source of analysis and case law by the courts that is sometimes inconsistent. However, a complete analysis of Article VIII 2(b) is beyond the scope of this book.[6]

Exchange Permissions and Consents. Exchange controls or moratoriums are addressed in the local law of the host country. The project sponsor will need to verify that it has the right under local law to convert local currency into the desired foreign exchange. Also, the project sponsor will want to ensure that it possesses the related right, discussed below, to make payments to the project lender.

Most countries impose central bank registration requirements on external loan transactions. In such countries, conversion rights are unavailable unless the loan is registered. The local law and regulations of the host country must be carefully examined to determine the rights granted. In a few countries, registration is not available until after the loan disbursement. In those countries, the project lenders will require that registration takes place as soon as possible.

---

[3] Articles of Agreement of the International Monetary Fund, Done at Bretton Woods, 1944, as amended 1969 and 1978.

[4] Articles of Agreement of the International Monetary Fund, art. VIII 2(b).

[5] *Id.*

[6] *See generally* PHILIP WOOD, THE LAW AND PRACTICE OF INTERNATIONAL FINANCE (1990).

Several types of conversion rights should be included in the conversion registration. The tolerance of any individual country for broad advance approval varies. For example, in some countries, the conversion rights registration cannot be made until after the loan is disbursed. Also, the scope of the conversion rights should be examined closely to determine whether the rights extend to all obligations under the loan agreement, such as principal, interest and fees, gross-up payments, yield protection and other indemnity payments, expenses, acceleration of the debt, and proceeds from foreclosure of local collateral.

Reducing Exposure to Exchange Controls. To reduce exchange control exposure, there is no substitute for the guidance and advice of local lawyers in the host country. Their expertise will be crucial to avoiding problems.

Protections can be included in the development stage of the project to reduce later problems and delays. These include making exchange control consents a condition to the effectiveness of contracts; including exchange control approvals, or statements of governmental cooperation on exchange controls, in the implementation agreement or letter of intent with the host government; and making the scope of exchange control requests as broad as possible.

[4] Currency Devaluation Risk Caused by Fluctuations in Foreign Exchange Rates

Generally. The *currency devaluation risk,* or *rate of conversion risk,* is the term used to describe the difficulties encountered by a foreign borrower or foreign affiliate in making future payments due in a currency other than the currency in which revenues are earned. It is also called the *currency devaluation risk.*

An example of this risk is the situation in which a loan is made in a foreign currency, such as U.S. dollars, and repayment is made by a borrower with earnings only in local currency. The risk is that the local currency depreciates to a point where the borrower is unable to generate sufficient local currency for the conversion necessary for debt service. In short, any significant local currency devaluation requires a corresponding increase in project cash flow so that foreign currency debt and other foreign currency obligations can be satisfied. This risk is particularly prevalent in countries with developing economies.

The maze of project finance contracts and the lengthy term of both the project contracts and the underlying project debt make the devaluation risk in a project financing particularly severe. Fluctuations in currency exchange rates can affect what comes into and out of a project: the amount of revenue generated by a project, the price of inputs, and the returns on equity.

This risk manifests itself in other ways, as well. For example, the exchange rate fluctuation could take place after the payment in the local currency is made but before the payments in foreign exchange are made to the project's lenders, contractors, or suppliers.

Protections against this risk are limited. It is not covered under insurance policies that protect a project against political risk.

Mitigation of this risk is possible in a variety of natural and synthetic approaches, however, including indexing purchase prices under off-take contracts to inflation or to fluctuations in the exchange rate; revenue payment in hard currency; raising debt in the local currency; and using derivatives.

Indexing Revenues. Indexing involves linking the amount of payments made in a local currency to the rate of inflation or to a hard currency. For example, a turnkey construction contract with a foreign equipment supplier might provide for an automatic price adjustment upon the occurrence of a currency rate fluctuation.[7]

Matching Revenue Currency to Debt Currency. In some projects, where long-term, fixed-price contracts govern cash flow, revenue streams cannot be adjusted to offset a detrimental change in exchange rates. However, this risk can be improved by structuring contracts to match the revenue currency with the debt currency.

---

[7] Larry Wynant, *Essential Elements of Project Financing,* HARV. BUS. REV., May–June 1980, at 168. As an example, a joint mining venture in Australia eventually collapsed because of effects of output contracts based on U.S. dollars in a revaluation of the Australian dollar and increased oil costs.

For example, in an energy infrastructure project, the power purchase agreement and other off-take contracts could be denominated in U.S. dollars or other hard currency. The host government could then assure that payments under these contracts would be actually paid in dollars. Although some operating costs would not be denominated in hard currency, the bulk of the risk would be covered. This approach is based on an important assumption, however; the off-take purchaser must be able to generate sufficient profits to cover the devaluation risk it absorbs by agreeing to an index. In situations in which devaluation risk materializes in a project, economic forces could combine to make it impossible for the off-take purchaser to pass on higher costs to its own customers.

Raising Debt in Local Currency. Alternatively, project debt could be raised in the same local currency in which the revenues will be received and expenses will be paid. This option will have limits determined by the capital available in the host country, among other factors.

Derivatives. Another option is using derivatives to cover the risk. These include forward contracts, currency options, and money-market hedging techniques. A large market exists in listed currency derivatives. In addition, banks are typically willing to develop customized hedging products. This type of protection is not inexpensive. Unfortunately, these products are not typically available in developing countries.

FORWARD CONTRACTS. A forward contract is a market hedging technique in which a bank agrees to make a future payment in a designated currency, in exchange for another currency delivered at the time of payment. Generally, contracts are available for payments due no more than 180 to 360 days in the future.

For example, if a payment is due in U.S. dollars in thirty days, the project company would contract with a bank that upon delivery to the bank of a specified amount of foreign currency in thirty days, the bank will make the required payment in U.S. dollars irrespective of the rate of exchange between the two currencies on that thirtieth day. If the project company does not receive the underlying payment from its obligor,

it must still deliver the specified amount of foreign currency to the bank.

CURRENCY OPTIONS. A currency option provides one party the right, but not the obligation, to buy or sell a specified amount of currency at a specified rate of exchange, on or before a certain date. There is no risk of loss for the purchaser. That is, if the exchange rate moves in favor of the option issuer, the option holder is not obligated to exercise it.

Sharing of Risk. To the extent the foregoing alternatives are not viable, the currency devaluation risk may need to be shared by the project participants, including the lender. Another alternative is the host-country guarantee, in which the host-country government guarantees to make up any shortfall in debt service and operating costs to the extent a devaluation renders the project company unable to satisfy those obligations.

[5] Offshore Accounts

If the project receives foreign exchange from sale of the products produced, creation of an offshore account is sometimes required by the project lender and is often a prudent structure for the project company even without a lender requirement. Under an offshore account structure, the project's off-take purchaser, pursuant to an agreement between the off-take purchaser and the project company, makes payments in foreign exchange directly to the offshore account, an account offshore from the country in which the project is located. If the account is required by the project lender, the offshore account is part of the lender's collateral for the loan and includes reserves for debt service and operating costs payable in foreign exchange. Periodically, amounts on deposit in the offshore account are used to pay interest and principal on project debt and fund reserve accounts, and the balance is distributed to the project sponsors.

Typically, the host-country central bank will need to approve the amount of foreign exchange that can be retained offshore. The amount is usually related to the amount of operating costs and debt service payments that must be made in foreign exchange over a brief period of time (three months to one year is the customary range). All governmental approvals for creating and maintaining the offshore account must be obtained.

Where the project faces the nonconvertibility and transfer of currency risks, an offshore account can be used to alleviate these risks. All foreign exchange revenues can be deposited into this account, and a reasonable debt service reserve and reserve for foreign currency operating accounts can be retained in it. This strategy can provide the project lenders with additional time to work through a risk problem.

Whenever an offshore collateral account is used, the project lender will want to ensure that all legal risks associated with that account are addressed. These include the following: (i) secure all host-country foreign exchange approvals for creation and maintenance of the account; (ii) create and perfect (to the extent available for perfection) a security interest in this account in the host country, in the country or countries where necessary for the project output purchaser, and where the account is physically located; (iii) notification to, and acceptance by, the project output purchaser that all revenues will be deposited in this account; and (iv) where the host country controls the project company, consider obtaining a waiver by the World Bank of its negative pledge provision.

[6] Special Currency Problems in Large-Scale Projects

Large-scale projects, involving large operating costs and debt service requirements, place extra stress on a developing country's currency conversion and exchange rates. For some very large projects in countries with a small foreign exchange market, payment of quarterly debt service or monthly operating costs can affect a significant percentage of the markets for that day. To avoid stress on the market, amortization of principal, payment dates for interest, and payment dates for bank fees must be considered carefully.

Operation and maintenance expenses must be similarly considered. It might be necessary to pay these costs in a local currency and the debt service in another currency. Otherwise, operation and maintenance expenses, typically paid in priority before debt service, increase the burden on the local currency and the devaluation risk intensifies.

[7] Advance Approvals

Exchange controls can apply to almost every aspect of a project, including repayment of project loans from foreign lenders; equity investment by foreign lenders; imported services, supplies, raw materials, and fuel; and payment of technology license fees to foreign licensors. A case-by-case approach to seeking host governmental exemption for this wide variety of transactions is not prudent. Such an approach is costly, time consuming, and likely to result in project delays. Rather, blanket consents and exemptions for a project should be obtained where possible.

Consent. An exchange control consent is generally subject to revocation by the issuing governmental authority. The revocation is in its discretion.

Exemption. Preferable to a consent is an exemption. An exemption provides permanent relief from transferring funds described in the exemption. It is not generally revocable. An example of an exchange control exemption is one that applies to proceeds from export sales held in an account with a project's foreign lender.

Debt Repayment. The project lender will require that the project company have the rights necessary to convert local currency into the currency used for debt repayment (principal and interest) and lender fees. This is typically a condition precedent to the first advance of the project loan. Also, the lender will require that an opinion of attorneys licensed to practice law in the host country verify that these rights are obtained and in full force and effect.

[8] Summary of Currency Risk Minimization Techniques

Payment in Hard Currency. Payment in hard currency is the best technique to avoid exchange risk. Although there is a risk that hard currency may not be available, this technique virtually eliminates the currency risk. This may be the least favorable approach for the off-take purchaser because it places on the purchaser the obligation to obtain foreign exchange.

Foreign Exchange Risk Insurance. Foreign exchange risk insurance, available from bilateral and multilateral agencies, is also an available alternative. This is discussed in Chapter 20.

Indexed Local Currency Payments. Another technique is to index payments due in local currency under off-take contracts so that the project company is compensated for currency depreciation. This places no obligation on the off-take purchaser for foreign exchange availability. The additional costs could be passed on by the off-take purchaser to its customers.

§ 3.03 PERMIT, CONCESSION, AND LICENSE RISK

[1] Permits

The project company must apply for, obtain, and maintain in full force and effect, all governmental permits necessary for the ownership, development, construction, start-up, operation, and financing of a project. The need for these is particularly significant in large infrastructure projects, such as energy production facilities and mining or other natural resource exploitation projects. To the extent that any significant permit is not obtained or maintained, the project will likely be unable to operate, thereby producing a shortfall in revenue, default under debt instruments, and possibly subject the project to damage payments under project contracts, such as off-take and fuel agreements or complete termination.

The transnational project, however, goes beyond this classic description of the project finance permit risk. In a transnational project, the very government that supports the project could, indirectly, remove support later by slowing the permit process to a crawl or outright denying the issuance of a needed permit. To reduce the likelihood of this occurring, protections in an implementation agreement, discussed in Chapter 14, are typically negotiated.

In an implementation agreement, among other things, the host government agrees that it will do one or a combination of the following: waive all permit requirements, to the extent it is able legally to do so; pay the project sponsor any increased costs incurred due to a delay, to the extent the failure to issue the permit can be cured by money; or guarantee that a list of agreed-upon permits, if completely and accurately applied for by the project company, will be issued.

Post-issuance permit risks within the control of the government, such as permit revocation, requiring additional permits at a later date, failure to renew permits, and imposition of adverse terms and conditions on a project after a permit is issued, can be addressed in the implementation agreement in a similar manner. To the extent these types of post-issuance risks are within the control of the project company, they can be managed to the extent the government does not use this right in a way discriminatory to the project or as a form of indirect expropriation.

The implementation agreement approach is not without problems. Serious legal issues arise about whether a governmental agency can waive all permit requirements. Local law must be consulted to determine whether such a commitment is legal and enforceable.

[2] Concessions and Licenses

The right granted by a host government to a foreign entity to develop, own, construct, and operate a project is sometimes granted by the host government in a concession or license.[8] The terms are often used interchangeably.

A concessions agreement is used in a build-own-transfer (BOT) project finance structure.[9] Under this structure, a private entity is awarded

---

[8] *See generally* Alejandro P. Radzyminski, *Private Investment in Infrastructure Concessions: Legal Obstacles and Incentives* (Inter-Am. Dev. Bank), Sept. 15–16, 1977; Viktor Soloveytchik, *New Perspectives for Concessions Agreements: A Comparison of Hungarian Law and the Draft Laws of Belarus, Kazakhstan, and Russia*, 16 Hous. J. Int'l L. 261 (1993).

[9] *See generally* Marc Frilet, *Some Universal Issues in BOT Projects for Public Infrastructures*, 14 Int'l Construction L. Rev. 499 (1997); Tore Wiwen-Nilsson, *Underlying Conditions for Successful Infrastructure BOT Projects*, 14 Int'l Construction L. Rev. 513 (1997).

the right to build and operate a project that would otherwise be developed, owned, and operated by the host government. It is a temporary privatization in the sense that at the end of the concession, the project is transferred to the government.

The BOT structure is typically founded in a concessions agreement among the host government (or a government entity), the project company, and, in some cases, the project sponsors. The concessions agreement gives the project company the concession to develop, construct, and operate the project. Also, the government might agree to provide certain negotiated support to the project, ranging from infrastructure development to central government guarantees of its agency's obligation to purchase facility output.

The concessions agreement allows the government to retain control over the management of the project. In doing so, the host government might require various protections in the concessions agreement. These include service requirements from the project company throughout the concessions term; rate regulation over facility output; a sufficient operation, maintenance, and repair procedure so that the project transferred at the end of the concessions term retains value; milestone dates that must be achieved, such as construction completion dates; and rights of the host government to terminate the concession if certain events occur to the project company or to project sponsors.

Because of the role of the host government in a successful project financing, project sponsors and project lenders require certain assurances from the government, either in a concession, license, law, or separate agreement. These include the following: assurances of raw material supply; work visas for management; acquisition of necessary real estate rights; and resolution of the risk allocation for the types of political risks discussed below, including expropriation and repatriation of profits.

In addition, depending upon the terms of the concession or license, it might be prudent to secure the approval of the host government of the underlying project arrangements. For example, if the term of the concession is tied to the achievement of an agreed-upon equity return for the project sponsor, which is determined by the financing arrangements, approval by the host

government of the financing terms might alleviate later disputes over the achievement of the target return.

Other considerations include approval of development and construction plans; whether the project lender is permitted to take a security interest in the concession or license; the lender's ability to operate the project upon a default; the ability of the project lender to cure defaults by the project company under the terms of the concession or license; and whether a transfer of the concession or license by the project lender following a foreclosure requires further consent.

The host government might not be able to provide complete assurances on these concerns, however. Constitutional prohibitions, limitations in laws, and political necessities and conveniences limit actions for most governments. To that extent, project sponsors and project lenders must accept some political risk, such as these. Despite these restrictions, however, governments can agree in advance to attend meetings and cooperate with the project sponsor and project lender in resolving project difficulties.

§ 3.04 EXPROPRIATION RISK

Nationalization by the host country of project assets or rights, or the equity ownership of the project, in an arbitrary, discriminatory way, or without just compensation, is the expropriation risk. It can be accomplished in a single, sweeping governmental seizure, although this is increasingly rare.

More threatening to a project is the type of expropriation that can take place over time, in a series of so-called creeping acts that collectively result in an expropriatory act. Creeping expropriation is, perhaps, the most feared risk, by which the host government uses a combination of taxes, fees, and other charges and devices to increase its share of the project's profits.

Failure to pay "just compensation" for such a taking is considered a violation of international law. The determination of what is just compensation is an evolving concept. For example, the U.S. view has been that compensation is just when it is "prompt, adequate and effective." This standard is emerging as the international standard, as well.[10]

Under this standard, the equity holders would be entitled to a payment equivalent to the "value of the expropriated property as a 'going concern.'" The payment would be in convertible currency. Often, any debt outstanding on the expropriated property is assumed by, or kept current by, the expropriating government, in an effort to maintain good lending relationships.

The expropriation risk should be analyzed carefully in projects that are particularly vulnerable to expropriation.[11] These include energy production projects, oil and gas pipeline projects, roads, railways, airports, and seaports. The ability to obtain assurance against the expropriation risk varies with the government concerned. Mitigation of this risk through sovereign guarantees is discussed in Chapter 20.

An offshore collateral account can be used to alleviate the expropriation risk. An offshore account, funded with a sufficient debt-service reserve account, may give the project lenders a more lengthy time to work with the host country to change the expropriation. Other approaches that may be useful include co-financing the project with multilateral or bilateral agencies, and requiring a host-country agreement where the host country agrees not to take expropriatory actions. Offshore collateral accounts are discussed in Chapter 26.

§ 3.05 EXPATRIATION

Expatriation is the term applied to the risk that the profits earned in connection with project operation cannot be removed from the host country and repatriated in the home country of the project sponsors. This is a particularly significant risk in countries that prefer to retain the capital in the country, thereby providing financial resources for further investment and economic growth. In some countries, percentage limitations are imposed on the ability to take out profits, while in other countries, the profits must remain in the country for a time.

§ 3.06 CHANGE OF LAW RISK

The change of law risk is the risk that a governmental body, whether legislative, judicial, or executive, will change the legal, regulatory, or judicial frameworks in which a project was developed. The risk is that a *legal* governmental action will affect the ability of the project to service debt or make the project unprofitable. Examples of a change in law that may affect a project include import and export restrictions, taxation, and changes to environmental standards requiring capital improvements.

Because the governmental action is legal, political risk insurers do not typically insure against this risk. However, the host country may be willing to contract with the project sponsor that certain actions will not be taken. If so, such political risk insurance providers may be able to insure against the risk that the contract is repudiated or abrogated.

[1] Import Tariffs
Imposition of import tariffs on project inputs by the host government during the construction or operation phases of a project could increase the project construction costs or operating costs. This is a risk of particular importance where domestic sources are not adequate substitutes, or where the very nature of the project is to process foreign raw materials. The project company should secure all necessary governmental approvals for all importing and exporting countries. Also, an agreement with the host country may be necessary to help guard against future actions.

[2] Export Tariffs
Similarly, export tariffs, quotas, and prohibitions can reduce the revenue of a project where the project output is sold outside of the host country. These types of expenses and restrictions diminish the ability of the project to mitigate losses during a period of uncertainty, economic or political, in the host country. Similar to import restrictions discussed above, the project company should

---

[10] *See* RESTATEMENT (THIRD) OF THE FOREIGN RELATIONS LAW OF THE UNITED STATES § 712 (1987).

[11] *See generally* Frank C. Shaw, *Reconciling Two Legal Cultures in Privatizations and Large-Scale Capital Projects in Latin America*, 30 LAW & POL'Y INT'L BUS. 147 (1999).

secure all necessary governmental approvals for all importing and exporting countries, and consider a host-country agreement to help guard against future actions.

[3] Production or Consumption Controls

The host government could decide to limit production or consumption of natural resources to the extent necessary to achieve short-term economic goals. Also, trade alliances, informal government agreements, trade sanctions, Organization of Petroleum Exporting Countries (OPEC) quotas, and the like may result in these measures being imposed on the project.

[4] Taxes

Generally. The power to tax is the power to destroy. Tax policy is a particularly tempting tool for a government to eliminate, or force renegotiation of, a project. Alternatively, host-government financial difficulties could be improved, in part, by special taxes imposed on the project, or on the entire industry in which the project operates. These taxes may be politically attractive where the project is owned primarily by foreign investors, or financed by foreign lenders, in which case taxes on repatriation of profits and interest earnings are concerns.

Tax policy, whether manifest in income tax, stamp taxes, mortgage taxes, or tax withholding, may affect a project's economics. Besides new taxes, the effect of cancellation or modification of favorable tax treatment (tax holidays, reduced tax rates) must also be considered. International tax treaties, and the effect and likelihood of changes to them, must also be analyzed.

Project viability, including the amount of the economic return on a developer's investment in a project, can be affected by the level of taxes, duties, levies, and similar governmental charges. Project developers attempt to structure the development company so that local taxes are minimized. Also, the structuring process will include analysis and use of double taxation treaties, bilateral trade treaties, and multilateral trade treaties. Typically, duties, levies, and other charges are paid by the development entity but included as a cost of business, which increases the price of the goods or services produced at the project.

Taxes on Income. The project entity will be structured in the way most appropriate to minimize payment of income taxes, minimize withholding, and maximize the use of tax concessions. In general, foreign income taxes can be credited to the project sponsor in the developer's home country. To the extent the taxes paid in the host country are more than the tax rates applicable in the home country, no credit or carry forward is typically allowed.

To the extent taxes cannot be offset by a tax credit in the home country of the sponsor, the cost of the good or service produced will necessarily be increased. This is also the case if the tax rate in the sponsor's home country is less than the tax rate in the foreign country because no credit or carry forward is typically allowed. Thus, foreign taxes may become an additional cost to the project sponsor, which is passed on to the offtake purchaser or user in the form of higher costs.

Customs Duties. Customs duties, which are amounts imposed on imported and, less commonly, exported goods, are typically paid by the project company. The costs are then included in the cost of goods produced at the project and passed through to the customer or user in the form of a higher cost.

Withholding Tax on Payment of Interest. In structuring the financing, it is important to determine the extent of tax withholding on the payment of interest by the project company to its lenders. In some situations, tax treaties can form the basis of eliminating or minimizing liability, through use of a bank's branches in other countries.

Generally, interest paid to governments or agencies of governments, such as export-import banks, are exempt from withholding liability. But, withholding of taxes on interest income is applicable to a commercial lender. A commercial lender, in turn, requires that the borrower reimburse it for any withholding. This withholding, even if later returned to the lender, could cause the financial feasibility of the project to deteriorate.

Nondiscrimination. It is useful to place the project on an equal level with other projects that might follow. A nondiscrimination clause can assist the project in not being legislated out of existence. An example follows:

Nondiscrimination. The [*Host Government*] covenants with the [*Project Company*] that it shall not enact any law, rule, or regulation the effect of which is to discriminate against the project in any manner whatsoever, it being the stated intention, policy, and agreement of the [*Host Government*] that all projects [*describe project purpose/output*] shall be treated equally, irrespective of location, pricing, participants, lenders, or any other factor. The scope of this provision shall include any tax, whether franchise tax, excise tax, income tax, profits tax, dividend tax, sales tax, purchase tax, occupation tax, property tax, or any other tax howsoever calculated or applied; any duty, whether customs, minerals, fuels, or any other duty howsoever calculated or applied; and any other burden of taxation whatsoever now existing or imposed in the future.

[5] Environmental Controls

Project capital costs, operating expenses, and production can all be affected by the imposition of more stringent environmental regulation by the host government. In some cases, these changes could render certain technologies or fuel sources no longer effective economically.

[6] Regulation and Deregulation

For projects in countries with regulatory regimes in place that offer predictability in off-take pricing, deregulation to market pricing, or a less stringent regulatory scheme, could result in a decrease in project revenues. Conversely, regulation of a formerly unregulated economic sector or industry can have a similar negative effect on a project.

[7] Price Controls

The imposition of price controls by a host government could negatively interfere with project success. The practical implications of price controls should be included in project economic projections. Where appropriate, a host-country agreement in which the government agrees not to impose price controls, may be necessary.

[8] Privatization of Suppliers or Purchasers

In a project where output is sold to a governmental or quasi-governmental agency or where fuel or other inputs are purchased from a government or governmental agency, the project company should consider the effects of a governmental privatization on the contract obligations of these entities. An agreement with the host country that expressly addresses the effect on the project of a privatization program should be seriously considered.

[9] Change in Foreign Laws

In some projects, foreign input suppliers or output purchasers are important to the project success. In these cases, the effects of a change in the laws of the jurisdiction where these entities are located must be examined.

§ 3.07 POLITICAL VIOLENCE, CIVIL UNREST, WAR, AND OTHER POLITICAL FORCE MAJEURE EVENTS

The risk of political violence, whether manifested in civil war or revolution, regional or world war, insurrection or civil strife, sabotage or terrorism, can affect a project's construction or operation, ability to service debt or even the very existence of the project. Political risk insurance for this type of risk is discussed in Chapter 20.

§ 3.08 POLITICAL COLLAPSE AND SUCCESSION

In most countries, political succession and the concomitant transfer of power is a risk all too often overlooked. The risk is that the party achieving power, whether central, state, or local, will seek to undo some portion or all of the predecessor party's work in connection with support of a project.

For project finance transactions, particularly infrastructure projects important to the host government's economy, there are possible warning signs that might suggest this risk is more likely. These include a lack of support for privatization programs; failure of the governing party to maintain a consensus on bidding and contracting programs; corruption; no competitive bidding program; the degree of perceived openness of government in awarding contracts; contracting that does not appear to reflect terms received in similarly situated countries; press criticism of other projects in operation or development; degree of nationalist sentiment; historical experience in governing party transfer of political power; and stability of power where family members of a ruler receive preferential economic treatment.

Political succession risk can lead to a reversal of previous decisions. The basis for the reversal could be a means of correcting perceived corruption or cronyism, to solicit "contributions," and to reward political supporters. The risk can occur as a result of violent overthrow or election.

It is improbable that a project sponsor will be much more effective at guessing election results than political professionals. Perhaps the most sound way to avoid major project problems from succession risk is to avoid exclusive close ties to one politician or party; diversity in support should be garnered. Also, "clever," one-sided agreements, real or perceived, should be avoided by negotiating competitive, market-based terms. Competitive bidding programs can help relieve the appearance of impropriety. These broad protections will help ensure that a project can escape, but not avoid, scrutiny after a political succession.

Indeed, changes to contracts negotiated by a previous government in a developing country cannot be completely avoided in most circumstances. In some countries, where legal systems are only now developing, this is particularly true. As protection against this risk, termination provisions and termination payments could be an important protection for the project sponsor.

§ 3.09 PREEMPTION AND PRIORITY

In certain, limited situations, the host government could require preemption or priority rights in connection with raw materials, fuel, and project output. These rights are usually related to energy and fuel access or use during emergencies. These rights should not extend to economic or social policy making or other undefined or loosely defined situations.

§ 3.10 SOVEREIGN RISK

Sovereign risk is the term generally applied by credit-rating agencies to certain debt payment risks. One is the risk that, in a project issuing debt in the cross-border capital markets, a country may impose exchange controls or put other restrictions on the ability of a project to pay foreign debt holders. Another is the ability of a project to service debt denominated in the currency of the project's location. These risks are discussed in greater detail earlier in this chapter.

§ 3.11 BREACH OF UNDERTAKINGS (CONTRACT REPUDIATION)

The host government is a party to at least one of the contracts necessary to develop a project, particularly in developing countries. Examples include obligations of the host government in implementation agreements, concession agreements, and sovereign guarantees. The undertakings range from a commitment to improve roads to financial guarantees of a government-owned company. As with any contractual undertaking, there is a risk that a party will not perform the contract.[12] Unlike contracts between private parties, however, political influences can affect the ability and willingness of the host government to carry out undertakings. This is particularly evident when political power changes and a new regime is faced with unpopular agreements negotiated and signed by its predecessor. The doctrine of sanctity of contracts[13] and repudiation of contracts is discussed at length in Chapter 18

§ 3.12 COLLATERAL RISK

In domestic projects in such countries as the United States and Great Britain, the laws governing debtor-creditor relations, the creation

---

[12] *See* Danielle Mazzini, *Stable International Contracts in Emerging Markets: An Endangered Species?*, 15 B. U. Int'l L. J. 343 (1997) (conflict between Enron Corporation and the Indian state of Maharashtra, which unilaterally terminated its power purchase agreement with an Enron affiliate).

[13] Nagla Nassar, Sanctity of Contracts Revisited: A Study in the Theory and Practice of Long-Term International Commercial Transactions 35 (1995).

and perfection of security interests, the granting and registration of mortgages, and the bankruptcies of borrowers are highly developed and highly protective of creditors' rights. Lenders to projects in developing countries face a much more uncertain legal environment.[14]

Civil law countries generally do not recognize the floating charge and do not provide for security over inventory, receivables, or other moveable assets. Many countries do not permit mortgages to be registered in foreign currency, and the value of the collateral can therefore be significantly eroded by devaluations. In addition, many countries place significant restrictions on the ability of foreign entities to operate or purchase projects upon foreclosure, especially projects that are important to the country's economic development plans.

The legal infrastructure of many developing countries is emerging and is changing rapidly. Even where collateral laws are in place, there is no long history of their use or certainty on court interpretation.

Given these problems, project financings in developing countries often require lenders to live with a degree of uncertainty as to effective remedies upon default that is much different from a domestic transaction. This is particularly troublesome in a nonrecourse project finance transaction where the collateral assumes such importance. Lenders with experience in these types of financings have learned to accept that liens on the project assets are often more important for their strategic negotiation value when things go wrong, rather than for their realizable liquidation value upon default.

[1] What Type of Collateral Security Does the Sovereign Government Allow?

The first consideration for the lender or contracting party to understand before entering into project development is the type of collateral security permitted by the laws of the sovereign. Generally, common law countries provide that a lien can be taken for collateral purposes over all assets. Both fixed and floating charges are available. A

floating charge is a lien that attaches to specific assets at the time the charge is enforced. By contrast, civil law countries generally do not provide for security over collateral that attaches on enforcement; therefore, no floating charges are available. Types of collateral grants and enforcement that might present difficulties for the project lender in projects located in developing countries include inventory (moveable assets), accounts receivable (book debts), cash flows, and contract rights.

[2] Are All Local Formalities Complied With?

Local law and practice will require certain formalities be adhered to in connection with lien recording. For example, some civil law countries require protocolization of all security agreements. This is generally accomplished by a local notary translating the collateral agreement into the local language and inserting the agreement into the notary's protocol book, which is kept at the local registry office. An accompanying fee is charged; in some countries, the size of the fee is significant.

[3] What Is the Priority of Lien?

The lien priority rules should be clearly understood. Of particular importance are so-called hidden liens. These are liens that do not appear as a matter of record but are statutory in origin. These include governmental liens, particularly tax liens.

[4] How Is the Lien Enforced?

Beyond seeking the advice of local lawyers and obtaining an opinion of local lawyers that the lien is enforceable, practical questions about enforcement should be explored. For instance, the actual costs of enforcement should be understood. These include legal costs, court taxes, and other costs that may make the liens economically unenforceable.

[5] How Does the Foreclosure Process Work?

Beyond enforceability, the mechanics of the foreclosure process are important. Among the questions that should be posed to local lawyers include the following: whether any restrictions exist on a lender's right to purchase the collateral at foreclosure; whether a lender can use debt owed to it (instead of cash) to bid for the collateral

[14] Richard Walsh, *Pacific Rim Collateral Security Laws: What Happens When the Project Goes Wrong*, 4 STAN. J. L. BUS. & FIN. 115 (1999).

at a foreclosure sale; and whether a private sale is permitted instead of a public sale.

Practical questions of enforcement that are unique to project financings must not be overlooked. For example, usually the only practical ability of a lender to be repaid is if the foreclosed project can continue to operate and be made operable at a profit. Local law should be consulted to determine whether the lender can operate the project upon foreclosure. Related questions include whether permits and governmental approvals for the operation of the project are assignable to the lender; and whether there are restrictions on foreign ownership or operation of the project that affect foreclosure value.

Finally, the costs and time to undertake and complete a foreclosure proceeding should be understood. In some countries, foreclosure proceedings may take as long as ten years. In other countries, the risk is not length of time, but the immensity of court and other costs associated with a foreclosure.

[6] Collateral Trusts

It is often prudent for one lender to hold all security interests in project collateral for all lenders. This simplifies the closing process, reduces transaction costs, allows for easy transferability of loan interests to new lenders, and provides for efficient credit administration. Nonetheless, the local law of the host country might not recognize this and similar trust arrangements. Local lawyers should be consulted to determine whether this or alternate structures for collateral can be used and enforced.

[7] Real Property

The ability of a foreign lender to take a security interest in real property in the host country, or to own it after a foreclosure, is not necessarily available in every country. Indonesia and some states in India are examples of jurisdictions where foreign ownership is restricted. Local law should be examined to determine the flexibility of the lender. In some situations, a bank in the host country can be used as a collateral trustee for the other project lenders.

[8] Interaction Among Risks

The interaction between the collateral risk and other risks discussed in this chapter is impor-

tant. For example, a currency risk exists in every foreclosure proceeding if the lender cannot sell the collateral for hard currency but, instead, must receive the local currency. Also, any required foreign exchange approval must include authorization for proceeds from the sale of collateral.

Currency risk can also exist in other ways. For example, in countries that require a lender to denominate the value of a mortgage in local currency, devaluation risks exist and can erode the value of the lender's collateral. Although the loan agreement can require the borrower to deliver a new mortgage if the value is exceeded because of currency devaluations, the risk of intervening mortgages could sabotage this solution. A recourse obligation may be needed in such situations.

§ 3.13 LAW AND LEGAL SYSTEM RISKS

Additional risks are associated with foreign investment, lending, regulatory and other laws, or the lack of them, and differing legal systems and cultures.[15] The local laws[16] of the jurisdiction where the project is located should be carefully examined by the project participants, particularly the project sponsor and lenders, early in the structuring and documentation process. Advice of local lawyers should be obtained, as is discussed more completely in Chapter 30.

The legal systems of most emerging countries continue to be less developed than in industrialized countries.[17] This results in a degree of uncertainty as to the legal environment the project must be constructed and operated in. It also provides uncertainty to the project lenders, if compelled to enforce their rights. Significant considerations include access of foreign entities to the judicial system, enforceability of foreign

---

[15] See generally Shaw, supra note 11; Ken Miyamoto, Measuring Local Legal Risk Premium in Project Finance Bonds, 40 VA. J. INT'L L. 1125 (2000).

[16] See Don Wallace, Jr., Host Country Legislation: A Necessary Condition?, 24 FORDHAM INT'L L. J. 1396 (2001); Wallace, UNCITRAL Draft Legislation Guide on Privately Financed Infrastructure Projects: Achievements and Prospects, 8 TUL. J. INT'L & COMP. L. 283 (2000).

[17] Michael Gordon, Of Aspirations and Operations: The Governance of Multinational Enterprises by Third World Nations, 16 U. MIAMI INTER-AM. L. REV. 301 (1984).

judgments, whether arbitration is permitted for dispute resolution, and enforceability of arbitration awards.

Requirements for a change in law are not without precedent. Sometimes projects cannot move forward past the development phase to the financing phase without a change in the local law. An implementation agreement is the usual document where changes in law are described and required as a precondition to project construction. Whether any particular project can obtain legislative relief depends upon such factors as the size of the project, its social and economic importance to the sovereign government, and the political and public support for it. In infrastructure projects, uncertain legal structures also result in increased cost to the host-country citizens, who ultimately bear the cost of the risk premium added to the cost of project output. This risk premium is an attempt to compensate the project lender (through loan terms), or project investor (through higher output prices), for the legal risks taken.[18]

[1] Choice of Law

Financing documents are seldom governed by the sovereign law of the jurisdiction where the project is located. Rather, the law of a financial center, such as New York or London, is selected. This is because the commercial laws and legal precedents in those centers tend to be more settled than in other locations, and the lenders are therefore more comfortable with them. The local law of the sovereign must be examined to determine if that choice of law will be enforced in the local courts.[19]

[2] Agent for Process and Submission to Jurisdiction

Beyond securing a choice of law provision that is enforceable, project finance lenders should also consider the following: appointment by the borrower of an agent for the service of process *in the lender's country*; and a submission by the borrower to the jurisdiction of the courts of the lender's country.

[3] Dispute Resolution

Contracts used in a project financing are often governed by the law of the sovereign. These include the construction contract, off-take contract, and fuel agreements. The dispute resolution procedures in these agreements are important and should be carefully analyzed with local lawyers. Dispute resolution is discussed in Chapter 31.

[4] Fees, Approvals, and Filings

Local law sometimes requires governmental approval of the borrower's performance under the financing agreements. These include exchange control approvals, which are discussed elsewhere in this chapter; registration with the agency responsible for regulating lenders; registration of loans; and so-called alien's landholding licenses that are required if a foreign lender obtains any interest in local property, including a mortgage. Failure to obtain these approvals may result in unenforceability of the collateral documents or voiding of the loan transaction. Also various fees may need to be paid in connection with loan transactions, such as filing fees and stamp duties.

[5] Legal Expertise and Experience

The expertise and experience of local lawyers and judges are sometimes less developed than project sponsors and lenders are accustomed to in industrialized countries. This is not a reflection on the abilities of these lawyers but, rather, a reflection of a lack of sophisticated commercial transactions in these countries and a lack of experience with the type of issues in a dispute that arise in them.

[6] General Business Law and Regulation

Besides laws relating to the collateral and the enforcement of liens, general laws applicable to business and the predictability of the business environment are not necessarily available in all countries. The availability and substance of laws and regulations concerning competition, intellectual property protection, and similar business protections should be examined and

---

[18] *See* Note, *Measuring Local Legal Risk Premium in Project Finance Bonds*, 40 Va. J. Int'l L. 1125 (2000) (exploration of differences between investment grade ratings in civil law and common law countries on issue of legal system risk).

[19] *See generally* Raymer McQuiston, *Drafting an Enforceable Guaranty in an International Financing Transaction: A Lender's Perspective*, 10 Int'l Tax & Bus. Law. 138 (1993).

understood as part of the project development process.

[7] Waiver of Sovereign Immunity

In agreements with the host-country government and with entities controlled by the government, a waiver of sovereign immunity is important. Sovereign immunity precludes an allegedly wronged party from bringing a cause of action, valid as it may be, against a government unless the government consents. It is generally agreed that any agreement with a government should contain a waiver of the doctrine of sovereign immunity. Such a clause permits the nongovernmental party to commence litigation before an independent body, and if wronged, to receive a judgment against a government.

[8] Legal Cultures

A clash of legal cultures is common in project finance transactions. The interplay of investors and attorneys experienced in common law legal traditions, on the one hand, and their counterparts experienced in civil law traditions, on the other, can require a reconciliation of goals, expectations, and risk allocation with the realities of a different legal climate for project development to proceed successfully.[20]

§ 3.14 ILLIQUIDITY OF EQUITY INVESTMENT

Equity investments in infrastructure projects are not necessarily as liquid as projects in other industries. This is particularly true in developing countries, where equity markets are only now emerging. Some governments impose equity sales restrictions on project sponsors, particularly in the early years of a project, to help ensure sponsor support, financial stability, and management experience for the project. Also, where governments want the ownership ultimately in local hands, equity transfers will be restricted until a sufficient local investment base develops to purchase interests in the project.

[20] For an excellent overview of the challenges presented by differing legal cultures, and an examination of how those cultures are being reconciled in Latin America, *see* Shaw, *supra* note 11.

§ 3.15 FREEZING OR BLOCKING ORDERS

Freezing or blocking orders are designed to block currency exchange to protect national interests or to maintain national defense. Examples are those imposed against Iraq, Iran, and Libya. This type of governmental action is not easily predictable but could be damaging to a project.

§ 3.16 EXPORT PROHIBITIONS

Wherein a project exports all or part of its production to another country, limitations on the sale of that production could alter project feasibility. Consequently, the history of relations with the country or region to which the production is sold should be analyzed. In addition, a governmental commitment not to prohibit exports by the project could be helpful. However, during periods of war or national security emergency, governments have prohibited exports.

§ 3.17 PRICE CONTROLS AND REGULATION

The risk that the government could impose price controls on the product produced at the project, or otherwise regulate the price of the product, is an important one. It is particularly important in the infrastructure area, where governments are more likely to consider price controls necessary to stabilize inflation or other economic problems. Energy prices, for example, have been used in developing countries to control inflation.

To control this risk, the government's commitment to free-market action should be gauged. If the prices of product output are subject to price regulation, such as through a tariff, the tariff should be well developed and the procedure for changing the tariff well understood by the project developer.

§ 3.18 COMMERCIAL OR POLITICAL – IT MAY BE BOTH

It is always tempting in a book such as this to over-classify, and thereby oversimplify, descriptions of risks. Where a project involves the host government, or an entity controlled by the host government, distinctions between commercial risks and political risks are blurred.

For example, in a privately owned electrical generation project in a developing country, it is common for a state-owned utility to purchase all power produced at the project. If the state-owned utility defaults on its obligation to purchase the project output, it will be difficult, if not impossible, to determine whether the default is politically motivated or not.

The classification of the risk is of more than academic interest. If the reason for the default is political, such as where the government fails to perform under a standby funding agreement designed to guarantee the utility's payment obligations, political risk insurance may cover the associated losses. If, on the other hand, the default is based on a lack of funds due to mismanagement, the risk is a commercial one. As such, it is not likely to be covered by any insurance.

Yet, the reason for the default could be partially political, and partially commercial. For example, the utility's payment breach could be based, in part, on a change in government tariff policy that reduced the revenues earned by the utility. However, that same breach could also be commercial in nature if the utility failed to respond to lower revenue expectations with labor cuts and other cost-savings measures.

CHAPTER FOUR

PROJECT FINANCE COMMERCIAL RISKS

§ 4.01 INTRODUCTION TO COMMERCIAL RISKS

Besides the transnational risks discussed in the preceding chapter, commercial risks also exist in a transnational project financing. These risks are not limited to international projects but, rather, exist in both domestic and international project financings.

An exhaustive list of potential commercial risks would result in many pages of print and would doubtless miss many risks individual to particular industries. A fully developed business acumen is unnecessary to understand that identification of many risks is dependent upon an understanding of the specific project, in the specific industry, at a specific site, and so forth. The following discussion will assist both the novice and experienced project financier with more than a serendipitous approach to risk identification.

[1] Probability of Risk Evolving Into a Project Problem

The potential for a risk actually occurring is not small. Results of a published study that 82 percent of projects financed encountered *some* form of trouble are perhaps the best argument for a risk identification approach to project financing coupled with a complete due diligence process. The study revealed the following problems and frequency of occurrence: construction cost overruns (71%), completion delays (59%), inaccurate cash flow projections (35%), market problems (one project), political risks (one project), and project inefficiencies (one project). Nine of the seventeen projects (53%) in the study were described by the researcher as in "severe trouble," with two projects ending in bankruptcy and six incapable of generating sufficient cash to cover principal payments.[1]

[2] Due Diligence

Due diligence in a project financing is an important process for risk identification. It is an inter-disciplinary process of legal, technical, environmental, and financial specialties, designed to detect events that might result in total or partial project failure. Participants involved in this process, besides the project sponsors, are lawyers, engineering firms, fuels consultants, market consultants, insurance consultants, financial advisors, and environmental consultants. The level of due diligence undertaken involves considerations of time available, cost, and the type of project.

[3] Feasibility Study in Risk Identification

In many project financings, project development has progressed beyond the feasibility study, which gives details about whether the project is financially viable, when lawyers are instructed to prepare necessary documentation. In some projects, however, lawyers participate in or comment on the feasibility study. Typically, these internal studies consider the availability and cost of basic project requirements, such as the market for the product produced, raw material supply, site acquisition cost and suitability of the site, construction costs, operating costs, and financing costs, all to determine whether projected cash flow from the operation of the project is sufficient to pay debt, operating expenses, and an attractive investment return. Lenders prepare independent feasibility studies to augment the study prepared by the project sponsor.

The feasibility study is a useful mechanism for setting forth a description of the project, the goals

of the project sponsor, sensitivities of the project to various construction, start-up, and operating risks, an analysis of financing alternatives, and credit enhancement. It will include estimated capital needs, debt service capabilities, revenue projections from output sales, operating costs, and market projections. Typically, variables such as fuel cost fluctuation, interest rates, currency exchange rates, and others are examined in alternative scenarios. The study enables the sponsor and lenders to analyze the potential of the project before any party unnecessarily commit resources when the project is not economically feasible. The resultant study, of course, must conclude that the project will have sufficient viability to pay debt service, operations and maintenance costs, provide a return on equity, and, if necessary, provide for contingencies.

[4] Categories of Commercial Risk

There are nine categories of commercial risks attributable to failed projects. Three causes for project failure exist during the design engineering and construction phases of the project: a delay in the projected completion of the project and the resultant delay in the commencement of cash flow, an increase in capital needed to complete construction, and the insolvency or lack of experience of the contractor or a major supplier. The other six basic risks generally exist in the start-up and operating stages of a project: technology failure or obsolescence, changes in law, uninsured losses, shifts in availability or price of raw materials, shifts in demand or price of output, and negligence in project operation. The mere presence of these risks does not prohibit the financing of the project on a nonrecourse basis, however. As discussed in Chapter 20, proper selection of credit enhancement and monitoring methods can combine to improve or eliminate these risks.

§ 4.02 CREDIT RISKS

Allocation of risks to other parties in a project financing is only a useful exercise if the parties assigned the risk are creditworthy; that is, they must have the financial resources, both now and in the future, to perform the obligations

---

[1] Grover R. Castle, *Project Financing – Guidelines for the Commercial Banker*, J. COM. BANK LENDING, Apr. 1975, at 16.

undertaken. In the project finance equation, the project company's lack of creditworthiness, therefore, is exchanged for the creditworthiness of the other project participants.

Among the project participants that must be creditworthy, include the project sponsors, to the extent they provide completion or support guarantees; the contractor, operator, and fuel supplier for performance of the construction contract, operating agreement, and fuel supply contract, respectively, and the damages payable under each contract; the off-take purchasers and users of the project, which in many projects are the foundations of the project financings; the host government, to the extent it undertakes financial support pursuant to guarantees or support agreements; and insurance companies, reinsurers, title insurers, and payment and performance sureties, to perform their obligations under the insurance policies and bonds issued by them.

§ 4.03 INCREASE IN CONSTRUCTION COSTS

The risk that construction of the project will cost more than the funds available from the construction loan, other debt sources, and equity is perhaps the most important risk for the participants in a project financing. Construction costs exceed estimates for various reasons, including inaccurate engineering and plans, inflation, and problems with project start-up.[2] This cost overrun risk may result in increased debt service costs during construction, unavailability of sufficient funds to complete construction, and even if funded, in the inability of the project owner to pay increased interest and principal that result from the additional debt required to complete construction.

Improvement of the cost overrun risk is possible even where the contractor has not assumed that risk in a fixed-price turnkey contract. For example, in the case of a cost overrun, contractual

undertakings can provide the infusion of additional equity by the project sponsor, other equity participants, or standby equity participants. Similarly, standby funding agreements for additional financing, either from the construction lender or subordinated debt lent by project participants or third parties, can be used. Another alternative is the establishment of an escrow fund or contingency account under which the project sponsor establishes a fund that is available to complete the project in case of a cost overrun.

§ 4.04 DELAY IN COMPLETION

Likewise, a delay in project completion may result in an increase in project construction costs and a concomitant increase in debt service costs. The delay may also affect the scheduled flow of project revenues necessary to cover debt service and operations and maintenance expenses. In addition, a delay in project completion may result in damage payments payable under, or termination of, project contracts, such as fuel supply and output contracts. Probably no better example of the potential impact of a delay in construction on project revenues and expenses is the nuclear power plant experience.[3]

Completion risks can be allocated or mitigated in the following ways: fixed price, firm completion date construction contracts; performance bonds; project sponsor completion guarantees; selection of proven technology with which the contractor and operator have experience; host-government guarantees; funding of reserves to cover cost overruns and other completion costs; and output purchase agreements and input contracts that provide flexibility in project commencement.

§ 4.05 FORCE MAJEURE IN CONSTRUCTION CONTRACTS

International projects are structured with, and negotiated among, many diverse parties, often from different countries. Sometimes, the

---

[2] Larry Wynant, *Essential Elements of Project Financing*, HARV. BUS. REV., May–June 1980, at 167 (site modification requirements caused an increase in construction costs of $200 million for project financing of a copper mining development).

[3] *See* Witten & Hecht, *Whoops, There Goes Washington: Is California Next?*, 15 PAC. L.J. 955 (1984).

underlying project contracts are negotiated by separate teams of negotiators and lawyers, resulting in uncoordinated force majeure provisions. This could result in a situation, for example, in which the contractor is excused from its obligation to complete the project by a date certain, whereas the off-take contract does not give the project company similar relief. The result could be a terminated off-take contract. Even where the inconsistencies are not of such dramatic proportions, the effect on the project's schedule or economics may be significant.

Inconsistent force majeure provisions can be cured with a so-called resurrection clause, in which the contractor agrees with the project company that where force majeure inconsistencies exist between contracts, the contractor will not receive relief greater than the relief available to the project company under other relevant contracts. In the earlier example, the contractor could not have been excused from performance to the extent such excuse would have resulted in a project delay of such length that the off-take contract would be terminated. However, a less extensive delay would be permissible.

§ 4.06 EXPERIENCE AND RESOURCES OF CONTRACTOR

The experience, reputation, and reliability of the contractor, subcontractors, and suppliers for a project should ensure the timely completion of the project at the stated price. Similarly, the contractor, subcontractors, and suppliers must possess the financial resources necessary to support contractual provisions relating to liquidated damage payments, workmanship guarantees, indemnities, and self-insurance obligations. An important part of this analysis is the record of the contractor in completing projects on time and at required performance levels.

The contractor must possess sufficient human and technical resources necessary to satisfy contractual requirements. The potential risk is that the contractor or a major subcontractor or equipment supplier will be unable to perform a contractual obligation because of a low commitment to the industry, insufficient resources, or lack of knowledge or experience.

In an international project, the contractor should be particularly adept at working with the local labor force. Local construction site managers, with local experience, are particularly beneficial in reducing the risk of local labor problems.

§ 4.07 BUILDING MATERIALS

A project finance risk often overlooked in industrialized countries is the risk of unavailability of building materials necessary for project construction. Although theoretically any material is available at the right price, the price and time necessary to manufacture or transport the material can affect project economics in a manner similar to cost overruns and delays. Of particular concern is the impact of import and export laws when the project is either located abroad or where imported materials are contemplated for construction. Local law should not be overlooked regarding the availability of construction materials.

§ 4.08 FACILITY SITE

Pre-existing conditions on the project site can affect both construction and long-term operations, especially if the site has hazardous waste problems. Examples of site condition problems that can affect the project price, construction schedule, and operations include geological formations, ongoing mining, and other underground site conditions that affect the cost or schedule for construction.

§ 4.09 TECHNOLOGY

Project finance participants cannot ignore new technologies because new technologies can result in profitable project financings. Nevertheless, without credit enhancement to cover the risk that the new technology will not perform as expected, project financings do not often involve new technologies because unproven technologies are not sufficiently predictable and therefore form an unstable basis for a project financing. An example of this risk is exemplified by the early technology difficulties in solid-waste resource recovery projects. New technology, however, can be used in a project financing provided the obligation to repay project debt is supported by a guarantee of technological performance from the creditworthy participant that owns or licenses the technology, such as the equipment supplier or contractor.

In general, technology used in a project financing must have a good record of performance; the contractor must have experience with the technology; the technology guarantee must be adequate to support the underlying debt; and maintenance and overhauls must be cost-effective. Also, the technology must be able to satisfy the performance requirements for the project, in availability and efficiency.

Often, the only operating and performance data available for a new technology is from a small test facility. Although the data from such a facility is instructive on technology performance, it is not always conclusive, particularly where the ultimate project constructed is planned to be much larger in size.

Technology risk is also present in circumstances where the technology is of such a proprietary nature that it is unmarketable, nontransferable, or otherwise inflexible in a foreclosure proceeding. In such circumstances, the project lender is unable to continue project operation after a foreclosure and must choose whether to sell the project at a distressed price or sell it to the technology owner.

The technology risk can be covered by completion guarantees and other credit enhancement. These are discussed in Chapter 20.

§ 4.10 CONSTRUCTION OF RELATED FACILITIES

International projects, particularly in developing countries, often require the simultaneous construction of facilities related to the project. Large gas pipelines, docks, railways, manufacturing facilities, and electrical interconnection and transportation facilities may be required. Each of the related facilities will affect the success of the underlying project and each must therefore be examined to determine the risks involved. Construction synchronization is perhaps the most important initial concern to the sponsors of the underlying project.

Of equal concern is compatibility of systems. For example, rail beds, roads and docks must be adequately designed to conform to the requirements of the project. Even existing infrastructure must be examined to determine whether the existing facilities can satisfy project requirements.

Although an engineering firm or project sponsor personnel can initially certify that existing and planned facility design will satisfy the requirements for the project, changes may occur. The project sponsor may want to contract with the developers of the related facility, or the government, to ensure that existing and planned facilities will not be modified to a less desirable standard.

§ 4.11 SHORTFALLS IN MINERAL RESERVES

For minerals projects, sponsors and lenders receive exploration surveys that estimate the amount of production that can be expected from project operations. If the actual production is significantly less than the survey projections, less revenue will be available to service the debt.

§ 4.12 RAW MATERIAL SUPPLY AND UTILITIES

Similar to the role of building material supply dependability in production of revenue, the project must be assured of a supply of raw materials and utilities at a cost within the acceptable ranges of financial projections. The formality of the commitments for the supply depends on the availability of the materials in the project area. For example, a supply of wood chips necessary for a waste wood-burning energy project in the Pacific Northwest may be sufficiently assured that no need exists to contract for a 100 percent supply. Yet, under various scenarios, such as the limitation of forest processing because of economic conditions in the lumber industry, alternate sources may be needed. In addition, costs of import or export fees, transportation charges, storage costs, stability of product, monopolies, and finance costs, all are potential risks in determining whether an adequate supply exists.

In many projects, long-term requirements contracts are developed to provide the necessary raw material supply at a predictable price to reduce this risk. Less frequent are supply-or-pay contracts, in which a supplier is dependent on some aspect of the project and agrees to either provide the needed raw material or pay a fee to the project. With both contracts, however, the credit of the supplier must be sufficient to ensure performance of the contract.

§ 4.13 CREDITWORTHINESS OF OFF-TAKE PURCHASER

In nonrecourse and limited recourse project financings, lenders base credit appraisals on the projected revenues from the operation of the facility. Because the ability of the project sponsor to produce revenue from project operation is the foundation of a project financing, the contracts constitute the framework for project viability and control the allocation of risks. Revenue-producing contracts, such as off-take agreements, are critical.

The off-take purchaser must be creditworthy; that is, it must have sufficient cash to pay its bills, as proven by past, present, and expected future financial performance. To the extent this is not present, credit enhancement, such as a guarantee by a creditworthy central government or multilateral support, is needed.

In determining creditworthiness of the off-take purchaser, many factors are considered. These include the off-take purchaser's industry ranking; line of business and product lines; sensitivity to price fluctuations; and overall business practices and reputation.

An alternative to credit enhancement is replacement of the off-take purchaser with another off-take purchaser, who in turn must be creditworthy. In remote locations, however, this might not be possible.

§ 4.14 MARKET FOR PRODUCT OR SERVICE

Once produced, of course, the project needs to generate revenue from sales of the product or service. Market risk comes in two forms: price and access to purchasers for sale of the project's output.

Although market studies are performed to estimate the market for the project's output, a crystal ball is sometimes just as helpful unless conservative assumptions are made. These studies include price and market projections. Market forces, over which the project sponsors have little practical control, can undermine the need for the project's output. These include competition from similar projects; tariffs and trade barriers; market access; obsolescence of technology or production processes; emergence of new technologies and processes; and, in government subsidized markets, a willingness of the populace to pay increased, nonsubsidized rates at the level necessary to support a project financing.

Many project financings are based on long-term, take-and-pay contracts, in which one or more purchasers agree to accept the production of the project at a firm or predictable price. (Similarly, *throughput contracts* are used in pipeline projects and *tolling agreements*[4] are used in some energy and processing plant projects.) Provided the credit of the purchaser is adequate, a market exists for the product and the cash flow to the project is assured if the project operates. Yet, product risk does not disappear simply because a long-term take-and-pay contract is executed. Market competition from other producers of the same or similar products or services, new technologies, obsolescence, changing demand, increased operating costs, increased

---

[4]An example is a tolling plant. A tolling plant can be structured with a tolling agreement between a fuel supplier and the project. The fuel supplier has the contractual right to decide when to sell fuel, when to produce power, or when to allow the plant to remain idle. Generally, the fuel supplier pays the project a capacity payment and receives a power price netback from the project.

In another tolling plant structure, it is the power customer who decides when to use fuel, generation quantity, and what market price it will accept. The power customer pays the capacity charge, together with a pass-through of fuel costs and a fee for generation.

production costs, changes in the needs of the purchaser, and other events can combine to render the contract less valuable to the project or to the purchaser.

Where there exists only one potential user of a project's output, such as an electric utility that purchases the output of an electrical generation project, the market risk exists. Typically, the utility will enter into a long-term power purchase agreement. Under that agreement, the utility agrees to purchase the electrical output of the project at an agreed price, thereby creating the market for the output. These agreements are discussed in greater detail in Chapter 19.

In emerging markets, demand projections are particularly difficult to make. In these economies, demand for natural resources, energy production, and other types of project output, as well as need for infrastructure projects, are directly dependent upon the overall growth in these markets. Yet, the ability of these markets to grow and create demand for a project's output is dependent upon the development of increased wage and business earnings. Still, this increased earning power is often dependent on the project being built. Increased, reliable electricity production, for example, enables the development of new and more efficient factories, which in turn increases jobs and wages, which in turn allows the population to pay for power.

Historically, in developing countries, electricity is subsidized by the government. That is, consumers, and sometimes businesses, pay less for power than it costs to produce. This adds a new dimension to the problem of determining demand for an energy project's output. If the electricity was previously subsidized, the consumer expects that subsidy to continue, and may be unable or unwilling to pay the increased rate for power necessary to support the project. This adds another dimension to the demand study – at what price can the project output be sold if it previously was free or subsidized.

§ 4.15 SHORTFALLS IN ANTICIPATED CAPACITY, OUTPUT, AND EFFICIENCY

Failure of the project to perform as expected is a risk for project participants. Performance areas include capacity, output, and efficiency. Failures in any of these areas might result in decreased revenues, increased operating costs and even termination of project agreements.

§ 4.16 OPERATOR EXPERIENCE

The operation of the facility in an efficient, reliable manner is essential to the long-term success of the project. No matter how well designed the project or how well constructed, the project will work only as well as the operator performs. This is particularly true in projects employing new technology, and in a project where fuels management is important.

The entity operating the project, typically pursuant to a long-term operating agreement, must possess sufficient experience to operate the project at the levels necessary to generate cash flow at projected levels. Similarly, the operator must possess the financial ability to support operating guarantees and other obligations under the operating agreement.

§ 4.17 GENERAL OPERATING EXPENSES

Operating expenses greater than estimates is another risk to the project. These inaccuracies arise from errors in design engineering, excessive equipment replacement, unscheduled maintenance, incorrect assumptions about the amount of spare parts inventory needed, failure to design equipment redundancies, poor productivity of labor, incorrect assumptions concerning the labor force required to operate, and other operating problems.

§ 4.18 SPONSOR COMMITMENT

The project sponsor must possess the requisite commitment to a project to manage it through construction and start-up. Commitment is typically measured by how much equity project sponsors invest in the project. Generally, the higher the equity, the more committed the project sponsor is to its success. Also, technical and financial resources available to the project are important indicators of a sponsor's commitment.

§ 4.19 MANAGEMENT EXPERIENCE

Similarly, the project sponsor must have the requisite experience to manage the project in areas other than actual project operation. Day-to-day decisions about the project are essential to the success or failure of the project, including the repayment of project debt. Thus, the personnel, resources, and experience of management must be sufficient to address those tasks.

§ 4.20 PERMITS AND LICENSES

The risk that a project does not have, or might not obtain, permits necessary for the construction or operation of the project are, of course, a significant concern to all project participants. Generally, permits for the project must be obtainable, without unreasonable delay or expense. At the time of construction funding for a project financing, permits are classifiable in three categories: permits already obtained and in full force and effect, which are not subject to appeal, further proceedings, or to any unsatisfied condition that may result in a material modification or revocation; permits that are routinely granted on application and that would not normally be obtained before construction; and permits other than those in full force and effect and those routinely granted on application. The last category of permits is, of course, the relevant concern for project participants. The application and approval process for the last category must be carefully examined to determine the likelihood of issuance, the cost associated with possible conditions attached to permit approval, and similar issues.

Necessary permits vary depending on the site, technology, process, and a host of other variables. In any particular financing, the various governmental agencies with jurisdiction can range from the local level to the central government level. The processes of determining which permits are required is typically a role of the project sponsor working with the contractor and operator.

§ 4.21 POLITICAL ENVIRONMENT

If the project is located abroad, the political climate of the host country must be analyzed carefully to discover the sentiments about foreign investments in the host country. The risk of, and the consequences resultant from, a change in the political environment where a project is located is best exemplified by the experience of project finance lenders in India. The risk of expropriation by developing countries is obvious. Less obvious is the negative effect on project economics of indirect governmental action in the form of tax increases or demands for equity participation.

§ 4.22 INTEREST RATE

Where interest rates vary over the term of the financing, the risk of unrealistic interest rate projections can affect the ability of the project revenues to service debt. The interest rate projections are typically a component of the feasibility study, which must show that the project economics can adapt to interest rate variations. If not, interest rate hedging must be obtained, such as interest rate swaps, caps, and collars for a significant portion of the debt.

§ 4.23 FORCE MAJEURE

Force majeure is the term used generally to refer to an event beyond the control of a party claiming that the event has occurred, including acts of nature, fire, flood, earthquakes, war, and strikes. Acts of nature (sometimes called "acts of God" in Western culture), a subset of force majeure events, are events occasioned exclusively by nature, without human interference. The party who will bear the risk is always a subject of negotiation, and often rests with the party best able to control (by, for example, obtaining insurance) each particular force majeure risk.

Whether a force majeure is found to have occurred depends upon the perspective of the parties. As between a project company and an offtake purchaser, an expropriatory act by the host government may be a force majeure, because it is beyond their control. As between the government and the project company, however, the act is not a force majeure (the act is within the host government's control), although it might be a breach of a governmental obligation to the project company.

A force majeure event typically excuses performance obligations, including payment of damages, by the parties to a contract. Generally, there is an obligation to attempt to resolve the effects of the force majeure as soon as possible, so that contract performance can resume.

§ 4.24 ECONOMIC PROJECTION AND FEASIBILITY REPORT INACCURACY

The risk that economic projections and feasibility reports are inaccurate relates to each risk discussed in this section. An inaccuracy in the appraisal of equipment, for example, relates to the amount of insurance coverage necessary, which in turn relates to ability to operate the project and achieve projected cash flows.

Project lenders typically select a competent, experienced engineering firm to review the technical and financial aspects of the project, and the other risks described in this book. For an unbiased review, the project lender insists on the independence of the firm from the project sponsors. Experience in advising lenders, and experience in projects of similar type, size, and location of the one proposed, are also important to the lender.

§ 4.25 ENVIRONMENTAL

Environmental protections through governmental laws and regulations can impose significant liability risks on a project. Risks include governmental fines and penalties, and liabilities to third parties injured by environmental problems created by a project. In addition, cleanup costs and treatment costs can be expensive. Apart from financial risks, permit conditions, if violated, can result in permit revocation.

Changes in environmental laws can result in additional capital costs necessary to retrofit existing facilities for environmental protection. Also, new requirements for environmental equip-

ment can increase operating costs and operator fees.

§ 4.26 CONTRACT MISMATCH

Project finance participants sometimes consider a project finance transaction as a giant jigsaw puzzle assembled in the dark. The number of contracts makes it difficult to ensure that all the pieces fit. Each contract in a project financing must fit together. For example, the loan document payment dates must match the date range in which project revenues will be received. Also, the commencement of fuel supply deliveries under the fuel contract must match the commencement date of the other operating agreements. Minor mismatches are not fatal to project financing.

§ 4.27 CONTRACT RISKS GENERALLY

In the final analysis, project financings are dependent on contracts. As such, they are governed by contract law. Contracts must be carefully reviewed to determine whether the contract terms negotiated by the parties are enforceable. For example, a commitment of one party to prepay the project debt if it breaches a contract may not be enforceable as *liquidated damages*. If the parties desire that a particular contract be performed by a particular party, the laws of *specific performance* must be examined to determine whether that can be enforced.

§ 4.28 COMMERCIAL RISK MITIGATION

As discussed in Chapter 2, project finance risks generally are allocated to the project participant best able to manage those risks. The device used to allocate the risk is called a risk mitigation instrument, tool, or technique. The types of risk mitigation tools used in a project financing transaction are best discussed in the context of risk periods: construction and operation. Chapter 20 contains more exhaustive discussion of this topic.

[1] Construction Period Risk Mitigation

During the construction period, four general risk mitigation tools are used: contractual undertakings, contingency reserve accounts, equity and other funding commitments, and insurance. The scope of each of these varies with the extent of the perceived risk.

Contractual Undertakings. Contractual arrangements, including guarantees, are common risk mitigation instruments used during the construction period of a project. Contracts provide a variety of risk allocation alternatives and a full spectrum of mitigation alternatives.

In a project finance construction contract, for example, construction risks are allocated between the project company and the contractor. A common risk allocation is that the contractor is responsible for the timely completion of project construction, for a fixed price, which operates at negotiated levels of performance or quality.

Failure to achieve those contractual obligations typically results in an obligation by the contractor to compensate the project company for the damages it suffers because of the late completion or unsatisfactory performance. This obligation is in the form of a liquidated damage provision.

Liquidated damages are of two general types: delay liquidated damages and buy-down liquidated damages. Delay liquidated damages, due for late project completion, compensate the project company for additional interest during construction that results from the contractor's failure to satisfy the completion schedule agreed to in the construction contract.

Buy-down (also called performance) liquidated damages compensate the project company for decreased revenue and increased operating costs associated with the failure of the contractor to meet the agreed-upon performance criteria. These are often used to prepay the project company's debt to offset the expected decline in project output (and the associated cash flow) due to the failure to satisfy those standards. Typically, the amount of the buy-down is designed to prepay an amount of debt sufficient to maintain the debt service coverage ratio that would have otherwise been achieved.

Because of the potential magnitude of liquidated damage payments, the total exposure under the contract is usually limited. The limitation is determined by the market for construction services, taking into account the technological challenges of the project. A damage cap of between 10 and 30 percent of the total construction contract price is not atypical.

The creditworthiness of the contractor determines the strength of contractual undertakings as a risk mitigation instrument. If the contractor is not financially strong, it is less likely that it will pay the liquidated damages when due. Consequently, project lenders sometimes require that these financial undertakings be supported by a payment guarantee from a creditworthy entity or a performance bond or other surety instrument.

Contingency Reserve Funds and Equity and Other Funding Commitments. A risk mitigation–structuring tool used to mitigate the cost overrun risk is the construction budget contingency reserve fund. This fund is a line item in the construction budget, supported with loan or equity commitments, to pay cost overruns during the construction period. Subordinated debt commitments and letters of credit provided by project sponsors can also support such a contingency.

Insurance. A common risk mitigation instrument is insurance. During construction, construction all-risk insurance is obtained to protect the project construction against property damage.

[2] Operation Period Risk Mitigation

Contractual Undertakings. Material, workmanship, and equipment guarantees are important risk mitigation instruments during a project's post-construction phase. These are typically time-limited to periods of one or two years.

Contractual Arrangements. Contractual arrangements to manage risks are the most common risk mitigation tool used during the project's operation phase. Take-or-pay, take-and-pay, put-or-pay, and pass-through structures are used to assure revenue streams to the project company. Each of these is discussed in Chapter 20.

Contingency Reserve Funds. During the operations phase, contingency reserve accounts can be used to mitigate the risk that insufficient revenue will be available to pay operating costs, planned and extraordinary equipment overhauls, and debt service. These can take the form of operating cost reserve accounts, overhaul reserve accounts, and debt service reserve accounts, respectively. Loan proceeds and project operating revenue are the typical funding sources for these accounts. They can also be unfunded, provided backup credit support exists to provide the funds if needed, such as through a letter of credit.

Cash Traps. Because of the benefits of a nonrecourse debt structure, project companies are typically structured as single-purpose entities, with no assets other than the project. Consequently, profits are not retained at the project company level but are distributed to project sponsors on a periodic basis. Project sponsors usually want these distributions made more frequently than project lenders permit.

The cash trap is a risk mitigation technique that is sometimes used to balance the competing concerns of owner and lender. Under this technique, profits can be distributed to project sponsors as long as a negotiated debt service coverage test is satisfied or other conditions are met. If not, all excess cash not needed for project operation or debt service is held (trapped) in a collateral account. The funds on deposit in this account can be applied by the project lender for debt service, and ultimately debt prepayment, if project difficulties are not resolved.

Insurance. Insurance is also used as a risk mitigation tool during the operations phase. Casualty and liability policies, in addition to loss of revenue from machinery breakdowns, are common forms.

PART THREE

PROJECT FINANCE STRUCTURES

CHAPTER FIVE

PROJECT FINANCE PARTICIPANTS AND THEIR ROLES

§ 5.01 PROJECT SPONSOR

The *project sponsor* is the entity, or group of entities, interested in the development of the project and that will benefit, economically or otherwise, from the overall development, construction, and operation of the project. It is sometimes called the *developer*. The project sponsor can be one company or a group of companies.

§ 5.02 PROJECT COMPANY

The *project company* is the special-purpose entity that will own, develop, construct, operate, and maintain the project. The precise nature of organization for this entity is dependent upon a myriad of factors.

Of foremost concern is the local law of the country in which the project is based. The local law must be examined to determine, for example, whether a form of organization is prescribed; whether a foreign entity can do business in the host country; whether a foreign entity can own real property in the host country; the extent to which liability limitations, such as is enjoyed by a corporation or limited liability partnership, is permissible; requirements for local investor participation in the entity organized in the host country; and similar concerns.

Other factors also influence the selection of the form of organization for the project company. These include tax laws in the host country, tax treaties, and foreign exchange rules of the host country.

§ 5.03 BORROWING ENTITY

The borrowing entity in a project financing is most often the same as the project company. However, in some transactions, another borrower or multiple borrowers are used. For example, in a project financing of a mine, the mine owner, the operator, and the major off-take purchaser might form a joint venture to develop the project. Each could enter into borrowing transactions to fund their own individual commitment to the project, whereas the joint venture itself would have no project debt.

§ 5.04 COMMERCIAL LENDER

Commercial lenders, including banks, insurance companies, credit corporations, and other lenders, provide debt financing for projects.[1] These institutions might be based in the host country or in another country.

Sometimes, the lenders are strategically selected from a range of countries. The purpose of this syndicate diversity is to discourage the host-country government from expropriatory acts or other discriminatory action. If the host government elected to do so, it could thereby endanger economic relations with the home country of each lender.

Lenders in the host country are also sometimes included in the lending group for the purpose of restraining the host government from expropriatory acts or other discriminatory action. Also, in countries that limit a foreign entity's right to take a security interest in project assets, selection of a local bank to receive the security interest for all lenders could be important.

The lenders might provide different types of debt to the project. For example, some lenders could provide debt with a right of payment senior in priority to other, subordinated lenders. Also, some lenders might provide a tranche of debt with specific interest rates, amortization, and terms different from the tranche provided by other lenders.

[1] Arranging Bank

The amount of debt required in many large project financings requires that several lenders join to provide the debt facility. The lenders act together because any one lender individually does not have the capacity to provide the entire project loan or because it wants to limit its risk exposure in the financing. The resulting group of lenders is often called a *syndicate*, while the lead bank that arranges this type of cooperation is called the *arranging bank*.

[2] Managing Bank

The *managing bank* is typically a title assigned to one or more banks in a syndicate to reflect the status of the bank as one of the major syndicate members. It is primarily a title for marketing purposes and does not usually signify that the bank has accepted any increased responsibilities or duties to the borrower or to the other syndicate members.

[3] Agent Bank

By contrast, the *agent bank* is a role with responsibilities. It is the bank responsible for administration of the credit and the collateral. It coordinates loan drawdowns, monitors covenant compliance by the borrower, issues and receives notices to and from the borrower, and is a clearinghouse for information. It polls the bank group members in situations in which a vote is required, such as whether to declare a default or approve amendments to the credit documentation, and communicates decisions to the borrower.

[4] Engineering Bank

The *engineering bank* is responsible for compliance with technical performance covenants and progress. It coordinates with technical consultants and project engineers and reports this information to the bank group.

[5] Security Agent

The *security agent*, or *collateral agent*, as it is sometimes called, is responsible for holding security interests as agent for the project lenders. It also monitors lien filings and other steps necessary to protect the security interests of the lenders. In some transactions, this role is fulfilled by the agent bank.

§ 5.05 BONDHOLDERS

Another source of debt in international project financings is from *bondholders*, who purchase project debt in the form of bonds. The bondholders are represented by a bond trustee, a financial

---

[1] For a discussion of bank capital adequacy requirements and project finance, *see* Michael P. Malloy, Symposium, *Markets in Transition: Reconstruction and Development: Part Two – Building Up to a Drawdown: International Project Finance and Privatization – Expert Presentations on Lessons to be Learned: International Project Finance: Risk Analysis and Regulatory Concerns*, 18 Transnat'l Law. 89 (2004).

institution that acts as the representative for the bondholders in managing the debt transaction. This financing structure, of increasing importance in international project finance, is discussed in Chapter 21.

§ 5.06 INTERNATIONAL (MULTILATERAL) AGENCIES

The World Bank, the International Finance Corporation, regional development banks, and other international agencies provide significant credit support for projects financed in developing countries. These agencies are discussed in Chapter 21.

§ 5.07 BILATERAL AGENCIES

Unlike multilateral agencies, bilateral agencies are designed to promote trade or other interests of an organizing country. They are generally nationalistic in purpose and nationalistic and political in operation. Funding for bilateral agencies generally comes from their organizing governments.

Bilateral agencies are generally of two types: developmental agencies and export-import financing agencies. Developmental agencies are designed to provide grants or concessional financing to promote economic and political goals of the organizing government in developing nations. An example in the United States is the U.S. Agency for International Development.

The most common type of bilateral agency is an export-import bank. Many sources of financing are available from governments for exporting goods and services. Government-supported export financing includes pre-export working capital, short-term export receivables financing, and long-term financing. These are discussed in Chapter 21.

§ 5.08 RATING AGENCY

Where projects are financed through access to public debt markets, *rating agencies* are con-

sulted to provide credit ratings for the underlying debt.[2] These agencies are typically involved at very early stages of project development so that credit concerns can be addressed and structured in an efficient, timely manner.

§ 5.09 SUPPLIER

The *supplier* provides raw materials, fuel, or other inputs to the project. Because of the importance of inputs to the project, the project sponsors and lenders are concerned with the underlying economic feasibility of supply arrangements, the economic terms of the contracts, and the ability of the suppliers to perform the contracts.

§ 5.10 OUTPUT PURCHASER

The *output purchaser* is the purchaser of all or some of the product or service produced at the project. In most nonrecourse and limited recourse project financings, the off-take purchaser provides the credit support for the underlying financing.

The output purchaser's financial commitment to the project depends upon how much interest it has in a long-term supply that is priced based on the project's cost rather than market forces. This interest also determines to what extent the output purchaser will be willing to provide credit enhancement, such as guarantees, to assist in the financing process.

§ 5.11 CONTRACTOR

The *contractor* is the entity responsible for construction of the project.[3] It bears the primary

---

[2] Fitch, Moody's, and Standard & Poor's have each developed rating criteria for project finance debt. *See, e.g.,* Fitch, Inc., *Project Finance Criteria Approach, Rating Approach to Project Finance* (Aug. 12, 2004); Moody's, *Project Finance Sourcebook* (Feb. 23, 2006); Standard & Poor's, *Global Project Finance Yearbook 2007* (Feb. 2006).

[3] *See generally* Daniel Chao & Michael Selvin, *Project Development and Finance: The Evolving Role of the Engineering/Construction Contractor*, in PROJECT FINANCE YEARBOOK 1994/5 1 (Adrian Hornbook ed., 1994).

responsibility in most projects for the containment of construction-period costs.

§ 5.12 OPERATOR

The *operator* is the entity responsible for the operation, maintenance, and repair of the project. In some projects, this role is filled by one of the owners of the project company. In others, the operator role is undertaken by a third party under an operating agreement.

§ 5.13 FINANCIAL ADVISOR

The *financial advisor* is retained by the project sponsor to provide financial advisory services to the sponsor. These services include preparing the information memorandum. The information memorandum includes a detailed summary of project technical and economic feasibility; the proposed financing structure and proposed terms; a description of the experience of participants; a summary of the underlying project risks; and a description of each of the project contracts and credit support. The financial advisor also provides advice to the project sponsor on the host country, currency concerns, structuring the transaction, and possible debt sources. Many commercial banks provide financial advisory services.

§ 5.14 TECHNICAL CONSULTANTS

Technical experts, such as fuel consultants, insurance consultants, engineers, and environmental consultants, are retained to advise the project sponsor and lenders on highly technical matters, about which the sponsor and lenders have limited knowledge or that they want to confirm. In many financings, these consultants will each prepare reports, such as feasibility reports, for the project sponsor and lenders. During the project, these experts might be retained by the sponsor or lenders to confirm project progress and to analyze the technical aspects of disputes.

§ 5.15 PROJECT FINANCE LAWYERS

Project finance lawyers represent clients by combining experience with nonrecourse and limited recourse financial structures, experience with the underlying industry, and knowledge of project contracts, debt and equity documents, credit enhancement, and international transactions. These lawyers provide specialized assistance to project sponsors, host governments, lenders, investors, and the other project participants in risk identification and risk mitigation techniques.

Project finance lawyers provide advice on all aspects of a project, including laws and regulations; permits; organization of project entities; negotiating and drafting of project construction, operation, sale, and supply contracts; negotiating and drafting of debt and equity documents; bankruptcy; tax; and similar matters. Opinions on various legal matters are issued by these lawyers in connection with the financial closing process.

§ 5.16 LOCAL LAWYERS

Local lawyers in the host country of the project are typically needed by all participants. These lawyers assist in local legal and political matters, which are often coordinated by the project finance lawyers. Local lawyers also issue opinions on various local legal matters in connection with the financial closing process.

§ 5.17 HOST GOVERNMENT

The *host government* is the government of the country in which the project is located.[4] As such, the host government is typically involved as an issuer of permits, licenses, authorizations, and concessions. It also might grant foreign exchange

---

[4] For a discussion on contracts between a state and a foreign company, *see* Jean-Flavien Lalive, *Contracts Between a State or State Agency and a Foreign Company*, 13 INT'L & COMP. L.Q. 503 (1962); Frederick A. Mann, *State Contracts and International Arbitration*, 42 BRIT. Y.B. INT'L L. 1 (1967).

availability projections and tax concessions. In some transactions, it is the borrower.[5]

The host government can be the owner of the project, whether majority or minority, or can become the owner of the project at the end of a specified period, such as in a build-own-transfer (BOT) structure. It might also be involved as an off-take purchaser or as a supplier of raw materials or fuel.

Where infrastructure or other development is necessary in support of a project, such as roads, railways, and ports, host-government involvement can significantly reduce project costs. Yet, such governmental responsibility and participation may be detrimental, as well.

For example, if the project is dependent on new infrastructure for success, both must be completed on a coordinated schedule. Ideally, the project company will be intensely involved in all aspects of the new construction, including the schedule. Yet, the host government will want control over the construction and ultimate operation of the infrastructure because it is paying for it. If the risk of cost overruns is on the government, it will want to reduce its financial risks by managing the construction process. These competing perspectives need to be resolved in a mutually acceptable way to ensure project success.

The host government's ability to benefit from the project varies with its economic stability, natural resources, tax base, and other factors. In general, it may have any or all of the following objectives in cooperating in a project's development: quick and efficient development of needed infrastructure provided by the project; economic development; in developing countries, satisfying multilateral institutions of its development success and economic growth; proper, safe, and efficient operation; minimizing use of its own funds or credit for economic growth; obtaining project ownership after private participants receive an agreed equity return; taking control of the project if it is inefficiently operated or

otherwise fails; and providing regulatory stability for a project, while limiting restrictions on its ability to enact new laws and promulgate new rules affecting the business sector in which the project operates.

Whether the host government benefits from a project depends upon the allocation of risks between itself and the other project participants. As the discussion in Chapter 3 illustrates, the risks associated with infrastructure projects in a developing country often necessitates some form of host-government support, through a governmental guarantee or some other type of credit enhancement. Yet, governmental guarantees can undermine the benefits of private sector involvement (privatization). These guarantees can impose significant costs on the host country's taxpayers, and further erode the country's financial health.

Also, if the host government undertakes responsibility for the wrong risks, the project sponsors may lack sufficient incentives for efficient project operation. For example, a host-government guarantee of demand for a project's use or output can remove an important market incentive: the project sponsor's incentive to develop only those projects that are strong financially. In addition, the risk structure of a project can allocate too much risk to the host country, leaving the project company with insufficient financial responsibility for taking excessive risks.

The host country can, of course, endeavor to decrease the amount of credit support it must provide a project by undertaking a program of risk reduction. For example, if a host government is successful in maintaining stable macroeconomic policies, it is less likely that project sponsors will require exchange rate guarantees or assurances of currency convertibility or transferability. Similarly, a predictable regulatory framework, coupled with regulatory agencies that are reasonably independent from the political process, and an independent judicial system for dispute resolution, can combine to reduce the need for governmental guarantees. Finally, host governments that allow dispute resolution in international arbitration can ally fears of discrimination by the local courts, and reduce the

---

[5] See J. Speed Carroll, *Legal Aspects of Project Finance: The Borrower's View*, in SOVEREIGN BORROWERS – GUIDELINES ON LEGAL NEGOTIATIONS WITH COMMERCIAL LENDERS (Lars Kalderen & Qamar S. Siddiqi, eds. 1985).

need for government-provided credit enhancement.

Developed countries do not typically need to provide governmental guarantees for projects because the economic and political risks are satisfactory to project sponsors and lenders. This is not a benefit reserved only for developed countries, however. Some developing countries, such as Argentina, in its power industry, and Chile, in its telecommunications, power, and gas industries, have achieved an economic and political climate that permits infrastructure development and privatization without the need for governmental guarantees of project debt or performance.

Importantly, project financiers sometimes lose sight of the nature of a government; that is, a government must answer to a wide spectrum of often competing interests. As such, it is very difficult for a government to promise not to change the laws and regulations that affect a project, or if it does so, to compensate the project for the economic implications of such changes. For example, changes to environmental laws and regulations may be necessary to appease citizens, or to satisfy requirements imposed under treaties or by multilateral institutions. Similarly, new taxes may be needed to respond to changing economic conditions.

It is also sometimes difficult for a host government to control state-owned entities. For example, in an energy project, the purchaser of the project output is sometimes a public entity, controlled by a local or state government. The central government may not have sufficient control over such a public entity to provide a guarantee, however. The solution that may be preferable is for the government to undertake a privatization program, which removes the purchasing entity from many of the risks inherent in public ownership.

A host government is sometimes asked to bear project commercial risks, such as construction cost overruns and output demand risks. Yet, host governments often consider the project company as the entity better able to manage these risks; placing them on the host government can remove important incentives from the private sector for selecting sound projects for development and managing costs. The project company can be

rewarded, in part, for taking these risks by such solutions as lengthening the term of the concession awarded to it when demand is lower than projected or when the project fails to generate, on a present value basis, a negotiated revenue target.

Similarly, a host government may be unwilling to provide protection against exchange and interest rate risks. From the project company's perspective, this is necessary because the government controls these risks, and it encourages the government to maintain stable economic policies. Also, because project companies typically borrow adjustable rate debt in foreign-currency-denominated loans, project profits are sensitive to fluctuations in the interest rates and currency convertibility levels assumed in project feasibility studies. Yet, from the government's perspective, a government guarantee can encourage a project sponsor to borrow excessive debt in foreign currencies. Also, such guarantees can discourage governments from taking needed action to cure economic problems, such as a needed devaluation. Finally, currency depreciation is often coupled with a decline in income and the associated tax base, resulting in a decrease in funds available to a host government at precisely the time that the project company enforces the guarantee.

Ultimately, the private development and ownership of infrastructure projects is problematic for the host government because such services as roads, energy, and water have been traditionally provided by the government to its citizens and paid for with public funds, with either tax revenues or public debt. With public funds, the government has been traditionally free to change the rates charged for such services as economic situations develop. In an infrastructure project financing, however, such changes are unwelcome, even if economic developments place pressure on the government to change material terms of private infrastructure projects, including contract suspension and outright cancellation.[6]

---

[6] See generally Catherine Pedamon, Essay, How Is Convergence Best Achieved in International Project Finance?, 24 FORDHAM INT'L L.J. 1272 (2001).

§ 5.18 INSURERS

Insurance providers improve the risks inherent in project financings, whether casualty or political. *Insurers* typically work closely with the project sponsors and lenders to produce an insurance package that limits risks at an economical price. The acceptability of the insurance package is often confirmed by an insurance consultant, retained by the project sponsor and lenders.

CHAPTER SIX

PROJECT FINANCE STRUCTURES

§ 6.01 GENERALLY

Project finance structures are virtually unlimited by the creativity and flexibility of bankers and lawyers. Largely, the structures are influenced by the risk appetites of the lenders and investors involved in the financing and by the economic condition of the host country.

In general, these structures are based on one of three macro varieties: nonrecourse financing, limited recourse financing, and project output interest financing. Nonrecourse and limited recourse financing structures provide for debt repayment from the cash flows of the project. Output interest financing structures are centered on the purchase of an interest in the project output, which purchase price is used, in part, to finance the facility.

Within these three broad categories are countless other structures, on a micro level. The most frequently used of these, loan financing, export credit financing, lease financing, and bond financing are discussed in this chapter.

§ 6.02 COMMERCIAL LOAN FINANCING

The general structure of a loan financing in the project finance context is not unlike the structure used in other loan transactions. In the typical project finance transaction, funds are lent to the project company for the construction and operation phases of a project. The debt is repaid by the project company, together with payments of interest and bank fees.

In contrast to other types of loan transactions, however, the project finance loan is either nonrecourse or limited recourse to the project sponsors. The lender receives, as collateral, a security interest in all of the assets and cash flow of the project company.

The project finance commercial loan structure contemplates two phases: construction and operation. In some circumstances, the construction and operation phases are separated in two agreements, with one institution providing the construction loan and another institution providing the loan for the operations period. In others, the construction and operations phase loans are provided in the same agreement, with different terms applicable for each phase.

The project finance nonrecourse (or limited recourse) model is sometimes altered during the construction period. As discussed in Chapter 2, the construction period is a very risky period for the lender. To mitigate the effect of the potential risk during this period, the project sponsor sometimes agrees to accept all, or to share part, of the construction period risk. This might be accomplished in various forms, including full recourse to the project sponsor until the project is completed, or limited recourse during the construction phase for certain, specified agreed-upon risks, such as cost overruns.

[1] Construction Phase

During the construction phase (or the construction loan if a separate agreement and lender are used for the construction period), the lender will disburse funds for the construction of the project. Funds are typically advanced as required under the construction agreement, predicated on the submission of appropriate disbursement requests with supporting documentation. Because of the lack of operating revenue during the construction period, interest is capitalized; that is, interest otherwise payable on the funds advanced is paid from the construction loan proceeds.

[2] Operations Phase

At project completion, the operations phase of the debt program will begin. The so-called permanent lender will advance the entire amount of the loan on one day. This is typically disbursed soon after the first day of commercial operations for the project. Because operating revenues are generated by the operation of the facility, interest can be paid on the debt and the amortization can begin. The timing and amount of debt amortization are dependent upon the cash flow generated by the project.

In some transactions, the lenders will make available a working capital line of credit, as well. This type of facility gives the project working capital during periods of low cash flow.

§ 6.03 EXPORT CREDIT FINANCING

[1] Generally

Export-import financing agencies are designed to promote trade or other interests of an organizing country. Funding for bilateral agencies generally comes from their organizing governments. An example is the United States Export-Import Bank.

There are many sources of financing available from governments for exporting goods and services. In some countries, this type of financing is administered by the private sector. Government-supported export financing includes pre-export working capital, short-term export receivables financing, and long-term financing.

[2] Types of Export-Import Financing

The three general financing methods for an export-import bank to use in providing funds to an importing entity are direct lending, intermediary lending, and interest rate equalization.

Direct Lending. The simplest structure is a traditionally documented loan in which the borrower is the importing entity and the lender is the export-import bank. Most commonly, the loan is conditioned upon the purchase of goods or services from business in the organizing country.

Financial Intermediary Loans (Bank-to-Bank). Another structure is indirect lending. Under this structure, the export-import bank lends funds to a financial intermediary, such as a commercial bank, which in turn loans the funds (also commonly called *re-lending*, or *on-lending*) to the importing entity.

Interest Rate Equalization. Under an interest rate equalization structure, a commercial lender provides a loan to the importing entity at below-market interest rates. It is compensated by the export-import bank for the difference between the below-market rate and the rate the lender could otherwise obtain in the market.

§ 6.04 LEASE FINANCING

[1] Generally

Lease financing describes the separation of ownership and use interests in all or part of a project for financing a project. This structure is used to shift tax benefits from an entity that cannot use the benefits to another entity that can and to provide greater collateral protection for lenders in countries without adequate collateral security laws. Also, this structure is sometimes useful in overcoming the objection to interest payments in Islamic countries.

In the typical lease financing structure, a project company agrees to sell a project, typically at the end of the construction period, to a lease finance company. The lease finance company, acting as owner-lessor, leases the project back on a nonrecourse basis to the project company-lessee. As lessor, the lease finance company retains the ownership interest, including any tax benefits. The lessor is often a passive institutional investor.

The lease finance company enters into a lease financing arrangement with a lender to finance the costs of the project acquisition. The loan is repaid by the lessor from the rentals received under a lease agreement with the project company. The lease, which is assigned to the lender as collateral security, will contain the same types of covenants and defaults as are found in a project finance commercial loan transaction. In addition to an assignment of the lease, the lender is also granted a security interest in all of the underlying project assets.

At the end of the lease term, after the lessor receives its expected financial return and the debt is repaid, the project will be leased for a renewal period, transferred to the project company, or sold or leased to another entity by the lessor, with most of the additional rentals or sale price reverting to the project company as a commission. The ultimate disposition is highly dependent upon tax laws applicable to the lessor. The goal of the lessor and lessee is to satisfy those tax laws that allow treatment of the transaction as a true lease and not a conditional sale agreement.

[2] Advantages to the Project Company

A leveraged lease transaction benefits the project company (lessee) in several ways: control over the project is preserved, 100 percent financing is not atypical, lower financing costs are enjoyed, a tax deduction is available for rental payments, and it allows for a shifting of residual risk.

Control Over the Project. The lessee retains control over the use, operation, maintenance, and repair of the project. In most respects, the project is treated like other projects owned outright by the project sponsor and financed by a bank.

Total Financing. The project sponsor is able to achieve 100 percent financing for the project, together with the equity contribution by the passive investor. No separate equity investment by the project sponsors is required.

Lower Financing Costs. In many circumstances, the lease transaction will provide lower financing costs to the project company than a bank financing, particularly where the project company cannot take advantage of tax benefits (depreciation, interest deductions). In such circumstances, under a lease structure, the project company's effective lease cost is less than the project company's incremental cost of borrowing.

Tax Deductibility of Rent. A true lease structure provides the project company the ability to treat accrued rental payments as an expense.

Shifting of Residual Risk. Finally, the project company transfers the risk of a lower-than-expected residual value to the lessor. While the project company gives up the opportunity to enjoy a significant residual value increase, it simultaneously removes the risk of a decline in value.

Equity Risk Taker Replaces Lender as Financing Source. Typically, the institutional investor will be more willing than a commercial lender to accept equity-type risks in a project financing. Of course, a risk premium will be added to the financing costs to compensate the investor-lessor for the risks taken.

[3] Lease Financing From the Lessor's Perspective

The lessor enters the lease transaction with the goal of a fixed long-term return. This is accomplished through timely performance of the lease terms, liquidation of the assets at the residual value assumed in calculating the return, and realization of tax benefits. Any residual value of the project assets that exceed the projected value will increase the return to the lessor.

§ 6.05 BOND FINANCING

The bond financing structure is similar to the commercial loan structure, except that the lenders are investors purchasing the borrower's bonds in a private placement or through the public debt market. The bondholders are represented by a trustee that acts as the agent and representative of the bondholders.

§ 6.06 BOT

The build-own-transfer (BOT) structure is one of the most typical structures for infrastructure development in developing countries. Under this structure, the host government provides a concession (a right to build and operate some type of infrastructure) to the project sponsor, which agrees to build and operate the project for a specified number of years. At the end of the operations period, the project sponsor either transfers the project to the host government or renegotiates with the government for an extended period of operation.

BOT projects are beneficial to host governments seeking to achieve a variety of goals. Foremost of these is the ability to provide a needed project to its citizenry without an effect on the government's budget. It might also be useful in transferring a pool of local labor to the private

sector for training in modern, more efficient, operations. Foreign investment could also be increased through use of this structure.

The BOT structure is typically founded in a concession agreement among the host government, the project company, and, in some cases, the project sponsors. The concessions agreement is discussed more completely in Chapter 14.

§ 6.07 CO-FINANCING

The International Finance Corporation (IFC), the private sector lending institution of The World Bank, provides loans for projects on a nonconcessionary basis. Involvement by the IFC provides comfort to lenders that the host government will not fail to support the project, and this view attracts commercial lenders to IFC transactions.

Under the co-financing structure, the IFC makes an "A" loan and a "B" loan to a project company, through an investment agreement. Commercial lenders participate in the "B" loan portion of the financing, acting as "co-lenders," although they have no direct contractual relationship to the borrower. The IFC co-financing structure places control over covenant compliance and debt acceleration with the IFC. The commercial lenders participate through deposit agreements with the IFC.

Like participation agreements or syndication agreements among commercial lenders, the IFC will not accept liability for the value or appropriateness of the loan transaction. Thus, the participating lenders must agree that they have entered into the transaction exercising their own independent credit judgment, without reliance on the IFC or the World Bank.

§ 6.08 PRODUCTION PAYMENTS

Production payment project financing is a method of nonrecourse financing of a project through transfer to a special-purpose entity (a financing vehicle owned by the lender) of a proportionate share of project ownership in a natural resource (in the ground) and of a right to receive a share of proceeds from the sale of the natural resource. In return, an advance payment is made to the project company as compensation for the rights received.

The structure is similar to a loan. As the project company is able to generate production, payments from the sale of the extracted natural resource are returned to the special-purpose entity, together with an "interest" component. These funds are used to repay a loan made by a bank to the special-purpose entity. The banks take a security interest in the interest purchased. The special grant of the interest in the project by the project company to the special-purpose entity terminates when the "loan" is repaid.

This structure has been used in the United States as a financing structure for hydrocarbon projects. It has also been used as a structure for timber operations. Like other project financings, the lenders rely on the project's production for repayment of the loan; if there is no production, there is no repayment. This structure provides the lenders a complete ownership interest in a proportionate share of the project's production.

Although the special-purpose entity receives an ownership interest in the project, it is not responsible for operating costs or for sale of its share of the production. Typically, the production is sold by the production company as agent for the project company, at a market price, or more commonly, pursuant to take-and-pay contracts.

§ 6.09 FORWARD PURCHASE AGREEMENTS

A forward purchase structure is similar to a production payment structure. It is an agreement between the project company and a special-purpose financing entity created by the lenders, under which that entity makes an advance payment for the project's production. This advance payment is used to pay project development and construction costs.

The project sponsors typically guarantee to the special-purpose financing entity that the project company will perform under the forward purchase agreement. Another guarantee structure sometimes used is for the project sponsors to guarantee the obligations of the off-take purchaser under the take-or-pay contract. That guarantee is then assigned to the special-purpose financing entity, which in turn assigns it to the lenders as collateral for the loan.

After project completion, the project company delivers the good or service produced to the entity for which it has paid in advance of production. The output is then sold to repay the loan.

CHAPTER SEVEN

SELECTING THE PROJECT FINANCE OWNERSHIP STRUCTURE

§ 7.01 GENERALLY

Selection of the form of business organization for the project company is an important step in project development.[1] The type of entity selected affects many aspects of project development and financing, such as the drafting and negotiation of the project documentation and the regulatory permitting process.

For example, permits granted to the project sponsor and later transferred to a new project company may no longer be valid in some jurisdictions. This is because the ownership of the

---

[1] James F. Penrose, *Special-Purpose Entities in Project Finance Transactions,* 2 J. PROJECT FIN. 59 (1996).

project has changed. Also by example, a project contract that prohibits assignment of the contract from one entity to another may preclude a later transfer to the entity that will actually operate as the project company. Thus, the project company, whatever the form, should be organized as early in the development process as possible to avoid these concerns.

Where to organize the project company is also an important consideration: under the laws of the host country or under the laws of the project sponsor's organization. In making this determination, the advantages and disadvantages of each country's laws should be examined, as well as the tax treatment of the entity.

§ 7.02 PRE-DEVELOPMENT ACTIVITIES

[1] Generally
Before a project sponsor begins full development of a facility, a thorough examination of its feasibility is undertaken. During this period, both technical and financial feasibility are evaluated. To make this analysis worthwhile, a fair amount of time and resources must be invested. The factors considered in a feasibility study are discussed in detail in Chapter 8.

[2] The Development Agreement
If more than one project sponsor is interested in project feasibility, it is common for them to negotiate a project development agreement. In this agreement, each of the project sponsors agrees on how to proceed with an analysis of project feasibility, and how the project will be developed if it is to proceed. These agreements, while project-specific, contain common provisions, which are summarized below.

Definition of Project. The project must be completely and carefully identified in the development agreement. In most situations, the description will include the type of project, site, and identification of off-take purchasers. As complete a description as possible should be included so that the parties agree about the type of project that will be pursued. The description may change over time as development and feasibility studies proceed.

Exclusivity. Each participant will want a commitment from the other participants that all are exclusively bound to proceed with one another in development of the project. Otherwise, one party could leave the pre-development group to join another group, taking confidential or competitive information that could harm the original group.

Roles and Responsibilities. Each participant will bring different skills, experiences, and resources to the pre-development group. Consequently, it is important to specify clearly the roles and responsibilities of each member. For example, one participant could take primary responsibility for financial analysis, another for budgeting and projections, and another for managing relations with export credit agencies.

It is also possible at this stage to specify the roles of each participant if the project proceeds to development and financial closing. For example, one participant might be willing to pursue the project development only if it receives the construction work.

Tasks and Schedule. The tasks to be completed during the term of the agreement, and the schedule for accomplishing them, must be included. Each participant will have conflicting demands on its own resources, and such a listing of tasks and dates for their commencement and completion will assist all participants. Typical tasks include conducting a financial, technical, and contractual feasibility study; obtaining initial equity and debt commitments; negotiating and finalizing important project contracts; selecting a project structure; applying for and obtaining governmental permits and approvals; and selecting attorneys, financial consultants, and other advisors.

Cost Funding. Pre-development costs are significant, sometimes exceeding several million dollars. A clear framework must be established to provide for budgeting and funding of these costs.

Management and Voting. The manner in which decisions will be made about pre-development activities must be included. In general, all decisions will require a majority vote of the participants, with unanimity being required for the decision whether to proceed with the project. Because without unanimity a project could be abandoned, the project participants that want to proceed can usually purchase the interests of a participant that declines to proceed.

Withdrawal. The pre-development phase of a project can be several months or years long. During that time, a participant's view about a particular project, technology, host country, or resource commitment can change. Because of this, provisions are usually included to allow a participant to withdraw.

Abandonment. The complete abandonment of a project generally means that no one participant can proceed with it or that a competitive bid for the right to develop the project has been lost. On occasion, the decision to abandon a project is based on other factors, such as political actions, changes in tax treaties, and economic considerations in the home country of the participants.

Confidentiality. Each participant must agree to keep the pre-development effort confidential. This is important whether or not the project is a subject of a competitive bidding program. Beyond disclosure of the project budget, details about permitting strategies, land acquisition, and host government negotiations may be sensitive to an unauthorized disclosure.

Antitrust and Restrictive Trade Practices Considerations. The business regulation laws, such as antitrust[2] or restrictive trade practices,[3] of the home country of the project participants must be considered in the development agreement stage. The agreement could be subject to prior governmental approval or registration requirements.

§ 7.03 DETERMINING THE STRUCTURE TO USE

The important considerations in any formation decision will vary with the needs of the project

sponsors. Consequently, any discussion of the "typical" factors can only be illustrative of the thought process, not exhaustive of the considerations. Among the significant factors that may be considered in determining the ownership structure for a project financing include the following: whether there is a need for a high proportion of equity to debt; the grade of investment; tax laws of the host government and the government of the project sponsor and tax treaties; extent of project management control desired; accounting treatment and objectives; lender preferences; and the ease of transferability of equity interests in the project.

[1] Need for Leverage

One advantage of the project finance structure is the high debt-to-equity leverage that is possible. In projects where this is an important factor for the project sponsors, the form of organization of the project company needs to permit the contribution of additional equity if necessary for project construction or operation.

[2] Grade of Investment

Projects that are financially strong, from the standpoint of financial expectations, may need less flexibility for additional equity infusions. Thus, selection of the form of organization of the project company needs less attention to ease of entry of new investors.

[3] Tax Laws and Treaties

The tax treatment of the entity selected for project ownership should be carefully considered. This analysis should include such considerations as the taxation of the project company in the host country and in the home country of the owners of the project company.

[4] Project Management

The necessity for a large amount of project management by the project sponsors should be considered. Some forms of project ownership, such as a partnership, may provide more management flexibility than a corporate form.

[5] Accounting Treatment and Objectives

The accounting objectives of the project sponsors should also be considered when selecting

---

[2] Sherman Antitrust Act, 15 U.S.C. §1 (1976).
[3] Restrictive Trade Practices Act, 1976, c. 34 (Eng.).

the organizational form for the project company. Reporting income and loss for accounting purposes, among other accounting issues, varies based on the structure used.

[6] Lender Preferences

The preferences of the project lender need to be accommodated in the selection of the organizational form of the project company. Because, in general, the lender is indifferent, other lender concerns could be magnified by the selection of a particular entity over another. For example, a host country's laws might make it more difficult for a lender to take a lien on ownership interests in a partnership form of organization than a corporate form of organization.

[7] Transferability of Equity Interests

The ease of transferring equity interests in the project company should also be factored into the selection process. For example, in general terms, the more flexible an organization form is for equity transfers, the greater the pool of potential equity investors.

§ 7.04 AVOIDING PARENT COMPANY DIRECT INVOLVEMENT

It is a common goal of companies involved in the development of large-scale facilities that a parent company not be directly involved in a project in a host country. The goal extends to other project participants including the contractor, operator, or project sponsor.

Among the reasons for this view are the risks associated with subjecting the parent company to liability and regulation and the difficulty in allocating taxable income between multiple countries. In most circumstances, a special-purpose subsidiary is organized and used for the investment or other project activity.

§ 7.05 SPECIAL-PURPOSE NATURE OF PROJECT COMPANY

Classic nonrecourse and limited recourse project finance is based on the ability of the lender to analyze a defined project. This is most effective when a special-purpose entity is formed to own the project and no other assets. As a consequence, unrelated, non-project risk is segregated from the project financed. Such a structure makes it easier to reduce the risk that the project will become part of a U.S. bankruptcy proceeding's stay provisions if a related entity becomes bankrupt (the project company is then said to be *bankruptcy remote*). To maintain this protection, however, the organizational and finance documents must contain sufficient protections to ensure that the special-purpose status is maintained. These include restrictions on the entity's powers to undertake activities other than the project; debt limitations; restrictions on mergers or reorganizations; and maintenance of separateness, for purposes of both avoiding "piercing the corporate veil" and "substantive consolidation" attacks.

§ 7.06 HOST-COUNTRY INVESTMENT REQUIREMENTS

[1] Generally

Regulation of investment by foreign entities in a host country is determined by local law of the host country.[4] This regulation takes various forms, including prohibition on foreign ownership of real estate, local partnering requirements, and outright prohibitions of foreign investment in certain economic sectors. This regulation need not be negative in nature. Investment regulation sometimes takes a positive form, such as tax holidays, which provide tax benefits to foreign investors.

[2] Ownership of Real Estate

Some countries have requirements that no foreign entity own real property in the country. It may be possible to create structures to circumvent this type of prohibition. For example, a trust could be created to hold the real property interests necessary for a project, with the project company as beneficiary of the trust. Alternatively, a local partner could be included, whose purpose is to hold the real estate rights and lease those rights to the project company.

---

[4] There are some limited restrictions against investment barriers in the World Trade Organization Agreement on Trade Related Investment Measures.

[3] Local Participation

Other countries require a minimum level of local ownership in infrastructure and other projects. These requirements must be considered in the very early stages of project development and feasibility.

Of course, if a local partner is included, control issues must be considered. Local law must be examined to determine whether the requirement of local ownership is concerned with control, profit distribution, ownership allocation, or a combination of these. Once this is understood, control provisions can be negotiated for the project entity.

[4] Local Formation of Project Company

Some countries require that the project entity be incorporated, or otherwise formed if a partnership or other non-corporate entity, in the host country. The policy reason behind this type of requirement is sometimes based on nationalistic or political concerns. In other countries, it is based on the notion that these types of requirements provide the host government with better control over the project company, through regulation and taxation.

The project sponsors can also realize benefits through local formation in the host country. These include receiving benefits afforded local entities, not otherwise provided to companies formed abroad. Examples include local tax holidays and access to government-sponsored labor training programs.

§ 7.07 CORPORATION

[1] Generally

The single-purpose corporate subsidiary is perhaps the most common project financing structure. In this structure, the sponsor incorporates an entity, frequently wholly owned, solely to develop, construct, own, operate, and maintain a particular project at a specific site.

[2] Reasons for Selection

The corporate form of business entity allows the owners of the corporation to enjoy limited liability for the actions of the entity. This liability can be forfeited, however, if corporate formalities are not followed. Although a loss of this liability protection, called a piercing of the corporate veil, is relatively limited in England, it is a somewhat more troublesome problem in the United States.

Loss of limited liability may arise where an injured party seeks to disregard the corporate identity of the special-purpose subsidiary and sue the parent corporation directly for damages in personal injury or breach of contract actions. "Piercing the corporate veil," an equitable remedy, is applied by U.S. courts to rectify injustice caused by a perceived abuse of the corporate form. To determine whether the doctrine applies, courts consider whether the parent and subsidiary are viewed and treated internally by officers and directors, and externally by the public or parties dealing with these entities, as separate.[5]

---

[5] In general, a corporate entity will be recognized as such by a U.S. court unless the interests of justice require otherwise. *E.g.*, United States v. Milwaukee Refrigerator Transit Co., 142 F. 247, 255 (E.D. Wis. 1905). The seminal three-prong test of Lowendahl v. Baltimore & Ohio Railroad, 247 A.D. 144, 287 N.Y.S. 62 (1st Dep't.), *aff'd*, 272 N.Y. 360, 6 N.E.2d 56 (1936), requires proof of the following to pierce the corporate veil: control, not mere majority or complete stock control, but complete domination, not only of finances, but of policy and business practice in respect to the transaction attacked so that the corporate entity as to this transaction had at the time no separate mind, will, or existence of its own; such control must have been used by the defendant to commit fraud or wrong, to perpetrate the violation of a statutory or other positive legal duty, or a dishonest or unjust act in contravention of plaintiff's legal rights; and the control and breach of duty must proximately cause the injury of unjust loss complained of. *Id.* at 157, 287 N.Y.S. at 76. Some courts have condensed the *Lowendahl* formula into a two-prong test. In Automotriz del Golfo de California v. Resnick, 47 Cal.2d 792, 796, 306 P.2d 1, 3 (1957), the court required: "(1) that there be such unity of interest and ownership that the separate personalities of the corporation and the individual no longer exist, and (2) that, if the acts are treated as those of the [subsidiary] alone, an inequitable result will follow."

The first requirement, the control or instrumentality test, is addressed by determining whether the corporate subsidiary is merely an instrumentality of the dominant corporation. Factors for determining if one corporation is the instrumentality of another include whether the parent corporation owns all or most of the capital stock of the subsidiary; the parent and subsidiary corporations have common directors or officers; the parent corporation finances the subsidiary; the parent corporation subscribed to all the capital stock of the subsidiary or otherwise causes its incorporation; the subsidiary has grossly inadequate capital; the parent corporation pays the salaries and other expenses or losses of the subsidiary; the subsidiary has substantially no business except with the parent corporation or no assets except those conveyed to it by the parent corporation; in the papers of the parent corporation or in the statements of its officers, the subsidiary is

To avoid the piercing doctrine in a project financing, business of the subsidiary should be conducted by officers or representatives of the corporation in their name or capacity as such,

described as a department or division of the parent corporation, or its business or financial responsibility is referred to as the parent corporation's own; the parent corporation uses the property of the subsidiary as its own; the directors or executives of the subsidiary do not act independently in the interest of the subsidiary but take their orders from the parent corporation in the latter's interest; and the formal legal requirements of the subsidiary are observed.

In general, ownership of all of the stock of the subsidiary by the parent and existence of common directors or officers is insufficient to find that the subsidiary is in control of the parent. *E.g.*, Luckett v. Bethlehem Steel Corp., 618 F.2d 1373 (10th Cir. 1980). Neither has mere supervision by one corporation over another been sufficient to justify disregarding the corporate entity. *E.g.*, American Trading and Prod. Corp. v. Fischbach and Moore, Inc., 311 F. Supp. 412, 415 (N.D. Ill. 1970) (review of loan documents and guaranty of financial arrangements insufficient to pierce corporate veil).

Before the corporate veil is disregarded, U.S. courts require some showing of injustice in addition to finding that a corporation is a mere instrumentality of another. *E.g.*, Fidelity & Deposit Co. of Md. v. Usaform Hail Pool, Inc., 523 F.2d 744, 758 (5th Cir. 1975). Fraud need not be shown, however. *E.g.*, DeWitt Truck Brokers v. W. Ray Flemming Fruit Co., 540 F.2d 681 (4th Cir. 1976).

"Improper conduct" can also satisfy the injustice prong of the test. Conduct held to be improper includes inadequate capitalization; payment of excessive dividends, sale of products to the shareholder at a reduced price, or exacting unreasonable management charges; misrepresentation, commingling, and not holding out to the public that the enterprises are separate; and evading federal or state regulations through the use of wholly owned subsidiaries. Amfac Foods, Inc. v. International Sys. & Controls Corp., 294 Or. 94, 654 P.2d 1092 (1982); *but see* Consumer's Co-op of Walworth County v. Olsen, 142 Wis. 2d 165, 419 N.W.2d 211 (1988) (undercapitalization insufficient by itself to justify piercing).

Some U.S. courts require satisfaction of the third prong, or proximate cause requirement, of the test. This requires a showing that an act by the parent, through its subsidiary, served to wrong the plaintiff directly. In most cases, this is subsumed in the second prong of the test.

In contract cases, the injustice test is difficult for a plaintiff to satisfy, especially in a project financing wherein a plaintiff voluntarily entered into a contract with a subsidiary while fully aware of the subsidiary's financial and corporate status. Under these circumstances, mere undercapitalization is not enough to pierce the corporate veil. Instead, courts examine whether the corporation is adequately financed as a separate unit to meet its normal, foreseeable obligations. *E.g.*, Labadie Coal Co. v. Black, 672 F.2d 92 (D.C. Cir. 1982) (whether capitalization is adequate is a function of the type of business in which the corporation engages); Chengelis v. Cenco Instruments Corp., 386

rather than as officers or representatives of the parent. In addition, the subsidiary should be clearly identified as the contracting party and the nature of the relationship between the parent and subsidiary should be disclosed. If the subsidiary, and not the parent, is the entity to perform, no representation should be made, direct or implied, that the subsidiary's performance is supported by the parent or the parent's assets, unless by guarantee.

[3] Management

Management of a corporate entity is based primarily on statutory frameworks. In general, formal meetings of directors and shareholders are required, minority shareholder interests are protected, and financial reporting is required.

§ 7.08 GENERAL PARTNERSHIP

[1] Generally

A general partnership is a business entity created by and operated pursuant to contract, statute, or both, in which all partners share proportionately in the management and income (or loss) of the businesses undertaken. In selecting the general partnership form of business organization, it may be relevant to determine whether it is a separate form of legal business entity. In some states of the United States and in English commercial law, such separate status is not available.

[2] Liability

The general partnership structure does not afford nonrecourse or limited recourse liability. All partners must be willing to assume the associated joint and several liability resulting from any negligent operation of the project. In addition, all partners must be willing to be bound by the acts of

F. Supp. 862 (W.D. Pa. 1975) (parent corporation held not liable under a contract the plaintiff entered with wholly owned subsidiary because the plaintiff had negotiated with the defendant's subsidiary with full knowledge of the relationship between the two corporations and knew that the subsidiary was a wholly owned subsidiary of the defendant, none of the contracts in question provided that the parent guaranteed or bound itself under the obligations of its subsidiary, or represented that it would support the obligations of the subsidiary).

another partner, which is the general rule in the United States and England.[6]

Most investors that participate in a project organized in the general partnership form establish a special-purpose subsidiary that insulates them from joint and several liability. Although maximum liability exists at the partner level, this structure provides the equity investors maximum control rights over the project company.

[3] Reasons for Selection

When the partnership form is selected, the motivation is typically that the project sponsor has inadequate equity to pursue the project alone, all partners have similar tax positions, or all partners desire participation in project management and control. The partnership form, like the joint venture form discussed below, affords the members great flexibility in management and control.

[4] Collateral Considerations

The type of collateral that can be granted by a partnership to a project lender varies by jurisdiction. For example, the Uniform Commercial Code adopted in the states of the United States allows a project lender to receive a lien on the general assets of the partnership, including after-acquired property, perfected by a renewable filing. Also, project lenders can take an assignment of the various rights of the individual partners in the partnership, including the right to receive profits and the right to manage the partnership. These are extremely important rights for the project finance lender that must restructure a troubled project.

In England, however, the collateral situation for a partnership is more troublesome. A partnership floating charge can be registered under the Bills of Sale Act. Because new filings are required as new property is acquired by the partnership, the statutory scheme is somewhat unreliable in a project finance context.

The England partnership lien scheme is even more troublesome in the project finance context as it relates to liens on partnership interests. A lien or charge over a partner's partnership interest provides no priority protection over other creditors. Further, a charge on a partner's interest provides the chargee only with that partner's share in profits. Management interference by the chargee is impermissible.[7]

§ 7.09 LIMITED PARTNERSHIP

[1] Generally

A limited partnership is similar to a general partnership, except that it has both general partners and limited partners. This form of organization of a business entity is available both in the United States and in England.[8] However, they tend to be used somewhat rarely in England, while they are more commonplace among U.S. project sponsors.

A general partner is liable for all the debts and obligations of the limited partnership. Liability of the limited partners is limited to the extent of their capital contributions to the limited partnership.[9]

[2] Reasons for Selection

Because of the limited liability available to limited partners, the project finance limited partnership is a useful structure for the contribution of equity by passive project investors. For example, the structure is sometimes used as a mechanism for participants such as contractors and equipment suppliers to contribute needed equity to a project. These participants are motivated to make the capital contribution based on the desire to ensure that the project is financed so that construction and equipment profits are realized. Once the project is operational at acceptable performance levels, the limited partnership interests can be transferred or offered to other project owners for purchase.

[3] Management

Under a limited partnership structure, each limited partner shares in the project profits while enjoying the associated limitation of liability of a limited partner. They exercise minimal management rights.[10] Indeed, exercise of management

---

[6] *See, e.g.*, Partnership Act, 1890, § 5 (Eng.).

[7] Partnership Act, 1890, c. 39, § 31(1) (Eng.).
[8] *See, e.g.*, Limited Partnership Act, 1907, c. 24 (Eng.).
[9] *See, e.g., id.*   [10] *Id.* § 4.

rights by a limited partner can transform the limited partnership interest to one of general partner liability.[11]

§ 7.10 LIMITED LIABILITY COMPANY

Similar to a limited partnership is the limited liability company. Liability of the members of the company is limited to the extent of their capital contributions. Under a limited liability company structure, each member shares in the project profits while enjoying the associated limitation of liability. Unlike a limited liability partnership, the members need not abandon management control to enjoy the liability limitation.

§ 7.11 JOINT VENTURE

[1] Generally
Another established structure is the project finance joint venture. Loosely defined, a joint venture is a combination of entities to achieve a common purpose. It is a flexible form of business enterprise that allows the member companies great flexibility in how the venture will be managed and controlled.

[2] Reasons for Selection
A joint venture is formed for a project financing by a sponsor that has neither the financial nor management capability (or in some cases, the desire) to participate in the project alone, but that wants to join with other entities to combine financial, technology, and management resources and to share risks. However, the sponsor may have all of the qualifications, skills, and experience to develop the project but lacks local country expertise or political contacts. For example, a fuel supplier and a contractor might combine equity with a poorly capitalized local country entrepreneur to develop, construct, own, and operate a project promoted by the developer through the vehicle of a joint venture. Other factors that weigh heavily in favor of a joint venture structure include spreading risks, efficient allocation of tax benefits, and

avoidance of restrictive covenants in loan or other agreements. Thus, the venturers are companies with different components to contribute to a project financing.

[3] Types
Joint ventures can be equity joint ventures or contract joint ventures. Equity joint ventures, on the one hand, typically involve the creation of a separate entity, such as a partnership or corporation. Contract joint ventures, on the other hand, do not usually require the creation of a separate legal entity.

The most typical joint venture structure in a transnational project financing is operated pursuant to a so-called teaming agreement or joint development agreement.

[4] Project Management
Management or operation of the joint venture is usually controlled by the joint venture agreement. A managing partner or operating company is usually selected to manage the day-to-day activities of the venture, under the overall policy control of a managing body, termed a *management committee*, or *operating committee*, composed of representatives from all venturers. Voting authority, and responsibility for capital contributions and other cash calls, is usually allocated by ownership percentages.

[5] Conflicts of Interest
Conflicts of interest are inherent in the project finance joint venture because any venturer may have interests in pursuing other projects. The confidentiality of information is an important consideration. Each venturer should carefully consider the type of information available to the joint venture and the extent to which the other venturers must be contractually required to maintain confidential information. The venturers also must consider whether a provision should be added to the joint venture agreement relating to competition by any other venturer with the venture.

[6] Nature of Liability
A joint venture does not confer limited or nonrecourse liability to project sponsors. Joint venture

[11] *Id.* § 6(1).

members attempt to limit their liability to the amount of capital contributed to the joint venture. This is accomplished, in part, through use of limited liability partnerships or limited liability companies.

§ 7.12 EUROPEAN ECONOMIC INTEREST GROUPINGS (EEIG)

[1] Generally

A European Economic Interest Grouping is a relatively new business entity designed to improve economic cooperation in the European Community.[12] Loosely defined, the EEIG is a business organization of other entities formed under the laws of Member States of the European Community, and that are subject to administration in different Member States. The activities of the EEIG must be ancillary to the activities of its members. Although the EC Regulation that created the EEIG provides them with some elements of a separate legal entity (authority to execute contracts, sue and be sued, and perform other legal acts), each Member State determines whether it is a separate legal entity.[13]

[2] Nature of Liability

Each member of an EEIG is jointly and severally liable for the debts and obligations of the EEIG. Under the regulation, however, creditors are expected first to pursue their claims against the assets of the EEIG.[14]

[3] Management

Members of the EEIG are relatively free to develop management rules for the entity.[15]

[4] Collateral Considerations

Collateral concerns exist for the EEIG in a project financing. Although the regulation allows a member entity to create a lien on its ownership interest, the holder cannot become a member of the EEIG solely by virtue of that interest.[16]

§ 7.13 DEVELOPMENT CONSORTIUM

Similar to a joint venture is a consortium. A *consortium* is the term typically applied to a group of large, well-capitalized corporations that collectively develop a project. Some projects are so large and so complex that the collaboration of a consortium of companies is necessary to ensure success. In some cases, a governmental agency also participates through an equity interest.

A consortium agreement is used to define the relationship of the members and regulate day-to-day activities. Among the typical terms are ownership interests; capital contribution requirements; approval of project financing terms; liquidation; transfer of ownership interests; and miscellaneous provisions, including confidentiality and governing law.

The consortium structure is often too unwieldy. To make project development, construction, and financing more manageable, the member companies typically form a single company, organized in the host country, to develop the project. This provides not only an entity easier to manage but also the following additional advantages: risk isolation in a special-purpose entity; eligibility for local tax law holidays and other in-country benefits; a pre-arranged method of facilitating participation by any local investors required by law; and easier financing arrangements, particularly with the collateral.

§ 7.14 PRESERVING FLEXIBILITY

Although there is a need to establish the ownership structure as soon as possible to achieve the goals of the project sponsors, flexibility in transnational projects is equally important. To do so, the ownership structure should be kept flexible, allowing for participation by local private and state participants. In addition, flexibility should be preserved to allow for various levels of governmental involvement in the project, whether ownership or risk allocation. Finally, all available financing sources should be consulted for possible participation, including the following: equipment suppliers with access to export financing; multilateral agencies; bilateral agencies, which

---

[12] EC Regulation of 1985, Council Regulations (EEC) No. 2137/85.
[13] *Id.* arts. 1(2), 1(3). [14] *Id.* art. 24.
[15] *Id.* art. 19(3). [16] *Id.* art. 22.

may provide financing or guarantees; the International Finance Corporation or regional development banks that can mobilize commercial funds; specialized funds; institutional lenders and equity investors; and commercial banks, both domestic and international. Involvement of any of these sources might affect the ownership structure.

§ 7.15 FRAGMENTATION: THE MORE THE MERRIER

The complex nature of project-financed transactions, coupled with conflicting tax laws and accounting rules among countries, sometimes combines to make multiple project vehicles necessary. For example, a holding company is sometimes formed in a low-tax country for holding ownership interests in the project company.

These considerations are not limited to the project company and its owners. Other project participants, such as a multinational construction company, sometimes form onshore and offshore companies to participate in a single project. These separate entities provide different services to a project, often in exchange for payments in different currencies.

PART FOUR

TECHNICAL, POLITICAL, AND ECONOMIC FEASIBILITY

CHAPTER EIGHT

THE FEASIBILITY STUDY AND NEEDS ASSESSMENT

§ 8.01 PURPOSE OF FEASIBILITY STUDY

The purpose of the feasibility study is to provide an analysis of the technical, economic, contractual, governmental, and market aspects of the proposed project. It is useful as a report for the project sponsor in determining the best allocation of resources among proposed projects competing for limited developmental funds. Externally, the report is used by the project sponsor to explain the project to potential lenders, government officials, and potential equity investors.

In providing the relevant information, different reports might be prepared for each of these audiences. This allows for protection of the confidential information of the project sponsor, which might not be appropriate for disclosure to all recipients.

§ 8.02 GENERAL DESCRIPTION

The feasibility study generally begins with an overview description of the project. The location is specified, usually including a map of the project site, with details about the surrounding topography, weather, drainage, major landmarks, population density, access to transportation and housing, water and wastewater treatment facilities, and similar information that might affect cost, public support (or opposition), and environmental effects of the project.

§ 8.03 PROJECT SPONSORS AND PROJECT COMPANY

The project sponsors are described in the report. Ownership interests as well as management control in the project company are specified in detail.

The background and experience of the project sponsors are also important. Among the relevant discussions are experiences in the underlying industry or service area of the project, success in similar projects, credit ratings and access to capital, financial and operating performance and projections, and management experience.

§ 8.04 PROJECT PARTICIPANTS

Each of the project participants, including the contractor, operator, fuel supplier, off-take purchaser, local and central governments, and other major project participants are described in the study. Besides general descriptions of these participants, information is also included about the experience of the participants with similar projects, general financial information and available credit ratings, and similar information about the ability of the participants to perform the undertakings necessary for the project to succeed. To the extent detailed financial information about the participants is available, such as securities filings, this information is also included.

§ 8.05 TECHNICAL INFORMATION

The technical information section of the feasibility study provides an overview description of the proposed project and also explains the technology and processes that will be used. Equipment manufacturers and suppliers are also described.

If a new technology is proposed for use in the project, information about demonstration plants or other projects that use the technology will be described. Also, potential technological risks will be identified and explained.

In addition, all other technical aspects of the proposed project will be identified and analyzed. These include fuel sources (availability, storage, infrastructure needs for transportation, quality); utilities (type, sources, availability at the site); water (sources, quality, required treatment, transportation); roads, railways, ports, and docks (need, type, additional infrastructure needs); raw materials (sources and supply); local labor (availability and skills); subcontractors (availability, qualifications); construction and operation labor (training, housing needs); spare parts (availability, delivery time, on-site supply needs); and residue and other waste disposal (sites, transportation, liability).

A discussion of anticipated performance and completion tests proposed for the project is typically included. Also included are discussions about the technical aspects of applicable codes and standards and host government laws and regulations with which the project must comply.

§ 8.06 ECONOMIC INFORMATION

Economic information in the feasibility study provides a general description of the expected construction, operating, and financing expenses for the proposed project and an estimate of the investment return for the project sponsor. The assumptions made as a basis for the economic projections are explained and potential cost increases explored. Also, preliminary construction budgets and operations budgets are included.

§ 8.07 CONTRACTS

An overview of the proposed contracts and the preliminary credit enhancement structure is also provided in the feasibility study. Also, any agreements with the host-country government are explained.

Among the proposed agreements and credit enhancement described are agreements among the project sponsors, such as the development agreement, partnership agreement or joint venture agreement; the project management agreement; the construction contract; the operating agreement; any site leases or other real property contracts; fuel and raw material supply agreements; output sale agreements; waste-disposal agreements; host-country agreements; and any other significant project contracts.

The format for this section generally follows the outline of the proposed contract, with a summary of the important business terms. The important provisions include conditions precedent to contract effectiveness; cost and pricing; covenants and defaults; damages and liabilities, including liquidated damages; and agreements on arbitration and litigation. Beyond general information about these contracts, each description generally contains schedules for negotiating the contracts, details on current negotiations, major issues not yet agreed upon, and similar details of negotiation status.

§ 8.08 PROJECT SCHEDULE

The schedule for the development, construction, and initial operation of the project should be included with all important milestones. These include negotiation and execution of necessary contracts, issuance of needed governmental approvals and permits, commencement of construction, and commercial operations.

§ 8.09 GOVERNMENT

The host government is described in the study, together with information about the likelihood of its support for the project. Such issues as currency risks, political risks, and bilateral and multilateral interests are also described. Any proposed or existing agreements with the host government are described in detail in the study.

§ 8.10 MARKET

The market demand for the goods produced or services provided at the proposed project is also described. If a market study is prepared, the results of the study are also explained.

Market information typically includes descriptions of possible users of the project's production and the financial viability of these uses; competitors, both existing and possible; expected demand for the goods or services; governmental management of demand for the project's output and output from competing sources; pricing; importance of the product or service to the economy and to governmental policies for the economy; sector organization and analysis of plans for privatization of government-owned companies in the same sector; and industry trends that might affect the market for the project's output.

If the output will be exported, additional analysis is required. Among the factors that need to be analyzed are the specific geographic regions in which sales are feasible and legal, regulatory, and financial constraints to export and import of the output.

§ 8.11 PROPOSED FINANCING SOURCES

Although the final financing structure might not yet be known when the study is drafted, alternative financing sources should be outlined. Of particular interest should be availability of financing or other support from bilateral and multilateral institutions.

§ 8.12 PRIVATIZATION

[1] Generally

Privatization of state-owned assets has taken place in many governments around the world.[1] The effect of privatization on an economy and on an individual project is an important element to consider in determining the feasibility of a project. Proposals for future privatization should also be discussed if the implementation of such a proposal could affect the project.

[2] Types

Three types of privatization methods have evolved: total divestiture, partial unbundling, and greenfield-only. In a total divestiture program, such as is used in Argentina, all the assets of the government in a particular sector are sold to the private sector. In a partial unbundling, such as in Trinidad, only parts of the assets are sold by the government, which retains some ownership interests for sale at a later date or to fund social programs. Finally, in the most cautious approach, as in Colombia, infrastructure assets are retained by the government, but new infrastructure needs are provided by the private sector on a greenfield basis.

[3] Benefits

The benefits of privatization to a country depend on the unique economic situation of each country. In general, however, benefits include an infusion of foreign capital, technology, work

---

[1] *See generally* Ada K. Izaguirre, *Private Participation in Energy*, Public Policy for the Private Sector, World Bank Note No. 208 (May 2000); Ada Karina Izaquirre, *Private Participation in Telecommunications – Recent Trends*, in Public Policy for the Private Sector, World Bank Note No. 204 (Dec. 1999); Gisele F. Silva, *Private Participation in the Airport Sector – Recent Trends*, Public Policy for the Private Sector, World Bank Note No. 202 (Nov. 1999); Neil Roger, *Recent Trends in Private Participation Infrastructure*, in Public Policy for the Private Sector, World Bank Note No. 196 (Sept. 1999); Penelope J. Brook Cowen, *The Private Sector in Water and Sanitation – How to Get Started*, Public Policy for the Private Sector, World Bank Note No. 126 (Sept. 1997).

efficiencies and labor management; creation or expansion of local financial markets as new capital is created and traded; beneficial joint venturing arrangements between foreign and local companies; introduction of competition and free-market efficiencies to improve performance of the underlying economy; enabling competition of local companies in the global marketplace; and allowing limited capital for use in promotion or achievement of social goals, such as health, education, and sanitation.

[4] **Effect on Project Feasibility**

Several factors need to be considered in analyzing the effects of a potential privatization program on a project. First is whether there is a defined regulatory and legal framework for privatization. Privatization of infrastructure assets creates a radical change in the underlying economy, the results of which must be considered in laws and regulations. For example, where a developing country privatizes existing energy production assets, and has historically subsidized energy rates to consumers, the process for rate increases must be clearly articulated in laws and regulations. Otherwise, the participants in the energy sector (including the consumers) will not enjoy the advantage of the market setting of energy rates.

Second, the government must be committed to the changes brought about by privatization. To do so, the government must minimize intragovernment infighting and dissension and also provide a well-organized, efficient privatization process.

Third, any other industries or sectors still owned by the government must be willing to enter into contracts and business arrangements with the privatized sector. If new infrastructure development is financed under the project finance model, the other industries must be willing, and encouraged, to enter into financeable contracts. They may not understand the types of contracts needed in a project financing (long-term, fixed-price fuel contracts, for example) or be resistant

to promotion of the success of a privatization effort.

§ 8.13 NEEDS ASSESSMENT

A needs assessment is similar to a feasibility study. This is a report sometimes prepared by the off-take purchaser to determine the need for the product or service to be produced or provided by the project. The report typically includes a comparison of the cost of purchasing the off-take from the proposed project and from alternative, existing sources.

§ 8.14 THE INDEPENDENT ENGINEER

Project success depends upon the predictability of adequate cash flow to service debt, pay operating costs, and generate an equity return. This predictability involves more than laws, regulations, and contracts; an engineering evaluation of project design, construction, and operation helps establish technical feasibility.

It is customary for the project lenders to retain an independent engineering firm to review technical feasibility. From this review, the firm produces an engineering report that considers the feasibility of the project in the following seven areas: engineering and design, construction, project start-up, operation and maintenance, input supply, off-take production, and financial projections. The factors evaluated in the study vary with each particular project but may include the following: redundancy of equipment; local operating conditions; previous design vulnerabilities at similar projects; new technologies; the construction schedule and contractor incentives for timely project completion; operating budget contingencies; status of permits; project start-up risks; preventive maintenance plans; spare parts requirements; fuel handling; and suitability of assumptions in the financial projections.

CHAPTER NINE

HOST-COUNTRY BUSINESS ENVIRONMENT FOR PROJECT FINANCE

§ 9.01 INTRODUCTION

An understanding of the macroeconomic environment of a host country for a project is crucial to the success of a project financing. It must be *stable* enough to encourage long-term investments by developers and loans by financial institutions; stability is a crucial element of project finance. Countries that enjoy stable exchange rates and inflation and predictable political environments are more likely to foster successful project financings, without the need for multilateral support.

Also, the roles of foreign investors, foreign lenders, the host government, and the World Bank with respect to the project must be clearly understood by the local electorate and political leaders. In short, a consensus must be established in the country to promote the stability and foreign investment required in a project financing. Further, the laws and regulations of the host country must reflect that understanding in a clear and predictable way.

§ 9.02 POLITICAL CONDITIONS

Political risks in a cross-border project financing can emerge from several sources. Principally, these are

- the degree of political stability;
- government attitudes about foreign investment (whether through policies involving currency exchange, repatriation, taxation, private sector involvement in infrastructure (so-called privatization), or infrastructure need);
- the extent of government involvement in the economy of the host country; and
- the economic projections for the host country.

Political stability is an important ingredient for cross-border project financing success. Stability breeds financing and investment confidence. Investors, developers, and financial institutions must be reasonably confident about the stability of the political environment in a country before committing large financial resources to a project financing in that country.

Complete stability is, of course, utopian. Instead, a reasonable level of stability coupled with political predictability is the goal.[1]

Political predictability is subject to institutional and electoral influences. Predictability is strengthened by successful consensus building on important political and economic issues. To the extent the consensus cannot be established, whether because of institutional or electoral barriers, the requisite predictability is less likely to exist.

For example, developing countries have an enormous need for new infrastructure, yet possess little capital for its development. Before an infrastructure project financing with external debt and equity can be successful in such a developing country, the political apparatus of the

---

[1] "A party of order or stability, and a party of progress or reform, are both necessary elements of a healthy state of political life." JOHN STUART MILL, ON LIBERTY, ch. 2 (1859).

country must first decide upon the proper role of private investors in the country's infrastructure development, construction, operation, and ownership. Then, formal laws and regulations, and occasionally constitutional amendments, are needed to carry out these political decisions.

The electorate must support these reforms. Wholesale reform of the basic infrastructure in a country may result in electorate unhappiness, which may challenge the political institutions. For example, many emerging countries have subsidized energy costs for consumers, agriculture, or industries to keep power prices inexpensive. The decision to promote private-sector power development may be an unhappy outcome for subsidized energy consumers in the electorate. Regardless, it is often necessary that subsidies be eliminated for the feasibility of private power development. Unless a political consensus on private infrastructure development is achieved, political opposition could thwart reform efforts.

Among the political factors that should be understood before embarking on a project is the division of power and authority between the executive and legislative branches of government. This is particularly important to an understanding of what branch has the authority to enter into agreements and other commitments regarding the project.

Another consideration is the strength of opposition groups and parties. Although these groups might not have majority power at the central government level, they could have or develop such power at the local level where the project will be located. A related political factor that should be explored is how political opposition groups are treated and the foreseeable effect of that on the project.

Finally, the role of the host country in the region and internationally should be understood. The relative strength or weakness of its role might affect its ability to receive multilateral funds or other foreign government-related support.

§ 9.03 SOCIAL AND HUMAN RIGHTS CONDITIONS

Some legal commentators have begun to pose general questions about the social effects of project finance infrastructure projects.[2] This dialogue is centered on the potential negative effects of direct foreign investment in developing countries, in the form of infrastructure project finance, on nonconsenting third parties, typically the poor. However, these concerns are more accurately labeled as political risk and should in no way be viewed as unique to project finance. If a politically powerful group is likely to oppose a project, as in the Dabhol project or Indonesian projects discussed in Chapter 1, it will do so not because project finance is the financing technique chosen but because there is some other problem, typically either political corruption or economic decline.[3]

§ 9.04 LEGISLATIVE AND REGULATORY CONDITIONS

Besides predictable political stability, project finance requires the establishment of a legal framework required for ongoing business operation. At a minimum, this framework must include basic legal provisions applicable to the project financing, timely and reasonably predictable issuance of permits, enforcement of contracts, and reasonably efficient dispute resolution through arbitration.

Project financing requires that the laws be sufficiently predictable to ensure that the project is authorized by the government, that the project has clearly defined parameters in which to act, and that the economic cost associated with compliance does not render a project unfinanceable. Laws that should be in place and reviewed by project financiers include the following:

- role and responsibilities of the government agencies in the sector;
- issuance of licenses, permits and franchises;

[2] Michael B. Likosky, *Mitigating Human Rights Risks Under State-Financed and Privatized Infrastructure Projects*, 10 IND. J. GLOBAL LEG. STUD. 65 (2003); *see* Carl S. Bjerre, *Project Finance, Securitization and Consensuality*, 12 DUKE J. COMP. & INT'L L. 411 (2002); Lissa Lamkin Broome, *Framing the Inquiry: The Social Impact of Project Finance*, 12 DUKE J. COMP. & INT'L L. 439 (2002); Eric Marcks, *Avoiding Liability for Human Rights Violations in Project Finance*, 22 ENERGY L.J. 301 (2001).

[3] *Accord* Stephen Wallenstein, *Situating Project Finance and Securitization in Context: A Comment on Bjerre*, 12 DUKE J. COMP. & INT'L L. 449 (2002).

- price regulation and controls;
- general business regulation;
- intervention and control over businesses in which there are foreign investors;
- restriction of dividend payment to owners;
- rights, duties, and powers of off-take purchasers;
- rights related to easements and other real property interests;
- labor laws and regulations;
- environmental and safety laws and regulations;
- contract enforcement and repudiation;
- dispute resolution;
- real property rights; and
- tax obligations.

These basic laws should be sufficiently understandable and precise so that flexibility in regulatory interpretation is not a risk.

To be effective, the regulatory environment should be sufficiently defined that its operation is transparent. Regulatory objectives should be clearly articulated, regulations should be well developed with clearly understandable procedures, and the permit and license process should be as objective as possible.

Stability and predictability of regulations are strengthened by a developed system of publication. Publication of regulations, adopted and proposed, is important to provide the notice periods that give a project company time to plan for changes. Also, publication of regulations establishes a clearly articulated process of such things as permit applications and issuances, on which project participants can reach meaningful conclusions.

To the extent a country's laws and regulations are not sufficiently developed to support a project financing, the requisite stability can be based in contractual obligations of the host government to the project company. These terms can be set forth in an implementation agreement or similar document. Implementation agreements are discussed in Chapter 14.

§ 9.05 ECONOMIC CONDITIONS

Whereas the economies of the world seem to defy understanding, an understanding of the macroeconomic conditions in the host country needs to be analyzed to assist in a determination of project feasibility. Important conditions include price levels, domestic capital markets and domestic credit ratings (and the related foreign debt position), and interest rates. The governmental role in managing these conditions is also important.

§ 9.06 PROJECT FINANCE IN DEVELOPING COUNTRIES

The lack of capital in developing countries results in a need for foreign investment and lending to satisfy growing infrastructure needs. The stability and predictability favored in project financings make structuring project finance transactions difficult and expensive in the developing countries of the world because of the complexity of risk allocation among multiple parties (including lenders, political risk insurers, multilaterals, and bilaterals) and the higher returns required to compensate parties for the risks involved. Investors and project lenders, preferring predictability to uncertainty, must be assured that the economic assumptions underlying a project, including revenues, taxes, repatriation, and other economic factors, will not be disrupted by host-country action. These countries, of course, are by nature developing economic, labor, legislative, regulatory, and political frameworks for growth and prosperity, not yet as settled (or at least as predictable) as the developed world. Although project finance risk allocation is important in all countries, it is of particular importance in the developing world.

The business environment in a developing country is different in at least four major respects from the developed world: legislative and regulatory systems, political security, economic security and centralized infrastructure systems.

Legislative and regulatory systems are usually not as defined as in the developed countries. Environmental laws and policies, for example, have not yet been aggressively pursued in developing countries. Also, these countries might not have in place detailed systems for dealing with foreign lenders and foreign equity investors, on such matters as ownership of infrastructure projects, taxation, and repatriation of profits.

Political security is another area of uncertainty for project financings in developing countries.

It typically results in higher costs necessitated by the need for complex insurance programs and higher equity and debt rates. Political risks, including expropriation, civil unrest, war, expatriation of profits, nonconvertibility of currency, and breach of contractual or other undertakings by the host government, are all-important considerations. These are discussed in Chapter 3.

Economic insecurity arises in a project financing from the inability of the potential project users to support the project through use or purchases of the project's output or service. This risk might manifest itself in lower than expected demand, as with the Mexican toll road project financings, or an inability to pay, like the power project disaster in Indonesia. Infrastructure projects might provide a needed service but at a price that cannot be afforded by most of the population.

Either because of political theory, a lack of private capital, multilateral investments, or nationalization programs, most infrastructure is owned by the government in developing countries. This ownership structure eliminates the effects of competition and increases the likelihood of market inefficiencies. Consequently, developers of proposed infrastructure projects must consider the effect of this structure on the proposed project. Possible effects include competition with the existing government-owned projects, which are arguably more likely to reduce charges for output or use, in return for short-term political gains; eventual privatization of all government-owned infrastructure projects; and ongoing rigidity inherent in working with government bureaucrats responsible for existing facilities.

Each of these four differences results in a risk portfolio that potentially includes higher construction and operating costs (inflation, availability of foreign exchange, delays, cost overruns, reduced demand for project output or use, inability of the population to afford the project output or to use the project, limitations on transferability of profits, and a lack of safety of the investment from nationalization). These developing-country risks complicate the structuring of project financings and ultimately increase the associated costs. Because of them, nonrecourse and limited recourse project financings are considered extremely difficult to accomplish in the developing world and require intensive attention to risk mitigation.

CHAPTER TEN

ECONOMIC FEASIBILITY

§ 10.01 PURPOSE

The project sponsor must produce and analyze the financial information necessary to decide whether the proposed project is viable. This information will be needed by those financial institutions and equity investors considering participation in the project, for the purpose of determining whether to lend to, or invest in, the project company. In some circumstances, it must also be distributed to other important project participants, such as the host government and major off-take purchasers, so that these entities can verify that the project is viable.[1]

§ 10.02 CONSTRUCTION BUDGET

A major foundation for the economic analysis of the project is the anticipated cost of constructing the project. The construction budget is the estimate of these costs, including development costs; site acquisition; the construction contract price; construction permit costs; start-up costs, including fuel and other inputs needed to conduct performance testing at the end of the construction period; and interest payable to lenders during the construction period (so-called IDC, or interest during construction).

§ 10.03 OPERATING BUDGET

Similarly, the operating budget is an estimate of the costs necessary to operate the project. These costs include management fees, fuel, raw materials, operator fees, labor costs, insurance, disposal costs, and similar operating expenses.

§ 10.04 DEBT SERVICE

The debt service costs are typically analyzed as a separate category of costs. These costs include interest, fees, and other amounts payable to the lender. The amortization of principal is also analyzed.

The economic analysis will provide a general summary of the expected debt terms, including principal amount, fees, interest rate, drawdown schedule of loans during construction, and the amortization schedule.

§ 10.05 WORKING CAPITAL

A project financing is based on the ability of the project to generate sufficient cash flows to repay the debt. At the early operating stage of the project, however, no revenue will yet be received. A ninety- to sixty-day delay between the time the

---

[1] For an excellent discussion and analysis of valuation of project equity investments, *see* Benjamin C. Esty, *Improved Techniques for Valuing Large-Scale Projects*, 5 J. PROJECT FIN. 9 (Spring 1999). *See also* JOHN D. FINNERTY, PROJECT FINANCING – ASSET-BASED FINANCIAL ENGINEERING 110–134 (1996).

product is produced or the service is provided, and the receipt by the project of funds to pay for the product or service, is typical. Consequently, the project economic feasibility study will need to reflect a working capital availability to provide funds to the project until revenues are generated and during periods of low cash flow.

§ 10.06 ASSUMPTIONS

The economic analysis is dependent upon the assumptions made in the financial projections. Increases in interest rates, inflation, foreign exchange rates, prices for fuel and raw materials, and commodity prices for raw materials, are among the variables about which assumptions are made in the economic projections. Neither certainty nor guesswork is the criterion; rather, assumptions must be based on credible predictions, historical trends, and reasonable future expectations.

Financial assumptions are made more predictable if any of various hedging facilities are used to manage these risks. These include exchange rate and interest rate hedging facilities, in the form of currency or interest swaps, and interest rate caps, collars, and floors.

Similarly, the amortization schedule for the project debt can be adjusted by structuring the loan agreements to shorten or lengthen the term of the debt, or for interest rates to change, based on commodity pricing, inflation, prices for the goods produced at the project or similar factors. This technique allows for simultaneous

adjustments in reserve funding requirements based on these changes.

§ 10.07 RATIOS

The economic analysis typically sets forth the results of financial calculations designed to predict the ability of the project to service the debt and generate equity returns on the capital invested. These include debt service coverage ratios and return on investment. As with almost every aspect of the financial analysis, the usefulness of these ratios is dependent upon the definitions of those ratios and the assumptions made in their calculation.

§ 10.08 VALUATION

A valuation of the project finance investment is important in an analysis of a project. The standard valuation techniques are either to discount free cash flows, using the weighted average cost of capital and subtracting debt, or by discounting equity cash flows using the cost of equity.[2] Recently, these techniques have been challenged as producing incorrect results unless adjustments are made for the changing effects of debt leverage.[3]

---

[2] For an excellent discussion of valuing large-scale projects, *see* Benjamin C. Esty, *Improved Techniques for Valuing Large-Scale Projects*, 5 J. PROJECT FIN. 9 (Spring 1999).
[3] *See id.* at 13–22.

CHAPTER ELEVEN

ENVIRONMENTAL REGULATION AND
ENVIRONMENTAL FEASIBILITY OF THE PROJECT

§ 11.01 GROWTH OF ENVIRONMENTAL REGULATION

[1] Generally

Environmental issues are an important aspect of transnational project development, construc-

tion, and operation.[1] Increased project construction and operation costs, capital costs related to retrofitting equipment to satisfy new standards, civil and criminal penalties, and securities law violations can each have significant effects on a project and its sponsors.[2]

Environmental laws and regulations have applicability beyond the project itself. They can also apply to the products produced by the project and the waste and other byproducts generated.

[2] Host Country

Local, state, and central governments are increasingly protective of the environment, particularly in the areas of air and water pollution and waste disposal. The degree of implementation and enforcement of these protections varies.

[3] Multilateral and Bilateral Institutions

The World Bank and other multilateral and bilateral institutions, such as the African Development Bank, the Asian Development Bank, and the Inter-American Development Bank, consider protection of the environment a necessary component of their activities. As a result, many governments and multilateral and bilateral institutions require that the effect of a project on

---

[1] See Julia Philpott, *Keeping it Private, Going Public: Assessing, Monitoring, and Disclosing the Global Warming Performance of Project Finance*, 5 SUSTAINABLE DEV. L. & POL'Y 45 (2005); Edward D. McCutcheon, *Think Globally, (En)act Locally: Promoting Effective National Environmental Regulatory Infrastructure in Developing Nations*, 31 CORNELL INT'L L.J. 395 (1998).

[2] See generally Janis L. Kirkland et al., *An International Perspective on Environmental Liability*, in 1 ENVIRONMENTAL DISPUTE HANDBOOK: LIABILITY AND CLAIMS (David A. Carpenter et al. eds., 1991); THOMAS M. MACMAHON ET AL., INTERNATIONAL ENVIRONMENTAL LAW AND REGULATION (1991).

the environment be considered and approved before construction begins or money is lent to the project. Even where such advance consideration is not required, project sponsors must consider the potential risk that environmental laws and regulations might develop in the future with retroactive effect.

[4] International Treaties

Sometimes international treaties impose environmental regulation. For example, the North American Free Trade Agreement is accompanied by an environmental side agreement.[3] Of particular interest is a provision in the side agreement that allows nongovernmental entities to initiate procedures before the North American Commission for Environmental Cooperation for nonenforcement of national law.

[5] Home Country

Laws and regulations of the project sponsor's home country could affect the project sponsor as a whole, even when the project is not in the home country. In that regard, the potential for extraterritorial applicability of the environmental laws of a project sponsor's home country should be considered.[4] Similar applicability has been afforded securities laws and antitrust laws in the United States. For example, U.S. securities law requires consideration of contingent environmental liabilities incurred abroad.

§ 11.02 ENVIRONMENTAL IMPACT OF PROJECT

At the very early stages of a project's feasibility, the effect of the project on the environment must be considered. In some jurisdictions, this process contemplates the preparation of an environmental impact statement, a detailed statement in which the project is described, environmental

impacts noted, mitigation plans developed, and agencies with jurisdiction over the project identified. It becomes the basis for the environmental analysis.

Information and analysis included in the report or environmental impact statement vary with the type of project and governmental requirements. The types of information that may be required (and should be considered by the project sponsor even if not required) are summarized in the following discussion.

[1] Site

A description of the project site is a threshold factor in an environmental analysis of a project. The important elements for analysis include topography; soil type; contemplated topographical changes, such as filling or grading; possibilities of erosion or subsidence from construction or operation; and the site plan.

[2] Air

Of course, air emissions during construction, start-up, and operation should be considered in environmental planning. The environmental analysis also includes the processes for controlling air emissions.

[3] Water

The water needs of the project might affect the environment. Thus, the analysis applied must include the availability of groundwater, the quantity of its use, and the discharge of the water after use. The effect of the project on surface water, such as lakes, rivers and streams, through use, runoff, contamination, or needed diversions, should also be analyzed.

[4] Plant and Animal Habitats

The effect of the project construction or operation on the plant and animal ecology must be considered. This is of particular concern if the project could affect endangered plant or animal species.

[5] Health Hazards

Potential health hazards related to construction or operation of the project are of increasingly important significance in environmental analysis. This is primarily because of conflicting medical and scientific data about the health effects on humans of such things as air pollutant

[3] North American Free Trade Agreement between the government of the United States of America, the government of Canada, and the government of the United Mexican States, 1993; North American Agreement on Environmental Cooperation between the government of the United States of America, the government of Canada, and the government of the United Mexican States, 1993.

[4] See generally J. Turley, When in Rome: Multi-lateral Misconduct and the Presumption Against Extraterritoriality, 84 Nw. U. L. Rev. 598 (1990).

emissions, electromagnetic fields, and other potential health hazards. The health hazard risk also concerns obvious hazards, such as explosion, chemical, and hazardous material storage and spills.

[6] Noise

If the project is near a populated area, noise may be a concern. Any necessary noise abatement techniques, including management of noise levels during so-called quiet times (generally 6:00 p.m. to 7:00 a.m.), should be described in the environmental report.

[7] Aesthetics

Although aesthetics is not entirely an area of environmental protection, the aesthetics of project design is sometimes regulated by governments or is a necessary component to avoid public opposition.

[8] Historic and Cultural Significance

Similarly, if the project is near a culturally or historically important site, the effects of the project on it should be considered. Minimization techniques should similarly be analyzed.

[9] Transportation, Public Services, and Utilities

Analysis of the effect of the project on existing transportation, public service, and utilities and the potential for increased services, is also needed. To the extent additional transportation systems or roads, public services, such as fire control facilities or utilities are needed, the effect of the addition of these should also be analyzed.

[10] Indigenous People

If the project will require the relocation of indigenous people, this must be analyzed as part of the environmental analysis. Indigenous people are those for which the lands on which they live, and the natural resources on which they depend, are inextricably linked to their identities and cultures. Factors that should be considered include the timing and cost of relocation programs and whether acceptable areas for relocation exist.[5]

In 2005, the World Bank approved a revised policy on indigenous people.[6] This policy is designed to provide project-affected indigenous people with a consultation role. The World Bank will provide project financing only where "free, prior and informed consultation" results in broad community support and will not agree to physical relocation if they have not provided their broad support.[7]

§ 11.03 PERMITS

The environmental feasibility report, and, if required, the environmental impact statement, will include identification of all governmental permits necessary to construct and operate the project. Failure to obtain a necessary permit can result in both civil and criminal fines and penalties. However, the most damaging outcome of the failure to obtain or maintain a permit is the prospect of a prohibition of construction or operation until approval is obtained. Such a delay will increase project costs and, unless properly structured, may cause defaults under or termination of project contracts.

The permits required for a project vary with the type of project, location, government, technology, raw material used, discharges, and emissions. Examples of permits that could apply include permits for air emissions, wastewater discharges, ash disposal, hazardous waste disposal, and landfill construction and operation.

§ 11.04 PUBLIC OPPOSITION

Public opposition to a project is an effective mechanism to damage or destroy a project. The

[5] See Michael B. Likosky, *Mitigating Human Rights Risks Under State-Financed and Privatized Infrastructure Projects*, 10 IND. J. GLOBAL LEG. STUD. 65 (2003); *see* Carl

S. Bjerre, Project Finance, Securitization and Consensuality, 12 DUKE J. COMP. & INT'L L. 411 (2002); Lissa Lamkin Broome, *Framing the Inquiry: The Social Impact of Project Finance*, 12 DUKE J. COMP. & INT'L L. 439 (2002); Eric Marcks, *Avoiding Liability for Human Rights Violations in Project Finance*, 22 ENERGY L. J. 301 (2001).

[6] The World Bank Operational Manual, Bank Procedure 4.10 (2005). *See generally* Fergus MacKay, *The Draft World Bank Operational Policy 4.10 on Indigenous Peoples: Progress or More of the Same?*, 22 ARIZ. J. INT'L & COMP. LAW 65 (2005); Note, *The World Bank and the Internalization of Indigenous Rights Norms*, 114 YALE L. J. 1791 (2005).

[7] The World Bank Operational Manual, Bank Procedure 4.10 (2005).

usefulness of this tactic varies with the host country's tolerance for public opposition and its permit application and issuance procedures. Through procedural challenges of permits and approvals, public opposition can result in costly delays (both during development and construction), requirements for greater public participation in the project permit review stage, increased capital or operating costs to satisfy public concerns, and outright project abandonment. The feasibility study should consider the degree of public opposition as one factor in the chance for project success.

Public opposition may not necessarily be based in environmental issues. Nonetheless, environmental permit application and issuance procedures could be used as an indirect attack on a project opposed by the local population for political, labor, or other reasons. The risk of public opposition can be minimized but never eliminated. Potential risk mitigation techniques might include any of the following: building a base of local support for the project that clearly defines local benefits if the project succeeds; creation of additional community benefits, such as construction of schools, water-treatment facilities and similar infrastructure improvements; selection of a site that is less susceptible to opposition, even if more expensive; a careful approach to securing permits and approvals that cannot be effectively challenged or revoked; and maximizing environmental protections.

§ 11.05 WORLD BANK ENVIRONMENTAL STANDARDS

Multilateral institutions are uniquely situated to pressure project sponsors to control the environmental effects of a project,[8] by conditioning guarantees or loan availability on compliance with minimum environmental standards. Consequently, the World Bank is under pressure to improve environmental conditions in developing countries through its lending and investment activities. The International Finance Corporation

and the Overseas Private Investment Corporation also apply the environmental standards of the World Bank to their activities.

In the past, many bilateral lending institutions, such as the U.S. Export-Import Bank, applied separate environmental guidelines to financing activities. However, in 2003, the Organisation for Economic Co-operation and Development Export Credit Group agreed on the OECD Recommendation on Common Approaches on Environment and Officially Supported Export Credits. U.S. Export-Import Bank revised its environmental guidelines in 2004 to be consistent with the OECD document.

In the past, the World Bank applied a set of recommended environmental standards, which were collected and published in 1988, as guidelines for recipients of financing benefits.[9] In general, these guidelines are outdated and not protective of environmental goals in most developing countries.

The World Bank is in the process of issuing new environmental standards.[10] It is expected that these new standards will someday be applicable to all projects in which the bank is involved.

The new guidelines provide two types of environmental standards: performance standards, applicable by industry type, and generic standards, for specific pollutants and control technologies. In general, the new guidelines are more stringent than the former standards.

§ 11.06 ENVIRONMENTAL DAMAGE AND AUDITS

It is important to understand as much as possible about the site on which the project will be constructed. The prior use of the project site must be thoroughly understood, as researched through historical documents, land records, and similar information. In addition, tests designed

---

[8] See Homer Sun, *Controlling the Environmental Consequences of Power Development in the People's Republic of China*, 17 Mich. J. Int'l L. 1015 (1996).

[9] The World Bank considers environmental factors in its lending decisions through such mechanisms as Operational Directive 4.01. *See* R. J. A. Goodland, *The World Bank Environmental Assessment Policy*, 14 Hastings Int'l & Comp. L. Rev. 811 (1991).

[10] The World Bank Environment Department, Industrial Pollution Prevention and Abatement Handbook, Preliminary Version (July 1995).

to detect environmental hazards, such as toxic waste, should be considered, particularly if the site was used previously for military or industrial purposes in countries with minimal environmental protection laws and in former socialist countries where achievement of production goals surpassed environmental concern.

These precautions are necessary for several reasons. First, project construction or operation could disturb these materials, making the environmental hazard worse. Second, to the extent cleanup is necessary to proceed with or continue construction, cost overruns could result from the cleanup costs associated with undiscovered environmental problems. In addition, in countries such as the United States, any owner or operator of a site is responsible for the environmental cleanup of a site, even if the environmental conditions preceded the ownership or operation activities at the site.

The process of examining a site for environmental hazards is called an *environmental audit*. The audit is generally a two-phase process. The first phase involves an examination of the previous uses of the site and visual inspections. A report is then prepared and any additional environmental testing or examination is recommended. The second phase implements that recommendation and includes such things as soil borings and testing, groundwater-monitoring wells, waste storage analysis, chemical testing, and cleanup recommendations.

The possible exposure of a lender to liability under environmental laws because of its association with the project site is an important element of environmental analysis. Of particular interest to the lender will be whether the applicable law imposes liability on the lender if it forecloses and thereby becomes the owner of the project.

§ 11.07 FUTURE ENVIRONMENTAL REGULATION

Developing countries sometimes lack the type of environmental laws commonplace in the industrialized world. Whether these countries will enact more stringent environmental protections, at the insistence of its population or through World Bank requirements, is too speculative to answer.

It is likely, however, that these laws will develop during the operation period of a project. It is prudent for the environmental report to contemplate the projected technical and financial implications of such changes. These include capital additions, changes to the technology used, financing for changes, and the implications of higher operating costs to satisfy more stringent environmental controls. In negotiation of project contracts, the risk allocation for changes in governmental environmental laws and regulations should be an item clearly resolved in the documentation.

§ 11.08 THE EQUATOR PRINCIPLES

The Equator Principles, introduced in 2003 and revised in 2006, are a set of voluntary guidelines designed to provide lenders with a common way to assess and manage the environmental and social issues (indigenous peoples and cultural heritage) that arise in project financings.[11] The principles are based on, and incorporate, several policies and guidelines of the International Financial Corporation, the private-sector lending agency of the World Bank. Each lender (Equator Principles Financial Institution, or EPFI) that adopts these guidelines agrees to apply the principles to each new project in which they provide project financing. The guidelines fall into three categories: assessment, management, and documentation.

[1] Assessment

Each EPFI will classify projects according to the environmental and social risks presented. Project sponsors with proposed projects assessed as at a medium or high level of risk will be required to provide a satisfactory environmental assessment. The project risks are required to be assessed by referring to host-country laws and guidelines

---

[11] Note, *The Equator Principles: The Private Financial Sector's Attempt at Environmental Responsibility*, 40 VAND. J. INT'L L. 197, 200–3 (2007); *see* Elisa Morgera, *Significant Trends in Corporate Environmental Accountability: The New Performance Standards of the International Finance Corporation*, 18 COLO. J. INT'L ENVTL. L. & POL'Y 151 (2007).

of the World Bank and International Finance Corporation.

[2] Management

If a project presents a high level of risk (and, in some cases, if it presents a medium level of risk), the EPFI will require an Environmental Management Plan. The plan must detail how the risks identified in the environmental assessment will be mitigated, monitored, or managed and is required to have public input.

[3] Documentation

Project loan documentation will include a requirement that the project company comply with the Environmental Management Plan during the project term. Regular compliance reports from the project company (borrower) are also required. The project company will be required in the loan documentation to perform the obligations in the EPFI.

[4] 2006 Revisions

These Principles were revised in 2006. Among the 2006 revisions are the following: The principles will apply to all project financings with capital costs above US$ 10 million (lowered from US$ 50 million); the principles will also apply to project finance advisory activities; the principles now specifically cover upgrades or expansions of existing projects where the additional environmental or social impacts are significant; the approach in applying the principles to countries with existing high standards for environmental and social issues has been streamlined; each EPFI is now required to report on the progress and performance of Equator Principles implementation on an annual basis; and more comprehensive social and environmental standards, including more developed public consultation standards.

[5] Effects on Project Finance

The effects of the Equator Principles on project financing are not yet clear. A pessimistic view is that these are nothing more than an attempt by banks to manage social, environmental, and reputational risk and avoid costly litigation. However, the principles provide, at the least, a beginning of environmental regulation in developing nations.

PART FIVE

PROJECT FINANCE
DOCUMENTATION

CHAPTER TWELVE

AN OVERVIEW OF PROJECT DOCUMENTATION

§ 12.01 GENERALLY

Contracts are king in project finance. Perhaps no commercial contracts are more discussed and analyzed in the financing context than those used in project finance transactions. Because nonrecourse and limited recourse project finance are based on the predictability provided by the contract structure, project sponsors and lenders are all interested in the risk allocation and other contract terms.

It is not an overstatement to write that every term of a project finance document is significant for the project participants. Examples of important project finance provisions are

- restrictions on the use or sale of any project asset;
- restrictions on the right to receive or use project cash flows;
- grants of security interests or similar collateral security rights to any party other than the project lender;
- short cure periods for defaults or restrictions on automatic terminations without any cure periods;
- force majeure provisions; and
- transferability of project documents following a foreclosure.

The following chapters in this part of the book contain summaries of the significant documents in a project financing. Although the documents might seem to be a bit overdone, do not be too confused or disheartened. One author commented:

While the attainment of . . . [project finance] objectives leads to flights of legal ingenuity which one might think could be put to better purpose, it nevertheless explains the background which applies

in certain cases to some of the idiosyncratic contracts [used in a project financing]. . . . [1]

§ 12.02 TRANSNATIONAL CONTRACTING

Almost every country on the globe respects the
right of private parties to bind themselves in a
written contract. However, it is a mistake to conclude that the rules governing contract formation, enforcement, and interpretation are identical throughout the world.

[1] Governing Law
The first question that must be answered: What
law will govern the contract? In many contracts, a
choice of New York or English law is preferable to
the parties because both jurisdictions have well-
developed commercial law. Whether a court will
enforce such a designation must be addressed
by the parties.[2] Otherwise, the parties might not
receive the benefits of the deal negotiated.

In some countries, laws prohibit selection of
any governing law other than the local law. These
are typically justified on public policy or nationalistic grounds. In such situations, lenders might
require that specific exemptions be obtained,
if possible, to provide sufficient comfort to the
lender.

It is important that the parties resist the immediate temptation to have New York or England law
govern a contract. Thorough analysis, in which
local lawyer advice is solicited, may lead the parties to select the law of another country. This is
particularly true where the law of the host country provides an enforcement advantage.

[2] Forum
Equally important is the selection of the method
by which disputes will be resolved and where
those disputes will be resolved. These provisions
must make clear the parties' intent. Among the
considerations to address is whether the forum
selected for dispute resolution is mandatory or
merely permissive; whether all or only selected
disputes are to be resolved in the selected forum;
and whether the forum selection applies to disputes other than contractual disputes, such as
tort claims or causes of action based in a statute.[3]

[3] Contract Formation
The requirements for contract formation vary
from country to country. The parties must carefully follow the local requirements. These requirements, on a continuum, range from the infor-
mality of no writing requirement to the strict
formality of contract stamps and governmental
approvals.

[4] Contract Structure and Validity
Although many international contracts look
identical, local laws determine the elements necessary to ensure validity. A local lawyer will need
sufficient time to review the contract before it is
executed by the parties.

[5] Formalities
Similarly, local law review of the procedural
requirements should be obtained. Almost every
country, including the United States, imposes
procedural requirements on contracting parties.
Some contracts require governmental approval
before they are valid. Other contracts must be
notarized and witnessed. Other countries impose
similar procedural and substantive safeguards
and formalities for contracts.

[6] Enforceability of Risk Allocation and Remedies
A common mistake negotiating teams make in
the transnational project finance arena is in risk
allocation and remedies. A remedy for breach of
a contract, such as the payment of liquidated
damages by the contractor because of a delay in
project completion, may not be as enforceable
in other countries as it is in the United States.
Some contracting parties, such as host governments, may not be constitutionally permitted to
assume responsibility for certain risks. Consequently, the review of these provisions by local
lawyers is essential.

---

[1] PHILIP WOOD, LAW AND PRACTICE OF INTERNATIONAL
FINANCE, § 14.02[3] (1990).

[2] *See generally* SKADDEN, ARPS, SLATE, MEAGHER & FLOM,
PROJECT FINANCE: SELECTED ISSUES IN CHOICE OF LAW
(1996); *see also* EUROPEAN COMMUNITIES CONVENTION ON
THE LAW APPLICABLE TO CONTRACTUAL OBLIGATIONS (1980).

[3] *See generally* GARY BORN & DAVID WESTIN, INTERNATIONAL
CIVIL LITIGATION IN UNITED STATES COURTS (2nd ed. 1992).

[7] **Currency Issues**

Currency issues are discussed in detail in Chapter 3.

[8] **Government Action**

Government regulation and control of a project present unpredictable risks to project participants. This is particularly true in developing countries and in the emerging markets of the former Soviet block. This risk, often included in a force majeure clause, should not be overlooked.

[9] **Term**

The term of a contract is sometimes governed by local law. Both the term and termination provisions may present local law considerations for the participants.

[10] **Language**

Lastly, the parties should agree on the language in which the contract will be written and interpreted. Although it may be necessary or helpful for translations of the contract to exist, it is important that only one language be selected to control contract interpretation. This will avoid the disputes in contract interpretation that would otherwise exist in a multi-language contract.

§ 12.03 DOCUMENT TYPES

The following document list is an example of the types of documents that may be necessary in a nonrecourse or limited recourse project financing:

- *organizational documents*, such as a partnership agreement, joint venture agreement and shareholders' agreement;
- *agreements with the host-country government*, such as a concessions agreement, governmental license, sovereign guarantee, and implementation agreement;
- *real property agreements*, such as title documentation, leases, easements, and construction lay-down rights;
- *construction documents*, such as a construction contract;
- *technology documents*, such as a license agreement;

- *operation and maintenance documents*, such as an operating agreement and spare parts supply agreement;
- *fuel supply documents*, such as a fuel supply agreement;
- *utility documents*, such as electricity, oil, gas and water agreements;
- *off-take revenue agreements*, such as production sale agreements, energy sale agreements, and the like;
- *transportation documents*, such as equipment or fuel transportation agreements; and
- *financing documents*, such as loan agreements, intercreditor agreements, and collateral security agreements.

§ 12.04 AMENDMENTS, MODIFICATIONS, AND SUPPLEMENTS

If the project documents are unacceptable for use in a project financing, requiring amendments before lending any funds to the project company is common for lenders. Thus, besides negotiating documents that protect the interests of the project sponsors, they must also negotiate the documents in a way that will satisfy the requirements of the lending community.

This is a challenge, however, because in most deals the lenders are not selected before contract finalization. Indeed, the appropriate strategy in some negotiations may be to avoid controversial provisions that the project sponsors know the lenders will ultimately insist upon. After a lender is selected, the sponsor can ask that the contract be amended to facilitate financing. In other situations, however, the most prudent course is for the project sponsor clearly to articulate the requirements of the financial community and resolve the hard issues before executing the document.

§ 12.05 NONRECOURSE PROVISION

[1] **Introduction**

Classic nonrecourse project financing provides a structure that does not impose upon the project sponsor any obligation to guarantee the repayment of the project debt if the project revenues are insufficient to cover principal and interest payments. The nonrecourse nature of a project financing provides financial independence to each other project owned by the project sponsor (and other investors). It also provides protection of the sponsor's (and other investors') general assets from most difficulties in any particular project.

[2] Sample Provisions

A typical nonrecourse project finance loan provision provides that no recourse is available against the sponsor or any affiliate for liability to the lender in connection with any breach or default, except to reach project collateral. The lender, therefore, relies solely on the project collateral in enforcing its rights and obligations.

The nonrecourse nature of the debt in a project financing need not extend throughout the term of the financing. As discussed in Chapter 1, for example, a project financing may be structured to provide recourse liability to the project sponsor during a limited period of the project development.

An example of a nonrecourse loan provision for use in a project finance loan agreement is reproduced below:

Nonrecourse. The [*Owner – actual owner of Project Company*] shall not be personally liable for payment of the amounts evidenced by the Note executed by the [*Project Company*]. Nothing contained herein, however, shall (i) preclude the [*Lender*] or any holder of the Notes from exercising any right or enforcing any remedy under this Agreement, or the Note, whether upon an Event of Default or otherwise, under this Agreement, the Note, or any other Collateral hereunder or furnished as security for any of the indebtedness evidenced by the Note, or (ii) limit the [*Owner's*] liability hereunder in respect of any damages suffered by the Lender as a result of any inaccuracy of any representation in this Agreement or as a result of any fraudulent conduct on the part of the [*Owner*].

The nonrecourse provision is also a part of project finance documents other than loan documents. An example follows:

Nonrecourse. Any claim against the [*Owner – actual owner of Project Company*] that may arise under this Agreement shall be made only against, and shall be limited to the assets of, the [*Project Company*], and no judgment, order or execution entered in any suit, action or proceeding thereon shall be obtained or enforced against any partner of the [*Project Company*] or the assets of such partner or any incorporator, shareholder, officer or director of the [*Project Company*] or such partner or against any direct or indirect parent corporation or affiliate or any incorporator, shareholder, officer or director of any thereof for any purpose of obtaining satisfaction of any payment of any amount arising or owing under this Agreement.

§ 12.06 COOPERATION WITH FINANCING

[1] Introduction

In addition to protecting the interests of the project sponsors, project documents must also be negotiated in a way that will satisfy the requirements of the lending community. However, in most deals, the lenders are not selected before contract finalization.

One approach to this dilemma is to include a so-called financial cooperation clause in the project contracts. This provision allows the parties to execute the project contracts, yet agree to cooperate with the reasonable demands of a project lender that it imposes as conditions to financial closing. An example follows:

[2] Sample Provision

Cooperation for Project Financing. [*Contracting Party*] acknowledges that the [*Project Company*] wants to use the nonrecourse project finance financial structure for the financing of the project and further acknowledges that it understands the types of requirements imposed by project finance lenders on the underlying project contracts, such as this Agreement. [*Contracting Party*] agrees to cooperate with [*Project Company*] in the negotiation and execution of reasonable amendments or additions to this Agreement required by Lender as a condition to financial closing for the project debt, provided such amendment or addition does not result in a material adverse change to [*Contracting Party's*] rights and obligations hereunder. [*Contracting Party*] further agrees to provide such data, reports, certifications, and other documents or assistance as may be reasonably requested by Lender, provided such assistance does not result in a material adverse change to [*Contracting Party's*] rights and obligations hereunder.

§ 12.07 TERM

The term of most contracts used in a project financing is at least equal to the length of the underlying project debt. This is not universally the case, however. Construction contracts are of a brief term. Some supply contracts for inputs readily available at a reasonable price have short terms. However, most important project contracts that can affect the project's feasibility must extend for the term of the financing.

It is generally prudent for project finance contracts to extend beyond the stated maturity date of the debt. If unexpected delays occur in a project, or if the project debt requires a financial workout, the lenders will need additional time beyond the stated debt maturity date to resolve the problem. Interestingly, contracts can have a term that is too long. Contracts with the host government, for example, should probably not extend beyond a reasonable period of twenty-five to thirty years. Terms beyond that may provide an attractive target for successor governments to complain that they should have the right to change the transaction.

§ 12.08 COMPLETION

[1] Introduction

Another concept that applies in a variety of project contracts is project completion. It is sometimes also called *commercial operations*.

The occurrence of completion can have a triggering effect throughout the collection of contracts used in a project financing. Under the construction contract, completion determines if and when the contractor is liable for liquidated damages arising from construction delays or performance guarantees. Under the operating agreement, it determines the date the operator begins its responsibilities for project operation. Most supply obligations under input agreements, and purchase obligations under off-take

agreements, typically begin on completion, as well.

The debt documents also begin and end key obligations and rights based on the concept of completion. For example, interest rates and loan amortization are affected by completion, with interest rates sometimes decreasing on that date to reflect a termination of construction risk (with the associated risk premium to the lender for taking that risk) and commencement of loan repayment. Completion is usually the loan repayment date for construction loan providers and the loan drawdown date for term financing.

Equity commitment obligations sometimes mature on this date. This commitment can arise from the obligation to invest equity as originally contemplated in the sources and uses of funds for the project or to contribute additional equity due to cost overruns. Under a completion guarantee provided by the project sponsors, the definition of completion will determine when, and if, additional funds must be used to finish construction, or whether construction has occurred and the contingent liability terminated.

The occurrence of completion sometimes triggers multilateral and bilateral involvement in a project. For example, U.S. Export-Import Bank does not currently provide funds for construction financing of projects, instead awaiting completion to participate as a lender.

Because of the importance of the completion concept throughout the project documents, it is important that the definition of completion be thoroughly considered and used consistently in project documentation.

[2] Sample Provision

"Completion" shall mean the satisfaction of each of the following conditions: (a) the Project shall have been completed in accordance with the design specifications of the [*Construction Contract*], (b) the [*Contractor*] shall have completed all Start-up and Testing (as such terms are defined in the [*Construction Contract*]), (c) the terms of the Performance Guarantee (as so defined) shall have been fully satisfied by either successful completion of the Performance Test (as so defined) or the payment of all liquidated damages required under the [*Construction Contract*], (d) the Interconnection

Facilities (as so defined) shall have been completed, tested, and approved by the [*Output Purchaser*] as required by the [*Output Agreement*] and the [*Output Purchaser*] shall confirm its obligation to commence purchases, (e) all permits and other governmental approvals necessary to begin operations shall have been obtained, and shall be valid, binding, and in full force and effect; (f) all construction costs of the Project shall have been paid or the [*Project Company*] shall have made provision therefor; (g) each of [*list project contracts*] shall be in full force and effect, and there shall exist no default or event of default thereunder (whether with notice or the passage of time or both); and (h) [*insert references to other project contracts that require completion to occur before obligations commence*].

Drafting Note: Clauses (a) through (d) are typically used in a construction contract; clauses (a) through (h) are found commonly in a loan agreement.

§ 12.09 COME HELL OR HIGH WATER

Under a take-or-pay contract, the purchaser (off-taker) has an unconditional obligation to pay the contract amount even if no good or service is provided or producible by the project company. In projects that are based on take-or-pay contracts, a "hell or high water" clause is included. This provision makes clear that the off-taker has the absolute obligation to pay, and the project company has the absolute right to receive, the required payment, irrespective of any defense, counterclaim, set-off, frustration of purpose, or any other right or excuse available to the off-taker. The project company is thereby assured of payment, come hell or high water.

Even where a take-or-pay contract is not used, the lesson of such clauses is important. The entities contracting with the project company will have a legion of excuses for why they should be released from liability if the contract is breached. Although project participants will not agree to waive all of these rights and excuses to performance, it is possible to limit them. To the extent possible, the project company's obligations should be limited in every project contract, thereby limiting available excuses for nonperformance by the other parties.

§ 12.10 FORCE MAJEURE

The force majeure provision in a project contract must also be carefully considered. Inconsistent force majeure provisions among the project contracts can result in great risk to the project. For example, if the construction contract provides an extension of time for the contractor to complete the facility upon the occurrence of a force majeure, the same relief must be available under the off-take sales agreement. If not, and the off-take sales agreement requires that sales begin on a specified date with no extension permitted for a force majeure, the project company would be unable to comply with the sales agreement because the project would not be completed in time. The result could be a terminated sales contract. Even where the inconsistencies are not of such dire proportions, the effect on the project's schedule or economics may be significant.

Inconsistent force majeure provisions can be cured with a so-called resurrection clause, in which the contractor agrees with the developer that where force majeure inconsistencies exist between contracts, the contractor will not receive relief greater than the relief available to the developer under other relevant contracts. In the earlier example, the contractor could not have been excused from performance to the extent such excuse would have resulted in a project delay of such length that the off-take sales agreement would be terminated. However, a less extensive delay would be permissible.

In negotiating a force majeure provision for any project contract, understanding the local circumstances of contract performance is important. In short, the parties must understand what is uncontrollable *in that location*. For example, the nature of the construction trade in the United States allows contractors in a U.S. project, in most circumstances, to agree that a strike at the construction site by the contractor's employees or subcontractors is not a force majeure. However, a contractor may be less likely to accept this risk when it performs the contract in another country.

A similar problem arises with the *unforeseeability* of other risks. The phrase "unforeseeable weather conditions," for example, may have a different definition in a different country.

A particular type of adverse weather condition in one country may be sufficiently predictable and regular in another country to result in the word unforeseeable being inapplicable. Thus, a contracting party that routinely adds the phrase "unforeseeable weather conditions" to a force majeure clause used frequently in one country may find that the clause will not excuse it from performance in another country because the adverse weather is foreseeable in the other country.

Different legal systems can create havoc on well-planned, matched force majeure provisions. As discussed above, the choice of applicable law and the jurisdiction of disputes is a critical element in ensuring that the force majeure structure is respected and enforced.

Despite this careful planning, complete elimination of the risk of inconsistencies in force majeure provisions may not be possible. Rather than rely on contract provisions, project sponsors may need to seek alternate solutions, such as standby credit, dedication of reserve funds, employment of additional labor, and the like, to address inconsistent provisions.

§ 12.11 WHEN THINGS GO WRONG

[1] Generally

In the end, project financings are dependent on contracts. As such, they are governed by contract law. Contracts must be carefully reviewed to determine whether the contract terms negotiated by the parties are enforceable. For example, a commitment of one party to prepay the project debt if it breaches a contract may not be enforceable as liquidated damages. If the parties desire that a particular contract be performed by a particular party, the laws of specific performance must be examined to determine whether that can be enforced.

This legal obstacle course exists in every project financing. More often than not, litigation brought to force a party to perform a contract is a disaster for a project financing. Why, then, bother discussing remedies and enforcement at all? It is for two reasons: Disincentives must be given in the contract to guard against a breach, and potential remedies often provide negotiating strength if a problem does develop.

[2] Contract Damages

Unless the amount of damages is specifically provided for in the contract, the general rule is that a non-defaulting party is compensated for the loss the defaulting party should have reasonably contemplated (on the contract date) its breach would create. This concept is completely unworkable in the project finance context where a breach under an important project contract could result in an avalanche of damages. There is insufficient time to await the decision of a court or arbitral panel on such questions as foreseeability of the damage and whether the non-defaulting party has a duty to mitigate damages.

[3] Liquidated Damages

This is why liquidated damages are preferred in almost all project finance contracts. Liquidated damage provisions, sometimes considered sacred to project financiers, are not always respected by the courts, however. Uniform Commercial Code Section 2–718(1) provides an excellent summary of the law on liquidated damages in the United States:

> Damages for breach by either party may be liquidated in the agreement but only at an amount which is reasonable in the light of the anticipated or actual harm caused by the breach, the difficulties of proof of loss, and the inconvenience or non-feasibility of otherwise obtaining an adequate remedy. A term fixing unreasonably large liquidated damages is void as a penalty.[4]

Thus, liquidated damage provisions in contracts governed by U.S. law should not be considered beyond challenge.

The law is similar in the United Kingdom. If the damages are a negotiated estimate of loss, and not a penalty, these damages will be enforced under English law without the requirement to prove the loss first.[5] French law provides courts with authority to revise damage amounts after a finding that the damages are unreasonable.[6]

[4] Specific Performance

It would be much easier in a project finance transaction if the defaulting party would simply

---

[4] Official Uniform Commercial Code and Comments § 2–718(1) (1972).

[5] Joseph Chitty, On Contracts at 26–061 (1994).

[6] See, e.g., French Civil Code, art. 1152.

perform according to the contract. The remedy of specific performance is not always available, however, because it is in the discretion of the court. As a practical matter, it is not unusual for the non-defaulting party to want to replace the defaulting party in its project role. Thus, specific performance is not necessarily a panacea.

§ 12.12 INTERNATIONALIZATION OF CONTRACTS

Internationalization is the recently coined term to describe the technique in project finance contracts to place their interpretation and enforcement in the international arena. It is a technique that helps to avoid, or at least manage, some of the political risk inherent in transnational projects. It is achieved by pursuing the following: choosing a governing law other than the law of the host country; choosing a forum for dispute resolution other than a court or arbitration panel in the host country; involving the participation of bilateral and multilateral institutions in the financing or credit support for the project, where possible; placing collateral outside the borders of the host country, such as cash collateral accounts; execution of concession agreements with the host government; and requiring political risk insurance. As most project sponsors have learned, however, the best form of internationalization is a fair deal – fair in terms, both real and perceived.

CHAPTER THIRTEEN

REPRESENTATIONS AND WARRANTIES IN PROJECT FINANCE CREDIT AGREEMENTS AND CONTRACTS

§ 13.01 GENERALLY

Facts are important in any business transaction.[1] In a project financing, however, an understanding of the details of a project is crucial to proper structuring of each of the project contracts and the financing arrangements. Any unverified fact is the potential weakness of a project, for uncertain facts may lead to unpredictable results.

In contracts, facts are traditionally memorialized in the representations and warranties section. It is here that the contracting parties in a project financing can determine whether the elements necessary to support a project financing exist. Thus, the representation and warranty section of project contracts, including the project loan agreement, serves an important role in the project due diligence process.

[1] Definition

Representations and warranties form the basis of most business transactions, including a project financing. A representation is a statement by a contracting party to another contracting party about a particular fact that is correct on the date when made. A representation is made about either a past or a present fact but never a future fact. Facts required to be true in the future are covenants.

A warranty is sometimes confused with a representation, but in practice, the two terms are used together, the contracting party being asked to "represent and warrant" certain facts. As an oversimplification, a warranty is a duty created in a contract; a representation induces a party to enter into a contract and can exist even though no valid contract is created. A contractual warranty, therefore, is a guarantee that a given fact will exist as warranted at some future date.

Historically, a breach of a warranty could be enforced as a breach of contract; a misrepresentation could be enforced as a tort. A breach of warranty occurs when the contracting party fails to maintain compliance with the warranty. To be actionable, a misrepresentation must be an intentional false representation of a material fact, the contracting party must have had knowledge that the fact was false or the representation must have been made with reckless disregard for accuracy,[2] the contracting party must have been induced into the contract by that fact, and

---

[1] "She always says, my lord, that facts are like cows. If you look them in the face hard enough they generally run away." DOROTHY SAYERS, CLOUDS OF WITNESS, ch. 4 (1926).

[2] Under the Misrepresentation Act, liability exists even if the representation was made with reckless disregard for accuracy. Misrepresentation Act, 1967.

damages must be proximately related to the fact misrepresented.

Traditionally, the remedy for a breach of warranty is damages, although the contract remains binding. In misrepresentation cases, however, the remedy may be damages or rescission and restitution.

Because some courts blur the distinction between the two, the practice is to require the contracting party to "represent and warrant" the same facts and to state that the untruth of any representation or warranty is an event of default under the contract. Although there are practical differences between representations and warranties, this approach simplifies drafting and negotiation.

[2] Purpose

The purpose of a representation in a project finance contract is to set forth in the contract the factual basis under which each of the contracting parties is prepared to enter into the transaction. Each contracting party can thereby set out the basis of the project finance deal in the representation section of the contract.

In some instances, the representations will contain the key elements under which a board of directors or bank credit committee has authorized the transaction. In other instances, the representations are standard, commonsense, yet important, factual statements that are a part of every transaction.

Through the process of negotiation, a contracting party can discover whether the other contracting party can represent the facts that form the basis of the deal. This process aids each project participant in determining whether the essential elements of the project exist. If, for example, the project lender is basing its decision to lend funds partly on the assumption that the project company has obtained all necessary real property interests to build the project, and that is not yet the case, it will likely refuse to close and advance funds until the necessary interests are obtained.

[3] Role of Representations and Warranties in Project Finance

Because project financings are based on the financial merits of a project, including those embodied in the project contracts, representa-

tions and warranties are particularly important. In fact, representation and warranty sections in the typical project finance loan agreement do, and should, read like a checklist of the essential elements of project finance. Each element of the project must be verified to determine whether the necessary ingredients exist. This is the essence of due diligence and the purpose of the project finance representation section.

For example, project contracts that govern construction, operation, fuel supply, and output sales are important to the success of the project, including the ability of the project sponsor to service debt after operating costs are paid. If one of the contracting parties, for example, does not have a significant permit or asset, the project could experience delays in construction and concomitant increased costs, and the contract will fail in its credit support role. A properly drafted and negotiated representation and warranty section will assist the participants in verifying whether the contract provides the project with the necessary credit support.

§ 13.02 MECHANICS OF REPRESENTATIONS AND WARRANTIES

[1] Affirming the Basic Assumptions

Representations and warranties in a project contract or project finance loan agreement serve the purpose of affirming, in writing, the facts under which each contracting party bases its decision to enter the transaction. Months, and sometimes years, of discussions, feasibility studies, and projections culminate in a set of facts that form the foundation of credit approval by the project lender and selection of the contractor, operator, and fuel supplier by the project sponsor.

Many representations and warranties are common to all agreements, including legal status and authority to enter into the transaction. These are discussed immediately below.

Legal Status. The legal status of the contracting party is important because it determines the ability of the party to enter into the transaction and because it governs financial liabilities. A contract entered into with an unincorporated company affects the ability to enforce the contract against a presumed set of assets. Similarly, a limited partnership, the limited partners of which enjoy limited liability for partnership debts, is a very different contracting party from a general partnership, the partners of which have joint and several unlimited liability. Thus, such facts as due incorporation or organization, continued existence, good tax standing, and qualification to do business in foreign jurisdictions are each important.

Authority to Enter Into the Transaction. The ability of the contracting party to enter into the transaction is similarly important. Among the considerations are whether the party is subject to any corporate or partnership restriction relating to the transaction or whether any court or governmental agency order could have a material adverse effect on the party.

[2] Additional Facts Received in Negotiation Process

During negotiation of the contract, the representations and warranties are refined as the contracting parties disclose facts that may present potential problems. Typically, these result in changes to the representations and warranties and, of course, may modify the structure, price, or terms of the agreement, and the underlying project.

It is important in a project financing to disclose these problems early so that agreed upon resolutions are made without affecting the closing schedule. Although some project sponsors have been successful in hiding project problems, more often than not the problems rise to the surface creating larger problems.

For example, even though the project company has not yet received a required government approval, the project lender may agree to except that permit from the representation that the project company has all permits. Instead, the lender could modify the covenant section of the loan agreement to provide that the project company will apply for and diligently pursue the permit. Similarly, the default section can specify that the permit must be issued and in effect by a definite date.

[3] Date Representations and Warranties Are Made

Representations and warranties are typically made on the date the contract is executed. Some

contracts, especially loan agreements, provide that one contracting party is excused from taking a specified action, such as making further loans, if the representations and warranties are not true on the date the further action is permitted.

Thus, the contracting parties allocate the risk of the future correctness of representations and warranties by specifically assigning that risk to one of the parties. If, for example, a contractor represents in a construction contract that it has the personnel necessary to complete a project, and the representation and warranty is not required to be restated on each construction payment date, the project company has assumed the risk of low staffing by the contractor and will be required to pay the contractor. (Of course, other contract provisions may provide an excuse for the project company's obligation to make the payment.)

[4] Materiality and Knowledge Limitations in Representations and Warranties

In the negotiation process, contracting parties will sometimes desire to limit a representation and warranty by a materiality limitation or knowledge limitation. With a materiality limitation, the contracting party excepts from the scope of the representation and warranty those facts that are immaterial in effect. With a knowledge limitation, the contracting party limits the statement to only those facts now known; if the fact later becomes known as untrue, and the party had no knowledge of the untruth, no breach of the representation and warranty occurs. The significance of these limitations depends on the transaction involved and the assumptions made by the contracting party on which the transaction is based.

A materiality limitation is sometimes requested in situations in which a contracting party represents and warrants that it complies with laws and governmental orders, or that it is not in breach of any agreement. The contracting party may request that the representation and warranty be revised such that the contracting party is in compliance with all material laws, that it is in material compliance with all material laws, or that it is in compliance with all laws the failure to comply with which would have a material adverse effect on its business or operations.

The decision of the other contracting party to permit the materiality limitation is dependent on the importance of the representation and warranty to the transaction, and the ability of the party making the statement to verify the accurateness of the statement. If the representation and warranty is not exceptionally significant, then some form of the materiality exception is typically permitted. Similarly, if the contracting party to whom the representation is made can independently verify the facts underlying the representation and warranty, the materiality exception is often acceptable.

In a project financing, where operation of the project determines whether debt is repaid, the materiality limitation may be unacceptable to the lender in a loan agreement. This is because the lender will prefer to determine whether a breach of a representation is material *at the time* the inaccuracy becomes known.

In a project finance construction contract, however, it may be acceptable to permit the contractor to include a materiality limitation. This is because the contractor typically does business in a number of governmental jurisdictions, and it is probable that it is in violation of a law somewhere on some project, but the consequences of that violation are insignificant.

Similarly, the project finance lender may find a materiality limitation unacceptable when the project sponsor is asked to represent and warrant in the loan agreement that it is in compliance with all major project contracts. The lender, relying on the terms and conditions contained in these contracts in its decision to make loans to the project company, has a significant interest in determining whether any problems exist. Also, the project sponsor can obtain a consent from each of the contracting parties stating that no defaults exist, which makes it easier for the project company to then represent compliance to the project lender.

A knowledge limitation in a representation and warranty transforms the representation and warranty from a risk allocation mechanism to an antifraud provision. In effect, the limitation of the representation and warranty to the knowledge of the contracting party means that there can be no breach unless the party knew the fact was untrue and the other party can prove that the party made the representation knowing of its falsity. The limitation may be acceptable in limited situations in which the party is asked to represent a fact that is,

in part, known only to a third party. An example is the representation that there is no threatened revocation of a permit by a government agency.

§ 13.03 VERIFICATION OF REPRESENTATIONS AND WARRANTIES

It is not unusual for the contracting parties, particularly the project lender, to verify the representations and warranties made by the project company and the other project participants. The degree of this review depends on the sophistication of the parties, the nature of ongoing relationships between the contracting parties, and the financial risk in the transaction.

In general, project finance lenders conduct their own due diligence into the feasibility of the project, through such devices as feasibility studies by consultants, requiring legal opinions to verify the representations and warranties, and obtaining certificates from officers of the project sponsor. Another important due diligence item is the consent to assignment, obtained by the lender from the project participants as part of the financial closing process. The consent to assignment is discussed in Chapter 26.

§ 13.04 INTRODUCTION TO SAMPLE PROVISIONS

Section. The [*identity of party making representations and warranties*] represents and warrants to [*identity of party to whom made*] that:

The preamble to the representation and warranty section announces the representations and warranties made by one contracting party to another party. It also serves to remind the drafter that representations and warranties, not covenants, are to follow.

§ 13.05 FORMALITIES OF BUSINESS ORGANIZATION

[1] Generally
Among the first representations and warranties made in any transaction is the business organization representation, which concerns the form of

business organization of the contracting party, whether corporation, general partnership, limited partnership, limited liability company, or limited liability partnership.

This representation and warranty is significant in a project financing because of the importance of identifying and conducting a due diligence review of the parties involved. For example, as discussed in Chapter 15, in project financings, the contractor typically provides credit enhancement to the project through liquidated damages and other payments. The specific business organization of the contractor must be identified so that financial due diligence can be conducted on the contractor to determine whether the requisite creditworthiness exists to support the financial obligations it has undertaken.

Due Incorporation; Due Formation. Whether a corporation or partnership is duly incorporated or organized depends on the law of the jurisdiction in which the entity is formed. If the requisites of law were complied with on the date of formation, the corporation is said to be *duly incorporated.* A partnership, whether general or limited, is *duly formed* if the requisites of law were complied with on the day of partnership formation.

Valid Existence. Although duly incorporated or formed, a corporation or partnership may have lost its statutory or contractual existence. A corporation may be dissolved and its certificate of incorporation may expire if it was not formed with perpetual existence, or the jurisdiction of incorporation may revoke corporate existence. A partnership may cease to exist through statute or through operation of the partnership agreement.

Good Standing. Business entities are in good standing if they are in compliance with statutes relating to payment of fees and taxes and filings of annual reports. Failure to do so may restrict the entity from certain statutorily granted rights, such as access to the judicial system.

Power and Authority. A business entity has the power and authority to conduct business if such rights are granted in its documents of forma-

tion, whether the certificate of incorporation of a corporation or the partnership agreement of a partnership. Such organizational documents must be examined to determine whether an entity has the power to perform the contract it has executed.

Due Qualification. Statutes governing businesses generally require a foreign entity (an entity not formed in the jurisdiction) to qualify to do business in that jurisdiction. Failure to qualify may temporarily restrict the right of the entity to use the judicial system of the foreign state, although the right is often reinstated once back payments or filings are made. Some jurisdictions, such as a few states in the United States, deny access to the judicial system even after curative steps are made, however, with respect to contracts executed during the violation. Because of the importance of the underlying contracts in a project financing, the good standing of the project company should be carefully analyzed to ensure that important project contracts can be enforced.

[2] Corporation
Incorporation, Good Standing, and Due Qualification of Corporation. The [*Corporation*] is a corporation duly incorporated, validly existing, and in good standing under the laws of [*Jurisdiction*]; has the corporate power and authority to own its assets and to transact the business in which it is now engaged or proposed to be engaged; and is duly qualified to do business in each jurisdiction in which the character of the properties owned by it therein or in which the transaction of its business makes such qualification necessary.

[3] General Partnership
Formation, Good Standing, and Due Qualification of General Partnership. The [*General Partnership*] is a limited partnership duly formed and validly existing under the laws of [*Jurisdiction*]; has the partnership power and authority to own its assets and to transact the business in which it is now engaged or proposed to be engaged; is duly qualified to do business in each jurisdiction in which the character of the properties owned by it therein or in which the transaction of its business makes such qualification necessary; and the copy of the partnership agreement attached hereto as Exhibit _ is a true and

complete copy of such partnership agreement, and there have been no other amendments or changes to such partnership agreement.

[4] Limited Partnership

Formation, Good Standing, and Due Qualification of Limited Partnership. The [*Limited Partnership*] is a limited partnership duly formed and validly existing under the laws of [*Jurisdiction*]; has the partnership power and authority to own its assets and to transact the business in which it is now engaged or proposed to be engaged; is duly qualified to do business in each jurisdiction in which the character of the properties owned by it therein or in which the transaction of its business makes such qualification necessary; and the copy of the limited partnership agreement attached hereto as Exhibit _ is a true and complete copy of such limited partnership agreement, and there have been no other amendments or changes to such limited partnership agreement.

[5] General Partners of Limited Partnership

Incorporation, Good Standing, and Due Qualification of the General Partners. Each general partner of the [*Limited Partnership*] is a corporation duly incorporated, validly existing, and in good standing under the laws of [*Jurisdiction*]; has the corporate power and authority to own its assets and to transact the business in which it is now engaged or proposed to be engaged; and is duly qualified to do business in each jurisdiction in which the character of the properties owned by it therein or in which the transaction of its business makes such qualification necessary.

§ 13.06 POWER AND AUTHORITY

[1] Introduction

The power and authority representation and warranty concerns the contracting party's ability to enter into the specific transaction contemplated by the contract. Specifically, the contracting party confirms that all consents to the transaction by shareholders or partners have been received, it has the ability to enter into the contract under its governing documents and that all third parties, including governmental agencies and courts, have provided necessary approvals and consents to the transaction.

Authority to Enter Into and Perform Transaction. The contracting party's governing documents, such as the certificate of incorporation and bylaws of a corporation, or partnership agreement of a partnership, may impose limitations on certain transactions. For example, the certificate of incorporation may require shareholder consent for certain guarantees of a third party's debt or other obligations.

Corporate or Partnership Approval. Similarly, the governing documents may require shareholder or unanimous partner consent to the transaction.

Violation of Law or Judicial Order. The transaction contemplated may be prohibited or limited by a law or regulation, or by a judicial order, or may require a consent by a governmental agency or court. Also, the transaction may cause the contracting party to be in violation of a law or order, even though the transaction itself is not a violation.

The scope of this representation is not as far reaching as the representation that the project sponsor or other contracting party has all *project permits* necessary to construct or operate the project. That representation is discussed below. Rather, this representation is limited to the execution and delivery of one specific contract.

Breach of Existing Agreement. The transaction may also violate an existing agreement of the contracting party. Even though the violation of an agreement with another party is unrelated to the contemplated transaction, the violation may result in a default under that agreement, subjecting the contracting party to damages that may have a negative effect on the ability to conduct its business.

Creation of Liens. In some loan transactions, the lender includes a provision that prohibits the borrower from granting a security interest in its assets to another party unless the lender is also given a security interest. If the proposed contract includes a grant of security, this representation assists in determining whether such a grant creates a problem with the contracting party's lender.

[2] Sample Provision

Power and Authority. The execution, delivery, and performance by the [*Contracting Party*] of the [*Contract*] has been duly authorized by all necessary [*corporate / partnership*] action and does not and will not: (1) require any further consent or approval of the [*shareholders / partners*] of such [*corporation / partnership*]; (2) contravene such [*corporation's / partnership's*] [*certificate of incorporation or bylaws / partnership agreement / certificate of limited partnership or limited partnership agreement*]; (3) violate any provision of any law, rule, regulation, order, writ, judgment, decree, determination, or award presently in effect having applicability to the [*Contracting Party*]; (4) cause the [*Contracting Party*] to be in violation of or in default under any such law, rule, regulation, order, writ, judgment, injunction, decree, determination, or award or any such indenture, agreement, lease, or instrument; (5) result in a breach of or constitute a default under any indenture or loan or credit agreement or any other agreement, lease, or instrument to which the [*Contracting Party*] is a party or by which it or its properties may be bound or affected; or (6) result in, or require, the creation or imposition of any mortgage, deed of trust, pledge, lien, security interest, or other charge or encumbrance of any nature upon or with respect to the properties now owned or hereafter acquired by the [*Contracting Party*].

§ 13.07 LEGALLY ENFORCEABLE AGREEMENT

[1] Introduction

The representation and warranty that the contract is legally enforceable is not a legal opinion. Rather, the contracting party represents that the factual requisites of a contract are in place and therefore that the contract is legally enforceable. Thus, this representation affirms that a contract exists, that the validity of the contract is not in dispute, and that the contracting party has the legal ability to enter into the transaction contemplated and understands that the contract is enforceable through arbitration or the judicial system.

[2] Sample Provision

Legally Enforceable Agreement. This agreement is in full force and effect and, is a legal, valid, and binding

obligation of the [*Contracting Party*], enforceable against the [*Contracting Party*], in accordance with its terms, except to the extent that such enforcement may be limited by applicable bankruptcy, insolvency, and other similar laws affecting creditor's rights generally.

§ 13.08 FINANCIAL STATEMENTS, PROJECT BUDGET, AND PROJECTIONS

[1] Introduction

The financial statement representation is typically used in a project financing in the project credit agreement and relates to the project construction budget, projections of revenue and expenses during project operation, and the balance sheet of the project company. The type of representation required by the lender will vary depending upon whether the loan is for a project not yet under construction or whether the project is in operation. If the project loan is for construction, and the project company is a newly created entity, financial statements may be unavailable.

In some cases, other project contracts use this representation to set forth the creditworthiness of one of the project participants. This is particularly important where a project participant provides some form of credit enhancement for the financing, such as a contractor agreeing to pay liquidated damages under a construction contract. Because of the nonrecourse nature of project finance debt, this financial information is significant to the lender. The value of underlying contract obligations is determined by the balance sheet of the party providing the support.

In some situations, financial information of project participants is available from governmental agencies or public databases. For example, in the United States, a publicly traded corporation will have financial information on file with the Securities and Exchange Commission, copies of which are available to the public. In these situations, this representation is often not required.

[2] Sample Provision for Project Finance Credit Agreement for New Project

The financial statement representation for use in a project finance credit agreement for a project not yet under construction typically includes provisions relating to the project budget, project projections, and project liabilities.

Project Budget. The project finance lender must determine the construction cost of the project so that it can conclude whether the project revenue from operation will provide sufficient revenue to service debt and pay operating expenses. The representation will reference the project budget, typically either attached as an exhibit to the credit agreement or delivered separately at financial closing and state that the project budget fairly reflects the construction costs for the project.

Projections. Similarly, the project finance lender must determine the revenues that will be received by the project, as well as the project expenses incurred in operation of the project. The representation will reference these projections and state that the projections fairly represent anticipated revenues and expenses.

(a) *Project Budget.* The project budget was prepared using reasonable assumptions of the type typically used in projects similar to this project and the [*Project Company*] is not aware of any presently existing or threatened fact, condition, or event that indicates or could reasonably be viewed as indicating that the project will not be able to be completed in accordance with the project budget, and there are no liabilities of the [*Project Company*], fixed or contingent, which are not reflected in the project budget.

(b) *Projections.* The projections were prepared using reasonable assumptions of the type typically used in projects similar to this project and the [*Project Company*] is not aware of any presently existing or threatened fact, condition, or event that indicates or could reasonably be viewed as indicating that the project will not be able to be operated in accordance with the projections, and there are no expenses of the [*Project Company*], fixed or contingent, which are not reflected in the project budget.

(c) *No Other Business.* The [*Project Company*] has engaged in no business other than the project, and has no obligations or liabilities other than those incidental to its organization, and those incurred in connection with the project or its execution, delivery, and performance of this Agreement, all of which are set forth in the projections and project budget. The [*Project Company*] is solely in the busi-

ness of acquiring, developing, constructing, financing, owning, and operating the project.

(d) *No Material Adverse Change.* There has been no material adverse change in the condition (financial or otherwise), business, or operations of the [*Project Company*].

[3] Modification of Financial Statement Representation for Existing Project

If the project is in operation, the financial statement representation should be modified to reflect the availability of financial statements and the deletion of the project budget.

The financial statement representation should cover those statements upon which the bank relies in making its credit analysis. Typically, these include the borrower's last financial year reports, and the reports for the most recent financial quarter. The gap in time between the date of the last financial statement and the closing is addressed in a "no material adverse change" clause, which requires the borrower to represent that there has been no material adverse change in its condition, business, or operations since the date of the last financial statement.

Generally Accepted Accounting Principles. The borrower is required to affirm that the financial statements were prepared in accordance with those accounting standards generally accepted as standard accounting principles in the applicable country. In the United States, these are commonly referred to as *generally accepted accounting principles*, or GAAP). Often, these principles permit the use of different standards, so they must be consistently applied.

Fair Presentation of Financial Condition. The borrower is also required to represent that the financial statements fairly present its financial condition. Merely representing that the financial statements were prepared in accordance with generally accepted accounting principles may not necessarily result in a fair presentation of financial condition.

(a) *Projections.* The projections were prepared using reasonable assumptions of the type typically used in projects similar to this project and the [*Project Company*] is not aware of any presently existing or threatened fact, condition, or event that indicates or could reasonably be viewed as indicating that the project will not be able to be operated in accordance with the projections, and there are no expenses of the [Project Company], fixed or contingent, which are not reflected in the project budget.

(b) *No Other Business.* The [Project Company] has engaged in no business other than the project, and is engaged and only proposes to engage, solely in the business of owning and operating the project.

(c) *Financial Statements.* The balance sheet of the [Project Company] dated as at [date], and the related statements of income and retained earnings for the financial year ended [date], and the accompanying footnotes, together with the opinion thereon, dated [date], of [Accountants], independent certified public accountants, and the interim balance sheet of the [Project Company] as of [date] and the related statement of income and retained earnings for the [x]-month period ended [date] are complete and correct and fairly present the financial condition of the [Project Company] as at such dates and the results of operations of the [Project Company] for the periods covered by such statements, all in accordance with generally accepted accounting principles consistently applied, and since [date] there has been no material adverse change in the condition (financial or otherwise), business, or operations of the [Project Company].

[4] Financial Statement Representation for Contracting Party

Financial Information. The balance sheet of the [Contracting Party] dated as at [date], and the related statements of income and retained earnings for the financial year [date], and the accompanying footnotes, together with the opinion thereon, dated [date] of [Accountants], independent certified public accountants, and the interim balance sheet of the [Contracting Party] as of [date] and the related statement of income and retained earnings for the [x]-month period ended [date] are complete and correct and fairly present the financial condition of the [Contracting Party] as at such dates and the results of operations of the [Contracting Party] for the periods covered by such statements, all in accordance with generally accepted accounting principles consistently applied, and since [date] there has been no material adverse change in the condition

(financial or otherwise), business, or operations of the [Contracting Party].

§ 13.09 LITIGATION

[1] Introduction

The litigation representation is particularly important in a project financing because the existence of litigation could affect the project construction schedule, causing delays in project completion and increased construction costs as well as affect the long-term viability of the project. Threatened litigation is also typically included because the threat of litigation may slow project development or lead to an expensive settlement negotiation process.

The representation also covers litigation or proceedings that could affect the borrower. Many project financings are based on a predictable regulatory environment. Thus, the representation is required to ascertain whether any regulatory proceedings exist which, although not directly involving the project company, may nonetheless affect it.

[2] Litigation Representation When No Litigation Exists

Litigation. There is no pending or threatened action or proceeding against or affecting the [Contracting Party] [if a partnership: or any general partner] or any [Project Participant] before any court, governmental agency, or arbitrator, which may, in any one case or in the aggregate, materially adversely affect the financial condition, operations, properties, or business of the [Contracting Party] [if a partnership: or any general partner] or any [Project Participant] or the ability of the [Contracting Party] [if a partnership: or any general partner] or any [Project Participant] to perform its obligation under the [Project Documents] to which it is a party.

[3] Litigation Representation When Litigation Exists

Although it is unlikely that any pending or threatened litigation against or affecting the project sponsor will allow the project financing to close, litigation involving other project participants may be more palatable, though still bitter. If litigation exists or is threatened, or if a large, diverse company is involved, some limitation on the litigation representation may be requested.

Litigation. There is no pending or threatened litigation or proceeding against or affecting the [*Contracting Party*] before any court, governmental agency, or arbitrator which may, in any one case or in the aggregate, materially adversely affect the financial condition, operations, properties, or business of the [*Contracting Party*] or the ability of the [*Contracting Party*] to perform its obligations under this agreement.

§ 13.10 JUDGMENTS AND ORDERS

[1] Introduction
Even though no litigation exists, the project company may have completed litigation with an outstanding judgment that limits or prohibits participation in the project.

[2] Sample Provision
No Defaults on Outstanding Judgments or Orders. The [*Project Company*] has satisfied all judgments, and neither the [*Project Company*] nor any [*Project Participant*] is in default with respect to any judgment, writ, injunction, decree, rule, or regulation of any court, arbitrator, or federal, national, central, commonwealth, state, province, municipal, city, borough, village, county, district, department, territory, commission, board, bureau, agency or instrumentality, or other governmental authority, domestic or foreign, provided that, solely as to any [*Project Participant*], such default could have a material and adverse effect on such [*Project Participant's*] ability to perform its obligations under any [*Project Document*] to which it is a party. All [*Project Participants*] have satisfied all judgments and are in compliance with respect to all judgments, writs, injunctions, decrees, rules or regulations of all courts, arbitrators, or federal, national, central, commonwealth, state, province, municipal, city, borough, village, county, district, department, territory, commission, board, bureau, agency or instrumentality, or other governmental authority, domestic or foreign, where the failure to do any of the foregoing could affect the ability of any [*Project Participant*] to perform its obligations under any [*Project Document*].

§ 13.11 EXISTING AGREEMENTS

[1] Introduction
In addition to litigation, the project company may have entered into contracts that limit or prohibit participation in the project. Also, the organizational documents of the project company, such as the charter or partnership agreement, must permit the performance of the transaction. Thus, this representation complements the authorization representation discussed above.

The existing agreement representation is particularly significant in a project financing where the project company enters into a number of interrelated agreements, any of which, if breached, could negatively affect the financing.

Also, other project participants, such as the contractor or fuel supplier, could be parties to agreements that limit or prohibit the contemplated agreement. These agreements, which form the basis of the project economics, could similarly negatively affect the financing.

Finally, this representation assures that the project company is not in default under any agreements. This is particularly useful in a project financing since the continuing effectiveness of project contracts on the dates of construction loan draws is important.

[2] Sample Provision
Other Agreements. Neither the [*Project Company*] nor any [*Project Participant*] is a party to any indenture, loan, or credit agreement, or to any lease or other agreement or instrument or subject to any charter or corporate [*or partnership*] restriction which, if performed by all parties thereto in accordance with its terms, could have a material adverse effect on the business, properties, assets, operations, or condition, financial or otherwise, of the [*Project Company*], or on the ability of the [*Project Company*], or could reasonably be expected to have a material adverse effect on the ability of any [*Project Participant*], to carry out its respective obligations under the [*Project Documents*] to which it is a party. Neither the [*Project Company*] nor any [*Project Participant*] is in default in any respect in the

performance, observance, or fulfillment of any of the material obligations, covenants, or conditions contained in (i) in the case of the [Project Company], any agreement or instrument material to its business to which it is a party and, in the case of a [Project Participant], where a default under such agreement or instrument could have a material adverse effect on such [Project Participant]'s ability to perform its obligations under any [Project Document] to which it is a party, or (ii) any [Project Documents].

§ 13.12 FORCE MAJEURE

[1] Introduction
Force majeure is the term generally used to refer to an event beyond the control of a party claiming that the event has occurred, including fire, flood, earthquakes, war, and strikes. Which party will bear the risk is always a subject of negotiation.

On occasion, the phrase "acts of God" is used in connection with a listing of uncontrollable events. This phrase is probably best avoided. Nor is the addition of the phrase "act of God or of the public enemy" any more acceptable. It is offensive to some cultures and derogatory of some religious beliefs.

[2] Sample Provision
Force Majeure. Neither the business nor the properties of the [Project Company] or any of the [Project Participants] are affected by any fire, explosion, accident, strike, lockout, or other labor dispute, drought, storm, hail, earthquake, embargo, or other casualty (whether or not covered by insurance), materially and adversely affecting the business or properties or the operation of the [Project Company] or materially and adversely affecting the ability of any such [Project Participant] to perform its obligations under any [Project Document] to which it is a party.

§ 13.13 ASSET OWNERSHIP AND LIENS

[1] Introduction
The asset and lien representation is typically used in loan and project interest acquisition agreements. It states that the contracting party has ownership of its assets, free and clear of any liens other than those liens permitted by the agreement.

The representation is particularly important in project finance transactions because of the necessity to know whether all assets that are necessary for the development, construction, and operation of the project are owned by the project company. The absence of an essential element of the project could affect, at a minimum, the economic projections for the project, and quite possibly the overall success of the project.

[2] Sample Provision
Ownership and Liens. The [Project Company/Contracting Party] has good and marketable title to, or valid leasehold interests in, all of its properties and assets, real and personal, including, without limitation, the [Project Site] and the property and assets, real and personal, constituting a part of the project, and none of the properties and assets owned by the [Project Company/Contracting Party] and none of its leasehold interests is subject to any mortgages, deeds of trust, pledges, liens, security interests, and other charges or encumbrances, except such as are permitted herein.

§ 13.14 SUBSIDIARIES AND OWNERSHIP OF SECURITIES

[1] Introduction
Like the ownership and liens representation, this representation is typically used in loan and project acquisition agreements. It is used to confirm the subsidiaries of the project company and to make certain that all assets are owned that are necessary for the development, construction, and operation of the project.

[2] Sample Provision
Subsidiaries and Ownership of Securities. Exhibit __ sets forth a complete and accurate list of all subsidiaries of the [Contracting Party], the jurisdictions of incorporation, and the ownership of outstanding stock. All outstanding stock of each such subsidiary has been validly issued, is fully paid and non-assessable, and is owned by the [Contracting Party] free and clear of all mortgages, deeds of trust, pledges, liens, security interests, and other charges or encumbrances.

§ 13.15 OPERATION OF BUSINESS

[1] Introduction
Because a project financing is sensitive to undisclosed and undiscovered risks, it is often significant to determine that the project company and each important project supplier and off-take purchaser has all necessary rights to operate its business.

[2] Sample Provision
Operation of Business. Other than governmental approvals, the [*Contracting Party*] possesses all licenses, permits, franchises, patents, copyrights, trademarks, and trade names, or rights thereto, to conduct its business substantially as now conducted and, as presently proposed to be conducted, and the [*Contracting Party*] is not in violation of any valid rights of others with respect to any of the foregoing. Each of the [*list major contracting parties to each material project contract*] possesses all licenses, permits, franchises, patents, copyrights, trademarks and trade names, or rights thereto to perform its duties under the documents to which it is a party, and such party is not in violation of any valid rights of others with respect to any of the foregoing.

§ 13.16 PROJECT ASSETS AND NECESSARY ASSIGNMENTS

[1] Introduction
Sometimes important assets and contract rights that are essential to project success are not owned by the project company. Before financial closing, these assets and contracts must be transferred to the project company.

[2] Sample Provision
Assignments. Any and all assignments, consents, and transfers of property (real and personal), contracts, licenses, approvals, permits, and interest from [*describe assignor*] to the [*Project Company*] necessary for the construction of the Project by the [*Project Company*] are in full force and effect and are legal, valid, and binding on [*assignor*] and do not require any further approval by any Person or any Governmental Approval to become fully legal, valid, and binding agreements. There exist no liabilities or other obligations which have not been disclosed in writing to the [*Lender*] with respect to the purchase by the [*Project Company*] of all rights, title and interest of [*describe assignor*] to the Project.

§ 13.17 PROJECT CONTRACTS

[1] Introduction
Project finance lenders base credit appraisals on the projected revenues and anticipated expenses from the operation of the facility. Consequently, the terms, obligations, and liabilities in each contract to which the project company is a party must be reviewed and examined. Any amendments or modifications must also be disclosed to and examined by the lender. Finally, all conditions precedent under the project documents must have been satisfied or waived by the contracting parties so that there are no unacceptable conditions to contract performance. In particular, the project company must be in compliance with all milestone obligations, which require performance of specified obligations by negotiated dates.

[2] Sample Provision
Project Contracts. All Project Contracts are unmodified and in full force and effect, there are no defaults or events of default in any such Project Contracts or material breaches (if there are no definitions for defaults or events of defaults) under any such agreement, the [*Project Company*] is in compliance with all milestone obligations under each such Project Contract, and all conditions to the effectiveness and continuing effectiveness of each Project Contract required to be satisfied have been satisfied.

§ 13.18 DEBT

[1] Introduction
Project finance lenders rely on the project's revenue-producing contracts and off-take market for debt repayment. Therefore, the amount and terms of all debt obligations must be disclosed to the project lender. Generally speaking, only that amount of debt that can be serviced

(with a comfortable margin) can be outstanding at any time.

[2] Sample Provision
Debt. The only outstanding Debt of the [*Contracting Party*] is debt permitted under the terms of this Agreement.

§ 13.19 TAXES

[1] Introduction
Whether the project sponsor has complied with applicable tax laws may be important to a decision whether to extend credit. Exceptions are often allowed, however, if certain taxes are being contested in good faith and by proper proceedings and as to which adequate reserves have been maintained.

[2] Sample Provision
Taxes. The [*Contracting Party*] has filed all tax returns (federal, national, central, commonwealth, state, province, municipal, city, borough, village, county, district, department, territory, commission, board, bureau, agency or instrumentality, or other governmental authority, domestic or foreign) required to be filed and has paid all taxes, assessments, and governmental charges and levies thereon to be due, including interest and penalties except such taxes, if any, as are being contested in good faith and by proper proceedings and as to which adequate reserves have been maintained.

§ 13.20 REGULATORY AND LEGAL STATUS

[1] Introduction
A project financing is based on predictable regulatory environments, which combine to produce dependable cash flow. To the extent this predictability is unavailable or the risks of dependability are allocated unacceptably, credit enhancement is necessary to protect the lender from external uncertainties, such as fuel supply, product market instability, and changes in law. Because the regulatory status of a project is an important basis for a project, the regulatory and

legal status representation should be carefully drafted.

[2] Sample Provision
(a) The Project is a [*describe regulatory/legal status*] pursuant to [*describe statute or regulation*], and, as such, the [*Project Company*] is not subject to any laws or regulations respecting [*describe regulatory regime that is inapplicable to the Project Company; for example, the rates of public utilities or the financial and organizational activities of public utilities*].

(b) The [*Lender*] will not be deemed, solely by reason of any transaction contemplated by any of the [*Loan Documents*], by any federal, national, central, commonwealth, state, province, municipal, city, borough, village, county, district, department, territory, commission, board, bureau, agency or instrumentality, or other governmental authority, domestic or foreign, or other governmental authority having jurisdiction, to be subject to regulation under any federal, national, central, commonwealth, state, province, municipal, city, borough, village, county, district, department, territory, commission, board, bureau, agency or instrumentality, or other governmental authority, domestic or foreign, regulating [*describe project purpose; for example: the generation, transmission or sale of electricity*] under which the [*Lender*] would be deemed to be subject to regulation. [*Exceptions may be needed in the event the Lender becomes an operator of the project.*]

§ 13.21 PERMITS

[1] Introduction
The risk that a project company does not have, or might not obtain, permits necessary for the construction or operation of the project is, of course, a significant concern to all project participants. At the time of construction funding for a project, permits are classifiable into three categories: permits already obtained and in full force and effect, which are not subject to appeal, further proceedings, or to any unsatisfied condition that may result in a material modification or revocation; permits that are routinely granted on application and that would not normally be obtained before construction; and permits other

than those in full force and effect and those routinely granted on application. The last category of permits is, of course, the relevant concern for project participants. The application and approval process for the last category must be carefully examined to determine the likelihood of issuance, the cost associated with possible conditions attached to permit approval, and similar issues.

Necessary permits vary depending on the country, political jurisdiction, site, technology, process, and a host of other variables. The permits representation is designed to identify the necessary permits and the status of the applications for them.

[2] Sample Provision

(a) The Governmental Approvals set forth in Exhibit _ constitute all Governmental Approvals required (a) for design, construction, start-up, testing, and operation of the project, (b) for the execution, delivery, and performance by [Project Company] of its obligations, and the exercise of its rights, under the [Loan Documents], (c) for the grant by the [Project Company] of the liens created by the [Security Documents] and for the validity and enforceability thereof and for the exercise by the [Lender] of the remedies thereunder, and (d) for the transfer of any such Governmental Approvals to the entity responsible for obtaining or maintaining such governmental approval.

(b) The Governmental Approvals listed on Part 1 of Exhibit _ are all the Governmental Approvals required under applicable law to commence construction of the project and all such Governmental Approvals have been duly given, made, or obtained and are in full force and effect, and such Governmental Approvals are not subject to any pending or threatened judicial or administrative proceeding or appeal. None of such Governmental Approvals contains any terms, conditions, or provisions that could reasonably be expected to materially adversely affect or impair [Project Company]'s ability to build the project in accordance with project specifications set forth in the [Construction Contract].

(c) The Governmental Approvals listed on Part 2 of Exhibit _ have not been obtained as of the date hereof and are not required under applicable law

to be obtained as of the date hereof and cannot be obtained until commercial operation or performance testing of the project occurs.

(d) The Governmental Approvals listed on Part 3 of Exhibit _ have not been obtained as of the date hereof but (a) are not required under applicable law at the present stage of the project and (b) are of a nature that they can be obtained when required in the ordinary course of business from the applicable agency by the [Project Company].

(e) The Governmental Approvals listed on Part 4 of Exhibit _ have not been obtained as of the date hereof but are not required under applicable law at the present stage of the project.

(f) The Governmental Approvals listed on Parts 2, 3 and 4 of Exhibit _ are of a nature that they can be reasonably expected to be obtained upon timely and adequate application being made therefor and upon payment of prescribed fees.

(g) "Governmental Approvals" means any authorization, consent, approval, license, lease, ruling, permit, tariff, rate, certification, exemption, filing, or registration by or with any government or bureau, department or agency thereof.

§ 13.22 COMPLIANCE WITH LAWS

[1] Introduction

Compliance with applicable laws and regulations of each government with jurisdiction over a project participant is an important due diligence item.

[2] Sample Provision

Compliance with Laws. The existing and planned use of the project complies with all Legal Requirements, including but not limited to environmental laws, occupational safety and health, applicable zoning ordinances, regulations, and restrictive covenants affecting the [Project Site], as well as all ecological, landmark, and other applicable laws and regulations, and all Legal Requirements for such use have been satisfied, except where the failure to comply with a law, in any case or in the aggregate, could not reasonably be expected to materially adversely affect the [Project Site], the project or the ability of the [Contracting Party] to perform under any of the documents to which it is a party. No release, emission, or discharge into the environment of hazardous substances, or hazardous waste, or air pollutants, or toxic pollutants, as defined under any environmental laws, has occurred or is presently occurring or will occur in operating the project in its intended form in excess of permitted levels or reportable quantities, or other permitted concentrations, standards, or limitations under the foregoing laws or under any other federal, national, central, commonwealth, state, province, municipal, city, borough, village, county, district, department, territory, commission, board, bureau, agency, or instrumentality, or other governmental authority, domestic or foreign, laws, regulations, or Governmental Approvals in connection with the construction, fuel supply, water discharge, power generation and transmission, or waste disposal, or any other project operations or processes.

"Legal Requirements" means any and all federal, national, central, commonwealth, state, province, municipal, city, borough, village, county, district, department, territory, commission, board, bureau, agency, or instrumentality, or other governmental authority, domestic or foreign, statutes, laws, regulations, ordinances, rules, judgments, orders, decrees, permits, concessions, grants, franchises, licenses, agreements, or other governmental restrictions.

§ 13.23 INFRASTRUCTURE

[1] Introduction
Sufficient infrastructure for the project, such as roads, highways, railways, rail switching yards, piers, and docks, must be in place or planned at a level that will likely result in completion. For example, to the extent a road to the project site is not yet in existence, planning is necessary for financing and development of it.

[2] Sample Provision
Infrastructure. All [*identify necessary infrastructure: roads, access, highways, railways, rail switching yards, piers, docks*] necessary for the construction and full operation of the project for its intended purposes have either been completed or the necessary rights of way therefor have been acquired by

appropriate governmental authorities or dedicated to public use and accepted or otherwise approved by said governmental authorities, and all necessary steps have been taken by the [*Project Company*] and said governmental authorities to assure the complete construction and installation thereof no later than the earliest of the date required for their usage to construct and operate the project or any date required by any law, order, or regulation, or any document to which the [*Project Company*] is a party or by which it is bound.

§ 13.24 COMPLETION

[1] Introduction
A delay in project completion may result in an increase in project construction costs and a concomitant increase in debt service costs. The delay may also affect the scheduled flow of project revenues necessary to cover debt service and operations and maintenance expenses. In addition, a delay in project completion may result in damage payments payable under, or termination of, project contracts, such as fuel supply and output contracts. Consequently, the project company in the completion representation should estimate the completion date for the project.

The term *completion date* is a significant one. For a complete discussion of this term, and it far-reaching effects, see the discussion in Chapter 12.

[2] Sample Provision
Completion Date. The [*Project Company*], after reasonable investigation, estimates that the [*Completion Date*] will occur on or before [*date*].

§ 13.25 COLLATERAL

[1] Introduction
The ownership of any collateral given by the project company or another contracting party to the lender to secure its performance must be examined to determine whether the necessary assurances are in place for the enforceability of the collateral. Also, local law must be examined to determine whether the requisite filings are appropriately made.

[2] Sample Provision

Title; Security Documents. The [*Project Company*] has good and marketable title to the [*Real Estate*], and has good title to the other [*Collateral*] that exists as of the date of representation free and clear of all [*Liens*] other than [*Permitted Liens*]. The provisions of the [*Security Documents*] are effective to create, in favor of the [*Lender*], valid and perfected first priority security interests in and mortgage liens on such [*Collateral*]. All filings, recordings, registrations and other actions necessary or desirable to perfect and protect such security interests and mortgage liens have been duly effected or taken.

§ 13.26 FULL DISCLOSURE

[1] Introduction

A "catch-all" representation is often useful to help ensure that the contracting party has fully disclosed the details of its involvement in the project.

[2] Sample Provision

Full Disclosure. No written information, exhibit, or report furnished by the [*Project Company/Contracting Party*] to the [*Lender*] relating to the project in connection with the negotiation of this Agreement contained any material misstatement of fact or omitted to state a material fact or any fact necessary to make the statements contained therein not materially misleading after giving effect to the supplementation of such information, exhibits, and reports furnished by such parties. No information, exhibit, report, certificate, written statement, or other document furnished by the [*Project Company/Contracting Party*] relating to the project, to the [*Lender*] or to any appraiser or engineer submitting a report to the [*Lender*], or in connection with the transactions contemplated by this Agreement or the design, construction, start-up, testing, or operation of the project, contained any untrue statement of a material fact or omitted to state a material fact necessary to make the statements contained herein or therein not misleading under the circumstances in which they were made.

There is no fact or circumstance known to the [*Project Company/Contracting Party*] that materially adversely affects or could reasonably be antic-

ipated to materially adversely affect the properties, business, prospects, or financial or other condition of the [*Project Company/Contracting Party*] or any [*Project Participant*] or the ability of the [*Project Company/Contracting Party*] or any [*Project Participant*] to complete and operate the project as contemplated by the [*Loan Documents*] and project specifications and to perform its obligations hereunder as set forth in the [*Construction Contract*] or under the other [*Loan Documents*] to which it is a party.

§ 13.27 REPRESENTATIONS AND WARRANTIES MADE IN OTHER PROJECT CONTRACTS

[1] Introduction

It is often useful to include in an agreement, such as a project finance credit agreement, a representation and warranty that all the representations and warranties made in the other project contracts by the project company are true and correct as if fully set forth again in the agreement.

[2] Sample Provision

Representations and Warranties in Other Project Contracts. [*Project Company*] hereby restates each of the representations and warranties made to the respective parties to each of the [*Project Contracts*], as if each such representation and warranty were set forth in full herein on the date hereof.

§ 13.28 NO PRIOR BUSINESS ACTIVITY

[1] Introduction

Most project financings are undertaken by special-purpose entities formed for the sole purpose of development and ownership of a project. These entities have no other business activity that could interfere with the project or its ability to repay debt or perform project contracts. This representation is designed to verify that.

[2] Sample Provision

No Prior Business Activity. [*Project Company*] has not engaged in any material business activities except in connection with the development of the project and in matters specifically related thereto.

§ 13.29 COMPLETE PROJECT

[1] Introduction

A representation is made that all elements of the project are in place.

[2] Sample Provision

Complete Project. The work to be performed, the services to be provided, the materials to be supplied and the property rights to be granted pursuant to the [*Project Contracts*] are all of the rights and interests necessary for the development, construction, start-up, operation and ownership of the project.

CHAPTER FOURTEEN

PRELIMINARY HOST-COUNTRY AGREEMENTS

§ 14.01 INTRODUCTION

The host country for a project is involved,
knowingly or unwittingly, from the start of
project planning. Governmental involvement
can take many forms, ranging from enacting
laws that regulate a project to ones that encourage sector reform, such as through private
development, build-own-transfer (BOT) structures, or privatization. In the operation stage of
a project, government involvement continues,
through varying levels of continuing regulation
for some projects, and even non-regulation for
others.

Infrastructure projects – roads, railways, ports,
energy production, hospitals, and airports –
heighten the interest and involvement of the
government in the project's development, construction, operation, and financing. Projects less
tied to the country's infrastructure needs, such

as industrial projects, may involve government
interest and cooperation, but often at a less significant level. Even industrial projects sometimes
attract governmental interest beyond job creation and tax revenue, such as in projects where a
government-controlled fuel company will supply
project fuel.

The interest level of the host government in
a project will affect its ability and commitment
to execute support agreements for the project;
institute sector reforms, such as privatization;
and enact legislation needed to make a project
feasible. In this chapter, the processes governments use to solicit private-sector interest, and
the procedures and agreements typically used
by governments to support the development of
projects and encourage foreign investment, are
explained.

§ 14.02 BIDDING (TENDERING) PROCESSES

[1] Generally

A common way that host governments solicit
private-sector involvement in new projects, or
refurbishing of existing facilities, is through a bidding (also called *tendering*) process. A bidding
program is a competitive process undertaken by
a government that allows for the efficient selection of a provider of goods or services in a transparent manner, based on the selection criteria
formulated by the government, for the purpose
of selecting a low-cost provider best capable of
project completion and operation. The selection
criteria can be a simple, market-based price, or
it can make use of a complicated formula that
places differing weight on such considerations
as experience, financial strength, non-financial
resources, and price.

Project sponsors do not always look favorably
on bidding processes. Although bids limit renegotiation of contracts and help minimize public
perceptions of corruption and of higher than necessary infrastructure costs, they result in a costly
bid preparation and evaluation process and are
otherwise time consuming. As explained below,
as disadvantages to bidding programs, these programs are not always successful in meeting the
goals of their proponents.

[2] Advantages of Bidding Programs

Public bidding processes have several advantages for host governments. A bid process increases competition among potential providers of the goods or services, minimizes the cost of the solicited good or service,[1] and fosters public support and credibility for the project by avoiding the perception of corruption. In developing countries, the bidding process also helps government leaders overcome public resistance to previously free or subsidized infrastructure that will now be provided by the private sector. In a recent World Bank study, one-half of cancelled infrastructure projects between 1990 and 2001 involved allegations of corruption and impropriety and were not competitively tendered.[2]

Perhaps the best advantage of a bidding program is the innovation that it can encourage in the private sector. Capitalism breeds innovation, particularly as an outgrowth of competition. Entrepreneur risk taking and innovation will, in many cases, produce better, more cost-effective projects than can be produced by the public sector, which labors in a bureaucratic, political environment that often eschews creativity.[3]

[3] Disadvantages of Bidding Programs

The competitive bidding process can be thwarted, however, in a way that paralyzes these advantages. First, nonmarket elements can arise to thwart the companies selected for pre-qualification of bidders. For example, technical qualifications might be drafted to exclude potential bidders. These discriminatory provisions may be accidental or founded in a lack of knowledge or experience in the bid drafters.

Second, the successful bidder might underbid with the hope of later renegotiating the price

charged and the terms announced in the bid documents. This approach can completely circumvent the competitive advantages of a bid program and open the government to charges of corruption and unfairness.

Third, the process can be harmed by nonpublic opening of bids. This allows pre-negotiation sessions in which successful bidders are asked for more concessions or losing bidders are asked to lower the price bid. Although this may produce a lower price, transparency of selection is hampered, if not completely destroyed.

[4] Prequalification of Bidders (the RFQ)

The bidding process can be less burdensome on the bidders and the host government if a pre-qualification process is followed. It is during this process that the government determines who can submit a bid.

This process usually begins with issuance of a Request for Qualifications (RFQ) submitted to potential bidders. Typical qualifications considered include experience and performance in similar projects, experience, and performance in the host country, financial creditworthiness, technical expertise, technology type, and non-financial resources, such as technical experience of managerial, professional, and technical staff. Any subcontractors that will be used by the qualifying bidder should be similarly evaluated. In the aggregate, the returned responses to the RFQ constitute the qualifications to bid on, and if successful complete, the project.

The RFQ process limits the number of bidders, thereby helping to persuade the remaining small pool of bidders to commit resources to preparing and submitting a bid. Because of the qualification process, the possibilities of receiving inadequately prepared or non-conforming bids at the RFP stage are minimized, something bidders are tempted to do when there is a large group of bidders and the chances of winning the bid are comparatively small.

Another advantage of the RFQ process is the opportunity it provides to the bid preparer for refinement of the bidding process. The number and quality of responses to the RFQ can help determine whether the proposed project interests developers at an acceptable quality level of developer. If not, the project and bid elements can

---

[1] *See generally* Yves Alhouy & Reda Bousha, *The Impact of IPPs in Developing Countries – Out of the Crisis and into the Future*, PUBLIC POLICY FOR THE PRIVATE SECTOR, WORLD BANK NOTE No. 162, 5–6 (Dec. 1998) (study concludes that bidding reduced private power prices by 25% on average, with some exceptions).

[2] Clive Harris et al., *Infrastructure Projects – A Review of Canceled Private Projects*, PUBLIC POLICY FOR THE PRIVATE SECTOR, WORLD BANK NOTE No. 252 (Jan. 2003).

[3] *But see* Alhouy & Bousha, *supra* note 1, at 6–7 ("competition does not ensure financial efficiency if government exchange rate guarantees make the cost of loans much greater than the private cost to sponsors").

be redesigned to attract the appropriate interest level or be completely abandoned.

[5] Bid Design and Preparation of Bid Documents (the RFP)

Generally. For a bidding process to be successful from a competition perspective, bids need to be identical on as many project features as possible, including technology selection. While in some cases transparency can be achieved by limiting bid responses to price, other bidding programs will not be so simple to design. In these more common situations, the drafters of the bid documents should produce a detailed project description, settle on the regulatory structures that will affect the project, if any, and develop bid evaluation criteria and procedures that are as transparent as possible.

Also, the bidding process can be made more attractive to potential bidders if there is sufficient time for preparation of detailed bids, and if there is a clearly articulated procedure and timetable for bid evaluation and announcement of the winning bid.

Other elements of a bid are also important in bid design, including non-project terms. These include risk allocation, particularly risks passed to the host government; financial creditworthiness of the project company, including its financial capability to accept the risks allocated to it; and experience of the project sponsor.

Indeed, some flexibility should be provided to allow innovative solutions from bidders. Variant bids do not respond precisely to the bid requirements but do address the underlying needs through a technical innovation or operating efficiency that makes the bid worth considering. Otherwise, host governments begin to lose the advantages of working with the private sector: entrepreneur risk taking, innovation, and technology.

Finally, one of two general approaches to bid design must be selected: either the fixed or the negotiated approach. Under the fixed approach, the bid documents set forth a reasonably detailed list of project requirements, including contract terms, and the bidders respond with a fixed-price bid. Under the negotiated approach, a

preferred bidder is selected based on general price and technical, financial, and contractual terms, and then the actual contracts are negotiated.

Evaluation and Scoring. The two general approaches to evaluating and selecting a winning bid from the pool of bid responses are self-scoring and non-self-scoring.

SELF-SCORING. In the self-scoring option, a range of numerical values is created for characteristics in each category. The bidder then scores itself based on its response to each of the categories. This approach provides almost complete transparency in the selection process, although the scoring must still be checked to determine whether the scores assigned are correct. Other advantages include the ability to process many bids efficiently and expediently and the ability to immediately eliminate inferior bids.

There are disadvantages to the self-scoring model. This approach requires that the bidding program be adequately designed to produce the correct winning bid. Complicated projects are difficult to propose under this model because the complexity often precludes creation of segregated categories that can be easily scored. The self-scoring model does not completely eliminate use of scoring manipulation, through falsification or other means, and some response verification is needed.

NON-SELF-SCORING. The non-self-scoring approach requires bidders to submit documents specifying the characteristics of the proposed project. The method for selection of the winning bid is set forth in the bid documents.

Advantages of a non-self-scoring approach include the flexibility inherent in the bid design. It allows for submission of a wide range of creative and innovative proposals, a goal particularly important where a project is proposed for an immature industry or sector.

The most significant disadvantage is the potential lack of transparency in the selection process. It can also lead to inconsistent results in bid selection over a long bidding program. This approach tends to be more time consuming than the self-scoring model because it takes a longer period of time and resources to evaluate and score bids.

[6] Model Contracts
It is sometimes extremely helpful to include in the bid package prepared by the government and submitted for consideration to the bidders copies of the contracts that the government is prepared to execute with the project company. This is equally true in bidding programs prepared for private-sector projects. To the extent the bidders are unable to agree to any terms in these model agreements, comments should be solicited as part of the bid, and the comments should be considered in the bid evaluations. The use of model contracts will depend on the bid design, with use more typical in a fixed bidding process.

[7] Bid Meetings and Bidder Questions
Questions from bidders can arise in almost every bidding program, no matter how carefully the bid package is designed. Bid sponsors have the choice of not answering any questions, in favor of allowing the bid documents to be the sole information source. They also can decide to answer all questions and provide copies of the answers to all bidders.

Another alternative is for the bid sponsors to invite prospective bidders to a bid meeting. At the meeting, further information can be presented about the proposal, and questions can be answered, giving all bidders an opportunity to ask, and hear answers to, the questions.

Bid meetings have several advantages for a proposed bidding program. These include developing bidder interest in the project; creating an opportunity for the bid organizers to learn early about potential problems with bidding on the project; and an efficient, fair way to disseminate information about the proposed project.

[8] Security
It is often prudent to have bidders submit security with the bid response to ensure that the bidders are committed to honoring the bid submitted. Although various forms of security can be used, performance bonds and letters of credit are the most common types of security. If the bidder

does not honor the bid, the security can be drawn upon by the government to compensate for the delay and other costs incurred.

[9] Promotion of Public Bids by Multilateral Agencies
In 1951, the World Bank introduced International Competitive Bidding as the procurement procedure for use in projects it financed. These procedures, revised in 2004, establish nondiscriminatory specifications, selection criteria disclosure, and public bidding.[4] Failure to adhere to this process can result in cancellation of the World Bank financing.

[10] Bidding in the Project Finance Context

Generally. Properly structured and fairly administered, competitive bidding programs provide project companies with a reasonable level of assurance of stability. Because the project company has been selected as the best provider of the goods or services, based on the unique criteria used in the bidding process, there is less likelihood that the project will be criticized on price or other levels. The transparency afforded by a properly designed bidding process helps reduce political risk that might otherwise exist and lead to a later challenge of the project's pricing.

Special-Purpose Entities. The ownership and proposed structure of the company that will develop and own the project should be clearly described in the bid response. If not, the government could conclude that a parent corporation or other entity with substantial assets will own the project. In those situations in which financial criterion is part of the bid evaluation process, the bid award could be in jeopardy if a special-purpose entity is later substituted for a creditworthy, winning bidder. Because almost all project financings are structured using a special-purpose entity as the project owner, this problem is particularly significant. Conversely, if special-purpose entities are permitted to be used for project ownership,

[4] The World Bank, Guidelines – Procurement Under IBRD Loans and IDC Credits (May 2004).

that ability should be clearly authorized in the bid documents.

The Problem of Consortium Bids. Large-scale infrastructure projects often require development by more than one project sponsor. The financial needs and risk exposure may simply be too large for one company.

In such cases, a group of companies, or consortium, combines to develop a single project. It is common for the membership of the consortium to change over time, however, because the risks presented in a transnational project financing change over time and the individual risk appetites of consortium members are not identical. Yet, the selection of the consortium as the winner of a bidding program may make it unfair for change to be permitted.

One approach is to allow substitution of consortium members after the winning bid is selected. To be fair to all bidders, however, this right must be clearly set forth in the bid rules. Substitution can be limited to only those companies that possess at least the same level of financial creditworthiness, experience, and technical capability as the withdrawing consortium member.

When to Involve the Lenders. During preparation of a bid response, the project sponsor will consult with various lawyers, project lenders, multilateral agencies, bilateral agencies, and others to determine whether the bid is realistic in terms of lender requirements (is it "bankable") and agency programs requirements. The bid response will usually include a financing proposal, often with perspective lenders and agency programs listed in the bid. Review by a lender of the overall project proposal will help ensure that the submitted bid is as final as possible. Otherwise, the bid grantor can expect to see deal changes introduced after the bid is awarded, as lenders review the project risks and require changes for unacceptable ones.

This type of lender review is time consuming and expensive. After all, there is no guarantee that the lender's customer, the project sponsor, will even be awarded the bid. Lender requirements are somewhat fluid and are subject to change based on market, political, and general economic changes. Nonetheless, limited lender review of the overall bid response is helpful.

§ 14.03 LETTER OF INTENT AND MEMORANDUM OF UNDERSTANDING

In some projects, the first stage of project development is the negotiation of a letter of intent with the host government. It is sometimes also called a memorandum of understanding.

A letter of intent is a nonbinding written statement of a few pages in length that expresses the intention of the parties signing it to enter into a formal agreement or transaction at a later date. The transaction, and the role of the parties in it, is broadly described. This approach is useful in the project finance context where the host country may need to agree to certain changes to its laws, regulations, and policies, or to certain infrastructure or other investments for successful project development.

It should be made clear that the letter of intent is nonbinding. A sample provision is reproduced below.

Nonbinding Effect. This Letter of Intent is intended to be an expression by the parties to this letter of intent of their interest in negotiating in good faith the terms and conditions of the agreements the parties determine to be necessary in the development and financing of the [*Proposed Project*]. This letter sets forth the current status of negotiations among the parties and is not intended to be a contract of any type whatsoever.

The topics covered in a letter of intent vary based on the project and the host country. Generally, these include a description of the proposed project, including location and size; performance milestones, representing dates by which the project sponsors must satisfy certain levels of development; required governmental action; government cooperation in permit issuance; price and terms of any associated contracts with government agencies, such as fuel supply or offtake sales; governmental guarantees and other government-provided credit support; exclusivity of the project sponsors' rights to develop the project; payment and allocation of responsibility for developmental expenses should the project not reach financial closing; acceptable amounts of debt and equity of the project company, and acceptable rate of return on the project sponsor's equity; tax concessions; confidentiality; dispute resolution; and assignability of development rights to other parties.

§ 14.04 CONCESSIONS AND LICENSES

[1] Generally

The right to develop, own, construct, and operate a project is sometimes granted by the host government in a concession agreement.[5] The terms *concession agreement, license, service contract*, and *development agreement* are sometimes used interchangeably. Historically, the concession agreement developed in the oil exploration and development industry[6] and has expanded to a broader range of development projects.

[2] Concession Agreement

A concession agreement is entered into between the host government and the project sponsor (or, if already formed, the project company).[7] The agreement describes the project and provides the grant and terms of the governmental license for project ownership, development, construction, operation, and exploitation.

A typical concession agreement contains the following terms: term of the concession; description of project company's rights; permissible

equity structure for the project company; management of the project company; restrictions on foreign ownership and control of the project company; any fixed rate of return on equity permissible for the project sponsors; the manner by which the host government will be compensated for granting the license (for example, license fees with tax revenues or equity interest); terms for importation of equipment and supplies into the host country; applicability of tariffs and price controls to the project and the project sponsors; default provisions, by which the concession could be terminated; termination procedure; and concession renewal provisions. It has a dual role: It is a contract with business terms, yet is governmental in nature since it is a sovereign act.[8]

Terms From the Host Government's Perspective. The host government might require various protections in the concessions agreement. These include service requirements from the project company throughout the concession term; price regulation over facility output; a sufficient operation, maintenance, and repair procedure so that the project transferred to the host government at the end of the concessions term (if such a transfer is contemplated) retains value; milestone dates that must be achieved, such as construction completion dates; and rights of the host government to terminate the concession if certain events occur to the project company or to project sponsors.

Terms From the Project Company's Perspective. Because of the role of the government in a successful project financing, project sponsors, and project lenders require certain assurances from the government, in either a concession, license, law, or separate agreement. These include exclusive right to undertake and exploit the project; right to dispose of production; assurances of raw material supply; work visas for management; acquisition of necessary real estate rights; resolution of the risk allocation for the types of political risks discussed in Chapter 3, including

[5] "A concession agreement may be defined as a license granted by a sovereign government to a foreign corporation or business for the express purpose of exploiting a natural resource, developing a geographic area, or pursuing some particular venture, for which the government desires the corporation's expertise, assets, technology, or capital." Viktor Soloveytchik, *New Perspectives for Concession Agreements: A Comparison of Hungarian Law and the Draft Laws of Belarus, Kazakhstan and Russia*, 16 Hous. J. Int'l L. 261 (1993) (citing Kenneth W. Dam, Oil Resources: Who Gets What How 12–18 (1976)).

[6] *See* Ernest E. Smith, *From Concessions to Service Contracts*, 27 Tulsa L.J. 493 (1992); Note, *From Concession to Participation: Restructuring the Middle East Oil Industry*, 48 N.Y.U.L. Rev. 774 (1973); Kenneth S. Carlston, *International Role of Concession Agreements*, 52 Nw. U. L. Rev. 618 (1957).

[7] *See generally* Soloveytchik, *supra* note 5; J. Luis Guasch, Granting and Renegotiating Infrastructures Concessions – Getting It Right (World Bank Development Studies 2004).

[8] For a discussion of how France's, Germany's, and newly independent states' legal systems view this dual nature as it relates to enforcement and abrogation, *see id.* at 264–67.

expropriation and repatriation of profits; protections against force majeure and change in law, including tax law changes; currency protections, such as convertibility and exchange; assurances against nationalization of the project; and right to own and dispose of equipment and other site improvements.

Ongoing Consents and Approvals by the Host Government. In addition, depending upon the terms of the concession or license, it might be prudent to secure the approval of the host government of the underlying project arrangements negotiated by the project company. For example, the terms of the concession may limit the equity return of the project sponsors. Equity returns are, of course, affected by the project financing arrangements. Approval by the host government of the financing terms might alleviate later disputes over the achievement of the target return.

Other considerations include approval of development and construction plans; whether the project lender is permitted to take a security interest in the concession or license; the ability of the project lender to cure defaults by the project company under the terms of the concession or license; the lender's ability to operate the project after a default; and whether a transfer of the concession by the project lender following a foreclosure requires further consent by the host government. These rights are each important to the project lender.

The host government might not be able to provide complete assurances on these concerns, however. Constitutional prohibitions, limitations in laws, and political necessities and conveniences limit actions in almost all governments of the globe. To that extent, project sponsors and project lenders must accept some political risk, such as these. Despite these restrictions, however, governments may be able to agree in advance to attend meetings and cooperate with the project sponsor and project lender in resolving project difficulties.

[3] Example in a BOT Structure

A concessions agreement is used often in a BOT project finance structure. Under this structure, a private entity is awarded the right to build, own, and operate a project that would otherwise be developed, owned, and operated by the host government. It is a temporary privatization in the sense that at the end of the concession, the project is transferred to the government.

The BOT structure is typically founded in a concession agreement among the host government (or a government entity), the project company, and, in some cases, the project sponsors. The concession agreement provides the project company with the concession to develop, construct, and operate the project. The government might agree to provide certain negotiated support to the project, ranging from infrastructure development to central government guarantees of its agency's obligation to purchase facility output.

[4] Disputes

Host governments sometimes challenge concession agreements on the basis that they are non-binding on the government. This is sometimes justified under a claim of sovereignty,[9] which courts and arbitration panels have, generally, rejected.[10] Less clear, however, is whether a host government has the right to modify, amend, or terminate a concession agreement under international law or the host country's law.[11]

§ 14.05 LEGISLATIVE APPROVAL

In some countries, it may be prudent to seek legislative approval of the project before proceeding too far in the development process. Such approval could provide more certainty to the project sponsor on any number of development issues, such as currency convertibility, foreign ownership of local real estate, and access to natural resources needed for project success. This is particularly true of developing countries that have not yet been able to attract investors for a project financing of an infrastructure project.

At least two approaches are possible to address an inadequate investment climate. First,

---

[9] *E.g., Texaco Overseas Co. v. Libya,* 53 I.L.R. 329, 422 (I.C.J. Arb. 1977).

[10] *Id.* at 468–83 (interpreting stabilization clause).

[11] *See generally* Michael E. Dickstein, *Revitalizing the International Law Governing Concession Agreements,* 6 INT'L TAX & BUS. LAW. 54, 63 (1988); Georges R. Delaume, *State Contracts and Transnational Arbitration,* 75 AM. J. INTL L. 784 (1981).

necessary changes to tax and investment laws needed to support the project could be enacted by the legislature. Alternatively, an agreement could be entered into with the executive branch of the government, which would then be approved by the legislative branch, in which the government provides the necessary investment climate through agreement, rather than new laws. In civil law countries, action by the executive branch may be sufficient. In all countries, however, such agreements should be carefully considered with local lawyers.

§ 14.06 IMPLEMENTATION AGREEMENTS

[1] Generally

An implementation agreement is a contract between a project sponsor and a host government that addresses financial and political elements necessary in a project financing that are absent, or at least unpredictable, in the host country. Although the host government is a party, the governmental contracting entity varies by country but must include the government agencies that have the authority to provide the guarantees, support, and assurances necessary for project development, financing, and operation.

Thus, the implementation agreement is an effort to reduce risk and thereby encourage development efforts, capital investment, and debt in an uncertain environment. It is sometimes termed a *stability* or *support* agreement, recognizing the underlying stabilizing or supporting effect of the agreement on the uncertainties surrounding the proposed project.[12]

An implementation agreement addresses any or all of the following uncertainties: (i) sovereign guarantees; (ii) expropriation; (iii) permits and other governmental approvals necessary for the project; (iv) currency concerns; (v) tax benefits and incentives; (vi) legislative protection; (vii) war, insurrection, general strikes, and political violence; (viii) authorization to do business in the applicable sector, such as authorization of a project company to be a private power generator in an energy project financing; (ix) exclusivity

of right to develop the project; and (x) general cooperation between the host government and its agencies and the project sponsors. Each is discussed separately below. However, whether any or all of these are relevant in a particular host country, and whether it is necessary to address them in an implementation agreement will depend on the host country and the unique features of the project.

[2] Sovereign Guarantees

As discussed in Chapter 20, certain political, legal, regulatory, and financial risks within the host government's control must be addressed through a sovereign guarantee or some other form of credit enhancement. The sovereign guarantee, typically executed at financial closing, protects the project company against the risk that the government or a government agency fails to perform an obligation undertaken that is necessary for the success of the project.

For example, in an energy infrastructure project, the revenue source that will support the underlying project is, in many developing countries, a state-owned entity. These entities are often of uncertain, or at least questionable, credit standing. The project sponsor will desire that the sovereign guarantee the performance obligations of the underlying state-owned utility. This may present a problem for the sovereign. It has decided to privatize the infrastructure facility for the purpose of relieving itself of the burden of the associated financial obligations. A complete sovereign guarantee would circumvent that goal. Nonetheless, a compromise is often reached, ranging from a less than complete guarantee to a nonbinding comfort letter.[13]

[3] Expropriation

A fundamental assurance necessary in a project financing is that the government will not assert ownership over or otherwise take away the project assets from the project developer. The assurance is particularly important in

---

[12] For a sobering indictment of excessive concessions made to foreign companies, *see* E. EDUARDO H. GALEANO, OPEN VEINS OF LATIN AMERICA: FIVE CENTURIES OF THE PILLAGE OF A CONTINENT 12 (1973).

[13] *See generally* Thomas W. Waelde & George Ndi, *Stabilizing International Investment Commitments: International Law Versus Contract Interpretation*, 31 TEX. INT'L L.J. 216, 262 n. 196 (1996). In the "Pyramids" case, a state "approval" of a contract signed by one of its state enterprises was not determined to be a state guarantee. Pyramids Case, 8 ICSID-Rev.-F.I.L.J. 231, 264 (1993).

infrastructure projects developed in areas where private ownership of important resources is a new or developing concept.

A broad definition of expropriation is given in implementation agreements. In addition to an actual taking of assets, expropriation is typically defined to include less dramatic interference with a project. Also typically included are forms of "creeping expropriation," where a change in law has an indirect expropriatory effect.

The remedy available to the project sponsor for such a taking is not insignificant for the host country. In many situations, the remedy includes hard currency compensation sufficient to compensate the project sponsor for debt obligations and a reasonable equity return.

[4] Permits and Other Governmental Approvals

Responsibility for cooperation in the permitting process is also included in the implementation agreement. This cooperation is often manifested in an obligation that the host government and its agencies use best efforts to issue the permits and licenses needed by the project sponsor for construction and operation. This assurance also sometimes includes an undertaking in the implementation agreement that the host government will not revoke or modify permits and licenses without a justifiable reason and an opportunity to receive notice and be heard. In some situations, lenders will require that they be given prior notice and an opportunity to cure defaults before a significant permit or license is revoked.

[5] Currency Concerns

The implementation agreement will typically address a variety of country-specific currency issues. Currency issues that must be considered include convertibility of the currency, and whether sufficient foreign exchange is available to service the foreign currency obligations of the project, including debt, equity, and fuel payments.

The nature of the currency transfer risk varies based, in part, on the type of project. An infrastructure project in a developing country, for example, is unlikely to earn hard currency. The currency concerns for the project involve the inability to receive hard currency from customers, conversion of local currency receipts into hard currency, and transferring the hard currency abroad.

By contrast, if the project is a mining project in a developing country, the currency concerns are different because hard currency will most likely be generated from the export operations of the mine. Currency issues include the right of the project to retain the hard currency and apply it to debt and equity needs and the right to establish an offshore currency account for deposit of the export revenues.

To the extent these risks cannot be addressed adequately, insurance programs offered by the Overseas Private Investment Corporation and the Multilateral Investment Guarantee Agency should be considered.

Exchange controls can apply to almost every aspect of a project, including repayment of project loans from foreign lenders; equity investment by foreign lenders; imported services, supplies, raw materials, and fuel; and payment of technology license fees to foreign licensors. A case-by-case approach to seeking host governmental exemptions for this wide variety of transactions is not prudent. Such an approach is costly, time consuming, and is likely to result in project delays. Rather, blanket consents and exemptions for a project should be obtained where possible.

An exchange consent may be available to permit foreign currency to be retained in the form received. Host governments may permit foreign currency to be retained if it is received as loan proceeds, contributed or lent by equity investors, or generated from off-take sales and if it is needed by the project for project-related expenditures, such as payment of debt service, equity payments, equipment costs, and fees to service providers.

Currency and exchange risks are discussed extensively in Chapter 3.

[6] Tax Benefits and Customs Duties Relief

Generally. Any necessary reduction in host-country taxes, duties, and levies are also included in the implementation agreement. Often, these items are passed through by the project sponsor to the output purchaser through inclusion in the price of the good or service. If an increase occurs, the underlying price can increase to offset the tax increase.

It is particularly important that the entire project contract structure be included in the negotiation of this provision, so that tax or duty benefits extend to the contractor, operator, and fuel supplier. Otherwise, these entities will not enjoy the same benefits as the project sponsor, resulting in a pass-through of the taxes assessed against these entities to the project in the form of higher prices.

Tax Holiday. A tax holiday is an exemption from tax liability for a negotiated period of time. It is designed to provide temporary relief to a project that would not be feasible without the relief, or in recognition of other benefits the government is receiving because of the project development, such as jobs creation or associated infrastructure development paid for by the project that also benefits the country, such as roads and drinking water development.

Tax lawyers or accountants should be consulted in the preparation of a tax holiday provision. If not properly structured, the tax holiday in the host country could nonetheless result in tax liability when dividends are paid in the project sponsor's home country.

[7] Legislative Protection

Another risk that can be covered in an implementation agreement is the change of law risk. Protection is sometimes needed against a change in law or regulation that would have an adverse effect on a project. Assurances of nondiscrimination are essential in some countries. For example, Peru provides nondiscrimination protection to investors in the form of a stability agreement.

Project sponsors sometimes negotiate a "most favored status" protection. Such a clause provides the project with the prospective benefits of a favorable change in law that would otherwise not be available to it or that would result in anti-competitive effects favoring the project that enjoys the more favorable treatment.

[8] War, Insurrection, General Strikes, and Political Violence

Some form of financial protection is included in the implementation agreement in countries where war, insurrection or general strikes, or other uninsurable force majeure risks present risk to a proposed project. These provisions must be broadly drafted to encompass both international conflicts and internal domestic disturbances. This protection may take the form of a complete project buyout at an agreed-upon price after a certain period of time, or an agreement to pay project debt service and pay fixed operating costs during the force majeure event.

It can also be useful to require affirmative action by the sovereign to take any steps necessary to protect the project. This is particularly important in pipeline and transportation projects that are geographically large in scope and vulnerable to damage from demonstrations or sabotage.

[9] Authorization to Do Business

The role of the government in the industry in which the project operates must be clearly defined. Often, this role is addressed completely in the underlying laws and regulations applicable to the industry. However, in some cases the extent of governmental control over tariffs and equity return must be separately negotiated and documented. In any event, the implementation agreement should clearly state that the project sponsor has complete legal authority from the host government to produce and sell the good or service contemplated. It should result in the assurance that the project sponsor is entitled to rely on the benefits of the entire policy framework enacted by the government to promote the type of project under development.

[10] Exclusive Right to Develop Project

The implementation agreement should provide the project sponsor the exclusive right to develop the project for an agreed-upon period of time. Otherwise, the government could, knowingly or unknowingly, undertake simultaneous negotiations with other sponsors. After development and during the construction and operation phases, the sponsor should obtain from the host government a commitment that the government will not directly discriminate against the project in such a way as to support other, competing projects.

[11] General Cooperation for Project Development and Nondiscrimination

A variety of country-specific provisions can also be included in the implementation agreement. Cooperation with local lawyers is particularly helpful in ascertaining that these risks are identified. Examples include obligations by the host country to issue work permits that authorize the immigration and use of an adequate, trained work force; importation of equipment on a duty-free basis; development of infrastructure, such as roads and railways; assistance in site acquisition and assistance in fuel transportation.

While the government is in a spirit of cooperation, it is also useful to place the project on an equal level with other projects that might follow. A nondiscrimination clause, used aggressively in project financings of solid waste projects in the United States, can assist the project in not being legislated out of existence. An example follows:

Nondiscrimination. The [*Host Government*] covenants with the [*Project Company*] that it shall not enact any law, rule, or regulation the effect of which is to discriminate against the project in any manner whatsoever, it being the stated intention, policy, and agreement of the [*Host Government*] that all projects [*describe project purpose/output*] shall be treated no more favorably than the [*Project*], irrespective of location, pricing, participants, lenders, or any other factor.

[12] Good Citizenship
Some implementation agreements include obligations for the project company that benefit the health and welfare of the host government's citizens. These obligations include such things as development of infrastructure (such as water treatment) and environmental compliance (such as efforts to satisfy environmental performance levels that exceed local requirements).

[13] Enforcement and Dispute Resolution
Implementation agreements are generally considered as instruments difficult to enforce in a host country's own legal system. At a minimum, the host country must agree to a waiver of its sovereign immunity and other legal defenses. Enforcement problems can be further improved by choosing a governing law that is protective of creditor rights (e.g., New York or English law). It is also useful to require that disputes under the agreement be resolved in an offshore arbitration. Finally, it is helpful if the host government and the country in which arbitration is to take place have

signed the New York Convention on the Recognition and Enforcement of Foreign Arbitral Awards.

[14] Constitutionality Considerations of Implementation Agreements
The constitutionality of implementation agreements must be considered throughout the negotiation process. A determination must be made about whether another branch of government, such as the legislature, is legally required to approve the agreement. The specific provisions of the agreement must be considered carefully to ascertain whether the provisions are broader than that permitted by the constitution or other governing law. New or improved legislation may be necessary.

The problem of constitutionality is particularly acute in implementation agreements that include guarantees, change in law protection or tax concessions. In these situations, the freedom of the legislative body to create new laws and to raise and spend governmental funds are affected in a way that may require legislative authorization.

[15] Damages
Assurances and guarantees undertaken by the host government are often included to compensate the project if a political risk materializes or the government otherwise defaults on its obligations. These include such remedies as a buy-out of the project at an amount necessary so that the project sponsors can achieve a reasonable, minimal rate of return, and payment by the government of a supplemental amount or tariff designed to compensate the project company for the increased costs that result from governmental action.

[16] Contrast: Country Support Agreements
Two types of support agreements are used in transnational project financing: country and project. A country support agreement is negotiated and executed by a financing authority, such as an export financing agency or a bilateral risk insurer and the government. It is intended to address financing risks on a general, *multiple-*purpose level.

Alternatively, a project support agreement (implementation agreement) is negotiated and executed by the government and the sponsor of a *specific* project. It is necessary because of inherent inadequacies in the broad scope of the country support agreement, and to tailor risk allocation to the needs of a specific project.

In addition, country support agreements are negotiated to protect the financing agencies. Project support agreements, on the other hand, are negotiated to address risks to both the financing agencies, to the extent the risks are not completely covered in the country support agreement, and the project sponsor.

[17] Stabilization Clauses

Stabilization clauses, also called stabilization guarantees, have been used in contracts with host governments for many years, primarily in the exploitation of natural resources by foreign companies.[14] The purpose of the clause is to manage political risk; that is, to restrain a government, and increasingly a state enterprise, from abrogating or using its state powers to intervene in a contract entered into with a foreign company. This restraint applies to applicable law, the underlying fiscal regime, and the other investment conditions considered essential to the foreign entity's investment decision. Often considered extinct after the late 1970s as an unnecessary restraint on sovereign powers, the clause has reemerged to encourage and stabilize foreign investment for long-term infrastructure projects.

The stabilization clause strengthens the contract between the host country, or one of its enterprises, and the foreign company. Without it, investors fear that the foreign company is subject to the whims of the host government, particularly subsequent governments, and must rely on the terms of the contract, its enforcement, and arbitration to ensure contract performance.

Why would a government ever change its mind about the agreement reached with a foreign company? Nationalistic and socialistic concerns could re-emerge, of course, to upset the

concessions made or the privatization achieved. Eventually, the relative bargaining powers of emerging market countries can improve as political, currency, exchange, and other risks diminish and cause a concomitant increase in what they will be able to extract from the project and the foreign sponsors of it. In addition, the government could conclude that a change is necessary for any of the following reasons: The project becomes much more profitable than anticipated when the contracts were negotiated (particularly possible because project sponsors tend to make conservative projections about project profit potential); development of environmental concerns that did not exist at contract negotiation but could be addressed later by requiring that the project use new technologies or pay a special environmental tax; and unforeseen implications of the project, whether political, economic, or social. Of course, similar concerns could cause the foreign company to ask for changes to the deal; renegotiation is not only a governmental option.

In a project financing, the function of the stabilization clause is to freeze in place each of the significant investment assumptions made by the project company, over which the government has control. It is designed to mitigate *political* risk. This is particularly important in projects where the operating life extends over two or three decades, the duration of which increases the exposure to political risks.

If the underlying clause is breached, the available remedies are typically of two types. First, the foreign investor can be compensated through a renegotiation of the contract, in which the parties are placed back into their original positions after the effect of the new law or regulation is factored into the agreement. Second, the foreign investor, through cost recovery or cost accounting, is compensated by the state or state enterprise for the disrupted investment climate. Of course, should the state simply abrogate the contract through governmental fiat, then other remedies, such as creeping expropriation, can be pursued by the foreign investor.

[18] Sovereign Guarantees From the Government's Perspective

Whether the host government benefits from a project depends upon the allocation of risks

---

[14] *See generally* Waelde & Ndi, *supra* note 13, at 260–266; Esa Paasivirta, *Internationalization and Stabilization of Contracts Versus State Sovereignty*, 60 Brit. Y.B. Int'l L. 315 (1989); S. K. Chatterjee, *The Stabilization Clause Myth in Investment Agreements*, 5 J. Int'l Arb. 97 (1988); Rainer Geiger, *The Unilateral Change of Economic Development Agreements*, 23 Int'l & Comp. L.Q. 73 (1974).

between itself and the other project participants. As the discussion in Chapter 3 illustrates, the risks associated with infrastructure projects in a developing country often necessitate some form of host-government support, through a governmental guarantee or some other type of credit enhancement.[15] Yet, governmental guarantees can undermine the benefits of private sector involvement (privatization). These guarantees can impose significant costs on the host country's taxpayers, and further erode the country's financial health.

Also, if the host government undertakes responsibility for the wrong risks, the project sponsors may lack sufficient incentives for efficient project operation. For example, a host-government guarantee of demand for a project's use or output can remove an important market incentive: the project sponsor's incentive to develop only those projects that are strong financially. The risk structure of a project can allocate too much risk to the host country, leaving the project company with insufficient financial responsibility for taking excessive risks.

The host country can, of course, endeavor to decrease the amount of credit support it must provide a project by undertaking a program of risk reduction. For example, if a host government is successful in maintaining stable macroeconomic policies, it is less likely that project sponsors will require exchange rate guarantees or assurances of currency convertibility or transferability. Similarly, a predictable regulatory framework, coupled with regulatory agencies that are reasonably independent from the political process, and an independent judicial system for dispute resolution, can combine to reduce the need for governmental guarantees. Finally, host governments that allow dispute resolution in international arbitration can ally fears of discrimination by the local courts, and reduce the need for government-provided credit enhancement.

Developed countries do not typically need to provide governmental guarantees for projects, because the economic and political risks are satisfactory to project sponsors and lenders. This is not a benefit reserved only for developed countries, however. Some developing countries, such as Argentina, in its power industry, and Chile, in its telecommunications, power, and gas industries, achieved an economic and political climate that permits infrastructure development and privatization without the need for governmental guarantees of project debt or performance.

Importantly, project financiers sometimes lose sight of the nature of a government; that is, a government must answer to a wide spectrum of often competing interests. As such, it is very difficult for a government to promise not to change the laws and regulations that apply to a project, or if it does so, to compensate the project for the economic implications of such changes. For example, changes to environmental laws and regulations may be necessary to appease citizens, or to satisfy requirements imposed under treaties or by multilateral institutions. Similarly, new taxes may be needed to respond to changing economic conditions.

It is also sometimes difficult for a host government to control state-owned entities. For example, in an energy project the purchaser of the project output is sometimes a public entity, controlled by a local or state government. The central government may not have sufficient control over such a public entity to provide a guarantee, however. The solution that may be preferable is for the government to undertake a privatization program, which removes the purchasing entity from many of the risks inherent in public ownership.

A host government is sometimes asked to bear project commercial risks, such as construction cost overruns and output demand risks. Yet, host governments often consider the project company as the entity better able to manage these risks; placing them on the host government can remove important incentives from the private sector for selecting sound projects for development and managing costs. The project company can be rewarded, in part, for taking these risks by such solutions as lengthening the term of the concession awarded to it when demand is lower than projected, or when the project fails to generate, on a present value basis, a negotiated revenue target.

Similarly, a host government may be unwilling to provide protection against exchange and

---

[15] For a discussion on contracts between a state and a foreign company, see Jean-Flavien Lalive, *Contracts Between a State or State Agency and a Foreign Company*, 13 INT'L & COMP. L.Q. 503 (1962).

interest rate risks. From the project company's perspective, this is necessary because the government controls these risks and it encourages the government to maintain stable economic policies. Because project companies typically borrow adjustable rate debt in foreign-currency-denominated loans, project profits are sensitive to fluctuations in the interest rates and currency convertibility levels assumed in project feasibility studies. Yet, from the government's perspective, a government guarantee can encourage a project sponsor to borrow excessive debt in foreign currencies. Such guarantees can discourage governments from taking needed action to cure economic problems, such as a needed devaluation. Finally, a currency depreciation is often coupled with a decline in income and the associated tax base, resulting in a decrease in funds available to a host government at precisely the time the project company enforces the guarantee.

How can a host government make an informed decision about whether a guarantee is needed? It must measure the *expected* economic effects of a guarantee in its accounting system, and include these effects in its budget. The expected effects are difficult to project without a record of historical experience. However, economic models can be used to provide meaningful estimates. A financial analysis of a guarantee can assist the host government in determining whether to provide a guarantee, or, for example, a subsidy.[16]

§ 14.07 OTHER CONSIDERATIONS FOR PRELIMINARY AGREEMENTS

In exchange for providing cooperation for a project, or financial support through infrastructure investment or guarantees, the host government may require some additional agreements from the project sponsors. These can be included

in the implementation agreement, or be embodied in separate documentation.

[1] Infrastructure Development

Often, the host government agrees to provide or enhance the infrastructure in the area of the project to promote the project's success. This is the case in both industrialized and in developing countries.

Before the country begins to invest the resources to provide this infrastructure, however, it will desire a commitment by the project company to proceed with the project. This can be included in an implementation agreement, or can be part of a separate agreement.

Land and Air Transportation. Availability and access, cost, and regulation are the three major components of land and air transportation for project feasibility. Availability and access addresses the existence of transportation facilities, including air, road, and rail, and their proximity to the project. Cost addresses the cost payable by the project for their construction, maintenance or use. Regulation relates to the presence of cabotage.

AVAILABILITY. The availability of transportation to and from the project site is a significant feasibility consideration. A site visit can help determine the physical access to the project site. Less apparent is the available access to the transportation network beyond the project site. To the extent any necessary transportation component is lacking, governmental infrastructure investment may be needed.

COST. Short distance access roads or railways are common project development costs. Longer access to a project, whether by road or railway, is often considered an infrastructure cost more properly borne by the host government.

CABOTAGE. Cabotage is the regulation by a government of its transportation systems. The most common cabotage regulation is one that requires use of transportation vessels chartered in the country for movement of goods in the country. Similarly, bilateral treaties may require that transportation between two countries be allocated among vessels chartered in the two countries. In the absence of competition, of course, these internal and bilateral transportation costs may be

[16] *See generally* Christopher M. Lewis & Ashoka Mody, *Contingent Liabilities for Infrastructure Projects – Implementing a Risk Management Framework for Governments*, PUBLIC POLICY FOR THE PRIVATE SECTOR, WORLD BANK NOTE NO. 148 (Aug. 1998); Christopher M. Lewis & Ashoka Mody, *Risk Management Systems for Contingent Infrastructure Liabilities – Applications to Improve Contract Design and Monitoring*, PUBLIC POLICY FOR THE PRIVATE SECTOR, WORLD BANK NOTE NO. 149 (Aug. 1998).

excessive. Consequently, the project may desire to negotiate some waiver relief from these regulations and treaties allowing the project unfettered access to competitive rates.

Water Ports and Harbors. Some projects rely on water transportation of construction materials, fuels, raw materials, and other supplies. This is particularly true in geographic regions that offer no other efficient transportation alternative.

In many countries, ports and harbors are notoriously overcrowded and congested. To avoid delays and unanticipated operating costs, project sponsors sometimes prefer to build their own piers at existing ports and harbors, or to construct new facilities. Either action typically requires governmental approvals and cooperation, both of which should be included as topics of initial discussions with the host government.

Power. Electric power can be generated both internally in a country and imported into the country from external generating sources. As globalization of resources continues, it is likely that electric power will become more of an international commodity. Despite this emerging trend, however, it is important for the project sponsor to determine whether sufficient power exists in the host country for delivery to the proposed project site. If not, new generation capacity will need to be built. Also, if there is insufficient transmission capability to the project site, new transmission lines will need to be constructed.

A power purchase agreement between the utility and the project, for sale of electricity generated or distributed by the utility to the project company, will limit power price risk to the project. Unless governmentally approved and regulated power tariffs are in place, the project is subject to unregulated price increases by the utility, which may result in project operating costs that make the project infeasible.

The project company and the host government may find it more practical for the project company to construct its own electrical generation facility. This may be required irrespective of local generation and transmission capabilities and availability, however, if the project needs to purchase and use steam or heat in its manufacturing processes.

Whatever method is selected, sufficient power must be available over the life of the project, particularly over the term of the project debt.

Water. Process water (water used in connection with project production) and cooling water (water used to cool equipment) is important to many projects. Water quality, chemistry, accessibility, and availability are all considerations for the project company in siting a project and in estimating costs, whether the water is supplied by a utility or piped by the project from a nearby source.

The host government may be involved in supplying water to a project because either the water utility is owned by a governmental agency, or the government must approve the taking of water from navigable waterways. Other host-government considerations include the effect of the proposed project on water availability for future needs, including drinking water, and discharge of water into public water sources.

Waste Disposal. By-products of the project must be disposed of in adequately designed and maintained waste disposal facilities. To the extent these are unavailable near the project site, the project can either build its own facilities, or ask the government to construct them.

Communications. In many developing countries, cellular and digital communications systems are the most widely available infrastructure service. Yet, government cooperation may be needed to ensure that telephone service is available at the site.

[2] **Product or Service**
The host government may place restrictions on the types of goods or services produced at the project. For example, it may be significant to the host government whether the project's goods or services will replace goods or services currently imported. If the product will replace an imported product, the government may need to use this information to plan its foreign exchange and impose any necessary production restrictions.

[3] Milestones

It is not unusual for a host government to place completion deadlines on project sponsors. This helps assure that projects are completed within a reasonable time. These are often used in infrastructure projects. If a project is not proceeding on an appropriate schedule, the host government may want to impose penalties or cancel contracts with the project sponsor and select another developer.

Milestone dates are generally of three types: calendar, counting, and sunset. Calendar milestone dates are dates selected by the host government and project sponsor as the actual calendar dates by which certain events in project development must occur, such as financing and completion. With so-called counting dates, a number of days are assigned to each significant development activity and the project sponsor must complete the task within that number of days. A sunset date approach uses only one date, the completion date. If the project is not completed by that date, penalties or contract termination will result.

Whatever approach is used, time extensions are permitted for force majeure events, host-government fault, and other negotiated excuses. However, if a force majeure event occurs that continues for a long period, typically two to three years, then no further extensions may be permitted and the underlying contracts with the host government would terminate.

[4] Expansion Rights or Requirements

It is often prudent for the host government, project sponsor, or both, to negotiate project expansion rights at the time the initial project is negotiated. Economic efficiencies may exist for both the host government and the project sponsors for project expansion at any existing operating project site.

[5] Social Program Support

The host government may couple its approval of a project to a commitment by the project sponsors to participate in social programs in the country. This is particularly the case in projects that do not have any local ownership, and where the host government has a need to show that the project will benefit the local citizens. Examples include scholarship programs and expansion of water treatment facilities.

Training of local citizens is sometimes solicited by the host government. The project company will want to specify, however, that it alone is responsible for training and employment decisions.

[6] Option to Acquire Raw Materials in the Host Country

In some developing countries, offshore raw material supply is more predictable than in-country supply. Consequently, the project lenders may insist that raw material supply agreements be entered into with suppliers from other countries. If this adds costs to the project, it is possible to eliminate them when the in-country supply becomes more reliable. The framework for any later purchases of raw materials from the host country should be negotiated at the early stages of project development, when other host-country agreements are negotiated.

[7] Importation of Construction Equipment

A ready supply of, and access to, construction equipment is often taken for granted in the industrialized nations. In developing countries, however, specialized construction equipment must be brought into the country by the contractor, adding to construction costs. Also, in some situations, an equipment supplier in a host country may enjoy the exclusive right to import and supply specialized equipment to construction projects, further increasing the cost. Further costs arise from customs duties and sales or use taxes. Thus, in preliminary project agreement negotiations with the host country, the use and cost of construction equipment should be included.

It may be possible in such countries to receive a special construction equipment importation approval, which allows the contractor to import the construction equipment needed, free of importation duties, and sales and use taxes. This approval could be made subject to a requirement that the equipment be removed from the country after construction is complete, or if sold in the host country, that such sale be conditioned on payment of taxes based on the value of the equipment at the time of the sale.

[8] Price Regulation
The prices that can be charged for the output of the project are of fundamental importance to the project's feasibility. In many developing countries, however, price regulation and subsidization are time-honored traditions. For example, in many developing countries, residential electric customers have enjoyed unrealistically low electric rates that have been subsidized by the central government.

A project company will prefer to, and in most cases to ensure project viability must, charge market rates for its output, irrespective of central government social or political policies. A commitment by the government to allow market-based pricing, without imposing price ceilings or other controls, may be important.

A similar concern is present in projects that will export some or all of its output. With an export-oriented project, the host government has an interest in the project maximizing revenue. This results in higher tax revenues and foreign exchange receipts. In this type of project, a compromise may be to establish a price floor, below which the project company cannot price its output. Such a floor needs to be carefully structured so that the output price remains competitive with similarly-situated suppliers. One solution available is to establish a floor calculated as a percentage of a regional or international benchmark price or index.

[9] Government-Owned Natural Resources
In projects where the host country owns some or all of the sources of raw materials for the project, such as fuel or mining interests, it is important for the project company and the host government to agree on pricing terms at an early stage in project development. Otherwise, it will be uncertain whether the project is feasible. Even where the natural resources are in private hands, the government could still impose an extraction tax or fee on purchasers.

[10] Local Restrictions on Sale
Restrictions may exist that limit the project's ability to sell the goods or services produced. These may be imposed by law or regulation, in the form of a monopoly granted to a governmentally-owned entity, or by the physical constraints of

existing distribution systems, such as inadequate power distribution systems that require governmental approval for expansion. These shortcomings must be addressed to ensure project feasibility.

[11] Export Restrictions
Exports are commonly regulated by governments. If the project will export its output for sale, it is important to understand, with assistance from local lawyers, the effect of export laws on the project. Export laws may require licensing of the project, restrict the countries to which a project can sell its products, and impose export duties.

[12] Import Restrictions
Similarly, imports are the subject of governmental regulation. If the import restrictions are burdensome and import duties high, the project will be forced to rely on local supplies of needed project inputs. Of course, these inputs may not even be available in the host country. Consequently, an early investigation of the potential local sources, and the costs and availability of importing supplies, must be included in preliminary governmental discussions.

[13] Employees
Ninety-nine percent of the credit for controlling risk in some project financings should go to the site employees of the contractor, operator, and project company, and the remaining 1 percent to the project lawyers. Although this may be an exaggeration of the worth of lawyers, it is not an exaggeration of the contribution of employees. Consequently, the entry into a country of experienced, knowledgeable employees is significant to project success, and their entry and re-entry into a country should be assured.

In addition to entry and re-entry of these expatriates, provision should be made for the same treatment of their families. Also, they should be permitted to freely transfer salaries and wages out of the country, and be free of income taxes that are higher than the rate applied in the employee's home country. If not, project costs will increase for the project company as it or its contractor must pay employees for additional airfare costs for family visits, compensation for restrictions on income transfer and a gross-up in salary as compensation for higher income tax rates than would be applied by the employee's home country.

[14] Withholding Taxes on Loan Interest

It is important to determine the extent of tax withholding on the payment of interest by the project company to its lenders. In some situations, tax treaties can form the basis of eliminating or minimizing liability, through use of a bank's branches located in other countries.

Generally, interest paid to governments or agencies of governments, such as export-import banks, are exempt from withholding liability. But, the withholding is applicable to commercial lenders, which require that the borrower reimburse them for the effects of any withholding. The financial feasibility of the project could deteriorate if a significant percentage of interest payments are withheld.

§ 14.08 HOST-COUNTRY APPROVAL OF POLITICAL RISK INSURANCE

Before political risk insurance is provided to a project by an organization such as the Multilateral Insurance Guarantee Agency, approval must be obtained from the host country. Typically, the issuing agency obtains the necessary approval itself. Yet, it is helpful if this approval process is included in preliminary discussions with the host government. This is particularly true because insurance application must be made before an investment is made or irrevocably committed.

Approval of involvement in a country by a political risk insurer increases the likelihood of project success. It is generally believed that such an approval reduces claims exposure and loan default.

§ 14.09 THE PROBLEM OF BINDING FUTURE GOVERNMENTS TO ACTIONS OF PREDECESSOR GOVERNMENTS

[1] Introduction

In some countries, there is a risk that a new government achieving power, whether central, state, or local, will seek to undo some portion or all of the predecessor government's work in connection with support of a project. For project finance transactions, particularly infrastructure projects important to the host government's economy, there are possible warning signs that might suggest this risk is more likely. These include a lack of support for privatization programs; failure of the governing party to maintain a consensus on bidding and contracting programs; corruption; no competitive bidding program; perceived openness of government in awarding contracts; contracting that does not appear to reflect terms received in similarly situated countries; press criticism of projects in operation or development; degree of nationalist sentiment; historical experience in governing party transfer of political power; and stability of power where family members of a ruler receive preferential economic treatment. Each of these are early warning signs of potential problems should a successor government take power.[17]

It is improbable that a project developer will be much more effective at guessing election results than political professionals. Perhaps, the soundest way to avoid major project problems from succession risk is to avoid exclusive close ties to one politician or party; diversity in support should be garnered. One-sided implementation agreements, real or perceived, should be avoided by negotiating competitive, market-based terms, with attractive social and economic benefits for the host country.

Indeed, changes to contracts negotiated by a previous government in a developing country cannot be completely avoided in most circumstances. In some countries, where legal systems are only now developing, this is particularly true.

[2] The Effectiveness of Contracts With Host Governments as Risk Mitigation

The choice of a contract to address political risk mitigation is an admission that the underlying political process is too unpredictable to achieve the hoped for mitigation results. A contract, it is thought, is more useful in binding a sovereign government. In essence, it is hoped that the

---

[17] An example of action by a successor government to change a contract entered into by a predecessor government in the Dabhol project in India. That project is discussed in Chapter 18.

contract is an election, and a new law, neither of which can be changed, and both of which will be enforced. Yet, that hope may be less than certain.

Among the considerations that must be taken into account in determining whether the contract will be honored and enforced is whether the government has the legal authority to enter into it. Even if it does, there are often procedural requirements in the host country that must be carefully followed for the contractual obligation to be valid.[18]

[3] Contractual Damages and Assurances

As protection against this risk, termination provisions and termination payments could be an important protection for the project company. These damage payments would be due if the government breached a provision in a contract with the project company. In addition, it might prove beneficial to add a so-called statement of binding effect to an implementation or other agreement with the host country. An example of such a statement follows:

Statement of Binding Effect. The [*Host Government*] states that it is the intention, policy and purpose of the [*Identify Government*] that this agreement shall not be amended, annulled, modified, renounced, revoked, supplemented or terminated, nor its performance delayed or hindered, by any direct or indirect action or inaction by the [*Identify Government*] in any manner whatsoever or howsoever, whether by legislation (general or special), regulation, or administrative action. This statement shall bind all present and future executives, legislatures and administrative bodies, however termed, of the [*Identify Government*].

Whether any official or branch of the host government has the authority to enter into such a commitment must be examined with local lawyers. Nonetheless, should problems develop, it provides the project sponsors with useful arguments that compensation should be awarded for breach of contract, or that the equivalent of a nationalization of project rights has occurred.

[4] Sanctity of Contract Versus State Sovereignty

The legal status of contracts with governments in a project financing is not as settled as one would hope.[19] On the one hand, sovereign governments are considered to be free to enact new laws and regulations, change governments, and otherwise govern their people.[20] On the other hand, sovereign governments are considered to be free to enter into contracts stabilizing that inherent fluidity, and submit to international law, thereby encouraging foreign investment.[21]

§ 14.10 WAIVER OF SOVEREIGN IMMUNITY

[1] Generally

In agreements with the host-country government and with entities controlled by the government, a waiver of sovereign immunity is required.[22] *Sovereign immunity* precludes an allegedly wronged party from bringing a cause of action, valid as it may be, against a government unless the government consents. The doctrine began with the personal prerogatives of the Sovereign of England; no court was above the sovereign. Thereafter, it was extended to the state through some metaphysical somersaults best left to the law reviews.[23]

Project financings and other international transactions are left to deal with the doctrine today. It is generally agreed that any agreement

---

[18] *See generally* Waelde & Ndi, *supra* note 13, at 234–238.

[19] *See generally id.* at 243–246.

[20] *E.g.,* Texaco Overseas Oil Petroleum Co./California Asiatic Oil Co. v. Libyan Arab Republic, 21 I.L.M. 726, 735–36 (1982) ("The result is that a State cannot invoke its sovereignty to disregard commitments freely undertaken through the exercise of this same sovereignty, and cannot through measures belonging to its internal order make null and void the rights of the contracting party which has performed its various obligations under the contract."); Saudi Arabia v. Arabian Am. Oil Co. (Aramco), 27 I.L.R. 117, 168 (1963); Mobil Oil Iran Inc. v. Islamic Republic of Iran, 16 Iran-U.S. Cl. Trib. Rep. 3, 64–65 (1987).

[21] *E.g.,* American Indep. Oil Co. (Aminoil) v. Libyan Arab Republic, 21 I.L.M. 976, 1043 (1982).

[22] *See generally* Materials on Jurisdictional Immunities of States and their Property, U.N. Doc. ST/LEG/SER.B./20 (1982).

[23] *See generally* Georges R. Delaume, *The Foreign Sovereign Immunities Act and Public Debt Litigation: Some 15 Years Later,* 78 Am. J. Int'l L. 257 (1994).

with a government should contain a waiver of the doctrine of sovereign immunity. Such a clause permits the non-governmental party to commence litigation before an independent body, and if wronged, to receive a judgment against a government.[24]

[2] Foreign Sovereign Immunities Act of 1976 (U.S.)

Generally. Many countries have some form of sovereign immunity. In the United States, the Foreign Sovereign Immunities Act allocates to the courts the determination of sovereign immunity. In general, the statute provides that a foreign sovereign, or its agency or instrumentality, is immune from suit in the United States unless the Act otherwise permits the suit.[25] The Act is subject to overriding treaties and agreements. A corporation whose majority of shares are owned by a foreign state or political subdivision may also be considered a foreign state for the purposes of this Act.[26]

Exceptions to Immunity. The act provides, in Section 1605, exceptions to this immunity.[27] These include: (i) waiver; (ii) certain commercial activities; (iii) action where the taking is in violation of international law; (iv) action taken to confirm or enforce an arbitration agreement; (v) enforcement of maritime liens; and (vi) foreclosure of a preferred mortgage.[28]

WAIVER. First, the government can waive the immunity.[29] A waiver can be implicit or explicit. In *Morgan Guaranty Trust Co. v. Republic of Palau*,[30] the President of the Republic of Palau waived the Republic's sovereign immunity when he entered into loan agreements with United States companies regarding the construction of a power plant. The company sued the Republic to recover money paid under a guarantee when the Republic defaulted on loans. The court held that the Republic was required to reimburse the guarantors. By signing the agreement and backing the financing with the "full faith and credit of the Republic" the President waived immunity.[31]

CERTAIN COMMERCIAL ACTIVITY. The second exception arises from certain commercial activity: (i) commercial activity carried on in the United States by a foreign state, (ii) an act performed in the United States in connection with commercial activity of a foreign state elsewhere, or (iii) commercial activity of a foreign state outside the United States, which causes a *direct effect* in the United States.[32] Economic injury to a United States company as a result of a foreign state's commercial activity may satisfy the "direct effects" clause if the company is a primarily direct, rather than indirect, victim of conduct and if injurious and significant financial consequences to that company were foreseeable, rather than a fortuitous result of conduct.[33] Some courts have determined that the connection between

---

[24] *See, e.g.,* Texaco Overseas Co. v. Libya, 53 I.L.R. 389, 422 (I.C.J. Arb. 1977).

[25] Foreign Sovereign Immunities Act of 1976, Pub. L. No. 94–583, 1602, 90 Stat. 2891, 2892 (codified in 28 U.S.C. §§ 1602–1611 (1994)). *See generally* Delaume, *supra* note 23.

[26] Fore-most-McKesson v. Islamic Republic of Iran, 905 F2d 438 (D.C. Cir. 1990) (there must be a showing that the foreign state dominated the operations of the agency such that "a principal-agent relationship is created.").

[27] 28 U.S.C. 1605.

[28] There are other exceptions, not typically encountered in a project finance transaction: where rights in property in the United States acquired by succession or gift or rights in immovable property in the United States are in issue; money damages sought against a foreign state for personal injury or death, or damage to or loss of property, occurring in the United States and caused by a tortuous act of a foreign state.

[29] 28 U.S.C.A. 1605(a)(1).

[30] 702 F. Supp. 60 (S.D.N.Y. 1988).

[31] Morgan Guar. Trust Co. v. Republic of Palau, 702 F. Supp. 60 (S.D.N.Y. 1988).

[32] 28 U.S.C.A. 1605(a)(2). *See generally* Republic of Argentina v. Weltover, Inc., 504 U.S. 607, 614 (1992) (an activity is commercial "when a foreign government acts not as a regulator of a market, but in the manner of a private player within it."); MCI Telecommunications Corp. v. Alahdhood, 82 F.3d 658, 663 (5th Cir.) (*quoting* Callejo v. Bancomer, S. A., 764 F.2d 1101, 1108 n.6 (5th Cir. 1985)), *petition for cert. filed*, No. 96–434, 65 U.S.L.W. 3205 (Sep. 17, 1996) (commercial activity "is of a type that a private person would customarily engage in for profit"). *See also* MICHAEL GORDON, FOREIGN STATE IMMUNITY IN COMMERCIAL TRANSACTIONS §§ 3.01–4.03 (1991). Foreign courts have applied similar exceptions. F. A. Mann, *The State Immunity Act 1978*, 50 BRIT. Y.B. INT'L L. 43 (1979) (Great Britain).

[33] Gould, Inc. v. Pechiney Ugine Kuhlmann, 853 F.2d 445 (6th Cir. 1988).

the cause of action and the commercial activity must be material.[34]

PROPERTY TAKEN IN VIOLATION OF INTERNATIONAL LAW. A third exception to immunity arises where rights in property are taken in violation of international law and the property is (i) present in the United States in connection with foreign state and commercial activity or (ii) owned or operated by an agency of a foreign state and the agency is engaged in commercial activity in the United States.

CONFIRMATION OR ENFORCEMENT OF ARBITRATION AGREEMENT. Another exception is confirmation or enforcement of an arbitration agreement.[35] To qualify, (i) the arbitration must have taken place or be intended to take place in the United States; (ii) the agreement or award must be governed by a treaty or international agreement in force for the United States calling for recognition and enforcement of arbitral awards; or (iii) the underlying claim, except for the arbitration agreement, could have been brought in the United States under this section of the act (i.e., commercial activity).

MARITIME. Another exception is a suit in admiralty brought to enforce a maritime lien against a vessel or cargo of the foreign state.

PREFERRED MORTGAGE. Also providing an exception is any action brought to foreclose a preferred mortgage.

Counterclaims. Similar exceptions extend to counterclaims. With respect to counterclaims, in any action brought by a foreign state or in which a foreign state intervenes in the United States, a foreign state is not entitled to immunity with respect to any counterclaim: (i) for which the foreign state would not be entitled to immunity under Section 1605 had the claim been brought against the foreign state, or (ii) arising out of the transaction or occurrence that is the subject matter of the claim of the foreign state, or (iii) to the extent that the counterclaim does not seek relief exceeding in amount, or differing in kind from, that sought by the foreign state.

Extent of Sovereign Liability. Under the Act, if a foreign state is not entitled to immunity, the foreign state is liable in the same manner and to the same extent as a private individual under similar circumstances.[36] A foreign state (except an agency or instrumentality) is not liable for punitive damages.

Attachment of Sovereign's Property. The property of a foreign state is immune from attachment. However, property of a foreign state located in the United States and used for a commercial activity is *not* immune from attachment in aid of execution or from execution of an award if used for a commercial activity in the United States, and if: (i) the foreign state waived immunity from attachment; (ii) the property is used for commercial activity upon which the claim is based; (iii) the execution relates to a judgment establishing rights in property taken in violation of international law; (iv) the execution relates to a judgment establishing rights in property acquired by gift or succession, or immovable property in the United States except that which is used for purposes of maintaining a diplomatic mission; or (v) the judgment is based on an order confirming an arbitral award rendered against the foreign state.

Property used for commercial activity in the United States is not immune from attachment prior to an entry of judgment if: (i) the foreign state has explicitly waived immunity from attachment prior to judgment and (ii) the purpose of attachment is to secure satisfaction of a judgment that has been or may be entered against the foreign state and not to obtain jurisdiction.

Certain types of property are always immune from attachment. These are (i) property of organizations designated by the President of the United States as being entitled to enjoy privileges and immunities provided by the International Organizations Immunities Act; (ii) property of a foreign central bank or monetary authority, unless waived from attachment; and (iii) property which is or is intended to be used in connection with a military activity and is of a military character, or is under control of military authority.

The Act only deals with subject matter jurisdiction. Therefore, even if it is determined that

---

[34] *See* Stena Rederi AB v. Comision de Contratos del Comite Ejectivo, 923 F2d 380 (5th Cir. 1991).

[35] *See* Libyan Am. Oil Co., v. Socialist People's Libyan Arab Jamahirya, 482 F. Supp. 1175 (1980).

[36] 28 U.S.C. § 1606.

a foreign state is not immune, personal jurisdiction must still be established. This can be done rather easily by demonstrating that the foreign state has "minimum contacts" with the United States. Minimum contacts have included continuous and systematic activities in the United States, corporate agents regularly doing business in the United States, or evidence showing that the defendants have exercised privileges or benefited from protections of conducting business in the United States.[37]

Case Study: Waiver of Sovereign Immunity in a Project Finance Transaction. A short example of the application of the FSIA is helpful in understanding its application to project finance.[38] A typical project finance contract between a foreign government and a U.S. corporation is a power sales agreement. Under that agreement, the U.S. corporation develops, constructs and operates a power generation facility, and the foreign government (or an agency thereof) agrees to purchase and pay for the power produced.

In such a transaction, a sovereign's immunity could be waived under certain circumstances. If a sovereign expressly waived immunity in the power sales agreement, implementation agreement, or another document, sovereign immunity is directly waived.

Alternatively, sovereign immunity could be waived indirectly. If the claim brought against a sovereign is based upon its commercial activity, contracting for power supply may constitute a commercial activity, and sovereign immunity may be waived. That commercial activity must have a direct effect in the United States.

The Act gives little guidance on what constitutes a commercial activity and what is a direct effect. Furthermore, the case law surrounding this area is often inconsistent. However, the general rule is that a commercial activity is that which

a private party could engage in.[39] Stated in the obverse, commercial activity is activity that is not peculiarly sovereign. Under that rule, contracting for power supply may constitute a commercial activity, particularly since private sector entities contract for and purchase power. Further, noncommercial activities are usually only those which are sovereign in nature such as levying taxes or organizing the military.[40]

The *direct effect* standard is extremely fact specific.[41] However, in certain instances, injury to a United States corporation could be considered having a direct effect on the United States as a whole. Mere economic loss may be insufficient.[42]

Once it is determined that a waiver of sovereign immunity, direct or indirect, exists, the next step is to find property to attach. A sovereign's property used in a commercial activity in the United States could be attached under certain circumstances: attachment in aid of execution of judgment is waived if implicitly or explicitly waived, or the property is used for a commercial activity upon which the claim is based, or the property is used for a commercial activity and the judgment to be enforced is based on an order confirming an arbitral award.

Attachment prior to judgment is waived if the state has explicitly waived attachment, and the

---

[37] *See* Texas Trading & Milling Corp. v. Federal Republic of Nigeria, 647 F.2d 300 (2nd Cir. 1981) (litigation not unduly inconvenient where Nigeria agreed to International Chamber of Commerce arbitration that could take place anywhere); Gemini Shipping, Inc. v. Foreign Trade Organization for Chemicals & Foodstuffs (S.D.N.Y. 1980).

[38] *See* Danielle Mazzini, *Stable International Contracts in Emerging Markets: An Endangered Species?*, 15 B.U. Int'l L.J. 343, 363–369 (1997).

[39] Courts that have considered whether business activity is commercial activity include the following: Janini v. Kuwait Univ., 43 F.3d 1534 (D.C. Cir. 1995) (university teacher employment contract); Practical Concepts, Inc. v. Republic of Bolivia, 811 F.2d 1543 (D.C. Cir. 1987) (rural development); Segni v. Commercial Office of Spain, 835 F.2d 160 (7th Cir. 1987) (wine marketing contract); Callejo v. Bancomer S.A., 764 F.2d 1101 (5th Cir. 1985) (selling CDs and the breach of the sales contract were commercial acts); Texas Trading & Milling Corp. v. Federal Republic of Nigeria, 647 F.2d 300 (2nd Cir. 1981) (contract for sale of cement; letters of credit); Gemini Shipping, Inc. v. Foreign Trade Org. for Chemicals and Foodstuffs, 647 F.2d 317 (2d Cir. 1981) (grain shipping to government-owned company).

[40] *See* Janini v. Kuwait Univ., 43 F.3d 1534, 1537 (D.C. Cir. 1995) (university teacher employment contract).

[41] Republic of Argentina v. Weltover, Inc., 504 U.S. 607, 617 (1992) (direct effect found in the U.S. where Argentina bonds payments were to be made in New York); *but cf.* United World Trade, Inc. v. Mangyshlakneft Oil Production Ass'n, 33 F.3d 1232 (10th Cir. 1994).

[42] United World Trade, Inc. v. Mangyshlakneft Oil Production Ass'n, 33 F.3d 1232 (10th Cir. 1994) (contract required payment outside of U.S., with eventual transfer of funds to the U.S., held not a direct effect).

purpose is to secure satisfaction of a judgment, not to obtain jurisdiction.

If the United States is called upon to enforce an arbitration agreement, sovereign immunity is waived only if the arbitration took place or was intended to take place in the United States, or the underlying claim of the arbitration could have originally been brought in the United States.

Thus, the ability of a U.S. entity to litigate a claim against a sovereign government, and attach property of the sovereign government located in the United States, is extremely sensitive to the facts of the specific situation.[43] Full waivers, however, make such action much easier.

[3] State Immunity Act of 1978 (U.K.)

Generally. The State Immunity Act of 1978[44] in the United Kingdom is similar to the U.S. Act discussed above.[45] In general, the U.K. Act provides that a state is immune from the jurisdiction of the courts of the United Kingdom, and then establishes exceptions to that rule, as set forth in the Act.[46]

Exceptions to Immunity. Like the U.S. Act, numerous exceptions to sovereign immunity are included in the Act.[47] These include exceptions generally similar to those provided under the U.S. Act.

Application. The Act provides that the immunity applies to any foreign or commonwealth state.[48] References to a state include the sovereign or other head of that state in his public capacity; the government of that state; and any department of that government, but not any entity which is

distinct from the executive function of the government of the state, and capable of suing and being sued.[49]

§ 14.11 ACT OF STATE DOCTRINE (U.S.)

The *act of state doctrine* provides that U.S. courts will not consider whether the official acts of a foreign government, carried out in its own territory, are actionable.[50] It is a separate legal doctrine from sovereign immunity.[51]

The act of state doctrine represents a general distaste for judicial review of foreign government actions. Although the U.S. Supreme Court has never considered the question, lower U.S. courts have addressed the applicability of the doctrine to contractual disputes.[52] Perhaps the best generalization that can be made from these cases is that the lower courts will determine the applicability of the doctrine on a case-by-case basis. At least one commentator, in an excellent analysis of the subject, contends that the doctrine may be applicable in considering whether an investment contract with a sovereign government, typical in international project finance in developing countries, is enforceable in U.S. courts.[53]

The act of state doctrine can be addressed in a more flexible manner if arbitration is chosen as a dispute resolution method for the host-country

---

[43] The burden of proof is on the party alleging that the immunity is waived. Walter Fuller Aircraft Sales, Inc. v. Republic of the Philippines, 965 F.2d 1375, 1383 (5th Cir. 1992).

[44] State Immunity Act, 1978, ch. 33.

[45] *See generally* S. Bird, *The State Immunity Act of 1978*, 13 INT'L LAWYER 619 (1979); Georges R. Delaume, *The State Immunity Act of the United Kingdom*, 73 A.J.I.L. 185 (1979); F. A. Mann, *The State Immunity Act 1978*, 50 BRIT. Y.B. INT'L L. 43 (1979); Robin C. A. White, *The State Immunity Act 1978*, 42 MODERN L. REV. 72 (1979), D. W. Bowett, *The State Immunity Act 1978*, 37 CAMBRIDGE L.J. 193 (1978).

[46] State Immunity Act, 1978, ch. 33. § 1.(1).

[47] *Id.* § 1.(2)–(11).   [48] *Id.* § 14.(1).

[49] *Id.* § 14.(1)(a)–(c).

[50] *See* Underhill v. Hernandez, 168 U.S. 250, 252 (1897).

[51] Antonio Dolar, Comment, *Act of State and Sovereign Immunities Doctrines: The Need to Establish Congruity*, 17 U.S.F. L. REV. 110–16 (1982).

[52] *E.g.*, Ampac Group Inc. v. Republic of Honduras, 797 F. Supp. 973, 978 (S.D. Fla 1992) (enforcing cement company privatization contract against the government of Honduras); French v. Banco Nacional de Cuba, 242 N.E.2d 704, 709 (N.Y. 1968) (doctrine bars breach of contract claim against agency of Cuban government). *See generally* Michael Ramsey, *Acts of State and Foreign Sovereign Obligations*, 39 HARV. INT'L L.J. 1, 3 (1998).

[53] *See generally* Ramsey, *supra* note 52, at 22–45 (1998) (examining the doctrine in the context of power plant project finance and concluding that exceptions to or limitations on the doctrine do not completely remove enforcement of foreign sovereign contracts from its scope). *See also* Michael Gruson, *The Act of State Doctrine in Contract Cases as a Conflict-of-Laws Rule*, 1998 U. ILL. L. REV. 519 (foreign government interference in the context of contracts between two private parties).

agreement. Unlike litigation, this doctrine, as well as sovereign immunity, can be made inapplicable to agreements and disputes.[54]

§ 14.12 COOPERATIVE RISK MANAGEMENT

There is a danger for host governments and foreign investors in project finance political risk management that should be carefully avoided: In the zeal of lawyers and investors to manage and allocate political risks, the host government or its citizens perceive that the government has been bullied to accept risk mitigation alternatives that are not in the interests of the host government. This can create a new project risk.

Host governments are often completely understanding about the concerns of foreign investors. At the highest levels of developing country governments, officials are well aware of foreign investors' preference for timely debt repayment, rapid return of investments, tax concessions, exchange guarantees, and the like. Yet, these preferences may be unavailable to domestic firms. This creates an atmosphere in the host country of preferential, discriminatory treatment of foreign investors at the expense of local firms. At a minimum, political criticism of the host government will arise. This may lead to allegations of corruption by the negotiators or in the entire negotiation process. Coupled with fears of excessive capitulation to foreign demands, these

impressions can create an unhealthy climate for a project.

Although seemingly appropriate on paper, the implications of one-sided political risk mitigation may be unhealthy for the long-term success of the project. Once a project closes and construction begins, massive amounts of foreign capital have already been committed to the project. As the project proves successful, the bargaining position of the host government and the project changes, with the host government gaining in power. If a successor government, in an anti-foreign investment campaign, has second thoughts about the appropriateness of concessions made by the prior government, renegotiations can be a real threat.

Even apart from these concerns, the success of the project could be so in excess of the projections made at closing that allegations of unfairness arise. Similarly, host-government assumptions made at closing about the actual cost of infrastructure and related host-government obligations to the project could be wildly unrealistic, also fueling the fires of unfairness.

Rather than view the host government as an adversary, one author has suggested that it is in the best interests of the foreign investors to consider a cooperative approach to political risk management that recognizes that both the host government and the foreign investors can achieve benefits in political risk mitigation.[55] Indeed, foreign investors should be very wary of projects that have secured one-sided forms of political risk protection. They will likely not last.

[54] *See generally* Carsten T. Ebenroth and Thomas J. Dillon, Jr., *Arbitration Clauses in International Financial Agreements: Circumventing the Act of State Doctrine,* 10 J. Int'l Arb. 5 (1993).

[55] Waelde & Ndi, *supra* note 13, at 237.

CHAPTER FIFTEEN

CONSTRUCTION CONTRACTS

§ 15.01 GENERALLY

The construction contract in an international project financing serves to give the project company a fully completed and equipped facility. In addition, it provides for delivery by the contractor of a facility that satisfies specified performance criteria, for a fixed or predictable price, and completed on a specified date. To do so, the contract typically requires the contractor to provide all engineering and construction work, procurement of equipment and supplies, and start-up and testing.

The tension between the project company and contractor in a project financing is based on the turnkey nature of the construction contract: The contractor must deliver the project at a fixed or predictable price, on a date certain, warranted to perform at agreed levels. The contractor is, of course, concerned with the difficulty of predicting events that could delay project completion, increase the price, or reduce guaranteed performance. Thus, unless the contract price is extremely attractive (that is, the risk premium sufficiently high), significant objectives of the contractor in contract negotiation are to limit risks of any increase in the cost of the project, to ensure there are sufficient contractual excuses for late delivery, and to provide sufficient time to satisfy performance guarantees.

A customary reward to the contractor, in return for assuming these price, delay, and performance risks, is through a bonus payment. The project company pays a bonus payment to the contractor if the project is completed ahead of the scheduled completion date. In a project financing, the bonus concept must conform with the rights and obligations of the project company under the other project contracts.

As discussed below, the risk that construction costs will exceed the funds available to complete the project, from the construction loan, other debt sources, and equity, is a significant risk in a project financing. Increased construction costs may result in increased debt service costs during construction, unavailability of sufficient funds to complete construction, and even if funded by debt, in the inability of the project company to pay increased interest and principal during project operation. Because of the nature of the cost overrun risk, the project finance lender and its lawyers pay particular attention to the allocation of risks in the construction contract.

Project finance construction contracts typically contain each of the following provisions: a detailed, all-inclusive scope of work; a fixed price for all of the work necessary to complete the project; performance guarantees and warranties; liquidated damages for failure to satisfy performance guarantees and for late completion; performance tests to confirm completion within the performance guarantees; and assurances of financial creditworthiness of the contractor. Each of these is discussed later in this chapter.

§ 15.02 IMPORTANT CONSTRUCTION RISKS

The allocation of construction risks between the project company and the contractor is an important element of a financeable project. In general, the most significant construction risks in a project financing must be allocated to a creditworthy contractor.

[1] Increase in Construction Costs

The risk that construction of the project will cost more than the funds available from the construction loan, other debt sources, and equity is perhaps the most important risk for the participants in a project financing. Construction costs exceed estimates for various reasons, including inaccurate engineering and plans, inflation, and problems with project start-up.[1] This cost overrun risk may result in increased debt service costs during construction, unavailability of sufficient funds to complete construction, and even if funded by debt, in the inability of the project company to pay increased debt service during operation.

Improvement of the cost overrun risk is possible even where the contractor has not assumed that risk in a fixed-price turnkey contract. For example, in case of a cost overrun, contractual undertakings can provide the infusion of additional equity by the project sponsor, other equity participants, or standby equity participants. Similarly, standby funding agreements for additional financing, either from the construction lender or subordinated debt lent by project participants or third parties, can be used. Another alternative is the establishment of an escrow fund or contingency account under which the project company establishes a fund that is available to complete the project in case of a cost overrun.

[2] Delay in Completion

Likewise, a delay in project completion may result in an increase in project construction costs and a concomitant increase in debt service costs. The delay may also affect the scheduled flow of project revenues necessary to cover debt service and

operations and maintenance expenses. In addition, a delay in project completion may result in damage payments payable under, or with termination of, project contracts, such as fuel supply and output contracts.

To limit this risk, developing a project construction schedule, which will specify important milestones of the construction process, is important. This schedule should be included in the construction contract and should be updated regularly. Such a schedule can give the project company advance warning of a seriously delayed construction schedule. Further, the parties can tie some construction payments to this schedule, giving the contractor additional incentive to achieve timely construction progress.

[3] Performance Guarantees

Even if a project does not operate after completion at guaranteed levels, the project company will need to pay debt service and other contractual obligations. A common solution to this risk is a liquidated damage payment. A liquidated damage payment is an estimate by the contractor and project company of the consequences of deficient performance by the contractor on the project.

Performance (also called *buy-down*) liquidated damages compensate the project company for increased operating costs associated with the failure of the contractor to meet the agreed-upon performance criteria. These are often used to prepay the project company's debt to offset the expected decline in project output (and the associated revenue flow) due to failure to satisfy those standards. Typically, the parties design the amount of the buy-down to prepay an amount of debt sufficient to maintain the debt service coverage ratio that the project company would have otherwise achieved.

Because of the potential magnitude of liquidated damage payments, the total financial exposure of the contractor is usually limited. The market for construction services and lender requirements together determine the limitation, taking into account the technological challenges of the project. A damage cap of between 10 and 30 percent of the total construction contract price is not atypical.

The creditworthiness of the contractor determines the strength of the contractual

---

[1] Larry Wynant, *Essential Elements of Project Financing*, HARV. BUS. REV., May–June 1980, at 167 (site modification requirements caused an increase in construction costs of US$200 million in a copper mining project financing).

undertakings as a risk mitigation instrument. If the contractor is not financially strong, it is less likely that the contractor will pay the liquidated damages when due. Consequently, project lenders sometimes require that these financial undertakings be supported by a payment guarantee from a creditworthy entity, a letter of credit, or a performance bond or other surety instrument.

[4] Force Majeure in International Construction Contracts

International projects are structured with, and negotiated among, many diverse parties, often from different countries. Sometimes, separate teams of businesspeople and lawyers negotiate the underlying project contracts, resulting in uncoordinated force majeure provisions. This could result in a situation, for example, in which the contractor is excused under a force majeure provision from its obligation to complete the project by a date certain, while the off-take sales agreement does not give the project company similar relief. The result could be a terminated off-take sales agreement. Even where the inconsistencies are not of such disastrous proportions, the effect on the project's schedule or economics may be significant.

Inconsistent force majeure provisions can be cured with a so-called resurrection clause, in which the contractor agrees with the project company that where force majeure inconsistencies exist between contracts, the contractor will not receive relief greater than the relief available to the project company under other relevant contracts. In the earlier example, the contractor could not be excused from performance to the extent such excuse would result in a project delay of such a length that the utility would end the power contract. However, a less extensive delay would be permissible.

In negotiating a force majeure provision for a construction contract, understanding the local circumstances of contract performance is important. In short, the parties must understand what is uncontrollable *in that location.* For example, the nature of the construction trade in the United States generally allows contractors in a U.S. project to agree that a strike at the construction site by the contractor's employees or subcontractors is not a force majeure. However, a contractor may be less likely to accept this risk when it performs the contract in a foreign jurisdiction.

A similar problem arises with the *foreseeability* of other risks. The phrase "unforeseeable weather conditions," for example, may have a different definition in different countries. Adverse weather conditions may be sufficiently predictable and regular to result in the word *unforeseeable* being meaningless in some areas of the world, such as the Philippines.

Different legal systems can create havoc on well-planned, matched force majeure provisions. As discussed in Chapter 12, the choice of applicable law and the jurisdiction of disputes is a critical element in ensuring that the force majeure structure is respected and enforced.

Despite this careful planning, complete elimination of the risk of inconsistencies in force majeure provisions may not be possible. Rather than rely on contract provisions, a project company may need to seek alternate solutions, such as standby credit, dedication of reserve funds, employment of additional labor, and the like.

[5] Experience, Reputation, and Resources of Contractor

The experience and reputation of the contractor, subcontractors, and suppliers for a project can help ensure the timely completion of the project at the stated price. Similarly, the contractor, subcontractors, and suppliers should possess the financial resources necessary to support contractual provisions relating to liquidated damage payments, workmanship guarantees, indemnities, and self-insurance obligations.

The contractor should possess sufficient human and technical resources necessary to satisfy contractual requirements. The risk is that the contractor or a major subcontractor or equipment supplier will be unable to perform a contractual obligation because of a low commitment to the industry, insufficient resources, or lack of knowledge or experience.

In an international project, the contractor should be particularly adept at working with the local labor force. Local construction site managers, with local experience, are particularly beneficial in reducing the risk of local labor problems.

The reputation of a contractor for high reliability will result in fewer requirements from project lenders for construction-related credit enhancement. In determining whether the requisite level of reputation exists for a lender to forgo credit enhancement protection, it considers such things as experience in similar projects; financial strength, either in the capitalization of the contracting entity or at the parent level through a guarantee; the size of the contractor, both as to employees and technical resources; abilities in problem solving, particularly because a fully operating project is infinitely more valuable to a project lender than contract damages; and participation in the industry of the project, through ownership or operation of similar facilities.

[6] Building Materials

A project finance risk sometimes overlooked in industrialized countries is the risk of unavailability of building materials necessary for project construction. Although theoretically any material is available at the right price, the price and time necessary to manufacture or transport the material can affect project economics in a manner similar to cost overruns and delays. Of particular concern is the impact of import and export laws when the project is either located abroad or where the parties contemplate use of imported materials for construction.

[7] Construction of Related Facilities

International projects, particularly in developing countries, often require the simultaneous construction of facilities related to the project. Also potentially required are large gas pipelines, docks, railways, manufacturing facilities, and electrical interconnection and transportation facilities. Each of the related facilities will affect the success of the underlying project and each must therefore be examined to detect the risks involved. Construction synchronization is perhaps the most important initial concern to the project sponsors.

Of equal concern is compatibility of systems. For example, rail beds, roads, and docks must conform with the requirements of the project. Even an examination of the existing infrastructure is required to learn whether the existing facilities can satisfy project requirements.

Although an engineering firm or project company personnel can initially certify that existing and planned facility design will satisfy the requirements for the project, changes may occur. The project company may want to contract with the developers of the related facility, or the government, that existing and planned facilities will not be modified to a less desirable standard.

[8] Raw Material Supply and Utilities

Similar to dependability of building material supply in production of revenue, the project must be assured of a supply of raw materials and utilities at a cost within the acceptable ranges of financial projections. The formality of the commitments for the supply depends, in part, on the availability of the materials in the project area. For example, a supply of necessary wood chips as fuel for a waste-wood-burning energy project in the U.S. Pacific Northwest may be sufficiently assured that no need exists to contract for a 100 percent supply. Yet, under various scenarios, such as the limitation of forest processing because of economic conditions in the lumber industry or environmental pressures, the project may need alternate sources. In addition, costs of import or export fees, transportation charges, storage costs, stability of product, monopolies, and finance costs all are risks in determining whether an adequate supply exists.

In many projects, the project company develops long-term requirements contracts to provide the necessary raw material supply at a predictable price to reduce this risk. Less frequent are supply-or-pay contracts, in which a supplier is dependent on some aspect of the project and agrees to provide either the needed raw material or pay a fee to the project. With both contracts, however, the credit of the supplier must be sufficient to ensure performance of the contract.

[9] Excuses for Contractor Nonperformance – The Owner Did It

It is usual for a contractor facing liquidated damage liabilities in a project finance transaction to blame the project company for the problems. Construction delays and an inability to satisfy performance obligations may indeed be the fault of the project company. Potential problems caused by the project company include failure to provide needed information on a timely basis, failure to satisfy obligations clearly allocated to the project company in the construction contract, failure to obtain permits, and supply of inappropriate fuel for testing.

To increase the likelihood that such allegations by the contractor will not excuse performance responsibility, several contract provisions can be included in the construction contract. First, the contract should clearly and precisely identify the responsibilities of both the project company and the contractor. The responsibilities of the project company should be kept to an absolute minimum.

Second, to the extent that the contractor will be excused from liability for late completion or cost overruns, the project company should condition the excuse on receipt of written notice from the contractor, with an acceptable period to remedy the failure. If no one gives the notice, the right of the contractor to use the alleged failure as an excuse to liability would be waived. A provision similar to the notice procedure given for a force majeure is a preferred approach.

[10] Coordination

Two or more contractors construct some projects, each fulfilling a different construction role for the project, without single-point responsibility. Hydroelectric projects are an example of this type of practice. Risks relating to construction coordination arise in this structure, however. Without coordination, risks of construction delays and cost overruns increase. In addition, without coordination, each contractor can place blame on the other for delays and cost overruns. Consequently, the project company, acting as construction manager, must carefully monitor project construction under this approach. At a minimum, it is very useful if each construction contract includes an acknowledgment by the contractor that it has reviewed the terms, including construction schedules, of the other construction contracts. This acknowledgment should be coupled with a representation that the contractor has not identified any scheduling or other deficiencies between the contracts.

§ 15.03 CREDITWORTHINESS

Risk allocation in a project finance construction contract is only effective to the extent the contractor is creditworthy. It must have sufficient financial resources, both at the time of contract execution and during performance, to undertake the obligations in the contract. These include payment of liquidated damages payable if the contractor delays the facility and if the contractor has not constructed the facility to perform according to the performance guarantees. The contractor must be able to absorb any losses it might incur if the actual construction costs exceed the amount guaranteed to the project company as the fixed construction price. To the extent the financial resources do not exist, and no adequate credit enhancement is available at a reasonable cost to improve this credit risk, such as parent guarantees, letters of credit and payment, and performance bonds, the contract will not be financeable and another contractor must be found.

§ 15.04 TYPES OF CONSTRUCTION-RELATED CONTRACTS

Engineering, procurement, and construction, together with testing and start-up, are the four broad, general phases of project construction. It is not surprising therefore that the types of construction-related contracts are generally structured to cover these phases. There are three general types of construction-related contracts used in a typical project financing: engineering, procurement, and construction. A fourth, called commonly an EPC, is one contract that covers all three phases – engineering, procurement, and construction. The latter type is often called a *fast-track* construction contract.

[1] Engineering Contract

The engineering contract provides a project company with professional assistance in project design, bidding and review, and administration of the work. Specifically, it provides for the preparation of preliminary and general project designs; preparation of specifications; preparation of initial cost estimates; preparation, solicitation, and analysis of bids for work and supplies;

preparation of detailed drawings for bidding purposes; review of detailed drawings produced by suppliers; scheduling of work; inspection and testing; and during the construction phase, administration of the construction contract for the project company.

It is not used often in a project financing. This is primarily because all project construction work, including engineering work, is included in a broad, turnkey construction contract in which the contractor is a single point of responsibility for all construction phases. From a practical perspective, funds are typically not available for construction work until a financial closing occurs. At that point, because interest on the debt is accruing without revenue to pay it, construction work must proceed quickly.

[2] Procurement Contract

The procurement contract provides for the orderly procurement of work and supplies for a project. The contract includes provisions that require the architect/engineer to establish bidding procedures for machinery, equipment, material, and supplies; to perform an economic analysis of the bids; to coordinate export licenses and other governmental authorizations necessary for the export or import of materials, supplies, machinery, and equipment to the project site; schedule and monitor delivery dates; make transportation arrangements for delivery of materials, supplies, machinery, and equipment to the project site; and coordinate financial matters, such as scheduling cash needs, reviewing invoices, and administration of accounting records.

A separate procurement contract is not used often in a project financing, for the same reasons that a separate engineering contract is not used. That is, all procurement work is included under the scope of the turnkey construction contract, and funds are typically not available for procurement work until a financial closing occurs.

[3] Construction Contract

The construction contract is the contract that governs the complete construction of the project. As such, the contractor agrees in the construction contract to provide all construction-related services, including construction supervision, labor

and management, construction facilities, tools and supplies, site investigation, and field engineering.

[4] EPC Contract

The EPC (engineering, procurement, and construction) contract combines the three stages of construction under one contract. It is sometimes called a fast-track contract, in that it enables progress on a project to proceed on an overlapping basis, at a faster pace than if the three stages followed in series.

§ 15.05 FIXED-PRICE CONTRACT

A fixed-price construction contract requires the contractor to construct a project, or part of a project, for a fixed sum. Sometimes, the fixed sum is subject to adjustment based on an agreed-upon index. This is particularly helpful to the contractor in countries that experience rapid inflation, although the project lender may insist on a cap on such adjustments.

As discussed elsewhere in this chapter, the tension between the project company and contractor in negotiating a fixed-price construction contract is based on the nature of the construction contract: The contractor must deliver the project at a fixed price. The contractor is, of course, concerned with the difficulty of predicting events that could result in delivery of a project at a cost to the contractor that is higher than expected. Typically, the contractor will include a contingency in the fixed construction price to ensure that adequate cushion exists for uncertainties in the cost calculation process. Generalizing in this area is difficult, but a risk contingency of between twelve and 20 percent is common.

Even in a fixed-price contract, however, the fixed price is subject to adjustment for certain negotiated contingencies, such as force majeure events, delays caused by the project company, changes requested by the project company, and other excluded events or conditions, such as unexpected site conditions. The extent of the adjustment varies. Sometimes, such as where a force majeure event has a delaying effect but no monetary implication, no price increase is permitted. Instead, an extension of the time for construction completion is granted to the contractor. In other situations, such as where the project company delays the construction, an equitable price adjustment is generally agreed to. Finally, for changes requested by the project company, the parties negotiate any price increase.

§ 15.06 COST-PLUS-FEE CONTRACT

Another approach to a construction contract is the cost-plus-fee contract. As the name implies, the project company pays the contractor the costs of construction, plus a fee. The contractor is assured of earning a fee and enjoying the income attributes of the fee, while the project company is more likely to receive the lowest construction cost. In contrast to the fixed-price construction contract, the project company avoids payment of the contingency risk premium but assumes the risk of an increase in construction costs beyond the amount assumed in the project construction budget.

§ 15.07 COST-PLUS-FEE CONTRACT WITH MAXIMUM PRICE AND INCENTIVE FEE

The cost-plus-fee contract is modified by adding a maximum price and an incentive fee payable to the contractor based on cost performance. Provisions are included that provide the contractor an incentive to keep costs low, such as penalties charged and bonuses earned based on budget performance. If costs exceed the maximum price guarantee, the contractor typically absorbs these costs, up to the amount of its construction fee. To the extent there is a savings as compared with the maximum price guarantee, the contractor and the project company typically split the savings on a shared basis.

§ 15.08 PROJECT FINANCE TURNKEY CONTRACT

A project finance transaction is based on predictability, including the predictability of the construction price, construction schedule, and project performance. From this need for predictability, a hybrid construction contract has developed that requires the contractor to provide the complete scope of construction work for a project, for a fixed price, and for completion and delivery by a date certain, which performs at agreed-upon levels. All the project company has to do is pay the construction price and "turn the key."

In return for this predictability, the contractor will charge a risk premium. The risk premium is charged because the contractor is concerned with the difficulty of predicting events that could result in delivery of a delayed project, at an increased price, that does not perform as expected. Besides the risk premium, the contractor seeks in contract negotiation to limit risks of any change in the cost of the project, to ensure there is sufficient contractual excuse for late delivery, and to provide sufficient time to satisfy performance guarantees.

A customary reward for the contractor in return for assuming the risk of completion on a date certain for a fixed price is through a bonus payment, which the project company pays to the contractor if the project is completed before the scheduled completion date. In a project financing, the bonus concept must relate to the other project contracts. For example, this is necessary so that if the facility is completed earlier than the scheduled date, the other contracts permit or contemplate an earlier commencement of operation. The obligation of the project company to pay a bonus to the contractor could otherwise result in an obligation to pay money not matched with an ability to earn revenue, or to obtain needed project inputs. If the project does not contemplate early operation, then funds necessary to pay a construction bonus will need to come from additional equity contributions or subordinated debt, or be included as part of the construction budget and reserved in a contingency account.

As discussed earlier in this chapter, the risk that construction costs will exceed the funds available from the construction loan, other debt sources, and equity is a significant risk in a project financing. Increased construction costs may result in increased debt service costs during construction, unavailability of sufficient funds to complete construction, and even if funded, in the inability of the project company to pay increased interest and principal that results from the additional debt required to complete construction.

§ 15.09 TYPICAL PROVISIONS IN PROJECT FINANCE TURNKEY CONSTRUCTION CONTRACTS

Construction contracts generally contain the following key provisions: technical scope and specifications, commonly called the *scope of work*; a detailed listing of each of the contractor's and the project company's responsibilities, compensation and payment terms, subcontracts, acceptance and performance testing, changes in the work, rejection of work, warranties, title to work, remedies for breach, performance and warranty bonds, insurance, dispute resolution, indemnification, assignment, suspension of work and termination, and force majeure. These typical construction contract clauses are discussed below.

§ 15.10 SCOPE OF WORK

[1] Introduction
The scope of work is in many respects the most important provision in a project finance construction contract. This section, with references to accompanying schedules, describes in detail the design and engineering criteria and technical specifications for the project. In addition, this section of the contract identifies major pieces of equipment. It is an important part of the construction contract because it describes the scope of the contractor's obligations, which determines the type of facility that will be constructed for the agreed-upon price. Unless this section describes all the work and equipment necessary to construct the facility, the fixed price set forth in the contract will be illusory. Additional work not specified in the scope of work will result in contract amendments called *change orders* and can cause price increases.

[2] Sample Provision
Scope of Work. Contractor shall perform the work hereunder in accordance with the Contract Documents.

Contract Documents means this Construction Contract and all exhibits hereto, including the Scope of Work attached hereto as Exhibit __, it being the intent of the parties hereto that such scope shall include (i) all design, procurement, construction, installation, equipping, start-up, and performance testing of the facility; (ii) the provision of all equipment and supplies required by the Contract Documents; (iii) the provision of necessary construction forces, including all supervisory field engineering, quality assurance, support service personnel, and field labor; and (iv) preparation and delivery to the [*Project Company*] of operation and maintenance manuals.

§ 15.11 CONTRACTOR'S RESPONSIBILITIES

[1] Introduction
Among the terms included in the contractor's responsibility section are the types of services that will be provided, such as design, engineering, procurement, construction, and supply. Other typical responsibilities include staffing, training, security, personnel conduct, coordination of training, and turnover to the project company and operator, and permit application and prosecution responsibilities.

[2] Sample Provision
Independent Contractor. Contractor is an independent contractor and shall maintain control over its employees and all Subcontractors. Contractor shall perform all Work in an orderly and workmanlike manner.

Project Manager. (a) Before starting the Work, Contractor shall designate a Project Manager as its representative to represent Contractor and shall notify [*Project Company*] of the name, address, and telephone number (day and night) of such representative, and of any change in such designation.

(b) The Project Manager shall be present or be duly represented at the Site at all times when the Work is actually in progress and, during periods when the Work is suspended, arrangements mutually acceptable to the Parties shall be made for any emergency Work that may be required. All requirements, instructions, and other communications given to the Project Manager by [*Project Company*] shall be as binding as if given to Contractor.

Supervision. Contractor shall supervise and direct the Work. Contractor shall be solely responsible for all construction means, methods, techniques, sequences, and procedures, and for coordinating all portions of the Work under the Contract.

Access. Upon reasonable prior notice, Contractor shall provide [*Project Company*], Lender and [*Project Company*]'s Representative with reasonable access to the Work; provided, however, that Contractor may require such representative to be accompanied by an escort and to follow any of the procedures which Contractor, in its sole discretion, deems necessary or advisable. Contractor shall provide the representatives of any governing or regulatory agency having jurisdiction over the Work with similar access.

Emergencies. In the event of any emergency endangering life or property on or about the Work or the Site, Contractor may take such immediate action as may be reasonable and necessary to prevent, avoid, or mitigate damage, injury, or loss, and shall report to [*Project Company*], as soon as reasonably possible, any such incidence including Contractor's response thereto.

Compliance With Laws. Contractor shall meet and shall see that the Project shall meet all applicable requirements of federal, national, central, commonwealth, state, province, municipal, city, borough, village, county, district, department, territory, commission, board, bureau, agency or instrumentality, or other governmental authority, domestic or foreign, laws, codes, and regulations governing construction of the Project in existence as of the date of this Contract. The effect of changes in such laws, codes, and regulations after the date hereof shall be determined pursuant to Article ___.

Contractor Permits. Contractor shall secure, pay for, and maintain the Contractor Permits.

Notices. Contractor shall give all notices and comply with all material laws, ordinances, rules, regulations, and lawful final orders of any Governmental Agency bearing on the performance of the Work. If Contractor observes that any of the Contract Documents are at variance therewith in any material respect, it shall notify [*Project Company*] in writing, and any necessary Changes shall be made by appropriate Change Order.

Security. Contractor, at its expense, shall provide the following security for the Project: [*describe any planned fencing, watchmen, and/or procedures*].

Records. Contractor shall maintain at the Site for [*Project Company*] one record copy, and, at [*Project Company*]'s expense, shall furnish additional copies thereof to [*Project Company*], if requested, of all Contract Documents, drawings, plans, specifications, copies, addenda, test reports, Change Orders, and modifications, in good order and marked to record all changes made during performance of the Work; these shall be delivered to [*Project Company*] as a condition of final payment.

Cleaning Up. Upon completion of the Work and before final payment is made, Contractor shall, or shall cause Subcontractors to, remove rubbish and unused Product from the Site and leave the Site in an orderly condition.

§ 15.12 PROJECT COMPANY'S RESPONSIBILITIES

[1] Introduction
Conversely, the project company's responsibility section describes the responsibilities of the project company. These include required conditions for the project site, access to the site, permits, fuel for testing and start-up, utilities, and waste disposal.

Failure of the project company to perform these obligations might delay or otherwise impair the contractor's ability to perform the contract at the fixed price and by the scheduled completion date. Consequently, the project company and the project lender will desire that the responsibilities be kept to a minimum and include only those areas with minimal risk of nonperformance by the project company.

[2] Sample Provision
Project Company Responsibilities. (a) The [*Project Company*] shall investigate, determine, secure, pay for, and maintain any and all Permits required for [*Project Company*]'s ownership and commercial operation of the [*Project*] and for the performance of the Work (the "[*Project Company*] Permits"), including: federal, national, central, commonwealth, state, province, municipal, city, borough,

village, county, district, department, territory, commission, board, bureau, agency or instrumentality, or other governmental authority, domestic or foreign, environmental, water, sewer, and land use Permits, including those [*Permits*] described in Exhibit __. [*Project Company*] shall further be responsible for obtaining and maintaining all easements or other real property rights necessary for performance of the [*Work*]. Contractor shall cooperate with [*Project Company*] (or with such other effected party as [*Project Company*] may designate, for and on behalf of [*Project Company*]) to provide such pertinent data and information as [*Project Company*] or effected party may request to permit [*Project Company*] to obtain the [*Project Company*] Permits.

(b) In addition to other requirements contemplated by this Contract, [*Project Company*] shall furnish within [*Project Company*]'s property limits as and when reasonably necessary for the purposes of this Contract, upon the request of Contractor, access to: (i) the areas on the [*Site*] required for new construction, lay down areas, construction offices, temporary roads and utilities; (ii) designated Contractor parking areas; (iii) designated areas of existing buildings as reasonably required in conjunction with the [*Work*]; and (iv) areas at the property boundaries for junction or other work relating to electrical power, natural gas and oil lines, water, sewer, telephone, and other utility connections.

(c) [*Project Company*] will provide at the Site and pay for kW power for use by Contractor in its performance of the [*Work*].

(d) [*Project Company*] shall provide at the [*Site*] and pay for: (i) fuel and consumables, such as lube oils, lubricants, filters, chemicals, and other related costs as specified by Contractor for start up, debugging, Performance Testing, environmental testing and Commercial Operation otherwise in performance of the Work; (ii) connections at the points specified in Exhibit __ for water, sewer, electricity, telephones, and other public works; (iv) any water required for use by Contractor in its performance of the Work; (v) any special or supplementary operating equipment required for operating and maintaining the Project, such as fuel analyzing and temperature, performance, and supply output monitoring equipment with operating supplies, all as further specified on Exhibit __ attached

hereto; (vi) all rolling stock and Residue removal and disposal of all effluents from the Project during testing, Provisional Acceptance and Commercial Operation; (vii) mobile equipment, if any, required by the Project and not specifically described in the Scope of Work; and (viii) operation and maintenance of the Project.

(e) Contractor shall obtain the Permits described in Exhibit __ ("Contractor Permits"). [*Project Company*] shall promptly sign any application for such Contractor Permits which require [*Project Company*]'s signature. In no event shall Contractor have any liability or responsibility for the failure of any Governmental Agency to grant or act upon any application for a permit, license, exemption, or approval, or for the cost of, or the terms or conditions made applicable to, any permit, license, exemption or approval to be obtained by [*Project Company*].

§ 15.13 THE NOTICE TO PROCEED AND COMMENCEMENT OF CONSTRUCTION

[1] Introduction

It is usual for the construction contract to be negotiated and executed several months before the financial closing occurs. Because the project company has only minimal assets, unless the project sponsor contributes capital to the project company to fund construction, there will not be sufficient funds for the contractor to be paid for construction at the time. Consequently, the prudent contractor will want to delay its obligations to commence construction until the financial closing occurs. Otherwise, because the project company has no assets, it assumes the risk of non-payment.

The notice to proceed is a written notice from the project company to the contractor authorizing the contractor to commence work. The contractor will typically include conditions on its obligation to accept the notice to proceed and begin work. These include evidence of financial closing, receipt of necessary construction permits and other governmental approvals, environmental auditing, and completion of any necessary remediation, and immediate availability of funds to the project company under the financing documents in an amount necessary to complete construction. In addition, the contractor is interested in provisions assuring that the financing documents require the lender to make payments directly to the contractor, limit the conditions to advancing funds under the financing documents to a default by the project company (except for disputes under the construction contract), and require notification of the contractor by the lender if an event of default exists under the loan documents. The contractor is not always successful in obtaining all of these protections.

[2] Sample Provision

Notice to Proceed. Contractor shall achieve Commercial Operation of the Project no later than (__) months after receipt of an effective written notice in the form attached in Exhibit __ (the "Notice to Proceed") from [Project Company] to commence the Work (the "Completion Date"); provided, however, that [Project Company] may not deliver the Notice to Proceed unless at least five (5) business days prior to such delivery it has provided Contractor with (i) certified copies of the permits described in Exhibit__ in final, non-appealable form, (ii) evidence reasonably satisfactory to Contractor that [Project Company] has entered into a loan agreement with a lender or lenders which individually or collectively have assets in excess of U.S. $2 billion and shareholder's equity in excess of U.S. $100 million (the "Lender") and that such loan agreement (the "Construction Loan Agreement") provides that (a) the total amount available for borrowing by [Project Company] (the "Construction Loan") includes at least [Contract Price] that can be used for no other purpose by [Project Company] other than to fulfill its obligations under this Contract; (b) all payments to be made by [Project Company] to Contractor pursuant to Article __ shall be made directly by the Lender by wire transfer, so as to be beyond the reach of [Project Company]'s creditors other than Contractor and the Lender; (c) the Construction Loan Agreement shall obligate the Lender to make or cause to be made all payments to Contractor to which it is entitled in the event of any termination of this Contract; (d) the Construction Loan Agreement may not be amended or terminated except upon terms that assure that Contractor shall receive all payments to which it is entitled under this Contract; (e) the Lender will accept payment and/or performance by Contractor,

in lieu of [Project Company], to cure any default by [Project Company] under the Construction Loan Agreement, but without the obligation on the part of Contractor to make any such payment or provide such performance; and (f) the Lender will provide Contractor with written notice of any default by [Project Company] and the same period of time in which to cure such default as [Project Company] is entitled to; and (iii) [Project Company] has closed the Construction Loan and the funds to be borrowed thereunder are available for use in accordance with the provisions of the Construction Loan Agreement. Notwithstanding the curing by Contractor of any default by [Project Company] under the Construction Loan Agreement, Contractor shall retain any rights and remedies it may have against [Project Company] by reason of any such default by [Project Company] and shall be subrogated to any rights and remedies the Lender may have against [Project Company] pursuant to the Construction Loan Agreement.

§ 15.14 PRICE

[1] Introduction

The construction contract will contain a fixed, all-inclusive price for the costs, charges, and expenses necessary for construction of the facility. This requires the contractor to be diligent in the preparation of the price, while the project company must be diligent in the review of the scope of work, which sets forth the type of project that the contractor will build and deliver.

Examples of costs, charges, and expenses that generally would be included in the construction price in a project finance construction contract include the following: labor; compensation and governmental employment-related taxes; materials, supplies, and equipment to be made part of the facility and transportation to the project site; materials, supplies, and equipment to be used in construction, but not made part of the facility, and transportation to the project site; subcontract charges; equipment rental and mobilization; credit enhancement costs, such as insurance premiums and performance and payment bond premiums; taxes, fees, and duties; license fees and royalties; and site cleanup and debris removal.

In some industries, the cost-plus construction contract is used rather than the fixed-price structure used in nonrecourse and limited recourse project financings. Cost-plus contracts provide the project company the opportunity to save construction costs because the contractor does not need to increase its price to include a risk premium to cover the risk of cost overruns that might be incurred. However, cost-plus contracts are seldom used in a project financing. To the extent they are, completion guarantees from the project sponsors are required by the project lenders to cover the risk that the construction price exceeds the budget.

[2] Sample Provision

Firm Price. [*Project Company*] shall pay to Contractor in respect of the [*Work*], the amount of ($), subject to price adjustment only in accordance with this Contract (the "Contract Price").

§ 15.15 PAYMENT AND RETAINAGE

[1] Introduction

If a cost-plus contract is used, payment is made periodically over the construction period. The amount is equal to the amount of costs reasonably incurred, plus agreed-upon amounts for indirect costs and a construction fee.

In the more typical fixed-price contract, the construction price is paid over time to the contractor based on progress made toward project completion, calculated on the value of work installed or delivered, accomplishment of milestones, or in compliance with an agreed construction payment schedule. Restrictions are typically placed on the ability of the contractor to receive payments earlier than expected by the project company, even if the work is performed. This helps assure the project company will not incur cost overruns by higher capitalized interest than provided for in the construction budget. If milestone payments are used, payments to the contractor are customarily withheld in an amount equal to the value of work not yet completed.

Some construction contracts permit that the contractor receive payments in advance. This contract structure provides the contractor with

funds to purchase materials, equipment, and supplies.

If so, the risk exists that the funds might not be returned. To protect against this risk, an advance payment guarantee is used. This is a guarantee given to the project company, in which the contractor agrees to return advance payments made under the construction contract if not earned within a specified time or the construction contract is not otherwise performed by the contractor.

It is typical for the project lender to retain an independent engineer, or use the services of its own engineering staff to monitor construction progress and the right of the contractor to receive the payment requested. To do this, the independent engineer will review the work completed and approve the payment requisition. This requires that the construction contract payment provisions be consistent with loan disbursement procedures under the project company's loan agreements.

Withheld from each payment is a percentage amount of the construction price, called *retainage*. Retainage is withheld by the project company to provide the contractor a financial incentive to complete the work; retainage is paid only upon final completion. Otherwise, the financial and lost opportunity cost to the contractor of completing minor elements of the work may outweigh the receipt of the final, often minimal, payment. Retainage typically is 5 to 10 percent of each payment. Alternatives to retainage include letters of credit and retention money guarantees.

[2] Retention Money Guarantee

In many construction contracts, the project company is entitled to withhold a percentage of payments otherwise due the contractor, called *retainage*. Retainage, typically in a range of 5 to 10 percent, provides motivation to the contractor to finish the work, because it is usually not payable until completion of the project.

If the contractor desires the full payment when each progress payment is made under the construction contract, the project company can require that the contractor provide a so-called retention money guarantee, or retainage guarantee. This guarantee, provided in lieu of retention, gives the project company the right to receive payments equal to the amount that would otherwise have been retained, if the project is not completed or defects are discovered within an agreed upon period.

[3] Liens

Suppliers, vendors, and subcontractors to the contractor generally have the right to place a lien on the project if they are not paid for the work performed or equipment supplied. In many situations, the project company could find itself paying the same amount twice: once to the contractor, and again to the contractor's supplier, vendor, or subcontractor.

A labor and material payment bond can be required of the contractor to guard against the risk. This bond requires a surety to pay the unpaid supplier, vendor, or subcontractor amounts due it from the contractor that are unpaid.

[4] Sample Provision

Retainage. [*Project Company*] shall withhold from each payment of the [*Contract Price*] due Contractor hereunder an amount equal to __ (__%) percent as retainage, to be paid to Contractor only upon achievement by it of [*Final Completion*].

§ 15.16 COMPLETION DATE GUARANTEES, PERFORMANCE GUARANTEES, AND LIQUIDATED DAMAGES

[1] Introduction

The contractor must achieve three performance dates in a project financing: mechanical completion, substantial completion, and final completion. In addition, to limit the risk of delay, it is important to develop a project construction schedule, which will specify important milestones of the construction process. This schedule should be included in the construction contract and updated regularly.

[2] Mechanical Completion

Mechanical completion is achieved when all mechanical components of the facility have been delivered, constructed, and installed to such an extent that, apart from minor work that does not affect safe operation, the facility is ready for start-up and testing. Minor items include painting, landscaping, grading, and similar work. If the contractor does not achieve this date, damages are typically due.

[3] Substantial Completion

Substantial completion is reached when the contractor is able to satisfy certain agreed-upon performance guarantees. These vary with the type of project. Irrespective of the type of project, in general the contractor is required to demonstrate that the facility is capable of producing a level of output that is necessary to produce revenue to service the project debt and to satisfy the agreements the project company has reached with the output purchaser.

In an energy project, the contractor is typically required to demonstrate achievement of performance guarantees and availability guarantees. Performance (or capacity) guarantees are designed to demonstrate that the facility is capable of operating at negotiated levels of power output (an output guarantee of a minimum net electrical output); fuel use (an efficiency guarantee or a guarantee of limits on fuel consumption); limits on consumption of other feed materials or utilities, such as auxiliary electric consumption or limestone (an input guarantee); and within environmental emission limits, other environmental restrictions, and other requirements of applicable law (environmental guarantee). Availability guarantees, also called *reliability guarantees*, cover the ability of the facility to operate on and sustain a reliable level of operations over a test period of a negotiated length.

Failure to achieve these guarantees generally results in the obligation of the contractor to pay so-called *buy-down* liquidated damages, the sole remedy available to the project company against the contractor. These damages are calculated to buy-down, or prepay, a portion of the project debt, which preserves an agreed-upon debt service coverage ratio for project debt. This is necessary because the project is not able to operate at the levels of production, or using the level of fuel or other inputs, necessary to service the outstanding debt.

The total exposure of the contractor to these types of liquidated damages is generally limited to a percentage of the construction contract price. For example, capped liability of between 25 and 40 percent is not unusual in construction contracts for energy projects. Typically, the contractor has the option of taking corrective action and retesting the facility for a negotiated period of time before it has the obligation to pay the liquidated damages.

Payment of liquidated damages is generally an insufficient remedy for the environmental guarantee. At a minimum, the permit authorities will likely block further operation of the project if environmental permits are violated. Consequently, the contractor is typically required to undertake corrective action necessary to satisfy the environmental guarantee.

Similarly, if the project does not achieve the availability guarantee, liquidated damages are often an insufficient remedy because the off-take sales agreement will likely be breached. As with the environmental guarantee, the contractor is typically required to undertake corrective action necessary to make the facility more reliable in operation.

At substantial completion, the contractor turns the facility over to the project company. The project company begins to operate the project at this point, and the warranty period begins.

[4] Final Completion

Final completion occurs after substantial completion and is achieved by the contractor when all the standards for facility completion are reached, or to the extent not, then all liquidated damages have been paid. The facility is transferred to the project company for operation at this point, and the final construction payment, including retainage, is paid.

[5] Correction

In many construction contracts, the contractor will include the ability to attempt to correct the facility so that it is capable of achieving the performance guarantees. During this period, the facility will likely need to be operated either to satisfy the obligations under debt documents or other project contracts or as a way to mitigate the total damages that the contractor must pay. The contractor will need to pay the project company damages resulting from the extended construction period, including an amount equal to

the shortfall in facility revenues necessary to pay debt service, operating and maintenance costs at the budgeted levels, and performance damages under other contracts. The contractor must complete its correction efforts in a way that does not unreasonably interfere with facility operation. To the extent the contractor is successful in its correction efforts, the contractor might be able to reduce its damages, or if liquidated damages have been paid, to recover some portion of the damage.

The correction period will only be available to the contractor to the extent the major project contracts, such as revenue-producing off-take contracts, permit this flexibility. It is not unusual, however, for off-take contracts to require the completion and performance guarantees be reached by a definite date. If so, the extended construction period will not be available to the contractor for any meaningful purpose other than in an effort to correct the facility so that operating costs to the project company are reduced.

[6] Delay Liquidated Damages

To the extent the contractor does not achieve the mechanical completion, substantial completion or final completion dates, delay liquidated damages must be paid to the project company. Delay liquidated damages are designed to compensate the project company for the costs it incurs, on a daily basis, for the delays. The costs include additional debt service costs arising from the extended construction period, damages under off-take contracts, fuel contracts and other project contracts that assess a daily delay for the failure of facility operation by an agreed date, and any additional operating and working capital costs incurred because of the delay, such as payment for demobilization costs of the operator. Delay liquidated damages, together with performance guarantee liquidated damages, are usually subject to an aggregate, maximum amount, ranging from 25 to 45 percent of the contract amount.

[7] Testing

Because of the importance of the various dates and guarantees described above, the test criteria and procedures must be agreed upon. In addition to the technical features of the tests, agreement must be reached on such things as who bears the costs of testing, and who is responsible for labor and needed inputs, such as fuel.

[8] Bonuses for Early Completion

Early completion of the project provides the project company with the opportunity to earn revenue earlier than expected and reduce debt service costs. It also provides a basis for the contractor to benefit from expedient work. The calculation and amount of the bonuses vary, ranging from a lump-sum payment per day of early completion, calculated on the debt service savings, to a share in the profits generated during the early operation period. All project contracts, such as fuel contracts, output contracts, and operating agreements, must be structured to permit early operation.

Payment of bonuses must be provided for in the construction budget. These can be paid from contingency fund savings, from capitalized interest savings, and from additional revenue generated by early project operation. In some cases, bonuses are paid only out of project revenues, after payment of operating costs and debt service.

[9] Environmental Guarantees

As discussed above, the contractor will need to show that the project is capable of operating within the emissions and other environmental standards required by permits, laws, and regulations, and in some cases, standards imposed by multilateral and bilateral financing agencies, such as the World Bank. These requirements sometimes change over time and, in some cases, change during the construction of a project. The allocation of which party will bear the risk for changes in environmental standards during the course of construction is an important one.

Unless the change is proposed by the responsible agency at the time of negotiations and is reasonably expected to be imposed on the project, the contractor typically views the change in law risk as an equity risk. However, if the contractor is using the best available technology for environmental controls, it may be able to accept this risk. However, the construction price

might increase to the point that the project is no longer competitive with other projects that do not employ the best available environmental control technologies.

[10] Exceptions to Guarantees

Contracting parties do not like to provide guarantees without some opportunity to escape them, and a contractor is no different. This is particularly true in the context of a project finance construction contract, where the potential liability for liquidated damages is large.

Guarantees are subject to the following types of exceptions: changes in law; interference by the project company; breach of the project company's obligations; changes in the design or construction of the facility requested by the project company that are not approved by the contractor; and force majeure, including political risks, war, and civil disobedience. Responsibility for strikes and labor disturbances are commonly not excuses to performance of guarantees, because the contractor is thought to be in the best position to control these acts. Unexpected subsurface conditions are the subject of negotiation and are sometimes accepted as risks by the contractor.

[11] Alternatives to Guarantees

As discussed above, the consequences of the failure of the contractor to satisfy guarantees have cost implications for the project. A portion of these risks can sometimes be addressed through other types of protections, including performance or completion bonds, builder's risk insurance, and systems or efficacy insurance. Performance or completion bonds must be carefully reviewed to determine the exact construction risks covered. Builder's risk insurance, provided by a casualty insurer, covers certain casualty risks, and compensates the project company for debt service that results from a delay caused by a covered casualty. Systems or efficacy insurance, of limited availability and costly, may be available to cover delay risks and performance shortfalls that arise from events not covered by builder's risk policies.

Another alternative is to allocate some of the costs of delay or underperformance to other project participants in return for price concessions. For example, an off-take purchaser may decide to bear some of these risks in return for a lower price for output produced by the project.

[12] Sample Provision

Drafting of liquidated damage provisions is highly dependent upon the unique facts and circumstances of the particular transaction involved. The following is one example of a delay damage and buy down provision.

Delay Damages; Buy Down. If the [*Facility*] has not achieved [*Commercial Operation*], including satisfaction of the performance guarantees, by the [*Completion Date*], the [*Completion Date*] may be extended for an additional period of time not to exceed ____ if Contractor continues to pay delay liquidated damages equal to ____ for each day such date is so extended. In the event that [*Facility*] still has not achieved [*Commercial Operation*] at the end of any extension of the [*Commercial Operation Date*], Contractor shall pay to [*Project Company*] on demand liquidated damages calculated in accordance with Exhibit [*typically, a formula based on the estimated damages to the Project Company of the delay and of the failure of the Facility to perform at levels guaranteed in the Performance Guarantees*].

§ 15.17 WARRANTIES

[1] Introduction

Whereas a guarantee addresses the ability of the project when new, a warranty is designed to provide protection against defects in design, workmanship, and components over a negotiated period. The contractor typically provides several warranties to the project company.

First is that the engineering, materials, and workmanship used in the design and construction of the project satisfy an agreed-upon standard, and to the extent they do not, the contractor agrees to repair or replace any portion of the work found defective within a negotiated period. Typical standards are that the design and construction of the facility is free from defects, or that the contractor has complied with generally accepted design and construction practices. The contrac-

tor will usually make the same warranty on behalf of its suppliers and subcontractors to the project company.

Next is a statement that all materials and supplies are new. To the extent any used or refurbished equipment or supplies are used, these should be specifically mentioned in the contract.

A third is that the contractor has free and unencumbered title to supplies and materials. The contractor warrants that, to the extent there are any processes or equipment that are protected by patents or intellectual property rights, the contractor has the right to use the processes or equipment and that those rights will be transferred to the project company.

The contractor will also warrant compliance with negotiated standards of care. A typical warranty is that the contractor has used good and workmanlike care in the construction process.

A warranty is included that the contractor is in compliance with the specifications incorporated into the contract. Typically, this is made with reference to the scope of work in the construction contract, as modified by any change orders.

The contractor will warrant that the facility is constructed in accordance with all applicable laws, regulations, codes, requirements of agencies that issue permits, and industry codes and standards. Because legal requirements sometimes change over time and, in some cases, change during the construction of a project, the parties must determine who will bear the risk for changes in laws during construction. Some changes are proposed at the time the construction contract is signed and are well known. Others, even if proposed, are unknown to the parties. Because of this uncertainty, the contractor typically views the change in law risk as an equity risk.

[2] Sample Provision

Warranty. For a period of one year, Contractor warrants to [*Project Company*] that the [*Work*] will be free from defects in material and workmanship (the "Warranty"). However, the Warranty is subject to the following terms and conditions:

(1) The term "defects" shall not include damage arising from [*Project Company*]'s or any other

Person's misuse or reckless disregard, force majeure events, normal wear and tear, failure to comply with generally approved industry practices, or failure to follow written storage, maintenance, or operating instructions.

(2) The Warranty does not apply to defects caused by conditions more severe or adverse than those ordinarily or customarily experienced by like facilities or structures or to defects in design, material or workmanship furnished by [Project Company], its separate contractors, licensors, vendors of material, fabricators, or suppliers.

(3) All duties under the Warranty shall be discharged by repair or replacement of the defect at Contractor's option.

(4) [Project Company]'s failure to allow Contractor to make such tests or perform such remedial services as Contractor may deem appropriate shall relieve Contractor of its Warranty obligations with respect to the subject of such test or service. Contractor shall make such tests or perform such remedial services at such times as are reasonably mutually convenient.

Subcontractor and Vendor Warranties. With regard to any product or portion of the [Work] performed by or acquired from subcontractors, suppliers, or vendors, in the event Contractor obtains for the benefit of [Project Company] a warranty from such subcontractor, supplier, or vendor of at least equal or comparable coverage and duration to the Warranty, then the Warranty shall not apply to such product or portion of the [Work] and Contractor shall have no liability whatsoever for design and/or material and workmanship defects therein. Nothing in this Section shall be construed to obligate Contractor to attempt to obtain any such warranties.

§ 15.18 CHANGES

The change in work section sets out the procedure for changes in the terms of the contract. Even though all project participants attempt to develop an all-inclusive scope of work, changes are likely as construction proceeds. Examples of the types of changes contemplated by this section are work agreed to in the technical scope and

specifications, changes in price, and changes in the time for performance.

§ 15.19 TITLE TO WORK

[1] Introduction
It is typical for the title to each component of the project that is installed or delivered to the project site to pass to the project company upon payment.

[2] Sample Provision
Title to the Work. Title to each item of equipment or work in progress/construction services will pass to [Project Company] upon receipt by Contractor of payment therefor.

§ 15.20 REMEDIES FOR BREACH

[1] Introduction
If the contractor fails to perform one of its obligations under the construction contract, the remedies available to the project company vary based on the harm incurred. As discussed above, performance shortfalls or completion delays generally are compensated to the project company through liquidated damages. Other breaches can be addressed through various remedies, ranging from the right of the project company to stop work and replace the contractor to money damages for non-liquidated damage claims.

In project financings with contractual obligations requiring project operation by a definite date, the remedy section is particularly important. The project company should have the ability to replace the contractor, or finish the work itself, should the contractor not perform on schedule.

[2] Sample Provision
Events of Default. Either Party may terminate this Contract for default by the other Party as provided below. A Party shall be considered in default of its obligations under this Contract upon the occurrence of an event described below:

Insolvency. The dissolution or liquidation of a Party; or the failure of a Party within ___ (__) days to lift any execution or attachment of such consequence as may materially impair its ability to perform the

[*Work*]; or a Party is generally not paying its debts as such debts become due; or a Party makes an assignment for the benefit of creditors, commences (as the debtor) a voluntary case in bankruptcy under the [*describe relevant bankruptcy statute*] (as now or hereafter in effect) or commences (as the debtor) any proceeding under any other insolvency law; or a case in bankruptcy or any proceeding under any other law is commenced against a Party (as the debtor) and a court having jurisdiction enters a decree or order for relief against the Party as the debtor in such case or proceeding, or such case or proceeding is consented to by the Party or remains undismissed for a period of ____ (__) days, or the Party consents to or admits the material allegations against it in any such case or proceeding; or a trustee, receiver, custodian, liquidator or agent (however named) is appointed for the purpose of generally administering all or part of the property of a Party of such property for the benefit of creditors;

Failure to Perform. The failure by a Party to observe or perform any material covenant, condition, agreement, or undertaking hereunder on its part to be observed or performed for a period of thirty (30) days after notice specifying such failure and requesting that it be remedied is given to such Party, unless the other Party shall agree, in writing, to an extension of such time prior to its expiration;

Misrepresentation. Any representation or warranty of a Party herein is false or misleading or becomes false or misleading in any respect that would materially impair the representing or warranting Party's ability to perform its obligations under the Contract Documents.

Remedies on Default; Termination. Upon the occurrence of any of the foregoing, the non-defaulting Party shall notify the defaulting Party in writing of the nature of the default and of the non-defaulting Party's intention to terminate this Contract for default (a "Notice of Default"). If the defaulting Party does not cure such default immediately, in a default relating to payment of money due, or commence and diligently pursue cure of such default, in the case of any other default, within thirty (30) days from receipt of such notification (or sooner reasonable period if safety to persons is involved), or if the defaulting Party fails to provide reasonable evidence that such default does not in fact exist, or will be corrected, the non-defaulting Party may,

upon five (5) days written notice, in the case of a default in the payment of money, or seven (7) days written notice, in the case of any other default, to the defaulting Party and, in the case of the Contractor, its sureties, if any, terminate the non-defaulting Party's right to proceed with the Work (a "Notice of Termination").

Notice to Lender and Right to Cure. No Notice of Default or Notice of Termination sent by Contractor to [*Project Company*] pursuant to this Contract shall be deemed effective against the [*Project Lender*] until a copy of such notice shall have been received by the [*Project Lender*]. The [*Project Lender*] shall have the same rights as [*Project Company*] to cure any default of [*Project Company*]. Cure by the [*Project Lender*] shall include, but not be limited to, (a) causing [*Project Company*] to cure, (b) curing itself, or (c) finding a suitable replacement for [*Project Company*] and permitting such replacement to cure within the time provided herein.

Right to Possession of Site and Contract Documents. Upon termination of the contract by the [*Project Company*] due to a default by the Contractor, Contractor shall provide immediate possession of the [*Site*] to the [*Project Company*] and deliver to the [*Project Company*] all [*Contract Documents*], plans and specifications, drawings, equipment, materials, and tools at the [*Project Site*] related to the [*Work*].

§ 15.21 SUSPENSION OF WORK AND TERMINATION

[1] Introduction
The construction of the project must be carefully structured and monitored. Delays might result in damages under or termination of other project contracts and in increased debt service costs. Consequently, the project company must be able to react swiftly to any construction problem. One available remedy should be the ability to suspend work or terminate the contract. The project company must preserve the ability to assume project construction and complete the work.

[2] Sample Provision
Right to Complete Work. In the event the Contractor's right to complete the Work under the terms

of this contract is terminated, [*Project Company*] may complete the Work or have it completed by others. Provided [*Project Company*] continues the [*Work*], Contractor shall not be entitled to further payment until the Work has been completed. If the unpaid balance of the Contract Price exceeds the cost of completing the [*Work*], Contractor shall be entitled to such excess. If the cost of completing the [*Work*] exceeds the unpaid balance, Contractor shall be obligated to pay the difference to the [*Project Company*] on demand.

§ 15.22 PAYMENT AND PERFORMANCE BONDS

[1] Introduction

Performance Bond. A performance bond, used as credit enhancement to support a contractor's obligations in a construction contract, is issued by a surety to a project company, and is usually assigned to the project lender as part of the project collateral. It is callable if the contractor fails to perform the terms of the construction contract. If it does not, the surety will cause the performance of the contract so that the project is completed.

Payment Bond. A payment bond is issued by a surety to a project company, and is similarly assigned to the project lender as part of the project collateral. It is callable if the contractor fails to pay some amount that is due under the terms of the construction contract, such as liquidated damages for late performance. If it does not, the surety will make the payment.

Warranty Bond. Another form of performance bond is a warranty bond. Also called *maintenance bonds*, warranty bonds are provided by the contractor to the project company as a safeguard against the risk that the contractor will not make repairs or replacements during the project warranty period under the construction contract for defective work. It is also typically assigned to the project lender as collateral. In some situations, this protection is provided within the scope of the performance and payment bonds.

Money Retention Bonds. As discussed above in this chapter, construction contracts routinely provide that a portion of the periodic payments to the contractor under a construction contract are withheld – retained – pending completion. Rather than forgo the use of this money, contractors sometimes provide retention money bonds to the project company as security for project completion. It can then receive the money that would otherwise be retained. If construction is not completed, the project company can receive the contingency amount covered by the bond for project completion.

[2] Sample Provision
Bond. Contractor will provide to [*Project Company*] a [*performance/payment/warranty*] bond in a form acceptable to the [*Project Company*]. Such bond shall list [*Project Company*] and [*Project Lender*] as beneficiaries thereof as their interests may appear, and be issued by a surety acceptable to [*Project Company*].

§ 15.23 INSURANCE

[1] Introduction
During the construction phase, project finance contractors are typically required to obtain property damage insurance such as "all-risk" builder's risk insurance to pay for direct loss or damage occurring to the work during construction, however caused, whether at the manufacturer's premises, during transit, or on-site. It generally terminates on acceptance of the project. The builder's risk policy applies to all perils that are not specifically excluded, including the damage consequences of a defective design, material and workmanship, and protection during start-up and testing. It does not extend to coverage of losses that result from contractual indemnity or liquidated damage payments for late delivery or completion.

[2] Sample Provision
Property Damage Insurance. Contractor shall provide and maintain All Risk Builder's Risk insurance covering usual risks of physical loss or damage to the [*Work*] to the full replacement value of the [*Project*], from the start of activity at the [*Site*] until

the [*Final Completion Date/Commercial Operation Date*]. [*Project Company*] and the [*Project Lender*] shall be named as additional insureds and such policy shall be endorsed to waive subrogation against [*Project Company*] and the [*Project Lender*]. The [*Project Lender*] shall be named as loss payee as its interests may appear.

Contractor shall procure a "delayed opening" endorsement to the above All Risk Builder's Risk insurance policy with limits of $__ subject to a deductible of __ days' delay. This coverage shall provide for payment of construction loan interest expense up to $__ per day, attributable to delay caused by damage to project property. It is agreed and understood that any proceeds from this "delayed opening" insurance shall first be applied to mitigate Contractor's obligation to pay liquidated damages under Section __ [*delay liquidated damages section*].

Certificates of Insurance; Policy Endorsements; Etc. Contractor shall furnish to [*Project Company*] certificates of insurance that evidence the insurance required hereunder is being provided by insurance carriers authorized to do business in [*insert name of jurisdiction*]. Each certificate shall provide that at least 30 days' prior written notice shall be given to [*Project Company*] and the [*Project Lender*] in the event of cancellation or material change in the policy to which it relates.

§ 15.24 FORCE MAJEURE

[1] Introduction

As discussed elsewhere in this chapter, it is important that force majeure provisions in the construction contract be coordinated with force majeure provisions in other project contracts. Otherwise, the situation could arise in which, for example, the contractor is excused from its obligation to complete the project by a date certain, while the off-take sales agreement does not provide the project company with similar relief. Inconsistent force majeure provisions can be cured with a so-called resurrection clause, in which the contractor agrees with the project company that, where force majeure inconsistencies exist between contracts, the contractor will not receive relief greater than the relief available to

the project company under other relevant contracts.

[2] Sample Provision

Adjustment for Delay. If the performance of all or any portion of the [*Work*] is suspended, delayed or interrupted by a [*Force Majeure Event*] or by an act of [*Project Company*] or by its failure to act as required by the [*Contract Documents*] within the time specified therein (or if no time is specified, within a reasonable time), an equitable adjustment will be made by [*Project Company*] to the [*Contract Documents*], including without limitation the [*Contract Price*] and the [*Completion Date*] for any increase in the cost or time of the performance of the [*Work*] attributable to the period of such suspension, delay, or interruption. Contractor shall give [*Project Company*] written notice of Contractor's claim as a result thereof specifying the amount of the claim and a breakdown of how the amount was computed. Any controversy concerning whether the delay or suspension was unreasonable or any other question of fact arising under this paragraph will be determined pursuant to arbitration, and such determination and decision, in case any question shall arise, will be a condition precedent to the right of Contractor to receive any payment or credit hereunder. Notwithstanding the foregoing, Contractor will in no event be permitted an extension of the [*Completion Date*] beyond that date required under the [*Off-Take Sales Agreement*].

§ 15.25 COORDINATION CONCERNS

[1] Introduction

In construction projects where other contractors are performing work at the facility site, coordination provisions are included in the construction contract. Construction work by these other contractors must not interfere unreasonably with the progress of the work. If it does, the contractor might seek a delay in the scheduled completion date or insist upon an increase in the construction price.

Similar concerns arise in so-called inside-the-fence projects. In these projects, constructed on the site of an operating industrial company or other entity with ongoing operations, construction coordination is particularly important, and the risk of contractor interference is particularly acute.

[2] Sample Provision

Interface and Coordination. During the progress of the [*Work*] other contractors may work in or about the [*Project*], including_____. [*Project Company*] is responsible for overall interface and coordination between or among the contractors at the [*Site*] and only [*Project Company*] shall have the authority to effect such coordination among contractors at the [*Site*]. No such authority shall be exercised by [*Project Company*] that will require Contractor to incur any additional expense or cost in connection with performance of the [*Work*]. [*Project Company*] shall so arrange and schedule the work of such other contractors so that Contractor is able to complete the [*Work*] without interruption or delay.

§ 15.26 TRAINING

[1] Introduction

The contractor is in the best position to train operating personnel about the project. Consequently, it is important that it undertake to train personnel to operate and to prepare and supply operation and maintenance manuals for long-term use at the project.

[2] Sample Provision

Training. Contractor shall train the operating staff of [*Project Company/Operator*] with respect to the operation and maintenance of the [*Project*]. In the course of such training, Contractor shall prepare and submit to [*Project Company*] operation and maintenance manuals for the [*Project*].

§ 15.27 SUBCONTRACTORS

[1] Introduction

After performing due diligence on the contractor, thereby assuring itself that the contractor has the ability and resources to perform, the project company does not want to find itself dealing

with subcontractors. Rather, the contractor must agree to be responsible for its subcontractors and stand behind their performance obligations. Further, cost increases, delays, or performance shortfalls caused by the subcontractors do not excuse the contractor from its obligations to the project company.

Even so, it is not unusual for the project company to require that the contractor seek its approval of all major subcontractors and vendors. Even though the contractor is responsible, the project company still has an interest in the quality of the subcontractor's or vendor's work.

Further, if the contractor defaults under the construction contract, the project company may decide to assume the contractor's obligations to its subcontractors so that the work can proceed. It is often advisable for the project company to require that all subcontracts contain a provision permitting the subcontract to be assigned to the project company in the case of a construction contract default.

[2] Sample Provision

Subcontractors, Suppliers, and Vendors. (a) Nothing contained in the Contract Documents shall create any contractual relationship between [*Project Company*] and any subcontractor, supplier, or vendor. The Contractor shall be solely responsible for the acts and omissions of all subcontractors, vendors, and suppliers retained by, through or under the Contractor in connection with the [*Work*].

(b) Provided Contractor has been paid for the applicable portion of the [*Work*], Contractor shall promptly pay each subcontractor, vendor, or supplier the amount to which the subcontractor, vendor, or supplier is entitled. [*Project Company*] shall have no obligation to pay or to see to the payment of any monies to any subcontractor, vendor, or supplier.

(c) Without in any way limiting Contractor's liability and responsibility under paragraph (a), all major subcontractors, vendors, and suppliers proposed to be retained by, through or under the Contractor in connection with the [*Work*] shall be subject to the prior written approval of the [Project Company].

§ 15.28 LIABILITY LIMITATIONS

[1] Introduction

A limit is typically applied to the contractor's maximum liability under a construction contract. In most cases, this is limited to a percentage of the construction price. Because the implications of a late performance by the contractor will likely be greater than a percentage of the construction price, the project company will want other rights, such as the ability to terminate the contract and replace the contractor, so that it can protect the viability of the project in a delay scenario.

The limit of liability does not apply to all obligations of the contractor, however. Exclusions are the contractor's obligation to reach mechanical completion for the fixed fee, liability covered by insurance, and liability resulting from willful misconduct. It is typical for both the contractor and the project company to reject liability for special, punitive, and consequential damages.

[2] Sample Provision

Limitation of Liability. (a) Contractor's aggregate liability on all claims of any kind, whether based on contract, warranty, tort (including negligence of Contractor or any subcontractor or supplier), strict liability, or otherwise, for all losses or damages arising out of, connected with, or resulting from this Contract, or for the performance or breach thereof, or for services or equipment or materials covered by or furnished pursuant to this Contract (including remedial warranty or performance achievement efforts) shall in no case exceed the [*Contract Price*]. [*Project Company*] shall not assert any claims against Contractor unless the injury, loss, or damage giving rise to the claim is sustained during the Contractor's warranty period, and no suit or action thereon shall be instituted or maintained unless it is filed in a court of competent jurisdiction within three (3) months after the cause of action accrues.

(b) Except for the damages specifically provided in this Contract, in no event (except if and to the extent the liquidated damages provided for it may cover such damages, whether as a result of breach of contract, warranty, indemnity, tort (including negligence), strict liability, or otherwise), shall Con-

tractor or its subcontractors or suppliers be liable for direct, indirect, special, incidental, consequential, or exemplary damages including, but not limited to, loss of profits or revenue; loss of use of the equipment or any associated equipment; cost of capital; cost of substitute equipment, facilities or services; down time costs; cost of purchased or replacement steam or electric power; or claims of customers of [*Project Company*] for such damages.

§ 15.29 SITE CONDITIONS

[1] Introduction

The condition of the site is a potential cause of construction cost overruns and delays. Consequently, the contractor must be familiar with the site and the site conditions, so that these do not excuse its performance obligations under the contract.

[2] Sample Provision

Site Familiarity. Contractor represents and warrants to [*Project Company*] that it has examined the [*Site*] and is familiar with the condition, topography, weather conditions, and access to and from the [*Site*]; and that it has undertaken such studies of surface and subsurface conditions as it has deemed necessary and is satisfied with the results of such studies.

§ 15.30 THE SPECIAL PROBLEM OF COMPLIANCE BY THE CONTRACTOR WITH THE OTHER PROJECT CONTRACTS

[1] Introduction

Because of the interrelatedness of all project contracts, the contractor should receive copies of, and be familiar with, the material project contracts. This will help ensure that the contractor is aware of the possible effects of its performance or nonperformance on other contracts and the project generally.

[2] Sample Provision

Project Contracts. Contractor represents and warrants to [*Project Company*] that it has received copies of and reviewed each of the [*Project*

Contracts] in the form in effect on the date hereof, and agrees that it shall construct the [*Project*] in such a manner as is required by the [*Project Contracts*], and further agrees not to cause any cost increase, breach, violation, or default thereunder.

§ 15.31 UNRAVELING THE PROJECT FINANCE DEAL: TERMINATION FOR CONVENIENCE

The construction contract is often signed before the financing is arranged for the project. This approach allows the project company to obtain a firm construction price for use in project budgeting. If the financing cannot be obtained, however, the project sponsors will want to terminate the construction contract without liability, or with limited liability.

One approach to this problem, a notice to proceed, is discussed above. Another technique is to include a provision allowing the project company to terminate the agreement at any time for its convenience. The contractor is often paid the costs and expenses incurred for work requested by the project company that is performed before the termination date.

§ 15.32 COMPLIANCE WITH CONCESSION TERMS AND CONDITIONS

[1] Introduction
It is important that the contractor agree to satisfy the requirements of any concession agreement that applies to the project. Often, concession agreements include the requirement that the project sponsor satisfy dates of performance for such milestones as commencement of construction, completion, and start-up. Concession agreements are discussed in Chapter 14.

[2] Sample Provision
Compliance With Concession Terms and Conditions. Contractor represents and warrants that it has received a true, correct, and complete copy of the Concession and that it shall satisfy each of the terms and conditions therein relating to project construction, completion, and start-up, as follows: [*describe*].

CHAPTER SIXTEEN

INPUT CONTRACTS

§ 16.01 INTRODUCTION

Because the ability of the project company to produce revenue from project operation is the foundation of a project financing, the contracts constitute the framework for project viability and control the allocation of risks. Contracts that represent the cost of fuel and other inputs to the project company are of particular importance because these contracts affect cash flow.

Inputs needed for a project vary with the type of project. As such, the terms of input contacts vary widely. Nonetheless, some generalizations, discussed in this chapter, can be made.

Input contracts must not interfere with the expectation of debt repayment from project revenues. If risks are allocated in an unacceptable way from the project lender's perspective, credit enhancement from a creditworthy third party is needed, such as letters of credit, capital contribution commitments, guarantees, and insurance.

To the extent expense predictability is unavailable or the risks of dependability are allocated unacceptably, credit enhancement is necessary to protect the lender from external uncertainties, such as supply, transportation, product market instability, and changes in law. Sometimes, however, the project exists in an uncertain environment that subjects the project lender to some unallocated risks. The tolerance of the capital and debt markets for this type of residual uncertainty varies over time with changing market conditions.

Project financings generally require a long-term, supply-or-pay contract for essential inputs, such as fuel. As discussed below, in some projects, the long-term contract is not necessary because supply and transportation are widely available.

Where needed, a supply-or-pay contract is often the contract structure used. In a supply-or-pay contract, the supplier agrees to provide goods, such as fuel, or services, such as fuel transportation. If the supplier is unable to fulfill that obligation, it must generally provide either the goods or services from an alternate source at its expense or pay damages to the project company for expenses incurred by the project company in securing the goods or services itself. The supplier's obligations are subject to negotiated excuses, such as force majeure events and breaches by the project company.

Supply contracts, whether necessary to operate the facility (as with industrial projects) or to convert to the output of the facility (as with energy production projects), have three main concerns in a project financing: supply reliability, transportation reliability, and cost. Each of these concerns must be addressed in a way that provides the requisite predictability required by a project financing.

§ 16.02 WHEN INPUT CONTRACTS ARE NOT NEEDED

In some projects, the supply and transportation of fuel, or other goods and services necessary for the project, are not concerns. Wide availability, little price risk, and no transportation problems combine to make spot purchases more beneficial to the project than long-term contracting. In such cases, the responsibility for obtaining adequate supplies is imposed on the project operator. These are rare projects indeed. Contracts for assured supplies of critical project inputs, such as fuel, at costs consistent with financial projections are usually essential to project financings.

If contracts are thought not to be needed for a project, several risks need to be considered before rejecting their importance completely. These include an examination of the sources and availability of the fuel or other input by a market analysis projection of current and future availability and price; if the fuel or other input is imported, a consideration of the import and export political risks, including changes in import and export duties; and availability and cost of transportation, including whether any transportation service is the only available mode of transportation.

§ 16.03 IMPORTANT INPUT RISKS

[1] Increase in Input Costs

Project inputs, such as fuel costs, are historically very volatile. Consequently, a fixed-price fuel contract, adjusted periodically based on a negotiated index, is the typical way to address the price increase risk. To the extent this arrangement is not available, other risk avoidance structures can be used. For example, the project company could require that part of the fuel cost be subordinated to debt service payments. Alternatively, payment of costs above a ceiling price could be deferred through a tracking account mechanism until all debt is repaid. Finally, the project company could purchase the fuel reserves in advance, thereby fixing the cost of fuel supply.

[2] Delay in Completion of Transportation Facilities

In a captive fuel project, fuel is available at the project site. For example, a project could be built at the mouth of a coal mine, which would not require huge expenditures to build transportation facilities. At the most, a conveyor system or areas for truck loading and unloading would be the basic transportation needs.

In other projects, however, the fuel or other input must be transported over a mix of pipelines, railways, and roads, and from seaports and river docks. Sometimes facilities for these types of transportation must be newly constructed. In others, major upgrades are needed to satisfy a project's needs. Construction or upgrade programs must be carefully scheduled so that they are completed and available for use to transport a project's input requirements at the time needed for start-up and testing and eventually commercial operations.

[3] Availability of Supply

The input supply available for a project must be sufficiently determinable so that the supply available can be confirmed. If the input is abundant over the long term, then supply is assured, although a price risk remains. There are several ways to address the risk of insufficient supplies of needed inputs. The most conservative approach is for the supplier to dedicate a proven field or mine as the source for the project's supply. Less conservative is a guarantee of supply from a creditworthy supplier. Other alternatives include acquisition of supply sources by the project company, and entering into multiple, partially redundant supply agreements with multiple suppliers.

[4] Disruption to Transportation

Often the fuel needed for the project must be transported to the project site. Although some projects, such as electricity generation projects at a mine mouth, are not dependent on transportation risks, most projects are located in areas where fuel must be transported.

The fuel transportation risk can be addressed in several ways. The most conservative approach is for the project company to own all infrastructure needed to transport fuel to the project site. As an example, the project company could own

railways and rail equipment needed to transport coal to a project.

Less expensive is a guarantee of transportation from a creditworthy transporter. Other alternatives include entering into multiple, partially redundant, transportation agreements with multiple transporters.

[5] Force Majeure in International Input Contracts

The force majeure risk in a fuel contract is significant to the risk allocation structure of the financing and the price of project output. In short, the focus of negotiation of a force majeure provision is which party will bear the risk that an unexpected and uncontrollable occurrence will disrupt the input supply or input transportation to the project. Like many risks in a project financing, the risk can be allocated to the supplier or transporter, the project company, or the off-take purchaser. Force majeure provisions are discussed in greater detail below.

[6] Experience and Resources of Input Supplier and Transporter

The fuel supplier and transporter must have sufficient experience and resources to perform the obligations under the fuel contracts. Minimum requirements include adequate financial resources, labor and technical qualifications, and management experience in managing production and deliveries.

[7] Fuel Management and the Fuel Manager

Where the fuel program selected for the project is complicated in any area, such as scheduling deliveries, mixing fuels, price control, or similar decisions, it is important that the project company prepare a fuel management program for implementation by the operator, or to employ or contract with a fuel manager to control these decisions.

[8] Quality

Variations in fuel quality, particularly Btu (British thermal unit) value, moisture content, and other factors, can affect the electricity generated and therefore the revenue earned by the project. This risk can be assigned to both the fuel supplier, to the extent the quality concern is based in the fuel supply, and to the fuel transporter, to the extent the transportation affects fuel quality.

Typical remedies include a decrease in the price paid by the project company for the fuel supply or transportation service; contract damage payments, to the extent the project incurs damage liability to the off-take purchaser for lower deliveries caused by input quality problems; pass-through of higher operating costs, to the extent costs increase; and termination of the contract.

[9] Linking Project Inputs to Outputs

The danger inherent in a long-term input contract is that the contract price paid by the project company under the contract will be more than the future market price. In a competitive marketplace for the project output, this could result in a reduction in project revenues, because project competitors, experiencing the same lower commodity costs, can charge less. In common terms, there is the absence of a linkage between project inputs and outputs. Long-term commodity projects should generally include provisions that permit the commodity price to be renegotiated, within certain limitations, to maintain the pricing margins necessary for a successful project. Alternatively, the price of the output can be tied (or linked) to the price of the underlying inputs, thereby reducing materially the sensitivity of the project to fluctuations in input cost increases.

§ 16.04 TYPES OF INPUT CONTRACTS

[1] Fixed Amount

Input contracts can be for supply or transportation of a fixed amount. Under this type of contract, the supplier or transporter agrees to supply or transport a specific amount of the needed input to the project, and the project company agrees to purchase a specific amount. This gives both parties certainty but leaves no room for changes to the amount available or required.

[2] Requirements

A requirements contract enables the project company to purchase only those supply and transportation services it requires. It generally has no duty to have any requirements, which places the supplier at a disadvantage. The project company

maintains flexibility with this type of contract, because if the facility is not capable of operation, or if the project company chooses not to operate the project, no damages are due to the supplier or transporter. The supplier or transporter takes the risk that its supplies or transportation capacity are sufficient to meet the needs of the project's requirements.

To make a requirements contract more useful in a project financing, changes are needed. A common change is to require that the supplier meet the requirements of the user, but the requirements cannot exceed a specified maximum amount. Also, there is a requirement that the project company purchase a minimum amount of the input. To allow for planning and flexibility, a detailed notice provision is added for the project company to give the supplier advance notice of changes in its requirements.

[3] Output

An output contract requires the supplier to supply and sell to the project all of its production or output, or all of its production or output from a specified source. In effect, the specified source becomes captive of the project. However, there is no assurance for the project company that the output will be sufficient to provide the requirements for the facility.

[4] Spot

Under a spot contract, the project company agrees to purchase supply or transportation services on the terms available in the market at the time of purchase. It generally does not provide the predictability necessary in a project financing. However, it can be successfully used in projects where supply is abundant and price is not volatile.

[5] Dedicated Reserves

In some situations, where the project feasibility is particularly sensitive to input costs, supply, or transportation availability, the supplier is required to set aside input reserves for use only by the project. Examples include coal and gas reserves. In some situations, the reserves must be purchased in advance.

[6] Firm Versus Interruptible

Firm and interruptible input contracts are exactly as the words imply. A firm contract requires that an input, such as fuel, be supplied and transported to the project without interruptions in favor of other customers. An interruptible contract permits the fuel company to favor the needs of firm contract holders.

The type of contract required for a project depends upon the project's needs. If the project can stop operations temporarily without damage liability to the off-take purchaser, it can probably save money by entering into an interruptible contract. Similarly, an interruptible contract may be permissible if the project can shift to a different input source during interruption periods.

[7] Subordination of Project Costs to Debt Service

A technique used to address project input price risk is the subordination of certain project input costs to the project debt. For example, a supplier of a project input, such as fuel, may be asked to forgo the receipt of a portion of its payment in certain negotiated scenarios. These subordinated costs would be paid, if at all, in the future when debt service payments and funding of reserve accounts are no longer in jeopardy. The terms of the subordination are carefully negotiated.

[8] The Commodity Supplier as Project Partner

The project owned by a commodity supplier, or the project in which such a supplier is a partner, can greatly reduce input price risk. The commodity supplied can be priced at or near production cost, with profits generated at the output level of the project.

One type of arrangement, called a tolling agreement, is discussed in Chapter 19.

§ 16.05 EXCUSES TO PERFORMANCE

Generally, courts in the United States hold parties to their contractual agreements. This is equally true in the fuel supply context. For example, in *Iowa Electric Light & Power Co. v. Atlas Corp.*,[1] the court required a supplier of uranium to perform the contract it had entered with a utility, though the price of uranium to the supplier had increased substantially.

Of course, contractual provisions can be added to the contract to excuse performance upon the occurrence of negotiated events, such as price increases.[2] This, however, may introduce a degree of operating cost uncertainty that might be unacceptable in a project finance transaction. If so, the contract should be clearly drafted so that price adjustments are not allowed for changes in market conditions, including fluctuations in availability and price.

§ 16.06 CREDITWORTHINESS

Because of the long-term nature of the supply contract, the reliability and creditworthiness of the supplier or transporter are extremely important to the project company. Each must have sufficient financial resources, both at the time of contract execution and during performance, to undertake the obligations in the contract. These include payment of liquidated damages due if the supplier delays the supply or transportation of the input, or if the input quality does not conform to contract requirements. To the extent the financial resources do not exist, and no adequate credit enhancement is available at a reasonable cost to improve this credit risk, such as parent guarantees, letters of credit, and payment and performance bonds, the contract will not be financeable and another supplier or transporter must be substituted.

§ 16.07 TYPICAL PROVISIONS IN PROJECT FINANCE INPUT CONTRACTS

Input supply and transportation contracts generally contain the following provisions: quantities and commencement of deliveries; price; payment; scheduling, metering, and weighing;

---

[1] 467 F. Supp. 129 (N. D. Iowa 1978), *rev'd on other grounds*, 603 F.2d 1301 (8th Cir. 1979), *cert. denied*, 445 U.S. 911 (1980).

[2] *See* Eastern Air Lines, Inc. v. McDonnell Douglas Corp., 532 F.2d 975 (5th Cir. 1976) (force majeure doctrine is inapplicable where a future event was specifically provided for in the contract).

quality and rejection; title and risk of loss; term; force majeure; default; and remedies for breach.

§ 16.08 QUANTITIES AND COMMENCEMENT OF DELIVERIES

[1] Introduction
Predictability of input supply is an important element in a project finance transaction. The project must be assured of the supply quantity that will be required. This should be set forth in a clear contract provision, obligating the supplier to deliver a specified quantity, or to deliver within a range of specified quantities.

The contract must also set forth a definitive date on which the delivery obligation begins. In many projects, inputs must be delivered to the project site ahead of commercial operation. Such supplies are used for facility testing or to establish an input stockpile at the project site.

[2] Sample Provision
Quantity; Commencement of Deliveries. Supplier shall deliver the [*Product*] to the [*Project Site*] in the following quantities: [*set forth quantities required*] per [*hour/day/week/month/year*]. Such deliveries shall begin on the date specified by [*Project Company*] in a notice to Supplier, which date shall be no earlier than the date [*number*] days after receipt of such notice by Supplier.

§ 16.09 PRICE

[1] Introduction
Predictability of price over the life of the project is critical to the feasibility and success of a project financing. The agreement should contain a clear articulation of price; allocate responsibility for taxes, duties, and governmental charges; and the basis, if any, for price adjustments.

[2] Sample Provision
Price. The price of each [*unit/pound/ton*] of the input delivered to the [*Project Site*] shall be [*describe price or provide formula for calculation*]. Such price shall include all taxes, duties, fees, royalties, production payments, and other

governmental (whether central, state or local) charges.

Adjustments. The price of any delivery of [*input*] hereunder shall be adjusted based on the quality of [*input*] delivered by Supplier as follows: [*list adjustments necessary to offset the additional costs for processing the lower-quality input*].

§ 16.10 PAYMENT

[1] Introduction
The agreement should specify when payments are due, whether on receipt of the seller's invoice, or after testing is successfully completed. Also, the mechanics for payment should be specified.

[2] Sample Provision
Payment. [*Project Company*] shall pay [*Supplier*] for all input delivered in conformity with the terms hereof on the last day of each month during the term hereof, commencing on the [*Initial Delivery Date*]. The amount due shall be that amount set forth in an invoice prepared by the Supplier and delivered to the [*Project Company*] no later than the __ day of the immediately preceding month.

§ 16.11 SCHEDULING, METERING, AND WEIGHING

[1] Introduction
It is important that the input agreement ordering, delivery, and scheduling provisions conform to the purchase schedules of the off-take sales agreement. For example, ordering requirements under the input contract must be delivered on a schedule consistent with production and delivery schedules under the off-take agreement. Also, the agreement should include a clear and detailed description of how and where the input will be metered, measured, or weighed. If the necessary meters, or scales, are not already constructed or in service, the agreement should specify the party responsible for the purchase, installation, maintenance, and repair of them. The agreement should include provisions for reviewing the measurement data, observing calibration tests, and otherwise monitoring the process as well as

provisions for resolving disputes about the measurement process.

[2] Sample Provision

Scheduling. Supplier and [*Project Company*] shall cooperate to schedule deliveries of the [*input*] on a schedule consistent with the [*Off-Take Contract*]. Annually the [*Project Company*] shall provide to Supplier a schedule of deliveries, which Supplier shall follow, consistent with the terms hereof.

Metering and Weighing. Each delivery hereunder shall be weighed on the scales maintained by the [*Project Company*] at the [*Project Site*]. Upon request, not to be unreasonably made, Supplier shall have the right to have the calibration of such scales tested by [*entity*]. Any error in the calibration shall be resolved by the parties pursuant to the arbitration provisions herein.

§ 16.12 QUALITY AND REJECTION

[1] Introduction

Input quality is an important element of risk in a project financing. For example, low fuel quality could increase operating costs or prevent a facility from meeting permit requirements. If the fuel does not meet or exceed the specifications under which the facility was designed, it may not operate at the performance levels needed for a successful project. Consequently, the agreement must set forth a detailed specification of the fuel quality and characteristics requirements.

Similarly, where the fuel is used in an energy production facility, the Btu value of the fuel should be specified. Some variations in Btu value can be handled by adjusting the fuel price paid to the supplier. Yet, at some point, the project company will want to reject deliveries and either seek damages or replace the supplier.

Besides a clear statement of the fuel quality and characteristics, a procedure is needed for testing the fuel delivered to the facility. This may be accomplished through an independent laboratory or by operating personnel at the delivery site. A determination should be made about which party is to bear the cost and frequency of testing and which party is responsible for the testing. Finally, a dispute resolution procedure is helpful

in resolving disputes relating to compliance with these specifications.

[2] Sample Provision

Quality. The [*input*] delivered by Supplier hereunder shall be of the quality and shall have the characteristics and specifications set out in Exhibit _ hereto. [*Project Company*] shall have the right to reject any delivery not in conformity with such characteristics and specifications.

§ 16.13 TITLE AND RISK OF LOSS

[1] Introduction

The title to the fuel, and the party who will bear the risk of loss, must be set forth in the contracts. In general, the title to and risk of loss of fuel passes from the seller to the project company at a delivery point determined by the mode of transportation.

[2] Sample Provision

Title; Risk of Loss. Title and risk of loss to all [*input*] shall pass to the [*Project Company*] upon delivery to the [*Project Site*].

§ 16.14 TERM

[1] Introduction

The term of the input supply agreement typically has a length at least equal to the term of most of the underlying debt. This helps ensure that the input costs are sufficiently predictable for a project financing. The commencement of the term should be delayed to the extent a force majeure or other event beyond the control of the project company delays the commencement of facility operations. For maximum flexibility, it is often helpful for the supplier to grant the project company the ability to delay commencement of deliveries if the project company pays a delay fee. Renewal terms should also be considered. Renewal or extension of the initial term may be required, or advisable, depending upon the length of the initial term and the expected life of the project.

[2] Sample Provision

Term. The term of this agreement shall commence on the date hereof and terminate on the date of the twentieth anniversary of the [*Commercial Operation Date*].

§ 16.15 FORCE MAJEURE

[1] Introduction

Force majeure is an event outside the reasonable control of the effected party to a contract, which it could not have prevented by good industry practices or by the exercise of reasonable skill and judgment, which typically excuses certain negotiated portions of contract performance during its pendency. The effected party is obligated to take all reasonable actions necessary to restore performance as soon as possible.

Narrowing the application of force majeure events in the input contract is important. Force majeure relief typically applies only to specific, well-defined events listed in the contract; is available only if contract performance is substantially and adversely affected; applies only to extraordinary events, not normal business risks or insurable events; and the relief is limited to the effects of the force majeure.

[2] Uncontrollable Events

In general, performance is excused by a party upon the occurrence and during the continuance of a force majeure, outside a party's reasonable control, that makes performance impossible. These include acts of war, unusual or catastrophic weather events, and the like.

[3] Change of Law

The effects of a change of law should also be considered. In developing countries, both the underlying economy and the country's laws, are emerging. Consequently, it is probable that over the twenty-year course, or so, of a project, new laws will be applied, such as environmental laws that are more costly to comply with than existing laws. The economic implications of a change of law need to be allocated to one of the two parties.

[4] Sample Provision

Force Majeure. If the performance of all or any portion of the delivery obligations of Supplier hereunder, or of [*Project Company*] to accept deliveries

hereunder, is suspended, delayed, or interrupted by a [*Force Majeure Event*], such party's obligations shall be suspended hereunder during such event. The party experiencing the [*Force Majeure Event*] shall give [*Project Company*] written notice of the event and the consequences as a result thereof. Any controversy concerning whether the delay or suspension was unreasonable or any other question of fact arising under this paragraph will be determined pursuant to arbitration. Notwithstanding the foregoing, no party will be permitted to have its obligations suspended hereunder for a period in excess of [*specify*].

§ 16.16 DEFAULT

[1] Termination Events Generally

Because the supply and price of the needed input are important to project feasibility and success, it should not be easily terminable by the supplier. Termination events must be precisely drafted, with sufficient advance notice that project lenders and other interested parties can cure the related default events.

[2] Termination by Supplier

From the perspective of the supplier, the input agreement is typically subject to termination for the following events: nonpayment of amounts owed by the project company to the supplier; bankruptcy, acceleration, or liquidation of the project company; abandonment of the project (unless it is the supplier's fault); termination or material amendment of certain agreed-upon project contracts (other than for good cause or default by the other party); sale of project assets; failure to achieve milestones, including commercial operations, by a definite date; contract repudiation or other action that implies the project company does not intend to perform the contract; and other breaches of material provisions of the agreement.

[3] Termination by Project Company

From the perspective of the project company, the input agreement is typically subject to termination for the following events: nonpayment of amounts owed by the supplier to the project company; bankruptcy, acceleration, or liquidation of the supplier; contract repudiation or other action that implies the supplier does not intend to perform the contract; the project company is unable to complete construction or operate the project because of a force majeure or supplier fault; and other breaches of material provisions of the agreement. If the supplier is a government entity, whose obligations are guaranteed by the host government, the agreement will be terminable if the government, as guarantor, defaults under the guarantee.

[4] Sample Provision

Events of Default. Either Party may terminate this Contract for default by the other Party as provided below. A Party shall be considered in default of its obligations under this Agreement upon the occurrence of an event described below:

Insolvency. The dissolution or liquidation of a Party; or the failure of a Party within sixty (60) days to lift any execution, garnishment, or attachment of such consequence as may materially impair its ability to perform the Agreement; or a Party is generally not paying its debts as such debts become due; or a Party makes an assignment for the benefit of creditors, commences (as the debtor) a voluntary case in bankruptcy under the [*describe applicable bankruptcy statute*] (as now or hereafter in effect) or commences (as the debtor) any proceeding under any other insolvency law; or a case in bankruptcy or any proceeding under any other insolvency law is commenced against a Party (as the debtor) and a court having jurisdiction enters a decree or order for relief against the Party as the debtor in such case or proceeding, or such case or proceeding is consented to by the Party or remains undismissed for a period of one hundred twenty (120) days, or the Party consents to or admits the material allegations against it in any such case or proceeding; or a trustee, receiver, custodian, liquidator or agent (however named) is appointed for the purpose of generally administering all or part of the property of a Party of such property for the benefit of creditors;

Failure to Perform. The failure by a Party to observe or perform any material covenant, condition, agreement or undertaking hereunder on its part to be observed or performed for a period of thirty (30) days after notice specifying such failure and requesting that it be remedied is given to such Party, unless the other Party shall agree, in writing, to an extension of such time prior to its expiration;

Misrepresentation. Any representation or warranty of a Party herein is false or misleading or becomes false or misleading in any respect that would materially impair the representing or warranting Party's ability to perform its obligations under the Agreement.

§ 16.17 REMEDIES FOR BREACH

[1] Introduction

Generally, the above list of termination events does not automatically result in contract termination. Rather, the party in default is typically given time to cure its breach. If it fails to do so, termination may then result. If termination is not selected or available as a remedy, a damage payment may be due, or the defaulting party might be forced to perform the contract. Remedies vary based on negotiations and the unique setting of each project.

[2] Termination Payments

The amount of a payment due on termination of the contract will vary based on the cause of termination. If the input contract is terminated for convenience, or because of a default, the party terminating for convenience or in default should generally pay a high termination payment.

If the supplier terminates the agreement for convenience or the contract is terminated because of a supplier default, the project company will need to consider how project debt will be paid and how it will recover some investment return for the lost opportunity associated with contract nonperformance.

[3] Specific Performance

If the supplier provides one of the only sources of input supply or transportation for a project, with other alternatives too costly to form serious alternatives, or where the price is crucial to project success, the only remedy that may be acceptable to the project company is that of specific performance. Specific performance would require the party in default to perform the contract as agreed. Local counsel should be consulted to learn whether this is an available remedy.

[4] Alternative Inputs

Another remedy is to require that the supplier supply and transport the needed input to the project from other sources if it is unable to perform the contract.

[5] Sample Provision

Remedies on Default; Termination. Upon the occurrence of any of the foregoing, the non-defaulting Party shall notify the defaulting Party in writing of the nature of the default and of the non-defaulting Party's intention to terminate this Contract for default (a "Notice of Default"). If the defaulting Party does not cure such default immediately, in a default relating to payment of money due, or commence and diligently pursue a cure of such default, in the case of any other default, within thirty (30) days from receipt of such notification (or sooner reasonable period if safety to persons is involved), or if the defaulting Party fails to provide reasonable evidence that such default does not in fact exist, or will be corrected, the non-defaulting Party may, upon five (5) days written notice, in the case of a default in the payment of money, or seven (7) days written notice, in the case of any other default, to the defaulting Party, terminate the Agreement (a "Notice of Termination").

Notice to Lender and Right to Cure. No Notice of Default or Notice of Termination sent by Supplier to [Project Company] pursuant to this Contract shall be deemed effective against the [Project Lender] until a copy of such notice shall have been received by the [Project Lender]. The [Project Lender] shall have the same rights as [Project Company] to cure any default of [Project Company]. Cure by the [Project Lender] shall include, but not be limited to, (a) causing [Project Company] to cure, (b) curing itself, or (c) finding a suitable replacement for [Project Company] and permitting such replacement to cure within the time provided herein.

Right to Possession of Supply Site and Transportation Documents. Upon termination of the Agreement by the [Project Company] due to a default by the Supplier, Supplier shall provide immediate possession of the [Supply Site] to the [Project Company] and deliver to the [Project Company] all [Transportation Documents] related to the [Supply]. [Project Company] shall thereupon have the right to [describe right of Project Company to take over mine or production facilities and supply the input to the Project.]

§ 16.18 RESERVES AND MINING OR PRODUCTION PLANS

The source of the input, in most project financings, must be clearly identified to the project company and the lenders. The input supplier must clearly set forth the source of the input and its mining or production plans for mining or production throughout the term of the supply contract. This may take the form of a representation in the contract, coupled with such drilling, sampling, and other geologic data and mining or production plans as is necessary to confirm the existence of the input and the cost and ability to mine or produce it. In addition, evidence must be submitted to confirm that the reserves can be economically recovered. This data should be updated annually and submitted to the project company.

In some projects, where the input source is new and must be developed through infrastructure or other investment, it is prudent to require that the input supplier satisfy milestone events by negotiated dates. These might include dates for opening new mines, deadlines for geological studies, and reports and similar requirements.

Stockpiles are another important risk area in input supply. Stockpiles are of two types: input stored or piled at the supplier facilities and input stored or piled at the project by the project company. In general, the input supplier should be required to maintain an input stockpile at the project or at its own facilities, such as at a mine, to cushion any production problems it experiences, or because of disruptions in delivery. A supply of from one to three months may be required.

CHAPTER SEVENTEEN

OPERATION AND MAINTENANCE AGREEMENTS

§ 17.01 GENERALLY

A project sponsor has two options for project operation. It can decide either to operate the project itself, without an operating agreement, or retain an operator to operate the project for it. If the project company retains an operator, it is sometimes an affiliate of a project sponsor.

[1] Operating Agreement

Similar to the project finance construction contract, operation and maintenance agreements in international project financings must serve to provide the project sponsor with a facility that performs within certain agreed-upon performance criteria, and that operates at a fixed or reasonably predictable cost. Similar to the contractor's responsibility in a project, an operator should likewise be responsible for all aspects of project operation and maintenance.

As discussed below, the risk that operating and maintenance costs will exceed the budgeted estimate and the funds available from project revenues is a significant risk in a project financing. If operating costs exceed estimates, the additional money needed for project operation will need to come from reserve accounts, if there are any, or from funds that would otherwise be used to pay debt service or distribute to the equity owners.

Project finance operation and maintenance agreements typically contain each of the following provisions: a detailed scope of work; a fixed or variable (but predictable) price for all of the work necessary to operate the project; performance guarantees; liquidated damages for failure to satisfy performance guarantees; and a showing of financial creditworthiness of the operator.

In at least one respect, the operation and maintenance agreement is not as critical to the project as is the construction contract: The operator can be replaced without major consequences. However, the flexibility of the project company for replacement varies with the difficulty of operating the project and the availability of replacement operators. Replacement of operators in projects relatively simple to operate, using proven technology, and without fuel-handling or feedstock-handling difficulties, pose the least concern.

[2] Self-Operation

Instead of an operating agreement between the project company and an operator, project sponsors sometimes elect to operate the project themselves. This is particularly the case where one project sponsor is experienced with operating facilities similar to the project. Even if self-operation is selected, the project lenders or other project sponsors may insist upon a written operating agreement between the project company and the related entity that will operate the project.

§ 17.02 IMPORTANT OPERATION RISKS

The allocation of operating risks between the project company and the operator is an important element in the determination of whether a project is financeable. For an operating agreement to be effective in a project finance transaction, the most significant operation risks must be allocated to a creditworthy operator.

[1] Increase in Operating Costs

The risk that operation of the project will cost more than the amount of funds available from revenue is an important risk for the participants in a project financing. Operating costs exceed estimates for various reasons, including construction defects, use of a new technology, and input difficulties, such as fuel handling. This cost overrun risk may result in the inability of the project company to pay interest and principal on the project debt.

The operating cost overrun risk can be managed and its effects reduced even where the operator has not assumed that risk in a fixed-price operating and maintenance agreement. For example, if there are higher than expected operating costs, contractual undertakings can provide for the infusion of additional equity by the project sponsor, other equity participants, or standby equity participants. Similarly, standby funding agreements for additional financing, either from the project lender or subordinated debt lent by project participants or third parties, can be used. Another alternative is the establishment of a contingency account under which the project company establishes a fund that is available to pay increased operating costs.

[2] Performance Guarantees

If a project does not operate after completion at guaranteed levels, the project company will still need to pay debt service and other contractual obligations. Unfortunately, the revenue may not be available so to do.

One approach to this risk is a liquidated damage payment. A liquidated damage payment is an estimate by the operator and project company of the consequences of deficient operation by the operator of the project.

Performance liquidated damages compensate the project company for increased operating costs or reductions in revenues associated with the failure of the operator to meet the agreed-upon performance criteria. Amounts paid are used for such expenses as damage payments due to the off-take purchaser, increased operating costs, and debt service costs that cannot be paid otherwise because of the decline in project revenue.

Unlike the use of liquidated damage payments in a construction contract, the liability exposure of the operator is comparatively very small. It is usual, for example, for the operator to limit its maximum liability for liquidated damages to an amount equal to one or two years' profit received under the agreement. However, the project company can replace the operator with another entity, thereby, it is hoped, improving performance.

The creditworthiness of the operator determines the strength of the contractual undertakings as a risk mitigation instrument. If the operator is not financially strong, it is less likely that it will pay the liquidated damages when due. Consequently, project lenders sometimes require that these financial undertakings be supported by a payment guarantee from a creditworthy entity, a letter of credit, or a payment bond or other surety instrument.

[3] Force Majeure in International Operation Contracts

Project finance contracts are interrelated. A breach under one contract can cause a breach under another, setting off a chain reaction of problems for the project company. For example, if the operator is excused from operating the facility under a force majeure clause, but the project company is not similarly excused of its obligations to deliver under an off-take agreement, the project could lose its revenue stream.

Inconsistent force majeure provisions can be cured with a so-called resurrection clause. This contractual provision cures inconsistencies in force majeure clauses found in project contracts, providing that the operator will not receive relief greater than the relief available to the project company under other relevant contracts, particularly the off-take contract.

In negotiating a force majeure provision for an operation and maintenance agreement, understanding the local circumstances of contract performance is important. In short, the parties must understand what is uncontrollable *in that location*. This is particularly true in international projects, where labor, transportation systems, and infrastructure can vary greatly from the operator's home country.

Different legal systems can create havoc on well-planned, matched force majeure provisions. As discussed elsewhere in this book, the choice of applicable law and the jurisdiction of disputes is a critical element in ensuring that the force majeure structure is respected and enforced.

Despite this careful planning, complete elimination of the risk of force majeure may not be possible. Rather than rely on contract provisions, project sponsors may need to seek alternate solutions, such as standby credit, dedication of reserve funds, employment of additional labor, and the like.

[4] Experience and Resources of Operator

The experience and reputation of the operator must help ensure the efficient operation of the project at the levels of operating costs set forth in the project budget. Similarly, if the operator has adequate financial resources necessary to support its contractual obligations, then provisions relating to liquidated damage payments, guarantees, indemnities, and self-insurance obligations will provide protection to the project company.

Like the project contractor, the operator must possess sufficient human and technical resources necessary to satisfy its contractual undertakings. The risk is that the operator will be unable to perform a contractual obligation because of a low commitment to the industry, insufficient resources, or lack of knowledge or experience.

In an international project, the operator should be particularly adept at working with the local labor force. Local site managers, with local experience, are particularly beneficial in reducing the risk of local labor problems.

[5] Raw Material Supply and Utilities

The project company must be assured of a supply of raw materials and other inputs and utilities at a cost within the acceptable ranges of financial projections. Responsibility for managing these supplies often rests with the operator. The formality of the commitments for the supply depends on the availability of the materials in the project area, and the ability of the operator to manage supply needs effectively.

[6] Excuses for Operator Nonperformance – The Contractor Did It; The Owner Did It

It is not unusual for an operator facing liquidated damage liabilities in a project finance transaction to blame the contractor or the project company for the problems. Inability of the operator to satisfy performance obligations may indeed be the fault of the contractor or project owner. Potential problems caused by the contractor include defective construction. Problems sometimes caused by the project company include failure to provide needed information on a timely basis, failure to satisfy obligations clearly allocated to the project company in the operation and maintenance agreement, failure to obtain permits, and supply of inappropriate fuel or other inputs.

To increase the likelihood that such allegations by the operator will not excuse performance responsibility, several contract provisions can be included to the agreement. First, the agreement should clearly and precisely identify the responsibilities of both the project company and the operator. The responsibilities of the project owner should be kept to an absolute minimum.

Second, to the extent that the contract excuses the operator from liability for inadequate performance or cost overruns, the operator should be required to deliver a written notice to the project company of perceived problems. The operating agreement often provides a period to remedy the failure. If the notice is not given, the right of the operator to use the alleged failure as an excuse to liability is waived. A provision similar to the notice procedure given for a force majeure is a preferred approach.

[7] Coordination

Projects usually begin operation when the contractor is still completing work, typically minor items sometimes referred to as *punch list* work. Even if the construction work is completed, the operator must still coordinate its operation activities with other activities at the site, such as at a site used by a manufacturing company and the project.

Without coordination, risks of construction delays and operating cost overruns increase, and the contractor and operator are each able to blame the other for delays and cost overruns.

Consequently, project construction and operation must be carefully monitored by the project company, which must serve as construction manager to that extent. Also, at a minimum, it is very useful if each contract includes a provision in which the contracting parties acknowledge that they have reviewed the terms, including schedules, of the other contracts, and acknowledging that they have not identified any scheduling or other deficiencies between the contracts.

One way to avoid conflicts between the contractor and operator is to retain the contractor as the operator of the project, at least for the initial years of the project operation. This approach has several benefits. First, it avoids problems during the testing phase of the project when both the contractor and operator are on the site. Second, it avoids finger-pointing duels about who – contractor or operator – is responsible for a problem. Finally, it should make it more likely that the contractor will construct and operate the facility at a high performance level because the contractor, as operator, is familiar with its own construction.

§ 17.03 CREDITWORTHINESS

Risk allocation in a project finance operation and maintenance agreement is only effective to the extent the operator is creditworthy. It must have sufficient financial resources, both at the time of contract execution and during performance, to undertake the obligations in the contract. These include payment of liquidated damages due if the facility is not operated to meet the performance guarantees. Also, the operator must be able to absorb any losses it might incur under the agreement. To the extent the financial resources do not exist, and no adequate credit enhancement is available at a reasonable cost to improve this credit risk, the contract will not be financeable and another operator must be found.

§ 17.04 FIXED-PRICE CONTRACT

Ironically, a fixed-price operations and maintenance agreement is extremely rare in project finance. Such a contract requires the operator to operate a project, or part of a project, for a fixed sum. Sometimes, the fixed sum is subject to adjustment based upon an agreed-upon index.

The tension between the sponsor and operator in negotiating a fixed-price operations and maintenance agreement is based on the nature of the agreement: The operator must operate the project at a fixed price. Yet, almost none of its underlying costs can be fixed with much confidence over a fifteen- or a twenty-year contract term. Escalation indices provide some protection but are not perfect at mimicking the actual economic conditions affecting a project.

§ 17.05 COST-PLUS-FEE CONTRACT

A much more common approach to an operation and maintenance agreement is the cost-plus-fee contract. As the name implies, the owner pays the operator the actual costs of project operation incurred by the operator, plus a fee. The operator is assured of earning a fee, while the owner is more likely to receive the lowest operating costs. In contrast to the fixed-price construction contract, the owner avoids payment of the contingency risk premium.

§ 17.06 COST-PLUS-FEE CONTRACT WITH MAXIMUM PRICE AND INCENTIVE FEE

In a related approach, the cost-plus-fee contract is modified by adding a maximum price and an incentive fee payable to the operator based on cost or budget performance. Provisions are included that provide the operator with an incentive to keep costs low, such as penalties charged and bonuses earned based on budget performance. If costs exceed the maximum price guarantee, the operator absorbs these costs, or alternatively, the owner has the right to replace the operator and terminate the agreement. To the extent there is a savings as compared with the maximum price guarantee, the operator and the owner might split the savings on a shared basis.

Incentive fees, or bonuses, can also be awarded for a variety of operating needs. For example, the project company could award a bonus for quickly and efficiently bringing the facility to full operation. It could also be awarded for such things as good community relations.

Bonuses could also be offered during periods in which financial results are higher than projected. This provision must be carefully drafted so that performance is rewarded. A mere increase in revenue is an insufficient determinant because revenues could increase for a variety of reasons, including inflation or fluctuations in the cost of fuel or supplies.

§ 17.07 TYPICAL PROVISIONS IN PROJECT FINANCE OPERATION AND MAINTENANCE AGREEMENTS

Operation and maintenance agreements generally contain the following key provisions: a detailed listing of each of the operator's and the owner's responsibilities, compensation and payment terms, subcontracts, performance testing, changes in the work, warranties, remedies for breach, insurance, dispute resolution, indemnification, assignment, suspension of work and termination, and force majeure. These typical operation and maintenance agreement clauses are discussed below.

§ 17.08 OPERATOR'S RESPONSIBILITIES

[1] Introduction

Among the terms included in the operator's responsibility section are the types of services that will be provided, such as operation, maintenance, and repair. Other typical responsibilities include staffing, hiring, and training of personnel; purchasing supplies; maintaining an adequate spare parts inventory; scheduling and carrying out maintenance, including routine inspections, preventive maintenance, and scheduled overhauls; performing all maintenance needed to keep vendor warranties in effect; security, fire prevention, and emergency planning; personnel conduct; financial and operating result reporting;

maintenance of operating logs, operations manuals and maintenance reports; and the obtaining of and maintaining of permits necessary for operation.

The operator must operate the facility in compliance with the other project contracts, warranties, and applicable laws and regulations. The operating agreement typically contains a provision that requires the operator to acknowledge that it has received and reviewed copies of the important project contracts.

The services are usually divided into three phases: mobilization, pre-operations, and operations. During the mobilization phase, the operator provides input into the preparation of budgets and projections, makes equipment recommendations, and reviews the project contracts. During the pre-operations phase, the operator recruits and hires personnel, develops tool and spare parts requirements, procures inventories, develops operation procedures and maintenance plans, trains personnel, and supports the contractor in start-up and testing. During operations, the operator controls and monitors operations, performs preventative maintenance, performs scheduled maintenance, prepares operating budgets and plans, and helps maintain community relations.

[2] Sample Provision

Operator's Responsibilities. (a) Operator shall operate and maintain the [*Project*] in accordance with (i) generally accepted practices for the operation and maintenance of similar facilities; (ii) the [*Operation and Maintenance Manual*]; (iii) the [*Permits*]; (iv) [*Governmental Requirements*]; and (v) the [*Off-Take Sales Agreement*].

(b) Operator shall provide the labor, materials, and services necessary for it to perform the foregoing. Operator shall train employees to operate and maintain the [*Project*] in accordance with generally accepted practices for training employees for similar facilities.

(c) Operator shall perform the foregoing services in three phases: mobilization, pre-operation, and operation, as further described in detail in the scope and timing of services set forth in Exhibit ___.

§ 17.09 PROJECT COMPANY'S RESPONSIBILITIES

[1] Introduction

Conversely, the project company's responsibility section describes the responsibilities of the project company, as owner. These may include access to the site, permits, fuel for operations, utilities, and waste disposal.

Failure of the project company to perform these obligations might delay or otherwise impair the operator's ability to perform the contract at the agreed-upon price and at the performance levels contemplated. Consequently, the project company and the project lender will want the responsibilities kept at a minimum and include only those areas with least risk of nonperformance by the project company.

Operating agreements sometimes contain a provision that places responsibility on one party for obligations necessary for the successful operation and maintenance of the project that are not expressly set forth in the contract. Such a provision is reproduced in the sample provision immediately below.

Both parties resist this, however, because of the ability afforded to one party to place blame or financial responsibility on the other. With proper diligence, such a clause can be used, because the elements of the project operation will be clearly understood by both parties before the contract is executed.

[2] Sample Provision

Project Company Responsibilities. (a) *Input Supply.* [*Project Company*] will provide Operator with a sufficient quantity and quality and type of [*describe inputs*] to permit operation of the Project in accordance with this Agreement.

(b) *Project Permits.* [*Project Company*] shall, at its sole expense, procure and maintain in effect all [*Permits*].

(c) *Access.* [*Project Company*] shall provide Operator with all access to the [*Site*] required by Operator.

(d) *No Interference by Third Parties.* [*Project Company*] shall not permit any third parties to have access to the [*Project*] that would interfere with the performance of Operator's obligations hereunder.

(e) *Other.* Any obligations necessary for the successful operation and maintenance of the [*Project*] not described in this Agreement shall be [*Project Company/Operator*]'s responsibility.

§ 17.10 OPERATING STANDARD

[1] Introduction
The operating agreement imposes on the operator a duty to fulfill a standard of care when operating the facility. Standards used include "standard industry practices" and "in a manner that will achieve maximum revenues consistent with prudent operating practice."

In transnational projects, reference is sometimes made in the operating standard to similar facilities in the country. Take care when using this reference, however, unless the parties thoroughly understand the operating conditions at those facilities.

[2] Sample Provision
Operating Standard. Operator shall operate and maintain the [*Project*] in accordance with generally accepted practices for the operation and maintenance of similar facilities, in such a manner so that maximum revenues will be achieved, consistent with prudent operating practice.

§ 17.11 PRICE AND PAYMENT

[1] Introduction
The cost of operation and maintenance services is discussed earlier in this chapter. Alternatives include fixed price, cost-plus-fee contract, and cost-plus-fee contract with maximum price and incentive fee.

The operating costs are paid periodically to the operator, usually monthly. Methods of payment vary. Operators generally prefer to receive some portion of the payment in advance, so that they have sufficient funds to pay for operating supplies and raw materials.

[2] Sample Provision
Price provisions vary based on the technology used, the sensitivities of project economics to various risks, the ownership of the project company, whether the operator is an affiliated entity, and many other factors. Therefore, a sample or model provision is not very helpful to the reader. Rather, the author sets forth below an example of a fixed-fee provision.

Fixed Fee. (a) For each Operating Year, [*Project Company*] shall pay to Operator, for the performance of the services described herein, an annual amount equal to [*amount*], invoiced in monthly installments beginning on the [*Commencement Date*], and on the first day of each calendar month thereafter. Monthly invoices shall be due __ days after receipt thereof. Each such invoice shall be in an amount equal to 1/12 of such annual sum; provided, however, in the event that the [*Commencement Date*] is on a day other than the first day of the month, the first such invoice shall be in an amount equal to 1/365 of such annual sum multiplied by the number of days from the [*Commencement Date*] to the last day of the calendar month in which the [*Commencement Date*] occurs and the last such invoice shall be an amount equal to 1/365 of such annual sum multiplied by the number of days from the first day of such last month through the last day of the term hereof.

(b) Beginning in the first Operating Year, the annual sum shall be increased or decreased, as the case may be, by the percentage increase or decrease in the [*Escalation Index*] during the preceding Operating Year or, in the case of the first Operating Year, from the calendar year of the date hereof.

(c) When any [*Direct Costs – specify*] are incurred by Operator, including the insurance required hereunder; or any central, state, or other sales, use, value-added, gross receipts, duty, fee, or similar tax or charge with respect to the services hereunder, [*Project Company*] shall pay such tax or, if Operator is required to pay same, Operator shall include such amount in the next monthly invoice rendered.

§ 17.12 PERFORMANCE GUARANTEES AND LIQUIDATED DAMAGES

[1] Introduction
Liquidated damages are payable by the operator to the project company if the performance

guarantees negotiated are not achieved. These vary with the type of project. In general, the operator may be required to guarantee that the facility will be operated to produce a level of output that is necessary to generate revenue to service the project debt and to satisfy the agreements the project company has negotiated with the output purchaser.

In an energy project, the operator is typically required to prove that the facility operates at negotiated levels of power output and fuel use. Availability guarantees cover the ability of the facility to operate on a reliable level.

Failure to achieve these guarantees generally results in the obligation of the operator to pay so-called performance liquidated damages, the sole remedy available to the project company against the operator. These damages are calculated to pay debt service shortfalls, increased operating costs, or contract damages under other project contracts arising from the operator's inadequate performance. The total exposure of the operator to these types of liquidated damages is generally limited to a percentage of the operator's fee for a one- or two-year period.

[2] Sample Provision
Performance Guarantees and Liquidated Damages.
(a) Beginning on the [*Commencement Date*], Operator shall guarantee that in each Operating Year the [*Project*] will produce __ (the "Guaranteed Output").

(b) Operator shall pay [*Project Company*] liquidated damages of $__ for each [*quantity shortfall*] by which the actual output of the [*Project*] during any Operating Year is less than [*specify guaranteed amount*].

(c) [*Project Company*] shall pay Operator a bonus of $__ for each [*quantity overage*] by which the actual output of the [*Project*] during any Operating Year is more than [*specify guaranteed amount*].

(d) In the event that a Force Majeure Event occurs, the actual output of the [*Project*] shall be corrected by adding the output that the [*Project*] would have been capable of producing during such time period but for such Force Majeure Event.

§ 17.13 CAPITAL CHANGES

[1] Introduction
During the operating period, it is not unusual for the project company or operator to suggest capital changes for the project that will improve operations. These changes are typically outside the scope of the operator's general responsibilities under the operating agreement. Because of the familiarity of the operator with the project, it is often preferable for the operator to either manage the improvement, or perform the work itself. The capital change section sets out the procedure for these changes. Whether or not the operator performs the work, it must be included in the process if the project will continue to operate while the capital improvement is under way.

[2] Sample Provision
Capital Costs. The services Operator is obligated to provide hereunder do not include the repair or replacement of structural components of the [*Project*] or of major pieces of equipment of the [*Project*]. If [*Project Company*] desires that Operator perform any such services, Operator agrees to consider such request and provide [*Project Company*] with its decision within 30 days after such request.

§ 17.14 REMEDIES FOR BREACH

[1] Introduction
If the operator fails to perform one of its obligations, the remedies available to the project company vary based on the harm incurred. As discussed above, performance shortfalls generally are compensated to the project company through liquidated damages. Other breaches can be addressed through various remedies, ranging from the right of the project company to replace the operator to money damages for non-liquidated damage claims.

[2] Sample Provision
Events of Default. Either Party may terminate this Contract for default by the other Party as provided below. A Party shall be considered in default of its

obligations under this Contract upon the occurrence of an event described below:

Insolvency. The dissolution or liquidation of a Party; or the failure of a Party within sixty (60) days to lift any execution, garnishment, or attachment of such consequence as may materially impair its ability to perform the [*Services*]; or a Party is generally not paying its debts as such debts become due; or a Party makes an assignment for the benefit of creditors, commences (as the debtor) a voluntary case in bankruptcy under the [*describe applicable bankruptcy statute*] (as now or hereafter in effect) or commences (as the debtor) any proceeding under any other insolvency law; or a case in bankruptcy or any proceeding under any other insolvency law is commenced against a Party (as the debtor) and a court having jurisdiction enters a decree or order for relief against the Party as the debtor in such case or proceeding, or such case or proceeding is consented to by the Party or remains undismissed for a period of one hundred twenty (120) days, or the Party consents to or admits the material allegations against it in any such case or proceeding; or a trustee, receiver, custodian, liquidator, or agent (however named) is appointed for the purpose of generally administering all or part of the property of a Party of such property for the benefit of creditors;

Failure to Perform. The failure by a Party to observe or perform any material covenant, condition, agreement, or undertaking hereunder on its part to be observed or performed for a period of thirty (30) days after notice specifying such failure and requesting that it be remedied is given to such Party, unless the other Party shall agree, in writing, to an extension of such time prior to its expiration;

Misrepresentation. Any representation or warranty of a Party herein is false or misleading or becomes false or misleading in any respect that would materially impair the representing or warranting Party's ability to perform its obligations under the Contract Documents.

Remedies on Default; Termination. Upon the occurrence of any of the foregoing, the non-defaulting Party shall notify the defaulting Party in writing of the nature of the default and of the non-defaulting

Party's intention to terminate this Contract for default (a "Notice of Default"). If the defaulting Party does not cure such default immediately, in a default relating to payment of money due, or commence and diligently pursue cure of such default, in the case of any other default, within thirty (30) days from receipt of such notification (or sooner reasonable period if safety to persons is involved), or if the defaulting Party fails to provide reasonable evidence that such default does not in fact exist, or will be corrected, the non-defaulting Party may, upon five (5) days written notice, in the case of a default in the payment of money, or seven (7) days written notice, in the case of any other default, to the defaulting Party, and terminate (a "Notice of Terination").

Notice to Lender and Right to Cure. No Notice of Default or Notice of Termination sent by Operator to [*Project Company*] pursuant to this Contract shall be deemed effective against the [*Project Lender*] until a copy of such notice shall have been received by the [*Project Lender*]. The [*Project Lender*] shall have the same rights as [*Project Company*] to cure any default of [*Project Company*]. Cure by the [*Project Lender*] shall include, but not be limited to, (a) causing [*Project Company*] to cure, (b) curing itself, or (c) finding a suitable replacement for [*Project Company*] and permitting such replacement to cure within the time providedt herein.

§ 17.15 SUSPENSION OF SERVICES

[1] Introduction

The project company often wants the flexibility to suspend project operations. It may do so as part of an agreement with the off-take purchaser or may find that operation is no longer economically feasible. In such situations, the project company will want the ability to suspend operations temporarily or terminate the agreement.

However, the operator will not want to be terminated without cause, and lose the ability to earn the profit it expected to receive. This is particularly true where the operator has assumed operating risks under the risk of liability for inadequate performance, thereby providing a necessary element for project financing. To address these concerns, the operator might require that there be no such termination, without a penalty, during the first five to ten years of operation.

[2] Sample Provision

Suspension of Services. At any time on and after the ___ anniversary of the [*Commencement Date*], [*Project Company*] shall have the right to terminate the Agreement upon not less than ___ days' advance notice to Operator. Such option shall be exercisable without liability to Operator, other than for those amounts due for the performance of services hereunder through the date of termination and for reasonable demobilization costs.

§ 17.16 PROCEDURE AT END OF AGREEMENT

[1] Introduction
The procedure for terminating an operation and maintenance agreement must include consideration of passing on to the project company the knowledge, records, and techniques of the former operator. On termination, the operator should be obligated to transfer operating information, records, and manuals to the project company or the new operator. Sometimes it may be prudent for the old operator to be obligated to train the new operating personnel.

Other obligations of the operator at the end of the term include transferring spare parts, assigning vendor warranties, and licensing any needed technology to the new operator or the project company. In some situations, conducting an environmental audit of the site and facility to determine whether any environmental liability exists that should be paid for by the operator may be prudent for the project company.

[2] Sample Provision
Turn-Over Upon Termination. Upon termination hereof, Operator shall immediately provide to [*Project Company*] access to the [*Project Site*]. Operator shall further immediately provide to [*Project Company*] all operating information, records and manuals; transfer to [*Project Company*] spare parts; assign to [*Project Company*] any vendor

warranties, and license any technology used at the [*Project*], to the [*Project Company*].

§ 17.17 INSURANCE

[1] Introduction
Insurance is an important credit enhancement tool in a project financing. Project risks during operation that are not otherwise mitigated are typically addressed in an insurance program required under the operating agreement. The insurance requirements will include policy deductibles set at realistic levels, self-insurance amounts set at levels that cannot undermine the operator's financial strength, and minimum creditworthiness and stability of insurance underwriters. Insurance is discussed at length in Chapter 20.

[2] Sample Provision
Insurance. (a) During the term of the Agreement, Operator shall maintain in effect the following insurance from an insurance company licensed to write insurance in [*jurisdiction*] in at least the following amounts: [*specify: workers' compensation; employer's liability; comprehensive general liability (including premises/operations, products and completed operations, broad form property damage (including products and completed operation), coverage for collapse, explosion, and underground hazards, employees as additional insureds, independent contractor coverage, cross-liability and severability endorsement, personal injury, incidental medical malpractice, occurrence policy form, and blanket contractual liability extended to include hold harmless and indemnification agreement); automobile; umbrella liability; "all risk" property insurance (including flood, earthquake, and collapse); comprehensive boiler and machinery insurance including production machines and electronic data processing equipment used in connection with the operation of the Project*].

(b) Operator shall furnish to [*Project Company*] certificates of insurance signed by its insurance carriers that evidence the insurance required hereunder, and upon request by [*Project Company*], it shall also furnish [*Project Company*] copies of the actual policies. Each certificate shall provide that at least thirty (30) days' prior written notice shall be given to [*Project Company*] and [*Project Lender*] in the event of cancellation, suspension, or material change in the policy to which it relates.

§ 17.18 FORCE MAJEURE

[1] Introduction

As discussed elsewhere in this chapter, it is important that force majeure provisions in the operating agreement be coordinated with force majeure provisions in other project contracts. Otherwise, the situation could arise in which, for example, the operator is excused from its obligation to operate the project, while the off-take sales agreement does not give the project company similar relief.

[2] Sample Provision

Adjustment for Delay. If the performance of all or any portion of the [*Services*] is suspended, delayed, or interrupted by a [*Force Majeure Event*] or by an act of [*Project Company*] or by its failure to act as required by the Agreement within the time specified herein (or if no time is specified, within a reasonable time), an equitable adjustment will be made by [*Project Company*] to the Agreement, including without limitation the [*Annual Fee*] for any increase in the cost or time of the performance of the [*Services*] attributable to the period of such suspension, delay or interruption. Operator shall give [*Project Company*] written notice of Operator's claim as a result thereof specifying the amount of the claim and a breakdown of how the amount was computed. Any controversy concerning whether the delay or suspension was unreasonable or any other question of fact arising under this paragraph will be determined pursuant to arbitration, and such determination and decision, in case any question shall arise, will be a condition precedent to the right of Operator to receive any payment or credit hereunder.

Notwithstanding the foregoing, Operator will in no event be permitted relief beyond the type permitted to [*Project Company*] under the [*Off-Take Sales Agreement*].

CHAPTER EIGHTEEN

PROJECT FINANCE OFF-TAKE SALES CONTRACTS

§ 18.01 NECESSITY FOR OFF-TAKE CONTRACTS

Off-take agreements are the agreements that provide the revenue flow to a project. They are the agreements by which the project company sells its product or service. Truly, they are the linchpins of project finance transactions.

Long-term contracts in which a creditworthy purchaser agrees to purchase the output of a facility are not always necessary for a nonrecourse or limited recourse project financing. Instead of this arrangement, the project company and the project lenders rely on the demand produced by the market for the credit support. This type of structure works effectively where the need for the project is well established and the price for the project output will remain generally stable throughout the term of the project debt. Nonetheless, the project company and project lender assume risks related to output price fluctuations, obsolescence, competition, and other market risks.

§ 18.02 TYPES OF OFF-TAKE CONTRACTS

[1] Great Confusion
There is confusion over the definitions of two terms: *take-or-pay* and *take-and-pay*. Yet, the

difference between the two terms is straight-forward: take-and-pay requires a payment only if the product is produced, whereas take-or-pay requires a payment unconditionally.

[2] Take-or-Pay

A *take-or-pay contract*,[1] in general, refers to a contractual obligation between a purchaser of a facility's output and a project company in which the purchaser agrees to make payments to the project company for the good or service producible at the facility in return for maintaining the capacity to produce and deliver the good or service.

Under this structure, the off-take purchaser makes payments for capacity *whether or not* the project company actually generates the good or service at the purchaser's request. The payment obligation of the buyer for the capacity component is *unconditional*.

The parties typically structure the contract with two components to the purchase price: fixed (or capacity) costs and variable costs. The fixed cost, which must always be paid whether or not the project can produce the product contracted for, represents the cost of project debt service, fixed operating costs, and a minimum equity return. The variable cost must only be paid if the purchaser wants to buy the product and represents variable operating costs. This allows a minimum amount to be paid by the off-take purchaser, without providing a windfall to the project company for variable expenses only incurred if the project company actually produces a product.

These agreements are sometimes referred to as having "hell-or-high-water" obligations. Even if the project company produces nothing or delivers nothing, or even if the project is incapable of producing or delivering anything, the payment obligation exists.

This obligation results in a characterization of take-or-pay contracts as a form of a guarantee. In most situations, it is reportable as a guarantee of a third party's debt on financial reports and information of the purchaser.

Because this type of agreement is a guarantee, the off-take purchaser may need to receive approval from its own lenders to enter into the contract. Most loan agreements restrict the ability of a borrower to provide indirect guarantees of a third party's debt without consent.

[3] Take-and-Pay

The *take-and-pay contract* requires the purchaser to take and pay for the project output or to pay the project company as if it did take the output. However, the buyer is only obligated to pay *if* the project company has actually produced and delivered the product or service. If the purchaser does not want to buy the output, it is not required to do so, *provided* the project company is incapable of producing the product contracted for. It is sometimes called a *take-if-offered* contract.

Like the ironclad take-or-pay contract, this version is typically structured with two components to the purchase price: fixed and variable. The fixed cost, which the off-take purchaser must always pay if the project can produce the product contracted for, represents the cost of project debt service, fixed operating costs, and a minimum equity return. The off-take purchaser must pay the variable cost only if the purchaser wants to buy the product and represents variable operating costs. The risks that the project company will sell sufficient off-take to satisfy debt obligations, operating costs, and an equity return are firmly with the project company.

This arrangement may not sound different from a long-term sales agreement, discussed below. The distinction is that in a take-and-pay agreement the purchaser has an option to refuse deliveries if it pays a capacity charge, which reflects the producer's fixed costs. In a long-term sales agreement, undetermined contractual damages could be awarded to the seller for a breach of the buyer's purchase obligations.

[4] Blended

Off-take contracts are sometimes structured to include aspects of both take-and-pay and take-or-pay contracts. In a blended contract, payments of the purchaser are required in specified cases of service interruption. Such payments can be loans or advance payments, which the project

---

[1] A. F. Brooke II, *Great Expectations: Assessing the Contract Damages of the Take-or-Pay Producer*, 70 TEX. L. REV. 1469 (1992).

company then credits against service provided later.

[5] Long-Term Sales Agreements

A long-term sales agreement is an agreement between the project company and a purchaser for the purchase and sale of specified quantities of the project's output. The term of the agreement is usually one to five years.

The purchaser has the obligation to purchase the contract quantity only if it is produced and delivered and meets the contract quality requirements. If it does not buy conforming goods, contract damages may be payable to the project company. The purchaser has no obligation, however, to make minimum payments to support the project debt.

[6] Spot Sales

The least useful project finance off-take arrangement is a spot sale at the market price existing at the time of sale. Such sales are sometimes pursuant to a contract or purchase order. The purchaser is not obligated to make additional purchases, pay capacity charges, or otherwise support the project debt if the purchases are not made.

§ 18.03 CONTRACTUAL RISK – THE VALUE OF CONTRACTS TO THE PROJECT COMPANY AND AS A CREDIT SUPPORT

Two legal considerations contribute to the value of project finance contracts to the project company and to the lender as the basic credit support for a transaction. Because the usefulness of the contract to both the project company and the lender depends upon enforceability, the fundamentals of contract law must be applied. Moreover, the viability of the contract as collateral if the transaction results in economic difficulties must be considered.

From the project company's perspective, the project contracts are the basis for project earnings and expenses. Similarly, from the lender's perspective, the salient collateral in a project financing is the collection of contracts entered into by the project company for the development, con-

struction, and operation of the project, which are each crucial to the credit assessment of the lender.

Generally, each project finance contract is an executory contract: one of the project participants has yet to perform or finish performing for entitlement to the full benefits of the contract, and the other party has yet to pay in full for the goods or services.[2] Executory contracts present unique risks to the project that affect the value as collateral. The risk to the project finance lender is based on this executory nature. Neither the project company nor the other contracting party (the "obligor") will have performed any significant contractual obligation at the time of the closing of the project finance loan. Moreover, ongoing performance obligations will exist throughout the life of the project because project finance contracts typically have terms of fifteen, twenty, and as long as thirty years. A legion of excuses will exist to give the obligor defenses to the requirement to perform the contract, including payment of any revenue due the project.

For example, the obligor may have a defense to performance or payment that arises under the terms of the contract, or the obligor may have a right of setoff arising independently of the project financing. Because each project contract operates in a changing, not static, environment, the contract is subject to modification by formal amendment or waiver of rights or remedies. A project financing is therefore distinguishable from accounts receivable financing: The collateral is subject to many problems that arise from the executory nature and that interferes with the ultimate collateral value.

§ 18.04 RISKS IN CONTRACT TERMS AND DEFENSES

In a book about international transactions, it is a challenge to present information applicable

---

[2] See generally BARKLEY CLARK, THE LAW OF SECURED TRANSACTIONS UNDER THE UNIFORM COMMERCIAL CODE at § 11.01 [2] (1993) (citing Scott L. Hoffman, *A Practical Guide to Transactional Project Finance: Basic Concepts, Risk Identification, and Contractual Considerations*, 45 BUS. LAW 181 (2006)).

throughout the globe, while recognizing that most law is developed on a country-by-country basis. With that apology, the following discussion is based primarily on the Uniform Commercial Code, as it is in effect in the various states of the United States. The rights of the project company in a contract are, of course, subject to the contract terms and many defenses, claims, and other offsets. These subject the project finance lender to a variety of risks resulting from the project company's contract performance, misconduct and the enforceability of the contract.

One solution is for the secured party to obtain in the consent a "cutoff" pursuant to U.C.C. §§ 9–403 and 9–404 that the other contracting party will not assert claims, defenses, or offsets against the secured party.[3] Such an agreement is unenforceable, however, where the secured party knew of the defense or did not act in good faith.[4] Further, the contracting party would not be considered to have waived the contractual defenses that relate to capacity, such as fraud and lack of authority.[5]

If a cutoff agreement cannot be obtained or a consent otherwise negotiated, the secured party can still benefit by giving the other contracting party notice of the assignment. U.C.C. § 9–404 provides the secured party with the ability to stop the other contracting party from raising defenses or claims against the secured party that accrue after notice is given that are related to other transactions between the project company and the other contracting party.[6]

In addition, or as an alternative to an agreement with or notice to the obligor, the lender will examine the contracts for validity and enforceability. This due diligence investigation typically takes the form of opinions and review by counsel.

[1] Commercial Impracticability

The common law doctrine of frustration of purpose relieves an obligor of its duty to perform where a failure of some basic assumption results in extreme difficulty or expense.[7] Changed circumstances that frustrate or render impracticable a purchaser's performance obligations under a project output sales agreement could therefore result in the avoidance of the agreement by the purchaser. The general test is "whether the cost of performance has in fact become so excessive and unreasonable that the failure to excuse performance would result in grave injustice."[8]

Alternatively, a project participant may avoid performance of contractual obligations through the doctrine of commercial impracticability. The doctrine, embodied in U.C.C. § 2–615,[9] provides that performance under a contract will be excused if the party has not assumed the risk of some unknown contingency, the nonoccurrence of the contingency had been a basic assumption underlying the contract, and the occurrence of the contingency has made performance commercially impracticable.

Section 2–615 is generally applied when an unforeseeable contingency has altered the essential nature of the performance. U.C.C. Comment 4 states that "the severe shortage of raw materials or of supplies due to a contingency such as war, embargo, local crop failure, an unforeseen shutdown of major sources of supply or the like . . . " may entitle a party to relief under § 2–615.[10] The section does not excuse a party from its contract obligations merely because of a rise or collapse

---

[7] RESTATEMENT (SECOND) OF CONTRACTS, §§ 261, 265 (1981).

[8] Gulf Oil Corp. v. Federal Power Comm'n, 563 F.2d 588, 599 (3d Cir. 1977). Although commercial impracticability has been successfully invoked in long-term supply contract cases, e.g., Aluminum Co. of Am. v. Essex Group, Inc., 499 F. Supp. 53, 70 (W. D. Pa. 1980), International Minerals & Chem. Corp. v. Llano, Inc., 770 F.2d 879, 887 (10th Cir. 1985) (natural gas purchaser held unable to receive gas because of imposition of state environmental rule), it has not been accepted with extensive success. See, e.g., Iowa Elec. Light and Power Co. v. Atlas Corp., 467 F. Supp. 129 (N. D. Iowa 1978), rev'd on other grounds, 603 F.2d 1301 (8th Cir. 1979), cert. denied, 445 U.S. 911 (1980) (increase in cost of uranium); Superior Oil Co. v. Transco Energy Co., 616 F. Supp. 98 (W. D. La. 1985) (increase in cost of natural gas); Eastern Air Lines, Inc. v. Gulf Oil Corp., 415 F. Supp. 429 (S. D. Fla. 1975) (energy crisis price increase and impact on long-term, fixed-price fuel contract).

[9] U.C.C. § 2–615. Although Section 2–615 expressly refers only to a seller, Comment 9 to that Section provides that, in certain circumstances, a buyer may be entitled to relief. See J. WHITE & R. SUMMERS, UNIFORM COMMERCIAL CODE 128 (2d ed. 1980).

[3] U.C.C. §§ 9–403; 9–318(1)(a); see generally CLARK, supra note 2 at § 11.04[4].

[4] U.C.C. § 9–404. For applicability of this clause to assignable agreements other than sales contracts, see CLARK, supra note 2 at § 11.04.

[5] U.C.C. § 9–404.   [6] U.C.C. § 9–404.

[10] U.C.C. § 2–615, Comment 4.

in the market, however, because that is "the type of business risk which business contracts made at fixed prices are intended to cover."[11] Thus, courts have declined to excuse the buyer from performance merely because resale market prices fall severely after contract execution.[12]

Frustration of purpose and commercial impracticability are generally not major risks for the project participants. The nonrecourse limitations on debt repayment require that project contracts contain detailed force majeure provisions to allocate risks associated with contract performance. Thus, the project company can limit a project participant's recourse to the doctrine of commercial impracticality by enumerating in the contract the sole contingencies that will excuse performance. Comment 8 to § 2–615 provides that the applicability of that Section is "subject to greater liability by agreement."[13]

[2] General Contract Theories

Other legal theories that can be invoked to abrogate project contracts include mutual mistake about the basic assumptions of the transaction[14] and "unconscionability" arising out of onesidedness.[15] In addition, each project contract is subject to the terms of performance set forth in the contract, including such provisions as warranties[16] and conditions to performance. Thus, a court may provide relief from unanticipated commercial risks, despite the collateral impact on financing.

[3] An Example of Project Contract Risks: Output and Requirements Contracts

Although a complete analysis of contract law is well beyond the scope of this book, an example of the potential issues that could appear to frustrate the expectations of the project participants will suffice. In analyzing a project financing, the structure of the contractual obligations in supply and sales agreements, such as whether a supply of goods contract is either an output contract or a requirements contract, is important to the credit analysis by the lender. Excuses to performance under these contracts that the U.C.C. permits can affect the operation of the project and the predictability of cash flow.

A requirements contract is an agreement in which the project company promises to sell and deliver all the buyer's requirements of specified goods, and the buyer promises to refrain from buying comparable goods from any other supplier. In an output contract, the project company promises not to sell specified goods to any other customer, and the buyer promises to accept and pay for all of the goods that the project produces for sale.

Generally, the buyer in a requirements contract has no duty to have any requirements, and the seller in an output contract has no duty to have any output. A good faith standard applies

---

[11] *Id.*

[12] U.C.C. § 2–615, Comment 9.

[13] U.C.C. § 2–615, Comment 8.

[14] The doctrine of mutual mistake provides relief if a mistake is made by both parties about a basic assumption on which the contract is formed, which had a material effect on the agreed performance, and was a risk not undertaken by the breaching party. *See* RESTATEMENT (SECOND) OF CONTRACTS § 152 (1981). *E.g.,* Aluminum Co. of Am. v. Essex Group, Inc., 499 F. Supp. 53, 69 (W. D. Pa. 1980) (long-term supply contract; attempt to tie a contract price to other prices permits reformation in light of unforeseen increases in electricity prices brought about by rising oil prices); *but see* Exxon Corp. v. Columbia Gas Transmission Corp., 624 F. Supp. 610 (W. D. La. 1985) (assumption that contract price would provide profit held not sufficient basis for modification of purchase contract).

[15] U.C.C. § 2–302. In general, a presumption of conscionability in contracts exists between two parties in a commercial setting. *E.g.,* Consolidated Data Terminals v. Applied Digital Data Sys., Inc., 708 F.2d 385, 392 (9th Cir. 1983). Courts have applied the unconscionability doctrine as a basis for refusing to enforce a commercial agreement where unequal bargaining power exists. *E.g.,* Pittsfield Weaving Co. v. Grove Textiles, Inc., 121 N H. 344, 430 A.2d 638 (1981). *See* Cal. Civ. Code § 1670.5 (West 1979), which extends the doctrine of unconscionability to all contracts.

U.S. courts are consistently adverse to an unconscionability defense based on inflation because unconscionability is determined at the time the contract is signed, not performed. *E.g.,* Kerr-McGee Corp. v. Northern Util., Inc., 673 F.2d 323, 328 (10th Cir. 1982), cert. denied, 459 U.S. 989 (1982) (rejection of utility claim that an indefinite price escalation clause in a natural gas sales agreement was unconscionable); Compania de Gas de Nuevo Laredo v. Entex, Inc., 686 F.2d 322, 328 (5th Cir. 1982) (application of clause providing for pass-through of cost increases was not unconscionable).

[16] U.C.C. §§ 2–313 (express warranties), 2–314 (implied warranty of merchantability), 2–315 (implied warranty of fitness for a particular purpose), 2–316 (exclusion and modification of express and implied warranties).

to both, however.[17] The U.C.C. defines good faith as "honesty in fact and the observance of reasonable commercial standards of fair dealing in the trade."[18]

The U.C.C. also provides that no quantities unreasonably disproportionate to any stated estimate, or in the absence of a stated estimate to any normal or otherwise comparable prior output or requirements, may be tendered or demanded.[19] This proviso applies only to increases in requirements or output, not reductions.[20] Thus, a drastic reduction, even to the point of termination, is not precluded if made in good faith.

From the project company's perspective, the good faith termination standard allows the buyer to escape from contractual obligations. A buyer, for example, may end its requirements by a good faith decision to use a substitute good for that supplied under the contract, such as the substitution of natural gas for coal in the buyer's production process.[21] Also, a buyer's discovery of a less expensive substitute may constitute a good faith excuse for terminating all of its requirements.[22] Similarly, where the buyer can prove that continued operation would cause severe economic loss, courts will permit termination of a product line or production segment.[23] Thus, even if the buyer's needs decrease, the project may lose sufficient revenue to amortize the loan.

Contractual provisions can be included to render the termination issue more predictable.[24] For example, the buyer can agree to have future requirements through a minimum quantity term in the contract, thus obligating the buyer to purchase that minimum quantity of goods, even if the buyer decides to terminate operations.[25] An additional protection is to require an assignment of the requirements contract to the successor-in-interest upon the consolidation, merger, or sale of the requirements business.[26]

An output contract will shift the risks of business termination and quantity variations to the buyer of the project output. Because in an output contract, the buyer agrees to accept and pay for all of the goods that the project produces for sale, the buyer, not the project, bears the risk of uncertainty.

§ 18.05 REVENUE CONTRACTS IN TRANSNATIONAL PROJECTS

In some countries, a project financing, which is based on the underlying cash flow from the revenue-producing contracts of the project, is a new concept. Until recently, financings based on contracts committed to repayment of project debt were relatively unknown in developing countries. Thus, key project finance contract provisions that are standard in the United States and Great Britain are not yet developed in these countries. Examples of these standard provisions, considered essential to a successful project financing, include definitive obligations for purchases of a project's output at a defined price, defaults, and remedies.

§ 18.06 ENFORCEMENT OF REVENUE CONTRACTS IN TRANSNATIONAL PROJECTS

Reliable methods for enforcing a revenue-producing contract on which a project financing is based must be carefully considered. These include the following factors: (i) access to judicial

---

[17] *E.g.*, Fort Wayne Corrugated Paper Co. v. Anchor Hocking Glass Corp., 130 F.2d 471, 473 (3d Cir. 1942); *see also* U.C.C. § 2–306(1).

[18] U.C.C. § 2–103(1)(b).   [19] U.C.C. § 2–306(1).

[20] *See* R.A. Weaver and Assoc., Inc. v. Asphalt Constr., 587 F.2d 1315, 1322 (D. C. Cir. 1978); Michael S. Finch, *Output and Requirements Contracts: The Scope of the Duty to Remain in Business*, 14 U.C.C. L.J. 347, 351 (1982).

[21] Paramount Lithographic Plate Service, Inc. v. Hughes Printing Co., 22 U.C.C. Rep. 1135 (Pa. C. P. 1977), aff'd w/o opinion, 337 A.2d 1001 (Pa. Sup. 1977), citing McKeever, Cook & Co. v. Cannonsburg Iron Co., 138 Pa. 184, 16 A. 97, 20 A. 938 (1888, 1890).

[22] *Id.*

[23] Fort Wayne Corrugated Paper, 130 F.2d 471 (3d Cir. 1942); HML Corp. v. General Foods Corp., 365 F.2d 77, 81 (3d Cir. 1966). Conversely, if the contract is fixed-price, and the market price for the good or service increases, the project loses the ability to recover the increase in value. *See* U.C.C. § 2–306 Comment 2.

[24] *See, e.g.*, Monolith Portland Cement Co. v. Douglas Oil Co. of Cal., 303 F.2d 176 (9th Cir. 1962); *see also* In re United Cigar Stores, 8 F. Supp. 243 (S.D.N.Y. 1934).

[25] Utah Int'l, Inc. v. Colorado-Ute Elec. Ass'n, Inc., 425 F. Supp. 1093, 1096–97 (D. Colo. 1976)(dictum).

[26] *See* Finch, *supra* note 20; cf. Texas Indus., Inc. v. Brown, 218 F.2d 510, 513 (5th Cir. 1955) (similar contract provision construed to reinforce court's conclusion that leasing of plants to another party did not release requirements buyer from contract obligations).

system, (ii) length and cost of judicial process, and (iii) enforcement of arbitration provisions.

If the enforcement of such contracts is lengthy, costly, or otherwise unpredictable, the project could still be considered creditworthy. This is because the underlying economic conditions affecting the project output, and need for the output, could justify a project financing even without a firm output purchase contract in place.

§ 18.07 ASSIGNMENT OF REVENUES TO THE PROJECT LENDERS

Because of the importance of revenue produced by off-take contracts to repayment of project debt, it is typical for all payments to be made to the project lender, for credit to the project company's account. The consent of the off-take purchaser to this arrangement is discussed in Chapter 26.

§ 18.08 SELECTED PROVISIONS IN OFF-TAKE CONTRACTS

Off-take contracts are negotiated to reflect the underlying goals of the project participants. Consequently, these contracts, more than any other contract used in a project financing, tend to be unique for each transaction. There are some basic common provisions, however, which are discussed and sampled in the sections that follow.

§ 18.09 AGREEMENT FOR ALLOCATION OF A PORTION OF PRODUCTION CAPACITY

[1] Introduction

The allocation of all or a specified portion of the output capacity of a project gives a purchaser supply certainty. This allocation assures the purchaser that it has manufacturing or other production capacity available to it, though it does not actually own the production facilities.

At the same time, this allocation provides sales predictability to the project company. Either the allocated capacity will be used for production and sale to the purchaser, or the purchaser will pay a capacity or other charge to the project company in return for reserving, but not using, capacity.

[2] Sample Provision

The [Project Company] allocates to the Purchaser a percentage of the total output capacity of the [Project] equal to [___] percent, per calendar [month/quarter/year].

§ 18.10 OPTION CAPACITY

[1] Introduction

If there is more than one purchaser of a project's output, any purchaser wishing to be excused from its purchase obligation could probably escape liability if the other purchasers can purchase the capacity output no longer needed by the withdrawing purchaser. Off-take contracts will typically require that the withdrawing purchaser's capacity be offered to other purchasers. If another purchaser agrees to take the capacity, the withdrawing purchaser will be released of any obligation to pay capacity and standby charges to the project.

[2] Sample Provision

The Purchaser shall have the option, exercisable on [specify period]'s advance notice, to increase such percentage to an additional percentage of up to [___] percent.

§ 18.11 RESERVE CAPACITY

[1] Introduction

Often a project's actual capacity is greater than its designed, or nameplate, capacity. Off-take purchasers sometimes want to have the first option to purchase the excess capacity. This is particularly true in projects based on take-or-pay contracts, where the purchasers indirectly guarantee the underlying project debt.

[2] Sample Provision

If at any time the [Project Company] determines that the actual capacity of the Project is in excess of the Nameplate Capacity, and the [Project Company] determines to operate the Project to take advantage of such additional capacity, which such decision shall be in the sole and absolute discretion of the [Project Company], then it shall make available to the Purchaser an option to purchase such reserve capacity. The Purchaser shall have the option, exercisable on [*specify period*]'s advance notice, to increase its purchased capacity hereunder to an additional percentage of up to [___] percent of the total reserve capacity.

§ 18.12 STANDBY CHARGE

[1] Introduction
A standby charge is the penalty under a take-or-pay contract equal to a project's fixed costs. If the purchaser does not purchase the contracted output of the project, it must pay the standby charge. If the project company is able to sell the output to another purchaser, the amount of the standby charge payable by the nonpurchasing entity is reduced.

[2] Sample Provision
If the Purchaser does not purchase and pay for the Minimum Quantity during any calendar month, it shall pay to the [*Project Company*] the Standby Charge. The Standby Charge means an amount equal to the difference between (A) the sum of (i) the Debt Service Costs, (ii) the Fixed Operating Costs and (iii) the Minimum Equity Return, and (B) the total sales price of any Minimum Quantity sold to another purchaser (but only that portion of the sales price representing the costs described in (A)(i) through (iii)).

§ 18.13 SANCTITY OF CONTRACTS

[1] Introduction
Often project financings are based on firm cash flows founded on governmental action, such as a contract, or backed by governmental support, such as a law or regulation, or both of these. This foundation for a project financing is often crucial in many countries, particularly in those with emerging economies where such governmental action is often necessary.

An example from the United States is instructive of the problem. In its Public Utility Regulatory Policy Act of 1978[27] (PURPA), the United States required utilities to purchase electric power at state-established rates. The statute gave a project company a firm cash flow on which to structure a loan because, in general terms, once the project company produced electricity to sell to a utility, the utility was required under PURPA to buy it.

Even with this greater level of predictability over cash flow, project participants generally required that the PURPA purchase obligation be memorialized in a contract. This was because specific price, delivery, warranty, and default provisions are each significant to a financing based solely upon project revenues.

Despite the contractual form, the U.S. experience is that the governmental support that produces this firm cash flow is nonetheless subject potentially to post-contract public policy considerations. The risk is that legislatures or regulatory agencies will be pressured to improve unfavorable effects of the contract that, when negotiated and approved under then applicable economic circumstances, was reasonable to the contracting parties and the legislature or governmental agency. If the contract is altered, the effect on the sufficiency of project revenues to support debt service may be negative on, or fatal to, project viability.

[2] Analysis Under U.S. Law
The ability of a U.S. state to interfere with an existing project finance contract is governed by the law applicable to that state. For example, the constitutional prohibition on enacting any law that will substantially impair the obligation of contracts is based on the Contract Clause in the U.S. Constitution.[28] The U.S. Supreme Court has generally analyzed Contract Clause cases by balancing the rights of contracting parties against the needs of the state; all impairment is not prohibited.[29]

---

[27] 16 U.S.C. § 824a-3.

[28] "No state shall . . . pass any . . . Law impairing the Obligation of Contracts. . . ." U.S. Const. art. I, § 10, cl. 1.
  Although the authors of the U.S. Constitution intended the clause to restrict the ability of the states to enact debtor relief laws, it has been expanded by the courts. *See generally* L. Levy, Original Intent and the Framers' Constitution 124–36 (1988); B. Wright, The Contract Clause of the Constitution (1938); Felix Frankfurter, The Commerce Clause Under Marshall, Taney and Waite (1937). The clause does not apply to the federal government.

[29] The ability of a state to interfere with an existing contract may also be limited by Congressional pre-emption, which renders federal jurisdiction exclusive in that area. *See, e.g.*, National Gas Pipeline Co. v. Railroad Comm'n of Texas, 679 F.2d 51 (5th Cir. 1982).

The Contract Clause does not obliterate state police power, however. Utilities and other industries dedicated to a public purpose are subject to state police power legislation.[30] A contract with a utility is therefore not immune from a state order changing or superseding existing rates.[31]

In *Energy Reserves Group, Inc., v. Kansas Power & Light Co.*[32] the U.S. Supreme Court applied a two-prong test to determine whether a particular state action is permissible under the Contract Clause. The Court required a state to have: (i) a significant and legitimate public purpose behind the regulations and (ii) adjusted the rights and responsibilities of contracting parties based upon reasonable conditions and a character appropriate to the public purpose justifying the state action.[33]

Kansas Power & Light Co. and its gas supplier, Energy Reserves Group, Inc., had entered into two intrastate natural gas supply contracts, which included two types of indefinite price escalator clauses. One provision provided the supplier the option for redetermining the sale price no more than once every two years. The other clause provided for increases in the sale price based on increases in governmental gas price ceilings.[34] After the contract was executed, Congress deregulated gas sales, and authorized the states to regulate intrastate gas prices.[35] In response, Kansas enacted price controls.[36] The utility refused to adjust the contract price based on a provision in the Kansas statute that prohibited the enforcement of the price redetermination clause.[37] Noting that the statute was not discriminatory to the gas supplier, but instead applied to all gas suppliers, the Court opined that the law was narrowly crafted to promote an important state interest in protecting utility ratepayers from market price fluctuations caused by federal deregulation of gas.[38]

Significant to the Court was the foreseeable impact of the governmental regulation on the gas contracts. Kansas had regulated natural gas sales for many years.[39] Moreover, the natural gas contracts were explicitly subject to state regulation.[40]

In *Keystone Bituminous Coal Assn. v. DeBenedictis*,[41] the U.S. Supreme Court ruled that a Pennsylvania statute that restricts mining operations to prevent subsidence damage does not violate the Contract Clause. The statute requires coal mine companies to leave in place sufficient coal for support of publicly used buildings, cemeteries, and perennial streams,[42] and regulations require the companies to pay repair costs if any damage is caused, although surface owners previously waived any claims to damages.[43] Stating that the Court will not second guess the state legislature's conclusion on how to resolve the problem, the Court ruled that no violation of the Contract Clause was found because the state has a strong public interest to prevent subsidence damage.[44]

The *Energy Reserves* and *Keystone* decisions suggest that project financings based on predictability in contract terms are not necessarily predictable. Areas that government highly regulates are subject to continuing regulation, and possibly contractual abrogation, without a violation of the Contract Clause.

[3] Retroactivity and Settled Expectations – The Effect of Governmental Actions on Existing Contracts

The question of the retroactive effect of governmental actions on existing project finance

---

[30] Contracts are generally subject to the state power "to safeguard the vital interests" of the people of a state. Energy Reserves Group, Inc. v. Kansas Power & Light Co., 459 U.S. 400, 410 (1983) (quoting Home Bldg. & Loan Ass'n v. Blaisdell, 290 U.S. 398, 434 (1934)). Supercession and annulment of existing contracts is permissible if the state action is based on a valid public purpose. *E.g.*, Exxon Corp. v. Eagerton, 462 U.S. 176, 190 (1983); Allied Structural Steel Co. v. Spannaus, 438 U.S. 234, 241–42 (1978).

[31] *See* Block v. Hirsh, 256 U.S. 135, 137 (1921). *See also* Munn v. Illinois, 94 U.S. 113, 133–34 (1876) (dedication of private property to a public use subjects the property to public regulation).

[32] 459 U.S. 400 (1983).   [33] *Id.* at 411–13.

[34] *Id.* at 403–405.   [35] *Id.* at 405–406.

[36] *Id.* at 407–408.   [37] *Id.* at 408.

[38] *Id.* at 421.

[39] *Id.* at 414 n.8; compare Allied Structural Steel v. Spannaus, 438 U.S. 234 (1978) (law under Contract Clause scrutiny affected an area not typically regulated by the state).

[40] *Id.* at 416; *see, e.g.*, Hudson County Water Co. v. McCarter, 209 U.S. 349, 357 (1908) ("One whose rights, such as they are, are subject to state restriction, cannot remove them from the power of the State by making a contract about them.").

[41] 480 U.S. 470 (1987).   [42] *Id.* at 476.

[43] *Id.* at 477.   [44] *Id.* at 506.

contracts and transactions concerns project lenders and other participants, especially when legislatures and executive agencies question the appropriateness of existing laws and regulations in light of changing economic conditions.[45] In the United States, the question arises in both Contract Clause cases, which are discussed above, and in the context of a taking of property without due process under the Fifth[46] and Fourteenth[47] Amendments to its Constitution.

In general, the U.S. courts are opposed to retroactive legislation, traditionally basing this opposition on a need for stability[48] and on a reluctance to permit the legislatures to affect selective classes of citizens.[49] Where the retroactive legislation involves an emergency, the U.S. Supreme Court has traditionally tolerated the retroactive impact.[50] Similarly, the Court tolerates the retroactive effect of legislation that ratifies prior governmental conduct or adjusts an administrative action.[51]

In other types of retroactive legislation, however, the Court closely examines the impact to determine whether the legislature has overcome the general judicial distaste for retroactive laws.

If the law affects a remedy and not a property right, or if the law bears a rational relationship to a governmental purpose, the retroactive impact is generally upheld.

For example, in *Chase Securities Corp. v. Donaldson*,[52] the plaintiff was barred from bringing a Blue Sky Law action because of a lapse of the statute of limitations. During a retrial and appeal, the Minnesota legislature removed the statute of limitations from certain categories of Blue Sky Law violations, including the type of violation about which the plaintiff complained.[53] The plaintiff reasserted its claim, and the defendant contended that the retroactive law violated the due process protections of the Fourteenth Amendment.[54] The Court rejected the defendant's contention, basing its decision on the distinction between the plaintiff's right to seek recovery, which was not affected by the law, and its remedy for doing so, which was the focal point of the law.[55]

Where property rights are involved, the Court applies a type of rationality test to determine the constitutionality of the retroactive effect. In *Railroad Retirement Board v. Alton Railroad Co.*,[56] a substantive due process decision, the Court voided legislation that required railroad companies to establish pension funds for workers no longer employed by the companies. The Court presumably concluded that the right of a company to terminate employment relationships and the associated liability outweighed the governmental interest involved.

The precedential value of *Alton Railroad* is limited, however, because of the decline of substantive due process, evidenced recently in the Court's decision in *Usery v. Turner Elkhorn Mining Co.*[57] In *Usery*, the Court considered the constitutionality of the black lung benefits legislation. The legislation required mine operators to pay benefits to miners who were no longer employed before the effective date of the law.[58] The Court upheld the legislation under a due process challenge, noting that retroactive legislation is not unconstitutional simply "because it upsets otherwise settled expectations."[59] Applying a rational relationship

---

[45] *See generally* Charles Hochman, *The Supreme Court and the Constitutionality of Retroactive Legislation*, 73 Harv. L. Rev. 692 (1960); W. David Slawson, *Constitutional and Legislative Considerations in Retroactive Lawmaking*, 48 Calif. L. Rev. 216 (1960); Ray Greenblatt, Judicial Limitations on Retroactive Civil Legislation, 51 Nw. U. L. Rev. 540 (1956); Seeman, *The Retroactive Effect of Repeal Legislation*, 27 Ky. L.J. 75 (1938); Elmer Smead, *The Rule Against Retroactive Legislation: A Basic Principle of Jurisprudence*, 20 Minn. L. Rev. 775 (1936).

[46] U.S. Const. amend. V. *E.g.*, Norman v. Baltimore & O. R. Co., 294 U.S. 240, 304–5 (1935); *see generally* Hochman, *supra* note 45, at 693–94.

[47] U.S. Const. amend. XIV. *E.g.*, Chase Sec. Corp. v. Donaldson, 325 U.S. 304, 315–16 (1945); *see generally* Hochman, *supra* note 45, at 693–94.

[48] *See* J. Rawls, A Theory of Justice 238 (1971).

[49] *See* Hochman, *supra* note 45, at 692–93.

[50] *E.g.*, Lichter v. U.S., 334 U.S. 742 (1948) (Fifth Amendment challenge to Renegotiation Act of 1942, which permitted the federal government to renegotiate existing contracts with private citizens to avoid profiteering from wartime conditions); *but see* Louisville Joint Stock Land Bank v. Radford, 295 U.S. 555 (1935) (emergency depression measure held invalid).

[51] *E.g.*, FHA v. The Darlington, Inc., 358 U.S. 84 (1958) (ratification of Federal Housing Administration policy by Congress found not violative of Fifth Amendment); Anderson v. Mt. Clemens Pottery Co., 328 U.S. 680 (1946) (retroactive law which cured defect in existing law upheld).

[52] 325 U.S. 304 (1945).   [53] *Id.* at 307.
[54] *Id.* at 308.   [55] *Id.* at 311.
[56] 295 U.S. 330 (1935).   [57] 428 U.S. 1 (1976).
[58] *Id.* at 8–9.   [59] *Id.* at 16.

test, the Court concluded that the law justifiably allocated mine work health costs to mine operators.[60]

Similarly, there are no substantive due process restraints on the power of Congress to legislate under the Commerce Clause, absent an express Constitutional limit on that power such as a reservation to the states of the power to regulate.[61] The power of Congress to legislate under the Commerce Clause extends to the power to abrogate existing contracts.[62]

The ability of U.S. legislatures to affect contractual arrangements, as evidenced by *Usery*, is somewhat unsettling in the project finance context because a project financing is based on "settled expectations." The traditional U.S. judicial bias toward retroactive legislation can be overcome and upset the reliability of assumptions upon which the financing is based. Although property rights are affected, if legislation bears a rational relationship to a governmental purpose, the U.S. Supreme Court will presumably uphold the retroactive effect of the legislation.[63]

[4] Lessons for International Project Finance

The experience of the United States with the sanctity of project finance contracts is as much based in its unique laws as it is in its economy. The real lesson of this experience is that, with certain qualifications, governments and off-take purchasers may have significant incentives to escape from, or allow others to escape from, less than successful business arrangements. The challenge for project finance participants is not only to examine the laws that could interfere with the predictability of contract arrangements (their sanctity), but also to examine the underlying economics to understand if the contractual terms are justified over the life of the project.

[5] Stability of Contracts in Emerging Markets – The Dabhol Project

After years of work to structure, negotiate, finance, and close a project finance transaction, renegotiation of key project contracts seems incongruent to the basic principles of project finance – stability and predictability. Yet, project participants often return to the bargaining table during the deal, either to cure an unanticipated problem, or to respond to changing economic or political situations in the host country.[64] Renegotiation can also take place where one of the participants has defaulted under one of its project obligations.

These words came alive in India in 1995. The breach of a long-term power purchase agreement between the Indian state of Maharashtra and an affiliate of Enron Corporation, a U.S. energy company, presents a clear example of the risk of the loss of a contract in a project financing caused by state action.[65]

In that project, the state of Maharashtra agreed to purchase electrical power produced at the US$2.8 billion facility at a negotiated rate, and to assume the foreign exchange risk. Enron was

---

[60] *Id.* at 19.

[61] U.S. Const. art. I, § 8, cl. 3; *see, e.g.,* Gibbons. v. Ogden, 22 U.S. 1, 196–97 (1824); Nebbia v. New York, 291 U.S. 502 (1934).

[62] Norman v. B & O. R. Co., 294 U.S. 240, 307–10 (1935).

[63] Abrogation of such a contract is not an unconstitutional taking under the Takings Clause. U.S. Const. amend. V. Although economic regulation may destroy value, if there is no physical invasion of property, and the regulation is in the public good, there is no "taking." Nor is the abrogation a violation of the Equal Protection Clause. U.S. Const. amend V. *See, e.g.,* Hodel v. Indiana, 452 U.S. 314, 331 (1981) (economic regulations will not be invalidated if rationally related to a governmental purpose unless a fundamental right is abridged or a suspect class created).

[64] *See* Jeswald W. Salacuse, *Renegotiating International Project Agreements,* 24 Fordham Int'l L. J. 1319 (2001); Abba Kolo and Thomas W. Walde, Renegotiation and Contract Adaptation in International Investment Projects, 1 J. World. Inv. 5 (2000).

[65] *See generally* Enron Corp. Unit Receives Green Light for a Power Plant in India, Wall St. J., Aug. 11, 1994; Marcus W. Brauchli, *A Gandhi Legacy: Clash Over Power Plant in India Reflects Deeper Struggle With Its Economic Soul,* Wall St. J., Apr. 27, 1995, at A1, A6; Marcus W. Brauchli, *Enron Project is Scrapped By India State,* Wall St. J., Aug. 4, 1995, at A3; Miriam Jordan, *Enron Pursues Arbitration in Dispute Over Project Canceled by Indian State,* Wall St. J., Aug. 7, 1995, at A9B; John Bussey, *Enron Sees Compromise on India Plant: Company Offers to Revise Pricing Pact But Keeps Its Legal Options Open,* Wall St. J., Aug. 23, 1995, at A8; Miriam Jordan, *State Government in India to Rethink Enron Power Plant,* Wall St. J., Sept. 25, 1995, at A9; *Enron and AES Unit Progress on Stalled Projects in India,* Wall St. J., Oct. 31, 1995, at A15; *Enron Begins Talks With an Indian State on Big Power Project,* Wall St. J., Nov. 6, 1995, at A19F; Miriam Jordan, *Enron, Indian State Revive Power Project,* Wall St. J., Nov. 22, 1995, at A4; Terzah Ewing, *Enron Resumes Building Dabhol Plant in India, Finishes a Phase of Financing,* Wall St. J., Dec. 11, 1996, at A4; Miriam Jordan, *Enron of U.S. Settles India Power Dispute,* Wall St. J., Jan. 9, 1996, at A6.

promised a 16 percent rate of return on its investment in the facility.

Soon after a power purchase agreement was negotiated and signed, the financial closing occurred, and construction began, the makeup of the government of Maharashtra changed. In essence, the new government justified the action by asserting that the prior government had negotiated a bad deal for India (expensive power prices; project too costly and awarded without competitive bid; environmentally unsound). Seemingly, the new government failed to recognize the complexities of project finance and the purpose of long-term contracts to support project financings. Alternatively, perhaps, it was a politically centered move in which the infrastructure needs of India were subordinated to short-term political gains. Perhaps it was simply that India, like many emerging countries, was still finding its way from colonialism to industrialization.[66] In any event, the move succeeded in halting infrastructure development and finance in India – the unilateral termination of the contract by the government sent shock waves throughout the project finance industry. Enron filed for arbitration of the dispute, but offered to renegotiate the contract.

By the end of 1996, renegotiations had culminated in the settlement of the dispute and the resumption of construction. The renegotiated project resulted in a reduction in the capital cost and the power price. Also, the state received an equity interest in the project.

What are the lessons learned from this project? Although principles of international law likely required that the state of Maharashtra perform the contract,[67] the state made allegations about the negotiation process that, if true, could have excused the state from performance, or at least lessened its obligations. Yet, the lengthy process of determining this in the courts or arbitration would have destroyed the project. However, price concessions by Enron would suggest that Enron was making too much money from the project. Still, if the state were permitted to attack the project, a dangerous message would be sent to all emerging countries about the sanctity of contracts and the risk tolerance of project finance.

Enron made the correct choice. To a certain degree, Enron was the victim of a poorly planned national energy strategy by India. Much of the problem could have been avoided if a competitive bid program was used. Much of what Enron did was to apply an ex post facto bidding process to the project, thereby assuring the state (and the rest of the emerging countries) that the state received the same type of deal (perhaps better) than it would have received in a transparent arrangement.

Some have feared that Enron's action would chill project development, destroy stability in international contracts, and prove that Western developers are exploitive of emerging markets.[68] I suspect it did not. Rather, it was an intelligent response to the underlying problem of a basic lack of transparency in the process and a reassessment of risks that obviously led to price concessions in which Enron had confidence.

Will similar situations be avoided in the future? Likely yes, if competitive bidding arrangements and similar transparent processes continue to be developed, and as public confidence in those processes increases. Yet, at least one commentator has predicted a possible re-emergence of nationalistic, and perhaps socialistic, attitudes that will result in similar attacks by host governments.[69]

---

[66] Marcus W. Brauchli, *A Ghandi Legacy: Clash Over Power Plant in India Reflects Deeper Struggle With Its Economic Soul*, WALL ST. J., Apr. 27, 1995, at A1, A6.

[67] The legal doctrine of *pacta sunt servanda* holds that every international agreement, like the repudiated agreement in the Dabhol project, binds the parties thereto and requires that it be performed in good faith. The legal theory, based on Western European principles of natural law, is that no government should have the right to change an existing contract to further its own political, social, or economic goals. RESTATEMENT (THIRD) OF THE FOREIGN RELATIONS LAW OF THE U.S. 321 (1987); *see e.g.*, Sapphire Int'l Petroleums Ltd. v. National Iranian Oil Co., 35 I.L.R. 136, 181 (Arb. Award 1963); *see also* Terence Daintith & Ian Gault, *Pacta Sunt Servanda and the Licensing and Taxation of North Sea Oil Production*, 8 CAMBRIAN L. REV. 27 (1977). The doctrine extends to state-controlled companies, which are not insulated from liability. *E.g.*, McKesson Corp. v. Islamic Republic of Iran, 52 F.3d 346, 352 (D. C. Cir. 1995) (separate existence of state-controlled companies that carry out state roles or policies does not shield the state from liability).

[68] Danielle Mazzini, *Stable International Contracts in Emerging Markets: An Endangered Species*, 15 B. U. Int'l L. J. 343, 355 (1997). *See also* Bernard Wysocki, Jr., *Some Painful Lessons on Emerging Markets*, WALL ST. J., Sept. 18, 1995, at A-1.

[69] Thomas W. Waelde & George Ndi, *Stabilizing International Investment Commitments: International Law Versus*

There are several considerations that should be kept in mind when negotiating this type of project:

- the underlying contract must be carefully drafted to clearly obligate the off-take purchaser to take the project output, including provisions that clearly articulate if, when, and how contractual terms can be reconsidered (such as termination for cause, termination for convenience, termination for breach, changes in the capital facility, rights to operate or sell project after termination);

Contract Interpretation, 31 Tex. Int'l. L. J. 216, 217–18 (1996). *See also* Michael D. Ramsey, Acts of State and Foreign Sovereign Obligations, 39 Harv. Int'l L. J. 1 (1998).

- consider use of a stabilization clause, which expressly forbids the unilateral termination of the contract by the host government, other than based on those events expressly provided for in the contract;[70] and
- consider giving the host government an equity interest in the project, and ensure that the contract negotiation is a result of a competitive bid or some other process that ensures transparency.[71]

[70] Stabilization clauses are discussed in Chapter 14.

[71] For an excellent discussion of factors to consider in the renegotiation of international project contracts, *see* Selacuse, *supra* note 64.

CHAPTER NINETEEN

POWER SALES AGREEMENTS

§ 19.01 INTRODUCTION

In a power project, a power sales agreement, or power purchase agreement as the purchaser calls it, is the linchpin of an energy project financing. This agreement sets forth the obligation of the project company to produce power for sale and for the power purchaser to buy it. It is from this transaction that the funds flow to pay debt service, operating costs, and an equity return. It must fulfill, therefore, the dual role of financing document and operating document.

The funds, of course, will not flow unless the power purchaser is creditworthy; that is, the power purchaser must have sufficient cash to pay its bills, as proven by past, present, and expected future financial performance. To the extent that this is not present, credit enhancement, such as a guarantee by a creditworthy central government or multilateral support, is needed.[1]

§ 19.02 REVENUE CONTRACTS IN TRANSNATIONAL PROJECTS

In some countries, a project financing, which is based on the underlying cash flow from the revenue-producing power contracts of the project is a new concept. Project finance contract provisions that are standard in the United States and Great Britain are either not yet developed, or relatively recent in concept, in these countries. An example of this type of provision, considered essential to a successful energy project financing, is a definitive obligation for a utility's purchase of the project's energy output at a defined price.

§ 19.03 DEVELOPMENT OBLIGATIONS

Developmental activities for a project are often cumbersome. The acquisition of land and property rights necessary to install transmission lines and equipment, application for and issuance of permits, and other development activities are often fraught with uncertainties and delay. In some projects, it is often prudent for the power purchaser to undertake either to assist the project company in these functions or to obtain them for it. In some projects, the power purchaser also assists the project company in negotiating the underlying project contracts for such contracts as fuel supply and transportation. In the end, however, the project company must have in place, to its satisfaction, all the necessary elements of a project financing. Yet, as discussed in the next section, the power purchaser has an interest in the completion of the developmental tasks according to its needs.

---

[1] For an excellent overview of the risks presented in a power sales agreement, *see* John G. Manuel, *Common Contractual Risk Allocations in International Power Projects*, 1996 COLUM. BUS. L. REV. 37 (1996). *See also* William M. Stelwagon, *Financing Private Energy Projects in the Third World*, 37 CATH. LAW. 45 (1996).

§ 19.04 PERFORMANCE MILESTONES

[1] Generally

The completion of construction and availability of the energy facility to meet the power needs of a power purchaser by a date certain are important to the power purchaser. It may have cancelled or declined to negotiate other power purchase agreements, made capacity commitments to regulatory authorities, or postponed construction plans for other capacity construction. To the extent the power contracted for is not available, it will face capacity constraints and possibly monetary damages.

To safeguard the integrity of its planning decisions, the power purchaser typically requires the project company to meet "milestones." Milestones are a series of important events that must be completed by specified dates if the project is to be completed on time. Through proper due diligence, negotiation of milestones into the provisions of the construction contract, and the addition of reasonable time periods, the project sponsor can guard against risk for milestone delays.

Examples of milestones, also called *conditions precedent*, which must be satisfied after or contemporaneously with contract execution, include payment of a contract deposit to evidence commitment, evidence of ownership and control over the development of the project, and obtaining any preliminary governmental approval. Conditions precedent that will need to be satisfied before commercial operation of the facility include energy tariff or rate approval; securing important permits; execution of construction, fuel, and operating agreements; evidence of insurance; financial and equity closings; construction completion and satisfactory facility testing; and necessary documentation and data for the power purchaser to perform an interconnection study and to design and construct interconnection facilities. By the required date for commercial operation, operation at the contract-specified levels must be achieved.

Failure of the project company to satisfy these milestones can arise from a myriad of factors, such as construction delays. This failure often allows the power purchaser to delay the start of capacity payments to the project company. In addition, the power purchaser might be granted the right to benefit from any security deposited by the project company with the power purchaser, such as drawing on a letter of credit, to pay liquidated damages for delay. In some projects, a "sunset" date is included in the power purchase agreement that gives the power purchaser the right to terminate the agreement if the milestone of commercial operation is not achieved on a timely basis.

The project company is typically not responsible for all types of delays, however. If, for example, a political action of the host government delays the project, the project company is excused from its performance obligation for the period of time necessary to alleviate the cause of the delay. The power purchaser, particularly if it is owned by the government, is considered better able to control political risks than the project company.

[2] Approval of Project Contracts

One important aspect for the power purchaser in determining the viability of the project relates to the project contracts. A host of agreements will need to be negotiated and executed by the project sponsor before a project can proceed. Often, the power purchaser will want to review and approve the terms of these agreements, in addition to setting a milestone date for their execution. This is particularly true when the power purchaser is paying, in the power purchase price, a portion of the project's fuel and operating costs as a direct pass-through.

The power purchaser, it might be argued, need not analyze the contracts because the financing entity will do an adequate job of reviewing them. This is a fool's paradise for the power purchaser. Each of the power purchaser and the financing entity has different risks and rewards from a project financing. As an example, the power purchaser is likely to be in a long-term contractual relationship with the project company, well beyond the term of the underlying project debt. The long-term goals of the power purchaser may not be the same as the goals of the lender. Therefore, a power purchaser cannot safely rely on the lender for a project appraisal.

Any review of project contracts will need to be done expeditiously by the power purchaser. Consequently, provisions typically provide a limited time for comment, restrictions on arbitrary behavior, and deemed approval if the power purchaser ignores the contracts submitted for review and no comments are received.

[3] Financial Closing

Unless the project sponsor funds construction costs from its own financial resources, project construction will not proceed until financial closing has taken place and the project lender advances funds for that purpose. Consequently, milestones tied to the release of construction funds are important to the power purchaser. It is usual for the power purchaser to require that financial closing be achieved by a date certain or the agreement terminates.

[4] Penalties for Missed Milestones

Generally. If one of the project milestones is missed, the parties need a remedy to address the adverse effects of the failure. Possible remedies include reports to the power purchaser about the missed milestone and the course that will be followed to achieve it; a periodically paid damage amount (daily or monthly damage payments, refundable if the project is completed by a date certain) from a creditworthy entity; or even contract termination if the project is not or cannot be completed by a date certain.

Delayed Entry Into Commercial Operation. As discussed above, a delay in the completion of construction and availability of an energy facility to a power purchaser by a date certain can result in capacity constraints and possibly monetary damages for the power purchaser under other contracts. If the date is not achieved, the power sales agreement may require that penalty payments be due to the power purchaser from the project company. The project company is typically excused from meeting the completion date, however, for force majeure events and for delays caused by the power purchaser.

Third-party action or inaction can also delay project completion. However, it is customary that the project company not be excused from meet-

ing the scheduled completion date because of a delay caused by a third party. This is because the damages associated with such a delay can be recovered by the project company from the third party, particularly if it is a party to one of the other project contracts.

Failure to Construct Facility. If the project is never constructed, the power purchaser is sometimes compensated for this failure by the project company. Because the project company, as a thinly capitalized special-purpose entity, will have no financial resources to pay these damages, some form of financial security, such as a letter of credit or guarantee from a creditworthy entity, is needed.

Shortfall in Nameplate Capacity. If the capacity of the project to produce energy is less than the estimated nameplate capacity agreed to in the power purchase agreement, relief for the purchaser is generally provided. The target availability the project company generally commits to achieve is 82.5 percent to 85 percent of net nameplate capacity for a coal-fired power station and 90 percent or more of net nameplate capacity for a gas-fired power plant.

While the exact nature of the relief to the power purchaser for lower capacity is subject to negotiation, at a minimum some damages are payable while the project is repaired. After a period is afforded the project company to bring the capacity to its rating, and the project fails to do so, a damage payment is generally made to the power purchaser to compensate it for the consequences of the capacity shortfall. The payment is usually used to reduce the project debt because the project will be unable to generate sufficient revenues to service the debt outstanding.

[5] Commercial Operations

An important milestone is commercial operations. At this point, the project is able to provide safe, reliable power to the power purchaser. A procedure is typically established in the agreement that specifies the performance tests that determine when commercial operation is achieved. These tests confirm operating characteristics of the facility, the amount of reliable capacity, and safety issues.

If the project milestone of commercial operations is not satisfied by the date required in the contract, any of several negotiated consequences will apply. The contract could terminate completely, without liability of the project company to the power purchaser. Alternatively, liquidated damages could be due to the power purchaser for each day of delay, and if commercial operations were still not achieved after a period of time, the contract would terminate either with or without additional damages due.

A related topic is whether the project company is entitled to operate the project early. If so, the price charged for the power must be agreed upon. It might be an energy-only payment, in which the power purchaser compensates the project company for its operating expenses (plus a profit) but not fixed charges already included in the construction budget. Or, the power purchaser might decline to purchase the early power and agree that it can be sold to third parties. In some situations, a bonus could be justified, particularly where the power purchaser is buying power from other sources at a high cost or is generating its own power at a higher cost.

In some situations, such as economic or national emergencies, or in a scenario of temporary overcapacity, the power purchaser may want to delay commercial operations. If this flexibility is desired, the contract should contemplate the payments that will be due from the power purchaser to the project company as compensation for the delay and the amount of advance notice needed. Obviously, the further the project is in its construction schedule, the more expensive this option becomes for the power purchaser.

[6] Force Majeure

In general, a force majeure extends the date of required compliance under the contract, but this is not always the case. In some power purchase agreements, a maximum delay caused by a force majeure is established, beyond which no extensions can be made even if the force majeure continues to affect performance. This provides the power purchaser with the ability to pursue other sources of power in areas where there is no force majeure delay.

§ 19.05 OBLIGATION TO DELIVER POWER; OBLIGATION TO TAKE POWER

The structure of the obligation of the power purchaser to accept, and the project company to deliver, power is the most important provision in a power purchase agreement. This obligation forms the basis for the credit support of the project financing. Excuses for performance under these contracts can affect the operation of the project and the predictability of cash flow.

For this reason, the excuses to the power purchaser's obligation to purchase power are limited in scope. Force majeure events generally excuse the obligations of the parties. Other excuses include emergencies in the power purchaser's system and pre-emergencies. System emergencies are conditions on the power purchaser's system likely to result in imminent, significant service disruption, or to endanger persons or property. Pre-emergency conditions are conditions on the power purchaser's system, prior to an actual system emergency, that could reasonably be expected to result or lead to a system emergency.

Most power purchase agreements used in a project financing are output contracts. These contracts allocate the risk of business termination and quantity variations to the power purchaser. Because in an output contract the power purchaser agrees to accept and pay for all of the power that the project produces for sale, the power purchaser, not the project company, bears the risk of demand uncertainty.

The contract will specify the kind of power to be delivered. Options include intermittent energy, fixed energy, or capacity and dispatchable energy. Because demand for power fluctuates based on such things as weather conditions, these agreements often include dispatch provisions. The dispatch provisions permit the power purchaser to select the periods during which it will purchase power. Capacity charges, designed to compensate the project company for its fixed costs, are paid during the period the project is not dispatched, however.

In general, the power purchaser will agree to purchase all of the capacity available from the project, up to a specified level. To the extent the capacity is not available, penalties are generally imposed. Because of this, the capacity level needs to be set at a realistic level. Because energy demand fluctuates based on the time of day and the season of the year, the purchase obligation also varies according to the same variables.

§ 19.06 DELIVERY POINT AND INTERCONNECTION

[1] Delivery Point

The power contract must state the point of delivery of the power sold. Often, this is accomplished by adding a set of line drawings as an exhibit to the agreement that specifies the point of interconnection.

[2] Interconnection Facilities

The contract must allocate responsibility for design, construction, ownership, and maintenance of the interconnection facility and upgrades to the power purchaser's system needed to accept deliveries of power from the project. The project company will need all interconnection facilities to be operable when the project is complete so that deliveries can be made to the power purchaser.

[3] Power of Eminent Domain

Whether the utility has the legal authority to acquire land and other real estate interests at little or no cost is particularly important. This right is an important cost-savings tool for use in acquiring land for substations, transmission lines, and other necessary interconnection facilities.

Even where a power purchaser has this right, however, it may be reluctant to incur political or citizen opposition by actually using it. This is particularly true in developing countries where land in urban areas is overdeveloped and would require relocation of, and sacrifice by, impoverished people for the benefit of business interests. Attention to the rights of indigenous people in rural or undeveloped areas will also cause the power purchaser to be reluctant to exercise any rights it has.

[4] Wheeling

If it is not physically possible or technically feasible to interconnect directly with the power purchaser, wheeling arrangements will be necessary and should be addressed in the contract. Among the contractual considerations are responsibility for wheeling arrangements, wheeling costs, and transmission line losses.

[5] Land Rights

In addition to the power of eminent domain, other rights concerning land are important in a power purchase agreement. The agreement should include mutual rights for access to and use of real estate of the other party. Access may be necessary for repair and maintenance of property located on the other's real estate, including interconnection facilities. As discussed in Chapter 26, these important real property interests must provide for assignability to the project lender and any subsequent purchaser of the project from the lender.

§ 19.07 PRICE FOR POWER

[1] Introduction

A project financing of an energy project is based on the cash flow under the power sales agreement for power produced. The price established must provide a predictable revenue stream.

[2] The Political Side of Energy Rates – A Lesson Learned in the United States

An important lesson learned in the United States is that in its power industry energy rates are political and economic. To the extent they are uneconomic, political forces will move to upset them. It is the same in developing countries. Despite competitive bidding, well-crafted documents, and elaborate power contract pricing provisions, the ultimate rate charged for power to the ultimate users must meet economic realities. In short, the maximum price for power that the ratepayer can bear must be factored into the negotiation discussion.

[3] General Forms of Power Contract Price Provisions

Take-or-Pay. A take-or-pay contract is the term generally used to refer to a contractual obligation between a power purchaser and a power seller in which the purchaser agrees to make payments to the seller for energy capacity in return for maintaining the capacity to produce and deliver energy. Payments for capacity are made whether or not energy is actually generated at the purchaser's request. The payment obligation of the buyer for the capacity component is unconditional. Thus, even if no power is delivered, the payment obligation exists. If energy is produced, the purchaser pays for both the energy produced at the plant and the capacity of the plant.

Take-and-Pay. A take-or-pay contract is in contrast to a take-and-pay power contract. With a take-and-pay contract, the buyer is only obligated to pay if the product or service is actually delivered. If power is delivered to the purchaser, the purchaser is obligated to pay certain definite amounts to the project sponsor. The risk that sufficient power will be sold to satisfy debt obligations, operating costs, and an equity return are firmly with the project company.

[4] Capacity and Energy Payments Structure

The price for power in a power sales agreement used to support a project financing is typically divided into two components: a capacity payment and an energy payment. These components create the revenue stream necessary to support the financing.

[5] Capacity Payment

Capacity rates will be either fixed or variable. These rates might also be subject to a floor, front-loaded, or levelized. Each of these is discussed in detail below. Whatever the approach, in a project financing, the capacity payments required under the contract must be sufficient to enable the project sponsor to pay debt service payments and fixed operating costs.

The capacity payment is designed to provide financial support for the *fixed* costs of a project and the equity return on the project sponsor's investment. It also includes recovery of project development costs of the project sponsor. As the foundation of revenue to repay fixed project costs, the capacity payment is paid throughout the initial term of the power contract and is based on the capacity of the facility for energy production. If the facility is capable of producing power, the capacity charge is paid by the power purchaser, whether or not the power is actually purchased.

The rationale for this approach is that these costs represent expenses that the project company incurs whether or not the facility is dispatched. In fact, with minor exceptions, if the purchasing utility had built and owned the facility itself, rather than contracting with the project company to purchase energy from it, these costs would have been incurred by the utility.

The fixed costs include operating and maintenance expenses for the energy facility, such as maintenance and spare parts; fixed fuel costs, such as demand charges, pipeline costs and fuel transportation costs; financing expenses, such as principal, interest, letter of credit fees, and commitment fees; and insurance premiums for casualty, business interruption, and political risk insurance.

The return on equity investment is an important part of the capacity charge. The rate of return that is recovered by the project sponsor varies with the risks it assumes. In some countries, a maximum rate of return is established by government policy.

Finally, the recovery of project development expenses by the project sponsor is included as part of the capacity charge. Development expenses include construction costs of the facility, permitting costs, legal expenses, engineering services, and environmental development costs.

Fixed or Variable. Capacity charges can be based on a fixed amount for each year of the contract or vary with changing conditions. Variable capacity charges are not usually predictable enough to support a project financing.

Floor. Capacity charges, subject to variation over time based on changed circumstances or facility performance, are often subject to a floor. Adjustments cannot be made to the capacity charge to the extent the price would fall below this floor, which is typically an amount needed to service project debt. This provides sufficient certainty to support a project finance transaction.

Front-Loaded. At the beginning of commercial operations, a project company will have borrowed a large amount of debt, which needs to be serviced. In some situations, the capacity price for the power is structured to be greater in the early years of contract performance, when more debt is outstanding and debt service costs are higher, than the later contract years.

The front-end-loaded approach presents collateral security issues for the power purchaser. These are discussed in detail later in this chapter.

Back-Loaded. The opposite approach is to back-load the capacity payments. Under this pricing alternative, debt amortization schedules provide for higher principal amortization in the later years of the contract. This approach is used when energy prices are predicted to be higher in the later years of the contract term. Politically, this approach can be useful in developing countries that want to avoid large increases in power rates necessary to support project financings. Alternatively, equity contributions or distributions can be modified to offset the heavy interest payments in the early years of a project. Historically, however, the capital markets have not generally agreed to these solutions, favoring front-loaded power contracts, instead.

Levelized. The middle approach is levelized capacity payments. Under a levelized approach, capacity payments are the same (level) over time, regardless of the amount of debt outstanding. The payment amount is determined by calculating an average present value of a best-estimate, long-term projection of a project's fixed-cost expenditures and needs.

[6] Adjustment to Capacity Charges

The risk that will be taken for unexpected costs is important for the project company to consider in determining the amount of the capacity charge. These include increases in construction costs, foreign debt interest rate margins and maturities, operating and maintenance cost variations, inflation affecting operations, foreign exchange fluctuations, domestic financing rates and maturities, changes in law, and changes in taxes. To the extent the power company bears the risk, the capacity charge will increase. The goal of such an approach is to ensure that the project company is in the same position it was in under the contract had the change not occurred. To the extent the power purchaser bears the risk, no increase will be awarded.

The allocation of these risks varies from project to project. Where the power purchaser is a governmental entity, however, private-sector disciplines (an advantage of privatization) typically result in the project company bearing the risks of increases in construction costs, foreign debt interest rate margins and maturities, and operating and maintenance cost variations. The other costs are typically allocated to the power purchaser – inflation, foreign exchange rate fluctuations, domestic financing rates and maturities, changes in law, and changes in taxes.

For example, where a change in a governmental regulation increases the construction price, the power purchaser is obligated to pay a higher capacity rate. This is because the power purchaser is thought to be in a better position than the project company to control political events. Allocation of this risk to the power purchaser is particularly justified in developing countries where many power purchasers are still owned by the government.

[7] Energy Payment

In contrast, energy payments are payable by the power purchaser only if energy is produced. Like capacity payments, energy payments can be fixed or variable, floor rates, forecasted, or indexed.

Energy payments are calculated to cover the *variable* operating expenses of the energy facility, such as fuel costs and variable operating and maintenance expenses. Examples include sales taxes and maintenance costs determined by project operation.

The energy payment assumes project operation. It is paid throughout the term of the power contract, based on the actual energy output of the facility. No energy payment is due during periods in which the facility is not in operation.

The variability of the components that constitute the energy payment, such as fuel costs, is subject to change over time. Consequently, the project company desires to either pass through the increased costs of fuel to the power purchaser by charging a higher energy rate that matches the increase or adjust the cost of fuel pursuant to an appropriate index, such as inflation or cost of fuel in a particular market.

Fixed or Variable. Energy charges can be based on a fixed amount for each year of the contract or vary with changing conditions. Adjustments, or variability, are discussed below. A variable energy price, coupled with a fixed capacity rate, is a frequently used pricing formula for energy project financings.

Floor. Energy charges, subject to adjustment over time based on changed circumstances, are often subject to a minimum or floor amount. Adjustments cannot be made to the energy charge to the extent the price would fall below this floor, which is typically an amount needed to pay certain operating costs.

Forecasted. A forecasted approach bases energy prices on a forecast of future energy rates.

Indexed. Indexed energy rates adjust based on an agreed-upon index. Example indices include industry price indices, utility fuel price averages, and fuel costs. Where an indexed approach is used, it is wise to include a mechanism for the parties to change the index if it is no longer available, if it is modified in its components, or if it otherwise fails to track costs fairly.

[8] **Fuel Costs**
The allocation of price risk for fuel costs is typically placed on the project company. The assumption is that because fuel costs are not fixed but rather are variable, the project company is best able to manage the risk. Nonetheless, the power purchaser typically has the right to approve the fuel arrangements and underlying contracts because of their importance to the project's success.

However, some projects are captive, or tied, to a fuel supply. Examples include projects that obtain fuel from a dedicated coal mine or dedicated gas reserve.

The risk of fuel price increases is sometimes shifted to the power purchaser. If so, the power purchaser will take an active role in monitoring negotiation of the fuel contracts and minimizing take-or-pay obligations and other obligations that could increase the cost of fuel. To the extent take-or-pay obligations exist, the power purchaser will need to conclude that the price for power is sufficiently low that the power purchaser will purchase the project's power output. If so, the power purchaser minimizes the risk that the project will be idled because of high operating costs and the risk that the power purchaser will need to pay under a take-or-pay contract for fuel not burned.

[9] **Penalties and Bonuses**
The variability of the energy payment provides uncertainty for the power purchaser. At the same time, pass-through of operating costs provides the project company with minimal incentive for controlling these costs.

Yet, if the project company accepted the contractual risk of escalating operating costs and was denied the ability to pass these through to the power purchaser, it would need to increase the capacity charge to compensate for the additional risk taken. This is not an attractive alternative for most power purchasers. Consequently, the typical power sales agreement structure addresses this concern through negotiated penalty and bonus payments. Penalties are applied for excessive levels of operating costs and bonuses are awarded for operating cost savings.

It also provides for penalty and bonus payments in connection with the capacity charge. This is because the power purchaser is relying on the availability of the facility for energy production. Under the typical structure, to the extent the facility is not available because of late construction completion, forced shutdown of the facility operation due to improper construction, or operation and maintenance, then the power purchaser is excused from paying the capacity charge.

However, that remedy is not always sufficient to compensate the power purchaser for the lack of deliveries. It may incur additional costs for purchasing the power elsewhere or to generate additional energy at its existing facilities. Similarly, if the plant is operating at higher levels of capacity than the minimum set forth in the contract, the power purchaser might receive sufficient benefit from that additional availability to provide the project company a bonus for the additional performance.

Other penalties and bonuses that are available for negotiation concern the construction costs for the project. It is typical for the project sponsors to bear the risk of construction cost overruns from the construction price estimate used to calculate the capacity payment needed. If construction price increases from that estimate, the project company might not have the funds necessary to service the debt. However, the project company is in the best position to control those costs through proper estimating and negotiation of price increase protections in the construction contract. Consequently, the usual bargain reached is that to the extent the construction costs are less than the amount estimated when calculating the capacity charge, the project sponsor retains that portion of the capacity charge as a bonus, or it is shared in an agreed-upon percentage with the power purchaser.

A similar compromise is often negotiated concerning the capacity of the facility. It is assumed when the capacity charge is calculated that estimates the amount of capacity for energy production that the facility will have at construction completion and during operation. It is typical for the project company to bear the risk of capacity underperformance from the estimate used to calculate the capacity payment needed. If capacity is less, the project company might not have the funds necessary to service the debt. However, the project company is in the best position to control the delivered capacity through the construction contract and proper operation and maintenance practices. To the extent the delivered capacity is more than the amount estimated when calculating the capacity charge, the project company might receive a bonus or be able to credit it against shortfalls during operation.

As to risks that are outside the control of the project company, however, the purchasing utility typically retains the financial exposure. This is because the project company is unable to control the risks. Indeed, the power purchaser would have borne the risk if it had built and operated the facility. Examples include certain variable fuel costs and sales taxes.

[10] When Capacity Payments Begin
Capacity payments typically begin on the date the project company is able to produce electricity or when the power purchaser determines that electricity can be reliably produced at agreed-upon levels. If the power purchaser causes a delay in this date, capacity payments generally begin on the expected date of commercial operations. However, force majeure events, acts by third parties, and other events over which the power purchaser does not have control, generally do not otherwise result in commencement of capacity payments.

[11] When Capacity Payments End
Because capacity payment amounts are designed to include project debt service, they are subject to revision when debt is repaid or refinanced on more attractive terms. This requires monitoring of the project company and its borrowing position throughout the term of the power purchase agreement.

[12] The Problem of Equity Return for Developing Countries
Project finance lenders, cognizant of the higher risks in project financings for facilities located in developing countries, are more likely to insist upon high levels of equity investment by the project sponsors. These entities will want to know that the project sponsors will receive a relatively high rate of return on those equity investments. This is because the lenders want the project sponsors to have an economic reason to stay involved in the project and support it financially if problems develop. A large equity investment, coupled with a reasonably high rate of return, will help ensure the involvement of the project sponsors when the inevitable occurs.

For developing countries, this presents political and economic problems. First, power rates in these countries need to be increased to pay for the high-equity returns, which customers might not be able to afford. Second, the increases may be objectionable to the ratepayers, causing political repercussions. This may lead to a repudiation or renegotiation of the power agreement, either before closing, during construction, or well into the operation period.

[13] What If the Deal Turns Out to Be a Bad One?

The long-term nature of a power purchase agreement increases the possibility that one party will not enjoy the benefits it thought it would receive. If the loss is large enough, the disappointed party will seek to renegotiate the contract, or perhaps attempt to terminate it through litigation. The sanctity of contract doctrine is discussed at length in Chapter 18.

Local law needs to be consulted to determine whether a long-term contract will be enforced by the court system. In the United States, such agreements are. For example, in *Sioux City Foundry Co. v. South Sioux City*,[2] the city attempted to increase its rate for energy under a power sales agreement. It argued that the power sales agreement rate resulted in a loss to the city. The Eighth Circuit noted that "the City's real argument here 'is that in retrospect it finds it made a bad bargain.' This does not make the 1968 contract ultra vires."[3]

In *United States v. Southwestern Electric Cooperative, Inc.*,[4] a similar result was reached. Southwestern Electric Cooperative agreed to purchase all of its power from Soyland. The power price was tied to the costs of construction of Soyland's plant, which ballooned from an expected $360 million to $5 billion. It later tried to void that contract, claiming mutual mistake and frustration of purpose. The court ruled that the contract had to be complied with, stating that if "the buyer forecasts the market incorrectly and therefore finds himself locked into a disadvantageous contract, he has only himself to blame and so cannot shift the risk back to the seller by invoking impossibility or related doctrines."[5]

Of course, contractual provisions can be added to the contract to excuse performance upon the occurrence of negotiated events, such as price increases.[6] This, however, may introduce a degree of uncertainty that might be unacceptable in a project finance transaction. If so, the contract should be clearly drafted so that price adjustments are not allowed for changes in market conditions, including fluctuations in availability and price.

§ 19.08 SECURITY AND COMMITMENT OF PROJECT SPONSOR

[1] Security for Performance

Because of the importance of the revenue stream to the project company, and of the facility performance to the power purchaser, the credit position of both the project company and the power purchaser is important. If either cannot pay the amounts required in the contract, the terms so carefully structured and negotiated are worthless. Examples of credit support alternatives are guarantees from a creditworthy entity, such as a project sponsor or central government, letters of credit from financial institutions, performance bonds, and cash escrow accounts.

From the project company's perspective, its focus will be on the creditworthiness of the power purchaser. To the extent payment risk exists, the project company will insist upon any of several credit enhancement alternatives. These include central government sovereign guarantees, government subordination, irrevocable letters of credit, escrow accounts, multilateral bank participation in the project, and a pledge of receivables from creditworthy customers of the power purchaser. These alternatives are discussed in Chapter 20 .

[2] Project-Based Security

Project-based security involves the grant of a lien by the project company to the power purchaser on all or a portion of the project assets. This approach has the advantage of not burdening the project company with credit enhancement costs, such as letter of credit fees.

---

[2] Sioux City Foundry Co. v. South Sioux City, 968 F.2d 777 (8th Cir. 1992), *cert denied*, 113 S. Ct. 1273 (1993).

[3] 968 F.2d at 782.

[4] United States v. Southwestern Electric Cooperative, Inc., 869 F.2d 310 (7th Cir. 1989).

[5] *Id.* at 315.

[6] *See* Eastern Air Lines, Inc. v. McDonnell Douglas Corp., 532 F.2d 975 (5th Cir. 1976) (force majeure doctrine is inapplicable where a future event was specifically provided for in the contract).

However, project-based security complicates the financing. These liens give project lenders concerns about lien maintenance, priorities on collateral in foreclosure proceedings, and the like. Consequently, the power purchaser must be willing to subordinate its project-based lien and collateral rights to the liens and rights of the project lenders.

[3] Minimum Equity Undertaking

As discussed in Chapter 1, project finance lenders generally require a level of project sponsor equity invested in a project so that they will have an economic interest that will be difficult to abandon. This strategy helps ensure a high level of equity interest. Similarly, the power purchaser sometimes requires that the special-purpose entity be properly capitalized, with definite equity contributions, meaningful in amount, to ensure that the project sponsors will continue to support the project, even during financial difficulties. This is often seen in a requirement for an agreed minimum capitalization and retention of profits at the project company level for an agreed upon time.

[4] Cash and Letters of Credit

Sometimes power purchasers require that the project company provide a cash collateral account or an irrevocable, direct-pay letter of credit as security for contract obligations. Upon a breach of the agreement, the power purchaser would have the authority to withdraw the cash equivalent to its damages from the collateral account, or draw on the letter of credit.

Although both types of collateral provide maximum protection to the power purchaser, they are expensive options from the project company's perspective. If cash is deposited in a cash collateral account, the project company loses access to those funds, which would otherwise be distributed to the project sponsors as profit. If a letter of credit is used for collateral, the project company must pay a letter of credit commission to obtain it.

[5] Tracking Accounts – Front-End Loaded

At the beginning of commercial operations, a project company will have borrowed a large amount of debt, which needs to be serviced. In some situations, power contract price provisions are negotiated to reflect that debt service obligation. In such circumstances, the capacity price for the power is greater in the early years of contract performance, when more debt is outstanding and debt service costs are higher, than the later contract years.

This creates a potential risk for the power purchaser, however. When the price is reduced in the later contract years, the project company could decide to terminate the project because revenue does not provide a sufficient equity return. In such circumstances, the power purchaser has lost the opportunity to purchase cheaper power, a benefit it negotiated in return for the higher power price paid in the early contract years.

To safeguard the power purchaser from this risk, it is common for the power purchaser to require collateral from the project so that the power purchaser can be treated as a secured party, with access to a cash collateral account or liens on the project assets to recover its losses.

§ 19.09 FORCE MAJEURE

Force majeure is an event outside of the reasonable control of the effected party to a contract that it could not have prevented by good industry practices or by the exercise of reasonable skill and judgment. Such an event typically excuses certain negotiated portions of contract performance during its pendency. The effected party is obligated to take all reasonable actions necessary to restore performance as soon as possible.

The method for allocating the risk of force majeure varies from contract to contract, which is particularly true in the power sales agreement context. In power projects in emerging countries, project sponsors often attempt to place the risk for all force majeure events on the power purchaser. The usual outcome, however, is much more limited.

Force majeure relief typically applies only to specific, well-defined events listed in the contract; is available only if contract performance is substantially and adversely affected; applies only to extraordinary events, not normal business risks or insurable events; and the relief is limited to the effects of the force majeure.

[1] Political Risk

Political risks, such as civil unrest, general strikes, and similar events, are frequently allocated to the power purchaser. In state-supported projects, the power purchaser is the entity best suited to control these risks. Thus, if a general strike occurs, the milestone performance dates in the power purchase agreement will be extended based on the delay experienced. Or, if the project is in operation, capacity payments will continue to be paid by the power purchaser.

Where the central government or a state utility is not the power purchaser, however, the power purchaser might be unwilling to accept full responsibility for these risks. If the project company accepts these risks, it will typically charge a higher rate to receive compensation for the risks assumed. This may not be an attractive economic decision to the power purchaser, particularly because it likely would have the same risk if it had constructed and operated the facility itself.

The generally recognized relief for a political risk is to increase the capacity charge to compensate the project company for the consequences of the action. In some situations, however, the remedy might be to extend the date the facility must be in commercial operation.

[2] Uncontrollable Events

Uncontrollable events are less problematic for the power purchase agreement negotiation. In general, performance is excused by a party upon the occurrence and during the continuance of a force majeure, outside of a party's reasonable control, which makes performance impossible. These include acts of war, unusual or catastrophic weather events, and the like.

Exposure to these types of uncontrollable events can be limited with an effective insurance program. This type of insurance will be required under the financing documents for the project and is also typically required by the power sales agreement to protect the power purchaser against the risk that the facility will be inoperable and therefore unable to supply it with power. Typical insurance programs include payment of asset replacement and payment of debt service and fixed costs for a reasonable period.

[3] Change of Law

The effects of a change of law should also be considered. In developing countries, both the underlying economy and the country's laws, are emerging. Consequently, it is probable that over the twenty-year term or so of a project, new laws will be applied, such as environmental laws that are more costly to comply with than existing laws. The economic implications of a change of law needs to be allocated to one of the two parties.

§ 19.10 PAYMENT

The power purchase agreement also contains procedural provisions for the billing and payment of amounts due under the agreement. These provisions must be tailored to the other project contracts so that the revenue is received before the times needed to pay debt service, fuel costs, and operating expenses. Otherwise, a working capital facility, reserve fund, or access to withheld equity distributions will be needed to provide the necessary funds.

Payments are required to be made within a reasonable time after billing occurs, usually thirty days. If the payment is not made by that time, a cure period is permitted. Late payments bear interest at a rate designed to compensate the project company for the lack of the use of funds and as a disincentive to use the project company as a bank.

§ 19.11 CURRENCY CONVERTIBILITY

Currency convertibility is a concern to the project company and the project lender, whether it relates to the revenue received under the power sales agreement or from the credit enhancement used to support the power purchaser's obligations under the power sales agreement. Currency convertibility is discussed further in Chapter 3.

§ 19.12 TERM AND TERMINATION

[1] Term

The term of the agreement should at least extend to the maturity of the underlying debt. This is necessary so that the project lender will be assured that a revenue stream will exist throughout the debt term. Often, project lenders will require that the term extend for a few years beyond the debt maturity so that a revenue flow remains during any period of restructuring or workout.

[2] Termination Events

Because the power purchase agreement forms the basis for revenues in a project financing, it should not be easily terminable. Termination events must be precisely drafted, with advance notice so that project lenders and other interested parties can cure the related default events.

[3] Termination by Power Purchaser

From the perspective of the power purchaser, the power purchase agreement is typically subject to termination for the following events: nonpayment of amounts owed by the project company to the power purchaser; bankruptcy, acceleration, or liquidation of the project company; abandonment of the project (unless it is the power purchaser's fault); termination or material amendment of certain agreed-upon project contracts (other than for good cause or default by the other party); sale of project assets; sustained periods of reduced deliveries of power (unless it is the power purchaser's fault); failure to achieve milestones, including commercial operations, by a date certain; contract repudiation or other action that implies the project company does not intend to perform the contract; and other breaches of material provisions of the agreement.

[4] Termination by Project Company

From the perspective of the project company, the power purchase agreement is typically subject to termination for the following events: nonpayment of amounts owed by the power purchaser to the project company; bankruptcy, acceleration, or liquidation of the power purchaser; contract repudiation or other action that implies the power purchaser does not intend to perform the contract; the project company is unable to complete construction or operate the project because of a force majeure or power purchaser fault; and other breaches of material provisions of the

agreement. If the power purchaser is a government entity, whose obligations are guaranteed by the host government, the agreement will be terminable if the government, as guarantor, defaults under the guarantee.

[5] Project Lenders

In some financings, the project lenders agree with the power purchaser that if the power purchaser proposes to terminate the contract an alternative company be substituted for the project company. This substitution is typically subject to reasonable approval rights of the power purchaser based on operating experience, financial resources, and, in some cases, national security.

[6] Remedies

In general, the foregoing termination events do not automatically result in contract termination. Rather, the party in default is typically given time to cure its breach. If it fails to do so, termination may then result. If termination is not selected or available as a remedy, a damage payment may be due, or the defaulting party might be forced to perform the contract under the legal theory of specific performance. Remedies vary based on negotiations and the unique setting of each project.

[7] Termination Payments

The amount of a payment due on termination of the contract will vary based on the cause of termination. Where the power contract is terminated for convenience, or because of a default, the party terminating for convenience or in default will likely be required to pay a relatively high termination payment.

If the power purchaser terminates the agreement for convenience or the contract is terminated because of a power purchaser default, the project company will need to consider how project debt will be paid, and how it will recover some investment return for the lost opportunity associated with contract operation.

If, however, the project company terminates the agreement for convenience or the contract is terminated because of a project company default, the power purchaser will likely be more concerned with the right to acquire the power production facilities than a monetary payment. This is particularly true when the only source of termination payments is the project company, which, as a special-purpose entity, usually will not have any financial resources. As discussed next, the power purchaser's need for capacity may require it assume control of the facility.

[8] Power Purchaser's Right to Operate the Project

The power purchaser will typically insist upon the right to operate the project upon a project company default. This is because of the importance of the project to the power purchaser's system and supply requirements. The project lenders can suspend this right, however, if the lenders replace the project company with a suitable operator.

[9] Ownership of Project at Expiration of Term

As discussed above, it is typical that capacity charges over the term of a power agreement compensate the project sponsors for their expected equity returns. It is a matter of negotiation whether the power purchaser should become the owner of the project at the expiration of the contract term. If so, the contract must include provisions concerning the condition of the facility at expiration and detailed procedures for the transfer of ownership and operation.

§ 19.13 PENALTIES

Delivery of power to the power purchaser by the date agreed is a significant contractual responsibility. Power purchasers rely on the planned capacity in making or not making other business arrangements for power purchasers. Consequently, damage payments may be necessary to compensate the power purchaser for late commercial operation of the project and for a shortfall in the project's nameplate capacity.

Similarly, the power purchaser may have damages assessed against it if the capacity is not available when planned. If the power purchaser is responsible for the construction or installation of any portion of the interconnection system, then damages will typically be payable by the power purchaser for late completion of those facilities.

§ 19.14 TECHNICAL STANDARDS

The power purchaser typically establishes detailed technical specifications for the project to satisfy before commercial operations begin, including operating characteristics and power grid requirements. These standards ensure that the project will not affect the safety and reliability of the power purchaser's other facilities.

The agreement will include provisions for appropriate monitoring of construction and testing of the facilities. Possible monitoring provisions include allowing the power purchaser reasonable access to the construction site, and an obligation for the project company to provide monthly construction progress reports to the power purchaser.

During the operations phase, the agreement will specify ongoing technical standards for operation and maintenance. It will also allow changes to the standards throughout the operating period.

§ 19.15 OPERATING PROCEDURES

The operating procedures for the plant should be considered during contract negotiations. This is particularly true where the project is dispatchable and the power purchaser will have control over the plant's operation. Because the operating procedures will vary with the type of plant and the unique needs of each power purchaser, factors for consideration include scheduling procedures, notice to go from cold shutdown to operation, requirement to maintain the plant on warm standby, maintenance schedules and standards, and periods when scheduled outages are not permitted.

§ 19.16 METERING

Metering is primarily technical in nature. Provisions typically address which party is responsible for cost, installation, testing, and maintenance of the metering equipment. Also included is a remedy section, specifying the action required, in the future and retroactively, when the meters are found inaccurate.

§ 19.17 THIRD-PARTY SALES AND PROJECT TRANSFERS OF OWNERSHIP

[1] Generally
Whether the project company has the ability to sell power to other purchasers is a subject for negotiation and varies from project to project. If such sales are permitted, the project company receives the right to maximize project revenue. The power purchaser, however, might want the right to purchase the power, on a right-of-first-refusal basis, or preserve the option of contracting for it later.

[2] Right of First Refusal
A right of first refusal in a power purchase agreement typically provides the power purchaser with the first right to purchase excess facility output and the facility itself. These rights are based on the need of the power purchaser for the power capacity, coupled with the desire for reliable power. If the original project company is to be replaced, the power purchaser desires the opportunity to at least consider whether to purchase the facility at fair-market value and operate it itself.

If a right of first refusal is provided to the power purchaser, problems can be presented for the project lender. These include the effect of the provision on the lender's ability to purchase the project in a foreclosure, resultant delays in the foreclosure process, interference with the ability to sell the project for an amount at least equal to the outstanding loan amount, and a decrease in the number of potential purchasers willing to consider purchase of the project (and an unwillingness to dedicate resources to consider the purchase) as long as the power purchaser has the right to buy the project.

[3] Effects of Third-Party Sales
If third-party sales of excess power are permitted, the project company and power purchaser must consider the effects of this on the underlying power purchase arrangements. The obligation of the power purchaser to make capacity payments is generally designed to provide the project company with a minimum level of equity return, whether or not third-party sales are made. A portion of that is sometimes returned to the power purchaser to the extent unexpected profits

are realized from third-party sales. Similarly, the power purchaser often provides other support to a project company, including the credit support necessary to finance the project, project development contributions, and infrastructure costs, which should be considered before a project company is allowed to make third-party sales. A pro rata reduction in capacity charges and other purchaser-provided costs is sometimes used as the mechanism to allow the project company to make third-party sales, while returning to the power purchaser a portion of the benefits it contributed to the project's initial success.

§ 19.18 "REGULATORY OUT" PROVISIONS

If the power purchaser is subject to regulation by the host government, there might be a risk that the power purchaser would seek to amend directly or indirectly the contract based on an unfavorable regulatory act. Where the contract language permits this action,[7] a financing problem exists for the project company because the terms of the contract could be negatively affected by a regulatory change. Although limited regulatory changes may be acceptable, an unlimited regulatory change is likely unacceptable in a project financing. It may be determined to be acceptable, however, based on the unique circumstances of the host country.

It is possible to include a regulatory out clause[8] in the contract, without an effect on financing.

[7] A *regulatory out* clause is a contract provision that provides for renegotiation of the price for power under a power sales agreement or outright termination of the agreement, if a court or governmental agency impairs the purchasing utility's ability to recover its costs from ratepayers. *See, e.g.,* North American Natural Resources, Inc., et al., v. Michigan Public Service Comm'n, 73 F. Supp. 2d 804, 808 n.5 (W. D. Mich. 1999).

[8] Two recent U.S. court decisions discuss regulatory out clauses in power sales agreements. Agrilectric Power Partners, Ltd., v. Entergy Gulf States, Inc., et al., 207 F.3d 301 (2000) (regulatory out price adjustment clause in power contract is enforceable where both parties voluntarily agreed to the clause); North American Natural Resources, Inc., et al., v. Michigan Public Service Comm'n, 73 F. Supp. 2d 804 (W. D. Mich. 1999) (state agency enjoined from any action to deny, directly or indirectly, purchasing utility's ability to recover rates paid to a QF from the utility's ratepayers). *See also* Freehold Cogeneration Assocs., L.P. v. Board of Regulatory Comm'rs of New Jersey, 44 F.3d 1178,

Instead, the regulatory risk is placed on equity after the project debt is repaid. An example of such a regulatory out clause is reproduced below:

The parties recognize and hereby agree that if any government or regulatory authority should for any reason enter an order, modify its rules, or take any action whatsoever having the effect of disallowing the [*Power Purchaser*] the recovery from its customers of all or any portion of the payments for capacity hereunder (a "Disallowance"), then:

(a) if the Disallowance occurs before the 15th anniversary of the commercial operations date, the [*Power Purchaser*] shall continue to pay for such capacity at the rate set forth herein. Payments for capacity beginning on the 15th anniversary of the commercial operations date shall not exceed the amount unaffected by the Disallowance. Further, the [*Power Purchaser*] may, at its option, beginning on the 12th anniversary of the commercial operations date withhold up to [*percentage*] percent of the capacity payments until the earlier of (i) the 20th anniversary of the commercial operations date and (ii) the date the entire amount of the Disallowance is repaid to the [*Power Purchaser*] plus interest thereon at the [*interest rate*] from the date each part of the Disallowance was paid to the [*Project Company*]; and

(b) if the Disallowance occurs after the 15th anniversary of the commercial operations date, all future payments for capacity shall not exceed the amount unaffected by the Disallowance, and the [*Project Company*] shall repay the full amount of the Disallowance plus interest thereon at the [*interest rate*] from the date each part of the Disallowance was paid to the [*Project Company*] by the later of (i) one year from the date of such Disallowance and (ii) the 20th anniversary of the commercial operations date.

The parties agree that neither shall initiate a petition for Disallowance, and obligate themselves to establish, if practicable, an appeal and overruling of any Disallowance or a superseding order, approval of modified rules or tariffs, or other action so as to allow timely resumption of full, or failing that, adjusted payments hereunder.[9]

This provision does not address refinancing or a potential workout of loan arrangements if the project encounters problems, where the debt term is longer than the fifteen-year period assumed in the sample above.

§ 19.19 POWER PURCHASER RESPONSIBILITIES

The project company will desire that the power purchaser commit to certain responsibilities. First among these concerns the conditions that must be satisfied before the contract is effective or be satisfied within a limited period. These might include such things as governmental approval of the contract or infrastructure expenditures necessary for the project to proceed.

The power purchaser is typically responsible for providing construction power, if available in the area of the project site and, in some projects, constructing transmission lines and interconnection facilities.

§ 19.20 PROJECT COMPANY RESPONSIBILITIES

The project company's responsibilities to the power purchaser include operating the power

1191–92 (3d Cir. 1995) (a state agency cannot force a utility and a QF to renegotiate power rates or negotiate a contract buy-out); Independent Energy Producers v. California Public Utilities Commission, 36 F.3d 848, 858 (9th Cir. 1994) ("the fact that the prices for fuel, and therefore the Utilities' avoided costs, are lower than estimated, does not give the states and the Utilities the right unilaterally to modify the terms of the standard contract. Federal regulations provide that QFs are entitled to deliver energy to utilities at an avoided cost rate calculated at the time the contract is signed."); Smith Cogeneration Management v. Corporation Comm'n, 863 P.2d 1227, 1240 (Okla. 1993) (once a state approves an avoided cost rate in a QF's contract with a utility, the state "cannot later review the contract to reconsider avoided costs.")

[9] Another example of a regulatory out clause was considered by the court in Agrilectric Power Partners, Ltd. v. Entergy Gulf States, Inc., et al., 207 F.3d 301 (2000) ("The payments made by [Entergy] to [Agrilectric] under this Agreement shall not be greater than the amount [Entergy], during any recovery period, fuel adjustment or reconciliation hearing, or any other point in time or for any period in time during the term of this Agreement, shall be allowed to recover as an energy, fuel, or other cost, in all regulatory jurisdictions. In such event, the parties shall mutually agree to the adjustment of payments to [Agrilectric].")

project in accordance with good industry practices, all laws and regulations, permits, grid requirements, and the power purchaser's dispatch procedures. In practice, these responsibilities will be imposed on the project operator in the operating agreement.

Maintenance obligations are closely coordinated with the power purchaser because maintenance shutdowns affect the energy production availability of the project. Because of these implications for availability, the following considerations should be addressed: advance approval of annual maintenance plan by the power purchaser; requirements, if any, on what time of year scheduled outages should occur; reasonable flexibility for the power purchaser to make changes to the schedule; and limits on unscheduled maintenance.

§ 19.21 INSURANCE

The power purchaser generally requires that the project company obtain and maintain insurance. This is particularly the case where the power purchaser must pay the project company specified amounts whether or not the power is produced and delivered.

Insurance provisions will typically include minimum requirements, listing the types of policies necessary; a requirement to name the power purchaser as a named insured on liability policies; and the required use of insurance proceeds, such as for repairs. Because project lenders will require that they have the right to apply all insurance proceeds to repay debt, consideration should be given to whether the power purchase agreement should include a reduction in the capacity charge to the extent debt is reduced prematurely.

§ 19.22 SUCCESSORS TO THE POWER PURCHASER

Where the power purchaser is owned by a governmental entity, it is probable that, over time, the state-owned utility will be privatized. The power purchase agreement must contain provisions that require that the obligations of the power purchaser be transferred to the successor entity. The creditworthiness of the new purchaser should be considered in the agreement. It may be prudent to require new credit support arrangements if the new entity fails to satisfy minimal levels of creditworthiness.

§ 19.23 COMMON RISK ALLOCATION IN DEVELOPING COUNTRY POWER PURCHASE AGREEMENTS

[1] Construction

Construction risks in an energy project financing in a developing country are typically allocated among the project sponsor, contractor, and the power purchaser (and the host government). Risks are allocated between the project company and the contractor in the construction contract and between the project company and the power purchaser in the power sales agreement. There are three main construction risks: cost overrun, delay, and failure to satisfy performance standards.

Cost Overrun. An important negotiation issue in determining the amount of the capacity charge is who will bear the cost overrun risk. To the extent the power purchaser bears the risk, the capacity charge will increase, with the goal being to ensure that the project company is in the same position it was in under the contract had the change not occurred. To the extent the project company bears the risk, no increase will be awarded.

Typically, the project company bears the risk of increases in construction costs, which it then passes along to the contractor in a fixed-price construction contract. However, either some risks the contractor will not assume or, if the risks were assumed, the construction price would be too high for the project to be financed. These include political risks, such as changes in law and changes in taxes that increase construction costs.

Political risks are typically borne by the power purchaser. This is because the power purchaser is thought to be in a better position than the project company to control political events.

Delay. Also important is what party will bear the risk of construction delays. If power contracted for is not available to a power purchaser when expected, it could face capacity constraints. To ensure schedule certainty, the power purchaser typically requires the project company to complete construction by a negotiated date. The project company then negotiates a specific completion date with its contractor under the construction contract.

Failure of the project company to satisfy these milestones can arise from many factors, such as late equipment deliveries. If the date is not achieved, the power purchaser can delay the start of capacity payments to the project company and charge liquidated damages for delay. The project company then passes this risk along to the contractor.

The project company is typically not responsible for all types of delays, however. If, for example, a delay in the project is caused by political action of the host government, the project company (and the contractor) is typically excused from its performance obligation for the time necessary to alleviate the cause of the delay. As with construction cost overruns caused by political risks, the power purchaser is considered better able to control risks than the project company.

Failure to Achieve Performance Standards. Power purchase agreements often require the project company to achieve a target level of performance at the facility, determined from the facility's capacity and heat rate. Failure to achieve the agreed-upon levels results in a payment of liquidated damages by the project company. The risk of a failure to achieve these standards, for reasons other than delay or fault of the project company or power purchaser, are controllable by the contractor.

[2] Operating

Operating risks in an energy project financing in a developing country are typically allocated among the project sponsor, operator, and the power purchaser (and the host government). Risks are allocated between the project company and the operator in the operations and maintenance agreement and between the project company and the power purchaser in the power sales agreement. There are two main operating-period risks: cost overrun and failure to satisfy performance standards.

Cost Overrun. The majority of operating risks are allocated to the operator in the operating agreement. Typically, if operating costs exceed an annually approved budget, the operator pays liquidated damages, calculated based on the overruns. However, cost overruns that result from an event of force majeure or a political risk entitles the operator to relief and an increase in the operating budget is made.

As between the project company and the power purchaser, the power purchaser compensates the project company for operating costs in the energy component of the power purchase price. The energy component reflects an agreed-upon amount for operating and maintenance costs, which is adjusted for such things as inflation and exchange rates. To the extent the project's actual operating and maintenance costs exceed this agreed-upon amount, the difference is not paid by the power purchaser, rather, it is paid in the form of liquidated damages to the project company by the operator.

It is typical for the operator to bear this risk because it is in the best position to control cost overruns. If the cost overrun is caused by a force majeure event, a political risk, or the fault of the power purchaser, however, the power purchaser will typically compensate the project company for the additional operating costs realized as a result.

Operating Performance Shortfall. Power purchase agreements typically require the project company to achieve a target level of performance at the facility on an ongoing basis. Failure to achieve the agreed-upon levels results in a payment of liquidated damages by the project company, typically as a reduction in the capacity charge.

The performance standards most often used are the number of unplanned operational shutdowns experienced by the project, deration of the capacity of the project by the power purchaser because of reduced availability, and deterioration in heat rate. The risk of a failure to achieve these standards, for reasons other than delay or fault of the project company or power purchaser, or equipment failure, is borne by the operator. However, political risks are borne by the power purchaser, and other force majeure events are borne by the project company.

[3] Fuel

Fuel risks in an energy project financing in a developing country are typically allocated among the project sponsor, fuel supplier, and the power purchaser (and the host government). Risks are allocated between the project company and the fuel supplier in the fuel supply agreement. Risks are allocated between the project company and the power purchaser in the power sales agreement. There are three main fuel risks: price, supply, and transportation. In some projects, a separate agreement exists between the project company and the fuel transporter.

Price. The price risk allocation is dependent, in part, on whether the fuel supplier is owned by the government. If so, fuel costs typically flow through the project company to the power purchaser, which reimburses the project company for those costs.

If not government owned, the fuel supplier typically charges a fixed, negotiated amount that is subject to an inflation index. The fuel supplier is thought to be in the best position to control fuel costs, other than inflation. The same inflation index is used in the power purchase agreement to increase the amount of the fuel component of the energy charge paid by the power purchaser to the project company. Thus, the project company passes along the inflation risk to the power purchaser, who then can pass along the risk to the power users.

Supply. The allocation of the fuel supply risk in energy project financings is generally dependent upon whether the fuel is imported or domestic. If imported, the failure of the fuel supplier to supply the project's fuel typically results in liquidated damages payable by the supplier to the project company. The amount of the damages is generally intended to compensate the project company for the revenues lost because of the nonsupply of fuel and any damages payable to the power purchaser because of the inability to produce energy.

Force majeure events, however, excuse the fuel supplier from its supply obligations, placing that risk on the project company. Where the fuel supplier is government owned, however, political force majeure events do not excuse its performance.

Transportation. Similarly, the failure of the fuel transporter to transport the project's fuel typically results in liquidated damages payable by the transporter to the project company. The amount of the damages is generally intended to compensate the project company for the revenues lost because of the nondelivery of fuel and any damages payable to the power purchaser because of the inability to produce energy. Force majeure events, however, excuse the fuel transporter of its transport obligations, placing that risk on the project company. Where the fuel transporter is government owned, however, political force majeure events do not excuse its performance.

[4] Market

Market risks in a developing country energy project are allocated in the power purchase agreement between the power purchaser and the project company. Market risks, such as demand, price, and exchange rate fluctuations, are generally allocated to the power purchaser, who is considered best able to plan for, analyze and manage market risks.

Demand. The risk of demand for the power produced by the project company rests with the power purchaser through its obligation to pay the capacity charge. If demand falls, the obligation to pay the capacity charge remains in place. As discussed earlier in this chapter, this amount is designed to compensate the project company for its fixed costs.

Price. The risk of an inadequate market price for power – the price the power purchaser charges the ultimate energy user – is also borne by the power purchaser. That is, the contract price, made up of a capacity charge, representing fixed costs, and a variable operating charge, representing fuel and variable operating costs, could be greater than the price the power purchaser could charge its customers for power.

Inflation. Inflation risk is also addressed in the power purchase agreement through the capacity and energy charge components of the power purchase price. In general, the risk of price increases based on inflation are borne by the power purchaser, assuming the indices are representative of the economic effects *on the project* of inflation.

Typically, costs associated with goods and services obtained outside of the host country, such as operating fees paid to the operator, are adjusted for hard currency index changes. Those associated with goods and services obtained in the host country, such as costs of local labor, are adjusted based on a local index. Fuel costs, as discussed above, are typically adjusted based on a separate fuel index. Interest costs on the project debt, where variable, are not adjusted by an inflation index but, rather, are adjusted based on the actual change in the interest mode selected by the project company, such as LIBOR, as compared with the interest rate assumed at the time the contract was originally executed.

Exchange Rate Fluctuations. Energy projects in developing countries typically contain currency risk caused by the project company incurring obligations for debt, construction, and some operating costs in hard currency, while receiving payments in the soft currency of the developing country. A typical solution is to index amounts payable by the power purchaser to the project company under the power purchase agreement. The index is designed to reflect the shifting exchange rate between the hard and soft local currencies.

[5] Political

Political risks, such as change in law, currency inconvertibility or nontransferability, expropriation, and war and civil disobedience are generally addressed in an implementation agreement. These agreements are discussed in detail in Chapter 14.

Whether a government, the party best able to control political risks, will assume these risks for a project varies based on a myriad of factors. These include the importance of the project to the host government's political, social, and economic goals; the degree of local participation in the project; involvement of multilateral and bilateral agencies; and general creditworthiness of the government.

Assurances and guarantees undertaken by the host government to compensate the project if political risks materialize include a buyout of the project at an amount necessary so that the project sponsors can achieve a minimum rate of return,

and payment by the government of a supplemental tariff to compensate the project for the increased costs.

§ 19.24 TOLLING AGREEMENTS

In some projects, the power purchaser is responsible for fuel delivery to the facility. Once the fuel is delivered, the project company is then required to produce energy with the fuel, and sell the energy to the power purchaser. The agreement that governs this structure is called a *tolling agreement*.[10]

The use of a tolling agreement is primarily for risk control. Under this structure, the power purchaser is better able to control the historically volatile risks of fuel availability and price.

Many of the principal contractual provisions of a tolling agreement are identical to a power purchase agreement. However, some important differences are discussed below.

[1] Fuel Availability and Force Majeure

In power purchase agreements, an event of force majeure will usually occur when the party responsible for fuel delivery cannot provide it, through no fault of its own. In a tolling agreement, however, the power purchaser and fuel supplier are the same. If the power purchaser is excused from paying for the project in the event of a fuel force majeure event, then the project revenue will be reduced. Because of this, the power purchaser is usually required to make capacity payments during a fuel-related force majeure event.

[2] Efficiency and Fuel Use

In general, fuel efficiency is not a concern of the power purchaser in a power purchase agreement. In a tolling agreement, however, inefficient fuel use would result in the power purchaser providing more fuel to obtain the required generation. The project operator must therefore guarantee a minimum level for fuel efficiency (heat rate). Often, the operator receives a bonus for fuel efficiencies achieved.

[10.]The name is based on the toll paid by users of roads or bridges; in effect, the power purchaser/fuel supplier pays a toll for the right to pass fuel through the project and have it converted into energy.

PART SIX

CREDIT ENHANCEMENT

CHAPTER TWENTY

PROJECT FINANCE CREDIT ENHANCEMENT

§ 20.01 INTRODUCTION TO CREDIT ENHANCEMENT IN PROJECT FINANCINGS

In theory, a project financing can be structured in which there are no risks and the lenders are content to rely solely upon the revenue-producing project contracts to service debt. In reality, of course, the discussion of project finance risks described in Chapters 2, 3, and 4 evidences that mere reliance on those contracts is insufficient to protect the lender from equity risk. Credit support, or enhancement of credit as it is sometimes referred to, from a creditworthy source is necessary.

The purpose of credit enhancement is to improve the most severe equity and lender risks in a triage of project financing risks identified. Depending on myriad factors, the requisite support can take the form of direct guarantees by the project sponsor or the project participants, guarantees by third parties not directly participating in the project, and in some cases contingent guarantees and so-called moral obligations of the project participants.

The most obvious type of commercial risk in a project financing is the risk of nonpayment of the project debt. Commercial risks must generally be covered by credit support of the project sponsor or a responsible third party. Although the project sponsor is conceptually the fundamental risk taker, the nonrecourse nature of a project financing limits the ability to allocate risks to the sponsor. While a sponsor may be asked to accept directly some risks, it most likely will also be asked to provide additional equity contributions upon certain specified events, and to provide credit enhancement in the form of insurance, third-party guarantees, or letters of credit in others.

In evaluating the use of a particular form of credit enhancement, the utility of each type of credit enhancement device must be considered in relation to several factors, including the term of the device selected, the cost, and the difficulty of, and time necessary for, enforcement. For example, in determining whether to use insurance or a third-party guarantee to enhance the risk of a force majeure to the project, the premium price, short policy term, and length of time necessary for enforcement of insurance claims must be compared to the cost, term, and enforcement issues of a guarantee.

Thus, the objective of risk allocation in a project financing is to combine credit enhancement mechanisms to distribute the risks among the participants. This combination must produce a bankable project without burdening any single participant to the point that the project financing is converted into a recourse financing.

Credit enhancement is not limited to the realm of third-party guarantees, although such guarantees are an important component of many financings. Other credit enhancement mechanisms include limited, indirect, implied, and deficiency guarantees, comfort undertakings, insurance, letters of credit, surety obligations, liquidated damages, take-or-pay, through-put, and put-or-pay contracts, indemnification obligations, and additional equity commitments. This list need not be exhaustive; the types of credit enhancement are limited only by the imagination and creativity of those structuring the deals.

Each type of credit enhancement is typically embodied in a separate agreement and must be incorporated in the finance structure. Thus, to the extent credit enhancement is a necessary component of a deal, it will be a condition precedent to the loan closing that the credit enhancement documentation be in place. It will also be a loan default if it is no longer in place. Finally, the credit enhancement will need to be collaterally assigned to the project lender and be enforceable by it.

The type of credit enhancement necessary to satisfy a lender or equity investor that a risk is covered varies based on the financial community's perception of risks at any given point in time. A risk covered by a guarantee on one occasion might not be required several years later, as in the case of a technology that has developed a record of reliable performance. One not required in the past might suddenly be necessary because of changes to the political environment underlying the project, as in the case of a change in the host country's political attitude.

§ 20.02 GUARANTEES

[1] Generally

Like other credit enhancement devices, a guarantee shifts risks to entities that prefer little direct involvement in the operation of a project. A guarantee is also a mechanism that permits entities to invest capital without becoming directly involved in the operation of a project.

The value of a guarantee to the project is dependent upon the creditworthiness of the guarantor. It is also influenced by the guarantee language. Unless the guarantee provides a waiver of defenses and an absolute and unconditional obligation, the guarantee may not provide the credit enhancement necessary to comfort a lender that a creditworthy support is in place.[1]

[2] Sponsor

There are essentially two types of guarantors in a project financing: sponsor guarantors and third-party guarantors. The most common guarantor in a project financing is the sponsor itself. Typically, the sponsor establishes a special-purpose subsidiary to construct, own, and operate the project. The subsidiary, however, lacks sufficient capital or credit rating to support risks associated with the underlying loan obligation. To reach a loan closing, the project sponsor must arrange some form of credit enhancement to cover the identified risks. Often the requisite credit enhancement is provided in the form of a guarantee by the project sponsor of the obligations of the project company.

The sponsor guarantee can be structured in various forms to satisfy the objectives of the sponsor and the enhancement needs of the project. For example, a completion agreement is sometimes used in which the project sponsor is required to complete construction of the project. Once the project is completed to agreed-upon performance levels, the agreement terminates. On termination, the liability of the project sponsor is also extinguished. As a result, its balance sheet is freed to similarly guarantee other projects.

---

[1] See generally Peter A. Alces, The Efficacy of Guaranty Contracts in Sophisticated Commercial Transactions, 61 N. Car. L. Rev. 655 (1983).

In this context, the definition of the term *completion* is carefully negotiated. The determination of whether a project is complete might include independent engineer verification, through facility testing, of construction contract performance guarantees; satisfaction of conditions to completion in environmental permits; and certificates from the borrower of project completion.

If the sponsor guarantee is insufficient, in terms or credit, to support the risks identified, however, credit enhancement by a third party is needed. Each project finance participant is a potential third-party guarantor because each participant has an economic stake in the success of the project's development. The various project participants that may provide project finance guarantees include suppliers that have an interest in the fulfillment of purchase orders contingent on financing or that recognize that a project sponsor cannot compete in the marketplace without financial assistance. Other potential providers are output purchasers where supply of the output is of particular importance, and contractors that are interested in constructing the project and realizing construction profit.

[3] Third Party
Third-party guarantors are often reluctant to sign a direct, unconditional guarantee in a project financing. In some financings, a lender may be persuaded to accept a different type of guarantee, in which the obligations of the guarantor are more limited. These include limited and indirect guarantees.

In general, the principal source of guarantors for a project financing is participants in the project. These include the project sponsors, the host government, bilateral and multilateral agencies, input suppliers, equipment manufacturers, contractors, and output purchasers.

[4] Contrast to Put Options
Payments made by the guarantor under a guarantee generally do not extinguish the liability of the party (obligor) whose performance or payment is guaranteed. Instead, the guarantor is subrogated to the rights of the beneficiaries of the guarantee. In other words, the obligations owed by the obligor to the beneficiaries of the guarantee are

transferred to the guarantor. This is in contrast to a put option, described below, in which no continuing contractual obligation exists after the option is exercised and performed.

[5] Collateral
The usefulness of a guarantee to a beneficiary is, of course, dependent upon the current and future creditworthiness of the guarantor. It is therefore not uncommon for guarantees to provide the beneficiary with access to collateral, including special, dedicated bank accounts. Also not uncommon are various financial covenants that the guarantor must satisfy. If it does not, a default will occur, either a default of the project loan agreements, or a default under the guarantee itself. If the latter occurs, the guarantor might be required to post cash collateral, a letter of credit, or alternate collateral to protect the beneficiary against the risk of nonperformance by the guarantor.

§ 20.03 TRANSNATIONAL GUARANTEES

[1] Introduction
The success of international project financings is often dependent upon the agreement by a creditworthy party to promise to pay or perform the obligations of another project participant. The international guarantee is sometimes a condition to obtaining financing. In other situations, the project developer desires additional comfort to protect the equity investors from additional risk.

Special problems exist with international guarantees. These include varying interpretation of terms, payments and currency risks, tax implications, and foreign law.

[2] Varying Interpretation of Terms
The interpretation of terms such as *absolute* and *unconditional* are generally construed to mean that there is no condition to pursuing the guarantor for payment or performance. However, the use of these terms in an international financing should be carefully considered. In the international finance context, there is typically somewhat more negotiation of guarantee obligations and less use of standardized guarantee language

and forms. Clarification of these terms in the guarantee may improve enforceability and protect against inconsistent court rulings.[2]

[3] Payments and Currency Risks

If the guarantor must make a payment under the guarantee, it is important to consider the currency in which the payment is obligated to be made. Failure to specify the currency could result in a significant loss to the beneficiary of the guarantee if exchange rates are unfavorable.

If no currency designation is made, the governing law will be applied to interpret the guarantee. For example, in England, the chosen currency is the one most closely associated with the underlying contract.

Another provision that should be considered is a so-called multi-currency provision. This is a clause that seeks to prevent loss caused by a guarantor's payment in a different currency from that required to be paid by the party whose payment or performance is guaranteed. Payment in another currency should be expressly disallowed in a guarantee, unless otherwise agreed, or unless the guarantor agrees to indemnify the beneficiary against conversion losses.

Currency uncertainty can also arise in connection with a court action against the guarantor. A judgment of a foreign court in a foreign currency could result in a loss to the beneficiary. Similarly, an enforcement of a foreign judgment resulting in payment in the court's local currency could have a similar effect.

A beneficiary could suffer a financial loss if there is a lag between the date of the judgment (and the currency rate in effect) and the date of payment of the judgment (and the currency rate in effect on that date). An appropriately drafted indemnity clause can guard against this risk.

[4] Tax Implications

Local law should be examined to determine whether any tax withholding may be required as a result of the transactions involved. If so, the beneficiary of the guarantee should consider requiring the guarantor to indemnify the beneficiary for these amounts. Because tax laws and treaties change regularly, the beneficiary should consider such a clause even if there would be no withholding rights under existing law.

[5] Foreign Law

A choice of law provision is critical to the enforceability of the guarantee, both with respect to the choice of law to govern the guarantee and the submission to a jurisdiction's court system so that the guarantee can be enforced in a favorable court with jurisdiction over the guarantor.[3]

§ 20.04 LIMITED GUARANTEES

[1] Generally

Traditional guarantees represent direct, unconditional commitments by a guarantor to perform all the obligations of a third party. Guarantees limited in amount or time can be used to provide the minimum enhancement necessary to finance the project. This approach provides the necessary credit support to a project without considerable impact on the guarantor's credit standing and financial statements. Examples of limited guarantees include guarantees that are effective only during the construction phase of a project or that are limited in amount, whether calculable in advance or not. An example of the latter type of guarantee is a cost overrun guarantee in which the guarantor agrees to finance construction of a project to the extent design changes or changes in law require additional funds for project completion.

[2] Claw-back

A claw-back guarantee is provided by the project owners, including the project sponsors and any passive equity investors. It requires that they return cash distributions to the project company to the extent required by the project for such things as debt service, capital improvements, and similar needs.

---

[2] *See generally* Raymer McQuiston, *Drafting an Enforceable Guaranty in an International Financing Transaction: A Lender's Perspective*, 10 INT'L TAX & BUS. LAW. 138 (1993).

[3] For an extensive discussion of choice of law provisions in guarantee agreements, *see id.*

[3] Cash Deficiency

A cash deficiency guarantee requires that the guarantor contribute additional capital to the project company to the extent cash deficiencies exist. It is often provided by a project sponsor. In some circumstances, however, other project participants provide this guarantee.

[4] Completion

A completion guarantee, typically provided by the project sponsor, is designed to cover the cost overrun risk – the risk that the project is not completed and able to operate at the time required and at the budgeted price. Under this arrangement, the project sponsor agrees to take certain action regarding the completion of the facility. This action can include such things as the following: committing additional capital to the project company to the extent necessary to complete project construction and achieve commercial operations, or if it decides not to complete the project, to repay the project debt; committing to cost overrun financing through subordinated debt; or ensuring that financial tests are met, such as debt service coverage, on an ongoing basis, to the extent such failure is caused by construction cost overruns.

Construction costs typically covered by the scope of this guarantee include all capital, equipment, construction services, and any other construction-related cost, including construction period interest, necessary to reach "completion." The definition of completion is extremely important in the context of the completion guarantee. This concept is discussed in detail in Chapter 12.

The project sponsors do not bear this risk alone, however. In turn, the project sponsors can negotiate commitments in the construction contract, equipment supply contracts, and other construction documents, that pass this risk to the contractor, equipment supplier, and other construction-period participants to the extent they cause the cost overrun.

[5] The Risk With Unlimited Guarantees

In contrast to limited guarantees are open-ended guarantees. Although at first glance, such guarantees seem the ultimate risk mitigation technique, they seldom are. It is difficult to keep this type of blank check secret.

For example, an unlimited completion guarantee offered by a project sponsor is a tempting pool of cash for contractors, host governments, offtake purchasers, and other project participants. As a result, construction costs could increase to the point that the project is no longer profitable. An important protective shield of project finance – the efficiency of the limited construction budget – is thereby removed from the financing by a seemingly simple credit enhancement device. Thus, even though the lender has a completed project, the project sponsor may abandon it because it is unprofitable to operate, and the lender is left with an unpaid loan.

§ 20.05 INDIRECT "GUARANTEES"

In contrast to these direct but scope-limited guarantees are indirect guarantees, which are "guarantees" based on the underlying credit of one of the project participants. Indirect guarantees are not subject to defenses available to a guarantor under a guarantee agreement. The most common indirect guarantee in a project financing is one of the revenue producing contracts. This obligation is typically in the form of a take-or-pay contract, in the case of goods, or a through-put contract, in the case of services, or a take-and-pay contract.

[1] Take-or-Pay Contracts

A take-or-pay contract is the term generally used to refer to a contractual obligation between a buyer and seller in which the buyer agrees to make payments on certain dates to the seller in return for available deliveries of goods or services at specified prices. The payment obligation of the buyer is unconditional. Thus, even if no goods or services are delivered, the payment obligation exists.

The take-or-pay contract can be used in a variety of project settings. It may be a contract for the purchase and sale of goods, such as minerals; a contract for the purchase and provision of services, such as municipal solid waste incineration; or a contract for use of a ship, such as in an ocean vessel project financing.

In a project financing where the contract represents the sole revenue source, the payments required under the contract must be sufficient to enable the project sponsor to pay debt service payments, and operation expenses. Because the contract is effective over a long term, typically at least the term of the project debt, the price is subject to escalation for such variables as inflation.

[2] Take-and-Pay Contracts

A take-and-pay contract is similar to the take-or-pay contract except that the buyer is only obligated to pay if the product or service is actually delivered. Thus, a take-and-pay contract does not contain an unconditional obligation. For example, in a project financing of a small power production facility, a typical power purchase agreement with a utility provides a guaranteed stream of revenue to the project. If power is delivered to the utility, the utility is obligated to pay certain definite amounts to the project sponsor. Thus, the contract acts as an indirect guarantee, guaranteeing a stream of revenue to a project.

[3] Other Forms

Other examples of indirect guarantees include agreements to provide additional funds, note purchase agreements that require the purchase of a lender's notes on certain specified events, and agreements to purchase project assets. Each has in common the purpose of paying or reducing the project indebtedness if the project is not completed as required, or some other problem arises that affects the ability of the project to produce sufficient revenues to satisfy the obligations incurred.

§ 20.06 IMPLIED GUARANTEES AND UNDERTAKINGS

[1] Generally

An implied guarantee in a project financing is a means of providing assurances to the lender that the "guarantor" will provide necessary support to the project, presumably out of its underlying credit. Implied guarantees are often not legally binding, and, as such, do not require financial statement reporting.

Lenders are sometimes comforted that the sponsoring company will continue to support the project on the basis of the size of the equity investment made in the project by the parent corporation and by the size of the economic benefit that will be realized from project success.

[2] Comfort Letter

An example of an implied guarantee is a comfort letter, in which the "guarantor" addresses a risk concern of the lender. These include covenants of a parent corporation with an excellent credit rating to continue to own all of the stock of the borrowing entity, and an expression of an intent not to sell the project company; an expression of an intention to use a part of the parent's name in the name of the project company and not to change that name while the loan is outstanding; and a statement of its business policy that it will supervise the management of the project.

The comfort that a lender will take in any of these scenarios is a subjective matter. They are usually expressed as statements of intent or statements of business policy, which, of course, can change over time. Comfort letters are not guarantees.

§ 20.07 PUT OPTIONS

[1] Generally

A project finance put option is the term generally used to refer to an agreement between the project sponsors and specified parties (such as passive equity investors and project lenders), whereby the project sponsors agree to purchase equity interests or debt obligations, as the case may be, if certain contingencies (equity returns or debt repayment, for example) are not satisfied.

[2] Regulatory Put

A common put option in project financings is a so-called regulatory put. An example of this type of option is where a passive investor, desiring an agreed-upon equity return and extremely limited management control of the project company, does not want to accept any risk of regulation solely as a result of its equity ownership. Some laws and regulations, however, either existing or in the future, might impose regulatory constraints. If such a risk materializes, the investor will want the project sponsor to agree to purchase its interest so that the regulation can be avoided.

[3] Contrast to Guarantees

In a put option, no continuing contractual obligation exists after the option is exercised and performed. The debt instrument or equity interest is transferred for the agreed upon put price, extinguishing the rights of the lender or equity investor. This is in contrast to a guarantee where payments made by the guarantor under a guarantee generally do not extinguish the liability of the party (obligor) whose performance or payment is guaranteed. Instead, the guarantor is subrogated to the rights of the beneficiaries of the guarantee. In other words, the obligations owed by the obligor to the beneficiaries of the guarantee are transferred to the guarantor.

Depending upon the structure, the beneficiaries might also continue to have a contractual arrangement with the obligor, even after the guarantee is performed. In that situation, the guarantor might be required to waive any rights of subrogation until that contractual arrangement ends and all obligations of the obligor to the beneficiary are paid.

§ 20.08 LETTERS OF CREDIT

Another type of credit enhancement device is a letter of credit, which is an agreement that substitutes the payment obligation and creditworthiness of a more solvent party, usually a bank, for the payment obligation and creditworthiness of a less solvent party, such as an insufficiently capitalized project company. In a project financing, the standby or guarantee letter of credit is used to protect against the project company's failure to perform some obligation, such as a payment or performance obligation.

For example, an off-take purchaser may require the project company to procure a standby letter of credit from a bank to ensure payment of liquidated damages due if the project is not completed by an agreed-upon date. The letter of credit, in effect, "stands by" awaiting a default by the contractor under the construction contract or some other specific default with reference to which the letter of credit is directed.

§ 20.09 SURETY OBLIGATIONS

The commercial risk of project completion to the point that permits operation at a level consistent with expected revenue is typically covered by a completion guarantee. A completion guarantee provides that the project will be completed and will operate at a specified level of production and efficiency. This guarantee is typically provided by the contractor, but the risk is often also covered by a surety that issues performance and payment bonds.

[1] Bid Bonds

A bid bond is a bond delivered with a bid for a project or contract. It is used typically by a host government that desires to ensure that the project sponsor that wins a bid for an infrastructure facility actually proceeds with the project. The amount of the bid varies and is sometimes as much as one or two percent of the contract price.

[2] Performance Bonds

A performance bond is used most often in connection with credit enhancement of a construction contract. The performance bond is issued by a surety to a project company and is usually assigned to the project lender as part of the project collateral. It is callable if the contractor fails to perform the terms of the construction contract. If it does not, the surety will cause the performance of the contract so that the project is completed.

[3] Payment Bonds

A payment bond is also used most often in connection with credit enhancement of a construction contract. The payment bond is issued by a surety to a project company and is similarly assigned to the project lender as part of the project collateral. It is callable if the contractor fails to pay some amount that is due under the terms of the construction contract, such as liquidated damages for late performance. If it does not, the surety will make the payment.

[4] Warranty Bonds

Also called maintenance bonds, warranty bonds are provided by the contractor to the project company as a safeguard against the risk that the contractor will not make repairs or replacements during the project warranty period under the construction contract for defective work. It is also typically assigned to the project lender as collateral. In some situations, this protection is provided within the scope of the performance and payment bonds.

[5] Retention Money Bonds

As discussed in Chapter 15, construction contracts routinely provide that a portion of the periodic payments to the contractor under a construction contract are withheld (retained) pending completion. Rather than forgo the use of this money, contractors sometimes provide retention money bonds to the project company as security for project completion. The contractor can then receive and use the money that would otherwise be retained. If construction is not completed, the project company can apply the contingency amount covered by the bond for project completion.

[6] Labor and Material Payment Bond

Suppliers, vendors, and subcontractors to the contractor generally have the right to place a lien on the project if they are not paid for the work performed or equipment supplied. The nature of this lien is governed by the law of the host country.

In many situations, the project company could find itself paying the same amount twice: once to the contractor and again to the contractor's supplier, vendor, or subcontractor. A labor and material payment bond can be required of the contractor to guard against this risk. This bond requires a surety to pay the unpaid supplier, vendor, or subcontractor amounts due it from the contractor.

§ 20.10 COMMERCIAL INSURANCE

[1] Generally

Commercial insurance is an important credit enhancement tool in a project financing. Project risks not otherwise covered that are insurable at a reasonable price will be addressed in an insurance program, which includes the possibility for self-insurance of certain agreed-upon minimal risks. The insurance requirements will include policy deductibles set at realistic levels, self-insurance amounts set at levels that cannot undermine cash flows needed for payment

of debt service and operating costs, and minimum creditworthiness and stability of insurance underwriters.

[2] Commercial Insurance and the Project Lender

Because the insurance protection package is so important to the project lender, it will require protection against a loss of the coverage and certain additional rights. These are discussed below.

Additional Insured. An additional insured[4] is any entity, other than the project company, that receives certain contractual benefits of an "insured" under the policy. The mere designation of additional insured status does not burden the project lender with any obligation to pay premiums, although it can elect to do so to preserve its collateral.

Once the project lender is listed as such under the project company's policy, the lender is treated the same as if it was separately covered. Importantly, however, the lender would not be paid insurance proceeds under the policy unless it is also listed as the loss payee.

Loss Payee. Once listed as a loss payee, insurance proceeds payable as a result of an insured loss will be made to the project lender first.[5] Typically, the loss payee clause states that insurance proceeds are paid to the project company and the project lender, as their interests may appear. This structure provides the project lender with control of insurance proceeds, up to the amount of the debt. The debt documents will then determine whether the proceeds will be used to repair or rebuild the project or be used to prepay principal on the underlying project indebtedness. Of course, neither the project company nor the lender would receive proceeds under third-party liability insurance. As with additional insured status, loss payee status does not impose upon the lender any responsibility for premium payment.

---

[4] An *additional named insured* is the term sometimes applied to a beneficiary of an existing insurance policy, while *additional insured* is the term applied to a beneficiary included in the policy when the policy is first issued. They are often used interchangeably.

[5] Sometimes, the project debt documents allow a pre-agreed small amount to be paid directly to the project company for minor claims.

Non-vitiation Clauses. In addition to named insured and loss payee protections, the project lender will also require that commercial insurance contain a non-vitiation (or breach of condition) clause. In general, an insurer can void an insurance policy on the basis of misrepresentation, non-disclosure, or breach of warranty by the insured, or on the basis of mistake. Each of these is very difficult for the project lender to determine in its due diligence process and impractical to monitor during the term of the loan. A non-vitiation provision prevents the insurer from voiding a policy or refusing to make a payment to the lender as loss payee. These provisions are difficult to negotiate, and their availability is influenced greatly by changing insurance market conditions.

Reinsurance. Some emerging market countries require that project companies procure insurance within the host country. Alternatively, exchange controls in the host country may have the practical effect of requiring that insurance be obtained in the host country. However, the project lender may determine that the creditworthiness of the host country insurer is insufficient. Also, the laws, court system, or other local risks may make the lender similarly uncomfortable with a local insurer. In these situations, the project lender may require that all or most of the insurance program be reinsured in the international insurance marketplace.

A reinsurance program does not provide any contract rights between the reinsurer and the project company or lender. It is, in simplest terms, an indemnity agreement between the insurer and the reinsurer. For direct contract privity to exist, a reinsurance cut-through provision must be included as an endorsement to the project company's policy.

Cut-through endorsements are available in several varieties. The complete cut-through endorsement redirects the payment of reinsurance proceeds from the insurer to a named beneficiary. A cut-through guarantee endorsement redirects the payment in the same way, and also covers the payment of proceeds attributable to the exposure retained by the primary insured.

It is in an insolvency situation that the cut-through is of great importance. If the primary insurer becomes insolvent, this endorsement redirects payments to the project lender, not the primary insurer (and its creditors), subject to local insolvency laws.

Waiver of Subrogation. A waiver of subrogation clause is customarily required in project finance. In general, upon payment, an insurer becomes subrogated to all the rights that its insured had against a third party. That is, the insurer can pursue the third party responsible for the loss in order to recover the insurance proceeds paid to the insured. The project lender does not want the insurer to pursue any such claims against the lender or the project company.

Collateral Security. Finally, the project finance lender will require that the project company assign to it, as collateral security, all insurance proceeds and policies. This, of course, does not affect the insurer but does provide the lender with protection from any other creditors of the project company.

Other Insurance Issues. The project finance lender will also require that the project company comply with other matters related to insurance, such as submission of evidence of payment of premiums; agreement by the insurance company that it will provide the lender with advance knowledge of policy cancellation, nonpayment of premiums and policy amendment, pursuant to a notice of cancellation or change clause; and an agreement that the lender will have no liability for unpaid premiums, but will have the option to pay them if the project company does not.

[3] **Types of Commercial Insurance**
Several types of insurance policies are available to cover risks in project financings. Each of these is described below. Because insurance varies significantly from country to country, and over time, the following discussion may not be accurate for each situation.

Contractor's All Risks. During the construction phase, project finance contractors are typically required to obtain property damage insurance such as "all risk" builder's risk insurance to pay for direct loss or damage occurring to the work during construction, however caused, whether at the manufacturer's premises, during transit, or on site. It generally terminates on acceptance of the project by the project company. The builder's risk policy applies to all perils that are not specifically excluded, including the damage consequences of a defective design, material, and workmanship, and protection during start-up and testing. It does not extend to coverage of losses that result from contractual indemnity or liquidated damage payments for late delivery or completion.

Advanced Loss of Revenue. Advanced loss of revenue provides insurance protection against the financial consequences for loss of revenue because of a delay following an insured loss or damage during the construction period.

Marine Cargo. Marine cargo insurance is available to provide protection against loss or damage caused to equipment and materials during transit from the shipper to the project site. It includes protection for losses sustained during unloading.

Marine Advanced Loss of Revenue. Marine advanced loss of revenue provides insurance protection against the financial consequences for loss of revenue as a result of a delay following an insured loss or damage.

Operator's All Risks. Operator's all risks provides protection against loss or damage, however caused, occurring after commercial operation. The coverage also includes protection for equipment being overhauled or repaired off the site.

Operator's Loss of Revenue. Operator's loss of revenue coverage includes protection for a loss of revenue suffered because of physical loss or damage after completion of the project. It can be extended to cover loss of revenue arising from loss or damage at a supplier's site.

Third-Party Liability. Third-party liability coverage provides protection against damage and losses attributable to legal liability for bodily injury and property damage. There are several specific exclusions from the coverage of the standard comprehensive general liability policy.

These exclusions include contractual liability, which covers liabilities that arise under many types of contracts; employer's liability, which includes liability under worker's compensation, unemployment compensation, and disability benefits; automobile liability; pollution, which includes bodily injury or property damage resulting from pollutants, that is regularly discharged in the normal course of the insured's business; war; loss of use; property damage to the named insured's products arising out of such products; and explosion, collapse, and underground hazard.

Liabilities for catastrophic occurrences are covered by umbrella and excess liability insurance policies. An umbrella policy generally provides coverage protection in excess of coverage provided by primary policies. Excess liability policies provide increased monetary limits.

Employers' Liability/Workers' Compensation. The employers' liability or workers' compensation coverage protects against legal liability or compensation for death or injury to employees.

Finite Risk. Finite risk insurance provides access to insurance proceeds in a multi-year structure.

Trade Disruption. Trade disruption insurance is a marine coverage providing loss of revenue protection, as well as extra expense protection, for a wide variety of risks, including property, political, transit, and force majeure.

[4] The "Commercially Available in the Marketplace" Standard

It is sometimes tempting to defer consideration of the precise insurance that will be required in a contract by stating that the insurance will be required only to the extent "commercially available in the marketplace." In many countries, however, there is no established insurance market. Insurance companies in those markets might not possess the ability to deal with the complex risks inherent in a project finance transaction or to provide insurance in the coverage amounts required to protect the project participants. Consequently, if such a phrase is used, it is important that the insurance market be adequately defined as a viable insurance market.

[5] Exchange Controls

In some projects, insurance policies may need to be denominated in the currency of the host country. If so, and a loss occurs, it may be difficult to export the insurance proceeds out of the host country. If exported, a loss may occur because of exchange rate fluctuations. This is a particular concern where there is a decision not to rebuild a project after a casualty.

If the exchange of insurance proceeds can be approved in advance, then this should be done. Alternatively, it may be prudent to require the local insurer to re-insure the risk offshore and then have the proceeds payable under the re-insurance contract assigned to the project company for payment should a loss occur. Exchange controls are discussed more fully in Chapter 3.

[6] Export Financing Requirements

If part of the project financing is supplied by an export credit bank, it will typically require that the project obtain insurance on the goods financed. If so, it will likely require that the insurance be obtained from companies in the export bank's home country.

§ 20.11 POLITICAL RISK INSURANCE, B LOAN PROGRAMS, AND GUARANTEES

[1] Generally

Political risks can be mitigated in several ways. As discussed in Chapter 3, the project can be structured to capture hard currency revenue streams offshore, thereby reducing currency transfer and convertibility risk. As discussed in Chapter 21, the involvement in a project by a multilateral financial institution, such as the International Finance Corporation (IFC), can reduce host-government interference with a project's ability to repay private-sector debt. Another option is a loan repayment guarantee by a bilateral or multilateral agency, through a political risk insurance program, which can be used to address political risk.[6] Of these, Japan Export-Import Insurance Depart-

ment/Ministry of International Trade and Industry, and U.S. Overseas Private Investment Corporation are the largest. Finally, political risk insurance from a commercial company is another way to reduce this risk.

The use of the term *insurance* is somewhat misleading. The risk coverage is narrow in scope, and the claims procedure is cumbersome. These programs do not completely substitute for a project management program that is sensitive to local political customs and procedures.

As discussed in this section, both bilateral and multilateral agencies provide political risk insurance.[7] Bilateral agencies are adept at working with projects within a foreign country's borders. Those projects that cross borders, such as the Caspian Sea Oil Pipeline and the Bolivia-to-Brazil natural gas pipeline, increase political risks. Consequently, multilateral agencies may be better able to deal with these multi-country mega-projects.

[2] Multilateral Investment Guarantee Agency

Generally. The Multilateral Investment Guarantee Agency (MIGA), created in 1988 and headquartered in Washington, D.C., has 168 member countries as of July 2006.[8] It is an affiliate of the World Bank.

According to the convention that established MIGA, its purpose is to

encourage the flow of investments for productive purposes among member countries, and in particular to developing member countries, thus supplementing the activities of the International Bank for Reconstruction and Development...,

[6] *See generally* Kenneth J. Vandevelde, *The Bilateral Investment Treaty Programme of the United States*, 21 Cornell Int'l L. J. 201 (1988); Jurgen Voss, *The Protection and Promotion of Foreign Investment in Developing Countries:*

Interests, Interdependencies and Intricacies, 30 Int'l & Comp. L. Q. 686, 686–88 (1981).

[7] *See* S. Linn Williams, *Political and Other Risk Insurance: OPIC, MIGA, EXIMBANK and Other Providers*, 5 Pace Int'l L. Rev.59, 64 (1993); *see also* Rodney Short, *Export Credit Agencies, Project Finance, and Commercial Risk: Whose Risk Is It, Anyway?*, 24 Fordham Int'l L. J. 1371 (2001) (questioning whether export credit agencies should provide long-term commercial risk insurance).

[8] MIGA was created under the Convention Establishing the Multilateral Investment Guarantee Agency, *done* October 11, 1985, *entered into force* April 12, 1988, reprinted in 24 I. L. M. 1598 (1985); *codified in* Multilateral Investment Guarantee Agency Act, Pub. L. No. 100–202, Section 10(e) (1987), 101 Stat. 1329–34, 22 U. S. C. § 2901c *et seq.*

the International Finance Corporation and other international development finance institutions.[9]

MIGA is organized to encourage foreign investment in developing member countries by providing guarantees (insurance), including coinsurance and reinsurance, against non-commercial risks.[10] Based on this grant of authority, MIGA provides limited insurance against (i) currency inconvertibility and transfer; (ii) expropriation; (iii) war, revolution, and civil disturbances; and (iv) breach of undertakings by the host government. These coverages can be purchased individually or in combination.

Eligibility. Eligible investments are new investments originating in a member country, but outside of the country in which the investment is made,[11] for investment in any developing member country.[12] Also eligible are investments for expansion, modernization, or financial restructuring of existing projects in developing member countries. Privatization investments are eligible.

To be eligible for the insurance, the lender or investor must be organized in, and have its principal place of business in, a member country (other than the country in which the investment is made) or be majority-owned by nationals of member countries.[13]

Eligibility is further conditioned on MIGA determining that participation is justified based on economic viability, its developmental effect, compliance with local laws, and investment conditions in the host country.[14]

Coverage. MIGA insurance covers equity and debt. Debt covered includes medium and long-

term debt guaranteed by an equity investor; and medium and long-term debt provided by a commercial lender, which debt relates to an investment covered by MIGA.[15]

Before MIGA coverage is issued, approval must be obtained from the host country.[16] Typically, MIGA obtains the necessary approval itself. This procedure increases the likelihood that the host government will work with MIGA in a way that reduces claims exposure.

As of 2006, MIGA would insure up to US$4 of bank debt for every US$1 of equity investment. Investors may choose any combination of the four types of coverage. Equity investments can be covered up to 90 percent and debt up to 95 percent. MIGA may insure up to $200 million, and if necessary, more can be arranged through syndication of insurance. A country limit of US$620 million is also in place.

MIGA coverage cannot be cancelled by MIGA unless the insured entity defaults in its obligations. An insured can terminate the insurance on any anniversary date of the coverage after the third anniversary.

The rates charged for MIGA coverage vary with the risk and project. World Bank risk management currently limits the total exposure MIGA can take in any project, with an aggregate cap for exposure in any country.

CURRENCY INCONVERTIBILITY AND CURRENCY TRANSFER RISKS. MIGA provides currency inconvertibility risk coverage for losses due to the inability to convert local currency returns (profits, principal, interest, capital, and other amounts) into foreign exchange and the inability to transfer foreign exchange outside of the host country. This protection is available whether inconvertibility is due to excessive delays in acquiring foreign exchange caused by the host's government's action or inaction, adverse changes in exchange laws or regulations, or a lack of foreign exchange. These coverages do not extend to currency devaluation (depreciation) risks.

Compensation paid by MIGA under the guarantee is in the form of the currency chosen in the guarantee. Upon receipt of the blocked local currency, MIGA will make the conversion.

---

[9] Convention Establishing the Multilateral Investment Guarantee Agency, art. 2 (October 11, 1985).

[10] *Id.* art. 2(a).   [11] *Id.* art. 2(a).

[12] *Id.* art. 14. A "developing country" is a member country listed from time to time on a schedule to the convention. *Id.* art. 3(c).

[13] *Id.* art. 13.

[14] The eligibility factors are "(i) the economic soundness of the investment and its contribution to the development of the host country; (ii) compliance of the investment with the host country's laws and regulations; (iii) consistency of the investment with the declared development objectives and priorities of the host country; and (iv) the investment conditions in the host country, including the availability of fair and equitable treatment and legal protection for the investment." *Id.* art. 12(d).

[15] *Id.* art. 12(a), (b).   [16] *Id.* art. 15.

EXPROPRIATION. Expropriation coverage provided by MIGA insures against the risk of a total or partial investment loss caused by a taking by the host government of the project assets or investor control over a project, whether by expropriation, creeping expropriation – a series of acts that, over time, have an expropriatory effect, nationalization, or confiscation of funds or tangible assets. Government actions that are bona fide, nondiscriminatory actions are not covered if taken in the exercise of legitimate regulatory authority.

For total expropriation of equity interests, MIGA compensates the insured for the net book value of the investment. For expropriation of funds, MIGA pays the insured portion of the blocked funds. Partial expropriation is compensable at the net book value for non-fund assets, and up to the insured amount for funds. For debt, MIGA insures the outstanding principal and accrued and unpaid interest.

Before compensation is paid, MIGA requires an assignment to MIGA of all right, title, and interest in the expropriated investment.

WAR, REVOLUTION, AND CIVIL DISOBEDIENCE. Losses associated with physical damage, destruction, or disappearance to tangible assets, or a substantial interruption of business due to acts of war, revolution, insurrection, *coups d'état*, terrorism, or sabotage in the host country are also covered by MIGA insurance programs. The action must be politically motivated and result in damage or destruction of the property covered.

Coverage also extends to business interruptions that are essential to project viability caused by war and civil disturbances. This business interruption coverage extends for the period set forth in the insurance. It is effective only when a total loss is experienced.

For equity interests, MIGA compensates the insured for the least of the net book value, replacement cost, or repair costs of the assets damaged. For debt, MIGA will pay the outstanding principal and accrued and unpaid interest in default as a result of the damage caused by the war or civil disturbance.

BREACH OF UNDERTAKING BY HOST GOVERNMENT. Finally, MIGA insurance coverage is available to protect against the risk of breach or repudiation of a contractual undertaking by the host government in an agreement with the project company. The insurance covers losses associated with the breach.

If there is an alleged breach or repudiation, the coverage insures against the risk that the insured is denied access to an appropriate forum to adjudicate the dispute within a reasonable period, or is denied the right to enforce a judgment or arbitration award relating to the breach. The contract must permit the investor to invoke a dispute resolution procedure, such as an arbitration. MIGA insurance proceeds will not be paid until after an award for damages has been made by the appropriate dispute resolution forum and after a specified period of nonpayment by the host government. Proceeds will also be paid after a specified period of time in which the dispute resolution mechanism fails to function because of host government action.

LENGTH. MIGA coverage is for up to fifteen years (possibly twenty if justified by the nature of the project). MIGA cannot terminate the contract unless the guarantee holder defaults on its contractual obligations to MIGA, but the guarantee holder may reduce or cancel coverage on any contract anniversary date starting with the third.

[3] International Finance Corporation

The International Finance Corporation (IFC), affiliated with the World Bank, was created in 1956 to promote private enterprise in the developing world. It is headquartered in Washington, D.C. In contrast to the World Bank, which loans money only to governments, the IFC lends to, and makes equity investments in, private companies.

The IFC is favorably regarded as an entity whose participation in a project helps mobilize additional loan financing and equity investments. It is active in loan syndication and security underwriting activities.

CURRENCY INCONVERTIBILITY AND CURRENCY TRANSFER RISKS. The IFC co-financing program offers rates that are not concessionary. These rates are often high, which serves, in part, to attract commercial lenders to the co-financing program. Commercial lenders are also attracted by IFC involvement, believing that the host government will be more likely to support a project in its country because of the IFC involvement. In fact, one of the greatest benefits of IFC involvement is the ability of the IFC to mobilize other financing sources.

Under the co-financing structure, the IFC provides financing to a project, and sells participation interests in the "B" loans to commercial lenders. It retains the "A" loan portion. Under the IFC umbrella, the commercial bank "B" loans are treated in the same way as the IFC "A" loans: The IFC documents and administers the loans, and collects and distributes payments and collateral pro rata among itself and the "B" loan lenders. An "A" loan default is also a "B" loan default.

The IFC "B Loan" program provides some protection against the currency inconvertibility and currency transfer risks. A "B" loan is a loan made by the IFC, or any other multilateral agency, that is participated out to other lenders but administered by the multilateral agency. Because the IFC originates, closes, and administers the loan, it is perceived that the participant banks have the same type of "preferred creditor status" that multilateral agencies have.

IFC-financed projects are typically designed to benefit the economy of the host country. This is accomplished most often by increasing the country's ability to earn hard currency. Nonetheless, great emphasis is placed on the potential success of the project financed because government guarantees are not available to repay the debt.

In general, IFC borrowers are locally organized companies. If the laws of the host countries permit, however, foreign ownership of these local entities is allowed.

[4] World Bank Guarantees

The World Bank, or the International Bank for Reconstruction and Development, was originally formed after the World War II to provide financing for war-torn Western Europe. Its scope and activities have evolved since that time, and it is now active in a variety of projects throughout the world. It is a nonprofit international organization that is funded and owned by the various world governments. The World Bank is discussed more fully in Chapter 21.

The World Bank guarantees loans made by commercial lenders to the private sector in certain developing countries, provided the host country issues a counter-guarantee. Political risks covered include losses attributable to currency convertibility and transfer, breach of contract by the host government (and its agencies), and changes in regulations that affect debt repayment. There is no limit on the amount or term, although the counter-guarantee requirement has a restricting role, particularly with the IMF, on the maximum aggregate amount of counter-guarantees the host country can have outstanding without jeopardizing its economic future. The requirement for a host-country counter-guarantee has limited the number of World Bank guarantees issued in project financings.

CURRENCY INCONVERTIBILITY AND CURRENCY TRANSFER RISKS. The World Bank provides guarantees to commercial lenders against political risks. The coverage is up to 100 percent of the debt exposure. Political risks covered by the guarantee are negotiable. The guarantee program was previously offered under the Expanded Co-financing Operation program (ECO), administered through the Co-Financing and Financial Advisory Services Group.

EXPROPRIATION. No coverage is provided by the World Bank for the expropriation risk.

WAR, REVOLUTION, AND CIVIL DISOBEDIENCE. No coverage is provided by the World Bank for the war risk.

BREACH OF UNDERTAKING BY HOST GOVERNMENT. The World Bank offers protection against the risk of breach of a contractual undertaking by the host government in an agreement with the project company. The protection covers losses associated with the breach.

[5] Asian Development Bank

The Asian Development Bank (ADB) was formed in 1966. It has members in 47 Asian countries and 19 industrialized countries from outside Asia. Any project eligible for ADB financing is also eligible for political risk protection. No counter-guarantee from the host government is required for a maximum coverage amount of $150 million or 50 percent of the project cost, whichever is lower.

CURRENCY INCONVERTIBILITY AND CURRENCY TRANSFER RISKS. The ADB provides protection against a breach of a government commitment on currency convertibility and nontransferability.

EXPROPRIATION. Coverage is available against the risks of confiscation, expropriation, nationalization, or deprivation of project assets.

POLITICAL VIOLENCE. Coverage is provided against the risk of political violence.

BREACH OF UNDERTAKING BY HOST GOVERNMENT. ADB offers protection against the risk of breach of a contractual undertaking by the host government in an agreement with the project company. These include maintenance of an agreed-upon regulatory structure, delivery by state-owned entities of required raw materials or other inputs, failure by state-owned entities to purchase project outputs, failure to build infrastructure needed for the project, and similar commitments.

[6] Inter-American Development Bank

The Inter-American Development Bank (IDB) was organized in 1959 and is a major lender to Latin American and Caribbean member countries. It is currently the principal source of external finance for most Latin American and Caribbean countries. The forty-seven member countries include Latin American countries, the United States, and other industrialized nations.

The IDB can guarantee loans made by private financial sources to both the public and private sectors. Unlike the World Bank, the IDB can provide guarantees without counter-guarantees by the host country's government.

IDB guarantees loans made to the private sector in developing countries against breach of contract, currency inconvertibility, and transfer risk, and for other political risks. Coverage extends up to 50 percent of project costs or $150 million, whichever is less.

There are comprehensive all-risk credit guarantees available for loans made by a commercial lender. These guarantees cannot exceed 25 percent of total project costs (40% for projects in smaller economies), or $200 million, whichever is lower.

The IDB has recently created a US$1 billion Guarantee Disbursement Loan program that provides the option of disbursing loans in the form of an IDB guarantee. This guarantee structure allows a borrower to take all or a portion of a loan in the form of a guarantee and use that guarantee as credit enhancement for loan terms available

from the private sector. This guarantee can be used for such purposes as reducing the interest rate available from the private sector for project debt.

CURRENCY INCONVERTIBILITY AND CURRENCY TRANSFER RISKS. IDB provides currency inconvertibility/transfer risk coverage. This coverage does not extend to currency devaluation risks.

EXPROPRIATION. No coverage is provided by IDB for the expropriation risk.

WAR, REVOLUTION, AND CIVIL DISOBEDIENCE. No coverage is provided by IDB for the war risk.

BREACH OF UNDERTAKING BY HOST GOVERNMENT. IDB offers protection against the risk of breach of a contractual undertaking by the host government in an agreement with the project company. These include maintenance of an agreed-upon regulatory structure, delivery by state-owned entities of required raw materials or other inputs, failure by state-owned entities to purchase project outputs, failure to build infrastructure needed for the project, and similar commitments.

[7] Overseas Private Investment Corporation (U.S.)

The Overseas Private Investment Corporation (OPIC), located in Washington, D.C., is an agency of the executive branch of the United States government.[17] It is self-sustaining, operating at no cost to the taxpayers of the U.S.

Established in 1971,[18] OPIC is organized to assist participation by United States private companies in economic development of developing countries, emerging democracies, and fledgling

---

[17] The purpose of OPIC, as set forth in the enabling legislation, is

> [t]o mobilize and facilitate the participation of United States private capital and skills in the economic and social development of less developed countries and areas, and countries in transition from nonmarket to market economies, thereby complementing the development assistance objectives of the United States . . .

22 U. S. C. § 2191.

[18] OPIC is an independent corporation operating under the Foreign Assistance Act of 1961, 22 U. S. C. §§ 2191–2206b. Well before its creation, the United States provided inconvertibility coverage to U.S. investors after World War II as part of the Marshall Plan. Later, before the creation of OPIC, the U.S. Agency for International Development provided political risk insurance to U.S. investors with investments in developing countries.

free-market economies. Its mandate is world-wide.

OPIC is widely known for its political risk insurance program, in which it covers losses attributable to certain political risks, including inconvertibility, expropriation, and political violence. OPIC insurance obligations are backed by the full faith and credit of the U.S. government.

In general, OPIC insurance coverage is available for new investments, privatizations, and expansions or modernizations of existing facilities. Acquisitions of existing facilities are also covered, but only if the investor undertakes an expansion or modernization program at the facility. Eligibility for OPIC insurance is determined by the Foreign Assistance Act.[19] Only (i) citizens of the United States, (ii) U.S. corporations or other business entities substantially owned[20] by U.S. citizens, (iii) foreign business entities owned at least 95 percent by U.S. citizens, or (iv) an eligible U.S. business entity, qualify for OPIC programs. Although investments in about 150 countries are eligible for OPIC participation, policy considerations and statutory developments from time to time limit specific country participation.[21]

There is no requirement that the foreign facility be owned or controlled by U.S. investors, however. Where there is foreign ownership, only the part of the investment made by the U.S. investor is insured. Restrictions apply to investments in facilities in which majority ownership or control is vested in a foreign government.

The effect of the proposed investment on the U.S. economy is a part of the criteria. The

considerations include negative effects on U.S. employment, imposition of requirements by the host country that substantially reduce the potential U.S. trade benefits of the investment, and significant adverse effects on the U.S. balance of payments. If any of the foregoing will exist because of the project, coverage is denied.

Also, the effect of the investment on the host country determines eligibility. In general, OPIC supports projects that respond to development needs, and that improve private initiative and competition.

The United States and each host country enter into bilateral agreements that relate to the OPIC programs. Under these agreements, the approval of the host government must be obtained before the OPIC insurance is issued.

For equity investments, OPIC insurance provides coverage against currency inconvertibility, expropriation, and political violence for investments and returns. Equity investment coverage includes protection for a range of investments, including capital, in-kind contributions, parent company debt, and loan guarantees.

For debt, OPIC inconvertibility insurance coverage pays compensation for defaults on scheduled payments that result from deterioration in the ability to convert these payments from local currency to dollars or to transfer dollars outside the host country. In the case of expropriation or political violence, compensation generally is payable if the borrower defaults on a scheduled payment as a direct result of one of these events, and the default lasts three months (or one month in the event of subsequent defaults caused by the same event). Loans must have a tenor of at least three years, and borrowers must be private-sector enterprises in the foreign country.

CURRENCY INCONVERTIBILITY AND CURRENCY TRANSFER RISKS. OPIC provides coverage against the risks of inconvertibility and transfer, thereby substituting itself for the central bank. The project company must obtain and maintain the underlying legal right to convert and transfer the local currency, however.

Before issuing this insurance, OPIC analyzes a country's currency conversion and transfer laws, regulations, and procedures. Once it does so, it establishes a baseline against which coverage is measured. If there does not exist a legal and

[19] 22 U. S. C. § 2191.
[20] OPIC deems a corporation organized under the laws of the United States or its states and territories to be beneficially owned by U.S. citizens if more than 50 percent of each class of its issued and outstanding stock is owned by U.S. citizens, either directly or beneficially. Where shares of stock of a corporation with widely dispersed public ownership are held in the names of trustees or nominees (including stock brokerage firms) with addresses in the United States, such shares may be deemed to be owned by U.S. citizens unless the investor has knowledge to the contrary. OPIC also permits the beneficial ownership of U.S. corporations to be determined by tracing back through any foreign ownership of their shares to the ultimate beneficial owners.
[21] U.S. statutes and policies sometimes change the availability of OPIC programs in certain countries. For example, in 2006, following the election of President Ellen John Sirleaf and the conclusion of its long civil war, OPIC was "reopened" for Liberia.

effective procedure for conversion and transfer, OPIC will not offer the coverage.

OPIC insurance covers changes in laws, regulations, and procedures that impair convertibility. Also covered is "passive" inconvertibility, which results from conversion delays (in excess of that usual in the country at the time the coverage is issued) caused by applicable officials.

In countries where convertibility is a general problem, OPIC can structure coverage that is based on an offshore account. Under such a structure, hard currency revenue is deposited in an offshore account. OPIC will insure against the risk of abrogation, repudiation, or rescission of the consent to, or approval of, that structure by the host country, thus insuring its viability.

The inconvertibility coverage does not extend to project fuel or other project inputs. Thus, it does not cover convertibility of local currency to hard currency needed to purchase project inputs that are to be paid for in hard currency.

OPIC coverage does not guarantee an exchange rate. Also, it does not extend to currency devaluation.

EXPROPRIATION. OPIC coverage is available to protect against nationalization, confiscation, expropriation of an enterprise, and "creeping" expropriation. For OPIC purposes, expropriatory acts are illegal acts by a foreign governing authority that deprive an investor of fundamental equity rights or interests. This action must be in violation of principles of international law or a material breach of local law. Generally, these acts must be a total, not partial, expropriatory act.

Not covered are reasonable exercises of a government's legitimate revenue and regulatory powers, such as increasing tax rates (unless in direct violation of an agreement to the contrary); and actions of the host government provoked or instigated by the project company.

OPIC recognizes a distinction between governmental acts and commercial acts in project financings. Actions by the government in a role of a commercial party in a project, such as fuel supplier, purchaser, or investor are excluded from coverage.

For example, OPIC recognizes that *power* project finance transactions sometimes involve contracts between the project company and an entity of the host government. In such cases, it provides an exception to the government action exclusion. OPIC coverage requires that the dispute resolution procedures of the contract be complied with before any payment of insurance proceeds. To that extent, OPIC coverage is to insure the risk of noncompliance by the government with the agreed-upon dispute resolution procedures, and payment of any award resulting from those procedures.

A slightly different insurance program is offered for *oil and gas* projects. In such projects, OPIC insures against losses caused by material changes in project agreements unilaterally imposed on the project company by the host government. Examples include abrogation of contract, contract impairment or repudiation, and material breaches of important project contracts between the project company and the host government, including concession agreements, production sharing agreements, and service agreements. Unlike power projects, there is no requirement that the dispute resolution process be completed before the claim matures. Also, coverage can be obtained to guard against the risk of interference with operations that causes the cessation of operations for six months or more as a result of political violence.

In general, OPIC coverage requires an assignment of the entire rights of the insured to OPIC as a condition precedent to payment of proceeds. This allows OPIC to pursue the host government for reimbursement. Because it is likely that these interests are also pledged to one or more project lenders, intercreditor agreements need to address this possibility.

For lender coverage, OPIC will pay the scheduled payments of principal, together with accrued interest to the date of payment, that the lender would have received. OPIC generally has the option to make a full prepayment of the debt.

POLITICAL VIOLENCE. Political violence insurance coverage includes protection against property damage and loss of business income caused by violence motivated by political considerations. Examples include war (declared or undeclared), hostile acts by national or international forces, revolution, civil war, insurrection, and politically motivated civil strife. Terrorism and sabotage, if politically motivated, are other examples. Actions to promote student or labor goals are excluded, unless politically motivated.

Like other insurers, OPIC places limitations on the amount of compensation that will be paid for property damage and loss of business income. For example, property damage compensation is generally based on replacement cost or the lesser of original cost, fair-market value at loss or the cost of repair, subject to an overall cap. Replacement cost is limited to twice the original value and is paid only if the equipment is replaced in the host country.

Coverage for loss of business income is generally limited to one year. If the project has critical infrastructure off the project site, such as a rail link or transmission facility, OPIC can cover losses to these sites also.

For lender coverage, OPIC will pay the scheduled payments of principal, together with accrued interest to the date of payment, that the lender would have received.

Recognizing the unique nature of oil and gas projects, which do not diminish in value over time if not used, OPIC modifies the insurance program. If acts of political violence make it impossible or dangerous to operate such projects, OPIC will pay the project the net book value in exchange for an assignment of the rights in the project. The project sponsors can repurchase these rights for the price paid by OPIC if the political environment changes so that within five years of the date of the original disruption the project can be operated.

PROJECT CONTRACTORS AND EXPORTERS. Project finance lenders and equity investors are not the only participants that have these risks. OPIC insurance coverage can protect these participants against the wrongful calling of contractor guarantees (such as bid, performance, or advance payment), loss of physical assets and bank accounts due to confiscation or political violence, inconvertibility of equipment sale proceeds, and losses due to certain breaches by foreign buyers of contractual disputes resolution procedures.

BOND FINANCING IN EMERGING MARKET PROJECT FINANCE. As discussed below under a separate heading, in 1999 OPIC introduced a political risk insurance program to enhance bonds issued to U.S. investors. The program is designed to acknowledge the continuing use of bond financing for emerging-market project finance.

[8] United States Export-Import Bank

U.S. Export-Import Bank (USExim), an independent U.S. agency, is organized to assist the export of nonmilitary U.S. capital, goods, and services. In 1994, USExim established a project finance division designed to assist U.S. exporters to compete in new international infrastructure projects. USExim support is particularly important to U.S. exporters as more and more developing countries reduce sovereign-guaranteed borrowing.

USExim can support the political risks in a project with a political risk only guarantee. The bank undertakes a detailed due diligence risk review of the project before committing to issue the guarantee. USExim will consider the following questions:

- Are there aspects to the proposed project arrangements that could influence, precipitate, or cause an event to occur that could result in a claim being made under the guarantee?
- Are there industry specific issues that could result in greater political risk?
- If a claim is made on the guarantee, is the project capable of repaying the debt?
- Is the host country a party to an international convention or is there a project-specific agreement providing some other form of government support? (This could mitigate the risk of a claim being paid under USExim's coverage or increase the likelihood of recovery after a claim is made.)

In addition, the project must comply with OECD guidelines, the requirements of USExim's Engineering and Environment Division, and its policies and procedures regarding utilization.

[9] Japanese Bank for International Cooperation

The Japanese Bank for International Cooperation (JBIC) was organized in 1999 as a Japanese governmental financial institution. The activities of the former Japanese Export-Import Bank were merged into this new entity. JBIC is able to provide political risk insurance in limited situations.

[10] Export Credit Guarantee Department of the United Kingdom Department of Trade and Industry

The Export Credit Guarantee Department (ECGD) is a governmental agency of the United Kingdom that provides commercial and political risk protection to United Kingdom exporters, investors, and lenders. A number of political risk insurance coverages are available, with terms as long as fifteen years. Under its programs, a wide variety of political risks can be insured. For example, project lenders can be protected against nonpayment directly caused by reason of political causes, including war, civil war, and rebellion; prevention of, or delay in, the payment of external debt by the host government or by that of a third country through which payment must be made; cancellation or non-renewal of an export license; and expropriation where the host government is not a shareholder in the project. The exact coverage is determined on a project-by-project basis.

[11] Export Development Corporation (Canada)

EDC is a Crown Corporation that provides financing and risk management services to Canadian exporters and investors in up to 200 markets worldwide. In 2005, EDC's services and deal structuring capabilities helped to facilitate $57.5 billion in transactions for nearly 7,000 Canadian companies. EDC is financially self-sufficient and operates on commercial principles. EDC can provide political risk insurance, covering up to 90 percent of losses. Coverage is available for breach of contract risk, conversion risk, expropriation risk (including gradual or creeping expropriation), nonpayment by a sovereign obligor, political violence risk, repossession risk, and transfer risk.

[12] Other OCED Government Insurance Entities

Each member country of the Organisation for Economic Co-operation and Development[22] (OECD) has established political risk insurance programs similar to the United States OPIC program.

[13] Other OCED Export Credit Agencies

Each member country of the OECD has established export credit agencies similar to the export-import credit agencies discussed above. The loans are typically available in project financings to the extent proceeds are used to purchase goods or services originating in the home country of the export-import bank.

[14] Commercial Insurance

A small community of insurers offers complementary and alternative political risk insurance.[23] These include Lloyd's of London, Zurich-American, American International Underwriters, and Chubb.

Scope of Coverage. In general, these coverages are of a limited term of one to three years and do not typically match the term of the project debt. However, some private insurers are now able to provide cover for up to ten years, almost matching the typical project's debt term.

Private insurance companies are generally more flexible than OPIC, MIGA, or the export-import agencies because they are not constrained by public policy considerations. That is, private insurance companies can issue political risk coverage without regard to a project sponsor's nationality or the economic effect of the project in the sponsor's home country. In addition, they provide benefits of confidentiality and possible cost savings associated with negotiation of complete, single-source insurance protection for a project, including casualty, liability, and other insurance. Further, they are able to tailor insurance programs to the specific needs of a project and a sponsor's credit profile, whereas a public agency is not so flexible in its program offerings. However, commercial insurers rarely offer currency transfer and political violence coverage in developing countries and emerging economies.

---

[22] Current members are Australia, Austria, Belgium, Canada, Denmark, Finland, France, Germany, Greece, Iceland, Ireland, Italy, Japan, Luxembourg, the Netherlands, New Zealand, Norway, Portugal, Spain, Sweden, Switzerland, Turkey, the United Kingdom, the United States, and its territories (Guam, Puerto Rico, and the Virgin Islands).

[23] *See generally* Douglas A. Paul, *New Developments in Private Political Risk Insurance and Trade Finance*, 21 INT'L LAW. 709, 712 (1987).

MIGA Cooperative Underwriting Program (CUP). Multilateral and bilateral agencies are beginning to cooperate with the private insurance industry, in an effort to create insurance programs that better respond to the marketplace. MIGA, in response to a World Bank mandate to create additional political risk insurance capacity for the private market, created the Cooperative Underwriting Program (CUP). CUP provides a stimulus to private insurers when reluctant to participate in a particular deal or country alone but would offer coverage if a public agency participated. CUP participation provides the private insurer with more due diligence and country information than it can typically obtain internally. Also, participation by a multilateral or bilateral in an insurance product provides a large deterrent to government action or inaction that would otherwise lead to a claim.

Portfolio Political Risk Insurance. Some insurance companies are offering political risk insurance on a portfolio basis. This coverage provides political risk protection for a project sponsor's entire investment portfolio in a particular country.

[15] Assignment Rights

As discussed above, many political risk insurance providers require that the project company assign rights in the project to the insurer as a condition to payment of the insurance proceeds. Because of this, it is important that project contracts permit such an assignment without the consent of the contracting party. See Chapter 26 for a complete discussion of consents to assignment.

[16] Political Risk Insurance for Bond Financing in Emerging-Market Project Finance

The bond market continues to grow in importance as a vehicle for financing projects in emerging markets. In 1999, OPIC introduced a new political risk mitigation program designed to enhance emerging market bond issuances to U.S. investors. Under this program, OPIC will provide coverage to eligible investors in an amount up to US$200 million for any single project, for up to twenty years. The policy, called the Contract of Insurance for Fixed Income Securities, will pay 100 percent of the total policy coverage for claims.[24] It is available for new projects and for expansion or upgrade of existing projects.

OPIC requires that the project company or issuer of the bonds sign a "company support agreement" with OPIC. Under this agreement, the project company makes certain representations and warranties and also agrees to certain covenants. Examples of the covenants included are the following: compliance with anti-corruption laws and regulations; compliance with environmental laws and regulations, including applicable World Bank environmental guidelines; and an agreement not to take action to thwart employees from lawful organizing and collective bargaining. Failure to comply could result in OPIC declining to pay a claim, or the withdrawal and termination of the policy. Whether this requirement will affect the usefulness of the insurance is uncertain. In over twenty-eight years of operation, OPIC has declined about 10 percent of claims, including once for breach of an environmental covenant.

The new coverage is significant because it is the first political risk insurance to enhance project bonds. In addition, the coverage allows a project, with an otherwise investment-grade credit, to be assigned a sovereign foreign currency investment grade rating. This coveted rating allows an expanded universe of institutional investors to purchase project debt that are otherwise prohibited from buying debt without such a rating. Expanding the universe of potential bond purchasers usually has the effect of lowering borrowing costs.

Currently, the primary coverage is for inconvertibility of local currency and inability to transfer converted funds abroad. OPIC will make payment where there has been a delivery of inconvertible local currency or where local currency is not legally available for delivery. Exclusions from coverage include pre-existing

---

[24] Some political risk policies include a deductible of 5 to 10 percent of the policy amount, thereby providing the insured with an incentive to minimize claims. Currently, the bond policy requires a deductible if the policy benefits bondholders that are affiliated with the issuer of the bonds. The OPIC equity policy, discussed elsewhere in this chapter, also requires a deductible.

restrictions to convertibility and transfer on the policy effective date, failure of the insured to use reasonable efforts to convert and transfer the currency, and provocation by the insured that is the primary cause of the loss.

The calculation of the rate of exchange will be made at the official rate (net of governmental charges and taxes). If a convertible currency is not available at the official rate, yet exchanges are available through another legal and customary means, OPIC will use that rate.

Under the new policy, the claims settlement process is designed to avoid missed bond payments to holders. This is accomplished through the creation, in advance, of a debt service reserve fund by the bond issuer, funded at a level sufficient for timely bond payments during the claim application and determination process.

[17] Credit Evaluation of Political Risk Insurance Policies

A political risk insurance policy and supporting documents, must be carefully examined to determine the extent of risk mitigation provided by it in the overall project credit package. Among the factors to analyze are the following: the credit quality of the issuer, the exact type of coverage, the events that must occur before payments are timely made, the adequacy of the payments, the events under which the insurer could deny claims, the events under which the insurer could revoke the policy, and whether adequate project reserve funds are in place to pay debt service during policy waiting periods and claims determination periods. Important to this evaluation is an analysis of the underlying project documents for the purpose of coordinating revenue and operating agreements with the political risk insurance policy and other credit enhancement.

Also, an understanding of the scope of the insurance is important. Political risk insurance does not cover all of the risks associated with a project, particularly those that are commercial in nature. In that sense, political risk insurance is not a credit guarantee.

Coverage against risks of inconvertibility and nontransferability of funds are the easiest to define in a policy. As such, these types of claims enjoy timely settlement.

§ 20.12 WARRANTY

Warranties extend protection to the project after the project is completed. They are typically included in construction contracts, subcontractor contracts, equipment supply agreements, and operating agreements. The terms of the warranty vary from project to project and are dependent upon the price associated with the underlying service or equipment. Most, however, are limited to obligations to repair or replace the defective construction or equipment. Warranties are sometimes considered "quasi-insurance" because in some cases these provide compensation for defects not covered by insurance.

§ 20.13 LIQUIDATED DAMAGES IN FIXED-PRICE CONSTRUCTION CONTRACTS AND OTHER LIQUIDATED DAMAGES

If construction of a project is not complete to the point necessary to begin commercial operation, or the project does not operate after completion at guaranteed levels, the project company will nonetheless need to pay debt service and other contractual obligations. One solution to this risk is a liquidated damage payment. A liquidated damage payment constitutes an estimate by the contractor and project sponsor of the ramifications of late or deficient performance by the contractor on the project.

The effect of a liquidated damage clause is to avoid calculation of damages following a dispute. These clauses are particularly useful in a project financing because of the need for predictable results after a failure to perform. An often overlooked risk in a project financing is that liquidated damages clauses are not favored by courts.[25]

The enforceability of a liquidated damage clause, however, must be carefully considered,[26]

---

[25] E.g., Note, *Liquidated Damages Recovery Under the Restatement (Second) of Contracts*, 67 CORNELL L. REV. 862 (1982).

[26] See generally Rubin, *Unenforceable Contracts: Penalty Clauses and Specific Performance*, 10 J. LEGAL STUD. 237 (1981); Goetz & Scott, *Liquidated Damages, Penalties and the Just Compensation Principle: Some Notes on an Enforcement Model and a Theory of Efficient Breach*, 77 COLUM. L. REV. 554 (1977).

particularly in the international context. Not all jurisdictions recognize the concept of liquidated damages. Thus, any party would be entitled to seek a determination of liability at trial.

The seminal common law test in the United States for approval of a liquidated damages clause is that (i) the clause must have been intended as a calculation of damages, not as a penalty; (ii) the contract must have as its subject a situation in which it will be difficult to calculate damages or in which a pre-estimation of damages was not possible; and (iii) the damages must be reasonable when compared with a calculation at common law.[27]

The primary question for project finance participants is whether there is a reasonable relationship between the damages payable under the liquidated damage clause and under the law when no liquidated damages clause is provided. This is typically a factual question.

If the contracting parties guess wrong, the question arises whether the liquidated damage clause is the exclusive remedy. U.S. courts have generally held that a liquidated damage clause is optional, and not an exclusive remedy.[28]

Liquidated damages as credit enhancement are used in other project contracts also. For example, a fuel supply contract might provide that if the fuel supplier is unable to provide fuel to a project, it will pay the project company liquidated damages equal to any increased fuel costs it incurs because of purchases of fuel from another source.

§ 20.14 INDEMNIFICATION OBLIGATIONS

Another form of credit enhancement in a project financing is a contractual indemnification obligation, which allocates liability among those who may be liable for a loss, as contrasted to placing this responsibility with a court or arbitrator. Such an obligation is designed to protect another person against the consequences of action in certain agreed-upon circumstances. Because an indemnification provision results in a shifting of risk, the impact of the assumption of this risk on the credit analysis of a project financing is not insignificant.

The absence of an indemnification provision in a project finance contract does not necessarily relieve a party of indemnification liabilities. In some states in the United States, for example, indemnification liabilities are implied. The concept of implied indemnity has been abolished in some other states, however, and is of limited importance in states that have adopted comparative negligence. The concept of implied indemnity nevertheless exists in some jurisdictions to allow a sharing of losses among entities of differing responsibility for a loss.

§ 20.15 SOVEREIGN GUARANTEES

[1] Project

Certain political, legal, regulatory, and financial risks within the host government's control must sometimes be addressed through a sovereign guarantee.[29] These include an uncreditworthy power purchaser, an unfavorable political climate, and an unfavorable economic climate.

In a sovereign guarantee, the host government guarantees to the project company that if certain events do or do not occur, the government will compensate the project company. The scope of a sovereign guarantee depends on the unique risks of a project.

The sovereign guarantee section in an implementation agreement may take various forms, including (i) direct undertakings to the project company, such as a guarantee of an off-take purchaser's obligations under an off-take agreement; (ii) political risk buy-outs; (iii) "comfort" language, indicating the host government's support for the project; (iv) commitment to reform law and regulations to support private energy development; (v) setting tariffs that permit

---

[27] The U.C.C. liquidated damages provision is similar to the U.S. common law, although the U.C.C. does not require consideration of the intent of the parties. U.C.C. § 2–718. Rather, an objective test is applied to determine the reasonableness of the damages. The real distinction between the common law and the U.C.C. approaches is the time at which the reasonableness is determined: the common law determines reasonableness based on the contract date; the U.C.C. looks at the situation on the contract date and at the time of the breach.

[28] *E.g.*, Ralston Purina Co. v. Hartford Accident & Indem. Co., 540 F.2d 915, 919 (8th Cir. 1976).

[29] *See generally* Jonathan Inman, *Government Guarantees for Infrastructure Projects*, 68 PROJECT FIN. INT'L 36 (1995).

recovery of costs (for such risks as a change in law) and a favorable equity return; (vi) commitment to guarantee private debt needed for project development; and (vii) counter-indemnities benefiting multilateral or bilateral institutions that have themselves provided guarantees to project lenders. In some cases, the sovereign guarantee is a separate instrument, not a part of the implementation agreement.

In some projects, the sovereign guarantee is replaced with a private-sector guarantee. For example, where a project's off-take purchasers include both private (business) and public (government) sector entities, the private-sector entities could be sufficiently creditworthy to guarantee the public entity's off-take purchase obligations.

In countries where the infrastructure will be privatized in the future, the host government may be unwilling to provide a sovereign guarantee that extends over the term of an off-take agreement. In such instances, the terms and scope of the guarantee must be tailored to fit the possibility of privatization. One possible compromise is a reduction in the coverage of the guarantee based upon the creditworthiness of the privatized entity.

[2] World Bank
Similarly, World Bank financing for a project is always conditioned on receiving a repayment agreement from the host government. If the financing is in the form of a World Bank loan, the World Bank will receive a repayment obligation from the country for loans made to the host country, or from the country for loans made to other parties. If the World Bank provides a guarantee, a repayment indemnity is provided by the country to the World Bank.

[3] Are Sovereign Guarantees Useful Without World Bank Involvement?
As discussed in Chapter 21, one benefit of World Bank involvement in a project, such as through a World Bank guarantee, is its ability to persuade a country to support a project in which the World Bank is involved. Otherwise, the country could simply ignore its reimbursement obligation for draws under the guarantee arrangement.

This has led to the question whether sovereign guarantees are of any benefit in a project financing if the World Bank is uninvolved in the project. The commercial lender certainly lacks the leverage over the host country that is enjoyed by the World Bank. For example, with some exceptions, unlike the World Bank they generally lack the ability to influence governmental actions through cross-default provisions in loan agreements, and the ability to influence governmental actions through decisions about financing future governmental projects. Without this involvement and leverage, the commercial lender might not be able to enforce the guarantee effectively, and should at a minimum, consider these implications before placing too much reliance on the sovereign guarantee as credit support.

[4] Availability of Funds to Pay Guarantee Claims
It is possible that the sovereign will not have immediate access to the funds necessary to pay on a claim made under a sovereign guarantee. This may be due to a general shortage of funds at the time of the claim. Such a credit risk is not limited to sovereign governments only; there is a credit risk with any unsecured guarantee obligation.

Alternatively, the failure of the sovereign government to pay immediately a guarantee claim may be due to a legal restriction. An example is when funds for payment of a guarantee claim are not in the government budget. In such circumstances, special legislation may be needed to authorize the payment. Resultant delays can produce further economic problems for the project that relied on the guarantee for the very purpose of avoiding them.

[5] Are Sovereign Guarantees From the Host Government Always Necessary?
The risks associated with infrastructure projects in a developing country often necessitate some form of host-government support, through a governmental guarantee or some other type of credit enhancement. Yet, governmental guarantees can undermine the benefits of private-sector involvement (privatization). These guarantees can impose significant costs on the host

country's taxpayers and further erode the country's financial health. A discussion of the implications for the host government of providing a sovereign guarantee is discussed in Chapter 14.[30]

§ 20.16 OTHER FORMS OF GOVERNMENT CREDIT ENHANCEMENT

[1] Generally

A government can provide other types of credit support to a project company in an effort to reduce risks in contracting with a state-owned off-take purchaser. These are limited only by the creativity of the participants.

[2] Government Subordination

Rather than a sovereign guarantee, credit support can be based in government subordination. In some power project financings, the government is involved in ways other than as merely owning the state utility. It receives taxes, provides fuel from the state-owned fuel company, and assesses and collects fees. It sometimes provides part of the financing for the project.

A subordination agreement, among the government, project company, and the lenders provides the basis for a government subordination. If a risk materializes, rather than advancing money to the state-owned utility, the government could instead agree to defer collection of payments due from the project company to it, or to another state-owned company participating in the project, such as the state-owned fuel company. The amounts would not be forgiven but rather deferred in time, until, for example, the state-owned power purchaser is able to make the payment. This technique works particularly well for short-term cash flow pressures at the state-owned utility.

[3] Government-Funded Accounts

Another alternative to a sovereign guarantee is a government-funded debt reserve account. Such an account, in which the sovereign government deposits funds, is pledged to the project lenders, and available to them for withdrawals to the extent a state-owned off-take purchaser is unable to make the necessary payments to the project company.

The key to structuring a financeable government-funded account is to put in place an irrevocable, creditworthy structure for the replenishment of the account for the term of the off-take sales agreement or, at least, the term of the debt.

[4] Pledge of Receivables

To the extent the state-owned off-take purchaser resells the off-take to creditworthy companies in the host country, such as a state-owned utility buying power from a project and then reselling it to industrial customers, these funds the project is entitled to receive upon delivery of the output can provide credit enhancement for the project. Under this structure, accounts owed by these high quality customers are paid into an account that would be pledged to the project lenders, and available to them for withdrawals to the extent the state-owned utility defaults in its payment obligations to the project company.

Under this structure, the state-owned utility would direct a group of creditworthy, industrial customers to pay all amounts otherwise due the state-owned utility directly into an escrow account. The group would be selected to provide a monthly balance equal to the monthly amounts due by the state-owned utility to the project company, plus a negotiated amount to provide a reserve. If necessary, deposits into this account could be supplemented with an additional, agreed-upon percentage of total state-owned utility receivables, deposited directly by the state-owned utility.

This is a classic structure for improving the creditworthiness of a financially weak entity. It segregates assets for collateral purposes, such as an accounts receivable financing. This approach, however, is limited. Although it is useful for a few projects, the highest-quality receivables are quickly depleted, decreasing or eliminating its

---

[30] *See generally* Christopher M. Lewis & Ashoka Mody, *Contingent Liabilities for Infrastructure Projects – Implementing a Risk Management Framework for Governments*, PUBLIC POLICY FOR THE PRIVATE SECTOR, WORLD BANK NOTE NO. 148 (Aug. 1998); Christopher M. Lewis & Ashoka Mody, *Risk Management Systems for Contingent Infrastructure Liabilities – Applications to Improve Contract Design and Monitoring*, PUBLIC POLICY FOR THE PRIVATE SECTOR, WORLD BANK NOTE NO. 149 (Aug. 1998).

usefulness as a credit enhancement structure for other projects. The base of industrial customers also must be diversified so that credit problems with one customer, such as an industrial company, do not jeopardize the viability of the account. The customer base needs monitoring to ensure that the collateral objectives continue to be satisfied. Further, existing creditors of the state-owned utility might need to consent to the segregation and dedication of quality receivables to the benefit of private power. Finally, while providing a priority security interest in a state-owned utility's best receivables could significantly assist the financing of discrete private power projects, a direct consequence could be a corresponding reduction and degradation of the state-owned utility's financial status.

[5] Government Account Supported With Local Country Bank Letter of Credit

Instead of the project company taking the risk that the state-owned utility or an industrial company does not make the necessary funding into the account, a financial institution could take that risk by issuing a replenishment guarantee, such as an irrevocable letter of credit. In some instances, only a limited guarantee, covering a specific, limited risk, may be necessary. For example, a guarantee could be limited to the receivables due from a particular industrial customer, not all industrial customers.

As with the previous structure, problems include persuading the financial institution to accept the credit risk of the state-owned utility and the industrial credit pool. Local financial institutions, particularly those with existing credit arrangements with these high-quality customers, may be more willing to accept these risks than international money center banks.

[6] Use of State Devolution Account as Collateral

Similar to the structures discussed above, this structure would use an escrow account funded by the state-owned utility, for use in the event of an off-take purchase agreement default. However, in the event the escrow account is not funded or is deficient, the shortfall would be supplied by the state. The state would agree that the appropriate central government bank or agency would transfer devolution account funds (the annual allocation of funds to the state from the central government) directly to the creditor, rather than to the state.

This approach may be difficult politically because it could divert funds from other state obligations, including important social projects. Also, other state creditors may need to consent to this type of diversion. Finally, possible constitutional impediments may preclude its use.

[7] Replacement of the State-Owned Off-Take Purchaser With a More Creditworthy Purchaser

Similar to using industrial credit to enhance escrow funding credit, creditworthy industrial customers could be the off-take purchaser (rather than a less creditworthy state-owned off-take purchaser). Although this technique improves financeability, it could lead to the degradation of the state-owned off-take purchaser's creditworthiness through removal of creditworthy customers.

§ 20.17 IMPLEMENTATION AGREEMENTS

An implementation agreement is a contract between a project developer and a host government that, in an effort to reduce risk and thereby encourage development efforts, capital investment and debt, addresses the following topics: (i) sovereign guarantees; (ii) expropriation; (iii) permits and other governmental approvals; (iv) currency concerns; (v) tax benefits and incentives; (vi) legislative protection; (vii) war, insurrection, and general strikes; (viii) authorization to do business; and (ix) general cooperation. The governmental contracting entity varies by country but must include the government agencies that have the authority to provide the guarantees, support, and assurances necessary for project development, financing, and operation. It is sometimes termed a *stability*, or *support*, agreement, recognizing the underlying stabilizing or supporting effect of the agreement on the uncertainties surrounding the investment made.

Implementation agreements are discussed in greater detail in Chapter 14.

§ 20.18 RESERVE FUNDS

Reserve funds are one of the most common forms of credit enhancement, both in project finance loans and in traditional asset-based financing. A reserve fund is an account mandated by the loan documentation for the purpose of setting aside funds designed for use to ameliorate the effects of a project risk. The account can be funded from equity contributions, a draw on a letter of credit, a call on a guarantee, from project cash flow, or any combination of these sources. Funds on deposit can then be used to offset the effects on the project of some increase in cost, such as an increase in interest or fuel costs, or some shortfall in anticipated project revenue. The funds on deposit are typically unavailable for any other use unless the consent of the project lender is obtained. If funds are withdrawn from the account, the loan documents require that the account be replenished, until such time as the risk is minimized to the extent that the reserve account is no longer necessary. For example, as project debt is amortized to lower amounts, reserve account minimum balances are often decreased or eliminated entirely.

§ 20.19 CASH CALLS

A *cash call* is the informal term applied to a mandatory infusion of equity or subordinated debt to a project company for the purpose of offsetting the effects of a project risk that has materialized. The loan documents will require such a call when the effects of the change in the project jeopardizes the ability of the project company to pay debt service and operating costs. For example, if fuel costs for a project increase beyond a level agreed upon between the lender and project company, additional cash will be needed to offset the increase. The use of the proceeds of the cash call will depend on the specifics of the project and can take various forms, including funding of a reserve account, immediate payoff of a portion of the project debt, thereby reducing debt-service

obligations, or the simple application of the proceeds to pay the increased costs. The exact use of the proceeds of a cash call will depend upon such factors as the amount of debt outstanding, anticipated length of time the project will experience the increased cost, and the overall financial health of the project.

§ 20.20 SUBORDINATION OF PROJECT COSTS TO DEBT SERVICE

Another technique used to address project risk is the subordination of certain project costs to the project debt. For example, a supplier of a project input, such as fuel, or the operator of the project, may be asked to delay the receipt of a portion of its payment in certain negotiated scenarios. These subordinated costs would be paid, if at all, in the future when debt service payments are no longer in jeopardy. The terms of the subordination are carefully negotiated.

§ 20.21 HEDGING STRATEGIES

Various hedging strategies available in the derivative markets can be employed to reduce commodity-pricing risk. These include options, swaps, forwards, and futures. However, the cost of managing a hedging program at the project level is not insignificant.

§ 20.22 THE COMMODITY SUPPLIER AS PROJECT PARTNER

The identity and role of a one of the project sponsors can be another form of project credit enhancement. For example, the project owned by a commodity supplier, or the project in which such a supplier is a partner, can greatly reduce commodity price risk. The commodity supplied can be priced at or near production cost, with profits generated at the output level of the project.

PART SEVEN

DEBT AND EQUITY FINANCING

CHAPTER TWENTY-ONE

FINANCING SOURCES FOR THE PROJECT

§ 21.01 GENERALLY

As a project financing is structured, project sponsors and host governments should constantly monitor the availability of debt and equity, as affected by the unique goals and risks involved in the particular deal being pursued.[1] Lender and investor interest will vary depending on these goals and risks. Commercial lenders will pursue projects with predictable political and economic environments. Meanwhile, multilateral institutions, with less emphasis on political and economic stability, will seek involvement in projects where they can also promote technology, social goals, exports, and environmental goals.

Close attention to the potential debt and equity sources is also necessary because of the frequent changes in the goals and capacities of lenders and investors. A risk that materializes with an individual project in the same country as a project in development could temporarily delay all financings in the same country. Debt crises (like the 1998 Asian currencies instability and the Mexican peso crisis), philosophical changes at multilateral institutions (like increased attention to the effect of projects on the environment), and other factors can also influence loan and investment fund availability. Thus, it is sometimes prudent for the project sponsor to pursue simultaneously alternative financing schemes for the same project, such as pursuing commercial bank financing with bilateral or multilateral support, while pursuing a bond offering rated by a credit-rating agency.

Financing sources are also affected by the goals of host governments and of project sponsors. Host governments are increasingly unwilling to support infrastructure projects with unlimited financial guarantees.

Similarly, project sponsors are reluctant to undertake large-scale projects in a way that requires long-term project debt to be recourse. Most project sponsors, for income-reporting purposes, desire to limit the presence of long-term debt on their balance sheets over an extended period of time. These goals limit the flexibility for financial structures.

In general terms, flexibility for financing options should be preserved as long as possible. To do so, the ownership structure should be kept flexible, allowing for participation by local private and state participants. Also, flexibility should be preserved to allow for various levels of governmental involvement in the project, whether ownership or risk allocation. Finally, all available financing sources should be consulted for possible participation, including the following: equipment suppliers with access to export financing; multilateral agencies; bilateral agencies, which may provide financing or guarantees; the International Finance Corporation or regional development banks that have the ability to mobilize commercial funds; specialized funds; institutional lenders and equity investors; and commercial banks, both domestic and international.

§ 21.02 BANKS AND INSTITUTIONAL LENDERS

Commercial banks and institutional lenders are an obvious choice for financing needs. Commercial funds are available from banks located in the host country or in other countries. Domestic banks are typically less able to provide financing for projects because they generally have less ability to assess project risks. Interest of domestic banks sometimes increases, however, if international banks are involved in the financing.

Generally, funds are either from independent loans from a number of lenders or from syndicated loans, in which several banks provide debt on a pro rata basis under identical terms.[2]

These participants, as lenders, tend to be risk averse, however. Risk identification and management for commercial and institutional lenders often results in relatively expensive credit enhancement.

---

[1] *See generally* David Blumenthal, *Sources of Funds and Risk Management for International Energy Projects*, 16 Berkley J. Int'l L. 267 (1998).

[2] *See generally* Brian W. Semkow, *Syndicating and Rescheduling International Financial Transactions: A Survey of Legal Issues Encountered by Commercial Banks*, 18 Int'l Law. 869 (1984).

§ 21.03 THE EQUITY MARKETS

Equity is often raised in the stock markets and from specialized funds, discussed below. The price associated with capital reflects the risks assumed by the investor and fluctuates as the risks fluctuate.

[1] Domestic Equity Markets and Equity Placements

Domestic capital markets provide access to significant amounts of funds for infrastructure projects. Although capital markets in developing countries are only now beginning to emerge, the growth and success of these markets suggest that they will provide an important amount of funds for infrastructure development.

Potential sources of domestic capital include issuance and sale of equity interests on a stock market, sale of equity interests to institutional investors, such as insurance companies, and sale of equity to individual investors.

[2] International Equity Markets

International capital markets provide access to significant amounts of funds for infrastructure projects. However, this is generally limited to large, multinational companies. Access to international capital markets by companies in developing countries is generally limited because of legal restrictions on investments and a lack of reliable, accurate financial information.

Private placements of equity in the international market are somewhat easier. In the United States, Securities and Exchange Commission (SEC) Rule 144A allows qualified institutional investors to buy certain securities not registered with the SEC.[3]

Potential sources of international capital include issuance and sale of equity interests on a stock market, sale of equity interests to institutional investors, such as insurance companies, and sale of equity to individual investors.

§ 21.04 THE BOND MARKETS

[1] Generally

Bond purchasers are generally the most risk averse of all sources of potential financing for a project. Established bond markets are in Germany, Japan, the United Kingdom, and the United States. Other bond markets in Europe and Asia are emerging. In the United States, bonds are sold to individual investors and to institutional investors.

[2] Credit Ratings

Bonds issued to the public receive a rating by a recognized rating agency.[4] These are issued by such agencies as Standard & Poor's, Moody's, and Duff & Phelps.

Ratings of projects are a comparatively new area. In general, the rating of a project reflects the prospects for timely debt repayment. Among the factors that are considered in applying a rating to the debt for a transnational project are the following: (i) sovereign risk, (ii) currency risk, (iii) political risk, (iv) legal (contract) risk, and (v) market for output. Other factors important to a rating are evaluations of output agreements, credit strength of the output purchaser, overall projected financial results, input and feedstock arrangements, fuel risks, and technology risks.

The credit-rating process is time consuming. It is generally most successful when the process begins early. In emerging markets, the strength of the project, from a credit-rating perspective, will depend upon the structure of the important project contracts and whether all project elements are covered appropriately by the contracts.

The following discussion summarizes the credit analysis undertaken by a credit-rating agency in developing a rating. Rating standards and procedures change over time, however. Thus, it is important in the project development process to understand these early in that process.

Sovereign Risk Analysis. Generally, at least two aspects of sovereign-oriented currency risks are

---

[3] Rule 144A permits companies in developing countries to issue American Depository Receipts (ADRs) and raise equity with them in the U.S. market. ADRs are issued by a U.S. depository bank, and the shares backing the ADRs are held by a custodian. ADRs can be traded on a national stock exchange.

[4] *See generally* Peter V. Darrow et al., *Rating Agency Requirements*, in SECURITIZATION OF FINANCIAL ASSETS (J. Kravitt ed. 1991).

considered in the credit-rating process. The first focuses on sovereign risk limits that apply to the sovereign. The rating concern is that in a financial or other crisis, a sovereign might impose exchange controls or other restrictions on the ability of a project company to make debt service payments to foreign debt holders. Consequently, the rating agency will award a credit rating to a project that is, generally, no better than that applied to the sovereign.

The second risk relates to the ability of the project company to service debt denominated in the local currency of the host country. In the rating process, local currency is subject to a separate ceiling. Thus, a project bond in a foreign country might have two ratings, one for a dollar denominated portion and one for a local denominated debt.

Currency Risk Analysis. The currency risk analysis generally focuses on the potential for currency depreciation. This is particularly necessary in a project that cannot adjust revenues to offset exchange rate changes. Adjustments can be made in several ways, including inflation adjustments, matching foreign currency revenues with foreign currency debt service costs, and raising project debt in a currency tied in closely with the currency in which revenues are paid.

Political Risk Analysis. The host country's laws and regulations are also analyzed as part of the credit-rating process. Factors considered include the country's attitude toward privatization, and the effect of potential privatization on the project.[5]

Legal (Contract) Risk Analysis. The rating process will analyze both the legal terms of the revenue-producing contracts and the economic incentives (and political incentives) underlying contracts or concessions. Significant attention is focused on whether long-term revenue-producing contracts are used to support financings. If not, the rating will focus on the prospects for output sales, not the underlying contract revenue.

Market for Output. In addition to the legal terms of the revenue-producing contracts for a project, the project's underlying economic characteristics are examined in the credit-rating process. Attention will also be directed at the potential effects on the project if these economic characteristics change.

While in emerging countries, much of the focus is on construction of new infrastructure capacity, this is not the complete extent of the credit review. Analysis will also be made of the long-term effects of the project on the economy. For example, the rates charged to the ultimate users of a project's output must be affordable, or there will be pressure to renegotiate the rates charged by the project.

[3] **Advantages**

Project sponsors must consider the advantages and disadvantages of raising debt on the traditional public debt market, as compared to financing from commercial banks and other institutional lenders. Key differences exist.

Large and Liquid Market. The public debt market provides project sponsors with access to a large and liquid market. In contrast, limited bank and institutional funds are available for international projects.

Longer Term of Debt. The public debt market tolerates a longer average life for debt than does the private debt market. Commercial banks, and some institutional investors, have regulatory or internal restrictions on the term of debt.

Less Onerous Terms. Terms of public debt deals are less onerous and contain fewer restrictive covenants than do private debt deals. In general, private debt deals favor early intervention by the lender in the event of a situation that might be averse to the project. However, public debt deals generally favor later intervention because of the cumbersome procedure necessary to amend bond documents. In public deals, intervention generally awaits an event that threatens timely payment of debt service.

For example, in a public debt deal, amendments to or wholesale replacement of a project contract are permissible if subsequent cash flows

---

[5] Ken Miyamoto, *Measuring Local Legal Risk Premium in Project Finance Bonds*, 40 Va. J. Int'l L. 1125 (2000).

are not negatively affected. In a bank transaction, the bank typically has the right to review and approve any amendment or replacement of a project contract. Other examples include the following: In a public debt deal, additional debt can be incurred by the project company for repairs or capital improvements if debt service coverage ratios remain achievable, whereas in a private debt deal bank consent typically would be needed; longer cure periods for nonpayment of debt exist in public debt deals; and there are less burdensome acceleration terms in public debt deals, where acceleration will occur only if a negotiated level of indebtedness is exceeded, as opposed to an acceleration if other indebtedness is accelerated as is typical in a private debt deal.

[4] Disadvantages

Regulatory Oversight. However, public market deals in the United States require lengthy Securities and Exchange Commission registration processes, except for Rule 144A filings, discussed below.

Ratings. Credit ratings are necessary. These are time consuming to obtain and affect the structuring and risk allocation in project contracts.

Consents to Changes to Underlying Project Are Difficult. Amendments or other changes to, including restructurings of, a project are extremely difficult to negotiate and complete because of the passive nature of the investment. Numerous and dispersed debt holders, coupled with a reluctance of trustees to exercise discretion in dealing with project options, combine to challenge the usefulness of the public debt markets as a project financing source. This problem is particularly great during a project's construction period, when debt agreement amendments, waivers, and consents are often more frequent.

Negative Arbitrage. Further, unlike traditional loan arrangements with commercial banks, all the proceeds of the debt offering must generally be raised at one time. Thus, there will be negative arbitrage for construction financing because funds raised will incur interest charges. In a bank

deal, funds are only drawn as needed during construction, although, in some cases, a commitment fee might be charged on undrawn funds.

Expensive Transaction Costs. Transaction costs are very high for accessing the public debt markets. Consequently, transactions of less than $100 million cannot generally access this market.

[5] The Mini-perm and Amortizing Mini-perm

One solution to the disadvantages of the public debt markets is a mini-perm structure, an abbreviation for a short-term, permanent financing. Under this financing structure, construction and term debt is loaned by private institutions, with a contemplated refinancing by a public bond issuance at the end of the term. The term of the institution debt is typically five to seven years, repaid under a long-term amortization schedule (twelve to twenty-five years), with the remaining balance maturing at the end of the term. This balance due is often referred to as a bullet maturity. At maturity, proceeds from the bond issuance are used to repay the institutional debt.

Another alternative is the amortizing mini-perm structure. This structure eliminates the risk that the project will be unable, for whatever reason, to access the public debt markets successfully on attractive terms at the time of the maturity of the institutional debt. Under this structure, financing is provided by both the public debt market and institutional lenders, with the public debt market providing the most significant percentage (i.e., 85%). The debt is amortized so that all institutional debt is repaid within the initial short-term maturity schedule (five to seven years). During this time, the public debt holders defer to the default, consent, and waiver decisions of the private institutions. An exception is where a default exists that is of fundamental significance to the public debt holders, such as where the interests of the private institutions conflict significantly with the interests of the public debt holders.

There are two important advantages of the amortizing mini-perm structure to project finance. First, there is no refinancing risk, and the institutional lenders can charge lower rates and fees in the absence of that risk. Second, the public debt holders enjoy the project expertise of the institutional lenders, which monitor the project construction and performance, minimizing structuring costs and allowing for greater project flexibility.

The structure presents intercreditor issues that must be negotiated between the public and private debt. While liquidation proceeds are typically shared proportionately, the rights of the public debt holders are quasi-subordinated. This requires the consideration of such issues as careful definition of voting rights by the public debt holders on the occurrence of fundamental defaults.

Negative arbitrage can be a problem also. All the public debt is issued at once, at the beginning of construction. Because the debt will not all be needed at once, the project will pay interest on the unused proceeds. This can be offset, in part, by interest earnings on the unused portion.

§ 21.05 RULE 144A DEBT PLACEMENTS (U.S.)

The U.S. Rule 144A debt market has developed since 1990, when the Securities and Exchange Commission (SEC) adopted Rule 144A. Historically, the SEC restricted secondary trading of private placements. By providing flexibility in resales of securities issued in private placements, Rule 144A has created liquidity in the private placement secondary market, making the U.S. market more attractive to international issuers.

The rule provides a non-exclusive safe harbor from Securities Act registration requirements for resales of the underlying debt security at any time to a qualified institutional buyer (QIB). A QIB is an entity that owns and invests on a discretionary basis at least $100 million in securities of unaffiliated companies, including securities issued or guaranteed by the United States. Examples of QIBs include insurance companies and pension plans.

The typical structure for a Rule 144A offering is for an issuer to sell, in a traditional private placement,[6] its securities to an investment banking firm. The investment banking firm then resells the securities, in reliance on Rule 144A, to QIBs.

To be eligible for the exemption, the securities must be sold only to QIBs. Also, the securities must not, when issued, be of the same type as those listed or quoted on a U.S. exchange (or quoted in a U.S. automated interdealer quote system); the seller and the prospective purchaser must have the right to receive certain information about the issuer; and the seller must ensure that the prospective purchaser is aware of the seller's potential reliance on Rule 144A.

Project sponsors must consider the advantages and disadvantages to raising debt on the public debt market, as compared with financing from commercial banks and other institutional lenders. Key differences exist.

[1] Advantages

The advantages of the Rule 144A market for raising project debt are similar to those in the public debt markets, discussed above.

Large and Liquid Market. The Rule 144A market provides project sponsors with access to a large and liquid market, although not as large as the public debt market. In contrast, limited bank and institutional funds are available for international projects.

Longer Term of Debt. The Rule 144A market tolerates a longer average life for debt than does the private debt market. Commercial banks, and some institutional investors, have regulatory or internal restrictions on the term of debt.

Less Onerous Terms. In addition, terms of a Rule 144A deal are less onerous and contain fewer restrictive covenants than do private debt deals.

Limited Regulatory Oversight. Rule 144A deals, unlike public market deals, do not require lengthy Securities and Exchange Commission registration processes.

[2] Disadvantages

Consents to Changes to Underlying Project Are Difficult. Amendments or other changes to,

---

[6] Traditional private placements are exempt from registration requirements under Section 4(2) of the Securities Act, or Regulation D promulgated under the Securities Act.

including restructurings of, a project are extremely difficult to negotiate and complete because of the passive nature of the investment.

Negative Arbitrage. Further, unlike traditional loan arrangements with commercial banks, in most circumstances, all the proceeds of the debt offering must be raised at one time. Thus, there will be negative arbitrage for construction financing because funds raised will incur interest charges. In a bank deal, funds are only drawn as needed during construction, although in some cases a commitment fee might be charged on undrawn funds.

§ 21.06 INVESTMENT FUNDS

Investment funds mobilize private-sector funds for investment in infrastructure projects. These specialized funds may be sponsored by governments or the private sector.

The International Finance Corporation, an affiliate of the World Bank, discussed in detail below, is instrumental in forming specialized investment funds for lending and equity investment in developing country projects. For example, funds have been established with the IFC's involvement for infrastructure projects, such as the Global Energy Fund.

§ 21.07 THE WORLD BANK GROUP FINANCING SOURCES

[1] Global and Regional Multilateral Involvement

Multilateral institutions, including the World Bank, the IFC, and regional development banks, are organized to assist development of specific programs and projects throughout the world or in a specific region. The types of projects supported vary over time. Although the amount of financial support is limited, any involvement by these institutions is helpful to a project because of the importance of the institutions to finances, currency, and development in the member countries.

[2] The International Bank for Reconstruction and Development (IBRD)

Generally. The World Bank, or the International Bank for Reconstruction and Development,[7] was formed in 1944, toward the end of the World War II, to provide financing for Western European roads, communications, power systems, and other infrastructure left marred or destroyed after the devastating war.[8] It is a nonprofit international organization that is owned by the various world governments.[9]

The World Bank was originally operated as a vehicle for borrowing for member countries in the world capital markets and loaning the money back to those member countries needing foreign capital. It was structured as a financing intermediary for those countries that lacked the creditworthiness to borrow at attractive rates on their own. The main objectives of the bank, as stated in the articles of agreement, are

(i) To assist in the . . . development of territories of members by facilitating the investment of capital for productive purposes, including . . . the encouragement of the development of productive facilities and resources in less developed countries.

(ii) To promote private foreign investment by means of guarantees or participation in loans and other investments made by private investors; and when private capital is not available on reasonable terms, to supplement private investment by providing, on suitable conditions, finance for productive purposes out of its own capital, funds raised by it and its other resources.

[7] The terms *World Bank* and *International Bank for Reconstruction and Development* are used interchangeably. The term *World Bank Group* refers to the IBRD and its affiliated organizations (the International Development Association, the International Finance Corporation, and the Multilateral Investment Guarantee Agency).

[8] For a short history of the World Bank, *see* HOSSEIN RAZAVI, FINANCING ENERGY PROJECTS IN EMERGING COUNTRIES 34–37 (1996).

[9] In 2007, the total membership of the World Bank was 184 countries. The ownership share of each member country is determined by the size of its economic capacity as compared to the other member countries.

(iii) To promote the long-range balanced growth of international trade and the maintenance of equilibrium in balance of payments by encouraging international investment for the development of the productive resources of members, thereby assisting in raising productivity, the standard of living and conditions of labor in their territories.[10]

After the early period of granting loans primarily to Western European countries for their reconstruction, the bank's lending objectives changed. Beginning in the late 1960s, most loans have been granted to developing countries in Africa, Asia, and Latin America. The 1980s saw a period of bank attention to projects that provided such basic needs as housing, health care, clean water, safe waste disposal, energy, and education to the most impoverished people in developing countries. In addition, World Bank attention moved beyond providing financing to include elements of management training and institution building coupled with fostering an economic environment conducive to growth.

Most recently, the World Bank has shifted its focus to reduce the public sector role and increase that of the private sector by encouraging the development of free-market economies. At the same time, the bank is a proponent of projects that, in addition to economic and social development, address regulatory matters, pricing issues and environmental responsibility.

Thus, various factors must be addressed to determine whether a project will be attractive to the World Bank for participation by it. These include improvement of the business environment in a country, advancement of private-sector involvement, and improvement of environmental problems. Of course, the original objectives of the World Bank – reducing poverty and encouraging economic development – must also be achieved by the project.

The World Bank loans about US$17 billion to US$20 billion. Funds for loans are raised by the World Bank from member countries. It requires member countries to subscribe to shares based on the strength of its economy. As of June 30, 2006, subscribed capital equaled US$190 billion. However, only about 7 percent of the subscription of each member country is paid. The remainder is required to be paid into the bank only if the bank requires the money for debt payment. Profitable since 1947, such action has never been necessary.

The bank raises funds it needs through short, medium, and long-term borrowings on international capital markets. These funds are supplemented by debt service payments made on outstanding loans and by investment earnings.

The bank enjoys the highest credit rating and is therefore able to borrow funds at attractive rates. The low cost of funds can then be passed on to developing countries, which would otherwise be unable to borrow at these rates.

Loan Program. Loans are generally made to member countries to finance specific projects.[11] Eligibility is conditioned on a showing that the borrower is unable to secure a loan for the project from any other source on reasonable terms. It is therefore generally considered as the lender of last resort.[12] In addition, a showing must be made that the project is technically and economically feasible and that the loan can be repaid.[13] If the loan is made to a private entity, the bank requires that the applicable member government guarantee the loan.[14]

---

[10] International Bank for Reconstruction and Development, Articles of Agreement, art. I.

[11] Article III, § 4 of the IBRD Articles of Agreement provides that "[t]he Bank may guarantee, participate in, or make loans to any member of any political sub-division thereof. . . ." *Id.* art. III, § 4.

[12] Article III, § 4(ii) of the IBRD Articles of Agreement provides that IBRD can make a loan if "[t]he Bank is satisfied that in the prevailing market conditions the borrower would be unable otherwise to obtain the loan under conditions which in the opinion of the Bank are reasonable for the borrower." *Id.* art. III, § 4(ii).

[13] Article III, § 4(v) of the IBRD Articles of Agreement provides that "[i]n making or guaranteeing a loan, the Bank shall pay due regard to the prospects that the borrower, and, if the borrower is not a member, that the guarantor [(the member country)], will be in a position to meet its obligations under the loan; and the Bank shall act prudently in the interests both of the particular member in whose territories the project is located and of the members as a whole." *Id.* art. III, § 4(v).

[14] Article III, § 4 of the IBRD Articles of Agreement provides that "[t]he Bank may guarantee, participate in, or make loans to . . . any business, industrial, and agricultural enterprise in the territories of a member . . ." *Id.* art. III, § 4.

Guarantee Program. The World Bank is not limited to providing loan programs; guarantees are also permitted.[15] After the debt crises of the 1980s, and the decrease in commercial loans in developing countries, guarantee programs were established to improve access to financing sources. The World Bank Partial Risk Guarantee Program provides private-sector lenders with limited protection against risks of sovereign nonperformance and against certain force majeure risks. The program does not extend to loans made by other multilateral organizations or export-import banks, and does not cover equity investments.

Generally, sovereign nonperformance takes place in two ways. One way is for the sovereign to default under one of the agreements entered into between it and the project sponsor. The other way is for the sovereign to deny responsibility for, or otherwise default in its performance of, the concession.

If a World Bank guarantee is issued, the bank must receive in return an indemnity or counter-guarantee from the host country, often called a *counterindemnity*.[16] In return for issuing the guarantee, the World Bank must receive "suitable" guarantee fees.[17]

Under the guarantee program, the World Bank must receive the right to purchase the guaranteed loan from the lenders if there is a default that requires the World Bank to perform under the guarantee.[18] By exercising this option, the World Bank becomes the direct lender to the borrower, rather than continuing to act as a continuing guarantor. This provides the bank with more control to restructure and otherwise deal with the underlying credit.

General Requirements. Financial support, whether in the form of loans or guarantees, is preconditioned on a finding by the World Bank that the project serves a productive purpose[19] and that the Bank has reviewed the likelihood of repayment.[20] The former concerns the project, while the latter concerns the creditworthiness of the host country.

The economic evaluation of a project analyzes the economic costs and benefits of a project in the host country.[21] In this analysis, World Bank procedures contemplate a calculation of the discounted present value of project benefits, net of costs, and an expected internal rate of return. An acceptable project must satisfy two conditions: a positive expected present value of net benefits and the expected present value must be at least

---

However, Article III, § 4(i) of the IBRD Articles of Agreement provides that "[w]hen the member in whose territories the project is located is not itself the borrower, the member or the central bank or some comparable agency of the member which is acceptable to the Bank [must] fully guarantee . . . the repayment of the principal and the payment of interest and other charges on the loan." *Id.* art. III, § 4(i).

[15] Article III, § 4 of the IBRD Articles of Agreement provides that "[t]he Bank may *guarantee*, participate in, or make loans to any member of any political sub-division thereof and any business, industrial, and agricultural enterprise in the territories of a member." *Id.* art. III, § 4 (emphasis added).

[16] Article III, § 4(i) of the IBRD Articles of Agreement provides that "[w]hen the member in whose territories the project is located is not itself the borrower, the member or the central bank or some comparable agency of the member which is acceptable to the Bank [must] fully guarantee . . . the repayment of the principal and the payment of interest and other charges on the loan." *Id.* art. III, § 4(i).

[17] Article III, § 4(vi) of the IBRD Articles of Agreement provides that "[i]n guaranteeing a loan made by other investors, the Bank receives suitable compensation for its risk." *Id.* art. III, § 4(vi).

[18] Article IV, § 5(c) of the IBRD Articles of Agreement provides that "[g]uarantees by the Bank shall provide that the Bank may terminate its liability with respect to interest if, upon default by the borrower, the Bank offers to purchase, at par and interest accrued to a date designated in the offer, the bonds or other obligations guaranteed." *Id.* art. IV, § 5(c).

[19] Article III, § 4 of the IBRD Articles of Agreement provides that "[t]he Bank may guarantee, participate in, or make loans to any member of any political sub-division thereof and any business, industrial, and agricultural enterprise in the territories of a member." *Id.* art. III, § 4 (emphasis added).

[20] Article III, § 4(v) of the IBRD Articles of Agreement provides that "[i]n making or guaranteeing a loan, the Bank shall pay due regard to the prospects that the borrower, and, if the borrower is not a member, that the guarantor [(the member country)], will be in a position to meet its obligations under the loan; and the Bank shall act prudently in the interests both of the particular member in whose territories the project is located and of the members as a whole." *Id.* art. III, § 4(v).

[21] The Bank determines "whether the project creates more net benefits to the economy than other mutually exclusive options for the use of the resources in question." THE WORLD BANK OPERATIONAL MANUAL, OPERATIONAL POLICIES, OP 10.04, ¶ 1 (Sept. 1994).

equal to the expected net present value of mutually exclusive alternatives.[22]

The financial analysis undertakes to determine the financial viability of the project. In general, this analysis determines the likelihood that the project will generate sufficient revenues to pay debt service and operating costs and generate an acceptable level of return on the equity investment of the project owners.

The World Bank also considers the project in the context of the other developmental goals approved for the country. For example, economic policy or regulatory reforms might be needed to support a proposed project adequately.

The country's loan repayment history on other World Bank transactions will be considered as part of a decision to finance a proposed project. Bank policy restricts providing new financing to any country that is significantly delinquent in IBRD or IDA loan repayments.

Various other factors are analyzed by the World Bank in determining whether to proceed with a project financing.[23] These include such socioeconomic factors as environmental effects of a project, potential resettlement of people, effects of a project on indigenous people, and effects on international waterways.

The foregoing considerations all relate to whether the project serves a productive purpose. As mentioned above, the other main consideration is the creditworthiness of the host country.[24] Among the factors considered in determining a country's creditworthiness are its existing and prospective debt service obligations and the ability to generate foreign exchange to service them, its economic structure, infrastructure, industry, agriculture, and natural resources, its trade patterns and balance of payments, and the quality of its public administration.[25] The analysis includes the effects of the proposed project.

Countries that do not satisfy the World Bank creditworthiness requirements are generally eligible for concessional lending from the International Development Agency (IDA). These countries are sometimes referred to as "IDA-only" countries.

Enclave Projects. In extraordinary circumstances, loans are made by the IBRD to IDA-only countries. These circumstances have emerged in situations in which IDA resources are insufficient to meet the needs for the project in the host country. To satisfy the IBRD Articles, however, it must conclude that the risk of nonpayment is small.[26] To reach this conclusion, IBRD has relied upon three factors: the project must have an export-oriented operation to generate enough foreign exchange to service the debt, guarantees or other credit enhancement for the benefit of the IBRD must be in place, and project revenues must be capable of segregation for servicing of the IBRD loan. Where these conditions are available, the IBRD loan considers the project as distinct from the host country – an enclave operation.

Indirect Support. World Bank involvement in a project can be extremely important, even though the financial commitment is small. The World Bank has particular power and influence in the business sectors of emerging countries. In addition to providing loans and guarantees for projects in member countries, the World Bank also affects the availability of funds from other, non-World Bank–affiliated sources.

Negative Pledge. The IBRD position on collateral affects the structuring of projects in which it is involved. It also affects project financings that use non-IBRD funds and guarantees to the extent the IBRD is a lender to the host government and the project wants to take a lien on assets of the host government.

The IBRD does not generally require collateral for its loans to countries. Also, it does not generally require collateral for loans to private

---

[22] The World Bank Operational Manual, Operational Policies, OP 10.04, ¶ 2 (Sept. 1994).

[23] For a concise explanation of the factors used by the World Bank in analyzing a proposed project, *see* P. BENOIT, PROJECT FINANCE AT THE WORLD BANK 2–30 (1996).

[24] International Bank for Reconstruction and Development, Articles of Agreement, art. III, § 4(v).

[25] *See* International Bank for Reconstruction and Development, Information Statement (September 20, 1994).

[26] International Bank for Reconstruction and Development, Articles of Agreement, art. III, § 4(v).

borrowers.[27] However, it does impose a negative pledge on IBRD borrowers in its loan agreements. That provision typically requires that if the borrower creates a lien in favor of another lender, an equal and ratable security interest must be created in favor of the IBRD.[28]

[3] International Monetary Fund (IMF)

The International Monetary Fund (IMF) was created at the same time as the World Bank. The ownership of the IMF is the same as that of the World Bank, and it is thus a sister organization to the World Bank. Originally created to stabilize the international monetary system, that role was abandoned in the 1970s. Today, the IMF has emerged as the global institution that monitors economic policies of member countries, assisting in debt problems, inflation, unemployment, and balance-of-payments deficits. IMF loans are often coupled with calls for stringent economic and policy reforms that will result in stronger economies.

The IMF is not involved directly in project finance transactions. However, its policy interventions can affect project finance credit decisions and the underlying projects. The interventions can extend to tax, tariff, and pricing issues. For example, in countries where energy prices are maintained at artificially low levels, the IMF can pressure a member country to promulgate a market-based approach to energy pricing. That approach would strengthen an energy infrastructure project based on the higher rates for energy that could be charged by the project. Without these reforms, the project probably could not be developed.

A position taken by a country that is contrary to IMF policy recommendations can also affect a project financing. Because the IMF attitude about a country is important, the failure of a country to address the IMF concerns will affect the view of the financial community to the proposed project.

[4] International Development Association (IDA)

The IDA, established in 1960, is the World Bank's concessional lending affiliate. Its purpose is to provide development finance for the poorest of countries, which do not qualify for loans at market-based interest rates.

The main objectives of the IDA, as stated in the articles of agreement, are

> to promote economic development, increase productivity and thus raise standards of living in the less-developed areas of the world included within [IDA's] membership, in particular by providing finance to meet their important developmental requirements on terms which are more flexible and bear less heavily on the balance of payments than those of conventional loans, thereby furthering the development objectives of the [IBRD] and supplementing its activities.[29]

In considering whether to participate in a proposed project, the IDA evaluates the same issues as the IBRD, both developmental and country. The development effect of the proposed project is central to the IDA decision. In the country context, the IDA considers whether the proposed project is a priority activity for the country's development, the economic policies in effect, and whether any IBRD loan or IDA credit is significantly in default.

In contrast to the IBRD, the IDA does not consider country creditworthiness, nor the prospects for repayment. Because the IDA does not borrow funds on the credit markets, it does not base interest rates on its borrowing charges, as does the IBRD. Finally, IDA credits are provided without the negative pledge provision found in IBRD loans.

Like the IBRD, however, the IDA is a lender of last resort,[30] and like the IBRD, it has limited financial resources, with many projects competing for its funds.

The IDA currently has 165 member countries. Membership in the World Bank is required for membership in the IDA.

---

[27] The World Bank Operational Manual, Operational Policies, OP 7.20, ¶¶ 1,2. (Feb. 2001).

[28] General Conditions Applicable to Loan and Guarantee Agreements, § 6.02 (July 1, 2005). Section 6.02(c) exempts certain liens, such as purchase money liens.

[29] International Development Agency, Articles of Agreement, art. I.

[30] Id. art. V, § 1(c).

IDA loans are called *soft loans*, or credits, and are made for a term longer than those provided by the World Bank. A small service fee, rather than interest, is charged. IDA loans, made pursuant to development credit agreements are in contrast to World Bank loans (made pursuant to a loan agreement), which are not soft or subsidized.

The IDA receives funds on subscription from prosperous member countries and from the World Bank, rather than through access to the capital markets. These funds are then lent to developing country governments for poverty reduction programs and projects, such as energy, education, health, and welfare. Funds are raised every three years in a replenishment program, in which funds are raised for succeeding three-year periods.

[5] International Finance Corporation (IFC)

Generally. The International Finance Corporation, established in 1956, is the private-sector lending arm of the World Bank. It provides financing without state support requirements to private sector operations in developing countries. In contrast, the World Bank itself provides only public-sector financing.

IFC-financed projects are typically designed to benefit the economy of the host country. This is accomplished most often by increasing the country's ability to earn hard currency. In contrast to the World Bank approach to projects, great emphasis is placed on the potential success of the project financed, because government guarantees are not available to repay the debt.

Its articles of agreement provide:

The purpose of [IFC] is to further economic development by encouraging the growth of productive private enterprise in member countries, particularly in less developed areas, thus supplementing the activities of the International Bank for Reconstruction and Development.... In carrying out this purpose, [IFC] shall: (i) in association with private investors, assist in financing the establishment, improvement and expansion of productive private enterprises which would contribute to the development of its member countries by making *investments, without guarantee of repayment by the member government* concerned, in cases where

sufficient private capital is not available on reasonable terms.... [31]

Unlike the World Bank, the IFC is permitted to make investments of all types – loans, guarantees, convertible debt, equity – and is not limited to loans and guarantees.[32] In contrast to the World Bank, no sovereign guarantee of debt is required.[33]

The IFC is a lender of last resort. As its articles state, IFC participation is limited to projects "where sufficient private capital is not available on reasonable terms.... [34] To date, the IFC has been particularly important in the first project in an emerging market or where new legal and regulatory systems designed to support private investment in sectoral reform infrastructure projects have not yet been tested.

In general, IFC borrowers are locally organized companies. If the laws of the host countries permit, however, foreign ownership of these local entities is allowed.

The IFC currently has 178 member countries. Membership in the World Bank is required for membership in the IFC.

Loan Program. The IFC loan program is composed of two elements: "A" loans and "B" loans. "A" loans are financed by the IFC from its own sources. "B" loans are syndicated to commercial lenders.

Unlike the IDA, the IFC loan program offers rates that are not concessionary. Unlike the IBRD, the rates and terms of an IFC loan do not enjoy the benefits of the World Bank's favorable credit rating. IFC rates are often high, which serves, in part, to attract commercial lenders to the "B" loan (also called the co-financing) program.[35]

---

[31] International Finance Corporation, Articles of Agreement, art. I (*emphasis added*).

[32] *Id.* art. III, § 2 (the IFC "may make investments of its funds in such form or forms as it may deem appropriate in the circumstances").

[33] *Id.* art. III § 1 (investments only in "private enterprises," which may include an enterprise in which there is governmental participation).

[34] *Id.* art. I (*emphasis added*).

[35] *Id.* art. III § 3(v) ("[IFC] shall undertake its financing on terms and conditions which it considers appropriate, tak-

Commercial lenders are attracted to the "B" loan program by IFC involvement, believing that the host government will be more likely to support a project in its country because of the IFC involvement. In fact, one of the greatest benefits of IFC involvement is the ability of the IFC to mobilize other financing sources.

Under this co-financing structure, discussed in greater detail in Chapter 20, the IFC provides financing to a project and sells participation interests in the "B" loans to commercial lenders. It retains the "A" loan portion. Under the IFC umbrella, the commercial bank "B" loans are treated in the same way as the IFC "A" loans: The IFC documents and administers the loans and collects and distributes payments and collateral pro rata among itself and the "B" loan lenders. An "A" loan default is also a "B" loan default.

Equity Program. The IFC has the ability to take passive, minority equity interests in projects, in the form of traditional equity, preferred stock, convertible debentures, loans bearing interest that fluctuate based on performance, and other types of quasi-equity.[36] It is also able to mobilize other sources of financing and equity investment, primarily because its involvement in a project provides access to high-level policy makers.

The IFC is instrumental in forming specialized investment funds for lending and equity investment in developing country projects. For example, funds have been established with the IFC's involvement for infrastructure projects. It has also been instrumental in assisting companies in developing countries access international bond and equity markets and in developing local capital markets.

Guarantee Program. The IFC is able to provide guarantees to financial institutions. This activity is somewhat rare for the IFC, however.

Benefits of IFC Participation. In addition to the debt, equity, and guarantee programs, a number of secondary benefits arise from IFC participation in a project. As with World Bank involvement, perhaps the most significant of these is its role as a catalyst for participation by other entities, including commercial lenders. Other advantages include the political risk protection and comfort it brings to a project, its status as a last-resort investor, its ability to invest in the private sector, and its flexibility in investment form.

CATALYST FOR PARTICIPATION BY OTHER ENTITIES. Through the "B" loan program, the IFC is a catalyst for participation by commercial lenders. These lenders rely heavily on the due diligence and structuring accomplished by the IFC for syndicated loans.

POLITICAL RISK PROTECTION AND COMFORT. Because of its multilateral status, the IFC, like the World Bank, is in a unique position to protect lenders and investors from project political risks. Its relationships with host-country governments, which are also IFC members, and its affiliation with the IBRD and IDA, helps it to encourage performance of investment agreements by borrowers, even though no sovereign guarantee is required. It does not, however, provide direct political risk protection to its B loan syndicate banks.

STATUS AS A LAST-RESORT INVESTOR. In some cases, without the IFC a project would not proceed. This is because the IFC plays the important role of a last-resort lender, providing investment funds in the face of negative private sector views about a project.

ABILITY TO INVEST IN THE PRIVATE SECTOR. Unlike the World Bank, which is limited to financial arrangements supported by a sovereign government, the IFC is able to lend to the private sector. This is particularly beneficial where economies are transitioning to free market

---

ing into account the requirements of the enterprise, the risks being undertaken by [the IFC] and the terms and conditions normally obtained by private investors for similar financing. . . . ").

[36] *Id.* art. III § 3(iv) ("[IFC] shall not assume responsibility for managing any enterprise in which it has invested and shall not exercise voting rights for such purpose or for any other purpose which, in its opinion, properly is within the scope of managerial control. . . . "). Nonetheless, in a default or insolvency situation, the IFC is not precluded from taking appropriate action. *Id.* art. III § 4 ("Nothing in [the Articles] shall prevent [the IFC], in the event of actual or threatened default on any of its investments, actual or threatened insolvency of the enterprise in which such investment shall have been made, or other situations which, in the opinion of [the IFC], threaten to jeopardize such investment, from taking such action and exercising such rights as it may deem necessary for the protection of its interests.")

economies and in developing countries that lack sufficient credit to support the quantity of infrastructure projects needed.

FLEXIBILITY IN INVESTMENT FORM. As indicated earlier, the IFC articles allow the IFC, subject to certain restrictions, to participate in any investment. Unlike the World Bank, which is limited to loans and guarantees, the IFC can offer loans, guarantees, equity, and quasi-equity investments.

[6] Role of World Bank Group Credit in Project Financings

Project finance transactions are supported in different ways by the IBRD, IFC, and the IDA.[37] In connection with project financings, the IBRD provides financial support in middle-income developing countries, the IFC provides private sector support in any developing country, and the IDA provides financial support in the poorest of developing countries. The Multilateral Insurance Guarantee Agency, the political risk insurer that is an organization within the World Bank, is discussed in Chapter 20.

Financing From the IBRD and IDA. Debt financing is provided for project financings by both the IBRD, in the form of loans pursuant to loan agreements, and the IDA, in the form of credits pursuant to development credit agreements. Loans and credits have the attributes of any non-revolving debt financing: a loan commitment is given, funds are disbursed over time (provided there is no default), and the credit is subject to acceleration upon the occurrence of specified defaults (although this remedy has not yet been exercised by the IBRD or the IDA).

IBRD loans are made in one of two ways: direct loans to the project company, and an onlend, in which funds are loaned to the host country and then re-lent, or on-lent, to the project company. Under the direct loan structure, a loan agreement is entered into between the IBRD and the project country. The host country guarantees to the IBRD that the loan will be repaid.

Under the onlend structure, the host country, not the project company, is responsible to the IBRD for repayment. Here, a loan agreement between the IBRD and the host country evidences the primary loan, and a loan agreement between the host country and the project company evidences the project loan. In addition, a project implementation agreement is usually entered into between the host country and the project company, which sets forth the obligations between the host country and the project company for project development, construction, and operation.

IBRD Financing for Enclave Projects. As discussed above, IBRD can provide loans for projects in IDA-only countries, even though the host country is not creditworthy. This structure has not been in active use since the 1960s, primarily because of the creation of the IDA.

To qualify, the project must generate sufficient cash flow to repay the IBRD loan, must have an export-oriented element so that foreign exchange can be produced offshore, and must be separable from the host country so that assets and collateral can be segregated. IBRD has generally required third-party credit support for the loan, either in the form of direct guarantees or implied guarantees in the form of take-or-pay contracts. A guarantee by the host country is also needed.

In addition, IBRD has required the creation of a collateral structure that provides for payment of debt service from project cash flows in a reliable manner. To do so, IBRD accepts an offshore trust account structure. Project revenues, in the form of foreign exchange, are deposited into this account. Withdrawals from the account are then made, in order of an agreed-upon priority, for debt repayment.

Like other IBRD loans, IBRD enclave loans are made in one of two ways: direct loans to the project company with a host-country guarantee, and an onlend transaction, in which funds are loaned to the host country and then re-lent, or on-lent, to the project company. Under the direct loan structure, a loan agreement is entered into between the IBRD and the project country. The host country and the private-sector project sponsors each guarantee to the IBRD that the loan will be repaid. A separate agreement establishes and provides for the administration of the offshore trust account.

---

[37] *See generally* BENOIT, *supra* note 23, at 37–57 (1996).

Under the onlend structure, the host country, not the project company, is responsible to the IBRD for repayment. Here, a loan agreement between the IBRD and the host country evidences the primary loan, and a loan agreement between the host country and the project company evidences the project loan. In addition, a project implementation agreement is usually entered into between the host country and the project company, which sets forth the obligations between the host country and the project company for project development, construction, and operation.

IDA Credits. IDA credits, unlike IBRD loans, are made to the host country, not the individual project. Under an onlend structure, the host country can then lend the funds to a project. Under this structure, the host country, not the project company, is responsible to the IDA for repayment.

The document structure is the same as for an IBRD onlend arrangement. A loan agreement between the IBRD and the host country evidences the primary loan, and a loan agreement between the host country and the project company evidences the project loan. A project implementation agreement is usually entered into between the host country and the project company, which sets forth the obligations between the host country and the project company for project development, construction, and operation.

Equity Financing. Neither the IBRD nor the IDA makes equity investments in projects. However, the World Bank has provided financing for equity investments by making loans to countries.[38]

Debt Refinancing. IBRD support can be used to refinance project debt. For example, a sovereign government might agree to provide funds to refinance short-term project debt. An IBRD loan to the sovereign country would be made to support the sovereign's refinancing obligation. Proceeds of the IBRD loan would be used to repay the existing short-term debt. Because potential short-term debt providers are assured of a refinancing (subject to negotiated conditions), the

project can obtain the benefits of both short-term and long-term financing.[39]

[7] Role of World Bank Group Guarantees in Project Financings

IBRD Guarantees. The IBRD currently provides three types of guarantees: partial risk, partial credit, and policy based.[40]

The *partial risk* guarantee protects a lender from the risk of payment caused by nonperformance of a host country's contractual obligations. The types of risks covered by the partial risk guarantee are individually negotiated, but can include tariff risk, regulatory risk, collection risk, arbitration, changes of law, convertibility risk, transferability risk, and subsidy payments. The guarantee is used in the following document structure.

A loan is made by commercial lenders pursuant to a loan agreement. An implementation or other agreement between the host country and the project is entered into, specifying certain contractual obligations of the government to the project company. The IBRD issues a guarantee, protecting the lenders against all or some of the risks allocated to the host government in this agreement. The host country provides an indemnity (or counter-guarantee) to the IBRD for repayment of any advances made by the IBRD to the commercial lenders under the partial guarantee.

The *partial credit* guarantee protects a lender from the payment risk, but is limited to a specified tranche of debt. The tranches protected usually have later maturities than the other tranches of debt.

The *policy-based guarantee* is issued in support of policy initiatives of the Bank.

IBRD Indirect (Financed) Guarantee Coverage. Rather than providing direct guarantees to lenders on behalf of a sovereign or other party's obligations, the World Bank could provide a loan to the sovereign to finance draws under a sovereign or third party guarantee (such as a bank). Because the guarantee is given by the sovereign or third party, under this structure there is no direct

---

[38] *See generally id.* at 51–52.

[39] *See generally* BENOIT, *supra,* note 23, at 52–53.

[40] *See generally* The World Bank Operational Manual, Operational Policies, OP 14.25 (Dec. 2005); The World Bank Operational Manual, Bank Procedures, BP 14.25 (Dec. 2005).

recourse by the beneficiary of the guarantee to the World Bank; it is an indirect relationship.

If a sovereign guarantee is used, the World Bank would enter into a loan agreement with the sovereign government and commit to finance any claims made under the guarantee.

If a third-party guarantee is used, a commercial bank or other independent entity would provide the guarantee. The sovereign would then agree to reimburse the third party for draws under the guarantee (pursuant to a counter-guarantee or reimbursement agreement). Any draws on the guarantee would be financed by World Bank credit to the sovereign.[41]

When Are World Bank Guarantees Available? Several factors determine whether a World Bank guarantee is available in a project financing: the investment form, the type of obligation guaranteed, and the type of risks covered by the guarantee.

The IBRD can issue only guarantees of *loans*.[42] Project financings often require guarantees of other types of investments, however. If a guarantee of equity or another type of investment is needed, the World Bank could agree to finance any draws made under a sovereign guarantee.[43]

As to the type of obligation, because the IBRD can issue only guarantees of loans, only payment guarantees, as opposed to performance guarantees, are available. If a financing requires a guarantee by the sovereign with respect to some currency risk, the resultant sovereign guarantee would involve performance. If IBRD credit enhancement is needed to support the sovereign's obligations under the guarantee, it would need to come in the form of sovereign guarantee indirect financing by IBRD. Even then, the performance obligation would need to be reduced to a monetary obligation.[44]

Finally, the types of risks covered determine eligibility for IBRD guarantees. Although neither the IBRD nor the IDA articles relating to guarantees address the type of risks that can be covered in guarantees, policy currently does. In general, the World Bank limits the risks guaranteed to political risks and breaches of government undertakings, rather than commercial risks. This policy is based, in part, on the World Bank's ability to manage political and government undertaking risks, as opposed to commercial risks, through its direct involvement with the sovereign government, its debtor-creditor relationship with the sovereign, and its non-commercial orientation.

IDA Guarantees. The IDA does not currently offer a guarantee program. The IDA articles provide the IDA with authority to offer guarantee programs, however.[45]

Other Credit Support – Take-or-Pay and Take-and-Pay Contracts. The legal (guarantee of payment of loans only) and policy (political and governmental undertaking risks covered) framework of IBRD guarantees might limit the flexibility of the IBRD in project financings. Yet, the World Bank has shown increasing flexibility in its programs.

As an example, take-or-pay contracts are, in essence, credit enhancement devices in a project financing, similar to guarantees. They create an unconditional obligation on the part of the buyer to pay even if no good or service is provided by the seller. Thus, these assure long-term revenue flow.

If a sovereign government entered into such an agreement, could the IBRD finance the sovereign's obligations? Perhaps. If the goods are delivered, the contract is simply a purchase contract. The IBRD regularly provides financing for purchases.

However, if the goods are not delivered, and the sovereign must still pay the project company, the contract is more like a guarantee by the sovereign of the underlying project debt. As a guarantee, the IBRD could indirectly guarantee political and governmental undertaking risks through

---

[41] BENOIT, *supra* note 23, at 46–47.

[42] Article III, § 4 of the IBRD Articles of Agreement provide that "[t]he Bank may guarantee, participate in, or make *loans* to any member of any political sub-division thereof and any business, industrial, and agricultural enterprise in the territories of a member." International Bank for Reconstruction and Development, Articles of Agreement, art. III, § 4 (*emphasis added*).

[43] BENOIT, *supra* note 23, at 47–48.

[44] *Id.* at 48.

[45] International Development Agency, Articles of Agreement, art. V, § 5.

an agreement to finance any such guarantee-like payments under the contract. Commercial risks would need to be addressed through other credit support. Under this proposed structure, a loan by the IBRD to the sovereign government would be made to finance any required payments for covered risks, with proceeds paid directly to the project company under the contract.[46]

[8] Benefits of World Bank Involvement
In addition to the debt and guarantee programs, there are a number of secondary benefits that arise from World Bank participation in a project. Perhaps the most significant of these is based in its role as a catalyst for participation by other entities, including commercial lenders, other multilateral institutions, and bilateral institutions. Other advantages include its tremendous financial base; ability to lend to developing countries, ability to finance government investment, favorable maturities and interest rates on debt, political risk protection and comfort, ability to influence governmental actions through cross-default provisions in loan agreements, ability to influence governmental actions through decisions about financing future governmental projects, influence over macroeconomic policies that may affect a project, less emphasis on project risks, use of World Bank procurement policies, and use of World Bank management requirements.[47]

Catalyst for Participation by Other Entities. The World Bank is a catalyst for participation by commercial lenders, other multilateral institutions, and bilateral institutions. Many agencies coordinate involvement in projects with the World Bank, and primarily rely on World Bank credit decisions. Budgetary restrictions and a lack of staff at other agencies sometimes combine to limit the analysis that can be made on individual projects.

Financial Resources. The financial resources available to the World Bank are tremendous. Unlike commercial lenders, with finite resources for debt and risk, the IBRD is much more flexible.

Ability to Lend to Developing Countries. Because of its nature as a developmental lender, the

World Bank is generally more eager, if not just as eager, as commercial lenders to lend to developing countries. Coupled with its developing country lending experience and its ability to manage these loans, the World Bank is a significant source of funds to these countries.

Ability to Finance Government Investment. The World Bank is able to carry on a dialogue with key officials in a borrowing country that is unparalleled in the commercial loan sector. Consequently, it is better able to loan funds to a developing country for investing in a project, which commercial lenders are not generally prepared to do. Often, the governmental investment portion of a financing is difficult to obtain from any other source.

Favorable Maturities and Interest Rates on Debt. Loan maturity terms and interest rates provided by the World Bank are generally better than those offered in the private sector. IDA loans are concessional.

Political Risk Protection and Comfort. Because of its multilateral status, the World Bank is in a unique situation to protect lenders and investors from project political risks. As described above, the IBRD can provide political risk coverage in the form of an IBRD guarantee, or through financing a country's guarantee obligations.
   The mere presence of IBRD involvement in political risk coverage is generally considered an important element in reducing political risks. Its close ties to sovereign government officials, role as lender on a variety of projects in the sovereign country, and goal of avoiding a call on its guarantee, combine to persuade other lenders and investors that the risk of political events interfering with the project are minimized. Because draws under any IBRD guarantee arrangement must be repaid, the sovereign government has an interest in working with the IBRD to avoid such a draw and to avoid any effect on other loans the sovereign government hopes to obtain in the future.

Ability to Influence Governmental Actions Through Cross-Default Provisions in Loan Agreements. IBRD and IDA loan agreements with governments contain provisions that permit the

[46] BENOIT, *supra* note 23, at 50–51.
[47] BENOIT, *supra* note 23, at 59–67.

IBRD or IDA to suspend, and ultimately terminate loans, upon a breach. These agreements also contain a cross-default provision, which enables the World Bank to suspend loan disbursements under all loans if they are suspended under any one loan.[48]

Ability to Influence Governmental Actions Through Decisions About Financing Future Governmental Projects. Similarly, host governments must consider the effect an action might have on the World Bank's decision to lend money for future projects. Inappropriate political action with respect to one project might chill lending for years to come.

Influence Over Macroeconomic Policies That May Affect a Project. World Bank involvement in a project, or series of projects, is often tied to some type of economic policy reform, whether at the project, sector, or country level. This is called "policy conditionality" at the World Bank. This study by the bank, coupled with reforms, often provides significant comfort to lenders and investors.

Less Emphasis on Project Risks. World Bank risk analysis should not be confused with the risk analysis applied by commercial lenders. Commercial lenders focus on all types of project risks. Because the loan or guarantee is backed by a sovereign government's obligation to repay the World Bank, it places more emphasis on the host-country credit risks than the underlying project risks. This is not to imply that project risks are insignificant to the World Bank. Because of its developmental focus, the bank will analyze project risks to ensure that the project is reasonably viable.

Use of World Bank Procurement Policies. World Bank loans require borrowers to comply with the bank's procurement standards, which are generally more detailed than those required by commercial lenders.[49] The standards are designed to

promote economy and efficiency, and to provide nationals from World Bank member countries an opportunity to bid.[50] Procurement standards also apply to goods and services acquired with the proceeds of loans to be guaranteed by the IBRD.[51]

Use of World Bank Management Requirements. Similarly, World Bank standards for accounting, reporting, and auditing procedures are also applied to those receiving World Bank funds.[52]

§ 21.08 REGIONAL DEVELOPMENT BANKS

[1] Generally
Regional development banks are organized with goals similar to the World Bank, such as poverty reduction and promotion of economic growth. Rather than a global focus, however, these banks instead focus on a particular geographic region. They are owned and funded by the governments of the region and industrialized nations.

[2] African Development Bank
The African Development Bank (AfDB), which began operations in 1963, is a major source of public financing on the continent of Africa. The member countries include fifty-three African states and twenty-four other countries, most of which are industrialized nations. Annual lending is US$3 billion to US$4 billion in new loans and grants.

AfDB provides loans for projects at interest rates based on its own cost of funds. It also participates in technical cooperation, facilitating investment and loan operations through feasibility studies, project preparation, and implementation activities.

---

[48] IBRD General Conditions Applicable to Loan and Guarantee Agreements, § 6.02(d) (January 1, 1985).

[49] *Guidelines: Procurement Under IBRD Loans and IDA Credits* (Jan. 1995, rev. Jan. 1996, Aug. 1996, Sept. 1997, Jan. 1999). Article III, § 5(b) of the IBRD Articles of Agreement provides that "[t]he Bank shall make arrangements to ensure

that the proceeds of any loan are used . . . with due attention to considerations of economy and efficiency. . . . " International Bank for Reconstruction and Development, Articles of Agreement, art. III, § 5(b).

[50] *Guidelines: Procurement Under IBRD Loans and IDA Credits* (Jan. 1995, rev. Jan. 1996, Aug. 1996, Sept. 1997, Jan. 1999).

[51] *Id.* at ¶ 3.14.

[52] Financing Accounting, Reporting, and Auditing Handbook (Jan. 1995).

[3] Arab Fund for Economic and Social Development

Established in 1972, the Arab Fund for Economic and Social Development assists development in the member countries of the Arab League. The fund assists in financing of development projects.

[4] Asian Development Bank

Organized in 1966, the Asian Development Bank (ADB) is a lender for infrastructure development in Asian member countries. The sixty-six member countries include Asian countries and other industrialized nations.

The ADB loans about US$6 billion. Funds for loans are raised by the ADB from member countries. It requires member countries to subscribe to shares. However, only about 12 percent of the subscription of each member country is paid. The remainder is required to be paid into the bank only if the bank requires the money for debt payment. The ADB raises its other funds in the capital markets.

Although ADB historically focused on government-level public agency lending with a governmental guarantee, privatization in member countries has resulted in a private-sector mandate. Lending to private entities does not require a governmental guarantee.

[5] European Bank for Reconstruction and Development

The European Bank for Reconstruction and Development (EBRD) began operations in 1991. It was organized to provide assistance to those nations of central and eastern Europe that are committed to multiparty democracy, pluralism, and market economics, for transition to market-based economies. There are sixty member countries. EEC and European Investment Bank are also shareholders. It has loaned money and made investment exclusively in the countries of central and eastern Europe, including the former Soviet Union.

The EBRD raises funds from member countries. It requires member countries to subscribe to shares. About 25 percent of the subscription of each member country is paid. The remainder is required to be paid into the bank only if the bank requires the money for debt payment.

The EBRD raises its other funds in the capital markets.

The EBRD focuses on financing specific projects, particularly in the private sector. It charges market-based rates for the financings. The EBRD can provide financing, financing support, and investment in a variety of ways, including as a lender (in foreign or local currencies); an equity or quasi-equity investor; a mobilizer of co-financing from other sources; a guarantor; a treasury risk management provider of repurchase agreements and interest rate swap agreements, among others; and an underwriter of local or foreign debt securities.

[6] European Union

The European Union, organized in 1993, is an organization of twenty-five European nations. It provides grants to developing countries throughout the world, including Africa, Asia, the Caribbean, central and eastern Europe, Latin America, and the former Soviet Union.

[7] European Investment Bank

Organized in 1958, the European Investment Bank (EIB) provides financial support for development both in and outside Europe, and is the financing institution of the European Union. The members are the member states of the European Union.

The EIB raises funds from member countries. It requires member countries to subscribe to shares. However, only about 7.5 percent of the subscription of each member country is paid. The remainder is required to be paid into the bank only if the bank requires the money for debt payment. The EIB raises its other funds in the capital markets.

[8] Inter-American Development Bank

The Inter-American Development Bank (IDB) was organized in 1959 and is a major lender to Latin American and Caribbean member countries. It is currently the principal source of external finance for most Latin American and Caribbean countries. The forty-seven member countries include Latin American and Caribbean countries, the United States, and other industrialized nations.

The IDB loans about US$5 billion to US$7 billion. The IDB raises funds for loans from member countries. It requires member countries to subscribe to shares. However, only about 2.5 percent of the subscription of each member country is paid. The remainder is required to be paid into the bank only if the bank requires the money for debt payment. The IDB raises its other funds in the capital markets.

In general, loans are made to public agencies of member countries to finance specific projects. A government guarantee is required.

Loans may be made directly to private businesses without government guarantees on the basis of market-based pricing. Proceeds of private-sector loans are generally used for infrastructure projects and for export financing.

Inter-American Investment Corporation. Direct support to the private sector is made available by the bank through its affiliate, the Inter-American Investment Corporation (IIC). The IIC is the private sector affiliate of the ADB. It provides loans, makes equity investments, and issues guarantees for new projects, expansion or modernization of existing projects, and privatization. Although the amount of money that is available is limited, particularly for large-scale infrastructure projects, the IIC's multilateral status can assist in mobilizing other financial and equity sources.

The IIC provides a syndicated loan program similar to that offered by the IFC. It offers rates that are not concessionary. These rates are often high, which serves in part to attract commercial lenders to the syndication program. Commercial lenders are also attracted by IIC involvement, believing that the host government will be more likely to support a project in its country because of the IIC involvement. Under the cofinancing structure, the IIC is the lender of record and administers the loan. A loan default is considered a default to the IIC.

[9] Islamic Development Bank
The Islamic Development Bank (IsDB), established in 1974, is a multilateral organization of fifty-six countries. Its purpose is to promote economic development in member countries and in Muslim communities in non-member coun-

tries. The bank, operating within the principles of the Koran (Islamic Sharia),[53] provides interest-free loans for development projects and also finances lease transactions and installment sales and makes equity investments.

[10] Nordic Investment Bank
The Nordic Investment Bank (NIB) was formed in 1975 by Denmark, Finland, Iceland, Norway, and Sweden. It now has eight member countries. Its purpose is to finance investments in which its member nations are interested, both within the Nordic countries and internationally.

[11] Nordic Development Fund
Since 1989, the Nordic Development Fund (NDF) has provided credits to developing countries on concessional terms, primarily in Africa and Asia. In 2005, the member countries voted to close operations.

[12] OPEC Fund for International Development
The OPEC Fund for International Development, established in 1976, provides financial assistance to developing countries. Its members are twelve countries that are members of the Organization of Petroleum Exporting Countries.

§ 21.09 BILATERAL AGENCIES

[1] Generally
Unlike multilateral agencies, bilateral agencies are designed to promote trade or other interests of an organizing country. They are generally nationalistic in purpose and nationalistic and political in operation. Thus, to work effectively with a bilateral agency, it is important to understand who the agency's client is and what mandates it is established to achieve, such as promotion of a country's exports and assisting development in emerging market-based economies.

---

[53] *See generally* Michael J. T. McMillen, *Islamic Shariah-Compliant Project Finance: Collateral Security and Financing Structure Case Studies*, 24 FORDHAM INT'L L.J. 1184 (2001); Benjamin C. Esty, *The Equate Project: An Introduction to Islamic Project Finance*, 5 J. PROJECT FIN., No. 4, at 7–20 (Winter 2000).

Bureaucracy and budget constraints, like in any governmental agency, affect their efficiency and ability to respond to project financing needs. Funding for bilateral agencies generally comes from their organizing governments.

Bilateral agencies are generally of two types: developmental agencies and export-import financing agencies. Developmental agencies are designed to provide grants or concessional financing to promote economic and political goals of the organizing government in developing nations. An example in the United States is the U.S. Agency for International Development (USAID).

The most common type of bilateral agency is an export-import bank. There are numerous sources of financing available from governments for exporting goods and services. Government-supported export financing includes pre-export working capital, short-term export receivables financing, and long-term financing. Often, pre-commitment "indications of support" can be obtained for use in bid documents and marketing.

In addition to sources of financing, export-import banks also typically provide political risk insurance to projects. This is particularly important in mobilization of other debt, as lenders rely on the belief that a foreign government will not risk disfavor with a foreign bilateral agency in the government's interactions with a project. Political risk insurance is discussed in Chapter 20.

Bilateral agencies are, of course, creatures of governments. As such, programs, policies, and credit standards are well-defined and consistent. This is in sharp contrast to commercial lenders and private equity sources whose policies fluctuate, sometimes overnight, based upon competitive pressures, management decisions, and loan or investment loss experience.

[2] The OECD Consensus

Concessional financing by the world's governments for exports and imports affects competition, manufacturing efficiency and prices. In recognition of this, the member countries of the Organisation for Economic Co-operation and Development (OECD) signed the Agreement on Officially Supported Export Credits.[54] It is also called the OECD Consensus. The Consensus was revised in 2005.[55]

The OECD Consensus establishes guidelines and limits on the terms of export credit. Each of the member countries agrees in the OECD Consensus to limit export credit to no more than 85 percent of the contract value. Interest rates applicable to the financing cannot be less than the OECD interest rate schedules, which are semi-annually revised.

In 1998, the OECD announced an agreement to amend the Consensus Arrangement for Officially Supported Export Credits to allow agencies greater flexibility when supporting projects financed on a limited recourse basis.[56] The amendment was in response to the increasing share of project finance transactions in the portfolios of OECD members' export credit agencies, especially where such support is to non-OECD markets. It was one of the first multilateral agency responses to the barriers that existed to flexible, innovative, limited-recourse financing methods.

The amendment to the Consensus Arrangement enables export credit agencies to support credit terms that more accurately reflect project cash flows and makes it easier for them to work with banks and other financing institutions to co-finance complex project finance transactions. Until this agreement was reached, the credit terms that export credit agencies could support for overseas projects financed on a limited recourse basis were constrained by the general terms of the OECD Consensus.

---

[54] The OECD has thirty members, including Australia, Britain, Canada, France, Germany, Japan, Mexico, and the United States. The member countries agree to promote economic growth in developing nations while expanding world trade.
[55] Arrangement on Officially Supported Export Credits, Organisation for Economic Co-operation and Development, TD/PG(2005)38/FINAL (Dec. 5, 2005).
[56] *Project Finance: Understanding on the Application of Flexibility to the Terms and Conditions of the Arrangement on Guidelines for Officially Supported Export Credits in Respect of Project Finance Transactions, for a Trial Period,* Consensus (98)27 (1988). The Understanding defines project finance as "[a] financing of a particular economic unit in which a lender is satisfied to consider the cash flows and earnings of that economic unit as the source of funds from which a loan will be repaid and to the assets of the economic unit as collateral for the loan." *Id.* app. 1.

The project finance agreement[57] provides a maximum repayment term of fourteen years, except when official export credit support provided comprises more than 35 percent of the syndication for a project in a high income OECD country, wherein the maximum repayment is ten years.[58] The agreement also provides flexibility on repayment of principal and payment of interest. A surcharge on the appropriate commercial interest reference rate will apply when credit terms exceed twelve years.

[3] Methods of Export-Import Financing

There are three financing methods generally used by an export-import bank in providing funds to an importing entity, which are direct lending, intermediary lending, and interest rate equalization.

Direct Lending. The simplest structure is a traditionally documented loan in which the borrower is the importing entity and the lender is the export-import bank. Most commonly, the loan is conditioned upon the purchase of goods or services from business in the organizing country. Loan terms are within the parameters of the OECD Consensus.

If the loan is not conditioned upon the purchase of goods or services from business in the organizing country, a so-called untied loan, international competitive bidding can be used. Untied loans need not follow the OECD Consensus because competitive bidding replaces the need for its protections.

Financial Intermediary Loans (Bank-to-Bank). Another structure is indirect lending. Under this structure, the export-import bank loans funds to a financial intermediary, such as a commercial bank, which in turn loans the funds (also commonly called *relending* or *onlending*) to the importing entity.

Interest Rate Equalization. Under an interest rate equalization structure, a commercial lender provides a loan to the importing entity at below-market interest rates. It is compensated by the export-import bank for the difference between the below-market rate (often the OECD Consensus rate) and the rate the lender could otherwise obtain in the market.

[4] U.S. Export-Import Bank

The U.S. Export-Import Bank (USExim) operates as an independent U.S. agency. It has three guiding principles imposed on it by its governing statutes: support United States exports through financing, attain a reasonable assurance of repayment, and provide financing support where commercial finance cannot do so. In 1994, USExim established a project finance division designed to assist U.S. exporters to compete in new international infrastructure projects.[59] USExim support is particularly important to U.S. exporters as more and more developing countries reduce sovereign-guaranteed borrowing.

USExim loans provide financing for U.S. exports on a fixed interest rate basis. It can provide direct loans to foreign entities that purchase U.S. goods and services or intermediary loans to entities that provide the financing to foreign buyers, for up to 85 percent of the U.S. export value. If the export contains foreign-made components, USExim will finance or guarantee up to 100 percent of the U.S. content, provided that the total loan or guarantee amount does not exceed 85 percent of the export price and provided that the total U.S. content is not less than 50 percent of the export price. Repayment of USExim loans are consistent with OECD guidelines.

In addition, the USExim guarantee program provides credit support for private-sector loans made to foreign buyers, to protect against repayment risks.

Whether an export loan or a guarantee of a commercial loan, USExim does not accept the commercial risk of project completion. It therefore does not provide construction financing, although it can have an arrangement to "take out" the construction debt at completion, but only if certain completion tests are satisfied. It believes

[57] *Id.* at Annex X, Terms and Conditions Applicable to Project Finance Transactions, 78–80.
[58] *Id.* at 78, ¶ 2.
[59] Eduardo Lachica, *U.S. Export-Import Bank Builds Up Steam for Key Role in Project Finance*, WALL ST. J., May 8, 1995, at A9G.

these risks are best addressed by the private sector. During the construction period, the USExim political risk guarantee program is available, however.

USExim has articulated general requirements for projects in which it is asked to participate. In general, these requirements are included in any appropriately structured project finance transaction. They are the following: The project should have long-term contracts from creditworthy entities for the project's outputs and inputs, with terms longer than the USExim debt; the project should have an appropriate risk allocation, adequate debt service coverage ratios, project costs comparable to similar projects, market-based pricing of outputs and inputs, and mitigation of currency devaluation risks; project participants must possess the technical, managerial, and financial capabilities to perform their respective obligations within the project, and have proven and reliable technology; technical feasibility must be demonstrated; host-government commitment to the project must be demonstrated; and legal and regulatory analysis must demonstrate enforceable contractual relationships.

On a case-by-case basis, USExim could require a project incentive agreement with the host-country government. This type of agreement is required to address certain political risks and the method that will be used by USExim and the host-country government to resolve a conflict relating to those risks.

Eligibility requirements exist for participation in USExim programs. Generally, creditworthy U.S. exporters, U.S. financial institutions, and foreign financial institutions are eligible for programs, which support sales of goods and services by U.S. companies. Projects financed or loans guaranteed must offer reasonable assurances of repayment. In addition, unless the benefit to the U.S. economy outweighs the detriments, USExim is prohibited from participating in any project that produces a commodity that (i) will be surplus in world markets when the project becomes operable, (ii) competes with U.S. producers, or (iii) will result in substantial injury to U.S. producers.

Finally, the host government and USExim must have in place a bilateral agreement. This agreement must give USExim recourse to the government if a political risk event, such as political violence, expropriation, or inconvertibility occurs, and results in a default.

[5] Export-Import Bank of Japan

The Export-Import Bank of Japan (JExim) closed. Export financing is now provided by the Japan Bank for International Cooperation (JBIC). JBIC also provides financial assistance including concessionary long-term, low-interest funds needed for the efforts of developing countries, including social infrastructure development and economic stabilization. They account for 40 percent of Japan's official development assistance.

[6] Overseas Private Investment Corporation

The Overseas Private Investment Corporation (OPIC), located in Washington, D.C., is an agency of the executive branch of the United States government. It is self-sustaining, operating at no cost to U.S. taxpayers.

Established in 1971,[60] OPIC is organized to assist participation by United States private companies in economic development of developing countries, emerging democracies, and fledgling free-market economies. Its mandate is worldwide.

OPIC must be *open* in the host country. Thus, the U.S. and the host country must enter into a bilateral agreement that relates to the OPIC programs. Under a bilateral agreement, the approval of the host government must be obtained before the OPIC insurance is issued.

The effect of the proposed investment on the U.S. economy is a part of the criteria. The considerations include negative effects on U.S. employment (no net U.S. job loss), imposition of requirements by the host country that substantially reduce the potential U.S. trade benefits of the investment, and significant adverse effects on the U.S. balance of payments. If any of the

---

[60] OPIC is an independent corporation operating under the Foreign Assistance Act of 1961, 22 U.S.C. § 2191. Well before its creation, the United States provided inconvertibility coverage to U.S. investors after World War II as part of the Marshall Plan. Later, before the creation of OPIC, the United States Agency for International Development provided political risk insurance to U.S. investors with investments in developing countries.

foregoing will exist because of the project, the loan is denied.

Also, the effect of the investment on the host country determines eligibility. In general, OPIC supports projects that respond to development needs and that improve private initiative and competition.

OPIC is widely known for its political risk insurance program, in which it covers losses attributable to certain political risks, including inconvertibility, expropriation, and political violence. In addition to its political insurance program, OPIC can provide project financing on a limited recourse basis of foreign direct investment projects, through direct loans and loan guarantees.

The borrower must be either a wholly owned U.S. company or a joint venture in which the U.S. sponsor firm is a participant. The U.S. investor must have a significant risk exposure, generally through ownership of at least 25 percent of the project equity.

The private sector must own a majority of the voting ownership interests in the project. However, if an agreement is in place that requires private-sector management, and there is a strong showing of direct U.S. interest in other respects, this requirement can be waived. Projects wholly owned or controlled by governments are not eligible, because of the OPIC requirement for significant U.S. participation.

The minimum amount for a project finance loan is typically $100,000. Loans are available up to US$250 million or US$325 million for oil and gas projects.

The loan program is not available to projects that can obtain financing from commercial sources. It is designed to provide financing in countries where conventional financial institutions often are reluctant or unable to lend on such a basis. Since its programs support private-sector investments in financially viable projects, OPIC does not offer concessionary terms.

[7] Office National du Ducroire (Belgium)
Export credit programs in Belgium are administered by the Office National du Decroire. OND provides export credit insurance as the credit enhancement for commercial bank loans.

[8] Export Development Corporation (Canada)
The Canadian Export Development Corporation provides export financing and insurance support. The financing is in conformity with OECD guidelines.

[9] Eksportkreditraadet (Denmark)
The Export Credit Council (*Eksportkreditraadet*) is the Danish export finance organization. It provides only guarantees.

[10] Finnish Export Credit Limited (Finland)
The Finnish Export Credit Limited is a joint stock company, majority-owned by the government. It provides financing to exporters, buyers, and bank-to-bank credit.

[11] Compagnie Française d'Assurance pour le Commerce Extérieur (France)
Compagnie Française d'Assurance pour le Commerce Extérieur is France's export credit agency. It provides commercial and political risk insurance.

[12] Hermes Cover (Germany)
Export credits in Germany are provided by Euler Hermes Kreditversicherungs-AG.

[13] Instituto Centrale per il Credito a Medio Termine (Italy)
Italy's export credit program is administered by Instituto Centrale per il Credito a Medio Termine. Export credit commercial and political risk insurance is provided by Sezione Speciale per Assicurazione del Credito all' Esportazione (SACE), which formed a project finance group in 1997.

[14] The Netherlands
In the Netherlands, export financing is provided by commercial banks. The Nederlandsche Credietverzekering Maatschapij provides insurance against credit risks.

[15] Export Credit Guarantee Department (United Kingdom)
In the United Kingdom, export financing is provided by commercial lenders. The Export Credit Guarantee Department (ECGD) guarantees payment to a United Kingdom financial institution to support United Kingdom goods and services.

ECGD guarantees United Kingdom exporters against payment risks because of commercial and political risks. In addition, ECGD insures against expropriation, war, and currency inconvertibility for equity and loan investments made in a foreign country by a United Kingdom company.

[16] Export Finance and Insurance Corporation (Australia)

Export credit in Australia is provided by the Export Finance and Insurance Corporation (EFIC). EFIC provides export financing and commercial and political risk insurance.

[17] Oesterreichische Kontrollbank AG (Austria)

Export finance programs in Austria are administered by the Oesterreichische Kontrollbank AG.

[18] Garanti-Instituttet for Eksportkreditt (Norway)

The Garanti-Instituttet for Eksportkreditt (GEIK) in Norway provides loan guarantees to support export financings. Also, the Norwegian Agency for Development Cooperation, together with Eksportfinans, provides export credit. Eksportfinans is an export credit agency owned by commercial banks and GEIK.

[19] Swedish International Development Authority

The Swedish International Development Authority provides export credits. Guarantees are provided by the Swedish Export Credits Guarantee Board.

[20] Export Credit Insurance Company (Spain)

The Spanish Export Credit Insurance Company provides commercial and political risk insurance for export credits. Concessional export credits are provided by the Institute for External Trade.

[21] Export-Import Bank of Korea

Bilateral loans are provided in Korea by the Export-Import Bank of Korea.

[22] Other Bilateral Support

Bilateral agencies also provide other support to exporting entities and their lenders, particularly for projects in developing countries. Most common is insurance against export commercial and political risks. Guarantees are also available to protect against these risks.

§ 21.10 GLOBAL ENVIRONMENT FACILITY

The Global Environment Facility (GEF), established in 1991, is a trust fund established to provide grants and concessional financing for environmental projects and programs in developing countries. Projects that minimize global warming by reducing emissions of CO_2 and methane are favored. There are 176 member countries in this international program, which is administered jointly by the United Nations Environment Programme, the United Nations Development Programme, and the World Bank.

The GEF program is designed to finance projects that are made infeasible from an economic analysis because of environmental protections. This analysis allows so-called earth benefits to receive the same importance in project analysis as economic benefits.

§ 21.11 SUBORDINATED DEBT

[1] Generally

Subordinated debt is another form of financing used in project financings. It is a form differentiated in both terms and pricing. The form of the financing is much like other types of financing, except that the subordinated lender has rights junior to other lenders with respect to repayment and exercise of its rights to collateral. Subordinated lenders insist upon higher interest rates and fees to compensate them for the increased payment and collateral risks.

[2] Subordinated Debt Terms in Project Financings

Funding. The subordinated lender and project company must determine when the subordinated loans will be made to the project. Will the subordinated debt be funded pro rata with senior debt construction draws, or at term conversion? In some projects, where the subordinated debt is a substitute for an equity contribution, the senior lenders want all of the subordinated debt drawn during the construction period. While this reduces the amount of senior debt, it increases the amount of interest payable during the construction period.

Conditions to Funding. Alternatively, the subordinated debt can be funded pro rata with the senior construction draws. However, it is typical that the subordinated lender will have very little control over these conditions to funding. This is particularly true where the senior lender considers the subordinated debt a "hell or high water" commitment by the subordinated lender to fund without conditions.

Similarly, if the subordinated loan is funded at term conversion, the senior debt will want the funding conditions very limited. In some circumstances, limited conditions can be negotiated (such as a maximum level of senior debt), but these usually result in the senior debt looking to the project company to provide higher contingency reserves or similar protections.

Other Indebtedness. Senior debt will want flexibility to increase the amount of its debt, at least to the extent necessary to remedy construction and operational problems. The senior lenders sometimes are willing to negotiate a cap on this amount.

Payment Blockage Periods. Generally, senior lenders permit principal and interest payments to be made on subordinated debt as long as the senior debt payments are not unpaid, and as long as there is no default under the senior loan agreement. If a default occurs, senior lenders will want to block payments to subordinated lenders, often for an extended period.

Amendment of Senior Debt Documents. The senior lenders' ability to deal with a problem project is often very broad. Generally, senior lenders require the ability to increase the amount of principal outstanding, increase the interest rates or fees, and to accelerate the amortization schedule. Subordinated lenders often can cap the amount of this increase or acceleration, in return for other concessions to senior debt or from the borrower.

Amendment of Project Contracts. Senior lenders generally want flexibility to permit the project company to amend the project documents. Often, senior lenders will agree not to permit the project company to do so if the effect would be to increase the senior debt principal amount, or to change the net cash flow in a way detrimental to subordinated debt.

§ 21.12 DEVELOPMENT LOANS

[1] Introduction
Project finance participants sometimes overlook the development phase of a project as an area of risk analysis. Yet, significant risks exist for the project sponsors during the developmental period. In addition, project development is expensive. Estimates of the cost of developing a project range from US$2 million to US$20 million. Funds for project development come from one or all of three sources: governmental grants, developmental loans, and equity.

[2] Definition
A development loan is debt financing provided during a project's developmental period. It is an important source of financing for the project sponsor with insufficient resources to pursue development of a project, either because of undercapitalization or because cash is needed for other activities. The developmental lender, typically a lender with significant project experience, brings important strategic benefits (credibility, financial support, and experience) to the project sponsor's development of the project.

[3] Goals of Project Sponsor
Project sponsors typically desire to retain ownership of the underlying project or at least maintain a significant equity position. They also desire to maintain control of the developmental process, and to use the proceeds of the developmental funds at their discretion.

[4] Goals of Developmental Lender
However, developmental lenders, funding the project sponsor at a very risky stage of the project, desire some equity rewards for the risk taken, some control over how funds are used, and the

ability to foreclose on the project at some point and finish the development phase to the extent the project sponsor does not do so. It is not atypical for the developmental lender to secure rights to provide permanent financing for the project as part of the development financing arrangement.

The developmental lender's role varies with the type of project and the experience of the developer. A passive developmental lender will review development reports, approve loan drawdowns, and monitor progress. An active developmental lender, on the other hand, will provide expert advice to the project sponsor on contracts and financeability and actively provide input in the development process.

Developmental loans are typically structured with milestone dates by which the project sponsor must have achieved the required activity. These include dates for execution of off-take and feedstock agreements, securing permits, obtaining financing commitments, and the like. Usually these dates are set far enough in advance that the developmental lender, if necessary, can develop the project itself if the project sponsor is unsuccessful in doing so. Of course, the ultimate milestone date is the date by which the project must be in commercial operation.

Developmental loans are typically advanced to the project sponsor on a periodic basis, usually monthly. Advances are based on a budget prepared to cover the entire development stage of the project.

As collateral for the loan, the developmental lender will typically require liens on all project assets, including permits and project contracts. Project assets will vary based upon the stage of development in which the loan is made, so ongoing monitoring of assets is needed.

Repayment of the loan is typically from proceeds of construction financing. Liens taken by the developmental lender ensure that it will be repaid because the construction lender will not be content to make construction loans when the developmental lender's liens remain in place.

Developmental loans are extremely risky for the lender. There is no assurance that the project can be developed. External uncertainties, separate from the project sponsor's abilities, can result in a failed project. During project development, any of several risks could render the development efforts worthless. These include the following: permitting risk; political opposition; citizen opposition; lack of creditworthy, long-term off-take purchasers; unavailability of needed inputs on financeable terms, such a raw materials, fuel and water; and changes in law.

Also, these loans are risky because the value of the collateral is totally dependent on the ability to develop the project. That value can reduce to nothing at any point.

§ 21.13 FINANCING FROM PROJECT PARTICIPANTS

Financial support, of course, is not limited to actual loans that require funds be advanced. For example, the project contractor might be willing to provide a loan to the project in lieu of its right to receive the construction contingency at completion, to the extent funds are not available to pay the contingent amount. Similar deferrals in the form of debt could be committed by the equipment suppliers, the project operator, fuel suppliers and other participants. If this type of support is needed by the project company, these project participants are sometimes willing to provide these types of commitments rather than lose the business associated with the project.

§ 21.14 OTHER SOURCES

[1] Generally
The alternative and supplementary sources of financing necessary for a project are only as limited as the imagination. Special tranches of debt, deeply subordinated debt, and other structures are available to provide specific returns while managing risks to both project participants and third-party lenders.

[2] Host Government
The host government is one potential source of financing, in a direct or indirect manner. Directly, the government can loan funds to a project company. Indirectly, the government can provide financing assistance through tax relief, such as tax holidays, and minimization of customs duties for project equipment.

There are a number of advantages to host-country financing assistance in a project. These include leverage, subordination, a lessened foreign exchange burden, and increased host-government support that decreases political risk.

Host-government lending can help attract private capital. In extremely large projects in less creditworthy countries, government lending of a large portion of the project costs – 20 to 30 percent – increases the likelihood that private debt and equity will be involved in the project. Such a governmental lending level is far better, from the host government's viewpoint, than financing 100 percent of the project.

If the government loans are repayable in local currency, the need for foreign exchange is reduced. The larger the amount of the governmental financing, the lesser the project's foreign exchange needs.

Government financing can also assist a project to the extent the governmental loans are subordinate in payment and lien priority to the private sector debt. In return for this concession, the government can charge a higher interest rate on its portion of the debt.

A project with host-government financing or equity participation is probably less likely to suffer political opposition or attack than a project wholly owned by foreign entities. In addition to profit sharing, the host government would be more likely to be aware of the details of the project through the role of lender or equity investor, as the case may be.

[3] Contractor

Generally. Contractors are not lenders. If construction funding, in whatever form, is provided by the contractor, it is generally understood that the price for the financing will be higher than for financing from traditional sources. Yet, in some circumstances, the unique risks involved in a project financing require that the project company look to untraditional financing sources.

The contractor is a resourceful source of funding for a project. For example, unlike most equity investors that disdain equity investment prior to construction completion, contractors understand construction risks and are sometimes willing to invest equity in a project during construction. Similarly, a contractor's understanding of start-up risks makes it a source of mezzanine financing, providing financing during the final stages of construction.

The contractor can also be a subordinated lender. Contractors are sometimes asked to convert the retainage due at completion to subordinated debt, payable from the future revenues after payment of senior debt and operating costs. This avoids payment of retainage from construction loan or term loan proceeds.

Retainage as Financing. It is interesting to note that even if retainage is paid at completion, it has served as a form of financing for the project since there is no interest paid on the retained amount while it is withheld. This interest savings is a benefit for the project during construction. Of course, a prudent contractor includes the loss of the use of this money in its construction price.

No Right of Offset. With contractor financing, the opportunity exists for the borrower to offset amounts due the contractor under the financing documents with amounts it believes are owed from the contractor for construction deficiencies. Unless the borrower waives the offset rights, the contractor will be unable to sell the loan documents to another lender upon project completion.

A sample provision follows:

[*Project Company*] agrees that the obligations of the [*Project Company*] under this Agreement to repay the [*Contractor*] for Loans shall be unconditional and shall not be affected, modified, or impaired, upon the happening from time to time of any event arising under the Construction Contract, including any of the following:

(i) performance or nonperformance by [*Contractor*] of the Construction Contract;

(ii) the existence of any claim, setoff, defense, or other right that the [*Project Company*] may have at any time against the [*Contractor*];

(iii) the release or discharge by operation of law of the [*Project Company*] from the performance or observance or any obligation, covenant, or agreement contained in the Construction Contract; or

(iv) any other circumstance or happening whatsoever, whether or not similar to any of the foregoing.

§ 21.15 FINANCINGS CONSISTENT WITH THE KORAN

The Koran prohibits the charging of interest on
loans.[61] A similar restriction is found in the Chris-
tian and Jewish Bibles. The Koran does not prohibit equity investments that produce equity
returns, however. Thus, equity-like structures,
lease transactions, and installment sales are
the acceptable financing techniques in Islamic
financings.

Both Islamic countries and Western financial
institutions have devised financing structures
that fit within the religious constraints of the
Koran. Nonetheless, a committee will analyze the
structure to determine whether it is consistent
with Shari'a, the Islamic religious law.

§ 21.16 SECURITIZATIONS OF PROJECT CASH FLOWS

[1] Generally

Securitization is becoming an increasingly mentioned financing technique for companies with
unencumbered operating projects and for project
acquisitions. In a securitization, cash flows and
associated contract rights are isolated from the
underlying project sponsor. These cash flows are
then pooled together to provide credit support for
asset-backed securities sold in the capital markets to investors.

Stability and predictability of the underlying
cash flows are important to the success of a
project cash flow securitization. This is because
these cash flows enable the principal and interest
due on the securities to be serviced.

The underlying securities can be structured in
various ways. One option is for each security to

represent a pro rata share of the underlying cash
flow. Another option is for the securities to be
issued with different tranches, with each tranche
having access to a different asset pool.

Securitization of project cash flows is difficult to
achieve. In part, this is because the off-take contracts that generate the cash flow are not easily
assignable. A typical project is a complex business that requires active management, and is not
merely a passive cash generator.

Recently, securitization has been extended to
"whole business" securitization, which may permit securitization to be a more popular choice
in project finance. Whole business securitization
allows an entire line of business to be segregated
and securitized, rather than the cash flows only.
For example, in Europe, some large infrastructure
projects are being financed using securitization
and project finance, on a whole business basis.
While to date this financing technique has been
applied to acquisition financing, it may be used
in the future as a financing option for new project
development.

[2] Benefits of Securitization

Securitization can provide a less costly source of
long-term financing for some companies, particularly those with a rating that is below investment grade. These lower financing costs stem
from the segregation of project cash flows from
the project sponsor credit risks, thereby allowing a credit rating of project cash flows that is
segregated from the credit quality of the project
owner.

The financing terms can be less burdensome
than with traditional bank financing. Currently,
financial covenants and other financing terms are
generally more favorable in a securitization context, at least in perception.

Flexibility in default is another benefit. In a
default scenario, a securitization is administered
by a bond trustee. Unlike a traditional bank
financing, controlled by an agent bank and a
bank group, the bond trustee is generally considered more flexible in addressing default concerns, unhampered by a few dissenting bank
group members.

The project sponsor can also improve its balance sheet through a securitization of project
cash flows. By removing the securitized assets,

---

[61] "Those who consume interest shall not rise again, except as
one arises whom Satan has prostrated by the touch; that is
because they have said: 'Bargaining is the same as interest.'
God has permitted bargaining but has forbidden interest."
The Koran, Sura 2:275–276. *See generally* Mansoor H. Khan,
Designing an Islamic Model for Project Finance, 16 INT'L FIN.
L. REV. 13 (1997).

and their accompanying funding liabilities, the sponsor's balance sheet will generally reflect the benefits. In addition, the sponsor's financial covenant compliance in its debt documents may become easier to satisfy.

Finally, like a traditional project financing, a securitization allows a project sponsor to match a specific project's debt with that project's cash flow. In that way, a twenty-year cash flow under an off-take sales agreement can be specifically matched with project debt equal to the same term.

[3] Structure of Securitizations

The precise structure of a securitization will depend, in part, on whether it is a cash flow or a whole business securitization. Among the other factors that will influence the structure of a securitization is the following: the objectives of the project sponsor, the credit quality of the underlying cash flow, the type of credit enhancement necessary to address defaults by the underlying obligors (off-take purchasers), whether the securities will be offered in the private or public markets, tax issues, and regulatory issues specific to the underlying business.

Also, the bankruptcy of the project sponsor must not affect the securitization. To accomplish this requirement, the local laws must be applied to create a bankruptcy-remote entity. In the United States, for example, the requirements of a "true sale" must be satisfied. English law is more flexible, providing more emphasis on the legal structure selected by the parties.

CHAPTER TWENTY-TWO

THE OFFERING MEMORANDUM

§ 22.01 PURPOSE

As a first step in seeking commitments for project debt from financial institutions, the project sponsors prepare an offering memorandum. The memorandum explains the project to potential lenders. It includes the following general topics: experience of the project sponsors; the identity and experience of the major project participants, including the contractor, operator, suppliers, and off-take purchasers; information on the host government; summaries of the project contracts; project risks and how the risks are addressed; proposed financing terms; the construction budget; financial projections; and financial information about the project sponsors and other project participants.

§ 22.02 KEY PROVISIONS

This chapter sets forth a discussion of each of the major provisions of a debt offering memorandum used commonly in international project finance transactions.

An offering memorandum is sometimes used to raise equity for investment in the project. Such an offering memorandum is nearly identical to a debt-offering memorandum and emphasizes the proposed equity terms.

§ 22.03 PROJECT OVERVIEW

A brief description of the proposed project is included first in the memorandum. The overview includes the type of project, background on the host country, the status of development, and other significant information.

§ 22.04 BORROWER

The description of the borrower explains the form of organization (corporation, partnership, limited liability company) and place of organization of the borrower. It includes the ownership structure of the borrower.

§ 22.05 PROJECT SPONSORS

The identity of the project sponsors and their involvement in the project is also included. This section explains how each sponsor will participate in the project, whether as a contracting party, manager, or passive equity investor. Summary financial information about the sponsors is also included.

This section also specifies the management structure of the project company. For example, this may take the form of a management committee or managing general partner. If another entity will manage the project, it is typically pursuant to a management agreement, the major terms of which are outlined.

§ 22.06 DEBT AMOUNT

How much debt the project will need is described generally in this section. Also included is the currency in which the loan is to be made and repaid.

§ 22.07 USES OF PROCEEDS

The manner in which loan proceeds will be used is an important part of the memorandum. It identifies for prospective lenders whether, for example, the loan will be a construction loan, term loan, or both, and the project assets that will be purchased with the loan proceeds.

§ 22.08 COLLATERAL

Equally important is the type of collateral the project company will provide for the loan. This discussion includes the identity of collateral, whether the collateral is junior in lien priority to other debt, and any special collateral considerations.

Including a short description of the type of lien available in the host country is also helpful. This depends on the laws of the host country, and is discussed in Chapter 26.

Further, the lenders will be interested in an explanation of their right to enforce the obligation of equity investors to contribute equity to the project. This is discussed further below.

§ 22.09 SOURCES OF DEBT AND EQUITY

The total construction budget and working capital needs of the project, including start-up pre-operation costs, are outlined in this section. The sources of the funds needed for the project are explained, including debt and equity. This section also describes any bilateral or multilateral loans or investments in the project.

§ 22.10 EQUITY TERMS

The terms of the equity are more completely described in this section. Included are explanations of the type of equity investments; dates on which equity will be contributed; the manner in which equity will be funded, such as the entire amount at construction loan closing, side by side with construction loans, or at completion of construction; whether the commitment is absolute or subject to conditions, and if conditional, the reasons why equity may not be invested; and the general terms of the equity.

Also included is a description of the agreement that equity investors will execute to memorialize the equity contribution obligation. If this agreement will be enforceable by the project lenders, as is often required, an explanation of the right of the lender to do so is also set forth.

§ 22.11 COST OVERRUNS

Once the debt and equity sources are explained, the offering memorandum typically sets forth an explanation of how any cost overruns will be funded. The solution initially provided by the project sponsors in the offering memorandum may change during negotiations. However, an initial position may comprise any of the following: a contingency account; a completion guarantee by the project sponsors; an explanation of the fixed-price, date-certain turnkey construction contract; and an obligation by the contractor to convert its right to receive retainage to subordinated debt.

§ 22.12 OTHER SPONSOR GUARANTEES AND CREDIT ENHANCEMENT

Any other guarantees or credit enhancement that the project sponsors will provide are also described. This section should describe the manner in which the project sponsors are subject to liability for a risk appearing during construction, start-up, or operation.

§ 22.13 INTEREST RATE

The project company will not typically mandate the interest rate in the offering memorandum. Rather, the section is left blank, thereby inviting tenders from interested lenders, or the project company can set forth the interest rate options it wants, leaving the credit spreads blank. Typical interest rate options include a bank's prime (or reference) rate, being the rate typically offered to its best customers, LIBOR (London Interbank Offered Rate), Cayman (rates of banks with respect to Cayman Island branches), and HIBOR (Hong Kong Interbank Offered Rate). Rates can, of course, also be fixed.

§ 22.14 REPAYMENT AND DEBT AMORTIZATION; MANDATORY AND OPTIONAL PREPAYMENTS

This section describes the proposed repayment terms of the debt. This includes the term, final maturity date, and an amortization schedule for the principal amount of the debt.

This section also specifies the terms of any optional and any mandatory prepayments. If a prepayment fee is due with any optional prepayment, that fee is also specified.

§ 22.15 COMMITMENT, DRAWDOWN, AND CANCELLATION OF COMMITMENT

The total loan commitment that the project company desires is set forth in another section, with the contemplated drawdown schedule. If the project company does not draw the full loan amount at closing, a commitment fee will typically be charged.

In the project finance context, it is typical for construction loans to be drawn down over the entire construction period. However, term loans are typically drawn down at the term loan closing, with proceeds being used to repay construction loans.

§ 22.16 FEES

The fees offered to the lenders, including structuring fees, closing fees, underwriting fees, and commitment fees are described. Amounts are usually left blank and resolved during negotiations.

§ 22.17 CONDITIONS TO CLOSING AND DRAWDOWN OF FUNDS

Conditions to closing vary from project to project, although some are common to all project finance loan agreements. These are described in Chapter 24.

§ 22.18 CONDITIONS TO EACH DRAWDOWN OF FUNDS

Conditions to drawdowns also vary from project to project. These are described in Chapter 24.

§ 22.19 COVENANTS

Covenants also vary from project to project. These are described in Chapter 24.

§ 22.20 DEFAULTS

Defaults also vary from project to project. These are described in Chapter 24.

§ 22.21 GOVERNING LAW

In this section, the choice of law to govern the loan documents is listed. It is sometimes the law of the host country. However, as discussed in Chapter 12, that is not so in financings in developing countries, unless lenders in the host country provide all debt.

§ 22.22 LAWYERS, ADVISORS, AND CONSULTANTS

This section will identify the lawyers, advisors, and consultants involved in the project. The memorandum will sometimes propose an arrangement for approval of the lawyers to the lenders by the project sponsors. Often, a budget for legal fees is requested.

CHAPTER TWENTY-THREE

PROJECT FINANCE DEBT COMMITMENT LETTERS

§ 23.01 THE TERM SHEET

Most project finance credit transactions begin with the preparation of a term sheet. The term sheet sets forth, in outline form, the main deal to be negotiated between the lender and the borrower. A difference exists between a term sheet (sometimes called a *letter of intent* or *interest letter*) and a commitment letter. One area of project finance that is consistently misunderstood, by developers, credit officers, contractors, utilities, and other participants in a project financing, is the area of lender commitments, including the differences between a financing letter of intent and a formal commitment letter. This misunderstanding often leads to confusion over what a lender and project sponsor have agreed to, the terms of a financing, how much time the developer has to satisfy the conditions to closing, the relationship between the lender and the project sponsor on future deals, and similar concerns. This confusion is unfortunate because it surrounds the very beginning of a relationship between the lender and the project sponsor. The following discussion summarizes the loan process in a project financing, from loan application, through the letter of intent to the commitment letter.

[1] Approaching the Project Finance Lender for Business Advice

Sometimes, the project sponsor approaches lenders about the appropriateness of an investment in a potential project or a project in operation. Questions include such concerns as whether a contract is financeable, whether a particular project is economic, and whether a contractor has a good reputation for performing contracts. Ordinarily, U.S. courts do not recognize that any fiduciary duty is owed by a bank to a borrower or potential borrower. Banks are therefore generally free to talk to borrowers or potential borrowers about a potential financing or investment.

Some U.S. courts have been willing to apply a fiduciary duty to a bank regarding its customer, however. These situations are typically limited to cases in which unusual circumstances existed. For example, one court found that a bank had a duty to reveal a lien it held on property in which a customer was investing.[1] Another court found that the bank had breached its fiduciary obligation to a borrower in a situation in which the bank had actual knowledge about fraudulent activities connected to an investment.[2]

Usually, where a project sponsor-borrower asks advice from a project finance lender, the fiduciary relationship will not exist unless the lender benefits from the transaction at the expense of the project sponsor, or there is a relationship in which the project sponsor-borrower relies, over an extended period, on the lender for financial advice. This will be rare in a project finance situation in which project sponsors have retained lawyers and consultants to provide professional advice and are sophisticated businesspeople.

[2] The Project Finance Loan Application – When Should the Process Begin?

No lender has an obligation to accept a loan application for a project financing. Once the application is accepted, however, the lender has a duty to process and evaluate the request.

Custom in the project finance industry has been to avoid the use of a formal loan application.

In its place, project sponsors circulate to potential lenders offering memoranda describing the project to be financed, the proposed terms for the financing, and limited due diligence information, such as copies of important documents.

This process sometimes leads to confusion for the project sponsor. For example, the project sponsor may believe that the submission of the offering memorandum means that the lender is actively reading and considering the proposal. The lender may cause further confusion by stating to the project sponsor that the information is "in consideration," when, in fact, nothing has been done.

[3] The Letter of Intent – Showing Interest Without a Commitment

The letter of intent, or interest letter as it is sometimes called, is alive and well in the world of project finance. Many lenders use this type of letter to evidence interest in providing project financing to a project sponsor. They may do so even though internal guidelines have not yet been satisfied, such as presentation of the potential financing for approval by the lender's credit or investment committee. In such situations, the lender has intended the letter to do nothing more than show an interest in pursuing the loan application process.

In many situations, the lender uses this type of letter as a framework for credit committee approval. Typically, the project sponsor will agree with the lender on the basic terms for a financing and ask the lender to seek internal approval. It becomes a type of loan application. In this scenario, the interest letter looks very much like a commitment letter, although the text of the letter clarifies that the lender is not committing to provide funds, and the credit committee can make any such commitment only after internal guidelines are satisfied.

What, then, is the usefulness of the interest letter? For the project sponsor, it answers the important question of whether someone is actually analyzing the potential project financing presented to the potential lender. Although clear and effective communication between the parties can also answer this question, project sponsors sometimes feel that a written communication is better.

---

[1] First National Bank Lenox v. Brown, 181 N.W.2d 178 (Iowa 1970).

[2] Richfield Bank and Trust Co. v. Sjogren, 244 N.W.2d 648 (Minn. 1976).

In addition, the project finance due diligence stage is an expensive process. As discussed below, the project sponsor often agrees to reimburse the lender for the costs of legal and consultant review of the project and project contracts, whether or not the financial closing occurs. Consequently, this stage provides the project sponsor with an important initial indication of whether the lender is interested in the project on the terms proposed by the project sponsor.

For the lender, the interest letter provides some framework for the terms under which the borrower wants the credit officer to seek internal credit approval. The terms often vary from the aggressive (often), optimistic (sometimes) terms originally announced by the project sponsor in its offering memorandum. It also makes clear the terms under which loan approval is sought.

From the lender's perspective, this type of letter imposes upon the lender an obligation to pursue the application in a timely way. In addition, it affords the lender with an opportunity to violate internal guidelines if incorrect language is used. Therefore, lawyers should be consulted to ensure that the interest letter does not turn into a commitment letter.

[4] The Oral Commitment

As the lender and project sponsor continue toward negotiating a commitment letter, the project finance lender will be careful to avoid making an oral commitment to lend. For the project sponsor, the use of language that carefully avoids use of any definitive terms can be frustrating. However, credit officers realize that banks may be required to lend because of their oral commitment. A commitment need not be in writing; oral agreements can bind a lender.[3]

§ 23.02 THE COMMITMENT

Usually, the commitment letter is the document in which the bank makes its formal offer to its customer to lend money. Either the borrower then

accepts the offer by signing the commitment letter or negotiations continue until an acceptable commitment letter can be structured.

Commitment letters have many common elements. The following summary sets forth many typical clauses from a commitment letter and explains the purpose for the clauses.

[1] The Commitment and Its Scope

Introduction. This provision explains the scope of the commitment. The lender clarifies that it has not had the opportunity to perform due diligence on the underlying project and that the terms of the commitment may change based on that due diligence. The project sponsor, of course, will want this type of clause to be removed or limited in scope. However, the lender can only commit based on the facts it has before it. If a firm commitment is needed, the project sponsor must give the lender sufficient time to analyze the project finance proposal.

Sample Provision

[*Lender*] is pleased to deliver to you a commitment to provide financing in connection with your [*describe project*], all as set forth below. The terms for the commitment are outlined below. The proposed terms and conditions are based on a limited due diligence review. Accordingly, the terms and conditions herein are subject to our review of the [*Project*] (as defined below) and the relevant documents, legal review by our lawyers of all relevant documents (this includes legal acceptability), technical review by our technical consultant, and negotiation of final loan and collateral documentation.

[2] The Loan Amount

Introduction. The loan amount section of the commitment letter will specify the aggregate amount of the loans the lender is agreeing to provide to the borrower. In a project financing, this provision is sometimes divided into a construction loan commitment and a term loan commitment.

Sample Provision

The total principal amount of the loan commitment to be provided pursuant to the terms and

---

[3] *See, e.g.,* National Farmers Organization v. Kingsley Bank, 731 F.2d 1464, 1470 (10th Cir. 1984) (finding that a jury could fill in the deal on the following open areas: amount of the loan, time of loan, interest rate and repayment terms).

conditions of the loan agreement to be negotiated between the Borrower and Lender (the "Loan Agreement") shall be an amount not to exceed US$[000,000,000] (the "Loan Commitment").

[3] Use of Proceeds

Introduction. This provision specifies how the borrower can use the loan proceeds. It typically includes an explanation of how funds will be used to construct a project. Unlike other commitment letters, in a project financing, this section is usually very specific about proceeds use.

Sample Provision

The Loan Agreement shall provide that the [*Project Company*] will use the proceeds of the loan made by Lender under the Loan Agreement (the "Loan") for the development, construction and start-up of the [*Project*], as set forth in the construction budget attached hereto as Attachment___.

[4] Repayment Terms

Introduction. This provision is self-explanatory; yet, many commitment letters fail to cover one or more of the points set out in this provision. It is important to include the interest rate, method of interest rate calculation, frequency of repayments, the amount of repayments, the maturity date, and otherwise include the amortization schedule.

Sample Provision

The Loan Agreement shall provide that the loan shall be repaid in [*xx*] consecutive semiannual installments, commencing on [*date*], according to the following schedule: [*explain repayment schedule*].

The loan shall mature on [*date*]. All payments with respect to the loan shall be applied first to accrued and unpaid interest and then to principal. The Loan Agreement shall provide that the interest rate applicable to the loan shall be a [*fixed/variable*] rate per annum equal to the [*describe interest rate; example: Lender's Reference Rate (as defined below)*] plus [*xxx*] basis points (the "Interest Rate"). Interest shall be paid based on the amount of principal outstanding on the loan during the term of the loan. Inter-

est shall be payable [*describe payment date; for example: quarterly*], in arrears, on the first day of each [*describe months; for example: March, June, September and December*], commencing [*date*]. Interest will be calculated on a 360-day year basis for the actual number of days elapsed.

The Loan Agreement shall provide that the [*Project Company*] shall pay a default rate of interest equal to the interest rate plus [*xxx*] basis points, upon the occurrence of a default or event of default under the Loan Agreement.

[5] Representations and Warranties

Introduction. Often, project finance commitment letters contain a detailed listing of the representations and warranties that will be required in the loan documentation. Examples of representations and warranties found in project finance transactions are the subject of Chapter 13 and are not reproduced here.

As a general rule, provisions that state that representations and warranties "customary in a project financing" will be included in final documents should be avoided. Unfortunately, while a court could ultimately determine what is customary, the project company and lender may disagree, unnecessarily prolonging negotiations. However, if such a shortened approach is thought necessary, a representative provision is suggested below. Another approach is to attach a list of representations and warranties standard for a bank as an attachment to the commitment letter.

Sample Provision

The Loan Agreement shall include representations and warranties customary in financing a project, including without limitation, as to (a) organization and existence of the [*Project Company*], (b) financial condition and statements of the [*Project Company*], (c) the absence of litigation, (d) the absence of breaches of documents, (e) authorizing action, (f) governmental approvals, (g) no tax liens and payment of taxes, (h) title to assets, (i) creation and perfection of first liens, and (j) compliance with laws, and shall, in addition, include the following: (i) each of the [*Project Contracts*] (as defined below) are legal, valid and binding agreements, enforceable against the parties thereto in accordance with their terms; and (ii) all financial information regarding the [Project], including the capital budget, projections, operating budget, each major project participant and similar information, reflects the [Project Company]'s best and good faith budget and projections for the periods referenced therein.

[6] Covenants

Introduction. Similarly, the covenants contemplated for the project finance loan agreement are detailed in the commitment letter. Project finance loan covenants are discussed in detail in Chapter 24.

As with representations and warranties, terms such as "customary in a project financing" should be avoided. However, if time constraints require a shortened approach, important covenants can be specified and the general inclusive language can be used as a catchall.

Sample Provision

The Loan Agreement shall provide that the [Project Company] comply with affirmative and negative covenants customary in a project financing, and shall include the following:

Affirmative:

1. The [Project Company] shall provide for an adequate supply of fuel to the [Project] during the term of the loan.

2. The [Project Company] shall create a revenue account, into which account the [Project Company] shall deposit an amount equal to (i) gross revenue of the [Project], and from which shall be paid (ii) the sum of (a) the costs of fuel, operations, and maintenance of the Project and (b) debt service payable to Lender, which such funds may be applied by Lender, in its sole discretion, in the event of a default or event of default under the Loan Agreement.

Negative:

1. The [Project Company] shall not:

(a) incur any liens other than those permitted by Lender;

(b) incur any contingent liabilities relating to obligations of other persons/entities;

(c) incur any debt other than (i) the loan, (ii) subordinated debt approved by Lender in its sole discretion; and (iii) up to $[xxx] of debt incurred in the ordinary course of business.

2. The [Project Company] shall not sell, lease, assign, transfer or dispose of any of its assets, other than in the ordinary course of its business in excess of $[xxx] per event and/or $[xxx] per year (unless replaced by equipment of like kind, nature and condition).

3. The [Project Company] shall not merge into or consolidate with any person.

4. The [Project Company] shall not engage in any business other than in connection with operation of the [Project].

5. The [Project Company] shall not amend, modify or supplement or exercise any option under, any [Project Contract].

[7] Events of Default

Introduction

Similar to the representation and warranty and covenant section discussions above, this provision sets out specific events of default that will be included in the loan documentation. Early negotiation of these types of provisions accelerates the closing process.

Sample Provision

The Loan Agreement shall provide events of default and remedies customary in a project financing, and shall include the following:

1. Failure to pay any principal, interest, or fee under the Loan Agreement when due.

2. The bankruptcy or insolvency of the [Project Company] or any major [Project Participant].

3. A default or event of default by the [Project Company] under any agreement to which it is a party.

4. Any representation, warranty, statement, or certification made by the [Project Company] is false or misleading.

5. The breach of any covenant in the Loan Agreement.

6. Lender shall fail to have a valid and perfected first priority security interest in, and lien on, the collateral.

7. Any permit shall be revoked, terminated, withdrawn, suspended, modified or withheld, or cease to be in full force and effect, or shall fail to be obtained when necessary.

[8] Conditions to Closing

Introduction. The conditions to closing must be very specific from the lender's perspective because this provision will govern the time at which the lender is obligated to advance funds. In a project financing, these provisions are very broad. Once both the bank and the borrower sign the commitment letter, each has a duty to close the financing in good faith. If the borrower satisfies the conditions to closing set forth in the commitment letter, the bank must close the financing or it could be held liable for damages.

Sample Provision

The closing date shall take place upon satisfaction by the [*Project Company*] of the conditions precedent described below, in addition to those standard and customary for a project financing (the "Closing Date"), and shall be no later than [*closing date*]:

1. A favorable due diligence review of all documents necessary for the design, construction, operation and maintenance and fuel supply of the [*Project*] entered into by the [*Project Company*] and the respective parties thereto, with terms, conditions, guarantees, and credit enhancement, all in form and substance satisfactory to Lender and its lawyers (the "Project Contracts"):

2. Project design, engineering, operation plans, project economics (including the operating budget and project projections) shall be in conformity with the [*Project Contracts*], and shall be in form and substance satisfactory to Lender, its lawyers and technical consultant.

3. All permits, consents, and approvals from all governmental jurisdictions, agencies, or other entities thereof ("Governmental Permits") (i) required to construct the [*Project*] are obtained, are final and in full force and effect, are not appealable, are not the subject of or related to any pending or threatened litigation or governmental action that may result in the modification or revocation thereof, and are satisfactory in all respects to [*Lender*] and its lawyers, and (ii) no Governmental Permit necessary for operation of the [*Project*] is the subject of or related to any pending or threatened litigation or governmental action that may result in the failure of issuance thereof, and there is no reason to believe that any Governmental Permits necessary for the operation

of the [*Project*] will not be obtained, and those Governmental Permits necessary for the operation of the [*Project*] that are obtained are final and in full force and effect, are not appealable and are not the subject of or related to any pending or threatened litigation or governmental action that may result in the modification or revocation thereof, and are satisfactory in all respects to Lender and its lawyers.

4. The [*Project Company*] shall have granted to Lender, and shall have obtained, a first priority security interest in, or lien on, all collateral, all in form satisfactory to Lender and its lawyers.

5. No material adverse change in the condition of the [*Project Company*], the [*Project*] or any of the parties to the major [*Project Contracts*] shall have occurred since the date hereof.

6. There shall have occurred no default or event of default, or any event with which the giving of notice or the passage of time, or both, could result in a default or event of default, under any [*Project Contract*].

7. There shall be no pending or threatened litigation concerning the [*Project*].

8. An independent engineer's study shall have been prepared by [*Engineer*] and submitted to Lender, which such report shall be in form and substance acceptable to Lender.

9. An environmental audit of the [*Project*] shall have been submitted to Lender, which such report shall be in form and substance acceptable to Lender.

10. The Loan Agreement and all related documentation shall be duly authorized, executed and delivered by the [*Project Company*], and shall be in form and substance satisfactory to Lender and its lawyers.

11. A legal opinion satisfactory to Lender and its lawyers shall have been delivered opining as to the enforceability of the Loan Agreement and the other loan documents delivered in connection therewith, the enforceability of the documents related to the [*Project*], permit and regulatory matters, and such other matters as Lender may reasonably request.

12. Lender shall have received such certificates, opinions of lawyers and other closing documents as may reasonably be requested, all in form and substance acceptable to Lender and its lawyers.

13. Lender shall have received from the [*Project Company*] financial statements, capital budget projections, and base case projections, in form and substance acceptable to Lender.

[9] Term

Introduction. The project finance commitment letter generally contains an expiration date. That is, all of the conditions to closing must have been satisfied by the project sponsors on or before a specified date. If not, the commitment letter terminates and the project lender has no further duty or obligation, absent some action to the contrary, to continue to work toward a closing. The project sponsors continue to be liable for the lender's costs and expenses, however.

Sample Provision
This commitment will expire at [*time*], [*date*] if not agreed to and accepted by that date as evidenced by you executing a copy of this letter in the space indicated below and returning it to us by such time. Additionally, if the financial closing date does not occur by [*closing date*], the above terms and conditions will also no longer apply (except for Section x [*reimbursement of lender's expenses*], which shall survive termination hereof), unless mutually extended.

[10] Non-disclosure

Introduction. The confidentiality of the commitment letter is important to the lender. From a business perspective, the lender does not want the borrower to "shop" the commitment letter to other lenders, revealing confidential pricing information. From a legal perspective, the lender does not want to mislead third-party project participants, such as the contractor or utility, about whether or not the loan will close.

Sample Provision
This is a confidential communication, the contents of which may not be disclosed to any other person or entity without the prior written consent of Lender. This commitment is not assignable by the [*Project Sponsors/Project Company*] and may not be relied upon by any entity other than the [*Project Sponsors/Project Company*]. The com-

mitment, after acceptance by you, supersedes all prior oral discussions and written communications between us as to the subject matter hereof.

[11] Expenses

Introduction. Regardless of whether the financing closes, each of the project sponsors are usually jointly and severally responsible for all expenses incurred by the lender in negotiating and closing the project financing. These include the lender's out-of-pocket expenses and the expenses and charges of its consultants and lawyers.

The project sponsors will want to attempt to limit these costs. Uncontrolled, these costs can dramatically increase and represent a large amount by the time of closing.

Several Options Exist. The project sponsor can place a cap on the amount of these expenses. Once the cap is reached, all further expenses are for the account of the lender. If this approach is unacceptable to the lender, the project sponsor may be willing to rely on a budget of expenses prepared by the lender, with frequent reporting of actual expenses to the project sponsor. Another approach is to give the lender an agreed-upon fee amount, out of which the lender must pay (and control) these costs.

Sample Provision
Borrower will pay all reasonable expenses related to the drafting, execution, documentation, and administration of the loan. Such fees and expenses shall include but not be limited to reasonable out of pocket legal, consulting (including the lawyers and consultants referred to above), and reproduction costs incurred but will exclude Lender's related salary and general overhead expenses.

[12] Material Adverse Change

Introduction. The lender should include a material adverse change (MAC) clause, so that the lender can decline to close the financing, or at a minimum renegotiate terms, if a material adverse change occurs to the project sponsor, a major project participant (such as the contractor, supplier, or the off-take purchaser), or the project (through a change in law or other cause).

Sample Provision

The lender shall have no obligation to close hereunder if there shall occur any material adverse changes in the business, prospects, or condition (financial or otherwise) of the [*Project Company/Project Sponsors*], any affiliate thereof, the major [*Project Participants*], or the [*Project*], including, without limitation, the project budgets and cash flow projections.

§ 23.03 GENERAL RECOMMENDATIONS ON COMMITMENT LETTERS

In summary, reproduced below are a few guidelines for project finance commitment letters:

- The lender should be certain that the commitment letter is very detailed; the lender should avoid the use of phrases like "customary and reasonable covenants and events of default." As a general rule, the commitment letter should outline the major terms of a loan agreement.
- The lender, especially in a project financing, should include two dates: the first date is the date the commitment letter will expire if not accepted by the project sponsor; and the second date is the date by which either the transaction will close or the bank and project sponsor will have no obligation to try to close the transaction any longer.
- The lender should include a material adverse change (MAC) clause, so that the lender can decline to close the financing, or at a minimum renegotiate terms, if a material adverse change occurs to the developer, a major project participant or the project (through a change in law or other cause).
- The letter should be reviewed by project finance lawyers and other consultants.

CHAPTER TWENTY-FOUR

CREDIT AND RELATED DOCUMENTATION FOR PROJECT FINANCE TRANSACTIONS

§ 24.01 THE COMMERCIAL LENDER'S PERSPECTIVE

In a nonrecourse project financing, lenders base credit appraisals on the projected revenues from the operation of the facility, rather than the general assets or the credit of the project sponsors, and rely on the assets of the project, including the revenue-producing contracts and cash flow, as collateral for the debt. It is thus predicated on the economic and technical merits of a project rather than the credit of the project sponsor. Because the debt is nonrecourse, the project sponsor has no direct legal obligation to repay the project debt or make interest payments if the cash flows prove inadequate to service debt.

Contracts that represent the obligation to make a payment to the project company on the delivery of some product or service are of particular importance because these contracts govern cash flow. Each of the contracts necessary to construct and operate a project, such as the off-take agreement, site lease, and construction contract, must not interfere unduly with the expectation for debt repayment from project revenues. If risks are allocated in an unacceptable way from the lender's perspective, credit enhancement from a creditworthy third party is needed, such as letters of credit, capital contribution commitments, guarantees, and insurance. The project finance contracts must be enforceable and have value to the lender as collateral security.

A project financing is also based on predictable regulatory and political environments and stable markets, which combine to produce dependable cash flow. To the extent this predictability is unavailable or the risks of dependability are allocated unacceptably, credit enhancement is necessary to protect the lender from external uncertainties, such as fuel supply, product market instability, and changes in law. In many instances, however, the project exists in an uncertain environment, which subjects the project lender to some unallocated risks.

The classic project financing would result in no potential liability to the project sponsor for the debts or liabilities of an individual project. It would be *nonrecourse*. This is rarely the case. In most project financings, there are limited obligations and responsibilities of the project sponsor; that is, the financing is *limited-recourse*. The degree of recourse that is necessary is determined by the risks presented in a project.

§ 24.02 ANALYSES OF PROJECT RISKS IN THE CREDIT APPRAISAL PROCESS BY THE COMMERCIAL LENDER

Commercial lenders in a project financing conduct a detailed review and analysis of a proposed project before the decision to lend is made. While the intensity, scope, and methodology of the credit analysis varies from institution to institution, there are general fundamentals that almost every bank applies to the credit decision. These are summarized below.

[1] Experience and Reputation of Project Sponsor

The project sponsor's experience in similar projects in the host country is important to the lender. Although each project presents unique risks, similar experience is beneficial in project development, construction, start-up, and operation. Similarly, an industry reputation for project support and completion, even in the face of a financially uncertain outcome, is evidence of a "bankable" reputation.

[2] Experience and Reputation of Project Management Team

Similarly, the project sponsor must have the requisite experience to manage the project in areas other than actual project operation. Day-to-day decisions about the project are essential to the success or failure of the project, including the repayment of project debt. Thus, the personnel, resources, reputation, and experience of management must be sufficient to address those tasks.

[3] Experience and Resources of Contractor

The seasoned experience and good reputation of the contractor, subcontractors and suppliers should help ensure the timely completion of the project at the stated price. Similarly, the contractor, subcontractors, and suppliers must possess the financial resources necessary to support contractual provisions relating to liquidated damage payments, workmanship guarantees, indemnities, and self-insurance obligations.

The contractor must possess sufficient human and technical resources necessary to satisfy contractual requirements. The potential risk is that the contractor, major subcontractor, or equipment supplier will be unable to perform a contractual obligation because of a low commitment to the industry, insufficient resources, or lack of knowledge or experience.

In an international project, the contractor should be particularly adept at working with the local labor force. Local construction site managers, with local experience, are particularly beneficial in reducing the risk of local labor problems.

[4] Experience and Resources of Operator

The operation of the project in an efficient, reliable manner is essential to its long-term success. The entity operating the project, typically pursuant to a long-term operating agreement, must possess sufficient experience and reputation to operate it at the levels necessary to generate cash flow at projected levels. Similarly, the operator must possess the financial ability to support operating guarantees and other obligations under the operating agreement.

[5] Predictability of Price and Supply of Raw Materials to Be Used for the Project

The project must be assured of a supply of raw materials at a cost within the acceptable ranges of financial projections. The formality of the commitments for the supply depends on the availability of the materials in the project area. For example, a supply of used tires necessary for a waste tire burning energy project in a state with large tire piles and strict tire disposal laws may produce a sufficiently assured supply that no need exists to contract for a 100 percent supply. Yet, under various scenarios, such as processing of tires to produce other products, alternate sources may be needed. In addition, costs of import or export fees, transportation charges, storage costs, stability of product, monopolies, and finance costs, are all potential risks in determining whether an adequate supply exists.

In many projects, long-term requirements contracts are developed to provide the necessary raw material supply at a predictable price to reduce this risk. Less frequent are supply-or-pay contracts, in which a supplier is dependent on some

aspect of the project and agrees to either provide the needed raw material or pay a fee to the project. With both contracts, however, the credit of the supplier must be sufficient to ensure performance of the contract.

The effect of the various transnational risks, discussed in Chapter 3, on the ability of key suppliers to meet their obligations to the project must be examined. Among the questions for consideration are whether foreign exchange will be available to pay foreign suppliers and whether suppliers to the project are subject to export restrictions in their home countries.

[6] Predictability of Price and Supply of Energy to Be Used for the Project

Similarly, the utilities needed for project construction and operation must be available at the project site on reasonable terms. If not, the project must construct and operate its own utility services at the site.

[7] Market for Product or Service

Once produced, of course, the project needs to generate revenue from sales of the product or service. Many project financings are based on long-term, take-and-pay off-take contracts, in which one or more purchasers agree to accept the production of the project at a firm or predictable price. Thus, provided the credit of the purchaser is adequate, a financeable market exists for the product, and the cash flow to the project is assured if the project operates.

Yet, off-take risk does not disappear simply because a long-term take-and-pay contract is executed. Market competition with other producers, new technologies, changing demand, increased operating costs, increased production costs, changes in the needs of the purchaser, and other events can combine to render the take-and-pay contract less valuable to the project.

The effect of the various transnational risks, discussed in Chapter 3, on the ability of off-take purchasers to meet their obligations to the project company must be examined. Among the questions for consideration are whether off-take purchasers are subject to unacceptable import restrictions in their home countries.

[8] Terms and Enforceability of Off-Take Contracts

As the main source of project revenue, the lender is particularly interested in the off-take contracts negotiated for the project. The entire contract must be analyzed from a technical, financial, and legal perspective to determine what risks are involved in its performance. However, the lender's focus generally is twofold. First, the lender will want to assure itself that the payments under the contract will be adequate to pay operating costs, service the debt, and provide a reasonable equity return to the borrower. Second, the termination provisions must provide the lender with an adequate opportunity to cure defaults by the project company before the contract is terminated.

[9] Completion and Cost Overrun Risks Are Addressed

As discussed in Chapter 4, the risk that construction of the project will cost more than the amount of funds available from the construction loan, other debt sources, and equity is an important risk for the participants in a project financing. Construction costs exceed estimates for various reasons, including inaccurate engineering and plans, inflation, and problems with project start-up. This cost overrun risk may result in increased debt service costs during construction, unavailability of sufficient funds to complete construction, and even if funded, in the inability of the project company to pay increased interest and principal that result from the additional debt required to complete construction.

Amelioration of the cost overrun risk is possible even where the contractor has not assumed that risk in a fixed-price turnkey contract. Alternatives include infusion of additional equity by the project sponsor, other equity participants, or standby equity participants; standby cost overrun funding agreements for additional financing; and establishment of an escrow fund or contingency account under which the project sponsor establishes a fund available to complete the project in the event of a cost overrun.

[10] Technology

New, unproven technologies, by definition, make project performance unpredictable. Some form of credit enhancement to cover the risk that the new technology will not perform as expected is usually essential in the project financing.

[11] Real Estate

The real estate necessary for the construction and operation of the project must be in place at closing, in a form acceptable to the project lender. Examples of the types of real estate rights necessary include the ownership or lease of the project site; construction lay down space, access to roads and utilities, and easements and rights of way necessary to bring fuel and other supplies onto the site. In addition to real estate interests of the project sponsor, the lender will also want to verify that other project participants have the real estate interests necessary to perform their respective contractual obligations to the project.

[12] Construction of Related Facilities

International projects, particularly in developing countries, often require the simultaneous construction of facilities related to the project. Large gas pipelines, docks, railways, manufacturing facilities, electrical interconnection, and transportation facilities may be required. Each of the related facilities will affect the success of the underlying project and each must therefore be examined to determine the risks involved. Construction synchronization is perhaps the most important initial concern to the project sponsors. Of equal concern is compatibility of systems. Even existing infrastructure must be examined to determine whether the existing facilities can satisfy project requirements. Reasonable assurances may be needed to guarantee that future improvements to existing and planned infrastructure will not render the project incompatible.

[13] Permits and Licenses

The lender will review a project's permit status to analyze whether any permit application processes, or terms of issued permits, present any unacceptable risks. To undertake this analysis, the project company will supply the lender with a list of all permits necessary for the construction, start-up, and operation of the project and copies of all permit applications and copies of all issued permits.

The risk that a project does not have, or might not obtain, permits necessary for the construction or operation of the project is, of course, a significant concern to all project participants. Generally, permits for the project must be obtainable, without unreasonable delay or expense.

At the time of construction funding for a project financing, permits are classifiable in three categories: permits already obtained and in full force and effect, which are not subject to appeal, further proceedings, or to any unsatisfied condition that may result in a material modification or revocation; permits that are routinely and manditorily granted on application and fulfillment of applicable criteria and that would not normally be obtained before construction (ministerial permits); and permits other than those in full force and effect and those routinely granted on application (discretionary permits, the issuance of which are in the discretion of the issuing agency, and operating period permits not yet obtainable). The last category of permits (discretionary permits and operating permits not yet obtainable) is, of course, an important area of concern for project participants. The application and approval process for the last category must be carefully examined to determine the likelihood of issuance, the cost associated with possible conditions attached to permit approval, and similar issues.

Necessary permits vary depending on the country, site, technology, process, and a host of other variables. In any particular financing, the various governmental agencies with jurisdiction can range from the local fire department to the Army Corps of Engineers. The process of determining which permits are required is typically a role of the project sponsor working in conjunction with the contractor and operator.

[14] General Operating Expenses
Operating expenses in excess of estimates is another risk to the project. These inaccuracies arise from errors in design engineering, excessive equipment replacement and unscheduled maintenance, poor productivity of labor, incorrect assumptions concerning the labor force required to operate, and other operating problems.

[15] Political Environment
The political climate of the host country must be analyzed carefully to determine its sentiments to foreign investments. The risk of expropriation by developing countries is obvious. Less obvious is the negative effect of indirect governmental action in the form of tax increases or demands for equity participation on project economics. In certain countries, the lender will require that political risk insurance be obtained to protect against this risk.

[16] Currency and Exchange Risks
Currency and exchange risks are important to a lender in a transnational project. These risks are discussed in detail in Chapter 3 and are not repeated here.

[17] Timing and Certainty of Equity Contributions
In many project financings, equity contributions by project sponsors and passive investors are not contributed to the project company at the time of financial closing. These funds may be contributed *pari passu* with construction loan draws, or await investment until project completion. This contribution requirement is typically accelerated if an event of default occurs under the project loan agreements, however.

Equity contributions reduce the amount of debt necessary in a project financing and thereby reduce lender exposure. Consequently, the contractual arrangements for the timing and certainty of the equity funding are each significant to the lender.

[18] Equity Returns for Equity Owners
The project finance lender will want to verify that the project sponsors will earn a sufficient return on the equity invested to stay interested in the project. If not, there is a real risk that the equity investors will abandon the project, leaving the lender with a worthless project and unpaid debt.

[19] Value of Project and Project Assets as Collateral
In addition to the business strength of the underlying contractual arrangements, the project

lender will review the contracts to verify that they are each assignable. In the event of a foreclosure, the contracts will only have value to the lender if they can be assumed by the lender and later assigned to a purchaser of the project. Otherwise, the lender may have little ability to recover its unpaid loans because few projects have value without the underlying project contracts, particularly the off-take contract.

[20] Interest Rate

Where interest rates vary over the term of the financing, the risk of unrealistic interest rate projections can affect the ability of the project revenues to service debt. The interest rate projections are typically a component of the feasibility study.

[21] Force Majeure

Force majeure is the term used generally to refer to an event beyond the control of a party claiming that the event has occurred, including fire, flood, earthquakes, war, and strikes. The party who will bear the risk is always a subject of negotiation, and often rests with the party best able to control each particular force majeure risk. It is a particularly cumbersome part of negotiations because, by definition, none of the parties negotiating the provision would be responsible for the occurrence of the event.

International projects are structured with, and negotiated among, many diverse parties, often from different countries. Sometimes, the underlying project contracts are negotiated by separate teams of negotiators and lawyers, resulting in uncoordinated force majeure provisions. This could result in a situation, for example, in which the contractor is excused from its obligation to complete the project by a date certain, while the power contract does not provide the developer with similar relief. The result could be a terminated off-take contract. Even where the inconsistencies are not of such dramatic proportions, the effect on the project's schedule or economics may be significant.

Inconsistent force majeure provisions can be cured with a so-called "resurrection" clause, in which the contractor agrees with the developer that where force majeure inconsistencies exist

between contracts, the contractor will not receive relief greater than the relief available to the project company under other relevant contracts. In the earlier example, the contractor could not have been excused from performance to the extent such excuse would have resulted in a project delay of such length that the off-take contract would be terminated. However, a less extensive delay would be permissible.

In negotiating a force majeure provision for a construction contract, it is important to understand the local circumstances of contract performance. In short, the parties must understand what is uncontrollable *in that location*. For example, the nature of the construction trade in the United States allows contractors in a United States project to, in most circumstances, agree that a strike at the construction site by the contractor's employees or subcontractors is not a force majeure. However, a contractor may be less likely to accept this risk when the contract is performed in a foreign jurisdiction.

A similar problem arises with the *unforeseeability* of other risks. The phrase "unforeseeable weather conditions," for example, may have a different definition in a different country. Adverse weather conditions may be sufficiently predictable and regular to result in the word unforeseeable being meaningless in some areas of the world, such as the Philippines.

Different legal systems can create havoc on well-planned, matched force majeure provisions. As discussed elsewhere in this book, the choice of applicable law and the jurisdiction of disputes is a critical element in ensuring that the force majeure structure is respected and enforced.

Despite this careful planning, complete elimination of the risk of inconsistencies in force majeure provisions may not be possible. Rather than rely on contract provisions, project sponsors may need to seek alternate solutions, such as standby credit, dedication of reserve funds, employment of additional labor, and the like.

[22] Project-Specific Risks

The foregoing list is not exhaustive, of course. Projects have differences based on their own unique characteristics.

§ 24.03 PROTECTING THE LENDER FROM PROJECT RISKS

[1] Due Diligence

An important level of protection can be given to the lender by its counsel and consultants in the due diligence process. Due diligence is the term applied to the process of reviewing and analyzing the various project participants and contracts for the purpose of determining the risks present in a project.

The lender will want to verify the technical aspects of a project with professional consultants. These include engineering firms, fuel consultants, and technology experts. Such reviews, with conclusions acceptable to the lenders, are typically conditions to financial closing.

Technical feasibility includes a review of technical processes, plant design, permitting, construction budgeting, construction schedules, operations and maintenance costs, maintenance plans and schedules, and revenue projections. Fuel consultants undertake a similar review on the fuel aspects of a project. Technology specialists focus on the choice of technology for the project.

The project lender generally retains the independent engineer and other consultants, with costs paid by the project company. They are "independent" in the sense that they are disinterested parties, capable of rendering objective opinions.

[2] Assignments

The project contracts must be assignable to be useful as collateral. They must be assignable as collateral to the lender. In the event of a foreclosure, the contracts must be assumable by the lender and assignable to a post-default purchaser of the project. Otherwise, the lender may have little ability to recover its unpaid loans because few projects have value without the underlying project contracts, particularly the off-take contract.

[3] Control Over Excess Cash Flow

Lenders usually insist upon close control over money available for distribution to the project owners. This cash, termed *excess cash flow* or *distributable cash*, is typically defined as the project revenue remaining after operating costs and debt service are paid and contingency accounts are funded.

Generally, distribution of excess cash flow is only permitted on a periodic basis, and then only if the project company is not in default under the loan agreement and negotiated debt service coverage ratios are satisfied. Other project-specific conditions are often included as conditions that must be satisfied.

Upon the continuance of certain major defaults for a specified period, the excess cash flow is sometimes applied by the lender to prepay debt. These defaults generally relate to money, including operating costs in excess of the operating budget; construction cost overruns funded by the lender; and debt service coverage ratios below a negotiated level. This right provides the project sponsor with an incentive to remedy the underlying problems as quickly as possible, rather than contentedly watch as undistributed profits collect in a bank reserve account.

[4] Approval of Contract Amendments

After the lender has undertaken an extensive due diligence process, any change to the project contracts could interfere with the revenue, operating costs, and risk allocation on which the financing is based. Consequently, the project company is typically prohibited under the financing documents from making any change to any of the project contracts without the lender's consent. This restriction is sometimes eased by permitting immaterial changes.

[5] Restrictions on Sale of Project Interests

The lender bases part of its credit decision on the experience and reputation of the project sponsor. If the project sponsors were to sell all or a substantial portion of their investment in the project company, it is possible that they would then be more likely to abandon a project or not otherwise support it if financial or other problems arise. Lenders often restrict the amount of project interests that can be sold without lender consent.

§ 24.04 OVERVIEW OF PROJECT FINANCE CREDIT AGREEMENTS

The structure and content of project finance credit agreements for a transnational project are substantially similar to credit agreements used for other types of project finance transactions. They are also similar to non-project finance credit agreements used for secured commercial bank financing where the borrower is a foreign entity.

The standard type of project finance credit agreement in a transnational project contains these familiar provisions: mechanical provisions for the loan commitments and disbursement of loan proceeds; interest rates and provisions; lender protection against increased costs and illegality; representations and warranties, setting forth the factual assumptions upon which the financing is based; covenants, outlining the degree of regulation the lender will require over the construction, start-up, operation, maintenance, and ownership of the project; events of default; and miscellaneous provisions, including submission to jurisdiction. In addition, the credit agreement contains provisions that result from the transnational structure of the financing. These include waiver of sovereign immunity (to the extent the borrower is owned in whole or in part by a government); identification of the currency that will be accepted for debt payment; and "gross-up" provisions to protect the lender from foreign withholding taxes. Because of the non-recourse, or limited recourse nature of a project financing, the project finance lender will require a higher level of regulation of the borrower's business and contracts, in an effort to minimize the project risks. Yet, this regulation of the project finance borrower's project is easier drafted than employed as a guarantee of risk avoidance.

Unfortunately for the project finance lender, certain risks cannot be adequately guarded against in a credit agreement, including changes in political control and economic factors. Nonetheless, the goal of the project finance lender is to address the control over as many project risks as is possible. To the extent risks cannot be adequately regulated, these must be addressed in the interest rate and fee pricing of the credit.

§ 24.05 SIGNIFICANT PROVISIONS OF THE PROJECT FINANCE CREDIT AGREEMENT

The following sections of this chapter summarize the significant provisions of project finance credit agreements. Not every section is summarized; in general, those relating to pricing, interest rate definitions, agency, and the like, which are not unique to project finance, are not repeated here.

§ 24.06 CONDITIONS PRECEDENT TO CLOSING

[1] Generally

Before a lender agrees to advance funds to a project company, it will require that the borrower first comply with a set of conditions precedent. Once satisfied, the lender is obligated to make the loan.

Conditions to closing are designed to ensure that the closing does not occur unless and until each of the elements of a feasible project are in place or waived by the bank. These include economic and technical viability of the project, permit compliance, enforceable project contracts, and adequate collateral arrangements. As a whole, the conditions precedent are designed to include each of the conditions for lending imposed by the bank's internal credit approval process.

Conditions precedent in a project finance transaction include many of the same conditions found in asset-based loan transactions. These include execution and delivery of the note and security agreement, lien perfection, and priority, authorizing resolutions of the board of directors or other governing body of the borrower, incumbency certificates of officers executing the document, an opinion of counsel to the borrower, and delivery of a certificate of no default.

The other conditions precedent in a project finance transaction will be determined by the industry in which the project will operate, the identity of the host country, project economics, and the risk allocations made in the underlying project contracts.

[2] Organization and Existence of Project Company, Project Sponsors, Guarantors, and Other Major Project Participants; Copies of Governing Documents of Project Company, Project Sponsors, Guarantors, and Other Major Project Participants

Generally. The project company must be duly and legally established under the laws of the place organized. Copies of the organizational documents are typically provided to the project lender. This is more than routine due diligence in a project financing. The formalities of the organization and existence of the project entity must be assured because of the importance of the underlying permits and project contracts in the name of the project company.

Sample Provision
Organization of [Project Company/Project Sponsors]. Certified copies of the charter and by-laws (or equivalent documents) of the [Project Company/Project Sponsors] and all partnership or corporate action taken by each such [Project Company/Project Sponsor] approving the [Project Documents] to which such [Project Company/Project Sponsor] is or is intended to be a party (including a certificate setting forth the resolutions of the board of directors of, or the partnership action of, such [Project Company/Project Sponsor] adopted in respect of the transactions contemplated by this Agreement).

[3] Execution and Delivery of Credit Agreement and Related Financing Documents

Generally. The credit agreement between the project company and the lender must be executed and delivered on the closing date. In addition, other financing documents related to the project, typically referenced individually in the credit agreement, must also be executed and delivered on the closing date.

Sample Provision
Loan Documents. Each of the Credit Agreement and the other [Loan Documents] shall have been duly executed and delivered by the [Project Company] and the other parties thereto, and shall be in full force and effect, and no default (or any event that

with the lapse of time or the giving of notice would constitute a default) shall have occurred thereunder.

[4] Lien Filings and Possession of Certain Collateral

Generally. On the closing date, all filings or recordings necessary to evidence the liens of the lender in the assets of the project company must be accomplished. Similarly, to the extent necessary, collateral that cannot be perfected without possession, must be delivered to the lender.

Sample Provision
Liens. The [Lender] shall have received evidence that all filing and recording fees, and all taxes and other expenses related to such filings, registrations and recordings, necessary for the consummation of the transactions contemplated by this Agreement and the other [Project Documents], including for the perfection of the security interests granted pursuant to the [Security Documents], have been paid in full by or on behalf of the [Project Company].

[5] Availability of Funds

Generally. Sufficient debt funds must be committed on the closing date to provide the debt needed to finance the project. Thus, if other lenders are providing debt to the project, the requisite credit documents must be executed and delivered on or before the closing date.

Sample Provision
Availability of Funds. The [Export Financing Agreement] and the [Standby Subordinated Loan Agreement] shall have been duly executed and delivered by the [Project Company] and the other parties thereto, and shall be in full force and effect, and no default (or any event that with the lapse of time or the giving of notice would constitute a default) shall have occurred thereunder.

[6] Related Equity Documents and Availability of Funds

Generally. Similarly, all equity funds necessary for the project must either be contributed to the project company, or committed in capital contribution agreements (also called *investment agreements*) in a form acceptable to the lender.

Sample Provision

Equity Documents and Availability of Funds. The [*Capital Contribution Agreements*] shall have been duly executed and delivered by the [*Project Sponsors*], and shall be in full force and effect, and no default (or any event that with the lapse of time or the giving of notice would constitute a default) shall have occurred thereunder.

[7] Sponsor Support Documents

Generally. Any credit support provided by a project sponsor must be in a form acceptable to the lender, be authorized, executed, and delivered to the project company and lender, and be enforceable in accordance with its terms. Examples include standby capital contribution agreements for specified risk events, and completion guarantees.

Sample Provision

Sponsor Credit Enhancement. The [*Completion Guarantee*] shall have been duly executed and delivered by the [*Project Sponsors*], and shall be in full force and effect, and no default (or any event that with the lapse of time or the giving of notice would constitute a default) shall have occurred thereunder.

[8] Third-Party Support Documents and Credit Enhancement

Generally. Any credit support provided by a third party must be in a form acceptable to the lender, be authorized, executed, and delivered to the project company and lender, and be enforceable in accordance with its terms. Examples include performance and payment bonds, sovereign guarantees, and political risk insurance.

Sample Provision

Other Credit Enhancement. The [*Performance and Payment Bonds*] shall have been duly executed and delivered by the [*Surety*], and shall be in full force and effect, and no default (or any event that with

the lapse of time or the giving of notice would constitute a default) shall have occurred thereunder.

[9] Host-Government Concessions and Guarantees

Generally. All concessions and licenses necessary for ownership, construction, or operation of the project must be obtained and in full force and effect. Credit enhancement provided by the host government, such as a guarantee, must be authorized, executed, and delivered.

Sample Provision

Concession. The [*Concession*] shall have been duly authorized, executed, and delivered by the [*Government*], and shall be in full force and effect, and no default (or any event that with the lapse of time or the giving of notice would constitute a default) shall have occurred hereunder.

Host-Government Enhancement. The [*Government Guarantee*] shall have been duly authorized, executed, and delivered by the [*Government*], and shall be in full force and effect, and no default (or any event that with the lapse of time or the giving of notice would constitute a default) shall have occurred thereunder.

[10] Off-Take Agreements

Generally. The off-take agreement must be in a form acceptable to the lender, be authorized, executed, and delivered to the project company by the off-take purchaser, and be enforceable against the off-take purchaser in accordance with its terms. As discussed in Chapter 18, because of the importance of the project to the off-take purchaser, milestones are often included in off-take agreements. Failure to satisfy these milestones can result in reduced sales prices, contract damages, and contract termination. Consequently, the lender will be interested in whether all milestones have been satisfied and will typically require a letter or some other assurance from the off-take purchaser to that effect.

Sample Provision

Off-Take Agreement. The [*Off-Take Agreement*] shall have been duly authorized, executed, and delivered by the [*Off-Take Purchaser*] and the [*Project Company*], and shall be in full force and effect, and no default (or any event that with the lapse of time or the giving of notice would constitute a default) shall have occurred thereunder. All dates for performance by each party thereto shall have been satisfied.

[11] Supply Agreements

Generally. The supply agreements must be in a form acceptable to the lender, be authorized, executed, and delivered to the project company by the supplier, and be enforceable against the supplier in accordance with its terms.

Sample Provision
Supply Agreement. The [*Supply Agreement*] shall have been duly authorized, executed, and delivered by the [*Supplier*], and shall be in full force and effect, and no default (or any event that with the lapse of time or the giving of notice would constitute a default) shall have occurred thereunder.

[12] Construction Contract and Issuance of the Notice to Proceed

Generally. The construction contract must be in a form acceptable to the lender, be authorized, executed and delivered to the project company by the contractor, and be enforceable against the contractor in accordance with its terms.

As discussed in Chapter 15, there is typically a time between execution of the construction contract and actual commencement of construction. This is because the construction contract is often negotiated and signed well before the construction loan closing. The contractor usually insists upon waiting for the closing, and the related assurance of construction fund availability, before commencing work. The lender will want to assure that construction will indeed begin after loan closing, however. Consequently, the lender will require evidence that the notice to proceed has been given by the project company to the contractor and that the contractor has accepted it and acknowledges its obligation to begin work.

Sample Provision
Construction Contract; Notice to Proceed. The [*Construction Contract*] shall have been duly executed and delivered by the [*Contractor*] and the [*Project Company*], and shall be in full force and effect, and no default (or any event that with the lapse of time or the giving of notice would constitute a default) shall have occurred thereunder; evidence satisfactory to the [*Lender*] shall be delivered showing that the [*Project Company*] has issued the [*Notice to Proceed*] (as defined in the [*Construction Contract*]) pursuant to the [*Construction Contract*] contingent only upon the effectiveness hereof.

[13] Operation and Maintenance Agreements

Generally. The operation and maintenance agreement must be in a form acceptable to the lender, be authorized, executed, and delivered to the project company by the operator and be enforceable against the operator in accordance with its terms.

Sample Provision
O&M Agreement. The [*O&M Agreement*] shall have been duly executed and delivered by the [*Operator*] and the [*Project Company*], and shall be in full force and effect, and no default (or any event that with the lapse of time or the giving of notice would constitute a default) shall have occurred thereunder.

[14] Permits

Generally. The lender will require certified copies of all governmental actions, filings, permits, and approvals necessary for the ownership, construction, start-up, and operation of the project and the related facilities. These must be final, not subject to appeal, revocable only for clearly articulated defaults, and contain only such conditions and restrictions as are acceptable to the lender. Certified copies of the permit applications and correspondence between the governmental agencies and the project company must be submitted.

Not all of these will be issued or made by the construction loan closing date, either because they cannot reasonably be obtained or are not required until a later stage of construction or when operations begin. Consequently, the lender will not require those that (i) are routinely and manditorily granted on application and fulfillment of applicable criteria and that would not normally be obtained before construction (ministerial permits) and (ii) are not required to be obtained until a later stage of project development or when operation begins. The lender will carefully examine permits under the last category to determine the likelihood of issuance, the cost associated with possible conditions attached to permit approval, and similar issues. If the issuance of a permit is within the discretion of an issuing agency, and can be granted or denied based upon such things as the agency's view of the project or on public policy grounds, then it will receive extra attention from the lender, its counsel, and its advisors.

Sample Provision

Governmental Approvals. Copies of all [*Governmental Approvals*] referred to in Section ___ [*cross-reference to representation on permits*] and such other [*Governmental Approvals*] as the [*Lender*] may reasonably request and which, in the opinion of the [*Lender*] are necessary or desirable under applicable law and regulations in connection with the transactions contemplated by the [*Project Documents*], each of which shall have been duly obtained in the name of the Borrower and shall be in full force and effect and not subject to appeal.

[15] Insurance and Insurance Consultant's Report

Generally. The lender will require copies of all insurance policies required by the terms of the credit agreement and the other project documents. To verify that the insurance policies satisfy the requirements of the credit documents, the lender will either undertake a review of the policies using its own insurance department, or require a report of an insurance consultant. The report must verify that the project company has obtained all the insurance required by the credit agreement and that it is in full force and effect. It also must verify that the insurance is not can-

cellable except on advance notice to the lender and otherwise satisfy the requirements of the credit agreement.

Sample Provision

Insurance. A certified copy of the insurance policies required by [*Section ___*] (or, if copies of any thereof are unavailable to the Borrower, certificates of the issuers thereof evidencing the same), such policies to be issued by companies satisfactory to the Majority Banks, together with evidence that the payment of all premiums therefor is current, and a certificate of a nationally recognized insurance broker satisfactory to the Agent, or such broker's authorized representative, certifying that insurance complying with this Agreement, covering the risks referred to therein, has been obtained and is in full force and effect.

[16] Real Estate

Generally. Where available, it is customary for the lender to obtain land surveys of, and title insurance on, the project site and other real estate interests important to the project.

Sample Provision

Title Insurance; Survey. (1) A binding commitment to issue policy or policies of title insurance on forms issued by the [*Title Company*], in form and substance satisfactory to the [*Lender*], (i) insuring the [*Lender*] in an amount equal to $xxx,000,000 that good and marketable title to the [*Project Site and Other Project Real Estate Interests*] is vested in the [*Project Company*] and that the [*Mortgage/Deed of Trust*] constitutes a valid first priority mortgage lien on the [*Project Site and Other Project Real Estate Interests*] subject only to Permitted Liens and such exceptions set forth in the [*Title Policy*] as are acceptable to [*Lender*], (ii) providing full coverage against mechanics', workers', materialmen's, and similar liens, and (iii) containing such other coverages and endorsements as the [*Lender*] may reasonably require; (2) a survey of the [*Project Site*] by a licensed surveyor satisfactory to the [*Lender*], certified to the [*Lender*]; and (3) true, correct, and complete copies of all documents evidencing the [*Project Site and Other Project Real Estate Interests*].

[17] Financial Statements of Project Company, Project Sponsors, Guarantors, and Major Project Participants

Generally. The most recent financial statements of each of the project company, the project sponsors, guarantors, and each of the major project participants, such as the off-take purchaser and the contractor, must be submitted to the lender. These assist the lender in its determination whether these entities have the requisite creditworthiness to perform their respective obligations under the project documents.

Sample Provision
Financial Information. Financial statements of the [*Project Company*], each [*Project Sponsor*], the [*Contractor*], the [*Operator*], the [*Off-Take Purchaser*], the [*Supplier*], and [*others*], which shall be in form and substance acceptable to [*Lender*], including without limitation as to the creditworthiness of each thereof necessary, in the sole discretion of the [*Lender*] to finance the [*Project*] using nonrecourse/limited recourse project financing techniques and credit analysis.

[18] Construction Budget and Construction Drawdown Schedule

Generally. An important safeguard against cost overruns available to the lender is the project construction budget. Periodic reporting, often monthly during the construction period, provides the lender with important information on the constructions costs, the cost still needed to complete the project, and the funds available to complete the project.

Construction cost overruns develop from a host of conditions. These include construction contracts with improperly definitive descriptions of the scope of work, change orders, inaccurate budgeting processes, inadequate construction contingencies, uninsured losses, delays, labor problems, and an increase in the cost of non-fixed-price construction costs.

Once a cost overrun is identified the loan documentation must specify the corrective action to be taken. First, reporting the overrun is necessary, of course. Then, a source of funds for the overrun must be identified and contributed to the project. A typical source for additional funds is a completion guarantee from the project sponsor.

A construction drawdown schedule is either submitted separately or included in the construction budget. This schedule verifies the timing of construction draws and the need for interest during construction. If the construction drawdown schedule is front-loaded, the project will have higher interest costs during construction. Thus, the drawdown schedule affects the project's construction loan needs.

Sample Provision
Construction Budget; Drawdown Schedule; Milestones. A budget of [*Construction Costs*], a schedule of the dates upon which construction loan drawdowns will be requested and a milestone performance schedule shall be delivered.

[19] Revenue and Expense Projections

Generally. The revenue and expense projections are variously called the base case and the projections. However termed, these financial statements present the most reasonably anticipated, projected financial outcome for the project on an annual basis for the period beginning on the construction loan closing date and ending two to three years after the anticipated debt maturity date. Included are projected revenues and expenses, based on financial and operating assumptions about such things as project availability, inflation, currency values, and similar variables. These financial predictions will be reviewed and approved by the independent engineer and must be acceptable to the lender.

Sample Provision
Projections. A projection of the anticipated revenues and expenses of the project over the term of the financing.

[20] Engineering Report

Generally. A report prepared by an engineering firm acceptable to the lender must be submitted. This report analyzes the technical and economic feasibility of the project, including a review of technical processes, plant design, equipment selection, permitting, construction budgeting, construction schedules, operations and maintenance costs, maintenance plans and schedules, projected performance, and revenue projections.

Sample Provision
Engineering Consultant's Report. A report of the [*Engineer*] as to the technical and economic feasibility of the [*Project*], including a review of technical processes, plant design, equipment selection, permitting, construction budgeting, construction schedules, operations and maintenance costs, maintenance plans and schedules, projected performance, and revenue projections acceptable to the [*Lender*].

[21] Consultants' Reports

Generally. The need for the reports by other consultants varies with the type of project and risks involved. Consultants that are sometimes used include those experienced with fuel, transportation, mining, and hazardous waste disposal. In such circumstances, a report prepared by a consultant acceptable to the lender must be submitted on topics about which the lender is particularly interested.

Sample Provision
Consultant's Report. A report of the [*identify type of consultant*] as to [*identify scope of report*] acceptable to the [*Lender*].

[22] Environmental Review

Generally. In most countries, project lenders will require some form of environmental audit and report by an environmental consultant. The scope of the analysis and report may include an environmental audit and risk assessment, review of permit applications and issued permits, and evaluation of environmental risk mitigation plans developed by the project company or operator.

Sample Provision
Environmental Audit. An environmental audit of the [*Project Site*] prepared by an expert acceptable to the [*Lender*].

[23] Legal Opinions

Generally. Opinions of lawyers are intended as a mechanism to ensure that due diligence has actually been performed by competent, careful counsel. It is not a risk-shifting device or intended to serve as a guarantee for the underlying debt. Legal opinions address standard topics such as due organization, authorization, execution, and delivery of financing and project documents, enforceability, and no contravention of laws and contracts. Opinions of counsel are typically obtained for each jurisdiction selected as the governing law for the underlying documents and in the country in which the project is located.

Opinions will also confirm that judgments decided in one country will be honored and enforced in another country, that the relevant parties can be sued in litigation and that the various laws chosen to govern the documents will be applied and upheld, and the agreements to submit to the jurisdiction of particular courts are enforceable.

Opinions relating to the creation, perfection, and priority of liens are, of course, important. Also important are opinions that address the immunity of the host government from litigation, to the extent it or a company with partial government ownership or control is involved in the project.

In addition to these issues, local counsel will include in its opinions the status of governmental approvals and permits necessary for the project, including financing, construction, start-up, and operation. Local counsel will also discuss other issues governed by local law, including regulatory oversight and real estate matters.

Opinions of counsel are also required from parties other than the project company. These include major off-take purchasers and suppliers. This type of third-party opinion typically covers the legality, validity, binding effect, and enforceability of the documents to which it is a party.

Sample Provision
Legal Opinions. Legal opinions of [*identify lawyers*] in the form attached hereto as Exhibit ___; and such

other opinions as may be reasonably requested by the [Lender].

[24] No Material Adverse Change

Generally. On the closing date, there must be no material adverse change in the financial condition of the project sponsors, the project company, or any major project participant, or in the financial or technical feasibility or prospects for the project.

Sample Provision
No Material Adverse Change. There shall have occurred no material adverse change in the business, properties, or affairs of the [Project Company] or any [Major Project Participant], or in the feasibility, economic or otherwise, of the Project.

[25] No Defaults

Generally. There must not exist, on the closing date, any default or event of default under any of the project contracts. The borrower typically must deliver a certificate on the closing date to this effect. The lender may require that the major project participants certify, either in the consent (discussed in Chapter 26), or in a separate certificate, that it is not aware of any default or event of default under the contract between it and the borrower.

Sample Provision
No Default. No Default, and no default by the [Project Company] or by any [Major Project Participant] under any [Project Document], shall have occurred and be continuing or will result from the [describe credit event], which such status shall be certified by the [Project Company].

[26] No Litigation

Generally. There must be no litigation in existence, or any judgment, decision, or order rendered in litigation that is still subject to appeal, which relates to the project or the project company, or to the participation by any project sponsor or other major project participant in the project.

Sample Provision
Litigation. There are no legal or arbitral proceedings or any proceedings by or before any [Governmental Person], now pending or threatened against the [Project Company] or any [Major Project Participant].

[27] Other Conditions Precedent

Generally. The lender will include other conditions precedent required by the unique risks of the particular project under development.

Sample Provision
Additional Documents. Such other documents relating to the Project or the matters contemplated by this Agreement as the [Lender] may reasonably request.

§ 24.07 CONDITIONS PRECEDENT TO EACH CONSTRUCTION LOAN DRAWDOWN

[1] Generally
Once a project finance construction loan has closed and initial funds been disbursed, the lender typically has the ability to approve subsequent drawdowns (the initial drawdown usually occurs on the closing date) based on conditions precedent. Once satisfied, the lender is obligated to allow the drawdown of loan proceeds.

Conditions to subsequent loan drawdowns are designed to ensure that the project company is in compliance with the loan agreement at the time of the new disbursement. These include construction schedule compliance, construction budget compliance and absence of cost overruns, permit compliance, absence of liens, and continuing adequate collateral arrangements.

It is sometimes said that once a project lender disburses the first construction loan, it must continue to make loans. This is argued based on the premise that the only way to recover the money disbursed is to complete construction. This is not true, and indeed construction lenders do stop funding projects when problems develop.

[2] Recertification of Representations and Warranties

Generally. Each of the representations and warranties made on the closing date by the project company in the credit agreement and the related financing documents must be repeated on the loan drawdown date.

Sample Provision
Representations and Warranties. The [*Project Company*] shall deliver a certificate that each of the representations and warranties of the Borrower set forth in this Agreement and in each document delivered in connection herewith are true and correct on the date hereof and after giving effect hereto.

[3] No Change in Law

Generally. Between the closing date and the drawdown, there must not have occurred any change in law, rule, or regulation that affects the financial or technical feasibility of the project.

Sample Provision
Change of Law. The [*Project Company*] shall deliver a certificate that as of the date hereof there has been no change in or enactment or promulgation of any [*Governmental Rule*] from and after the [*Closing Date*] that [*describe change in law that could have a material adverse effect on the Project*].

[4] Permit Status

Generally. All governmental actions, filings, permits, and approvals necessary for the ownership, construction, start-up, and operation of the project and the related facilities in effect at closing must remain in full force and effect and not be the subject of any challenge or appeal. In addition, all such actions that by the drawdown date can be reasonably obtained or are required at the stage of construction, must have been obtained and be in full force and effect. Those that are not required to be obtained until a later stage of project development or when operation begins will not typically be required on the drawdown date.

Sample Provision
Governmental Approvals. Copies of all [*Governmental Approvals*] referred to in Section ___ [*cross-reference to representation on permits*] and such other [*Governmental Approvals*] as the [*Lender*] may reasonably request and which, in the opinion of the [*Lender*] are necessary or desirable under applicable law and regulations in connection with the transactions contemplated by the [*Project Documents*], each of which shall have been duly obtained in the name of the Borrower and shall be in full force and effect and not subject to appeal.

[5] No Default

Generally. There must not exist, on the drawdown date, any default, or event of default under any of the project contracts.

Sample Provision
No Default. No Default, and no default by the [*Project Company*] or by any [*Major Project Participant*] under any [*Project Document*], shall have occurred and be continuing or will result from the [*describe credit event*], which such status shall be certified by the [*Project Company*].

[6] No Material Adverse Change

Generally. On the drawdown date, there must be no material adverse change in the financial condition of the project sponsors, the project company, or any major project participant, or in the financial or technical feasibility or prospects for the project.

Sample Provision
No Material Adverse Change. There shall have occurred no material adverse change in the business, properties, or affairs of the [*Project Company*] or any [*Major Project Participant*], or in the feasibility, economic or otherwise, of the Project.

[7] No Litigation

Generally. There must be no litigation in existence, or any judgment, decision, or order rendered in litigation that is still subject to appeal, which relates to the project or the project company, or to the participation by any project sponsor or other major project participant in the project.

Sample Provision
Litigation. There are no legal or arbitral proceedings or any proceedings by or before any [*Governmental Person*], now pending or threatened against the [*Project Company*] or any [*Major Project Participant*].

[8] Construction Progress

Generally. The construction progress must be in conformity with the construction schedule provided by the project company to the lender at closing.

Sample Provision
Construction Progress. The progress of construction is in conformity with the [*Construction Schedule*].

[9] Construction Budget and Funds Available to Complete the Project

Generally. There must not be any construction cost overrun. The funds available to complete the project must be no less than the cost of completing the project, as calculated on the date of the drawdown.

Sample Provision
Cost Overrun; Funds Available to Complete the Project. There has occurred no [*Cost Overrun*], and the [*Funds Available to Complete the Project*] exceed the [*Cost to Complete the Project*].

[10] Lien Waivers

Generally. The borrower must deliver to the lender copies of receipts or other evidence that it has used the previous construction draws to pay project costs. No liens must exist on the project because of the borrower's failure to pay the contractor according to the terms of the construction contract.

Sample Provision
No Liens. No Liens other than Permitted Liens shall have been filed against or otherwise encumber or affect any assets, properties or revenues of the [*Project Company*].

[11] Other Conditions Precedent

Generally. The lender will include other conditions precedent required by the unique risks of the particular project under development.

Sample Provision
Additional Documents. Such other documents relating to the Project or the matters contemplated by this Agreement as the [*Lender*] may reasonably request.

§ 24.08 CONDITIONS PRECEDENT TO CONVERSION OF CONSTRUCTION LOAN TO A TERM LOAN

[1] Generally

Once construction is complete, the construction loan will be repaid and converted into a term loan by the same lenders, or will be repaid from the proceeds of a term loan provided by other lenders. If the loan is converted into a term loan by the same lenders, conditions precedent to that conversion must be satisfied by the project company. If the construction loan is paid from the proceeds of a term loan provided by other lenders, the other lenders will impose their own set of conditions precedent much like those discussed above as conditions to closing.

This section concentrates on the loan conversion. Upon satisfaction of the conditions precedent to closing, the lender is obligated to convert the loans from construction loans to term loans. This is important to the project company. Term loans typically bear lower interest rates than construction loans because the market considers construction risk to require a higher interest rate. Other advantages to the project company after conversion include a longer amortization schedule, the ability to receive distributions of profit, and the release of any unused construction contingency.

Typical conditions to loan conversion include receipt of all operating permits, satisfaction of performance tests, and continued economic viability of the project.

[2] Recertification of Representations and Warranties

Generally. Each of the representations and warranties made on the closing date by the project company in the credit agreement and the related financing documents must be repeated on the conversion date.

Sample Provision
Representations and Warranties. The [*Project Company*] shall deliver a certificate that each of the representations and warranties of the [*Project Company*] set forth in this Agreement and in each document delivered in connection herewith are true and correct on the date hereof and after giving effect hereto.

[3] No Change in Law

Generally. On the conversion date, there must not have occurred any change in law, rule, or regulation that affects the financial or technical feasibility of the project.

Sample Provision
Change of Law. The [*Project Company*] shall deliver a certificate that as of the date hereof there has been no change in or enactment or promulgation of any [*Governmental Rule*] from and after the [*Closing Date*] that [*describe change in law that could have a material adverse effect on the Project*].

[4] Permit Status

Generally. All governmental actions, filings, permits, and approvals necessary for the ownership, construction, start-up, and operation of the project and the related facilities must be in full force and effect and not the subject of any challenge or appeal.

Sample Provision
Governmental Approvals. Copies of all [*Governmental Approvals*] referred to in Section __ [*cross-reference to representation on permits*] and such other [*Governmental Approvals*] as the [*Lender*] may reasonably request and which, in the opinion of the [*Lender*] are necessary or desirable under applicable law and regulations in connection with the transactions contemplated by the [*Project Documents*], each of which shall have been duly obtained in the name of the Borrower and shall be in full force and effect and not subject to appeal.

[5] No Default

Generally. There must not exist any default or event of default under any of the project contracts.

Sample Provision
No Defaults. There shall exist no Default or Event of Default under any of the [*Project Contracts*].

[6] No Material Adverse Change

Generally. There must be no material adverse change in the financial condition of the project sponsors, the project company, or any major project participant, or in the financial or technical feasibility or prospects for the project.

Sample Provision
No Material Adverse Change. There shall have occurred no material adverse change in the business, properties, or affairs of the [*Project Company*] or any [*Major Project Participant*], or in the feasibility, economic or otherwise, of the Project.

[7] No Litigation

Generally. There must be no litigation in existence, or any judgment, decision, or order rendered in litigation that is still subject to appeal, which relates to the project or the project company, or to the participation by any project sponsor or other major project participant in the project.

Sample Provision
Litigation. There are no legal or arbitral proceedings or any proceedings by or before any

[*Governmental Person*], now pending or threatened against the [*Project Company*] or any [*Major Project Participant*].

[8] Completion

Generally. The construction of the project must be complete. The occurrence of completion can have a triggering effect throughout the collection of contracts used in a project financing. Under the construction contract, completion determines if and when the contractor is liable for liquidated damages arising from construction delays or performance guarantees. Under the operating agreement, it determines the date the operator begins its responsibilities of operation. The majority of supply obligations under input agreements and purchase obligations under offtake agreements typically begin on completion, as well.

Equity commitment obligations sometimes mature on this date. These can arise from the obligation to invest equity as originally contemplated in the sources and uses of funds for the project, or to contribute additional equity because of cost overruns. Under a completion guarantee provided by the project sponsors, the definition of completion will determine when and if additional funds must be used to finish construction, or whether construction has occurred and the contingent liability terminated.

Multilateral and bilateral involvement in a project is sometimes triggered by the occurrence of completion. For example, U.S. Export-Import Bank does not provide funds for construction financing of projects, awaiting completion to participate as a lender.

Because of the importance of this concept throughout the project documents, it is important that the definition of completion be thoroughly considered and used consistently in project documentation. A sample definition appears in Chapter 12.

Sample Provision
Completion. Completion shall have occurred, as certified by the [*Project Company*] and there shall be no facts or circumstances of which the [*Independent Engineer*] is aware that would cause the [*Independent Engineer*], in the exercise of its professional judgment, to believe that [*Completion*] has not occurred.

[9] Other Conditions Precedent

Generally. The lender will include other conditions precedent required by the unique risks of the particular project under development.

Sample Provision
Additional Documents. Such other documents relating to the Project or the matters contemplated by this Agreement as the [*Lender*] may reasonably request.

§ 24.09 REPRESENTATIONS AND WARRANTIES

Representations and warranties are discussed in Chapter 13.

§ 24.10 COVENANTS

[1] Generally
Covenants in a project finance transaction are designed (i) to ensure that the project company constructs and operates the project in the manner contemplated in the technical and economic assumptions that are the foundation of financial projections; (ii) to provide the lender with advance or prompt warning of a potential problem, whether political, financial, contractual, or technical; and (iii) to protect the lender's liens. These include covenants that the project will be constructed on schedule, within the construction budget and at agreed-upon performance levels, be operated in accordance with agreed standards, that project contracts will not be terminated or amended, and comply with operating budgets approved by the lender.

Covenants in a project finance loan agreement include many of the same covenants required by lenders in asset-based loan transactions. However, unlike asset-based transactions, project finance loan documents are designed to closely monitor and regulate the activities of the project company. These include obligations to provide the lender with periodic project operating information, copies of notices given the project company by the host government, and notices of default under material project agreements.

Other covenants in a project finance transaction will be determined by the industry in which the project will operate, the identity of the host country, project economics, and the risk allocations made in the underlying project contracts.

[2] Reports on Project Construction and Completion

Generally. Periodic reporting on the progress of construction provides important information to the lender on the ability of the contractor and project company to complete the project according to the construction schedule used as a basis for project economic projections. These reports typically contain information on construction progress generally; status of equipment orders, deliveries, and installation; minutes of construction progress meetings; force majeure events; and expected dates for completion.

The concept of completion is an important, albeit sometimes elusive, concept in project financing. It is from the date of completion that many financial commitments are made and released: project sponsor completion guarantees are terminated; loan pricing changes from rates reflective of construction risks to rates reflective of operating risks; because the project can now produce operating revenues, loan amortization begins; capital contribution agreements provide for the contribution of capital, or for the release of the obligation to do so; dividends and other payments are distributable to the project sponsors; responsibility for the project switches from the contractor to the operator; and so forth.

Failure to achieve completion can result in several remedies for the lender. These are default and foreclosure; additional equity contributions by project sponsors; and application of excess cash flow to debt repayment.

There are generally three levels of completion in a project finance transaction: mechanical com-

pletion, operational completion, and final completion. Each has a separate purpose in the loan agreement.

Mechanical Completion. Mechanical completion is achieved when the project is completed to the project specifications. This is confirmable by achievement of the tests outlined in the construction contract. These tests confirm safe operability, not necessarily performance guarantees.

Operation Completion. Operational completion is achieved when the project is operated at the levels guaranteed in the construction contract, and within environmental requirements. These tests confirm that the project is capable of operation at agreed-upon levels over an extended period. These periods vary based on the type of project but are always designed to confirm long-term reliability and performance within the assumptions made in project financial projections (operating costs, feedstock costs, labor requirements, maintenance costs, revenue produced).

Final Completion. Final completion is the point at which all provisions of the construction contract have been performed. Usually, these are minor obligations, such as completion by the contractor of minor portions of the work, usually referred to as "punch list" items, releases of minor liens, and similar requirements.

Sample Provision

At least once during each month occurring before the [Completion Date], [Project Company] shall provide to [Lender] a progress report setting forth in reasonable detail (1) the construction status of the Project, progress of start-up activities and the status of Contractor's adherence to the milestone schedule, (2) the status of [Governmental Approvals] necessary for construction of the Project, (3) the estimated [Completion Date], (4) a determination of whether sufficient funds remain available as [Construction Loans] and [Contingent Equity] in order to achieve [Completion] by the [Completion Date], and (5) any other critical event or circumstance that could have a material effect on the construction, completion, and/or cost of the Project.

[3] Reports on Project Operation

Generally. Similarly, the project company is typically obligated to provide periodic reports on the project's operation and maintenance. While the content of these reports varies with the industry involved, typical requirements include comparisons of project operation to prior periods, unusual operating conditions, details on unscheduled maintenance and repairs, casualty reports, force majeure reports, and other data.

Sample Provision
Within *xx* days after the end of each quarter ending after the [*Completion Date*], a report on the operation of the Project, in the form attached as Exhibit __.

[4] Notice of Certain Events

Generally. Advance warning of problems with the project is a significant benefit to the project lender. Project difficulties may take time to resolve, and the more advance notice of these that the lender obtains, the more comfortable it is with the risks in a project financing. Consequently, project finance loan agreements contain provisions obligating the borrower to provide notice of certain events, including the following: litigation against the project company; any default or event of default (whether with the giving of notice or passage of time, or both) under any project contract; and any default, termination, cancellation, amendment, supplement, or modification of any governmental permit, license, or concession.

Sample Provision
The [*Project Company*] shall provide [*Lender*] with notice of (a) all legal or arbitral proceedings, and of all proceedings by or before any [*Governmental Person*], and of any development relating thereto, affecting any [*Major Project Participant*] and (b) the [*Project Company*]'s obtaining knowledge of the commencement of any proceedings by or before any [*Governmental Person*] for the purpose of revoking, terminating, withdrawing, suspending, modifying or withholding any [*Governmental Approval*] necessary for the execution, delivery or performance by any [*Major Project Participant*] of its obligations, or the exercise of its rights or remedies, under the [*Project Documents*] to which such [*Major Project Participant*] is party, or for the construction or operation of the Project as contemplated by the [*Project Documents*].

[5] Maintain Existence

Generally. The borrower will agree to take all action necessary to preserve its existence. This includes such things as making required filings with governmental authorities and observing corporate or partnership formalities according to the laws of the jurisdiction of organization of the project company.

Sample Provision
The [*Project Company*] shall preserve and maintain its partnership existence in [*specify jurisdiction of formation*] and its rights, franchises and privileges in [*specify jurisdiction in which Project is located*] and in all jurisdictions where necessary in light of its business or properties.

[6] Maintain Interest in Project

Generally. The project company will be obligated to maintain its ownership of the project. It is also generally required that the project sponsors maintain either ownership interest in the project or voting control of the project company, for a negotiated period. This provides the lender with some comfort that the original equity investors will continue to be involved in the project, and that the lender can continue to transact business with the original sponsors.

Sample Provision
The [*Project Company*] shall maintain its ownership of the Project. The [*Project Sponsors*] shall maintain at least a 51% voting interest in the [*Project Company*].

[7] Pay Taxes

Generally. All taxes and other governmental charges must be paid when due and payable.

Exceptions are usually permitted for situations in which the project company is contesting the tax obligation in good faith, provided it has set aside a reserve for payment in the event it fails in contesting the liability.

Sample Provision

The [Project Company] shall pay and discharge or cause to be paid or discharged all taxes, assessments, and governmental charges or levies imposed on it or on its income or profits or on any of its property prior to the date on which penalties attach to its income, profits, or property, and all lawful claims that, if unpaid, might become a Lien upon the property of the [Project Company] (subject to the next sentence). The [Project Company] shall have the right, however, to contest in good faith the validity or amount of any such tax, assessment, charge, levy, or claim by proper proceedings timely instituted, and may permit the taxes, assessments, charges, levies, or claims so contested to remain unpaid during the period of such contest if: (a) the [Project Company] diligently prosecutes such contest, (b) during the period of such contest the enforcement of any contested item is effectively stayed, and (c) adequate security in the form of a bond or other security satisfactory to the [Lender] is provided by the [Project Company] to the [Lender] for the payment of any contested item such that enforcement of any contested item is effectively stayed and any Lien arising thereby is effectively removed. The [Project Company] will promptly pay any valid, final judgment enforcing any such tax, assessment, charge, levy, or claim and cause the same to be satisfied of record.

[8] Compliance With Laws

Generally. The project company will agree to comply with all laws applicable to it and to the project.

Sample Provision

The [Project Company] shall at all times comply with, and cause the Project to comply with, all applicable [Governmental Approvals] and [Governmental Rules].

[9] Obtain and Maintain All Approvals, Permits, and Licenses

Generally. Similarly, the project company will covenant that it will obtain and maintain all approvals, permits and licenses necessary or advisable in connection with: (i) development, construction, start-up, and operation of the project; (ii) execution, delivery, and performance of the project contracts and the credit documents; and (iii) taking of any action contemplated by these documents.

It is important that the project lender remain abreast of project developments. Consequently, it will require that the project company provide copies of all documents furnished to the project company by any governmental authority.

Sample Provision

The [Project Company] shall obtain all applicable [Governmental Approvals] as shall now or hereafter be necessary under applicable [Governmental Rules] for the construction, ownership, operation or maintenance of the Project or the execution, delivery and performance by the [Project Company] of any of the [Project Documents] and shall promptly furnish copies thereof to the [Lender].

[10] No Merger or Consolidation

Generally. The project company will agree not to merge with or consolidate with any other entity. This assures the project lender that it continues to lend money to the entity organized for the sole purpose of owning the project. This is particularly important in project finance transactions, where lenders base credit appraisals on the feasibility of a project.

Sample Provision

The [Project Company] shall not merge into or consolidate with any Person or sell, lease, transfer, or otherwise dispose of any of its assets other than sales of [describe off-take] pursuant to the [Off-Take Agreement], and equipment that is obsolete or no longer useful or necessary for the proper operation of the Project, and sales of assets in the ordinary course of its business having a fair market value not in excess of $xxx,000 for a single transaction or $xxx,000 in the aggregate for all such sales.

[11] Engineering Standards for Construction and Operation

Generally. The project company will covenant to satisfy an overall standard of care and operation consistent with the industry. An example is "in a proper manner in accordance with good industry practice."

Sample Provision
The [*Project Company*] shall cause the Project to be duly constructed and completed in accordance with the [*Construction Contract*] and all [*Governmental Approvals*] and in accordance with prudent engineering practices.

[12] Maintenance of Properties

Generally. The borrower typically covenants to maintain the project and the assets in good working order, making all repairs and replacements necessary to maintain and preserve the efficiency of the project.

Sample Provision
The [*Project Company*] shall maintain and preserve the Project and all of the [*Project Company*]'s other properties necessary or useful in the proper conduct of its business, in good working order and condition, ordinary wear and tear excepted, and in accordance with prudent and efficient utility practice.

[13] Environmental Compliance

Generally. Environmental compliance in the international context is complicated by the developing nature of environmental law. The project company typically agrees to comply with the laws of the jurisdiction in which the project is located, and to give notice promptly of any environmental hazard.

Sample Provision
The [*Project Company*] shall operate, maintain, and preserve the Project and all of the [*Project Company*]'s other properties necessary or useful in the proper conduct of its business, in strict compliance with all [*Environmental Rules*] and [*Governmental Approvals*].

[14] Insurance and Insurance Proceeds

Generally. The project company will be required to obtain and maintain insurance. The type of insurance coverage typically required is discussed in Chapter 20. The insurance must satisfy the requirements of the lender concerning form, creditworthiness of insurers, suitability of named insured, loss payee and subrogation provisions, and other concerns.

Insurance proceeds are typically payable to the lender. The use of casualty insurance proceeds after receipt is a subject of negotiation. Typically, the project company for project repair may use minor amounts. Major amounts can be used for repair but only after a showing by the project company that the project will continue to be feasible after the repair.

Sample Provision
The [*Project Company*] shall maintain, or shall cause to be maintained, the following insurance coverages with carriers authorized to cover risks and licensed to underwrite policies in the [*describe jurisdiction*] and having a [*Best's*] rating of __ or higher as are selected by the [*Project Company*] with the approval of the [*Lender*] (which approval will not be unreasonably withheld or delayed): [*describe insurance requirements*]. Also, the [*Project Company*] shall maintain, or cause to be maintained, all insurance required to be maintained pursuant to any other [*Project Document*].

All insurance policies required hereby covering loss or damage to the Project shall name the [*Lender*] as additional named insured under a lender's loss payable endorsement and shall provide that any payment under such policies for any loss or damage shall be made to the [*Lender*] and applied as provided in the [*Security Agreement*].

All liability insurance policies required hereby shall name the [*Lender*] and its assigns, subsidiaries and employees as additional insureds as their interest may appear, except for workers' compensation coverage and automobile liability coverage.

If the [Project Company] fails to maintain insurance as required above, then the [Lender], in addition to its other rights hereunder, may at its option maintain the required insurance and, in such event, the [Project Company] shall reimburse the [Lender] upon demand for the cost of such insurance together with interest on such cost at a rate per annum equal to [interest rate].

[15] Performance of Project Documents

Generally. The project company typically agrees to perform its obligations under, and otherwise comply with, each of the project documents, not to create any default thereunder, and to otherwise maintain them in full force and effect.

Sample Provision

The [Project Company] shall perform and observe each and every provision of the [Project Documents] in all material respects on its part to be performed or observed.

[16] Amendment, Modification, Termination, Replacement, and So Forth of Project Documents

Generally. The project company will agree not to take any action to amend, modify, or terminate, waive timely performance of, or replace or enter into any project contract without the consent of the project lender. In some situations, the project company is also precluded from electing any optional action under a contract.

Exceptions to this covenant are sometimes negotiated where, for example, a project contract is easily replaceable or where the amendment is not material in cost, effect, or technical implication to the project. A qualification typically requested by the project company is that it can take any of the foregoing action if the amendment, modification, termination, or waiver would not have a material adverse effect on the project.

Sample Provision

The [Project Company] shall not enter into or consent to any amendment, modification, or supplement of, or the exercise of any option under, any [Project Document] unless such amendment, supplement, or waiver, or exercise of option, could not have a materially adverse effect on the [Project Company], the Project, the [Project Company]'s ability to perform its obligations under the [Project Documents] or the rights or remedies of the [Lender]. The [Project Company] shall supply to the [Lender] copies of any such amendment, modification, or supplement promptly following the execution thereof. Notwithstanding the foregoing, the [Project Company] (a) shall not cancel or terminate any [Project Document] to which it is a party; (b) shall not sell, assign, or otherwise dispose of (by operation of law or otherwise) any part of its interest in any such [Project Document]; (c) shall not waive any default under or breach of any such [Project Document] or waive, fail to enforce, forgive, or release any right, interest, or entitlement, howsoever arising, under or in respect of any such [Project Document] or vary or agree to the variation in any way of any material provision of any such [Project Document] or of the performance of any material obligation by any other Person under any such [Project Document]; and (d) shall not petition, request, or take any other legal or administrative action that seeks, or may reasonably be expected, to rescind, terminate, or suspend any such [Project Document] or amend or modify any thereof.

[17] Change Orders

Generally. Changes to a project during the construction phase are inevitable. Small, insignificant changes are not usually subject to approval by the lender. Other changes, however, must be reviewed to determine whether the change affects the construction costs, construction schedule, operating costs, performance guarantees, and long-term reliability of the project. They must also be examined to confirm that they will not cause a default under any of the other project contracts.

Sample Provision

The [Project Company] shall not enter into change orders pursuant to the [Construction Contract] if such change orders, in the aggregate, (a) change the Technical Specifications in any material adverse respect; (b) increase the aggregate amount payable thereunder; (c) extend or cause an extension of the [*Scheduled Completion Date*]; (d) result, directly or indirectly, in any increase in any operation or maintenance expense in excess of $xx,000 in any year; or (e) require an amendment of any other provision of the [*Construction Contract*] that is materially adverse to the [*Project Company*], the Project or the rights or remedies of the [*Lender*].

[18] Engaging in Other Business

Generally. The project company will agree not to engage in any business other than the development, construction, start-up, and operation of the project. This restriction is important to the lender's credit decision, which is made on the assumption that the company will be solely operated as owner of the project.

Sample Provision
The [*Project Company*] shall engage solely in the business of production and sale of [*describe offtake*] at the Project.

[19] Indebtedness

Generally. Because the project lender is relying on the ability of the project revenues to repay the project debt, additional debt could impair the borrower's ability to make debt payments. Additional indebtedness is not permitted without the approval of the project lenders or, if permitted, in excess of negotiated amounts. The term *debt* is defined expansively to include all types of indebtedness.

There are typical exceptions negotiated to this covenant. They include indebtedness subordinated on terms acceptable to the project lender; current accounts and other amounts payable in the ordinary course of the project company's business if incurred for the construction or operation of the project; debt not in excess at any one time of a negotiated amount; and loans by project sponsors, unsecured, and subordinated on terms acceptable to the lender.

Sample Provision
The [*Project Company*] shall not incur or assume any Debt other than (a) Debt under this Agreement, (b) Debt under the [*Subordinated Loan Agreement*], (c) Debt in respect of equipment purchases up to but not exceeding $xxx,000 in the aggregate at any one time outstanding, (d) capital lease obligations permitted under [*specify section*], (e) Debt to the [*Project Company*] from [*partners/shareholders/owners*], and (f) other Debt in an aggregate principal amount not to exceed $x,000,000 provided that (i) Debt referred to in clauses (e) and (f) shall be evidenced by documents incorporating subordination provisions substantially in the form of Exhibit __ and otherwise in form and substance satisfactory to the [*Lender*].

[20] Liens

Generally. A typical lien covenant is that the borrower will not create, incur, or suffer to exist any lien on the project assets, other than permitted liens. Permitted liens are generally liens imposed by law, and liens that do not materially impair the project assets.

Sample Provision
The [*Project Company*] shall not create or suffer to exist any Lien on any of its assets securing any debt or other obligation of any Person, other than [*Permitted Liens*].

[21] Investments

Generally. The project company is not permitted to make investments in another entity, or to invest its own funds in any investment unless selected from a list approved by the lender.

Sample Provision
The [*Project Company*] shall not directly or indirectly invest funds held by the [*Lender*] pursuant to the [*Security Agreement/Disbursement Agreement/Accounts Agreement*], other than in [*Permitted Investments*] with maturities that will ensure that funds are available for payment of interest on a monthly basis without the incurrence of penalties. The [*Project Company*] shall not make any loan or advance (other than travel advances and the like to employees made, and account receivables created, in the ordinary course of business) to, or investment in, any Person, except for [*Permitted Investments*], or purchase or otherwise acquire the

capital stock of, all or a substantial portion of the assets of, or any obligations of or any interest in, any Person.

[22] Dividends and Restricted Payments

Generally. Release of profits and other distributions to the project sponsors is closely controlled by the project lender. Once the money is released, the funds are not typically available for use at the project. An exception exists where distributions are made contingent on delivery of guarantees by the project sponsors requiring that if funds are needed at the project for specified contingencies, such as operating cost overruns or capital costs, the funds will be returned as equity contributions in the project company.

Release of profits is typically conditioned on the following: at the time of the distribution, there must not exist any default or event of default; all amounts required to be on deposit in various reserve accounts, such as the debt service reserve account or maintenance account, have been fully funded; and that the debt service coverage ratio for the project satisfies a negotiated amount.

Sample Provision

The [*Project Company*] shall not declare or make any Restricted Payment; provided that the [*Project Company*] may, on [*specify distribution date*], declare or make a Restricted Payment if on such date (the "Restricted Payment Date"):
(a) no Default shall have occurred and be continuing;
(b) all [*Debt Service*] then due and payable shall have been paid in full;
(c) the balance in the [*Debt Service Reserve Account*] shall be at least equal to [*amount*];
(d) the [*Debt Service Coverage Ratio*] for the next quarter shall be greater than 1.x to 1.

[23] Maximization of Use of Export Financing, Sponsor Support, and Subordinated Debt

Generally. There is often a covenant of the project company to make maximum use of other debt sources available to the project. These can include export-import financing, equity contri-

butions from project sponsors, and subordinated debt.

Sample Provision

To the fullest extent permitted under the [*Export Financing Agreement*], the [*Project Company*] shall use all financing provided thereunder before requesting any loans hereunder.

[24] Mandatory Prepayment on the Occurrence of Certain Events From Excess Cash Flow

Generally. Project finance credit agreements typically contain mandatory prepayment sections to address unique project risks. These provisions allow the lender to block distributions of profits to the project sponsors, and use this excess cash flow to prepay debt.

Alternatively, the excess cash flow is deposited in a special reserve account. Funds in the reserve account remain on deposit for a negotiated period of time during which the borrower attempts to remedy the situation that results in the mandatory deposit of funds. If it cannot be cured or if the borrower fails to do so within the negotiated period, the funds on deposit are then used to prepay debt.

Examples of situations in which this remedy is used include the following: loss of an important project contract; loss of a project permit; operating budget cost overruns; and failure to satisfy a minimum debt service coverage test.

This mechanism allows the project lender to reduce its exposure and avoid the expense of foreclosure. It also provides the project sponsors with an incentive to correct the problem as promptly as possible.

Sample Provision

If the [*Debt Service Coverage Ratio*] for each of four fiscal quarters preceding each one year anniversary of the [*Completion Date*], is greater than or equal 1.x to 1 and less than or equal to 1.x to 1 then all [*Excess Cash Flow*] may be applied by the [*Lender*] for the purpose of payment and/or prepayment of the [*Loans*] (to be applied *pro rata* according to the outstanding installments of such loans).

[25] Financial Tests

Generally. Financial tests, such as debt service coverage ratios, minimum working capital requirements, net worth, and the like are the subject of negotiation. These are tailored to the specific risks of the project and the view of the credit officer structuring the transaction toward the efficacy of financial tests in a project financing. One view is that financial tests are not useful because at the time triggered, the project is already in serious difficulty. Others view them as helpful as early indications of difficulties and establish conservative tests for use as an early warning mechanism.

The debt service coverage ratio is a convenient mechanism for the project lender to monitor project performance and the likelihood for loan repayment. It is one meter for use in monitoring a project, however, and is seldom viewed by project lenders as the only necessary covenant. This is because many events can occur in the life of a project that do not have immediate negative effects. For example, an amendment of a project contract to reduce project revenues in the later years of a project would have no effect on the coverage ratio for the current fiscal period. Yet, in such a scenario, the project lender may want to begin reserving excess cash flow for later use.

Sample Provision
The [*Project Company*] shall not permit the [*Debt Service Coverage Ratio*], for any quarter, to be less than 1.x to 1.

[26] Special Milestones

Generally. Project due diligence may reveal one or more events that must be completed by specified dates if the project is to be feasible. Examples include dates that relate to construction deadlines, and termination dates under off-take purchase agreements if the project is not in commercial operation. These are incorporated into the loan agreement with covenants requiring the borrower to take the required action by the date specified.

It is typical for the loan agreement to establish a date for compliance that is well before the date specified in the underlying project contracts. This gives the lender time to cure the failure itself.

Sample Provision
The [*Project Company*] shall take all action necessary to achieve [*Commercial Operations (as defined in the Off-Take Agreement)*] at least [*specify number of months*] before the date required therein.

[27] Change in the Project

Generally. Prohibitions on the project company altering the project are sometimes overlooked. Participants incorrectly believe that by prohibiting changes to the underlying project documents, they have preserved the project unchanged. After completion, for example, it is possible to completely alter the project, however, by making changes to plant capacity, production schedules, and similar operating matters, without any contract changes.

The project company can agree that it will not make any change or addition to the project design or construction, or alter or reduce the project capacity, maintenance schedule or other operating procedures in a manner that is reasonably expected to reduce production below a negotiated amount.

Sample Provision
The [*Project Company*] shall not make any change in any plan or specification, or otherwise change any aspect of the Project from that described in the [*Construction Contract*] without the prior consent of the [*Lender*].

[28] Project Support

Generally. The project company covenants that it will support the project in all respects, including completion. It also agrees to resist any regulatory change that would have an adverse effect on the Project.

Sample Provision
[*Project Company*] shall diligently complete the project in accordance with the design specifications approved by the Lender; take all action required to meet the [*set forth description of*

milestone dates under Project Contracts and performance standards to be achieved]; provide administrative support and personnel to the Project; provide operational support and personnel to the Project; and otherwise support the Project in any manner reasonable or necessary to ensure that the [*Project Company*] complies with the Project Contracts. In addition, the [*Project Company*] agrees to use its reasonable efforts to resist any proposed regulatory change that is reasonably expected to have a material adverse effect on the Project.

[29] Financial Reporting

Generally. The project company covenants that it will provide the lender with annual audited financial information, certified by a nationally recognized accounting firm acceptable to the lender, and quarterly unaudited financial statements, certified by an officer of the project company, all prepared in accordance with generally accepted accounting principles consistently applied. It also covenants to provide the lender with access to accounting records for inspection purposes.

[30] Use of Proceeds

Generally. The project company will covenant that loan proceeds will be used only for the development, construction, start-up, and operation of the project. In addition, it will covenant that the proceeds of each construction loan drawdown will be used for the purposes requested. The project lender will want to avoid any use of proceeds for unapproved project changes or uses. If the construction lender approves a drawdown during construction, it desires that the payments due be made by the project company, not withheld for use as negotiating leverage to resolve a dispute between the project company and another contracting party.

Sample Provision
The [*Project Company*] shall use the proceeds of the loans solely to pay for the costs relating to the development, construction, construction management, financing, and performance testing and start-up of the Project in accordance with the

[*Project Documents*]. The proceeds of each requisition for funds during the [*Construction Period*] shall be applied as provided in the [*Construction Certificate*] delivered in respect of such requisition or borrowing.

[31] Security Documents

Generally. The borrower will covenant that it will take all action required to maintain and to preserve the liens created by the security documents and the priority of such liens. In addition, it covenants to provide consents to assignment in a form acceptable to the lender for any new project contracts.

Sample Provision
The [*Project Company*] shall take or cause to be taken all actions required or desirable to maintain and preserve the Liens created by the [*Security Documents*] and the senior priority of such Liens. The [*Project Company*] shall execute or cause to be executed any and all further instruments (including financing statements, continuation statements, and similar statements with respect to any of the [*Security Documents*]) requested by the [*Lender*] for such purposes.

[32] Operating Budget

Generally. The project company is typically required to submit an annual project operating budget for approval by the lender. Generally, the budget is submitted sixty days prior to the next operating year. Once approved, the project operating expenses cannot exceed the budgeted amount, plus a margin, without consent of the lender.

Sample Provision
The [*Project Company*] shall, not less than *xx* days prior to the beginning of each fiscal year, adopt a budget of [*Operating Costs*], divided into monthly operating periods, for each such fiscal year (each, an "Operating Budget"). Copies of a proposed Operating Budget, or an amendment to the Operating Budget for the remaining portion of the year covered by the most recently delivered Operating Budget, shall be delivered to the [*Lender*] not

less than *xx* days before the date on which the [*Project Company*] is required to deliver an Operating Budget pursuant to the preceding sentence or the date on which such amendment to the Operating Budget is to become effective, as the case may be. The [*Lender*] shall have the opportunity to review and comment on each Operating Budget and amendment thereto. If a Default shall have occurred and be continuing, the [*Project Company*] shall not adopt an Operating Budget, or any amendment thereto, without the prior written consent of the [*Lender*] (which approval shall not be unreasonably withheld or delayed).

[33] Accounts

Generally. As discussed in Chapter 26, it is typical for all project revenues to flow through a revenue control account maintained by the project company with the lender. All revenues generated by project operation, liquidated damage payments under project contracts, and other receipts are deposited into this account. The project company agrees to establish this account at closing.

The project company also agrees to apply the funds on deposit in the revenue account in the order of an agreed-upon priority. As an example, revenue in a project could be used in the following priority: payment of operating and maintenance expenses, payment of debt service, funding a standby capital repair account, funding a debt service reserve account, and profit distributions to the project sponsors. The mechanics of this procedure is discussed in detail in Chapter 26.

Sample Provision
The [*Project Company*] shall, forthwith upon the receipt of any [*Revenues*], pay the same in the same form as received by the [*Project Company*] (with any necessary endorsement) to the [*Lender*] to be held by the [*Lender*] in the [*Receipt Account*] subject to and in accordance with the provisions of the [*Security Agreement/Disbursement Agreement/Account Agreement*].

[34] Guarantee Obligations of Others

Generally. The project company will agree that it shall not guarantee the obligations of any other

entity, except for those that exist under the project contracts.

Sample Provision
The [*Project Company*] shall not enter into any guarantee agreement or otherwise guarantee the debt or obligations, performance or payment, of any other Person.

[35] Sale of Assets

Generally. Generally, no assets may be sold by the project company, except pursuant to the terms of the project contracts. An exception is permitted for assets sold in the ordinary course of business, if not in excess of a negotiated amount.

Sample Provision
The [*Project Company*] shall not sell, lease, transfer, or otherwise dispose of any of its assets other than sales of [*describe off-take*] pursuant to the [*Off-Take Agreement*], sales of equipment that is obsolete or no longer useful or necessary for the proper operation of the Project, and sales of assets in the ordinary course of its business having a fair market value not in excess of $xxx,000 for a single transaction or $xxx,000 in the aggregate for all such sales.

[36] Capital Expenditures

Generally. The project company is typically prohibited from making capital expenditures for the project, unless previously approved. Such a prohibition may seem counterintuitive. If the project sponsors want to invest additional equity to make changes at the project, it may be difficult to understand why this is not acceptable to a lender.

This type of prohibition is to avoid any changes inconsistent with the project contracts or the plans and specifications approved by the lender and its consultants. An exception is permitted if the expenditures enhance the project or to make repairs if such enhancement or repair would not have a material adverse effect on the project or performance by the project company of the project contracts.

Sample Provision
The [*Project Company*] shall not make any capital improvement that results in any change to any plan or specification, or otherwise changes any aspect of the Project from that described in the [*Construction Contract*] without the prior consent of the [*Lender*].

[37] Transactions With Affiliates

Generally. Because the lender places restrictions on when profits can be distributed to the project sponsors, indirect distributions are similarly disallowed. One indirect way to do so is through above-market transactions with affiliates. This covenant blocks those transactions.

Sample Provision
The [*Project Company*] shall not, except as expressly permitted by [*add cross-reference to the covenant that permits distributions*], enter into any transaction directly or indirectly with or for the benefit of any affiliate; provided that (i) the [*Project Company*] may enter into transactions with an affiliate if the monetary or business consideration arising therefrom would be as advantageous to the [*Project Company*] as the monetary or business consideration that the [*Project Company*] would obtain in a comparable arm's length transaction with a Person not an affiliate.

[38] Construction Cost Overruns

Generally. It is important to outline clearly the sources of money that can be applied if there is a construction cost overrun. A typical covenant obligates the project company to apply those funds in a particular order, often reserving for the last application the most expensive options for the project.

Sample Provision
If the [*Project Company*] shall, at any time prior to the [*Completion Date*], incur [*Construction Costs*] in excess of $xxx,000,000 ("*Construction Cost Overruns*"), the [*Project Company*] shall pay Construction Cost Overruns from the following sources in the following order of priority: (a) the first $x,000,000 from the [*Construction Contingency*], (b) the next $x,000,000 from the [*Construction Cost Overrun*

Guarantee], and (c) any other amount from the (c) [*Standby Equity Contribution Commitment*].

[39] Other Covenants

Generally. In addition to those listed above, the loan agreement will contain other covenants, including compliance with pension laws; to not enter into any lease agreement that in the aggregate exceeds a negotiated amount; to not enter into any sale and lease back arrangement; to not create any subsidiary; and to not sell, lease, transfer, or otherwise dispose of all or substantially all of the project company's properties to any other entity.

§ 24.11 EVENTS OF DEFAULT

[1] Generally
Many of the events of default in a project finance credit transaction are similar to the defaults in other loan agreements. These include failure to pay principal, interest, and fees; misrepresentations; breaches of the covenants discussed in this chapter; failure of lien creation, perfection, or priority; a judgment being entered against the project company in excess of a negotiated amount that is not vacated or paid; and insolvency or bankruptcy.

Events of default not common in other loan transactions include failure to complete construction by a date certain; termination of any project contract; bankruptcy or insolvency of major project participants; expropriation; project abandonment; and revocation of permits or governmental authorizations.

[2] Payment

Generally. Like other credit agreements, it is an event of default if the project company, as borrower, fails to make a required payment of interest or principal.

Unlike most other types of financing structures, the creditworthiness of third parties can affect the financing. Because of this, it is common for a payment default by another project participant under a project document to be included as a credit agreement default.

Sample Provision (Project Company)

The [*Project Company*] shall default in the payment of any principal of or interest on any [*Loan*] or any [*Reimbursement Obligation*] or any other amount payable by it hereunder when due.

Sample Provision (Project Participant)

The [*Contractor; Operator; Off-Take Purchaser*] shall default in the payment when due of any amount payable, or in the performance when due (giving effect to any applicable grace period) of any obligation to be performed, pursuant to the [*Construction Contract; O&M Agreement; Off-Take Purchase Agreement*].

[3] Breach of Covenants

Generally. A breach of one of the covenants set forth in the credit agreement is an event of default. The lender typically provides the project company a cure period for specified covenants that are capable of cure.

Similarly, because of the importance of the project contracts to the transaction, an event of default is included for breaches of the project contracts by major project participants. A materiality qualification is sometimes added to this default.

Sample Provision (Project Company)

The [*Project Company*] shall default in the performance of any of its obligations under Sections [*specify*] (other than Sections [*specify*]; or the [*Project Company*] shall default in the performance of any of its obligations under Sections [*specify*] and such default shall remain unremedied for a period of 10 days after notice of such default is delivered by the [*Lender*] to the [*Project Company*]; or the [*Project Company*] shall default in the performance of any of its obligations under Section [*specify*] and such default shall remain unremedied for a period of 30 days after notice of such default is delivered by the [*Lender*] to the [*Project Company*].

Sample Provision (Project Participant)

Any [*Major Project Participant*] shall fail to perform or observe in any material respect any term, covenant, or agreement contained in any [*Project Document*] other than this Agreement to which such [*Major Project Participant*] is a party on its part

to be performed or observed and such failure shall remain unremedied for 30 days.

[4] Breach of Representation or Warranty

Generally. A breach of one of the representations and warranties set forth in the credit agreement is an event of default. Because representations and warranties cannot be cured, no cure period is permitted.

A breach of a representation or warranty by a major project participant is sometimes also added as an event of default. The project sponsor sometimes objects, inaccurately believing that because it has no ability to verify those representations and warranties, it should not be a default. However, from the project lender's viewpoint, the representations and warranties made are as much a basis for the financing as those made by the project company. Any inaccuracy can affect, for example, the structure of the financing, or even the credit decision to close the financing. The project lender will often include a materiality standard to this default, however, so that no default will exist unless the inaccuracy could have a material adverse effect on the financial condition or operations, or the prospects or business taken as a whole.

Sample Provision (Project Company)

Any representation, warranty, statement, or certification made by the [*Project Company*] in this Agreement, any [*Project Document*] to which the [*Project Company*] is party or any certificate, financial statement, or other document furnished to the [*Lender*] by or on behalf of the [*Project Company*] shall prove to have been false or misleading at the time made (or deemed made) or furnished in any material respect.

Sample Provision (Project Participant)

Any representation, warranty, statement or certification made by or on behalf of any [*Major Project Participant*] other than the [*Project Company*] in any [*Project Document*] to which such [*Major Project Participant*] is a party or any representation, warranty, or statement in any certificate, financial statement or other document furnished to the [*Lender*] by or on behalf of such [*Major Project Participant*] shall prove to have been false or misleading at the time made (or deemed made) or furnished in any material respect, the effect of which could have a material adverse effect on the financial condition or operations, or the prospects or business taken as a whole, of the [Project Company], or which materially adversely affects, or could materially adversely affect, the [Project Company], the [Project] or the ability of such [Major Project Participant] to perform its obligations under the [Project Documents] to which such [Major Project Participant] is party.

[5] Filing of Bankruptcy Petition

Generally. If the project company, any project sponsor or any major project participant, such as the contractor, operator, off-take purchaser, or supplier, files a petition for bankruptcy or takes similar action, it is an event of default. A borrower-preferred qualification to this event of default is that such a filing by persons other than the project company shall not be an event of default unless it is reasonably expected to have a material adverse effect on the project or the borrower's ability to perform its obligations under the credit agreement or any of the project documents.

Sample Provision (Project Company)
The [Project Company] shall (1) apply for or consent to the appointment of, or the taking of possession by, a receiver, custodian, trustee or liquidator of itself or of all or a substantial part of its property, (2) make a general assignment for the benefit of its creditors, (3) commence a voluntary case under the [specify applicable bankruptcy code] (as now or hereafter in effect), (4) file a petition seeking to take advantage of any other law relating to bankruptcy, insolvency, reorganization, winding-up, or composition or readjustment of debts, (5) fail to controvert in a timely and appropriate manner, or acquiesce in writing to, any petition filed against it in an involuntary case under the [specify applicable bankruptcy code], or (6) take any corporate action for the purpose of affecting any of the foregoing.

Sample Provision (Project Participant)
Any [Major Project Participant] shall (1) apply for or consent to the appointment of, or the taking of pos-

session by, a receiver, custodian, trustee or liquidator of itself or of all or a substantial part of its property, (2) make a general assignment for the benefit of its creditors, (3) commence a voluntary case under the [specify applicable bankruptcy code] (as now or hereafter in effect), (4) file a petition seeking to take advantage of any other law relating to bankruptcy, insolvency, reorganization, winding-up, or composition or readjustment of debts, (5) fail to controvert in a timely and appropriate manner, or acquiesce in writing to, any petition filed against it in an involuntary case under the [specify applicable bankruptcy code], or (6) take any corporate action for the purpose of affecting any of the foregoing.

[6] Commencement of Bankruptcy Proceeding

Generally. Similarly, it is an event of default upon the commencement of a bankruptcy proceeding against the project company, any project sponsor or any major project participant, which continues undismissed for a specified period. A borrower preferred qualification to this event of default is that such a filing against persons other than the project company shall not be an event of default unless it is reasonably expected to have a material adverse effect on the project or the borrower's ability to perform its obligations under the credit agreement or any of the project documents.

Sample Provision (Project Company)
A proceeding or case shall be commenced, *without* the application or consent of the [Project Company], in any court of competent jurisdiction, seeking (1) its liquidation, reorganization, dissolution, or winding-up, or the composition or readjustment of its debts, (2) the appointment of a trustee, receiver, custodian, liquidator or the like of such [Project Company] or of all or any substantial part of its assets, or (3) similar relief in respect of such [Project Company] under any law relating to bankruptcy, insolvency, reorganization, winding-up, or composition or adjustment of debts, and such proceeding or case shall continue undismissed, or an order, judgment or decree approving or ordering any of the foregoing shall be entered and continue unstayed and in effect, for a period of [specify number of days] days; or an order for relief

against such [*Project Company*] shall be entered in an involuntary case under the [*specify applicable bankruptcy code*].

Sample Provision (Project Participant)

A proceeding or case shall be commenced, *without* the application or consent of the applicable [*Major Project Participant*], in any court of competent jurisdiction, seeking (1) its liquidation, reorganization, dissolution, or winding-up, or the composition or readjustment of its debts, (2) the appointment of a trustee, receiver, custodian, liquidator, or the like of such [*Major Project Participant*] or of all or any substantial part of its assets, or (3) similar relief in respect of such [*Major Project Participant*] under any law relating to bankruptcy, insolvency, reorganization, winding-up, or composition or adjustment of debts, and such proceeding or case shall continue undismissed, or an order, judgment, or decree approving or ordering any of the foregoing shall be entered and continue unstayed and in effect, for a period of [*specify number of days*] days; or an order for relief against such [*Major Project Participant*] shall be entered in an involuntary case under the [*specify applicable bankruptcy code*].

[7] Judgments

Generally

Final judgments rendered against the project company, any project sponsor, or any major project participant are considered an event of default. Generally, the judgments must be in excess of a negotiated minimum amount. Like other events of default that include entities other than the project company in scope, a borrower preferred qualification is that such a judgment filed against persons other than the project company shall not be an event of default unless it is reasonably expected to have a material adverse effect on the project or the borrower's ability to perform its obligations under the credit agreement or any of the project documents.

Sample Provision (Project Company)

A final judgment or judgments for the payment of money in excess of $xxx,000 in the aggregate shall be rendered by a court or courts against the [*Project Company*] and the same shall not be discharged (or provision shall not be made for such discharge), or a stay of execution thereof shall not be procured, within 30 days from the date of entry thereof and it shall not, within said period of 30 days, or such longer period during which execution of the same shall have been stayed, appeal therefrom and cause the execution thereof to be stayed during such appeal.

Sample Provision (Project Participant)

A final judgment or judgments for the payment of money in excess of $xxx,000 in the aggregate shall be rendered by a court or courts against any [*Major Project Participant*] and the same shall not be discharged (or provision shall not be made for such discharge), or a stay of execution thereof shall not be procured, within 30 days from the date of entry thereof and such [*Major Project Participant*] shall not, within said period of 30 days, or such longer period during which execution of the same shall have been stayed, appeal therefrom and cause the execution thereof to be stayed during such appeal.

[8] Final Acceptance Date

Generally. It is an event of default if the project completion date, typically called the final acceptance date, does not occur by a date certain. This date is selected based on the construction schedule agreed to in the construction contract and on the milestone dates in major project contracts, such as an off-take purchase agreement.

Sample Provision

The [*Final Acceptance Date*] shall not have occurred by [*specify date*].

[9] Government Approvals

Generally. An event of default also exists if the project company fails to obtain, maintain, renew, replace, or comply with all governmental approvals. The borrower will desire to limit the reach of this event of default to only those failures that could reasonably be expected to have a material adverse effect on the project, or the borrower's ability to perform its obligations under the credit agreement or any of the project documents.

Sample Provision

Any [*Governmental Approval*] required to be obtained shall be revoked, terminated, withdrawn, suspended, modified, or withheld, or shall cease to be in full force and effect, or shall fail to be obtained when necessary, and such revocation, termination, withdrawal, suspension, modification, withholding, cessation, or failure could have a materially adverse effect on the financial condition or operations, or the prospects or business taken as a whole, of the [*Project Company*], or which materially adversely affects, or which could materially adversely affect, the [*Project Company*], the Project or the ability of any [*Major Project Participant*] to perform its obligations under the [*Project Documents*] to which such [*Major Project Participant*] is party.

Any [*Governmental Person*] or any Person acting under governmental authority shall have taken any action to condemn, seize, or appropriate all or any substantial part of the property of the [*Project Company*] or to displace the management of the [*Project Company*] or to curtail its authority to conduct its business in any material respect.

[10] Project Contracts

Generally. An event of default will arise if (i) any person takes any action to terminate a project contract because of a default by the project company, (ii) any party to a project contract repudiates the contract or otherwise maintains it has no obligation to perform the contract in accordance with its terms, (iii) a default occurs under any project contract by any party thereto, or (iv) any project contract ceases to be in full force and effect prior to the stated termination date in such contract. The borrower will desire to limit the reach of this event of default to only those occurrences that could reasonably be expected to have a material adverse effect on the project, or the borrower's ability to perform its obligations under the credit agreement or any of the project documents.

Sample Provision

Any [*Project Document*] or any provision thereof shall at any time for any reason cease to be valid and binding or in full force and effect or any

party thereto (other than the [*Lender*]) shall so assert in any legal action in writing; or any material provision of any [*Project Document*] shall be declared to be null and void, or the validity or enforceability thereof shall be contested by any Person thereto (other than the [*Lender*]) or any [*Governmental Person*]; or any person not a party to a [*Project Document*] shall take any action to contest the validity or enforceability of such [*Project Document*] and as a result of such action any party to such [*Project Document*] shall be enjoined or otherwise prevented from performing its obligations thereunder; or any [*Major Project Participant*] shall deny that it has any or further liability or obligation under any such [*Project Document*], except upon fulfillment of its obligations thereunder.

[11] Abandonment

Generally. Abandonment of the project by the project company is an event of default. Typically, however, an exception is provided for a force majeure event that does not last longer than a negotiated period.

Sample Provision

The [*Project Company*] shall abandon construction of the Project or suspend, other than for Force Majeure (as defined in the Construction Contract) construction of the Project for a period exceeding [*specify*] months.

[12] Expropriation

Generally. An expropriation, whether a complete taking or an act of "creeping expropriation," discussed in Chapter 3, is an event of default. The lenders have structured the loan documents for a project that is owned and operated by the private sector, not a government. Therefore, the lenders will want the ability to take immediate action to protect the project loans. An example of the action a project lender might take pursuant to a pledge of ownership interests in the event of an expropriation is discussed in Chapter 26.

Sample Provision

Any [*Governmental Person*] or any Person acting under governmental authority shall have taken any action to nationalize all or any substantial part of the property of the [Project Company] or to expropriate (whether "creeping" or de facto) all or any substantial part of the property of the [Project Company] or to displace the management of the [Project Company] or to curtail its authority to conduct its business in any material respect.

[13] Ownership and Control

Generally. Failure of the project sponsors to maintain either an agreed-upon ownership interest in the project or voting control of the project company, for a negotiated period, is an event of default. This provides the lender with some comfort that the original equity investors will continue to be involved in the project, and that the lender can continue to transact business with the original sponsors.

Sample Provision

Project Sponsor] or a wholly owned subsidiary of [Project Sponsor] shall hold, beneficially and of record, directly or indirectly, less than [specify]% of the [general partnership interests; stock] issued by the [Project Company].

[14] Payment of Obligations

Generally. It is an event of default if the project company, any project sponsor, or any major project participant, such as the contractor, operator, off-take purchaser, or supplier, defaults in a payment obligation in excess of a specified amount. A borrower-preferred qualification to this event of default is that such a failure by persons other than the project company shall not be an event of default unless it is reasonably expected to have a material adverse effect on the project or the borrower's ability to perform its obligations under the credit agreement or any of the project documents.

Sample Provision (Project Company)

The [Project Company] shall at any time default in the payment when due of any principal of or interest on any of its [Debt] (other than the [Obligations] hereunder) aggregating at such time $xxx,000 or more; or at any time any event specified in any note,

agreement, indenture, or other document evidencing or relating to any such [Debt] aggregating at such time $xxx,000 or more shall occur if the effect of such event is to cause, or (with the giving of any notice or the lapse of time or both) to permit the holder or holders of such [Debt] (or a trustee or agent on behalf of such holder or holders) to cause, such [Debt] to become due prior to its stated maturity.

Sample Provision (Project Participant)

Any [Major Project Participant] shall default in the payment of any principal of or interest beyond any applicable period of grace on any of its [Debt] aggregating at such time $xxx,000 or more; or any event specified in any note, agreement, indenture, or other document evidencing or relating to any such [Debt] shall occur if the effect of such event is to cause, or (with the giving of any notice or the lapse of time or both) to permit the holder or holders of such [Debt] (or a trustee or agent on behalf of such holder or holders) to cause such debt to become due prior to its stated maturity.

[15] Breach of Credit Support

Generally. It is an event of default if any party to a credit support document, such as the sovereign under a sovereign guarantee, or any credit support obligation under a project contract, such as a liquidated damage payment obligation of the contractor under the construction contract, is not paid when due. Providers of subordinated debt and parties obligated to make capital contributions are included in the scope of this default.

Sample Provision

Any [Credit Support Document] or any provision thereof shall at any time for any reason cease to be valid and binding or in full force and effect or any party thereto (other than the [Lender]) shall so assert in any legal action in writing; or any material provision of any [Credit Support Document] shall be declared to be null and void, or the validity or enforceability thereof shall be contested by any Person thereto (other than the [Lender]) or any [Governmental Person]; or any person not a party to a [Credit Support Document] shall take any action to contest the validity or enforceability of such [*Credit Support Document*] and as a result of such action any party to such [*Credit Support Document*] shall be enjoined or otherwise prevented from performing its obligations thereunder; or any [*Credit Support Provider*] shall deny that it has any or further liability or obligation under any such [*Credit Support Document*], except upon fulfillment of its obligations thereunder.

[16] Security Documents

Generally

If any security document, such as a security agreement, stock pledge agreement or mortgage, ceases to be in full force and effect, or is no longer effective to create a first priority lien on the collateral, then an event of default occurs.

Sample Provision

The [*Lender*] shall fail to have a valid and perfected security interest in, and mortgage lien on, the [*Collateral*], subject to no prior or equal [*Liens*] (other than [*Permitted Liens*]);

§ 24.12 REMEDIES

Remedies are particularly troublesome in a project financing because of the need to preserve project operability, or to make the project operable in an expedient fashion. These are project-specific processes.

In general, project finance loan agreements have three types of remedy provisions: funding remedies, retention remedies, and foreclosure remedies. Each is crafted to address the degree of project difficulties encountered.

The funding remedies are designed to stop additional loan advances to the project until a problem is resolved. This remedy is particularly helpful during litigation or a permit dispute.

Retention remedies permit the lender to require the establishment of cash collateral

accounts by the borrower, mandate prepayments of debt, and otherwise restrict distributions by the project company to the project sponsors (dividends, fees, and similar amounts), pending resolution of the problem. These remedies are helpful with small problems because the project sponsors will have an incentive to cure them quickly and large problems where all available cash flow is needed to repay debt.

Finally, foreclosure remedies are available to the lender. These include traditional enforcement rights of any secured lender.

§ 24.13 GOVERNING LAW

Predictability is an important element of nonrecourse project financing. This can be increased in the context of the project finance credit agreement by providing that, irrespective of the location of the project, the agreement and related credit documents will be governed by the law of a jurisdiction with a developed commercial law, case law precedents, and experienced judges.[1]

§ 24.14 LIMITATIONS ON RECOURSE

Exceptions to nonrecourse provisions include limiting recourse to the construction and start-up period, withholding tax gross-ups, other tax indemnities, claims based on misrepresentation and fraud, and claims based on a failure of the security arrangements to create valid and perfected liens on the project assets. The extent of the recourse is sometimes capped at a negotiated limit or limited to the amount of dividends distributed to the project sponsors.

---

[1] *See generally* Kimmo Mettala, *Governing-Law Clauses of Loan Agreements in International Project Financing*, 20 INT'L LAW. 219, 236–40 (1986).

CHAPTER TWENTY-FIVE

EXPORT CREDITS DOCUMENTATION FOR PROJECT FINANCE TRANSACTIONS

§ 25.01 THE EXPORT LENDER'S PERSPECTIVE

[1] Generally

Commercial lenders and export-import financing agencies have a common perspective in project financings. Like commercial lenders, export-import financing agencies base credit appraisals on the projected revenues from the operation of the facility, rather than the general assets or the credit of the sponsor of the facility, and rely on the assets of the facility, including the revenue-producing contracts and cash flow, as collateral for the project debt. The credit appraisal of the export-import financing agency making a project finance loan is there- fore based on the underlying cash flow from the revenue-producing contracts of the project, inde- pendent of the project sponsor's assets.

Unlike a commercial lender, however, the export-import financing agency is a political creature. It is formed to promote trade or other interests of an organizing country and is gen- erally nationalistic in purpose and nationalistic and political in operation. Bureaucracy and bud- get constraints, like in any governmental agency, affect its efficiency and ability to respond to project financing needs. Funding for bilateral agencies generally comes from their organizing governments.

[2] The OECD Consensus

Concessional financing by the world's govern- ments for exports and imports affects compe- tition, manufacturing efficiency, and prices. In recognition of this, the member countries of the Organisation for Economic Co-operation and Development (OECD) signed the "Arrangement on Guidelines for Officially Supported Credits."[1] It is also called the OECD Consensus.

The OECD Consensus establishes guidelines and limits on the terms of export credit. In the OECD Consensus, each of the member countries agrees to limit export credit to no more than 85 percent of the underlying contract value. Interest rates applicable to the financing cannot be less than the OECD interest rate schedules, which are semiannually revised.

---

[1] Thirty countries have signed the OECD Convention, includ- ing Australia, Britain, Canada, France, Germany, Italy, Japan, Mexico, the Netherlands, and the United States. The member countries agree to promote economic growth in developing nations while expanding world trade.

The OECD Consensus was recently amended to provide bilateral organizations with greater flexibility in project finance transactions. Chapter 21 includes an explanation of the OECD Consensus and this amendment.

§ 25.02 METHODS OF EXPORT-IMPORT FINANCING

An export-import bank has three common financing methods to use in providing funds to an importing entity. These are direct lending, intermediary lending, and interest rate equalization.

[1] Direct Lending

The simplest structure is a traditionally documented loan in which the borrower is the importing entity and the lender is the export-import bank. Most commonly, the loan is conditioned upon the purchase of goods or services from businesses in the organizing country. Loan terms are within the parameters of the OECD Consensus.

If the loan is not conditioned upon the purchase of goods or services from business in the organizing country, a so-called untied loan, international competitive bidding is required by the export-import bank. Untied loans need not follow the OECD Consensus because competitive bidding replaces the need for its protection.

[2] Financial Intermediary Loans (Bank-to-Bank)

Another structure is based on an indirect lending model. Under this structure, the export-import bank lends funds to a financial intermediary, such as a commercial bank, that in turn loans the funds (also commonly called *relending* or *onlending*) to the importing entity.

[3] Interest Rate Equalization

Under an interest rate equalization structure, a commercial lender provides a loan to the importing entity at below-market interest rates. It, in turn, is compensated by the export-import bank for the difference between the below-market rate (often the OECD Consensus rate) and the rate the commercial lender could otherwise obtain in the market for its loans.

§ 25.03 EXPORT-IMPORT BANKS

Export banks are described in greater detail in Chapter 21. That chapter also contains a description of the export-import banks in the world.

§ 25.04 OVERVIEW OF PROJECT FINANCE EXPORT CREDITS AGREEMENT

The export credit agreement used in a project financing is very similar to the type of agreement used by a commercial bank. There are exceptions, however, related to the unique nature of this type of financing. These exceptions are summarized below.

§ 25.05 SIGNIFICANT PROVISIONS OF THE PROJECT FINANCE EXPORT CREDITS AGREEMENT

[1] Currency of Loan

The loan amount and repayment terms are generally denominated in the currency of the export credit agency. Because the purpose of the loan is to purchase goods and services in the export lender's country, such a denomination avoids some of the currency repayment risk in the transaction.

[2] Right to Prepay

Typically, the borrower has the right to prepay the loan anytime, without a penalty. In the commercial loan market, prepayment penalties are more likely, particularly with a loan from institutional lenders, such as pension funds or insurance companies.

[3] Conditions Precedent

Conditions to the drawdown of funds are similar to a commercial project finance loan. However, because of the unique purpose of export financing, conditions are included to assure the export bank that funds are used to purchase goods and services from its country. An example is a supplier's certificate, in which the supplier of the exported good or service verifies the country of manufacture or origination.

Conditions to closing are also typically similar to a commercial project finance loan. In addition, conditions are added for approval of the project by the project's host country; evidence of availability of additional debt or equity to pay the amount of the purchase price for the goods or services that exceeds the amount provided by the export bank (typically, 80–85% is provided by the export bank); evidence of availability of foreign exchange for loan repayment; evidence of insurance coverage on the goods financed, obtained from companies in the export bank's home country; and requirements for ocean shipping on a vessel flying the flag of the export bank's host country or similar requirements.

[4] Representations and Warranties

In addition to representations and warranties found in commercial loan agreements, export credit loan documents include some additional provisions relating to governmentally supplied funding. For example, where a tax or other treaty exempts interest paid to an export bank from withholding, a representation would be added to that effect.

[5] Covenants

Similarly, covenants are included that are similar to those used in commercial loan documents. Additional covenants relating to governmentally supplied funding are added, however. These include requirements that proceeds be used only for goods or services manufactured or originating in the host country and for obtaining required insurance only from insurers in the host country of the export bank, as well as other covenants required by the laws or regulations of the bank's host country.

[6] Events of Default

Events of default are similar to those contained in commercial loan agreements. However, these are often much less extensive.

PART EIGHT

COLLATERAL

CHAPTER TWENTY-SIX

PROJECT COLLATERAL

§ 26.01 THE ROLE OF COLLATERAL IN A PROJECT FINANCING

[1] Generally

The project finance structure, like most asset-based transactions, is centered on the assets of the borrower. Like all lenders, project finance lenders take collateral from a borrower so that if the loan cannot be repaid the collateral can be sold and the proceeds applied to loan repayment. In a project financing, the collateral documentation cannot be overlooked or its value minimized. Yet, the unlikelihood of disposition of a troubled project in a liquidation sale that recovers the full loan amount must be clearly understood.

[2] Collateral as a Defensive Tool

The project lender desires the right to take control of the assets necessary to finish construction, operate the project, or sell the entire project in a liquidation so that another entity can operate the project and apply the proceeds ahead of all other creditors to repayment of its loan. Preserving all the elements of a project is usually necessary to achieve this goal.

Project lenders have additional goals in taking a security interest in all of the project company's assets. The lender desires that the project assets not be sold or otherwise disposed of without its consent, thereby ensuring that important assets are available to operate the facility or are sold for a price that allows replacement. In addition, for the same reason, the lender does not want any third party to have rights to any of the project's assets.

Thus, although the project finance lender undertakes to achieve the ability to sell the collateral in a foreclosure proceeding for repayment of its loan, the collateral package for the lender is primarily *defensive* in nature. This is because in many types of project financings the lender has little expectation of realizing the full value of the loan in a foreclosure sale of the collateral.

Most projects have value only where the project is located and only if it is operating and producing revenue. High transaction costs and other "soft" costs make it extremely unlikely, in the early term of a highly leveraged project loan, that the project assets could be sold for the full value of the loan.

Even in the later years, if the project sponsors cannot profitably operate the project, it is unlikely that anyone else can either.

Projects located in developing countries may have a limited number of potential purchasers in a foreclosure sale. Not every project sponsor wants to own and operate a project in these countries. This is particularly true in situations in which the host country's political actions and economic policies have contributed to the project's demise.

[3] Collateral as an Offensive Tool

However, there is *offensive* value to the lender's collateral package. On occasion, projects are mismanaged in such a way that the project has value and can be sold to a third party at a price that permits the lender to recover the loan advanced. It is important to remember that most projects have value primarily because of the contracts negotiated to support the project and the underlying financing. By taking a lien on these contracts, and obtaining properly structured rights to keep the contracts in effect, the lender helps to ensure that the project has continuing value.

[4] Uncertainty in Collateral Protections Available to Lenders – You Can't Always Get What You Want

Beyond the value of the collateral, complicated issues exist relating to the creation of security interests in transnational projects. In their Uniform Commercial Code,[1] the states of the United States have one of the most developed, predictable security interest laws available to lenders. Lenders in transnational projects do not always enjoy the predictability offered in the United States. There is no collection of international laws that govern the creation, perfection, and priority of security interests.[2] It is the rare project financing that does not require compliance with the security laws of the host country, at least for part of the collateral. The risks presented by these laws must be understood and the requirements complied with.

---

[1] Uniform Commercial Code Official Text and Comments (1972).

[2] Exceptions exist for security interests in ships and aircraft, which are governed by multilateral conventions.

Also of significant concern to the project lender is whether the collateral laws in a host country permit the lender to foreclose on and complete construction of, or operate, a troubled project. Not every country allows secured lenders to take over and operate a company. This is particularly true with concessions.

§ 26.02 THE COLLATERAL PACKAGE

[1] The "Blanket" Lien

The project lender typically receives a so-called blanket lien, which covers all the assets of the project company. That is, each and every asset, real or personal, tangible or intangible, of the project company is pledged to the lender as collateral for the loan. In addition, each asset necessary for the ownership, development, construction, start-up, and operation of the project must be owned (or leased) by the project company, so that the lender has a complete collateral package.

[2] Project Cash Flow

Lenders usually take a security interest in the cash flows generated by the project under long-term off-take agreements. This is accomplished through a cash collateral account in which the off-take purchaser pays all revenue into an account established by the lenders. The lenders then apply this money to debt service, after operating expenses of the project are paid.

The value of a security interest in cash flow is not always of high significance. Where guaranteed payments to the project are made, such as in a take-or-pay contract where a third party pays the project company an agreed-upon amount whether or not the project operates, this approach is valuable. However, where payments are dependent upon the project operating, such as with a take-and-pay contract, the lien on cash flow is not very valuable if the project is not producing output; that is, cash flows only if the project operates.

[3] Personal Property

All personal (moveable) property of the project company is usually part of the project lender's collateral. Examples include equipment, com-

puters, vehicles, pipelines, transmission lines, and similar assets. In some situations, these assets have value and can be sold in a foreclosure setting, independent of the project.

In general, the Uniform Commercial Code (U.C.C.) in effect in the states of the United States provides secured parties a reasonable degree of freedom in choosing the law that will govern security interests. As discussed later in this chapter, this is not universally true for other countries.

Much less latitude is provided under the U.C.C. for choice of law in perfection of security interests, however. Various facts must be analyzed to determine which jurisdiction's law will govern.[3]

Intangible Assets. Intangible assets important to the project are included in the collateral. Examples of intangible assets include technology rights and technology licenses.

Permits, Licenses, and Concessions. An important part of the collateral package is the inclusion of permits, concessions, and licenses. Local law should be consulted to determine whether a security interest can be obtained in these rights. If so, it should next be determined whether the permit, concession, or license can be transferred to the lender or its transferee, and the project operated again, without additional consent of the issuing governmental body. Neither is necessarily permitted in all countries.

With permits, concessions, and licenses, the project lender will prefer that the issuing entity agree to provide it with advance notice and a reasonable cure period before an important right is revoked. However, project lenders are not always successful with this requirement because of constitutional issues and governmental interests in maintaining credibility of laws and regulations. In such cases, lenders must decide whether to assume the political risk involved.

In some situations, permit consultation and cooperation agreements are entered into between the lender and the sovereign. These agreements provide assurances that before a permit, concession, or license is modified or revoked, the issuing governmental authority will

---

[3] *See* RESTATEMENT (SECOND) OF CONFLICTS § 251 (1988).

attempt to notify the lender and provide it with opportunities to remedy any problems that the project may have. Neither the sovereign nor the lender undertake any liabilities under this type of agreement to the other; performance, in effect, is optional.

Contracts. All of the significant project contracts, including the revenue-producing off-take contracts, are made part of the collateral of the lender. These are discussed in a later section of this chapter.

Insurance Proceeds. The project company will be required to deliver to the lender an insurance program to protect the physical assets of the project from damage or destruction. Often, project lenders require that the borrower deliver a report of an insurance consultant to verify that the necessary insurance has been obtained and that the policies satisfy the requirements of the loan and project documents.

If insurance proceeds are payable, it is usually required that these proceeds be paid directly to the project lender. The project lender, pursuant to the terms of the loan documents, then either uses the proceeds to prepay debt or allows the project company to use the proceeds for repair or replacement of the damaged facility.

Surety Bonds. If performance bonds are required to be provided by the contractor pursuant to the construction contract, assignment of these bonds to the project lender will be required. The assignment provisions will ensure that payments of amounts demanded under these bonds are directly deposited with the lenders for debt prepayment or project completion.

Guarantees. Guarantees, whether from project sponsors, the sovereign government, or third parties, are also part of the collateral granted to the lenders. Any payments due under the guarantee are usually payable directly to the lenders as part of the collateral arrangements. Guarantees are discussed in Chapter 20.

Liquidated Damages. Similarly, to the extent liquidated damage payments are negotiated in construction contracts or operating agreements,

these payment rights are also part of the collateral granted to the lenders. As discussed in Section 12.11, liquidated damages are amounts payable by a defaulting party to the non-defaulting party, in an amount agreed upon in advance so that an arbitration or court proceeding in not necessary to settle a dispute.

Any liquidated damage payments are payable directly to the lenders as part of the collateral arrangements. The project lender, pursuant to the terms of the loan documents, then either uses the liquidated damages to service the debt, such as payment of construction period interest for construction contract completion delays; prepay debt, such as for liquidated damages paid because of inadequate facility performance levels; or make modifications to the underperforming facility.

As discussed in Section 12.11, the enforceability of liquidated damage contractual remedies must be researched under applicable law. Although many jurisdictions allow enforcement of liquidated damage provisions, laws vary.

Political Risk Insurance. Political risk insurance provided to the lenders is included in the collateral. This insurance provides protection against war, insurrection, or revolution; expropriation, nationalization, or requisition of assets; and non-conversion of currency and imposition of discriminatory exchange rates. Political risk insurance is discussed in Chapter 20.

Accounts. Finally, the project lender typically will insist on a pledge of the project company's interest in its bank accounts. This includes a pledge of its interest in the revenue account, into which all of the project's revenue will be directly deposited. The deposit and release of funds in these accounts is discussed below in the section on the disbursement agreement.

Project accounts can be established within the host country of the project and offshore, depending primarily on whether the project output is for use in the country or for export. If for export, an offshore account is typically used to reduce exchange and currency risks. Offshore accounts are discussed below in this chapter.

If the market for project output is domestic, an escrow or trust account is still helpful as a means of monitoring the project's use of cash flow. However, problems of foreign exchange availability and transfer of funds out of the country remain issues.

[4] Real Property

The lender also takes a lien on the real property interest associated with the project, through a mortgage, deed of trust, or similar real property interest document. The real property on which the project is located is usually crucial to the project's continued operation. There are exceptions, of course, such as electrical production projects located on moveable barges.

§ 26.03 COLLATERAL DOCUMENTS

[1] Generally

Collateral documents used in a project financing are designed, like collateral documents in other types of loan transactions, to safeguard the borrower's assets from other creditors in the event the collateral must be sold to recover the loans advanced. In the project finance context, however, the collateral is typically only useful to the extent the project can be operated. Consequently, the project lender will structure collateral documentation to ensure that it has the contractual rights to complete construction of an unfinished project, and to operate the project once finished, all in a manner consistent with the original plans of the project sponsor, or to sell the project to someone who will. To do so, of course, it must be given a lien on all of the assets of the project company, including a collateral assignment of the material project contracts.

[2] Personal Property Security Agreement

The structure and content of a project finance security agreement for a transnational project is substantially similar to security agreements used for domestic project finance transactions. These agreements are also similar to those used for secured commercial bank financings where the borrower is a foreign entity.

The standard type of project finance security agreement in a transnational project contains these familiar provisions: creation of a security interest; control and funding of collateral accounts; mechanical provisions for the maintenance and release of liens; representations and warranties; covenants; remedies and foreclosure on collateral; and miscellaneous provisions, including submission to jurisdiction. In addition, the credit agreement contains provisions that result from the transnational structure of the financing. These include provisions relating to foreclosure in the country in which the collateral is located.

All of the project's assets are included in the collateral given by the project company to the lender. These include equipment; accounts, onshore and offshore; revenue and the underlying off-take contracts; permits, licenses, authorizations, and concessions; and construction, operation, and supply contracts.

[3] Mortgage, Deed of Trust, and Indenture

The mortgage provides the project lender with a lien on the real property interests of the project company. If a deed of trust or indenture is used in the host country, the real property interests are conveyed to a trustee that holds the trust as beneficiary for the project lenders.

[4] Pledge of Ownership Interests

If a credit problem develops in a project finance transaction, the project lenders must have the ability to react quickly. As discussed elsewhere in this book, the only way for the project lender to receive repayment of its debt may be for the project to operate. Otherwise, the nonrecourse or limited recourse nature of the financing leaves no other source for repayment of debt.

For maximum ability to react quickly, project lenders often require a pledge of the project sponsor's ownership interest in the project company. If the project company is organized as a corporation, a stock pledge is required. If the project company is a partnership, a pledge of partnership interests is required.

It is the hope of the project lender that it can take control of the ownership interests of the project sponsors in the project company much more expediently than foreclosing on the project assets. This management control provides the project lender with the immediate ability to make decisions about a project at a time when the project sponsor may not be entirely cooperative.

For example, as discussed in Chapter 24, a project loan agreement will typically include an event of default for an act of expropriation. This event of default is generally coupled with the right of the lenders to accelerate the debt. Because the project debt is structured under the assumption that the project will be privately, not publicly, owned, this is an important right.

If the project lender has taken a pledge of the ownership interests in the project company, the lender will be able to use this pledge to protect its interests in negotiations over the compensation payable for the expropriatory act. At a minimum, such a pledge ensures that the lender will have a voice at the negotiations.

The project lenders may also want to require that project equity investors obtain political risk insurance to guard against expropriation. If so, the lenders will require an assignment in their favor of all political risk insurance proceeds (and take a security interest in the right to receive such payments). Otherwise, if the project owners do obtain political risk insurance, the political risk insurer will require that it receive its own pledge of ownership interests, unencumbered by lender liens. If the insurer exercises its rights under such a pledge, the project lender will find itself in a very complicated negotiation indeed.

[5] Voting Trust

Where a project sponsor is precluded under existing loan covenants from pledging its ownership interest in the project company to the project lender, a voting trust may be accepted by the project lender as an acceptable alternative. Under this structure, the ownership interests are placed in a voting trust. The project sponsors retain beneficial interest in the project company, and voting interest except in specified circumstances.

Upon the occurrence of a specified set of defaults, the project lenders could exercise the right to vote the ownership interests in a way to modify project management. The lenders would not have the right, however, to foreclose on the ownership interests or to receive dividends or other distributions arising from the ownership interests. Yet, management control is available.

[6] Offshore Accounts

Creation of an offshore account, and use of that account for deposit of project revenues, will in general terms, protect those funds from other creditors of the project company. In addition, as discussed in Chapter 20, offshore accounts and a waterfall of cash uses provide the project lender with regulation over the use of those funds.

The law governing creation and perfection of security interests in an offshore account is usually the law of the jurisdiction where the account is located. The local laws of the jurisdiction in which the project company is located should also be consulted, however.

[7] Disbursement Agreement

As discussed above, the project lender will typically take a pledge of the project company's interest in its bank accounts. The deposit and release of funds in the accounts is made pursuant to the disbursement agreement.

The project lender typically desires a great deal of control over the amounts deposited in the project company's accounts. The rights of the project company and the project lender to the deposit and disbursement of these funds is governed by the credit agreement and the security agreement. Alternatively, and increasingly more common, is the use of a completely separate document, the disbursement agreement, which governs the parties rights to amounts in the various bank accounts.

It is typical for all amounts received by the borrower as project revenue to be deposited in a bank account pledged to the project lender as collateral. Amounts on deposit in this account, typically called the revenue account, may be disbursed according to the priority and procedure in the credit documents.

This *priority* is generally referred to as a *waterfall*, or *cascade*, because the cash (water) flows downward into a series of pools, each below the others, in its downward journey to the project sponsors. Each pool represents a project cost that must be paid or a contingency for which amounts must be reserved. For example, water in one pool is used to pay operating costs then due, another to pay interest due, and another to fund a debt service reserve account. The number, purpose, and depth of the pools vary with the types of payment necessary and the risks that must be addressed.

As the water flows downward out of the revenue account, it fills each successive pool. Once a pool is filled, the excess water runs off the edge of the pool and continues down into the next pool until it is likewise filled, and so on. When all the pools are filled, any excess water continues to flow down and is given to the project sponsors as a profit distribution.

This waterfall approach ensures that the project company adequately manages its cash needs and prevents premature distributions of profit to project sponsors. The project company periodically verifies compliance with the procedure through submission of certificates to the lender.

§ 26.04 NEGATIVE PLEDGES

In some transnational project financings, it is not prudent, practical, or legal for the lender to require the grant of a security interest in certain types of the project company's assets. In such circumstances, the project lenders rely on a negative pledge to provide some form of protection. A negative pledge is an agreement between the lender and the project company that the project company will not create, directly or indirectly, any security interest, lien, or encumbrance in its assets for the benefit of any other entity.

A negative pledge provides the project lender with some comfort that no other lender or party will interfere with its rights to repayment. The negative pledge is not binding upon third parties. It does not provide legal protection to the lender over competing claims of other lenders or other creditors, does not provide the lender with a legal priority of payment over others, and does not confer upon the lender the right to foreclose, sell, or own the borrower's assets.

Although the negative covenant does provide the lender with a useful claim against the project company if it is violated, as a practical matter, it is only effective to the extent the project company fulfills its promise to the lender. This is because in most jurisdictions the security inter-

est granted to another entity is enforceable by the other entity against the project lender, even though the negative pledge is violated. Actual knowledge of the negative pledge by the entity receiving the security interest may, however, provide the project lender with a reasonable argument in court that the security interest is invalid. This is why, in part, lenders ask a borrower to represent that the giving of a lien does not violate any other agreements to which it is a party.

§ 26.05 THE FLOATING LIEN

Projects change over time; new assets are acquired and project documents are amended. The common law floating lien (which should not be confused with the floating charge, discussed below) enables a project finance lender to take a security interest in all of the project company's assets then existing or thereafter acquired, without the need for new documentation whenever an asset is sold or acquired. This concept is unavailable in many countries. In such countries, local law may provide alternate, although less satisfactory, mechanisms.

§ 26.06 OTHER COLLATERAL PROBLEMS

In addition to negative pledges and floating liens, other collateral security issues should be considered by the project lender. These should be understood and analyzed early in the structuring process because each will affect the transaction structure and could cause the lender to decline participation in the transaction.

[1] Types of Liens Allowed
The first consideration for the lender or contracting party to understand before entering into a project is the type of lien permitted by the laws of the host country and any other country that may be involved.[4]

---

[4] *See generally* American Bar Association National Institute on Multinational Commercial Insolvency (1993); International Loan Workouts and Bankruptcies (R. Gitlin & R. Mears eds., 1989).

Common Law Countries. Generally, common law countries provide that a lien may be taken for collateral purposes over all assets. A floating charge is a lien on all of a borrower's assets, including personal and real property. It transforms (*crystallizes*) into a so-called fixed charge when the debtor enters liquidation proceedings or upon enforcement of security rights by a secured party following an event of default. England, New Zealand, and Australia recognize floating charges.

While the lien floats, it is subordinate to liquidation expenses, certain taxes, and certain labor costs. Also, prior to crystallization of the lien, the borrower is free to sell or otherwise deal with the collateral, making the lien applicable only to assets owned at the time of crystallization.

Civil Law Countries. By contrast, civil law countries generally enact statutes to govern creation, perfection, and priority of security interests. These vary from country to country to such an extent that generalizations are unwise and unwarranted. A word of caution: Little comfort can be taken from experience learned in one country, even a civil law country, for application to another.

Developing Countries. In developing countries, much less certainty over creation, perfection, and priority of security interests may be available. Types of collateral grants and enforcement that might present difficulties for the project lender in projects located in developing countries include transportable assets, cash flows, and contract rights.

[2] Local Formalities

Local law and practice will require that certain formalities be adhered to in connection with lien recordation. For example, some civil law countries require protocolization of all security agreements. This is generally accomplished by a local notary translating the collateral agreement into the local language and inserting the agreement into the notary's "protocol book," which is kept at the local registry office. An accompanying fee, which can be significant, is charged.

[3] Denomination of Liens in Local Currency

Local law may require that the documentation contain a denomination of the lien amount in the local currency. This is contrary to the practice in the United States. As discussed in Chapter 3, this can present a currency risk to the lender if the currency of the debt is different from the currency listed in the lien document. Such a risk will materialize if exchange rate fluctuations create a deficiency in the stated lien amount in comparison to the debt outstanding that is denominated in another currency.

A value maintenance provision is a common remedy to this requirement. This provision imposes on the borrower an obligation to provide additional collateral to the lender if exchange rate fluctuations reduce the collateral value. Another approach available in some countries is an index clause, which automatically adjusts the lien value based on exchange rate fluctuations.

[4] Priority of Lien

The lien priority rules should be clearly understood. Of particular importance are so-called hidden liens. These are liens that do not appear as a matter of record but are statutory in origin. These include governmental liens, particularly tax liens.

[5] Enforcement

In addition to seeking the advice of local lawyers and obtaining an opinion of local lawyers that the lien is enforceable, practical questions about enforcement should be explored. For instance, the actual costs of enforcement should be understood. These include legal costs, court taxes, and other costs that may make the liens economically unenforceable.

In addition, as a practical matter, enforcement remedies may be almost nonexistent in some countries. Enforcement may be limited to public auction. Possession of the collateral as a remedy may not be permitted.

[6] Foreclosure

In addition to enforceability, the mechanics of the foreclosure process are important. Among the questions that should be posed to local lawyers, include the following: whether any restrictions exist on a lender's right to buy at foreclosure, whether a lender can bid in the debt at a foreclosure instead of cash, and whether a private sale is permitted in lieu of a public sale.

Practical questions of enforcement that are unique to project financings must not be overlooked. For example, in many cases, the only practical ability of a lender to be repaid is if the foreclosed project can continue to operate and be made operable. Local law should be consulted to determine whether the lender can operate the project upon foreclosure. Related questions include whether permits and governmental approvals for the operation of the project are assignable to the lender and whether there are restrictions on foreign ownership or operation of the project that affect foreclosure value.

The costs and time to undertake and complete a foreclosure proceeding should be understood. In some countries, foreclosure proceedings may take as long as ten years. India is an example of such a country. In other countries, the risk is not length of time, but the enormity of court and other costs associated with a foreclosure.

Similarly, the effect of foreclosure on an infrastructure project requires close examination. Whether a local government will provide full cooperation to a foreign lender's foreclosing on an important infrastructure project is, at best, uncertain.

Political realities of foreclosure must not be overlooked. It may not be possible in an infrastructure project, for example, for a lender to assume control of, or later sell, a concession. This right would need to be separately negotiated before the project finance closing.

[7] Real Property

Most countries permit a lender to take a lien on real property and enjoy priority treatment in a foreclosure sale. Although the mechanics of the process varies by country, it is almost universal that the law of the place where the real property is located will govern the lender's rights.

The ability of a foreign lender to take a lien on real property located in the host country, or to own it after a foreclosure, is not necessarily available in every country. Indonesia is an example of a country where foreign ownership is restricted. Local law should be examined to determine how foreign ownership restrictions affect the loan collateral. In some situations, a bank located in the host country can be used as a collateral trustee for the other project lenders.

[8] The Problem of Transferability of Project Ownership and Operation Rights

The transferability of the right to own and operate a project is important in nonrecourse and limited recourse project financing. Without these rights, the lender will have very limited ability to restructure a project in the event of financial problems. The value of the project as collateral will be affected to the extent there are significant limitations on transferability or operation.

The host government might impose substantial restrictions on what entity can own or operate the project; what entity has the right to receive project revenues; and what entity has the right to have the concession, franchise, license, or contractual right to operate the project. These restrictions are typically imposed by contract or are included in the underlying concession, franchise, or license. In addition, restrictions can be found in statute, regulation, or the host-government constitution.

[9] Limited Potential Purchasers of Collateral

There is not a large market of potential purchasers of projects in liquidation proceedings. In some countries, the project may be completely unmarketable, particularly where country risks materialized to cause the project company loan default.

[10] If You Think You're So Smart

Finally, the project lender, or its agent, may not be able to complete construction or operate the project any more quickly or efficiently than the project company. The annals of project finance include examples of projects foreclosed upon, or conveyed to the lender in lieu of foreclosure, with disastrous results. Except in extreme circumstances, all parties benefit when a mutually beneficial outcome is reached in which all the parties have a continuing economic interest in resolving the project's difficulties.

§ 26.07 COLLATERAL TRUSTS

It is often prudent for one lender to hold all security interests in project collateral for all lenders. This simplifies the closing process, reduces transaction costs, and provides for efficient credit administration. Lenders in a syndicate change over time, as lenders transfer participation interests or entire rights in a loan transaction. Nonetheless, the local law of the host country might not recognize this and similar trust arrangements. Local lawyers should be consulted to determine whether this or alternate structures for collateral can be used and enforced.

§ 26.08 SECURITY INTERESTS
IN PROJECT CONTRACTS

Each type of loan structure, including a project financing, requires some form of predictability of the effect of external events on cash flow and collateral. In a project financing, however, the recourse limitations of the loan necessitates the combination of contractual, regulatory, and other external elements that together form a transaction that will produce sufficient cash flow to service debt. The importance of project finance contracts to the transaction persuades the project finance lender to require a security interest in, or conditional assignment of, each significant contract in the financing.

The discussion that follows is based on U.S. law and assumes that U.S. law would apply to security interests taken by the project finance lender in the project contracts. Even where U.S. law does not apply, the following discussion is extremely important for an understanding of the interplay between collateral and the underlying project contracts.

[1] Contract Assignment and
Anti-assignment Clauses

The collateral assignment of project finance contracts is sometimes resisted by non-borrower project participants. In some cases, project participants are reluctant to agree that the lender, or the lender's transferee, is entitled to perform the contract after a default by the project company under the financing documents. For example, if project financial difficulties result in the lender's enforcement of the project finance collateral and transfer of project finance contracts to the purchaser of the project at a foreclosure sale, the other contracting parties may have important interests involved. These include such concerns as the financial posture of the transferee or the acceptability of the transferee from a business relationship viewpoint.[5]

The concerns of the third-party contractor are sometimes manifested in a contract clause prohibiting assignment of the contract.[6] A typical anti-assignment clause requires the lender to consider whether the project company can grant a security interest in that contract without violating the anti-assignment clause.[7] If prohibited, the project company may not have sufficient rights

---

[5] *See, e.g.*, Berliner Foods Corp. v. Pillsbury Co., 633 F. Supp. 557, 559 (D. Md. 1986).

[6] An assignment is a transfer of intangible rights under a contract, or a transfer of intangible rights in a claim, to the transferee. RESTATEMENT (SECOND) OF CONTRACTS § 317(1) (1981).

[7] The modern view is that assignments can be freely made. The Restatement (Second) of Contracts § 317(2) states that:

> A contractual right can be assigned unless
> (a) the substitution of a right of the assignee for the right of the assignor would materially change the duty of the obligor, or materially increase the burden or risk imposed on him by his contract, or materially impair his chance of obtaining return performance, or materially reduce its value to him, or
> (b) the assignment is forbidden by statute or is otherwise inoperative on grounds of public policy, or
> (c) assignment is validly precluded by contract.

RESTATEMENT (SECOND) OF CONTRACTS § 317(2) (1981). Anti-assignment clauses are typically narrowly construed. In general, these clauses are construed as imposing a duty on the assignor not to assign, but the assignment is not itself held invalid. *E.g.*, General Elec. Credit Corp. v. Xerox Corp., 112 A.D.2d 30, 490 N.Y.S.2d 407 (1985). The U.C.C. position is that an anti-assignment clause only bars delegation of duties of performance and not assignment of rights. U.C.C. § 2–210(3).

With respect to anti-assignment clauses, the second Restatement provides:

> (1) Unless the circumstances indicate the contrary, a contract term prohibiting assignment of "the contract" bars only the delegation to an assignee of the performance by the assignor of a duty or condition.

> (2) A contract term prohibiting assignment of rights under the contract, unless a different intention is manifested,

in the collateral to create a valid and enforceable security interest. Even if a security interest could be granted, the lender would need to consider whether the security interest could be enforced, or transferred in a foreclosure sale with other project assets, without violating the anti-assignment clause.

Under prior Uniform Commercial Code (U.C.C.) Section 9–318(4), any anti-assignment restriction in an account or a general intangible (such as a contract) consisting principally of a right to payment was ineffective if such a clause would have prevented the sale of the account or creation of a security interest in the general intangible. Thus, a project company could grant a security interest in the payments due under a contract, which could be enforced by the secured party, even if the terms of the contract prohibit the assignment.

The focus of this section, however, was on the payment of money. Many project contracts do not require the payment of money (at least, in primary part). Nonetheless, these other contracts are critical to the success of a project and are important parts of the lender's collateral. Notwithstanding the free alienability of contract rights that relate to payments due or payable under a contract, that former section did not extend this right to enforcing a security interest in the remaining contract rights, such as the right to perform the contract, or to assign the contract to the purchaser of project assets in a foreclosure

action.[8] Thus, the scope of the former section was limited.

The revision of Article 9 to the Uniform Commercial Code in the United States made some helpful changes to these problems, although did not make them go away.[9] Two separate sections now deal with anti-assignment clauses. Section 9–406[10] clearly provides that an anti-assignment clause is ineffective if it interferes with the creation, attachment, perfection, or enforcement of a security interest in a right to payment under either an account or a payment intangible.[11] It is now clear that the creation, attachment, perfection, or enforcement of a security interest in such collateral will not create a default under the contract, or provide an excuse for termination. In a typical power project, the project company's right to receive money for energy delivered is an account under this Section.[12]

Section 9–408[13] expands treatment of anti-assignment clauses beyond accounts, and is therefore a new inclusion for the U.C.C. Under this Section, anti-assignment clauses in a contract, permit, or license are ineffective to the extent the clause would interfere with the creation, attachment or perfection of the security

(a) does not forbid assignment of a right to damages for breach of the whole contract or a right arising out of the assignor's due performance of his entire obligation;

(b) gives the obligor a right to damages for breach of the terms forbidding assignment but does not render the assignment ineffective;

(c) is for the benefit of the obligor, and does not prevent the assignee from acquiring rights against the assignor or the obligor from discharging his duty as if there were no such prohibition.

RESTATEMENT (SECOND) OF CONTRACTS § 322 (1981).

The interplay of anti-assignment clauses with governmental prohibitions in regulations or statutes, and the ability of a debtor to create a security interest in the contract are discussed in BARKLEY CLARK, THE LAW OF SECURED TRANSACTIONS UNDER THE UNIFORM COMMERCIAL CODE § 11.06 (2006). See, e.g., King v. Gilbert, 569 F.2d 398 (5th Cir. 1978) (validity of assignment in face of Federal anti-assignment statute).

[8] U.C.C. § 9–318. Few secured parties were content to rely on the theory that anti-assignment clauses merely imposed a duty on the assignor not to assign the contract, and do not render the assignment invalid. RESTATEMENT (SECOND) OF CONTRACTS § 322(2)(b) (1981). Similarly, few desired to rely on the theory that a court would require the obligor to act reasonably in consenting to an assignment. E.g., Larese v. Creamland Dairies, Inc., 767 F.2d 716 (10th Cir. 1985).

[9] See generally Submitted Committee Report: Report of Finance and Transactions Committee, 23 ENERGY L. J. 541 (2002). See also Ryan E. Bull, Operation of the New Article 9 Choice of Law Regime in an International Context, 78 TEX. L. REV. 679 (2000); Carl S. Bjerre, International Project Finance Transactions: Selected Issues Under Revised Article 9, 73 AM. BANKR. L.J. 261 (1999); Neil B. Cohen, Internationalizing the Law of Secured Credit: Perspectives from the U.S. Experience, 20 U. PA. J. INT'L ECON. L. 423 (1999); Steven L. Schwarcz, Towards a Centralized Perfection System for Cross-Border Receivables Financing, 20 U. PA. J. INT'L ECON. L. 455 (1999).

[10] U.C.C. § 9–406 (d), (f).

[11] A payment intangible is a contract under which the contracting party's principal obligation is payment of money. Examples include rights to be repaid for a loan or rights to payment for funds sold in a foreign exchange transaction. Importantly, Section 9–406 does not apply to the sale of such a contract; that is covered in Section 9–408.

[12] U.C.C. § 9–102(a)(2)(v).   [13] Id. § 9–408.

interest.[14] Like Section 9–406, the creation, attachment, perfection, or enforcement of a security interest in such collateral will not create a default under the contract, permit, or license or cause its termination.

Importantly, enforcement is excluded in Section 9–408. Thus, an otherwise enforceable contract provision, or statute or regulation that limits the assignment of the contract, permit, or license on the enforcement of the secured party's lien is still effective.[15] This means, of course, that the project lender will need to require, as it has in the past, an agreement with the project contracting parties that provides the lender with negotiated rights to enforce its security interest in these types of collateral. These consents to assignment are discussed in the next section.

For project documents governed by English law, until 1999, a lender or other third party that wanted to assert rights under the contract could not do so. Before the new law's passage, such parties had to be a direct party to the project contract. The Contracts (Rights of Third Parties) Act 1999[16] permits contracting parties to create enforceable rights in favor of third parties. Nonetheless, it is likely the project finance lenders will continue to insist on a direct contractual relationship, either by becoming a party to the contract or through another contractual arrangement, rather than rely on a new statutory right.

Contracts executed for use in a project financing can be structured to anticipate the concerns of the lender by use of a project finance assignment clause. A sample clause is reproduced below:

Project Finance Assignment. This Agreement shall be binding upon and inure to the benefit of the respective successors, transferees, and assigns of the Parties. No assignment of this Agreement by either Party may be made without the prior written consent of the other Party and unless the assignee assumes the full obligations of the assignor; provided, however, that this Agreement may be assigned without the consent of Supplier to meet any requirements imposed in any development or construction financing documents, any

long-term financing or substitutions thereof, or any exercise of rights by any Lender in this Agreement pursuant to any collateral assignment or other security agreement; provided further that if any Lender requests Supplier to consent in writing to such an assignment for financing purposes even though such consent is not required hereunder, Supplier shall do so promptly. In the case of an assignment that does not require Supplier's consent, Developer's sole obligation under this Section is to provide Supplier with notice of such assignment.

Whenever a consent to an assignment or a transfer of a Party's interest in this Agreement is required, the assigning or transferring Party's assignee or transferee shall expressly assume, in writing, the duties and obligations under this Agreement of the assigning or transferring Party, and the assigning or transferring Party shall, prior to any such consent, deliver to the other Party a true and correct copy of such assignment or transfer and assumption of duties and obligations. This paragraph shall not be applicable to any Lender.

If either Party reasonably determines or is reasonably advised that any further instruments are necessary or desirable to carry out the intent of this Section, the other Party will execute and deliver all such instruments and take any action reasonable to effectuate the intent of this Section. The parties recognize that this Agreement is subject to review by financial institutions for purposes of the project financing of the facility. At the request of Developer, Supplier shall provide to any Lender, at the expense of the Developer, an opinion of lawyers addressed to any such Lender concerning such matters as such Lender requests, including that (i) the execution, delivery and performance of this Agreement is within Supplier's power, has been duly authorized, and is not in conflict with any agreement to which Supplier is a party or by which it is bound or affected; (ii) there is no law, rule, or regulation, nor is there any judgment, decree, or order of any court or governmental entity binding on Supplier which would be contravened by the execution, delivery, performance, or enforcement of the Agreement; and (iii) the Agreement is a legal, valid, and binding obligation of Supplier, enforceable against it in accordance with its terms.

---

[14] *Id.* § 9–408(a), (c).   [15] *Id.* § 9–408(d).

[16] Contracts (Rights of Third Parties) Act 1999 (England 1999).

[2] Consents to Assignment: Approving Assignments and Enhancing the Contract's Value as Collateral

The Secured Party's Perspective. Secured parties overcome the problems associated with the creation and enforcement of security interests in project contracts by requiring the third party contractor to consent[17] to the collateral assignment by the project company to the lender.[18] The documents used are usually referred to as consents, consents to assignment, or direct agreements. These documents are entered into by the project participant and the other contracting party. Often the project lender signs the document as well.

In addition to the consent to the collateral assignment, the consent serves additional purposes, all related to preservation of the value of the contract as collateral. First, it protects the lender from a contract termination through an agreement made by the other party that it will not take any action to terminate the underlying contract without first giving the lender notice and an opportunity to cure the breach. Second, in a project default and foreclosure situation, it provides the lender the right to "step into the shoes" of the project company and assume its contractual obligations or allow the transfer to a new project company that purchases the project from the lender. This is an extremely important right because of the significance of contracts to the overall project success. Without this right, the lender would face an immediate decline in the value of the project and be held hostage to the demands of the contracting party.

The executory nature of project contracts impairs their value as collateral.[19] For example, the collateral value of project contracts to the lender is dependent upon the terms of the contract and the defenses to payment and performance that arise under the contract. Thus, the lender must undertake due diligence to understand the contract terms and carefully monitor contract performance.

For example, as discussed in Chapter 18, because of the importance of the project to the off-take purchaser, milestones are often included in off-take agreements. Failure to satisfy these milestones can result in reduced sales prices, contract damages, and contract termination. Consequently, the lender will be interested in whether all milestones have been satisfied and will typically require verification in the consent to that effect.

The typical consent contains provisions relating to the modification or amendment of the contract. Because the secured party in a project financing is not a party to the underlying contract, the third-party contractor and the project company are free to amend and modify the contract. Thus, the secured party typically requires advance approval of all amendments to the contract and waivers.[20] Moreover, the secured party typically requires an agreement by the third-party contractor not to amend or otherwise modify the contract without obtaining the advance approval of the secured party and that no amendment or

---

[17] U.C.C. § 9–403(b) permits an agreement between the account debtor (third-party contractor) and the assignor (project company) that the third-party contractor will not assert against the secured party (project lender) any claim or defense it otherwise has against the project company.

[18] The general rule of assignments is that an assignee assumes the assignor's performance obligations. RESTATEMENT (SECOND) OF CONTRACTS § 328 (1981); U.C.C. § 210(4). *But see* Langel v. Betz, 250 N.Y. 159, 164 N.E. 890 (1928) (presumption that assignee does not assume performance obligations in a contract for the transfer of an interest in land). An exception applies to the assignment of a security interest in a contract. In such a case, the collateral assignment does not necessarily transfer the performance obligations (neither contract nor tort) to the secured party. RESTATEMENT (SECOND) CONTRACTS § 328 comment b (1981); U.C.C. § 9–402.

[19] *See generally* Roger D. Feldman & Scott L. Hoffman, *Basic Concepts of Project Finance Documentation: Risk Allocation, Drafting, and Regulatory Considerations for Power Sales and Fuel Supply Contracts,* in PROJECT FINANCING, 1987, at 433–34 (PLI REAL EST. L. & PRACTICE COURSE HANDBOOK SERIES NO. 297, 1987).

[20] *See* U.C.C. § 9–405, which gives effect to any modification or substitution made in good faith in accordance with reasonable commercial standards. The section also provides that the assignee-lender takes rights under the new or substituted contract pursuant to a modification between the obligor and the assignor (project company). Good faith means honesty in fact. § 1–201(19).

U.C.C. § 9–405 provides the secured party with "corresponding rights under the modified or substituted contract." Note that Comment 2 to former U.C.C. § 9–318(2) (new § 9–405) suggests that a modification of the contract also includes a termination.

modification will be valid without the secured party's consent.

Similarly, the typical consent contains a requirement that the third-party contractor provide notice to the secured party if an event of default occurs under the contract. Because the third-party contractor's performance requirements are subject to the adherence by the project company to the contract terms, the secured party must monitor the events that excuse the third-party contractor from performance.[21]

The secured party typically desires other goals in obtaining the consent to enhance the value of the contract as collateral. These include an allocation of responsibility for prior defaults by the project company and a series of representations related to the execution, delivery, validity, legality, binding effect, and default status of the contract at the time of the closing of the loan transaction. Also included are representations related to the terms and status of the contract, such as that all conditions precedent to contract performance are fulfilled, and that no prior assignments or collateral assignments have been made.

The Contracting Party's Perspective. The contracting parties typically are not keen on the idea of waiving rights, extending notice periods, awarding cure rights, and providing other protections to the project lenders without obtaining anything in return. They do benefit, of course, because these consents are a fundamental element of project financings and lenders insist upon them. In most cases, there will be no project unless the contracting party cooperates with the lender's requirements.

The Project Company's Perspective. Most of the project company's attention is directed to the credit agreement, which governs the rights of the lender following an event of default or acceleration. It often watches with nervous apprehension as the lender and the contracting parties negotiate the consent documents. Some, however, take

a more pro-active approach and stay involved in the negotiation of these documents.

The project company is not without risk in the consent. Consents must be carefully drafted so that the lender's rights are as limited as possible. For example, the lender will have an interest in the project and its contracts only as long as its debt is outstanding. Its step-in rights should therefore be limited to that period. After the debt is repaid, the agreements made in the consent should terminate.

The Host Government's Perspective. The host government has its own interests in the area of consents and step-in rights. As discussed in an earlier section of this chapter, project lenders desire the same types of collateral preservation protections in the area of permits, licenses, and concessions as they do with contracts.

If the project is particularly significant to the host country's infrastructure or economy, further complications arise. The host country will often also desire its own step-in rights to preserve the value of the project. A private off-take purchaser may have a similar concern if the off-take produced is important to its success.

In general, any of these entities may step into the shoes of the project company and operate the project. If the host government or off-take purchaser does so first, it typically must assume responsibility for, and repay, the project loans. If the lender steps in first, it must assume responsibility for, and perform, the agreement with the host government (the concession), or the off-take purchaser must perform under the off-take agreement), as the case may be.

[3] The Project Finance Lender's Rights Under U.C.C. § 9–406

In addition to a security interest in the project contracts, some project financings are structured to provide the lender with an immediate assignment of revenues due under the revenue-producing contracts as permitted by U.C.C. § 9–406.[22] Pursuant to that section, the secured party is typically required to notify the account debtor

---

[21] *See* U.C.C. § 9–404(a)(1), which subjects the secured party in a receivables financing to all terms of the underlying executory contract. *See e.g.,* James Talcott, Inc., v. H. Corenzwit & Co., 387 A.2d 350 (N.J. 1978). *Accord* RESTATEMENT (SECOND) OF CONTRACTS § 336(2) Comment C.

[22] U.C.C. § 9–406(a). If the account debtor fails to direct payments to the secured party, it has a risk of double liability, in which payments made incorrectly must be made again to the secured party. *E.g.,* Bank of Commerce v. Intermountain

(third-party contractor) to make all payments due the project company to a project operating account held by the lender for the project company. The lender is directed to transfer funds from the operating account to pay debt service and operating expenses. Excess funds are distributed to the project owners.

Section 9–406 is also significant to the project finance lender in the situation in which the lender desires to protect collateral at some date after the closing. The situation may develop in which the lender anticipates financial difficulties for the project and desires direct possession of the funds.

Although a complete discussion of financing executory contracts is beyond the scope of this book,[23] the major issues are briefly summarized. As discussed above, the U.C.C. generally provides that the other contracting party (the "account debtor") must pay the secured party amounts otherwise due the project company if the account debtor receives notice.[24] The concerns of the project finance lender with direct receipt of funds due under a project contract are similar to the concerns discussed earlier in the context of taking a security interest in the contract itself. That is, the other party to the contract may have excuses to performance that arise from the conduct of the borrower or otherwise from the contract terms,[25] including modification or amendment of the contract made in good faith and in accordance with reasonable commercial standards.[26] Further, the lender is subject to any "defense or claim" that arises independent of the contract and accrues to the account debtor (contracting party) before it receives notice of the assignment.[27] Diligence and security agreement provisions are therefore required to protect the lender from these risks.

With respect to subjecting the project finance lender to the terms of the contract, a prudent lender will apply a thorough knowledge of contract law, coupled with an understanding of the business risks of the industry involved in the contract, to analyze the risk. For example, a long-term open price contract for the project output, while enforceable under the U.C.C., may present an unacceptable business risk to the lender if price stability is not sufficiently predictable. Additional contract term risks are discussed in the next section.

The risk of contract modification or amendment is not limited to formal written documents. Because the U.C.C. contemplates modifications without consideration, the parties can change basic contract terms, such as the quality of the goods delivered, and thereby increase the lender's risks.[28] Because events of default can be drafted to guard against this risk, the practical protection is dubious. Similarly, the ability to persuade the third-party contractor to agree not to modify or amend the contract without the secured party's consent is not always present.

Perhaps the most significant risk concerns the defenses or claims that arise from the contract. For example, the secured party bears the risk that the project company delivers nonconforming goods or services. Unless the account debtor has agreed not to assert any defenses,[29] the revenue stream will be affected by a contract breach, either by nonpayment, asserting defenses to complete payment, or setoff against payments still due.

[4] The Project Finance Lender's Liability for Obligations Arising Under Assigned Contracts

U.C.C. § 9–402 provides that the secured party (project lender) is not subject to affirmative liability arising from the performance of the contract by the project company merely because of

Gas Co., 523 P.2d 1375 (Idaho 1974). There is no authority that clearly permits the secured party to sue the account debtor directly for funds due the assignee and not paid to either the assignee or the assignor. This issue is usually addressed in the security agreement and is included as a default in the loan agreement. *See generally* CLARK, *supra* note 7 at § 11.03.

[23] *See generally* CLARK, *supra* note 7 at §§ 11.01–11.08.

[24] U.C.C. § 9–406. After notice is received, the account debtor must make payments only to the assignee.

[25] U.C.C. § 9–404(a).   [26] *Id.* § 9–405.

[27] *Id.* § 9–404(a). *See e.g.*, Central State Bank v. State of New York, 73 Misc. 2d 128, 341 N.Y.S.2d 322 (N.Y. Ct. Cl. 1973).

[28] *Id.* § 2–209(1).

[29] *Id.* §§ 9–206; 9–404(a). For a discussion of the effect of a "cutoff" clause in which all defenses are waived by the other contract party, *see* In re O.P.M. Leasing Serv., Inc., 21 B.R. 993 (S.D.N.Y. Bankr. 1982).

the security interest.[30] Thus, the secured party is not responsible for damages owed to the account debtor (contracting party), such as consequential damages arising from defective goods delivered by the assignor to the account debtor.

There are a few decisions in which affirmative liability is imposed on a secured party for contract breach by the assignor.[31] In each decision, however, the secured party was actively involved in the contract administration and thereby had knowledge of the potential liability.[32]

§ 26.09 OFFSHORE COLLATERAL ACCOUNTS

If the project receives foreign exchange as part of the project revenue, creation of an offshore collateral account is sometimes required by the project lender.[33] Under an offshore collateral account structure, the project's off-take purchaser, pursuant to an agreement between the off-take purchaser and the project company, agrees, irrevocably, to make payments in foreign exchange directly to the offshore account. The offshore collateral account is part of the lender's collateral for the project loan. It is structured to include reserves for debt service and operating costs payable in foreign exchange. Periodically, amounts on deposit in the offshore account are

used to pay interest and principal on project debt and fund reserve accounts, and the balance is distributed to the project sponsors.

Typically, the host-country central bank will need to approve the amount of foreign exchange that can be retained offshore. The amount is usually related to the amount of operating costs and debt service payments that must be made in foreign exchange over a brief period of time (three months to one year is the customary range). All governmental approvals for creating and maintaining the offshore account must be obtained.

Creation of security interests in both the receivables due from off-take purchasers and the offshore collateral account, and perfection of the lien on that collateral, is an important consideration in structuring an offshore collateral account. A primary consideration is the law that will govern the creation and perfection of these security interests. Among the laws that may govern are the local law of countries in which the off-take purchasers are located and of the country where the account is physically located. It is preferable to take all steps necessary to perfect a security interest in all jurisdictions with a plausible interest in adjudicating conflicts over the collateral. In addition, the off-take purchaser that makes payments into the offshore account should irrevocably agree to make payments to the offshore account and acknowledge the security interest of the project lenders.

§ 26.10 INTERCREDITOR AGREEMENTS

[1] Generally
Intercreditor issues arise when two or more creditors are provided rights to receive payments of principal and interest from, or access to collateral owned by, the same debtor. In a project finance context, intercreditor arrangements are particularly important because of the likelihood of multiple lenders.

Even where multiple creditors do not exist at the early stages of a project, project financings are sometimes structured to contemplate the addition of other lenders to provide financing for working capital, cost overruns, or capital

[30] U.C.C. § 9–402. See, e.g.,, Michelin Tires (Canada) Ltd v. First Nat'l Bank of Boston, 666 F.2d 673 (1st Cir. 1981); Marron v. H.O. Penn Mach. Co., 518 F. Supp. 1069 (D. Conn. 1981).
[31] These decisions rely on a broad interpretation of the "defense or claim" language in former U.C.C. § 9–318. E.g. K Mart Corp. v. First Pa. Bank, 29 U.C.C. Rep. 701 (Pa. C.P. 1980) (supply contract; assignee required to return payments to account debtor); Farmers Acceptance Corp. v. DeLozier, 496 P.2d 1016 (Colo. 1972) (real estate construction contract; assignee required to return payments after breach by assignee); contra Phil Greer & Assoc., Inc., v. Continental Bank, 41 U.C.C. Rep. 659 (E.D. Pa. 1985) (supply contract).
[32] See Michelin Tires (Canada) Ltd. v. First Nat'l Bank of Boston, 666 F.2d 673 (1st Cir. 1981).
[33] If the project company is "controlled" by the host-country government, agreements between the host country and the World Bank should be consulted. Section 9.03 of the standard loan agreement of the World Bank contains a negative pledge that prohibits member countries from creating liens on "public assets," which are defined as assets of the member country or any entity controlled by the member country.

improvements. The terms of this type of financing can be structured into the documents, such as rights of foreclosure, maximum interest rates, and subordination, to name a few.

In projects with multiple lenders, either existing or contemplated, the parties need to address the creditor relationships if a default occurs. Issues include the right to receive payments of principal and interest, consent rights over changes to material project contracts and financing documents, standstill periods, waivers, acceleration, and foreclosure.

International project financings are often structured with a host of lenders, including multilaterals, bilaterals, commercial lenders, and bond owners. The funding priorities and rights of the parties are negotiated at the early stages of project financing.

[2] Goals of Lenders in an Intercreditor Relationship

The goals of lenders in an intercreditor arrangement are to protect their own individual autonomy, while creating a flexible structure that results in fast decision making. Because of the need of the project to operate, tactics that could result in one lender withholding a needed approval, or procedures that could result in expensive workouts, are avoided.

Some of the disputes in intercreditor relations can be avoided by deferring decisions to technical experts, where appropriate. Selection of an intercreditor agent, with authority to decide certain defined matters, can help minimize needless delays. Finally, the existence of a large creditor, with enough voting power to determine outcomes, might be beneficial to small creditors, as well as to the project company.

[3] Typical Intercreditor Arrangements

Generally. Intercreditor arrangements vary from transaction to transaction, depending on such factors as percentages of debt provided by each lending source, policies of multilateral, and bilateral participants, and whether subordinated debt is included in the financing structure. An intercreditor agreement is executed to set forth the

rights and priorities of the various lenders to the cash flow of the project company.

An intercreditor agreement in a project financing is similar to intercreditor agreements used in other types of multi-lender financing arrangements. The major differences relate to the following: (i) the nonrecourse or limited recourse nature of the financing and (ii) the importance of project contracts to the feasibility of the financing.

Nonrecourse Nature of Project Debt. Because the debt in a project financing is nonrecourse or of limited recourse to the lenders, they pay particular attention to the amount and terms of debt provided by all lenders. Any lender that increases the principal amount of its debt, thereby increasing project debt service costs, could affect the ability of the project to pay debt service to other lenders. A similar result could occur if a lender increases the interest it charges the project company. Consequently, project lenders pay more attention to blocking such changes than in many other types of financing.

Project Contracts. Similarly, because the underlying project contracts are important to project feasibility, the lenders will desire the right to consent to a change in any of the project contracts. The percentage of lenders that must consent varies, with 100 percent approval rare.

[4] Insurance

Where an insurer makes a payment on an insurance policy, intercreditor issues arise. This is because the insurer, as a condition to payment, steps into the position of the project company with respect to the claim made, either by assignment or subrogation. In a project finance context, however, this right of assignment or right of subrogation presents intercreditor problems. These include the right of the project lender to pursue the same claims; effects of existing liens in favor of the project lender on the right of the borrower to pursue claims; and possible conflicting provisions in other project contracts, such as a sponsor completion guarantee that excuses the project sponsor from completion obligations in exchange for a collateral assignment to the lender of the underlying claim. Issues such as these are particularly acute in large loss situations, such as by expropriation. In the expropriation context, the project participants will need to agree on how to share insurance proceeds, management of claims and decision making on claims settlements.

[5] General Terms of Intercreditor Agreements
Except as discussed above, the terms of intercreditor agreements used in a project financing are very similar to those found in other financings. These include the following: agreement on priority of use of funds and loan drawdown procedures; voting rights, waivers, and consents; sharing of payments, including optional and mandatory prepayments; sharing of collateral; cross-default rights; coordinated foreclosure procedures; and administrative powers in a single institution, as agent. The project collateral is held by one institution as collateral agent or trustee for all lenders.

§ 26.11 COMMERCIAL INSURANCE

The project finance lender will require that the project company assign to it, as collateral security, all insurance proceeds and policies. This, of course, does not harm the insurer but does provide the lender with protection from any other creditors of the project company.

Because the insurance protection package is so important to the project lender, it will require protection against a loss of the coverage and certain additional rights. These are discussed below.

Additional Insured. An additional insured[34] is any entity, other than the project company, that receives certain contractual benefits of an "insured" under the policy. The mere designation of additional insured status does not burden the project lender with any obligation to pay premi-

ums, although it can elect to do so to preserve its collateral.

Once the project lender is listed as such under the project company's policy, the lender is treated the same as if it was separately covered. Importantly, however, the lender would not be paid insurance proceeds under the policy unless it is also listed as the loss payee.

Loss Payee. Once listed as a loss payee, insurance proceeds payable as a result of an insured loss will be made to the project lender first.[35] Typically, the loss payee clause states that insurance proceeds are paid to the project company and the project lender, as their interests may appear. This structure provides the project lender with control of insurance proceeds up to the amount of the debt. The debt documents will then determine whether the proceeds will be used to repair or rebuild the project or be used to prepay principal on the underlying project indebtedness. Of course, neither the project company nor the lender would receive proceeds under third-party liability insurance, unless as reimbursement. As with additional insured status, loss payee status does not impose upon the lender any responsibility for premium payment.

Non-vitiation Clauses. In addition to named insured and loss payee protections, the project lender will also require that commercial insurance contain a non-vitiation (or breach of condition) clause. In general, an insurer can void an insurance policy on the basis of misrepresentation, non-disclosure, or breach of warranty by the insured or on the basis of mistake. Each of these is very difficult for the project lender to determine in its due diligence process and impractical to monitor during the term of the loan. A non-vitiation provision prevents the insurer from voiding a policy or refusing to make a payment to the lender as loss payee. These provisions are difficult to negotiate, and their availability is influenced greatly by changing insurance market conditions.

---

[34] An *additional named insured* is the term sometimes applied to a beneficiary of an existing insurance policy, while *additional insured* is the term applied to a beneficiary included in the policy when the policy is first issued. They are often used interchangeably.

[35] Sometimes, the project debt documents allow a pre-agreed small amount to be paid directly to the project company for minor claims.

Reinsurance. Some emerging-market countries require that project companies procure insurance within the host country. Alternatively, exchange controls in the host country may have the practical effect of requiring that insurance be obtained in the host country. However, the project lender may determine that the creditworthiness of the host-country insurer is inadequate. The laws, court system, or other local risks may make the lender similarly uncomfortable with a local insurer. In these situations, the project lender may require that all or most of the insurance program be reinsured in the international insurance market place.

A reinsurance program does not provide any contract rights between the reinsurer and the project company or lender. It is, in simplest terms, an indemnity agreement between the insurer and the reinsurer. For direct contract privity to exist, a reinsurance cut-through provision must be included as an endorsement to the project company's policy.

Cut-through endorsements are available in several varieties. The complete cut-through endorsement redirects the payment of reinsurance proceeds from the insurer to a named beneficiary. A cut-through guarantee endorsement redirects the payment in the same way and also covers the payment of proceeds attributable to the exposure retained by the primary insured.

It is in an insolvency situation that the cut-through is of great importance. If the primary insurer becomes insolvent, this endorsement redirects payments to the project lender, not the primary insurer (and its creditors), subject to local insolvency laws.

Waiver of Subrogation. A waiver of subrogation clause is customarily required in project finance. In general, upon payment, an insurer becomes subrogated to all the rights that its insured had against a third party. That is, the insurer can pursue the third party responsible for the loss in order to recover the insurance proceeds paid to the insured. The project lender does not want the insurer to pursue any such claims against the lender or the project company.

Other Insurance Issues. The project finance lender will also require that the project company comply with other matters related to insurance, such as submission of evidence of payment of premiums; agreement by the insurance company that it will provide the lender with advance knowledge of policy cancellation, nonpayment of premiums and policy amendment, pursuant to a notice of cancellation or change clause; and an agreement that the lender will have no liability for unpaid premiums, but will have the option to pay them if the project company does not.

PART NINE

PROJECT SPONSOR AND INVESTOR AGREEMENTS

CHAPTER TWENTY-SEVEN

GOVERNING THE PROJECT COMPANY: STOCKHOLDER, PARTNERSHIP, JOINT VENTURE, AND MANAGEMENT AGREEMENTS

§ 27.01 GENERALLY

A project company is often owned by more than one entity. This may be due to a need to combine several project participants, each with differing financial, management, operational, and technical resources and skills to develop a successful project. For example, one project participant could have excellent experience and skill in construction of the planned facility but no knowledge about the long-term market risks associated with the facility's output.

The need for large equity contributions in infrastructure projects may require that several companies unite to pool resources. The amount of equity that is required for a project, coupled with the political and other risks involved in the project, could strain the funding abilities of any one participant.

The decision to collaborate may also be based in a need to share equity ownership with local investors in the host country. In some countries, local law requires that a domestic equity partner must be included with foreign investors in a project. Irrespective of local law requirements, a local partner is often important to the success of a project, because if that entity is commercially experienced and well connected, it can help reduce political risks.

Aside from these necessities for multiple partner involvement, the addition of new equity participants increases the complexity of ownership. Each equity participant may have different investment goals for the capital contributed. These may include different accounting or tax concerns, different government regulation (a public company versus a private company, for example), risk appetite, and different investment and liquidation goals.

Whatever the reason for multiple equity owners, the equity participants will rarely have any common interest other than to maximize profits. Interest in management control, frequency of profit distributions, interest in maintaining residual value in the project, and concern over host-country regulation are among the varying interests that necessitate carefully structured agreements.

§ 27.02 STOCKHOLDER AGREEMENTS

A project financing may require an agreement among the owners of the corporation's shares (stockholders) to address various ownership issues. Flexibility is sometimes essential in these documents because the project may not be sufficiently developed at the time equity commitments are required. For example, stockholders may be permitted to delay decisions about such things as whether ownership will take the form of common stock or preferred stock, until a later time, such as at the financial closing of the project, or at project completion.

Among the provisions that may be included in a shareholder agreement are the following: management and voting, development stage financing and responsibilities, construction stage financing and responsibilities, operating stage financing and working capital financing, additional capitalization, rights to sell stock and rights of other stockholders to purchase stock from a selling stockholder, and restrictions on assignment or other transfer of stock.

§ 27.03 PARTNERSHIP AGREEMENTS

Where a general or limited partnership form of project ownership is selected by the project participants, the partnership agreement is similar to partnership agreements used in connection with other assets.

Among the provisions often included in partnership agreements are the following: name of partnership, nature and purpose of entity, ownership interests of each partner, management and voting, term, development stage financing and responsibilities, construction stage financing and responsibilities, operating stage financing and working capital financing, additional capital needs, rights to transfer partnership interests and rights of other partners to purchase interests from a selling partner, restrictions on assignment or other transfer of partnership interests, confidentiality and non-competition, and dissolution.

In many partnerships, particularly those structured as limited partnerships, one partner will act as the managing partner. However, some management decisions are considered too important to be left to the managing partner alone. In a project finance partnership, the managing partner is not permitted to incur additional debt, materially amend the project loan agreement, prepay debt, amend or modify important project contracts, waive rights or exercise options under important project contracts, compromise warranty or insurance claims, sell the project, or take similar actions without the approval of all or a specified number of the other partners. Exceptions are usually included for emergency situations.

§ 27.04 JOINT VENTURE AGREEMENTS

Where the project participants select a joint venture form of ownership of a project, the joint venture agreement will govern the interaction among the participants. It is, by nature, a contractual entity.

Among the provisions often included in joint venture agreements are the following: name of joint venture, nature and purpose of entity, ownership interests of each venturer, management and voting, term, development stage financing and responsibilities, construction stage financing and responsibilities, operating stage financing and working capital financing, additional capital needs, procedure for profit distribution, rights to transfer ownership interests and rights of other venturers to purchase interests from a selling venturer, restrictions on assignment or other transfer of interests, confidentiality and non-competition, and dissolution.

§ 27.05 MANAGEMENT AGREEMENTS

In some projects, management of the project entity is governed by a separate document in which a project manager is appointed to manage the project. The project manager may be an affiliate of one of the project owners or a completely separate entity.

The project management agreement typically imposes on the project company the following duties: preparation, dissemination, and administration of budgets; financial and technical record keeping and reporting; supervision of construction; disbursement of construction funds; collection and distribution of project revenues; processing of insurance and warranty claims; account management and expense payment; retention and management of legal, accounting, and other professional services; and maintenance of the insurance program.

PART TEN

SPECIAL TOPICS IN PROJECT FINANCE

CHAPTER TWENTY-EIGHT

BANKRUPTCY

§ 28.01 INTRODUCTION

Bankruptcy of a project participant with assets in the United States and another country or bankruptcy of a project participant with assets only in a host country presents a complicated risk for creditors. The risk includes the availability of ancillary proceedings in other countries and whether other countries recognize another country's bankruptcy proceeding. Unfortunately, there is no universal bankruptcy code.[1]

For international projects, bankruptcy reorganization in the sense common in the United States is not generally available. This is because one jurisdiction cannot typically assert overall control of the project's reorganization.

§ 28.02 TYPES

Two general theories of bankruptcy protection when a debtor's creditors, assets, or both are located in another country are universal and territorial.[2] An understanding of these theories assists in an understanding of the risks in transnational project finance.

[1] Universal
Countries that base their bankruptcy laws on a universal approach embrace the theory that the law of the country in which the bankruptcy is pending should be paramount. All of the debtor's creditors would therefore be required to participate in one proceeding. That proceeding's determinations are considered to have international effect.

[2] Territorial
At the other extreme, countries that embrace the territorial theory consider bankruptcy law to apply only within the borders of a country. Therefore, a debtor with multinational operations would pursue bankruptcy proceedings in several countries. The bankruptcy decisions rendered in other countries concerning the *same* debtor would *not* be applied.

[3] Universal and Territorial
Unfortunately, for creditors, most countries embrace both theories. They apply the universal

---

[1] *See generally* Richard Walsh, *Pacific Rim Collateral Security Laws: What Happens When the Project Goes Wrong,* 4 STAN. J. L. BUS. & FIN. 115 (1999); AMERICAN BAR ASSOCIATION NATIONAL INSTITUTE ON MULTINATIONAL COMMERCIAL INSOLVENCY (1993); INTERNATIONAL LOAN WORKOUTS AND BANKRUPTCIES (R. Gitlin & R. Mears eds., 1989).

[2] *See generally* 1 J. DALHUISEN, DALHUISEN ON INTERNATIONAL INSOLVENCY AND BANKRUPTCY § 2.03[3] (1986).

theory to local bankruptcy laws and the territo-rial theory to foreign bankruptcy laws. Under this approach, local bankruptcy law is supreme.

Almost every large government has enacted its own bankruptcy code.[3] However, although a few treaties on bankruptcy law exist, the progress in negotiating these is limited.[4] This is partially because bankruptcy law has developed as an insular body of law. As discussed above, most countries treat all creditors (local and foreign) of a local debtor in accordance with local law. Con-versely, with respect to local creditors and local assets of a foreign bankrupt, foreign bankruptcy law recognition is limited in a foreign debtor bankruptcy. Consequently, there is a minimum of international cooperation in bankruptcy law and policy.

§ 28.03 U.S. DEBTOR FILING FOR BANKRUPTCY PROTECTION IN UNITED STATES AND WITH FOREIGN ASSETS

Although the U.S. Bankruptcy Code[5] boldly asserts exclusive, global applicability, a U.S. Bankruptcy Court has limited ability to protect the assets of a U.S. debtor located abroad. The effectiveness of the bankruptcy stay over foreign assets is dependent upon the cooperation of the foreign court where those assets are located.

In this situation, foreign creditors with minimal U.S. contact could be free to pursue the foreign assets of a U.S. debtor unless stopped by the for-eign court. A U.S. creditor would be precluded from doing so because of the automatic stay pro-visions of the U.S. Bankruptcy Code. However, the foreign creditor would be precluded from receiv-ing a distribution in the U.S. bankruptcy proceed-ing until all U.S. creditors are paid an equivalent amount.[6]

The debtor must act quickly to protect its for-eign assets from foreign creditors. This is par-ticularly true where other project participants, such as an off-take purchaser, have taken a lien on project assets to secure the project company's performance obligations under the off-take con-tract. Whether the debtor can do so, and the pro-cess it must follow, is determined by the law of the jurisdiction where the assets are located.

§ 28.04 FOREIGN DEBTOR FILING FOR BANKRUPTCY PROTECTION ABROAD AND HAS U.S. ASSETS

Suppose the project finance debtor, with assets in the United States and in the host country, files for bankruptcy protection in the host country. Under U.S. bankruptcy law, the foreign bankruptcy pro-ceeding representative is permitted to begin a Section 304 ancillary proceeding.[7] In the pro-ceeding, the representative can ask the court to enjoin actions against the foreign debtor or its property, and to deliver to the foreign represen-tative the foreign debtor's property located in the United States. The court can also grant other relief, as appropriate.[8] In such a request, a U.S. Bankruptcy Court will be guided by what will ensure an economical and expeditious adminis-tration of the estate, consistent with several fac-tors.[9] These include just treatment of all hold-ers of claims against or interests in the estate,[10] protection of claim holders in the United States against prejudice and inconvenience in the pro-cessing of claims in the foreign proceeding,[11] prevention of preferential or fraudulent disposi-tions of property of such estate,[12] distribution of

[3] The bankruptcy laws of the Bahamas, Bermuda, Canada, the Cayman Islands, Ecuador, France, Hong Kong, Israel, Italy, Luxembourg, the Netherlands, Antilles, Sweden, and the United Kingdom have been found to be substantially similar to U.S. bankruptcy law. Linder Fund Inc. v. Polly Peck Int'l PLC, 143 B.R. 807 (S.D.N.Y. 1992) (United Kingdom); Petition of Brierly, 145 B.R. 151 (S.D.N.Y. 1992) (United Kingdom); In re Rubin, 160 B.R. 269 (S.D.N.Y. 1992) (Israel); In re Culmer, 25 B.R. 621 (S.D.N.Y. 1982) (the Bahamas); In re Koreag, 128 B.R. 705 (S.D.N.Y. 1991) (Sweden). Conversely, the bankruptcy laws of Australia, Spain, and Canada have been found not to be substantially similar. Interpool Ltd. v. Certain Freights of M/V Venture Star, 102 B.R. 373 (D.N.J. 1988) (Australia); Matter of Papeleras Reunidas, S.A., 92 B.R. 584 (E.D.N.Y. 1988) (Spain); In re Toga Manufacturing Ltd., 28 B.R. 165 (E.D. Mich. 1983) (Canada).
[4] R. Gitlin and E. Flaschen, *The International Void in the Law of Multinational Bankruptcies*, 42 Bus. Law. 287, 289–10 (1987); Kurt Nadelmann, *Bankruptcy Treaties*, 93 U. Pa. L. Rev. 58 (1944).
[5] 11 U.S.C. §§ 101–1330 (1994).

[6] *Id.* § 508(a).   [7] *Id.* § 304 (1994).
[8] *Id.* § 304(b). *See* Re Lineas Aereas de Necaragua, S.A., 10 B.R. 790, 791 (S. D. Fla. 1981) (foreign debtor's property turned over to foreign representative, with U.S. creditor's claim receiving priority).
[9] 11 U.S.C. § 304(c).   [10] *Id.* § 304(c)(1).
[11] *Id.* § 304(c)(2).   [12] *Id.* § 304(c)(3).

proceeds of the estate substantially in accordance with the U.S. Bankruptcy Code,[13] and comity.[14]

§ 28.05 SELECTION OF BANKRUPTCY FORUM FOR THE DEBTOR WITH MULTI-COUNTRY ASSETS

A debtor considering bankruptcy protection with assets in multiple countries will need to decide where to seek the protection; that is, where to file. The bankruptcy laws of each country where the debtor has assets will need to be examined to determine the appropriate jurisdiction for filing. Because some countries do not recognize a foreign bankruptcy proceeding, this initial analysis is important.[15]

A debtor with multi-country assets that decides to file in one country may be able to achieve bankruptcy protection in other countries by pursuing ancillary proceedings in the other countries. For example, Section 304 of the U.S. Bankruptcy Code permits an ancillary proceeding in the U.S. subsequent to a foreign bankruptcy protection filing.[16] Unfortunately, this approach is not without risk. There can be no guarantee that the U.S. Bankruptcy Court will enjoin U.S. creditors or order that the property located in the United States be given to the foreign bankruptcy representative.

As another alternative, the debtor could file for bankruptcy protection in multiple countries. Unfortunately, this approach is complex, expensive, and lengthy.

§ 28.06 STRUCTURING BANKRUPTCY SOLUTIONS BEFORE CLOSING

For international projects, bankruptcy reorganization as it exists in the United States is not generally available. This is because one jurisdiction cannot typically assert overall control of the project's reorganization.

One solution is a reorganization agreement. This is an agreement among the lenders and equity investors of a project, together with the major contracting parties, setting forth an overall procedure for a reorganization. Such an agreement can specify, for example, that no lender will begin an action to collect debt from a project company without an affirmative vote of a percentage of the creditors. This vote creates an environment that protects the creditors from the project company giving preferential treatment to any one creditor.

Of course, some mechanism must exist to encourage additional money, both debt and equity, to come into the project. Again, a vote of an agreed upon percentage of creditors could be the only authorization needed.

The terms for this debt and equity could be structured in advance. For example, additional debt could be permitted with preferential repayment terms. Additional equity could be encouraged by providing more liberal equity distribution covenants or not requiring all excess cash flow be used for mandatory debt prepayment.

In short, a procedure for a project finance reorganization could be agreed upon in advance, irrespective of the absence of a unified international bankruptcy structure. This approach is particularly important in a project financing. It is likely that the only way each participant achieves long-term goals is through project operation. Liquidation is not a viable option in project finance. The outstanding debt is typically greater than the asset value for a large portion of the debt term. The host government or off-take user desires project operation over receipt of a share of the foreclosure proceeds.

A reorganization is likely the best alternative in many troubled projects. Yet, unless this is accomplished pursuant to a unified bankruptcy code, which does not exist in international project finance, a pre-negotiated agreement is probably necessary if a reorganization is to occur. This is because the many diverse interests in a project financing – export banks, political risk insurers, commercial banks, a contractor, an operator, an off-take purchaser, a host government, and so forth – may make a structured reorganization impossible.

---

[13] *Id.* § 304(c)(4).   [14] *Id.* § 304(c)(5).

[15] Canada, Japan, the Netherlands, Peru, Paraguay, Panama, and Taiwan do not recognize foreign bankruptcy proceedings.

[16] 11 U.S.C. § 304.

CHAPTER TWENTY-NINE

UNITED STATES LAWS AFFECTING FOREIGN INVESTMENTS

§ 29.01 INTRODUCTION

The bribery of government officials is prohibited by many countries. In the United States, however, the prohibition extends to bribery of *foreign* government officials. Although the best-known U.S. prohibition of this activity is set forth in the Foreign Corrupt Practices Act of 1977, other U.S. statutes may also apply to a project financing.

These statutes, although enacted in the United States, are relevant to many project financings throughout the world because these statutes apply to companies organized in other countries with U.S. operations and to U.S. companies alike.

Many of the laws discussed in this chapter have no counterparts in other countries. Because of their reach, however, they must be generally understood in the project finance context.

§ 29.02 FOREIGN CORRUPT PRACTICES ACT GENERALLY

The U.S. Foreign Corrupt Practices Act of 1977[1] (FCPA) is an attempt by the United States to outlaw bribery of foreign officials. The statute has two components. It makes corrupt payments to officials and agents of foreign governments by U.S. persons an illegal business practice, and

---

[1] Foreign Corrupt Practices Act of 1977, Pub. L. No. 95–213, 91 Stat. 1494 (amended 1988, 1998), *codified at* 15 U.S.C. §§ 78dd-1, 78dd-2, 78ff(a), 78ff(c), 78m(b).

it requires accounting practices to accurately reflect payments to foreign officials and agents.

The FCPA was amended in 1998 as a result of the ratification by the United States of the Convention on Combating Bribery of Foreign Public Officials in International Business Transactions. It is ironic indeed that the United States was asked to strengthen the very law that stood for years as the only prohibition against foreign bribery. Prior to the amendments, there were differences between the Act and the Convention. Unlike the United States Foreign Corrupt Practices Act, the OECD Convention contemplates restrictions on "any person" acting in a country, not just domestic concerns. More broadly, the Convention covers payments made to secure "any improper advantage," while the FCPA address payments "to obtain, retain or direct business to any person." Finally, while the FCPA covers officials of a country's government, the Convention more broadly covers officials of public international organizations.

Interestingly, however, the Convention is more limited than the FCPA in at least one respect. The Convention, unlike the FCPA, does not restrict payments to political candidates, political parties, and their officials.

The 1998 amendments accomplish the following:

- the Act now covers persons acting in the United States other than U.S. persons;
- the Act now covers U.S. persons acting outside the United States;
- the prohibited payments have been expanded to include payments made to obtain "any improper advantage";
- the definition of "foreign officials" is expanded; and
- the exemption of various non-U.S. nationals from criminal penalties is removed.

Each of the amendments is discussed below.

[1] Anti-bribery Prohibition

The FCPA makes it unlawful to bribe foreign officials. It applies to four broad categories of entities and persons: issuers of securities regulated under Section 12 of the Exchange Act or that are required to file reports under Section 15 of the Exchange Act;[2] entities organized under federal or state law;[3] entities with their principal place of business in the United States;[4] and citizens, nationals, or residents of the United States.[5] It applies to any officers, employees, agents, or stockholders acting on behalf of a covered entity.

The 1998 amendments expanded the application of the FCPA to issuers organized under U.S. law and "United States persons," for acts committed anywhere in the world.[6] "United States persons" is defined as "national[s] of the United States . . . or any corporation, partnership, association, joint-stock company, business trust, unincorporated organization or sole proprietorship organized under the laws of the United States."[7]

This illegal activity includes any offer, payment, promise to pay, or authorization of the payment of money or anything of value to a foreign official for the purpose of obtaining or retaining business or directing business to any person. A similar prohibition applies to payments to a political party, an official of a political party, or a candidate for foreign political office.

Also illegal is the making of a payment of any type to any person, *while knowing* that all or a portion of the payment will be offered, given, or promised, directly or indirectly, to any foreign official (or foreign political party, candidate, or official) as a bribe for the purposes of assisting the firm in obtaining or retaining business. Because a person can know of a bribe, even though the bribe is not made by that person or while that person watches the transaction, the FCPA reaches indirect bribery.

[2] Accounting Provisions

The FCPA also requires issuers of securities to satisfy the accounting standards of the FCPA. These standards require that a corporation's books and records accurately and fairly reflect the transactions of the corporation. Internal accounting controls must be designed and implemented to

---

[2] 15 U.S.C. §§ 78dd-1, 78ff(a).
[3] *Id.* § 78dd-2.   [4] *Id.*
[5] *Id.*
[6] *Id.* §§ 78dd-1(g)(2), 78dd-2(i)(2).
[7] *Id.* § 78dd-2(i)(2).

prevent the diversion of assets or other prohibited uses of corporate funds.

[3] Multilateral Agency Anti-corruption Prohibitions

A recent wave of anti-corruption prohibition developments has taken place at multilateral agencies. Many have added protections against such activity to their lending programs. These developments are discussed in Chapter 32.

§ 29.03 ANTI-BRIBERY PROVISIONS OF THE FCPA

For an offense to exist under the FCPA, five elements must be found to exist: a corrupt intent; a use of interstate commerce; an offer, payment, gift, or promise of money or a thing of value; it must have been made to a foreign official or to another person while knowing that some or all of the money offered, given, or promised will be passed on to a foreign official; and it must have been made for the purpose of influencing the foreign official in his official capacity to assist the company in obtaining or retaining business. Each of these is explained below.

[1] Corrupt Intent

To be responsible under the FCPA, the person making or authorizing the payment must have a corrupt intent to use the mails or any means or instrumentality of interstate commerce in furtherance of an offer or payment of a bribe. Although corrupt intent is not defined in the statute, it is generally agreed that the offer, payment, promise, or gift must be intended to induce the recipient to misuse his official position to wrongfully direct business, or obtain favorable legislative or regulatory treatment.[8]

Corrupt intent is almost always present where the other elements of a FCPA ,offense exist. That is, a payment to a foreign official to influence the performance of official duties for the purpose of obtaining or retaining business will almost always be corrupt. However, this requirement acts to exclude small, token gifts, given to foster good relations, rather than influence actions.

The 1998 amendments expanded the scope of prohibited activities. Now, a FCPA violation occurs if a covered person bribes *to obtain any improper advantage.*[9]

[2] Interstate Commerce and Acts in Furtherance

The FCPA also prohibits the use of the mails or any means or instrumentality of interstate commerce in furtherance of the prescribed activity. In almost every conceivable situation, a telephone call or mail delivery will satisfy this requirement for prosecution under the Act.

The 1998 Amendments added a new anti-bribery provision. The FCPA now reaches any person when an act in furtherance of the offense is committed in the United States[10] In application, this provision is potentially broader than the interstate commerce provision applicable to domestic concerns and issuers.[11]

[3] Offer, Payment, Gift, or Promise of Money or a Thing of Value

There must have been an offer, payment, gift, or promise of money or a thing of value. This expansive phraseology includes almost any imaginable device necessary to alter human behavior.

---

[8] S. REP. No. 114, 95th Cong., 1st Sess. 10–11 (1977). The legislative history includes this explanation of the term "corruptly":

> The word "corruptly" is used in order to make clear that the offer, payment, promise, or gift must be intended to induce the recipient to misuse his official position in order to wrongfully direct business to the payor or his client, or to obtain preferential legislation or a favorable regulation. The word "corruptly" connotes an evil motive or purpose,

> an intent to wrongfully influence the recipient. It does not require that the act be fully consummated, or succeed in producing the desired outcome.

> *Id. See also* H.R. REP. No. 640, 95th Cong., 1st Sess. 8 (1977) (analogizing to the corrupt intent requirement of the federal statute that prohibits domestic bribery, 18 U.S.C. § 201(b)).

[9] 15 U.S.C. § 78dd-3.   [10] *Id.*

[11] *See* Commentaries on the Convention on Combating Bribery of Officials in International Business Transactions, art. IV (territorial nexus is to be interpreted expansively "so that an extensive physical connection to the bribery act is not required.").

[4] Foreign Official

The FCPA bribery prohibition extends to foreign officials, a foreign political party or party official, or any candidate for foreign political office. A foreign official means any officer or employee of a foreign government or any department or agency, or instrumentality thereof, or any person acting in an official capacity for or on behalf of any such government or department, agency, or instrumentality.[12] The 1998 amendments added officers, employees, or other persons acting on behalf of public international organizations,[13] as designated from time to time by the U.S. president.[14]

If an offer of money is made to someone other than a foreign official, but it is known that a foreign official will receive the money, the action is still unlawful. The knowledge required by the statute can be inferred to exist if a company's management is willfully blind or has an attitude of unwarranted obliviousness to acts, inaction, language, or other signals that reasonably alerts the management to a violation.[15]

The scope of the FCPA extends to reach persons retained by the foreign government to render services similar to employees. For example, an engineer, financial analyst, or fuel consultant retained by the foreign government to provide services in connection with a project finance transaction would be included in the foreign official definition. These persons are included to the extent they act in an official capacity for or on behalf of the government agency responsible for, respectively, engineering review of a project design or construction, financial analysis of a project, or fuels management.[16] In developing countries, where fuel supply companies, electric companies, and infrastructure is owned all or in part by some level of the government, the inclu-

sion of employees of these state-owned companies, is of particular concern.[17]

The Department of Justice has established a Foreign Corrupt Practices Act Opinion Procedure for questions about who is a foreign official.[18]

[5] For the Purpose of Influencing the Foreign Official, in His "Official Capacity," to Assist the Company in Obtaining or Retaining Business

Finally, the payment must be intended to induce the recipient to misuse his or her official position to wrongfully direct business to the company making the payment. An official acts in his official capacity when he performs the functions of his job or office. For example, persons in governmental positions can act as consultants to a company if their actions are unrelated to the authority or influence they have in their official governmental roles.[19]

The payment must have been made for the purpose of obtaining or retaining business. The scope of this phrase has not yet been resolved by the courts.[20]

The corrupt act actually does not need to *succeed* in influencing a decision. Rather, the mere act of making or authorizing the payment, with the requisite corrupt intent, is sufficient.

[6] Exceptions and Defenses

Exceptions to these broad and general prohibitions include facilitating payments, payments authorized by local law, and reimbursement of promotional expenses.

"Facilitating" Payments. Payments that are "facilitating" ("grease" payments, in the vernacular) or "expediting" in purpose to low-level

---

[12] 15 U.S.C. § 2929.
[13] *Id.* §§ 78dd-1(f)(1)(A), 78dd-2(h)(2)(A).
[14] 22 U.S.C. § 288.
[15] H.R. Conf. Rep. No. 576, 100th Cong., 2d Sess., at 919 (1988).
[16] Although no court has yet held in this way, the intent of the FCPA is consistent with such a result. *Cf.* United States v. Griffin, 401 F. Supp. 1222 (S.D. Ind. 1975), *aff'd without opinion* United States v. Metro Management Corp., 541 F.2d 284 (7th Cir. 1976) (construing the domestic anti-bribery statute to include private contractor that recommends suppliers for construction project).

[17] *See* FCPA Review Procedure Release No. 93–1 (Apr. 20, 1993) (commercial entity wholly owned and managed by foreign government is an instrumentality of the foreign government).
[18] 28 C.F.R. Parts 50–80.
[19] *See* FCPA Review Procedure Release No. 86–1 (July 18, 1986) (no prosecution of arrangement between American company and members of the British and Malaysian Parliaments where the relationship was fully disclosed and parliament members agreed not to use official capacities to influence decisions favorable to the company).
[20] U.S. v. Kay & Douglas, 200 F. Supp. 681 (S.D. Tex. 2002). *See* H.R. Rep. No. 640, 95th Cong., 1st Sess., at 8 (1977).

governmental employees that perform routine governmental actions are exempt from prosecution. Examples listed in the FCPA include obtaining permits, licenses, or other official documents; providing police protection or mail pickup and delivery; providing phone service, power, and water supply; loading and unloading cargo; protecting perishable products; and scheduling inspections associated with contract performance or transmitting goods across country. Actions "similar" to these are also covered. Clearly, routine governmental action does not include decisions by foreign officials to award new business or continue business with a particular party.

The 1998 amendments expanded the scope of prohibited activities. Now, a FCPA violation occurs if a covered person bribes *to obtain any improper advantage*.[21] It remains to be seen when a facilitating payment provides the payor an improper advantage.

Payments Authorized by Local Law. An affirmative defense to liability arises if the written laws and regulations of the foreign official's government permit the payment. This can be confirmed through an opinion of counsel or by using the Department of Justice Foreign Corrupt Practices Act Opinion Procedure review.

Promotional Expense Reimbursement. Also permissible under the FCPA are reasonable and bona fide payments in the nature of a reimbursement of the costs and expenses of a governmental official, which are directly related to the promotion, demonstration or explanation of products or services, or the execution or performance of a contract with a foreign government or agency thereof. The reimbursement cannot be made as a disguise for a corrupt payment made to influence an official act or inaction.

Payments by Subsidiaries of U.S. Corporations. Generally, the FCPA does not directly apply to a foreign subsidiary of a U.S. corporation. Exceptions exist, however, where the foreign subsidiary has its principal place of business in the United States, or is an "issuer" under the Exchange Act.

[21] 15 U.S.C. § 78dd-3.

Nonetheless, the reach of the FCPA is considerable. It applies to United States citizens, nationals, and residents and prohibits the use of the mails or any means or instrumentality of interstate commerce to further a corrupt payment. Even if a U.S. citizen, national, or resident is not involved; the U.S. mail is not used; and a telecopier or telephone located in the United States is not used, the FCPA may still apply. This is because it is unlikely that a foreign subsidiary could carry out a bribe without the parent corporation's knowledge if adequate internal accounting controls are in place. Failure to have such controls in place might be a violation of the FCPA by the parent corporation.

[7] Enforcement and Penalties

The Department of Justice is the chief enforcement agency for all criminal and civil enforcement of the FCPA. A coordinate role is played by the Securities and Exchange Commission (SEC), which is responsible for civil enforcement of the anti-bribery provisions related to issuers.

Criminal penalties of up to US$2 million may be imposed against firms for violations of the FCPA. Officers, directors, stockholders, employees, and agents are subject to a fine of up to $100,000 and imprisonment for up to five years.

Civil actions may be brought by the SEC or the attorney general. Penalties of up to $10,000 may be imposed on any firm, as well as directors, officers, and employees and agents of a firm or a stockholder acting on behalf of the firm. In an SEC enforcement action, an additional fine can be imposed, which cannot exceed the greater of (i) the gross amount of the gain as a result of the violation and (ii) a specified amount based on the egregiousness of the violation (ranging from $5,000 to $100,000 for a natural person and $50,000 to $500,000 for any other person).

In addition to these fines, federal criminal laws impose on individuals up to $250,000 (or up to twice the amount of the pecuniary gain or gross loss). In addition, a person or firm found in violation of the FCPA might be restricted from doing business with the federal government; be ruled ineligible to receive export licenses; result in suspension or bar by the SEC from the securities business or impose civil penalties; or result in suspension or debarment from Commodity

Futures Trading Commission and Overseas Private Investment Corporation programs. The unlawful payment is not deductible as a business expense for income tax purposes.

[8] Avoiding Violations of the FCPA

Because of the necessity for governmental permits and approvals, project development is particularly susceptible to temptations of bribery. This is particularly true in countries where bribery is the norm for advancement of permit applications and other governmental approvals.

Although directors, officers, and employees of project sponsors can be trained about the FCPA, the involvement of consultants and other agents presents problems to most companies doing business in other countries. Consultants and agents often promise to provide access to high-level governmental officials, help expedite processing of permit applications and other governmental approvals, and provide business introductions.

Due diligence on consultants and agents should be undertaken before they are retained to determine such things as reputation, experience, and qualifications. The scope of the work or service to be performed should be clearly articulated and understood and be commensurate with the fees paid. The fee should be of a level comparable to fees charged for similar services in that country. In addition, the consultant should be capable of performing the work or services described in the consulting agreement; it should not be a sham agreement.

After signing the agreement, the company should undertake good-faith efforts to ensure that consultants and agents comply with the FCPA. Of course, even with good-faith efforts, a consultant or agent could cause a violation of the FCPA.

Once misconduct is discovered, it is important that the misconduct be stopped and investigated. Employees, consultants, and agents should be considered for disciplinary action. If necessary, procedural and substantive safeguards should be established to avoid a repeat of the misconduct.

[9] The Problem of the Local Partner

Some countries require by law some portion of local ownership in an infrastructure project. Local participation is sometimes necessary for other reasons, as well. If the local partner makes a bribe to a government official, the U.S. company can be in violation of the FCPA, as a result. To guard against this possibility, U.S. businesses undertake background checks and hire special investigators to gather background information. Ongoing monitoring is important.

[10] Document Drafting Considerations

Document language in a consulting agreement cannot protect fully against violation of the FCPA. However, careful negotiation and drafting can help educate the parties about possible problems. Contract terms that should be considered are summarized below.

Representations. Representations about the FCPA assist in the establishment of a basic understanding of the FCPA for the consultant.

Each of the Project Company and the Consultant represent and warrant that: (i) it is familiar with and has read (or caused its legal counsel to explain to it) the United States Foreign Corrupt Practices Act, as amended; and (ii) none of the employees or personnel of Consultant are officials of or representatives of the Government of [*country*].

Conditions Precedent. Prior to the effectiveness of the consulting agreement, it might be helpful to obtain guidance on whether the agreement complies with the local law of the host country.

As a condition precedent to the effectiveness of this Agreement, the Consultant shall provide to the Project Company an opinion of counsel of attorneys acceptable to the Project Company opining that the Agreement and the payments contemplated thereunder for the services described therein are lawful under the laws of the [*country*].

Covenants. Certain promises between the project company and the consultant should help to overcome a potential FCPA violation.

Each of the Project Company and the Consultant agree that during the term hereof: (i) it shall take no action contrary to the FCPA; (ii) all payments shall be made by check or financial institution electronic transfer; Consultant shall not assign its rights under this Agreement without the prior written consent of the Project Company; (iv) Consultant shall provide immediate notice to the Project Company upon receipt of any oral or written notice of any violation of the laws of [*country*] related to the payments or services under this Agreement; (v) Consultant shall provide immediate notice to the general counsel of the Project Company of any request from any representative of the Project Company that the Consultant believes might or would constitute a violation of the laws of [*country*].

Termination. The agreement should provide flexibility for immediate termination upon a FCPA violation.

Each of the Project Company and the Consultant shall have the right to terminate this agreement at any time, without liability, due to (i) a breach by the other party of Sections [*list sections relating to FCPA*], or (ii) any other condition or event that could or does constitute a violation of the FCPA or the laws of [*country*].

Other provisions that should be considered include limitations on expenditures by the consultant for travel and entertainment expenses and record keeping requirements for the consultant with broad audit rights for the project company.

§ 29.04 THE SECURITIES EXCHANGE ACT OF 1934

The Securities Exchange Act of 1934[22] requires that publicly traded companies disclose "any material fact necessary in order to make statements made . . . not misleading."[23] In addition to financial information, information relating to the integrity of the company's management is also a subject of disclosure.

§ 29.05 THE MAIL AND WIRE FRAUD ACTS

The Mail and Wire Fraud Acts[24] make illegal the use of the mail or any interstate or interna-

tional electronic communication (including the Internet) to execute any scheme to defraud or to obtain money or property by means of false or fraudulent pretenses. These provisions are an excellent example of the U.S. efforts to ensure that its businesses do not attempt to corrupt foreign officials. In fact, the statutes have been used to prosecute U.S. companies on the theory that the citizens of a foreign country were defrauded of honest government by the bribery.

§ 29.06 THE INTERNAL REVENUE CODE

Section 162(c)(1) of the Internal Revenue Code (IRC) disallows deductions of payments made to foreign government officials if the payments would have been illegal under U.S. law had they been made to U.S. government officials. Sections 952 and 964 of the IRC treat bribes paid by a foreign subsidiary of a corporation as a dividend to the U.S. parent, thereby increasing the parent's income.

§ 29.07 THE CURRENCY AND FOREIGN TRANSACTIONS REPORTING ACT

The Currency and Foreign Transactions Reporting Act[25] requires the reporting of financial transactions involving sending or transporting over US$10,000 in currency value, whether U.S. or foreign, cash or check. Any suspicious activity by a customer in an attempt to circumvent this reporting threshold also triggers reporting requirements.

§ 29.08 THE FALSE STATEMENTS ACT

The False Statements Act[26] makes it a crime to knowingly make false, fictitious, or fraudulent statements to any department or agency of the U.S. government. The Act also applies to submission of false documents. Even in a transnational project financing, this statute is applicable whether U.S. agencies, such as the United States

---

[22] *Id.* § 78.
[23] 17 C.F.R. 240.136b2–2 (1996).
[24] 18 U.S.C. §§ 1341, 1343.

[25] 31 U.S.C. § 5311–5330.   [26] 18 U.S.C. § 1001.

Export-Import Bank or the United States Agency for International Development are involved.

§ 29.09 NATIONAL SECURITY AND RELATED POLITICAL CONSIDERATIONS

[1] Introduction

The United States, like many countries, has a complex collection of rules that restrict business arrangements by U.S. companies on geopolitical grounds. These include rules and regulations created to promote U.S. national security or promotion of a geopolitical policy.

In general, these restrictions restrict individual U.S. citizens, persons, or businesses within the United States, corporations, or other business entities formed in the United States, and any business that is owned or controlled by any of the foregoing. Civil and criminal enforcement are generally available if these rules and regulations are violated.

[2] Trade Embargo Regulations

The most typical restraint involves limitation on trade with other countries. In the United States, the Treasury Department's Office of Foreign Assets Control (OFAC) administers embargoes applicable to foreign destinations. Countries subject to current trade embargo regulations, as of July 1, 2006, are the Balkans, Belarus, Burma (Myanmar), Côte d'Ivoire, Cuba, Iran, Iraq, Liberia, North Korea, the Sudan, Syria, and Zimbabwe. The applicability of these regulations

varies by country and must be carefully analyzed against the project structure being considered.

[3] Terrorist States

U.S. trade restrictions exist for certain terrorist countries. As of July 1, 2006, these include Cuba, Iran, North Korea, Sudan, and Syria. Financial transactions with these countries are expressly prohibited. The prohibition applies to U.S. firms but not to subsidiaries formed under foreign law.

[4] Export Restrictions

The U.S. Commerce Department's Bureau of Export Administration (BXA) administers restriction of exports based on classes of goods, services, and technology. A complex set of regulations, referred to as the Commerce Control List, govern export restrictions, and export licensing requirements.[27]

[5] Exon-Florio Amendment

Section 721 of the Defense Production Act of 1950[28] (the Exon-Florio Amendment) gives the U.S. president authority to prohibit acquisition by a foreign person of a U.S. business if such acquisition could impair national security. The Interagency Committee on Foreign Investment in the United States, chaired by the Secretary of the Treasury, investigates such acquisitions and makes recommendations to the president.

[27] 15 C.F.R. Part 774.   [28] 50 U.S.C. § 2170.

CHAPTER THIRTY

LOCAL LAWYERS AND OVERVIEW OF LOCAL LAWS

§ 30.01 INTRODUCTION

The local law of the host country of a project is an integral part of project feasibility. Local lawyers are, of course, an excellent source of this information. In addition, summaries and overviews are available from publicly available information sources and libraries.

§ 30.02 LOCAL LAWYERS

[1] Need and Timing

Identification and selection of local lawyers for a project financing is important to the success of a project. An understanding of the local law during the structuring of the project and the importance of an understanding of these laws during negotiation with the host government and local participants require that local lawyers be interviewed and retained as early as possible in project development.[1]

In a country with a small number of competent law firms, competition among the various project participants for these firms is often intense. This requires that the local firm be retained very early in the project development process.

[2] Identifying Competent Lawyers

Identification of potential local law firms is often made by referrals from large law firms. This is an increasingly effective source of information as large law firms in industrialized countries have developed international capabilities and established local offices in foreign countries, merged with foreign law firms, or established correspondent arrangements or other informal alliances. However, because of the nature of these alliances as marketing arrangements among law firms, referrals are more likely to be based on the marketing arrangement made rather than the experience or skills of the lawyers referred.

Other sources include financial institutions and accounting firms located in, or doing business in, host countries. Historically, this is an effective source of information on competent lawyers.

Directories of local law firms are also available as important information sources. Examples include the *Martindale-Hubbell International Law Directory*, the *International Law List*,

---

[1] For a comprehensive checklist of questions about local law to submit to local counsel for explanation, see William F. Megevick, Jr., *Loan and Security Documentation in International Infrastructure Projects*, PROJECT FINANCING UPDATE 2004: REWORKING & BUILDING NEW PROJECTS IN DEVELOPING MARKETS (Peter F. Fitzgerald and Barry N. Machlin eds., PLI COMM. L. & PRACTICE COURSE HANDBOOK SERIES NO. A-866, 2004).

published by L. Corper-Mordaunt & Co., London; the *American Bar Association Guide to Foreign Law Firms,* by James Silkenat and Howard Hill; and country lists of lawyers available from U.S. embassies.

[3] Criteria for Selection

Among the criteria to consider in selecting local lawyers include the following: foreign language capabilities (both written and oral); experience in project finance; experience in the industry or business of the proposed project; experience with foreign clients; integrity, standing, and reputation in general and with local and central government officials; contacts with governmental officials; use of technology for easy accessibility; sensitivity to conflicts of interest; and sensitivity and methods to protect confidential information.

[4] Managing Local Lawyers

The most important method for control of local law firm costs is the preparation of a written scope of work. This document should clearly articulate the type of work that is required, the method of fee calculation (hourly rates or percentage of transaction financial size), and the treatment of out-of-pocket costs and disbursements. Frequent reports on progress and costs should be required.

§ 30.03 OVERVIEW OF LOCAL LAWS

Prior to consultation with local lawyers, review of a summary of local laws might assist business principals and lawyers in considering preliminarily the legal issues. There are several sources of these, including the Internet, corporate and tax law information published in booklets prepared by accounting firms, and summaries in the Martindale-Hubbell *International Law Digest.*

§ 30.04 LOCAL COUNSEL OPINIONS

The project sponsor will need to deliver an opinion of its local counsel at closing. The opinion, which will be addressed to the lender, gives the lender comfort that project matters governed by local law of the host country have been ade-

quately addressed and present no risks to the financing.

Although the exact requirements for the local opinion vary by country, in general, the lender will want to understand concession rights, obligations, and the procedure to cure defaults under the concession; permits necessary for project construction and operation and their status; and issues regarding how to obtain a lender interest in collateral and the mechanics for assuming control over, and possibly selling, the collateral should a loan agreement default occur. Because these issues are fundamental to the lender's ability to protect its interest in the loan, it is imperative that the local counsel explore these issues with the project sponsor very early in the project development process.

§ 30.05 OPINION OF COUNSEL ON PERMITS AND APPROVALS

[1] Purpose of Opinion

Projects require permits and approvals from the host country. They evidence the right of the project sponsor to own, develop, construct, start-up, and operate the project. Without permits, the project would be unfinanceable because it would exist in a state of uncertainty, subject to potentially unacceptable changes. Because of the importance of host-government permits and approvals to the project financing, lenders require that a permit and approval opinion be delivered at the financial closing by the local lawyers for the project company.

[2] Status of Permits, Approvals, and Concessions

The statements made in the opinion are usually based on the representation and warranty on permits and approvals that is in the credit agreement. That representation and warranty states that all permits and approvals necessary for the construction, start-up, and operation of the project have been obtained and are in full force and effect and not subject to appeal. At the time of financial closing for a project financing, permits are generally classifiable into three categories: permits already obtained and in full force and effect, which are not subject to appeal, further proceedings, or to any unsatisfied condition that may result in a material modification or revocation; permits that are routinely and mandatorily granted on application and fulfillment of applicable criteria and that would not normally be obtained before construction (ministerial permits); and permits other than those in full force and effect and those routinely granted on application (discretionary permits, the issuance of which are in the discretion of the issuing agency, and operating period permits not yet obtainable).

The structure of a project finance permits opinion is similar to other opinions of counsel: Law is applied to facts to reach a legal conclusion. The structure of the permits opinion is typically:

- description of facts;
- limitations, if any, on the opinions reached (such as extent of law firm's involvement in the permitting process, laws not addressed, assumptions made);
- legal opinions concluding that the project has all necessary permits and approvals; and
- qualifications on the opinions rendered.

The opinion must include a statement that the law firm has reviewed certified copies of the permit applications and correspondence between the governmental agencies and the project company. Among the considerations for counsel, include the following: whether the applications were properly completed and filed; whether the issuing authority acted within its power in issuing the permit; and whether all required public notices, and notices to other agencies, were made. This review is taken to confirm that the facts stated in the permit application, and the issuing agency's administrative process, resulted in a final, valid permit.

The lender will review a project's permit and approval opinion to analyze whether any permit application, or any permit, approval, or concession, presents any unacceptable risks. Important in this analysis is the confirmation that the project can be owned, constructed, and operated in conformity with local law. For the financial closing to be successfully completed, the lender must conclude that the project has all permits, approvals, and concessions necessary to own,

build, and operate the project or, to the extent not yet obtained, that such permits can be obtained in a time and manner, and with risks of nonissuance, appeal, or revocation, acceptable to the lender. Permits already obtained must be final, not subject to appeal or comment, revocable only for clearly articulated defaults, and contain only such conditions and restrictions as are acceptable to the lender.

To the extent this certainty cannot be given to the lender, then an analysis about the risks and possible solutions will be included in the opinion, with a discussion of the likelihood of success of those outcomes in resolving the problem identified.

[3] Change of Law
Although the legal opinion is not expected to predict whether laws will or will not change, to the extent a new law is effective, or if it is about to become effective, then the implications of that for the permits issued, or new permits to be required, must be disclosed.

[4] Rights of Lender
The lender will want the permit opinion to address how the lender can obtain a collateral interest in the concession, permits, and approvals and the procedure to cure defaults thereunder. Also, the permit opinion will need to address the mechanics for assuming control over, and possibly selling, the project together with these rights should a credit agreement default occur. This analysis is important because these issues are each fundamental to the lender's ability to protect its interest in the loan.

Often, the right of the lender to "step in" and cure permit problems, and to assign permit rights to a new project owner, is not always clear. In that case, the options available to the lender need to be discussed.

[5] Renewal
Many project permits are for a term shorter than the underlying project debt. Therefore, the project lender will need to consider accepting the risk that a project permit might not be renewed. The permit opinion can be helpful in explaining this risk if it clearly articulates the renewal requirements and any historical data available

about the likelihood that the permits will be renewed.

[6] Typical Problems Encountered and Disclosed

Although there are exceptions, some of the same issues tend to recur in projects when counsel considers the permit opinion. These include the following: some aspect of the project changes after a permit is received; the issuing agency fails to apply its regulations to the actual project proposed; an immaterial mistake is made by the applicant or the agency, which may or may not make the permit invalid; the agency lacks authority to take some action actually taken; and a lack of certainty on whether the permit is final.

CHAPTER THIRTY-ONE

DISPUTE RESOLUTION IN PROJECT FINANCE TRANSACTIONS

§ 31.01 INTRODUCTION

The amount of political risk associated with international project financings in unstable developing countries causes project participants to seek efficient and unbiased forms of dispute resolution.[1] Delays in the resolution of project disputes

---

[1] *See generally* Note, *International Arbitration and Project Finance in Developing Countries: Blurring the*

can negatively affect project economics, through lower project revenues and higher project expenses.

Multiple project documents, multiple parties, and potentially inconsistent treatment of the same or similar contract provisions can lead to unacceptable results. For example, two arbitration panels, determining whether a force majeure has occurred under two separate, but related, project contracts, might lead to inconsistent results. In transnational project financings, dispute resolution planning is particularly important because of conflicting laws, multiple forums with an interest in hearing a dispute, and varying tolerance for arbitration and enforcement of arbitration awards.

Within a project financing, these diverse parties have different tolerances for the acceptability of arbitration for dispute resolution. Although project sponsors and contractors in international project financings consider arbitration preferable to litigation for dispute resolution, project lenders and insurers often prefer litigation.[2]

§ 31.02 ON WHETHER TO LITIGATE OR TO ARBITRATE

There is general agreement on the benefits and disadvantages of litigation compared with arbitration. These are summarized below.

> *Public/Private Distinction*, 26 B. C. INT'L & COMP. L. REV. 355 (2003); Christopher Dugue, *Dispute Resolution in International Project Finance Transactions*, 24 FORDHAM INT'L L. J. 1064 (2001); James J. Myers, *Developing Methods for Resolving Disputes in World-Wide Infrastructure Projects*, 13 J. INT'L ARB. 101 (1996). *See also* Frank C. Shaw, *Reconciling Two Legal Cultures in Privatizations and Large-Scale Capital Projects in Latin America*, 30 LAW & POL'Y INT'L BUS. 147, 154–58 (1999); Georges R. Delaume, *State Contracts and Transnational Arbitration*, 75 AM. J. INT'L L. 784 (1981); Frederick A. Mann, *State Contracts and International Arbitration*, 42 BRIT. Y. B. INT'L L. 1 (1967).
>
> [2] *See generally* Mark Kantor, *International Project Finance and Arbitration with Public Sector Entities: When is Arbitrability a Fiction?*, 24 FORDHAM INT'L L. J. 1122 (2001); Otto Sandrock, *Is International Arbitration Inept to Solve Disputes Arising Out of International Loan Agreements?*, 11 J. INT'L ARB. 33 (1994); Kimmo Mettala, *Governing-Law Clauses of Loan Agreements in International Project Financing*, 20 INT'L LAW. 219, 236–40 (1986).

[1] Advantages of Arbitration

The commonly cited advantages to arbitration are quick, efficient resolution of disputes; lower legal fees; minimal pre-hearing discovery and motions; neutrality of the forum is permitted, which is particularly attractive in a multinational dispute, where any participant may be reluctant to resolve disputes in one participant's home country; arbitrators can be selected who have expertise over highly technical and complicated subject matter; one party cannot force dispute resolution into a local court; flexible and informal proceedings; and the privacy and confidentiality of proceedings.[3] Of course, these advantages only exist to the extent they are preserved in the arbitration clauses drafted for the contract, and to the extent the arbitration clauses are not challenged by litigation.[4]

In addition, foreign arbitration awards can be enforced easier under various conventions and bilateral treaties than is the case for enforcement of foreign judgments. These conventions and treaties are discussed in this chapter.

Although speed and efficiency are often cited as advantages of arbitration, it is not always the case in a project financing. The number of parties, documents, and overall complexity of a project financing can sometimes cause an arbitration to be as cumbersome as litigation.

[2] Advantages of Litigation

Litigation is selected as the forum for dispute resolution for the following reasons: Unlike arbitrators, courts base decisions on the facts and law, not compromise; even if an arbitration is used, judicial recourse may still be necessary, such as to compel arbitration or to enforce an arbitration award; arbitration has a limited or complete lack

> [3] Advantages to the selection of arbitration as a dispute resolution technique are not limited to this commonly cited list. For example, if a governmental entity is one of the contracting parties, an arbitration will circumvent the doctrine of "Act of State" as a defense under U.S. law. Carsten T. Ebenroth & Thomas J. Dillon, Jr., *Arbitration Clauses in International Financial Agreements: Circumventing the Act of State Doctrine*, 10 J. INT'L ARB. 5 (1993).
>
> [4] Paola Morales Torrado, *Political Risk Insurance and Breach of Contract Coverage: How the Intervention of Domestic Courts May Prevent Investors From Claiming Insurance*, 17 PACE INT'L L. REV. 301 (2005).

of discovery proceedings; court rules, developed over time, such as rules of evidence, apply; and interim relief [5] is more readily available.

[3] Can a Party Select Both?

Can a party to a contract have it both ways? For some contracting parties, it might be tempting to require the other party to always litigate but retain for itself the option to arbitrate or litigate. The U.S. courts are not aligned on whether so-called unilateral option clauses are enforceable in the arbitration context.[6]

[4] Alternatives to Arbitration and Litigation

There are other alternatives to dispute resolution.[7] Mediation is one option. It is a flexible, non-binding, confidential process where a neutral, third party assists the others with resolving a dispute through a series of meetings.

Another alternative is a mini-trial before executives representing each of the parties in dispute. This provides a confidential, flexible, inexpensive, and fast resolution of minor disputes.

Although these pre-arbitration, good-faith negotiation alternatives are sometimes helpful in resolving disputes, if the result can be appealed to a full arbitration panel, safeguards must be created so that the informal process is not used merely as a delay technique. The time allowed for an attempt to resolve disputes in this manner should be limited.

[5] Which Is "Best" for a Project Financing?

The question of which type of dispute resolution is best for a project financing cannot be answered in a vacuum. The answer will vary by project, with the parties, the type of project, its location, operation history, and other matters. In general, however, what is best is the method that will resolve the dispute as quickly as possible; project finance abhors delay.

The traditional advantages and disadvantages of arbitration and litigation are applicable generally to project finance transactions. Although arbitration offers some important advantages to project participants, however, it should not be selected for dispute resolution without careful consideration.

Project disputes are often highly technical in nature, involving multiple project participants. Arbitrators, unlike courts, can be selected based on level of expertise with the subject matter of the dispute, which can result in a more efficient decision-making process and a higher-quality outcome. This type of experienced arbitration panel can be more flexible in reaching a result that not only settles the immediate dispute but does so in a way that preserves the economic feasibility of the underlying project.

In addition, because project finance transactions involve participants from several countries, including the host country, arbitration allows for a more transparent, unbiased decision. A court, however, will be based in one of the participant's home country.

Yet, these advantages can place too much control with the arbitrators, making project lenders and insurers very uncomfortable, to say the least. Further, speed and efficiency – traditional advantages of arbitration – are not always present in a complicated project finance arbitration proceeding. Of particular concern, however, is whether arbitration is ever the best answer to resolve disputes in a project where governmental laws, regulations, concessions, and agreements, together with multiple project participants who are not part of the arbitration, combine to support an underlying project. For example, an arbitrator may have no meaningful control over a concession or regulation in a host country. Similarly, unless all important project participants are made parties to the arbitration,

---

[5] In the United States, arbitrators can order interim relief, but a court proceeding may be needed to enforce it. Federal courts will generally hear and grant motions for provisional remedies before an arbitration is decided. *See generally* Borden, Inc., v. Meiji Milk Products Co., 919 F.2d 822, 826 (2d Cir. 1990), *cert. denied*, 111 S. Ct. 2259 (1991) (preliminary injunction in aid of arbitration is consistent with powers under the New York Convention); Rogers, Burgun, Shahine & Deschler v. Dongsen Construction Co., 598 F. Supp. 754 (S.D.N.Y. 1984) (preliminary injunction granted pending arbitration completion). *See also* N.Y. Civ. Prac. L. & R. 7502(c) (McKinney's 1931) (attachment and preliminary injunctions).

[6] *Compare* W. L. Jorden & Co., Inc., v. Blythe Industries, Inc., 702 F. Supp. 282 (N.D. Ga. 1988) (enforceable) *with* Hull v. Norcom, Inc., 750 F.2d 1547 (11th Cir. 1985) (each party must make promise to arbitrate at least some disputes if one party is obligated to arbitrate all disputes).

[7] James J. Myers, *Developing Methods for Resolving Disputes in World-Wide Infrastructure Projects*, 13 J. INT'L ARB. 101, 102–108 (1996) (discussion of non-binding dispute resolution techniques).

the arbitrator may not be able to resolve a dispute in such a way that will ensure the underlying project will survive the decision.

Finally, an arbitration, unlike a court proceeding, may not be able to provide any meaningful interim relief that will allow the project to stay in construction or operation while the dispute is resolved. This type of relief is often integral to a project's success and helps ensure that one project participant will be unable to, in effect, hold a project hostage as it extorts relief.

One approach to this dilemma is the inter-party project arbitration agreement. This agreement, signed by the host-country government and all major project participants, is designed to make certain that a dispute under any one project agreement is resolved in such a way that the underlying project survives. In this way, all parties are able to be involved in forming, or approving, an acceptable solution. Interim relief can be provided, if agreed upon by the parties, so that project construction or operation can continue during arbitration. Necessarily, this type of agreement is extremely limited in scope to only those significant project issues that could have a severe effect on a project's viability. If such an agreement is not possible, then the disadvantages to arbitration in a project financing could render it unworkable as a meaningful tool for dispute resolution.

§ 31.03 INCONSISTENT PREFERENCES

As discussed above, the need for arbitration as a contractual dispute resolution device, and the selection of specific arbitration provisions, varies by project. Each project participant has different goals and risk tolerances that result in different negotiating positions for dispute resolution provisions in project contracts.

[1] Lender
Traditionally, financial institutions have abhorred alternate dispute resolution, such as arbitration. Instead, the lender prefers access to the courts where it can obtain strict and literal enforcement of loan and collateral documents. In addition, the court system traditionally provides quick provisional remedies for the lender, such as attachment and prelimi-

nary injunctions. Arbitration is viewed generally as more cumbersome for the lender, promoting compromise, rather than strict document interpretation.[8]

[2] Project Company
The efficient and timely resolution of disputes is generally the goal of all project participants, particularly the project sponsor. Disputes can translate into schedule delays, increased construction period interest, later completion of the project, possible termination of project contracts with deadlines for project completion (called *sunset* provisions), higher operating costs, possible credit agreement defaults, and a decrease in equity returns. Thus, project sponsors often favor dispute resolution by arbitration, rather than the court system.

[3] Contractor and Operator
Alternate methods of dispute resolution, such as arbitration, are familiar techniques for contractors and operators. These participants generally consider arbitration as a useful, efficient procedure for settling construction disputes. Consequently, arbitration provisions are often found in project finance construction contracts and operating agreements.

[4] Off-Take Purchaser
Off-take purchasers vary in attitudes about arbitration. Government-owned entities, such as government-owned fuel companies, often prefer to resolve disputes through the judicial system of the host government. The bias associated with this approach is often unacceptable to the project finance lender, however. The compromise is often to select arbitration in a neutral forum, outside of the host government.

§ 31.04 INCONSISTENT PROCEDURES

[1] Consistency
Proper structuring of a project finance transaction often requires consistency in the arbitration provisions among the various contracts. Otherwise, a tangle of procedures, dates, arbitration

---

[8] *See generally* Sandrock, *supra* note 2.

panels, and forums can hamper the resolution of disputes. Indeed, even if arbitration is not the selected form of dispute resolution, but rather litigation in the court system, inconsistent forum selection can wreak havoc. Inconsistency in dispute resolution choices and procedures, whether court litigation or arbitration, can result in delays, additional expense, and inconsistent results for the same dispute.

An example may be the best advocate for consistency. In an energy project, a contractor might allege that a force majeure occurred, entitling it to an excused performance delay. When the project sponsor notifies the off-take purchaser that the project completion will be delayed, however, the power purchaser maintains that the event was not a force majeure under the off-take contract; the project sponsor is not excused from performance. The lender, sensing disaster, declares a default under the loan documents. Three separate dispute resolutions are commenced: two arbitrations, each with separate rules, procedures, panels, governing law and forum, and the other in the court of the lender's home country. The result may be that the court action is stayed until resolution of the arbitrations.

Each of these project documents, the construction contract, off-take contract, and loan agreement, could foster inconsistency. To avoid unnecessary problems, these should be consistent, to the extent possible, in choice of law, choice of forum for resolution of disputes, and procedures for dispute resolution and selection of panels. However, the differing goals and preferences of the parties involved in a project financing do not always make this achievable.

[2] Uniformity
A technique preferable to consistency is uniformity in dispute resolution for all project documents. This can be most effectively accomplished through a dispute resolution agreement, executed by all major project participants.

[3] Consolidation
If multiple contracts require judicial resolution of disputes *in the same forum*, consolidation of those lawsuits can achieve many of the goals of uniformity. If different forums are involved, however, consolidation of the claims may be more

difficult. This problem is intensified in transnational projects. One way to avoid this problem is a dispute resolution provision that requires the parties to consolidate claims for certain, agreed-upon disputes.

If the dispute resolution is through arbitration, consolidation of the arbitration proceedings is not easy. This is because arbitration is essentially a contractual undertaking. Thus, arbitration provisions should include an agreement on the circumstances in which multiple arbitrations will be consolidated.

§ 31.05 CHOICE OF LAW

The selection of the law that will apply to an arbitration and the underlying project contract is significant. There are several considerations to be analyzed in selecting the law.

[1] Substantive Law
Laws vary depending upon the jurisdiction involved. Even with so-called uniform laws, the states of the United States apply varying provisions. In transnational projects, an understanding of the substantive law selected by the parties, with the assistance of well-informed local counsel, is crucial.

[2] Procedural Law
Similarly, the procedural law of the jurisdiction must be clearly understood, again with the assistance of local counsel. In some countries, selection of a jurisdiction's substantive law is also a selection of its procedural law on arbitration.[9]

[3] Renvoi
A jurisdiction's conflicts of law rules should generally be excluded from a choice of law provision. A sample provision is reproduced below:

This Agreement shall be construed in accordance with the laws of the [*identity jurisdiction*] without

---

[9] *See* Volt Information Services, Inc., v. Board of Trustees of the Leland Stanford Jr. University, 489 U.S. 468 (1989); Smith Barney v. Luckie/Merrill Lynch v. Menhard, 1995 NY LEXIS 233, 1995 WL 69301 (Feb. 21, 1995) (courts, not arbitrators, decide statute of limitation issues).

giving effect to the choice of law provisions thereof.

[4] *Lex mercatoria*

Lex mercatoria, Latin for law of merchants, refers to the rule of reason; that is, the principles of law and procedure of civilized countries. It is a body of law and custom of globally accepted principles of commercial law.[10]

In some countries, national pride and savvy negotiation techniques prohibit the selection of any law other than its own for contract enforcement. This, of course, sometimes places the project participants not based in that country at a disadvantage. Consequently, a compromise is the selection of *lex mercatoria* by the parties.

On the other hand, the *lex mercatoria* is not a certain, specific body of law. Rather, the arbitrators must decide what it is, based upon the arbitrator's own experiences and beliefs.

Allowing arbitrators to use *lex mercatoria* as a basis for arbitral decisions in a project finance dispute is dangerous. The parties should avoid giving arbitrators freedom to succumb to the easiest of all decisions when deciding a dispute: creating a solution that provides each party with one-half of what they want. Rather, the arbitrators should be required to reach all decisions in accordance with the document under which the dispute arose, yet be consistent with the concepts of project finance under which the transaction was structured.

[5] New York Law

The suggestion that New York law should apply to a contract in another country is often puzzling to participants in project finance transactions. Nonetheless, New York permits it, whether or not the contract "bears a reasonable relation to this state."[11] New York law is generally con-

sidered as having a well-developed body of commercial law, resulting from its location as one of the modern world's commercial and financial centers.

[6] Failure to Select a Law

If no law is selected, the decision is generally left to the arbitrators. In most instances, the law selected will be the location of the arbitration.[12]

[7] Flexibility for Application of Governing Law

Where a host country's laws are chosen as the governing law for a project contract subject to arbitration, some parties choose to provide the arbitrators with flexibility to deviate from that law. In such situations, the arbitration panel is free to deviate from a strict application of law where necessary to conform to the intent of the parties and the concepts of project finance. An example follows:

The arbitrators need not be bound to strict rules of law where they consider the application thereof to be inconsistent with the spirit of this contract and the underlying intent of the parties and as to such matters their conclusion shall reflect their judgment of the correct interpretation of all the relevant terms hereof and the correct and just enforcement of this contract in accordance with such terms.

§ 31.06 CHOICE OF FORUM

[1] Litigation

Courts in the United States generally permit contracting parties to select a forum for resolution of disputes. Yet, if the forum is selected because of its neutrality, the courts may not enforce it. Once again, New York provides assistance, permitting its courts to hear litigation where New York law is selected and the transaction is worth at least $1 million.[13]

[2] Arbitration – The New York Convention

The forum selected for arbitration of a dispute in a transnational project should be a signatory to the

---

[10] *See generally* D. Rifkin, *Enforceability of Arbitral Awards Based on Lex Mercatoria*, 9 ARBITRATION INT'L 67 (1993) ("an amalgam of most globally-accepted principles which govern international commercial relations: public international law, certain uniform laws, general principles of law, rules of international organizations, customs and usages of international trade, standard form contracts, and arbitral case law.").

[11] N. Y. GEN. OBLIG. LAW § 5–1401 (McKinney's 1931) (New York law can be used in a contract with a transaction value of $250,000 or more).

[12] 1980 Rome Convention.

[13] N. Y. GEN. OBLIG. LAW § 5–1402 (McKinney's 1931).

Convention on Recognition and Enforcement of Foreign Arbitral Awards, the so-called New York Convention.[14] Almost 120 countries, including the United States,[15] have signed the New York Convention.

The purpose of the New York Convention is to encourage and facilitate enforcement of international arbitration agreements and to standardize the enforcement of arbitration awards.[16] In general terms, the New York Convention mandates that signatory countries honor arbitration clauses in agreements subject to this convention; enforce arbitration of disputes covered by arbitration (unless the underlying agreement is null and void, inoperative, or incapable of being performed); and recognize and enforce arbitration awards made in other signatory countries without reviewing the arbitrator's decisions (subject to limited exceptions).

In almost all countries that have signed the New York Convention, laws implementing it have been enacted. These laws, together with the judicial decisions that interpret the convention and implementing laws, must be considered to determine whether the goals of the convention – enforcement of arbitration agreements and awards – are achieved. Even the U.S. courts lack uniformity.[17]

[3] Arbitration – Other Conventions

Two other conventions could be applicable to an arbitration in a project financing: the Inter-American Convention on International Commercial Arbitration (the Panama Convention)[18] and the International Convention on the Settlement of Investment Disputes (the ICSID Convention or Washington Convention).[19]

The Panama Convention includes many of the same protections found in the New York Convention, discussed above. As the name suggests, this convention applies to the United States, Mexico, and eighteen South and Central American countries.

The Washington Convention could apply to certain types of investment disputes in a project. To be applicable, the dispute must be between a government entity and a national of another state (that is a signatory of the convention).

[4] Arbitration – Bilateral Investment Treaties

Hundreds of bilateral investment treaties are in existence. These treaties could apply to a dispute in a project financing.

[5] Failure to Select a Law

If arbitration is selected as the form of dispute resolution, the forum should also be selected if predictable results are the goal of the parties. For example, in one court case,[20] where no forum was selected, the arbitrators chose the country. When one of the parties lost the arbitration and attempted to have the decision vacated in its own country, the home country court required that the motion to vacate be heard in the forum where the arbitration was decided.

[6] Developing Countries

The need to select the forum is particularly important in projects located in developing countries, where the law surrounding arbitration is still being established. If the selection is left to the arbitration panel, by the terms of the agreement or by deferral to the rules of the arbitrators,[21] the host country of the project could be selected, irrespective of whether the country will enforce its decision.

[14] Convention on Recognition and Enforcement of Foreign Arbitral Awards, September 30, 1970, 21 U.S.T. 2517, T.I.A.S. No. 6997. *See generally* ALBERT JAN VAN DEN BERG, THE NEW YORK ARBITRATION CONVENTION OF 1958 (1981).
[15] 9 U.S.C. §§ 1–16; 201–208 (2000).
[16] *See generally* Alan Rau, *The New York Convention in American Courts*, 7 AM. REV. INT'L ARB. 213 (1996) (no real consensus in U.S. courts about when the Convention is supposed to be applied); Gerald Aksen & Wendy S. Dorman, *Application of the New York Convention by United States Courts: A Twenty-Year Review (1970–1990)*, 2 AM. REV. INT'L ARB.65 (1991).
[17] 9 U.S.C. §§ 1–16; 201–208 (2000).
[18] Inter-American Convention on International Commercial Arbitration, Jan. 31, 1975, O.A.S.T.S. No. 42, 14 I.L.M. 336 (1975).

[19] Convention on the Settlement of Investment Disputes Between States and Nationals of Other States, Mar. 18, 1965, 17 U.S.T. 1270, 575 U.N.T.S. 159.
[20] International Standard Electric Corp. v. Bridas Sociedad Anonima Petrolera, 745 F. Supp. 172 (S.D.N.Y. 1990).
[21] *See, e.g.*, ICC Court of Arbitration Article 12.

§ 31.07 CHOICE OF PANEL

A number of arbitral tribunals are available to parties for dispute resolution. There are several factors to consider in determining which tribunal should be selected, such as the availability of qualified arbitrators, the institution's experience with the type of dispute and the industry involved, and the institution's reputation. These institutional alternatives are summarized in the following paragraphs.

[1] American Arbitration Association

The American Arbitration Association (AAA), headquartered in New York City, is the association often used by American companies for dispute resolution. The AAA provides administration, procedural rules, and appointment of arbitrators.

The Association has two sets of rules of interest to transnational project finance transactions. These are the AAA Commercial Arbitration Rules and the AAA Supplementary Procedures for International Arbitration.

[2] International Chamber of Commerce

The International Chamber of Commerce (ICC), based in Paris, France, is widely known and respected. It is generally regarded as more expensive than the AAA. It enjoys well-qualified, more experienced arbitrators. The ICC Rules of Arbitration govern the arbitration process.

In part because of continental law influence, great emphasis is given to documentary evidence and briefs. Testimony by witnesses is not given great weight.

The ICC provides for administration of arbitrations through its Court of Arbitration. It supplies procedural rules to provide decision-making guidance to arbitrators. There are no ICC arbitrators, although the ICC can confirm the neutrality of arbitrators chosen by the parties and appoint a third arbitrator.

[3] London Court of International Arbitration

The London Court of International Arbitration is based in London. The London Court of International Rules determines the procedure of arbitrations.

[4] United Nations Commission on International Trade Law

The United Nations Commission on International Trade Law (UNCITRAL) does not administer arbitration proceedings. Instead, UNCITRAL provides rules to govern arbitrations.

[5] Inter-American Commercial Arbitration Commission

The Inter-American Commercial Arbitration Commission (IACAC) issues rules and administers arbitration proceedings in the Americas.

[6] Stockholm Chamber of Commerce

The Stockholm Chamber of Commerce is a traditional arbitration choice for non-Western entities looking for an alternative to the ICC or LCIA.

[7] International Centre for Settlement of Investment Disputes

The International Centre for Settlement of Investment Disputes (ICSID), located in Washington, D.C., is part of the World Bank. It was established in 1966 as a public international institution and more than 100 countries have become members.

ICSID was created to give investors a forum to arbitrate issues related to investments in developing countries, such as expropriation, exchange controls, taxation, and similar investment concerns in these countries. Resolution of disputes by ICSID, through arbitration or conciliation, arises from agreement by the parties, either in the agreement or in a later submission.

Jurisdiction is based on a dispute that arises between a contracting member country (or an agency thereof) and a national of another contracting party. The dispute must be a "legal dispute arising directly out of an investment."[22]

[8] Others

Other alternatives include arbitrations in Switzerland and the Netherlands, which both have arbitration statutes governing international

---

[22] Convention on the Settlement of International Disputes Between States and Nationals of Other States Establishing an International Centre for the Settlement of Investment Disputes, 1965, 17 U.S.T. 120, 575 U.N.T.S. 159.

arbitrations; the British Columbia International Commercial Arbitration Centre; the Japan Commercial Arbitration Association; and the Hong Kong International Arbitration Centre.

[9] Ad Hoc

The contracting parties can decide to administer the arbitration themselves, on an ad hoc basis, rather than pursuant to an institutional model. The parties can select their own arbitrators, thereby ensuring maximum autonomy. Often, the UNCITRAL rules are used in ad hoc proceedings, which were designed for such ad hoc arbitrations. An ad hoc approach is best suited for transactions in which all parties are experienced with international arbitration, either through direct involvement with arbitrations in the past or where international arbitration has been historically supported by the host country.

An institutional proceeding is often the most useful in an international project financing, however. The complexity of project finance transactions, burdened with multiple parties and interests, may make use of an experienced institutional panel, acting under well-developed rules, the only practical means of efficient dispute resolution. Also, the contracting parties will usually have different levels of experience with arbitration and have different levels of comfort for it. In addition, differing cultural and geographical backgrounds may reduce comfort with an ad hoc approach. These same parties may have entered into their first transaction together, with the resultant lack of mutual trust in an ad hoc approach with which only one party has experience.

§ 31.08 DISPUTES INVOLVING PROJECT PARTICIPANTS NOT PARTIES TO THE CONTRACT IN DISPUTE

Project financings are a collection of contracts and parties. These financings involve parties that benefit from the contracts, even though they are not direct contractual parties. For example, a project company is not a party to a subcontract between the construction contractor and its supplier. However, the project company benefits from the performance of the subcontract.

In *Abbott Chemicals, Inc. v. ASEA AB*,[23] a project sponsor of a cogeneration facility claimed to be a third-party beneficiary of a subcontract between the contractor and its supplier. The project sponsor contended that design problems caused project delays and resulted in losses arising from the need to purchase electricity from alternate sources until the project was operational.

The construction contract contained liability limitation provisions for the benefit of the contractor. It also contained an arbitration clause, requiring the project sponsor to arbitrate "any controversy or claim arising out of" the contract in Sweden.

In an effort to avoid the construction contract limitations on liability, the project sponsor commenced litigation in Puerto Rico, site of the project, against the subcontractor, claiming that the project sponsor was a third-party beneficiary of the subcontract between the construction contractor and the subcontractor. However, the subcontract also contained an arbitration clause, consistent with the arbitration provisions of the construction contract. The provision in the subcontract stated that the arbitration form of dispute resolution was not limited to the parties to the contract. Thus, the court reasoned that because the project sponsor wanted to be a third-party beneficiary of the subcontract, it would need to adhere to the arbitration provisions and resolve its dispute in arbitration in Sweden, not in Puerto Rico.

§ 31.09 CHALLENGING ARBITRATION AWARDS

It is an overstatement to say that arbitrators have complete freedom and flexibility in deciding disputes. In general terms, arbitration awards can be overruled by a court, albeit in limited circumstances. These include corruption, fraud, or misconduct in procuring the award; partiality of an arbitrator appointed as a neutral; exceeding

---

[23] Abbott Chemicals, Inc. v. ASEA AB, Civ. No. 86–1305 (RLA) (D.P.R. Feb. 19, 1988). *See also* Coastal Steel Corp. v. Tilghman Wheelabrator, Ltd., 709 F.2d 190 (3d Cir.), *cert. denied*, 464 U.S. 938 (1983) (project owner bound by forum selection clause in subcontract between subcontractor and contractor under which the owner claimed rights).

the power given to the arbitrator; and "imperfectly executing" the power given to the arbitrator in such a way that a final and definite award is not made.[24] An arbitrator has a great deal of discretion; barring irrationality, the arbitrator can err in applying the law or in a contract interpretation without providing a justification to set aside the award.[25]

§ 31.10 ARBITRATION AND HOST-COUNTRY DISPUTES

[1] Generally

Respect for the outcomes of international arbitrations is not as firm as project participants sometimes believe. Although many countries have signed international treaties relating to enforcement of arbitration decisions, and modified local laws to provide for enforcement, the result has not always been predictable. Foreign governments can frustrate the administration of an arbitration proceeding, and take steps to attempt to deny the enforcement of the arbitration panel's decision.[26]

Several protections can be negotiated to lessen the ability of a host-country government to make arbitration less effective or even ineffective. First, despite the advantages of an ad hoc arbitration, it should be avoided when a foreign government is a party to the underlying contract. If an institutional arbitration is used, it will be much more difficult for the government to later allege that the arbitration process was corrupt or biased.

Next, it is necessary to confirm under the foreign government's local laws that the government, and the government entity that is actually a party to the underlying contract, has the ability to participate in an arbitration. If the government entity that participates in the arbitration has no lawful ability to commit the govern-

ment, the underlying arbitration is invalid or at least subject to approval.

Also, it is necessary to consider selecting a site for the arbitration that is outside of the host country. A country where all parties have neutral relations is preferable. This minimizes the temptation of the government to interfere with proceedings.

If the government is not a party to the New York or Panama Conventions, the parties can nonetheless agree that the arbitration award will be enforced in accordance with one of these conventions. In this situation, it may be useful for the local government (or the underlying state entity that is actually party to the agreement) to waive sovereign immunity.

In addition, it is necessary that the local counsel carefully draft and review the arbitration provisions of the contract. If a party wants to escape the necessity to arbitrate a dispute, it will most likely begin with the assertion that the subject matter of the dispute is not included in the contract arbitration clause. Consequently, the scope of the arbitration should include all types of disputes, acts, inaction, illegality, fraud, and misrepresentation directly or indirectly related to the underlying contract and its performance.

[2] *Pacta Sunt Servanda*, Private Contracting, and State Sovereignty

When negotiating an arbitration agreement with a host government (or an entity owned by the government), it is important for the parties to consider how the arbitrators might apply the legal doctrine of *pacta sunt servanda*. This well-established doctrine holds that every international agreement binds the parties and requires that it be performed in good faith. The legal theory, based on Western European principles of natural law, is that no government should have the right to change an existing contract to further its own political, social, or economic goals.[27]

---

[24] *See, e.g.*, NY CPLR § 7511 (McKinney's 1931).

[25] *See* Morales Torrado, *supra* note 4; H. Smit, *Substance and Procedure in International Arbitration: The Development of a New Legal Order*, 65 Tulane L. Rev. 1309, 1317 (1991).

[26] Mark Kantor, *International Project Finance and Arbitration with Public Sector Entities: When is Arbitrability a Fiction?*, 24 Fordham Int'l L. J. 1122, 1134–36 (2001).

[27] Restatement (Third) of the Foreign Relations Law of the U. S. 321 (1987); *see, e.g.*, Sapphire Int'l Petroleums Ltd. v. National Iranian Oil Co., 35 I.L.R. 136, 181 (Arb. Award 1963); *see also* Terence Daintith & Ian Gault, *Pacta Sunt Servanda and the Licensing and Taxation of North Sea Oil Production*, 8 Cambrian L. Rev. 27 (1977). The doctrine extends to state-controlled companies, which are not insulated from liability. *E.g.*, McKesson Corp. v. Islamic Republic

In general, this doctrine is consistently applied by arbitrators in international arbitrations. Whether its application will be as prevalent for disputes involving governments in infrastructure projects is not yet clear. Where the host-country government enters into a contract with a project company (either directly or through a government-owned entity, such as a utility), then the arbitrators can conclude that the government is acting as a private party to a contract and not as a government. The doctrine should apply, it would appear, and the host government should not be permitted to alter the contract, directly, or through legislation or regulation, without the consent of the project company.

However, in most project financings, the project is very important to the public. In addition, most of these projects are subject to ongoing governmental regulation. As such, the arbitrators may be tempted to allow the host government to change the underlying project contracts to which it is a direct or an indirect party, in a financial or political crisis, even if that action will affect the rights of a foreign contracting party.

When drafting an arbitration agreement for use with a host-country government (or an entity owned or controlled by it), the better practice is to clearly address this doctrine. The contract could, of course, specifically provide that *pacta sunt servanda* will be applied by the arbitration panel, even though the project directly affects the public health, safety, and prosperity. From a practical perspective, however, such a provision may constrain too firmly the sovereign right of the host country to govern and may be rejected by the arbitrators or invite judicial review.[28] It may very well be that the best practice is to include a provision that the doctrine will apply but also to arrange other protections, such as political risk insurance, in the event *pacta sunt servanda* is ignored by arbitrators or a court as too restrictive for infrastructure projects.[29]

§ 31.11 ARBITRATION IN DEVELOPING COUNTRIES

Project finance has provided developing countries with an attractive financing option for large-scale infrastructure development. At the same time, investors have access to lucrative new infrastructure markets that previously either did not exist or were financed solely by the government. With this new investment, however, comes the political risk inherent in developing countries. Arbitration can alleviate some of that political risk.

Developing countries have not always been as eager to forgo access to the judicial system, in favor of arbitration, to resolve disputes. Arbitration is based on the concept that contracting parties are free to develop their own rules and procedures for dispute resolution, without consideration for public concerns. This concept is problematic in infrastructure projects, however, because such services as roads, energy and water have been traditionally provided by the government to its citizens and paid for with public funds, either with tax revenues or public debt. With public funds, the government has been traditionally free to change the rates charged for such services as economic situations develop. In a project financing, however, such changes are unwelcome, even if economic developments place pressure on the government to change material terms of private infrastructure projects, including contract suspension and outright cancellation.[30]

Private investors in infrastructure projects in developing countries favor arbitration for several reasons. First, because of the public importance of these projects for basic needs, and the

---

W. Waelde & George Ndi, *Stabilizing International Investment Commitments: International Law Versus Contract Interpretation*, 31 Tex. Int'l L. J. 216, 244 (1996) (discussing conflict between *pacta sunt servanda* and domestic legislative rights).

[30] *See generally* Shalakany, *supra* note 28, at 465; Nagla Nassar, *Project Finance, Public Utilities and Public Concerns*, 31 Cornell Int'l L. J. 395 (1998). For a discussion about the tension between economic efficiency and public interest considerations in infrastructure projects, *see* Catherine Pedamon, *Essay: How Is Convergence Best Achieved in International Project Finance?*, 24 Fordham Int'l L. J. 1272 (2001).

---

of Iran, 52 F.3d 346, 352 (D.C. Cir. 1995) (separate existence of state-controlled companies that carry out state roles or policies does not shield the state from liability).

[28] Amr A. Shalakany, *Arbitration and the Third World: A Plea for Bargaining Bias Under the Specter of Neoliberalism*, 41 Harv. Int'l L. J. 419, 465–66 (2000).

[29] *See generally id.* at 459–60 (discussing application of *pacta sunt servanda* in Texaco-Libyan oil arbitrations); Thomas

accompanying temptation of local politicians to change the underlying contracts to meet changing economic realities, the privacy and confidentiality of an arbitration proceeding can help avoid a public dispute. This privacy can provide flexibility to the arbitrators in receiving evidence, and in developing compromises and awarding damages without destroying the project. This flexibility also allows the selection of an arbitration panel with experience in project finance and with developing country risks. With litigation, it is rare that a judge will have this experience.

Also, private investors prefer the use of arbitration because it is more adaptable to the complex structure of the financing, involving multiple contracts and parties, yet a single economic entity called *the project*. Disputes under one contract may arise from disputes under other contracts or even cause a default. Because the project is based on a collection of interrelated contracts, these investors prefer coordinated arbitration clauses in all contracts, so that it is clear how all project disputes will be mediated.

Despite these perceived advantages, the success of arbitration in project financings in developing countries is mixed.[31] Arbitrations in two Indonesian geothermal projects – Patuha and Himpurna – are examples. In both projects, the state-owned utility, PT Perusahaan Listruik Negara, agreed to purchase the power produced by the projects, and the state oil company, Pertamina, entered into contracts regarding operation of the geothermal fields. These contracts were approved by the Indonesian Minister of Mines and Energy on behalf of the government of the Republic of Indonesia. Moreover, the Indonesian Ministry of Finance delivered a letter to each project sponsor in which assurances were made that the contractual obligations of the two state-owned companies would be performed.

Arbitration provisions were included in these contracts, as well as in the Ministry of Finance letter. Disputes were to be resolved under UNCITRAL rules, in Jakarta. Careful attention was given in these documents to ensure that Indonesian law, the governing law chosen by the parties, could not be used by any party to circumvent the agreement to arbitrate disputes, including waiving the right to appeal arbitration decisions.

The project investors and lenders were sufficiently satisfied with the commitments of the Indonesian government and the arbitration provisions that debt financing was secured. The collapse of the Indonesian economy in 1997 (as a result of the Asian financial crisis discussed in Chapter 1) produced exchange rate fluctuations that ultimately caused the state-owned utility to announce that it could not perform the power sales agreements. The financial crisis also led to the fall of the ruling Suharto regime in 1998. At the same time, accusations surfaced that political corruption was involved in awarding contracts associated with energy projects in the country. When a new government came into power, it unilaterally "suspended" the two projects in response to economic adversity.

Following arbitrations,[32] the project companies were awarded an aggregate total of US$571 million, to be paid by the state-owned utility. When the utility failed to make the payments, a second arbitration was started, this time against the Indonesian government for failing to comply with the guarantees that the government provided in the contracts.

The state-owned utility then asked a court in Jakarta to vacate the arbitration award, which the court agreed to do. The state oil company also brought an action in court, arguing that it should have been included in the first arbitration proceeding. The court issued an injunction, suspending enforcement of the first arbitration award.

Meanwhile, the second arbitration proceeded, with the Indonesian government refusing to participate because the first arbitration was still unresolved. After the second arbitration panel

[31] Morales Torrado, *supra* note 4; R. Doak Bishop et al., *Strategic Options Available When Catastrophe Strikes the Major International Energy Project*, 36 Tex. Int'l L. J. 635 (2001); Note, *International Arbitration and Project Finance in Developing Countries: Blurring the Public/Private Distinction, supra* note 1.

[32] Himpurna California Energy Ltd. (Bermuda) v. PT. (Persero) Perusahan Listruik Negara (Indonesia), 14 Mealey's Int'l Arb. Rep., at A-26 (Dec. 1999); Patuha Power Ltd. (Bermuda) v. PT. (Persero) Perusahan Listruik Negara (Indonesia), 14 Mealey's Int'l Arb. Rep., at B-14 (Dec. 1999).

decided that the Indonesian government was responsible for paying the damages awarded in the first arbitration, pursuant to the guarantees it had signed, the government refused. Fortunately, the project companies had obtained almost US$300 million of political risk insurance from the Overseas Private Insurance Corporation (OPIC) and various syndicates, which was paid in late 1999.

The Indonesian experience with arbitration provisions suggests that arbitration may not be as efficient as hoped. The reasons for failure in Indonesia are complicated. Political corruption and government instability clearly affected the court decision to vacate the first arbitration award, and the economic collapse in the country certainly complicated the dispute resolution process.

Perhaps most importantly, however, is a lack of commitment in Indonesia and similar countries to respect private contracting in infrastructure projects that benefit the public and involve government contracts or guarantees. The developed world, in general, views the law as split between public law – the realm of the legislature, and private law – negotiation and performance of contracts. In developing countries, however, that distinction does not yet fully exist, if it ever will, when the contracts affect the public welfare. Where political stability is not as assured as in the West, governments in developing countries may be reluctant to allow arbitrators – in an inherently private lawmaking approach – to have the final decision in public infrastructure projects.

§ 31.12 ARBITRATION PROVISIONS

Project participants should avoid the use of all-purpose arbitration clauses; arbitration is too complicated to be dismissed in the boilerplate section of contracts. However, there are common provisions that should be considered.

[1] Final and Binding Arbitration
The contract must specify that arbitration is selected as the sole dispute resolution mechanism for all, or a carefully defined set of, disputes. The provision must specify in direct terms that

the results of the arbitration shall be final and that the results will be binding on all parties to the dispute.

[2] Scope of Arbitration
The parties must agree on the scope of the arbitration requirement. Thus, the contract must state which disputes will be subject to resolution by arbitration. Generally, an all-disputes clause should be included to describe the scope of the arbitration provision. Such a clause should specify that "each and every breach, dispute, claim, loss, damage, or controversy related to, arising from or otherwise occurring under the contract, including those based in fraud, illegality, or invalidity of the contract" are subject to final and binding resolution by arbitration. Local counsel should review the scope provision to verify that it adequately describes all disputes. To the extent this provision is insufficiently broad, any of the contracting parties may have the opportunity to escape arbitration by arguing that the dispute was not intended to be resolved by arbitration.

Similarly, where specific disputes are not intended to be resolved by arbitration, those disputes must be carefully described. Often, reference to specific contract sections, or specific legal areas, are necessary.

[3] Location of Arbitration (Choice of Venue)
The location where the arbitration decision will be deemed to have been issued should be carefully considered. It is perhaps the most significant decision to be made.

The legal system of the country chosen must be supportive of the choice of the parties to arbitrate disputes. Thus, it must compel arbitration where it has been chosen in a contract, and allow the arbitration to be conducted with minimal judicial interruption. Importantly, the laws of the country must permit the arbitrators to determine whether they have jurisdiction to hear the underlying dispute. Otherwise, resolution of the underlying dispute is delayed while the parties resolve in court whether the matter is properly decided by arbitration.

The venue must be a location that is a place where conventions or bilateral treaties will allow enforcement of the decision reached. As discussed earlier in this chapter, the conventions and treaties require support for arbitration as a dispute resolution method, and provide for the enforcement of foreign arbitration agreements and awards.

The status of these conventions and treaties in the country of venue must be carefully reviewed. For example, many countries, including the United States, require reciprocity by the local country in order for the enforcement provisions of the New York Convention and the Panama Convention to apply. The mere agreement to a convention is not enough; the enforcement provisions of the underlying treaty must be implemented under local law.

This location does not necessarily mean that all meetings and hearings related to the arbitration must take place there. In some cases, it may be useful to hold at least some of the meetings in the host country.

Where a foreign government is a party to the arbitration, however, the selection process must include consideration of whether the government will be likely to meddle or otherwise interfere in that location, and whether all parties will be confident that an unbiased, transparent decision has been reached in that geographical (and political) spot.

[4] Institution Selected for Arbitration

If the arbitration will use a specific institution for dispute resolution, that entity must be listed in the contract. For example, the ICC recommends the following: "All disputes arising in connection with the present contract shall be finally settled under the Rules of Conciliation and Arbitration of the International Chamber of Commerce by one or more arbitrators appointed in accordance with the said Rules." Alternatively, if an ad hoc approach will be used, the details of the process should be separately addressed.

[5] Selection of Arbitration Panel

The contract should specify the procedure for selection of the arbitration panel or the sole arbitrator if the parties decide not to use a panel. It is customary that either a sole arbitrator or a panel of three arbitrators conducts arbitration. If a panel is used, each party (if there are only two) typically selects an arbitrator, and then these arbitrators select a third panel member.

[6] Procedure

The procedure for the arbitration should be included in as much detail as possible. Among the provisions to consider are the following: how arbitration will be commenced, such as through issuance of a notice of arbitration to the other party; whether any rules of evidence or rules for discovery will be included; whether the decision will be confidential; and whether it will be in written form.

[7] Governing Language

Oddly, the failure to specify a language in which arbitration will be conducted is sometimes a source of friction among the parties. If not selected in the contract, it will be selected by the arbitrators. Including the designation of language in the contract will avoid unnecessary delays.

[8] Governing Law

As discussed above, the contract should specify the law that will govern the arbitration. This can be different from the law selected to govern the underlying contract.

Local counsel must be consulted to determine the ramifications of a choice of law. For example, many of the damages payable in a project finance transaction are liquidated damages. Laws relating to liquidated damages vary widely and must be considered in any choice of law decision. In addition, because laws change, the parties should consider use of a stabilization clause, which is a contract provision that requires application of the governing law in effect at the time of contract execution.

[9] Continuing Performance

An important consideration for a project financing is whether the parties must continue to perform the contractual obligations once an arbitration proceeding is commenced and while the arbitration proceeding is pending. In some situations, the parties agree to continue performance but not perform those obligations that are the subject of the dispute.

[10] Res Judicata

To the extent allowable by local law, the arbitration provisions should specify that final arbitration awards are final, binding, enforceable, and

DISPUTE RESOLUTION IN PROJECT FINANCE TRANSACTIONS

not subject to appeal. Otherwise, a disappointed party could pursue a new hearing in the judicial system.

This does not mean that an application to a court will never be needed. The parties should preserve the right to a court proceeding to seek temporary injunctive relief, to enforce an award for temporary or preliminary relief, to enforce an arbitral award demanding testimony of a witness or requiring submission of other evidence, and for registration of the judgment on the arbitration award.

CHAPTER THIRTY-TWO

MULTILATERAL AGENCY PROHIBITIONS ON ANTI-COMPETITIVE ACTIVITY

§ 32.01 INTRODUCTION

The word *bribery* carries with it different meanings, depending upon the values and practices of the country involved. In the West, bribery of governmental officials is viewed as economically inefficient, politically destabilizing, morally corrupt, and, of course, illegal. In other countries, bribery has been endemic – a necessary evil in accomplishing business goals. By 1977, the United States viewed bribery as no longer acceptable in the global marketplace. The U.S. Foreign Corrupt Practices Act,[1] which came on the heels of the Watergate and Lockheed scandals in the United States, made illegal the bribery of foreign officials to obtain or retain business. Yet, the United States stood alone in its efforts.

The effects of anti-bribery statutes are mixed. On the one hand, they provide an effective shield to a company against bribery attempts or threats; that is, the company can argue that bribes are illegal in its home country. Such illegality could potentially subject the officer or employee to criminal punishment, as well as embarrass the host country's government. On the other hand, unless parallel prohibitions are in place for foreign competitors, the prohibition places the company at a competitive disadvantage. At least one study suggested that U.S. companies lost almost $45 billion in contracts as a result of the prohibition.[2]

For these reasons, the internationalization of anti-bribery restrictions was a long-term goal of the United States, and later by other countries. By 1988, the U.S. Congress mandated that the United States attempt to negotiate anti-bribery restrictions at the multilateral level.[3]

---

[1] Foreign Corrupt Practices Act of 1977, Pub. L. No. 95–213, 91 Stat. 1494 (amended 1988, 1998), *codified at* 15 U.S.C. §§ 78dd-1, 78dd-2, 78ff(a), 78ff(c), 78m(b). The FCPA is discussed in Chapter 29.

[2] Statement of Michael Kantor, U.S. Trade Representative (Feb. 22, 1996).

[3] Omnibus Trade and Competition Act, Pub. L. No. 100–418, 102 Stat. 1107, 1415–25 (1988).

Ultimately, world opinion about the inefficiencies of bribery on economic and political systems, rather than Western business protestations or the mandates of the U.S. Congress, caused a call for curtailment of bribery and corruption, mandated by multilateral institutions.[4] In the early 1990s, scandals centering on extortion, bribery, and favoritism contributed to the instability of governments in many parts of the world. In Indonesia, for example, project finance utility deals supported by the ruling Suharto family were awarded without competitive bid or other transparency protections. World perceptions about bribery began to change. Rather than looking at anti-bribery laws as an attempt by the United States to export morals, bribery and political corruption became to be viewed as an irrational trade barrier that blocked access to new markets.

§ 32.02 PROCUREMENT GUIDELINES

[1] Generally
In general, competitive bidding is the preferred procurement procedure of multilateral agencies. Public bidding processes have several advantages for host governments. A bid process increases competition among potential providers of the goods or services, minimizes the cost of the solicited good or service, and fosters public support and credibility for the project by ensuring that the process is transparent and thereby free of bribes and other corruption. The competitive bid process, its advantages and its disadvantages, and the application of it to project finance, is discussed in Chapter 14.

[2] World Bank
In 1951, the World Bank introduced International Competitive Bidding as the procurement procedure for use in projects financed by it. These procedures, revised in the 1990s, establish nondiscriminatory specifications, selection criteria disclosure, and public bidding.[5] Failure to adhere to

this process can result in cancellation of the World Bank financing.

[3] Inter-American Development Bank
The Inter-American Development Bank strengthened its anti-corruption policies in 1998. The action reflected increased efforts by governments and multilateral institutions to fight against corruption as a part of the movement toward modernization of the state and consolidation of democratic rule.

The bank's procurement rules and procedures provide the IDB with the power to bar firms or individuals, temporarily or permanently, from future contracts if they have been involved in corrupt, fraudulent, coercive, or collusive behavior.[6] The bank can cancel or accelerate repayment of a portion of a loan or grant if there is evidence that the borrower or beneficiary has not taken adequate steps to halt corrupt practices.[7] To verify compliance, the bank added the ability to require that bidding documents include provisions that allow the IDB or its representatives to audit the records of suppliers and contractors participating in IDB-financed projects.[8] Finally, the bank has the right to accept "no bribery pledges," at the request of borrowing countries that commit contractors to comply with laws prohibiting corrupt practices in the country where the contracting takes place.[9]

[4] European Bank for Reconstruction and Development
Similarly, the European Bank for Reconstruction and Development issued guidelines in

---

[4] Paolo Mauro, *Corruption and Growth*, Q. J. Econ., August 1995, at 681, (comprehensive study relating corruption, investment rate, and growth).

[5] World Bank, *Guidelines: Procurement Under IBRD Loans and IDA Credits* (2004).

[6] Inter-American Development Bank, *Policies for the Procurement of Goods and Works Financed by the Inter-American Development Bank*, § 1.14 at 5–6 (2006). A *corrupt practice* is the offering, giving, receiving, or soliciting, directly or indirectly, of anything of value to influence the actions of another party. A *fraudulent practice* is any act or omission, including a misrepresentation, which misleads, or attempts to mislead, a party in order to obtain a financial or other benefit or to avoid an obligation. A *coercive practice* is impairing or harming, or threatening to impair or harm, directly or indirectly, any party or property of the party to influence the actions of a party. A *collusive practice* is an arrangement between two or more parties designed to achieve an improper purpose, including to influence improperly the actions of another party.

[7] *Id.* § 1.14(b) (iii) at 6.   [8] *Id.* § 1.14(d) at 7.

[9] *Id.* § 1.15 at 7.

1997.[10] These are guidelines only; they do not represent official policy. It is eight pages of text and sets forth a very concise summary of wise project development in any country. In addition to setting forth recommendations on relationships between a company and its customers, employees, suppliers, and its community, the guidelines discuss the proper relationship between a company and the government. The guidelines remind companies that the EBRD will require that they "deal with local and central government authorities in an arm's-length way without resorting to bribery or improper ways of influencing administrative decisions."[11] Its counsel on countries with emerging economies and countries in a state of "flux" are instructive:

> In countries where the laws, fiscal regimes and judicial systems are in a state of flux, these guidelines might sometimes be viewed as overly onerous or just not feasible. In such cases, it is better to engage in open and transparent dialogue with the authorities on the inappropriateness of certain provisions of the local laws than to take action that could create future liabilities and other problems.[12]

The restraint of the guidelines is remarkable, perhaps indicating a high level of confidence in the private sector to monitor itself and the governments in which they develop projects.

§ 32.03 ORGANIZATION OF AMERICAN STATES INTER-AMERICAN CONVENTION AGAINST CORRUPTION

The first international anti-corruption treaty was signed in 1996. Latin American countries joined to negotiate, and ultimately sign, the Inter-American Convention Against Corruption.[13] Effective in 1997, the treaty, which was subject to ratification, currently has thirty-four parties, including the United States.

The treaty, designed to combat corruption by governmental officials, requires member states to consider developing, maintaining, or strengthening its laws and regulations in relation to the following:

- Standards of conduct for the correct, honorable, and proper fulfillment of public functions. These standards shall be intended to prevent conflicts of interest and mandate the proper conservation and use of resources entrusted to government officials in the performance of their functions. These standards shall also establish measures and systems requiring government officials to report to appropriate authorities acts of corruption in the performance of public functions. Such measures should help preserve the public's confidence in the integrity of public servants and government processes.[14]

- Mechanisms to enforce these standards of conduct.[15]

- Instruction to government personnel to ensure proper understanding of their responsibilities and the ethical rules governing their activities.[16]

- Systems for registering the income, assets, and liabilities of persons who perform public functions in certain posts as specified by law and, where appropriate, for making such registrations public.[17]

- Systems of government hiring and procurement of goods and services that ensure the openness, equity, and efficiency of such systems.[18]

- Government revenue collection and control systems that deter corruption.[19]

- Laws that deny favorable tax treatment for any individual or corporation for expenditures made in violation of the anti-corruption laws of the States Parties.[20]

- Systems for protecting public servants and private citizens who, in good faith, report acts of corruption, including protection of their identities, in accordance with their Constitutions

---

[10] European Bank for Reconstruction and Development, *Guidelines for Sound Business Standards and Corporate Practices*, Publication No. 2829, 27/08/97 (Sept. 1997).

[11] *Id.* at 6.   [12] *Id.*

[13] Inter-American Convention Against Corruption, 35 I.L.M. 724 (March 29, 1996).

[14] Inter-American Convention Against Corruption, art. III, § 1, 35 I.L.M. 724, 728 (March 29, 1996).

[15] *Id.* § 2 at 728.   [16] *Id.* § 3 at 728.

[17] *Id.* § 4 at 728.   [18] *Id.* § 5 at 728.

[19] *Id.* § 6 at 728.   [20] *Id.* § 7 at 728.

and the basic principles of their domestic legal systems.[21]

- Oversight bodies with a view to implementing model mechanisms for preventing, detecting, punishing and eradicating corrupt acts.[22]
- Deterrents to the bribery of domestic and foreign government officials, such as mechanisms to ensure that publicly held companies and other types of associations maintain books and records which, in reasonable detail, accurately reflect the acquisition and disposition of assets, and have sufficient internal accounting controls to enable their officers to detect corrupt acts.[23]
- Mechanisms to encourage participation by civil society and nongovernmental organizations in efforts to prevent corruption.[24]
- The study of further preventive measures that take into account the relationship between equitable compensation and probity in public service.[25]

If a state party has not yet done so, it must adopt the necessary legislative or other measures to establish as criminal offenses under their domestic law any act of corruption.[26] "Acts of corruption," for this purpose and for purposes of the entire treaty is defined as:

a. The solicitation or acceptance, directly or indirectly, by a government official or a person who performs public functions, of any article of monetary value, or other benefit, such as a gift, favor, promise or advantage for himself or for another person or entity, in exchange for any act or omission in the performance of his public functions;

b. The offering or granting, directly or indirectly, to a government official or a person who performs public functions, of any article of monetary value, or other benefit, such as a gift, favor, promise or advantage for himself or for another person or entity, in exchange for any act or omission in the performance of his public functions;

c. Any act or omission in the discharge of his duties by a government official or a person who performs public functions for the purpose of illicitly obtaining benefits for himself or for a third party;

d. The fraudulent use or concealment of property derived from any of the acts referred to in this article; and

e. Participation as a principal, coprincipal, instigator, accomplice, or accessory after the fact, or in any other manner, in the commission or attempted commission of, or in any collaboration or conspiracy to commit, any of the acts referred to in this article.[27]

Recognizing the difficulty in proving the source of money or property as illegally obtained, the treaty includes the concept of "illicit enrichment," which it defines as "a significant increase in the assets of a government official that he cannot reasonably explain in relation to his lawful earnings during the performance of his functions."[28]

The treaty is transnational in effect. Each state is required to prohibit and punish bribes by its nationals, persons having their residence in its territory, and businesses domiciled there, to a government official of another member state, in exchange for any act or omission in the performance of an official's public functions.[29]

Interestingly, the treaty also offers direction to states party about additional protections that *should* be considered by them for addition as offenses under their laws. They are the following:

- The improper use by a government official or a person who performs public functions, for his own benefit or that of a third party, of any kind of classified or confidential information which that official or person who performs public functions has obtained because of, or in the performance of, his functions;[30]
- The improper use by a government official or a person who performs public functions, for his own benefit or that of a third party, of any kind of property belonging to the State or to any firm or institution in which the State has a proprietary interest, to which that official or person who performs public functions has access because of, or in the performance of, his functions;[31]
- Any act or omission by any person who, personally or through a third party, or acting as an intermediary, seeks to obtain a decision from

[21] *Id.* § 8 at 728.
[22] *Id.* § 9 at 728.
[23] *Id.* § 10 at 728.
[24] *Id.* § 11 at 729.
[25] *Id.* § 12 at 729.
[26] *Id.* § 7 at 730.
[27] *Id.* art. VI(1) at 729.
[28] *Id.* art. IX at 730.
[29] *Id.* art. VIII at 730.
[30] *Id.* art. XI, §1(a) at 730–31.
[31] *Id.* art. XI, §1(b) at 731.

a public authority whereby he illicitly obtains for himself or for another person any benefit or gain; whether or not such act or omission harms State property;[32] and

- The diversion by a government official, for purposes unrelated to those for which they were intended, for his own benefit or that of a third party, of any movable or immovable property, monies or securities belonging to the State, to an independent agency, or to an individual, that such official has received by virtue of his position for purposes of administration, custody or for other reasons.[33]

Each of the offenses is required to be extraditable offenses in any extradition treaty existing between or among the states parties.[34] If a state party makes extradition conditional on the existence of a treaty, and it receives a request for extradition from another state party with which it does not have an extradition treaty, the convention can form the legal basis for extradition.[35]

§ 32.04 COUNCIL OF EUROPE CRIMINAL LAW CONVENTION ON CORRUPTION

In 1999, the Council of Europe adopted a convention designed to stop corruption through bribes.[36] The convention requires each state party to criminalize intentional bribery, direct or indirect, whether of a governmental official or an official of an international organization.[37]

The convention adopts a very broad concept of corruption, as follows:

- when committed intentionally, the promising, offering or giving by any person, directly or indirectly, of any undue advantage to any of its public officials, for himself or herself or for anyone else, for him or her to act or refrain from acting in the exercise of his or her functions;[38]
- when committed intentionally, the request or receipt by any of its public officials, directly or indirectly, of any undue advantage, for himself or herself or for anyone else, or the acceptance

of an offer or a promise of such an advantage, to act or refrain from acting in the exercise of his or her functions;[39]

- the conduct referred to in Articles 2 and 3, when involving any person who is a member of any domestic public assembly exercising legislative or administrative powers;[40]
- the conduct referred to in Articles 2 and 3, when involving a public official of any other state;[41]
- the conduct referred to in Articles 2 and 3, when involving any person who is a member of any public assembly exercising legislative or administrative powers in any other State;[42]
- when committed intentionally in the course of business activity, the promising, offering or giving, directly or indirectly, of any undue advantage to any persons who direct or work for, in any capacity, private sector entities, for themselves or for anyone else, for them to act, or refrain from acting, in breach of their duties;[43]
- when committed intentionally, in the course of business activity, the request or receipt, directly or indirectly, by any persons who direct or work for, in any capacity, private sector entities, of any undue advantage or the promise thereof for themselves or for anyone else, or the acceptance of an offer or a promise of such an advantage, to act or refrain from acting in breach of their duties;[44]
- conduct referred to in Articles 2 and 3, when involving any official or other contracted employee, within the meaning of the staff regulations, of any public international or supranational organization or body of which the Party is a member, and any person, whether seconded or not, carrying out functions corresponding to those performed by such officials or agents;[45]
- the conduct referred to in Article 4 when involving any members of parliamentary assemblies of international or supranational organizations of which the Party is a member;[46]
- conduct referred to in Articles 2 and 3 involving any holders of judicial office or officials of any international court whose jurisdiction is accepted by the Party;[47]

---

[32] *Id.* art. XI, §1(c) at 731.   [33] *Id.* art. XI, §1(d) at 731.
[34] *Id.* art. XIII, § 2 at 731.   [35] *Id.* art. XIII, § 3 at 731.
[36] Council of Europe Criminal Law Convention on Corruption, European Treaties ETS No. 173, 38 I.L.R. 505 (January 27, 1999).
[37] *Id.* ch. 2 at 506.   [38] *Id.* ch. 2, art. 3 at 506.

[39] *Id.* ch. 2, art. 3 at 506.   [40] *Id.* ch. 2, art. 4 at 507.
[41] *Id.* ch. 2, art. 5, at 507.   [42] *Id.* ch. 2, art. 6 at 507.
[43] *Id.* ch. 2, art. 7 at 507.   [44] *Id.* ch. 2, art. 8 at 507.
[45] *Id.* ch. 2, art. 9 at 507.   [46] *Id.* ch. 2, art. 10 at 507.
[47] *Id.* ch. 2, art. 11 at 507.

- when committed intentionally, the promising, giving or offering, directly or indirectly, of any undue advantage to anyone who asserts or confirms that he or she is able to exert an improper influence over the decision-making of any person referred to in Articles 2, 4 to 6, and 9 to 11 in consideration thereof, whether the undue advantage is for himself or herself or for anyone else, as well as the request, receipt or the acceptance of the offer or the promise of such an advantage, in consideration of that influence, whether or not the influence is exerted or whether or not the supposed influence leads to the intended result.[48]

The convention seeks to cover money laundering of the bribery proceeds,[49] aiding and abetting the offenses described,[50] and committing, concealing or disguising the offences through record keeping or false or incomplete invoices.[51]

Importantly, the convention does not excuse corporations and their officials from responsibility. It requires that legal persons be held liable for the criminal offences of active bribery, trading in influence, and money laundering established under the convention:

- committed for their benefit by any natural person, acting either individually or as part of an organ of the legal person, who has a leading position within the legal person, based on:
  - a power of representation of the legal person; or
  - an authority to take decisions on behalf of the legal person; or
  - an authority to exercise control within the legal person;
- as well as for involvement of such a natural person as accessory or instigator in the above-mentioned offences.[52]

In addition, criminal liability applies where the lack of supervision or control by a natural person referred to in Paragraph 1 has made possible the commission of the criminal offences mentioned in Paragraph 1 for the benefit of that legal person by a natural person under its authority.[53] Thus,

as discussed in Chapter 29, local agents of a corporation, as well as employees, must be carefully controlled by businesses.

§ 32.05 ORGANISATION FOR ECONOMIC CO-OPERATION AND DEVELOPMENT (OECD) RECOMMENDATION OF THE COUNCIL ON THE TAX DEDUCTIBILITY OF BRIBES TO FOREIGN PUBLIC OFFICIALS

In 1996, the Organisation for Economic Co-operation and Development asked member countries to prohibit any favorable tax treatment of bribes.[54] Specifically, the council recommended that member countries that do not disallow the deductibility of bribes to foreign public officials deny this deductibility. The council stopped short of recommending that bribes to foreign public officials be treated as illegal.[55]

§ 32.06 ORGANISATION FOR ECONOMIC CO-OPERATION AND DEVELOPMENT (OECD) CONVENTION ON COMBATING BRIBERY OF FOREIGN PUBLIC OFFICIALS IN INTERNATIONAL BUSINESS TRANSACTIONS

Three years after the recommendations by the OECD to deny tax deductibility of bribe payments, the council adopted the Convention on Combating Bribery of Foreign Public Officials in International Business Transactions,[56] which entered into force on February 15, 1999.[57] The

---

[48] Id. ch. 2, art. 12 at 508.
[49] Id. ch. 2, art. 13 at 508.
[50] Id. ch. 2, art. 15 at 507.
[51] Id. ch. 2, art. 14 at 507.
[52] Id. ch. 2, art. 18, ¶ 1 at 509.
[53] Id. ch. 2, art. 18, ¶ 2 at 509.

[54] Organisation for Economic Co-operation and Development Council, Re: C(96)27/FINAL on the Tax Deductibility of Bribes to Foreign Public Officials, 35 I.L.M. 1311 (April 17, 1996). See 1996 Revisions to the International Chamber of Commerce Rules of Conduct on Extortion and Bribery in International Business Transactions, 35 I.L.M. 1306 (1996); Organisation for Economic Co-operation and Development Council Recommendation on Bribery in International Business Transactions, 33 I.L.M. 1389 (May 27, 1994).
[55] Id. at 1312.
[56] Organisation for Economic Co-operation and Development Council Convention on Combating Bribery of Foreign Public Officials in International Business Transactions; 37 I.L.M. 1 (Dec. 18, 1997).
[57] The twenty-nine members of the OECD are Australia, Austria, Belgium, Canada, Czech Republic, Denmark, Finland,

OECD Convention recommends that member states sanction *foreign* official bribery to obtain a business advantage.[58] Thus, it applies only to bribery of officials of non-member countries. It recommends that member countries regulate books and records so that the criminalization can be monitored.[59] Thus, it seeks to sanction active bribers and their accomplices, while establishing a system of preventative measures.

The convention defines bribery of a foreign public official as follows:

- Intentionally to offer, promise or give any undue pecuniary or other advantage, whether directly or through intermediaries, to a foreign public official, for that official or for a third party, in order that the official act or refrain from acting in relation to the performance of official duties, in order to obtain or retain business or other improper advantage in the conduct of international business;[60]
- Complicity in, including incitement, aiding and abetting, or authorisation of an act of bribery of a foreign public official shall be a criminal offence. Attempt and conspiracy to bribe a foreign public official shall be criminal offences to the same extent as attempt and conspiracy to bribe a public official of that Party.[61]

A *foreign public official* means "any person holding a legislative, administrative or judicial office of a foreign country, whether appointed or elected; any person exercising a public function for a foreign country, including for a public agency or public enterprise; and any official or agent of a public international organisation."[62] *Foreign country* includes all levels and subdivisions of government, from national to local.[63] The phrase "act or refrain from acting in relation to the performance of official duties" includes any use of the public official's position, whether or not within the official's authorized competence.[64]

§ 32.07 EUROPEAN UNION CONVENTION ON THE FIGHT AGAINST CORRUPTION INVOLVING OFFICIALS OF THE EUROPEAN COMMUNITIES OR OFFICIALS OF THE MEMBER STATES OF THE EUROPEAN UNION

The European Union has approved a Convention on the Fight Against Corruption Involving Officials of the European Communities or Officials of the Member States of the European Union, which is subject to ratification by the member countries.[65] The convention would criminalize passive and active corruption. *Passive* corruption is the deliberate action of an official, who, directly or through an intermediary, requests or receives advantages of any kind whatsoever, for himself or for a third party, or accepts a promise of such an advantage, to act or refrain from acting in accordance with his duty or in the exercise of his functions in breach of his official duties constitutes passive corruption. *Active* corruption is the deliberate action of whosoever promises or gives, directly or through an intermediary, an advantage of any kind whatsoever to an official for himself or for a third party for him to act or refrain from acting in accordance with his duty or in the exercise of his functions in breach of his official duties constitutes active corruption.

§ 32.08 UNITED NATIONS

The United Nations policy against bribery in international business transactions was announced in 1996.[66] The resolution calls on Member States to enact laws and regulations that cause

---

France, Germany, Greece, Hungary, Iceland, Ireland, Italy, Japan, Korea, Luxembourg, Mexico, the Netherlands, New Zealand, Norway, Poland, Portugal, Spain, Sweden, Switzerland, Turkey, United Kingdom, and the United States. There are five non-member signatories: Argentina, Brazil, Bulgaria, Chile, and the Slovak Republic.

[58] *Id.* art. 1(2) at 4.   [59] *Id.* art. 8 at 5.
[60] *Id.* art. 1(1) at 4.   [61] *Id.* art. 1(2) at 4.
[62] *Id.* art. 1(4) at 4.   [63] *Id.*
[64] *Id.*

[65] European Union Convention on the Fight Against Corruption Involving Officials of the European Communities or Officials of the Member States of the European Union, O.J. No. C195, 25.06.1997, 35 I.L.R. 1311 (May 26, 1997).
[66] UN General Assembly Resolution 51/191, 36 I.L.M. 1043 (Dec. 2, 1996) (UN Declaration Against Corruption and Bribery in International Commercial Transactions). *See also* UN General Assembly Resolution 51/59, 36 I.L.M. 1039 (Dec. 12, 1996) (Action Against Corruption) (1997); and UN General Assembly Resolution 3514 (XXX), 15 I.L.M. 180 (Dec. 15, 1975) (Measures Against Corrupt Practices of International and other Corporations, their Intermediaries, and Others Involved). *See* Draft United Nations Code of Conduct on Transnational Corporations, 23 I.L.M. 602 (June, 1984).

the criminalization of bribes for economic gain; to deny tax benefits for bribes;[67] to develop or maintain accounting standards that allow for the detection of bribes and that encourage transparency;[68] to examine establishing illicit enrichment by public officials or elected representatives as an offence;[69] to cooperate and afford assistance in connection with criminal investigations and other legal proceedings brought in respect of corruption and bribery in international commercial transactions;[70] to facilitate access to documents and records about transactions and about identities of persons engaged in bribery in international commercial transactions;[71] and to ensure that bank secrecy provisions do not impede or hinder criminal investigations or other legal proceedings relating to corruption, bribery, or related illicit practices in international commercial transactions, and that full cooperation is extended to governments that seek information on such transactions.[72]

The resolution defines bribery as follows:

Bribery may include, inter alia, the following elements:

a. The offer, promise or giving of any payment, gift or other advantage, directly or indirectly, by any private or public corporation, including a transnational corporation, or individual from a State to any public official or elected representative of another country as undue consideration for performing or refraining from the performance of that official's or representative's duties in connection with an international commercial transaction;

b. The soliciting, demanding, accepting or receiving, directly or indirectly, by any public official or elected representative of a State from any private or public corporation, including a transnational corporation, or individual from another country of any payment, gift or other advantage, as undue consideration for performing or refraining from the performance of that official's or representative's duties in connection with an international commercial transaction.[73]

§ 32.09 INTERNATIONAL CHAMBER OF COMMERCE RULES OF CONDUCT TO COMBAT EXTORTION AND BRIBERY

The International Chamber of Commerce has long been active in promoting the internationalization of anti-bribery and anti-corruption laws. In 1996, this body approved recommendations to governments on elimination of extortion and bribery in international business transactions.[74] The ICC called on governments to criminalize all aspects of both the giving and the taking of bribes including promises and solicitation of bribes and to enforce legislation in this area.

Its recommendations are interesting in that they are made from the perspective of the business community. For example, on economic authorizations, the ICC states:

When laying down any economic regulations or legislation, governments should, as far as possible, minimise [sic] the use of systems under which the carrying out of business requires the issuance of individual authorisations [sic], permits, etc. Experience shows that such systems offer scope for extortion and bribery. This is because decisions involving the issue of permits or authorisations are frequently taken in ways which make it almost impossible to ensure effective control and supervision. Where individual permits and authorisations remain in place, governments should take appropriate measures to prevent their abuse.

To misquote Shakespeare, "The first thing we do is kill all the permit officials."

The report also makes recommendations to the international business community. These Rules of Conduct are intended as a method of self-regulation by international business.[75] This voluntary code is reproduced at the end of this chapter. It should provide an effective checklist for project finance negotiators, who may find this easier to understand than the U.S. Foreign Corrupt Practices Act or the myriad of multinational conventions, treaties, and laws.

---

[67] *Id.* ¶ 4 at 1047.
[68] *Id.* ¶ 5 at 1047.
[69] *Id.* ¶ 7 at 1047.
[70] *Id.* ¶ 8 at 1047.
[71] *Id.* ¶ 9 at 1047.
[72] *Id.* ¶ 10 at 1047.
[73] *Id.* ¶ 3 at 1036.

[74] International Chamber of Commerce, Extortion and Bribery in International Business Transactions, 1996 Revisions to the ICC Rules of Conduct, 6–16, 35 I.L.M. 1306 (March 26, 1996).
[75] *Id.* at 1309.

INTERNATIONAL CHAMBER OF COMMERCE

RULES OF CONDUCT TO COMBAT EXTORTION AND BRIBERY

INTRODUCTION

These Rules of Conduct are intended as a method of self-regulation by international business, and they should also be supported by governments. Their voluntary acceptance by business enterprises will not only promote high standards of integrity in business transactions, whether between enterprises and public bodies or between enterprises themselves, but will also form a valuable defensive protection to those enterprises which are subjected to attempts at extortion.

These Rules of Conduct are of a general nature constituting what is considered good commercial practice in the matters to which they relate but are without direct legal effect. They do not derogate from applicable local laws, and since national legal systems are by no means uniform, they must be read mutatis mutandis subject to such systems.

The business community objects to all forms of extortion and bribery. It is recognised, however, that under current conditions in some parts of the world, an effective programme against extortion and bribery may have to be implemented in stages. The highest priority should be directed to ending large-scale extortion and bribery involving politicians and senior officials. These represent the greatest threat to democratic institutions and cause the gravest economic distortions. Small payments to low-level officials to expedite routine approvals are not condoned. However, they represent a lesser problem. When extortion and bribery at the top levels is curbed, government leaders can be expected to take steps to clean up petty corruption.

BASIC PRINCIPLE

All enterprises should conform to the relevant laws and regulations of the countries in which they are established and in which they operate, and should observe both the letter and the spirit of these Rules of Conduct.

For the purposes of these Rules of Conduct, the term "enterprise" refers to any person or entity engaged in business, whether or not organised for profit, including any entity controlled by a State or a territorial subdivision thereof; it includes, where the context so indicates, a parent or a subsidiary.

BASIC RULES

Article 1: Extortion

No one may, directly or indirectly, demand or accept a bribe.

Article 2: Bribery and "Kickbacks"

a. No enterprise may, directly or indirectly, offer or give a bribe and any demands for such a bribe must be rejected.

b. Enterprises should not (i) kick back any portion of a contract payment to employees of the other contracting party, or (ii) utilise other techniques, such as subcontracts, purchase orders or consulting agreements, to channel payments to government officials, to employees of the other contracting party, their relatives or business associates.

Article 3: Agents

Enterprises should take measures reasonably within their power to ensure:

a) that any payment made to any agent represents no more than an appropriate remuneration for legitimate services rendered by such agent;

b) that no part of any such payment is passed on by the agent as a bribe or otherwise in contravention of these Rules of Conduct; and

c) that they maintain a record of the names and terms of employment of all agents who are retained by them in connection with transactions with public bodies or State enterprises. This record should be available for inspection by auditors and, upon specific request, by appropriate, duly-authorised governmental authorities under conditions of confidentiality.

Article 4: Financial Recording and Auditing

a) All financial transactions must be properly and fairly recorded in appropriate books of account available for inspection by boards of directors, if applicable, or a corresponding body, as well as auditors.

b) There must be no "off the books" or secret accounts, nor may any documents be issued which do not properly and fairly record the transactions to which they relate.

c) Enterprises should take all necessary measures to establish independent systems of auditing in order to bring to light any transactions which contravene the present Rules of Conduct. Appropriate corrective action must then be taken.

Article 5: Responsibilities of Enterprises

The board of directors or other body with ultimate responsibility for the enterprise should:

a) take reasonable steps, including the establishment and maintenance of proper systems of control aimed at preventing any payments being made by or on behalf of the enterprise which contravene these Rules of Conduct;

b) periodically review compliance with these Rules of Conduct and establish procedures for obtaining appropriate reports for the purposes of such review; and

c) take appropriate action against any director or employee contravening these Rules of Conduct.

Article 6: Political Contributions

Contributions to political parties or committees or to individual politicians may only be made in accordance with the applicable law, and all requirements for public disclosure of such contributions shall be fully complied with. All such contributions must be reported to senior corporate management.

Article 7: Company Codes

These Rules of Conduct being of a general nature, enterprises should, where appropriate, draw up their own codes consistent with the ICC Rules and apply them to the particular circumstances in which their business is carried out. Such codes may usefully include examples and should enjoin employees or agents who find themselves subjected to any form of extortion or bribery immediately to report the same to senior corporate management. Companies should develop clear policies, guidelines, and training programmes for implementing and enforcing the provisions of their codes.

CHAPTER THIRTY-THREE

MERCHANT FACILITIES – PROJECT FINANCE WITHOUT CONTRACTUALLY ASSURED REVENUE FLOWS

OVERVIEW

§ 33.01 DEFINITION OF MERCHANT FACILITY

The term *merchant facility* is generally used to refer to a facility financed using project finance principles, except that long-term off-take contracts are not used to eliminate the market risk. Rather, project viability is based on the market for project output and forecasts of future market conditions because project output is sold into the commodity market and sold at a price at or below the market price.[1] As a facility financed using project finance techniques, the project company will be a special-purpose, stand-alone entity that does not have access to the balance sheet of its owners. The highly leveraged, nonrecourse nature of project finance, coupled with commodity risk and the inherent inability to stockpile electricity, combine to make these pure merchant power plant investments speculative.

Interestingly, projects financed as nonmerchant facilities often face these risks. For example, a project financed with a long-term contract involuntarily becomes a merchant plant if that contract is terminated. Similarly, a project that loses a regulatory benefit because of a change in law or a failure to comply with regulatory requirements can also become subject to merchant power risks.

In the United States, power projects are sometimes financed without firm, long-term power purchase contracts in place. Instead, the project sponsor and lender rely on demand in the U.S. power market to produce demand for the project output. In some cases, short-term power purchase contracts are used to mitigate some of the market risk.

There are several market conditions in the United States that have combined to allow some development of merchant power plants. Foremost is the attractiveness of peak margin opportunities. Other factors include electric utility industry deregulation, more open (transparent) wholesale power pricing, load growth and predicted new capacity shortfalls, the uncertainty surrounding nuclear power, inefficient and unreliable existing peaking generation, and transmission bottlenecks. News of power shortages during peak periods and extreme climate conditions are not uncommon in the United States. The challenge for the financier of the merchant power project is whether these conditions are

---

[1] *See generally* Peter N. Rigby, *Merchant Power Plants: Project Financing Criteria*, 5 J. PROJECT FINANCE 27 (Spring 1999); Christopher M. Dymond & Richard A. Sturges, *Financing Merchant Power: USGen's Portfolio Approach*, 5 J. PROJECT FIN. 43 (Spring 1999).

near-term, high-margin opportunities or whether the market conditions will continue to exist in the long term to the degree needed to ensure project viability.

The degree of market risk associated with a merchant project varies based on the type of power project. For example, a peak-load facility has an extremely high degree of revenue uncertainty. Demand for a peak-load facility's power is dependent on such unknowable (although arguably predictable using statistical analysis) factors as weather, maintenance schedules and unplanned maintenance of other power plants, and downed transmission lines.

Similarly, merchant power plants have been financed in the United Kingdom, Latin America, and Australia. The nature of risks and financing structures varies by the extent of deregulation of the electricity sector and the way independent power is developing in each country.

The recent experience with financing of merchant power plants has revealed the speculativeness of these projects. Highly leveraged projects without long-term power contracts continue to be difficult to finance on a project finance basis. This difficulty is reflected in the higher probability that merchant power projects will receive a speculative-grade debt rating, with higher debt costs. These higher costs may result in a merchant project that is simply noncompetitive in some markets. As a result, some developers have proceeded to finance these projects on their balance sheets, not with project finance debt structures.

§ 33.02 MARKET RISK

Market risk is one of the most difficult risks to analyze in a project financing. There are myriad market inputs that are known to affect demand and price for a project's output. These known factors are dwarfed by the potential future risks. For these reasons, classic project finance techniques require that long-term, fixed-price contracts with a creditworthy entity be in place to ensure revenue predictability. In a merchant project, however, such contracts are not used.

The stability of long-term contracts is exchanged for a business model that analyzes market risk and reaches conclusions that are sufficiently predictable to permit a financing or investment. The analysis of market risk for a merchant project is similar to that used in any new business model. That is, the market is analyzed to determine the price, supply, and demand for the product, and the effect of various inputs on that price, supply, and demand. Because the analysis is forward-looking, seemingly pessimistic analysis is needed.

Short-term power purchase contracts are sometimes a part of the model. These contracts, which may have a term of two to five years, reduce market risk for a portion of the project's output. For example, project debt documents can require that short-term contracts be in effect, with a term of two to five years on a rolling basis, throughout the term of the debt. The documents could be structured so that the revenue associated with these contracts match the project's operating costs, debt service, or some other desired cost, thereby providing the project with less market risk.

In addition to the use of short-term contracts, other structures exist to reduce market risk. For example, some merchant power projects rely on a captive host for part of the project's viability. Long-term energy service agreements, under which the project supplies the host with steam and electricity, help stabilize the cash flow available to pay operating costs and debt service. If the host is creditworthy, and significant contractual protections exist to protect the project if the host closes its plant, this technique can reduce market exposure significantly. This is particularly true when the contract covers most of the debt term, thereby subjecting the project lender to significant merchant risk only during the later years of a project, when debt amortization should be significantly less burdensome.

§ 33.03 MANAGEMENT OF COMMODITY RISK

[1] Generally

Many merchant projects are presented with the challenge of managing commodity risk. *Commodity risk* is the general term for the uncertainty that accompanies a project's inputs for project operation and the output produced. Examples include the products necessary for project operation, such as fuel, and the product or service actually produced and sold by the project, such as electricity. Various techniques to manage these risks include contractual protections, such as long-term hedges, and linking inputs to outputs. Also financial protections can be used for risk management, such as reserve funds for commodity costs, subordination of limited project expenses to debt service, and mandatory capital contributions by project sponsors based on increases in commodity costs (so-called cash calls).

[2] Long-Term Contracts

Of course, the primary mechanism for managing commodity risk is the long-term, fixed-price contract. These are discussed in Chapter 16.

[3] Linking Inputs and Outputs

The danger inherent in a long-term commodity input contract is that the contract price paid by the project company under the contract will be more than the future market price. In a competitive marketplace for the project output, this could result in a reduction in project revenues because project competitors, experiencing the same lower commodity costs, can charge less for the output. In common terms, there is the absence of a linkage between project inputs and outputs. In a merchant project, long-term commodity contracts should generally include provisions that permit the commodity price to be renegotiated, within certain limitations, to maintain the pricing margins necessary for a successful project. A merchant project does not typically enjoy the same linkage protections that are found in a classic project financing with long-term output purchase agreements, where the price of the output is tied (or linked) to the price of the underlying inputs.

[4] Reserve Funds

Reserve funds are one of the most common forms of credit enhancement, both in project finance loans and in traditional asset-based financing. A reserve fund is an account mandated by the debt documentation for the purpose of setting aside funds designed for use to ameliorate the effects of a project risk. The account can be funded from the construction budget, equity contributions, a draw on a letter of credit, a call on a guarantee,

project cash flow, or any combination of these sources. Funds on deposit can then be used to offset the effects on the project of some increase in cost, such as an increase in interest or fuel costs, or some shortfall in anticipated project revenue. The funds on deposit are typically unavailable for any other use unless the consent of the project lender is obtained. If funds are withdrawn from the account, the loan documents require that the account be replenished, until the risk is minimized to the extent that the reserve account is no longer necessary. For example, as project debt is amortized to lower amounts, reserve account minimum balances are often decreased or eliminated.

[5] Cash Calls

A *cash call* is the informal term applied to a mandatory infusion of equity or subordinated debt to a project company for the purpose of offsetting the effects of a project risk that has materialized. The loan documents will require such a call when the effects of the change in the project jeopardize the ability of the project company to pay debt service and operating costs. For example, if fuel costs for a project increase beyond a level agreed upon between the lender and project company, additional cash will be needed to offset the increase. The use of the proceeds of the cash call will depend on the specifics of the project and can take various forms, including funding of a reserve account; immediate payoff of a portion of the project debt, thereby reducing debt service obligations; or the simple application of the proceeds to pay the increased costs. The exact use of the proceeds of a cash call depends upon such factors as the amount of debt outstanding, anticipated length of time the project will experience the increased cost, and the overall financial health of the project.

[6] Subordination of Project Costs to Debt Service

Another technique used to address project risk is the subordination of certain project costs to the project debt. For example, a supplier of a project input, such as fuel, may be asked to forgo the receipt of a portion of its payment in certain negotiated scenarios. These subordinated costs would be paid, if at all, in the future when debt service payments and funding of reserve accounts are no longer in jeopardy. The terms of the subordination are carefully negotiated with project lenders.

[7] Hedging Strategies

Various hedging strategies available in the derivative markets can be employed to reduce commodity-pricing risk. These include options, sways, forwards, and futures. However, the cost of managing a hedging program at the project level is significant.

[8] The Commodity Supplier as Project Partner

Finally, the project owned by a commodity supplier, or the project in which such a supplier is a partner, can greatly reduce commodity price risk. The commodity supplied can be priced at or near production cost, with profits generated at the output level of the project.

§ 33.04 MANAGEMENT OF COMMODITY OUTPUT RISK

The marketing and pricing of output produced at a merchant facility is fundamental to the success of the project because the project output is not priced at closing under a long-term contract. In a merchant power plant, for example, the project sponsors must have access to a trading and marketing strategy that reduces volatility of project revenues. Where the project sponsors are not expert in this area, a viable out-sourcing strategy must generally be in place.

§ 33.05 LOAN COVENANTS FOR THE MERCHANT PROJECT

Because of the cash flow risks inherent in the market price uncertainty of merchant projects, merchant project lenders require protective covenants designed to address market and commodity risks specifically. These covenants are generally more restrictive than those typically required for non-merchant plant project financings. They include higher debt service coverage ratios before profit distributions can be made to project sponsors, as well as cash traps and reserve accounts designed to protect the project from revenue shortfalls that result in less cash flow available to service debt.

A CHECKLIST OF DUE DILIGENCE CONSIDERATIONS FOR A PROJECT FINANCING

Every project finance transaction presents its own risks and areas of needed due diligence. This checklist is designed to provide a general, yet inclusive, list of areas that should be considered as the project is developed and financed.

The Project Sponsor

1. Who are the project sponsors, what are the ownership interests in the project company, and what is their financial status?

2. Are any of the project sponsors governmentally owned? multilateral or bilateral agencies?

3. What experience does each project sponsor have with the development, construction, start-up, and operation of similar projects? in the host country?

4. What will each project sponsor contribute to the project? equity? development experience? construction and start-up expertise? technology? operating abilities? host-government experience?

5. What management control does each of the project sponsors have in the project company? What are the vote allocations? Is there one partner with veto power?

6. What are the income, loss, and capital contribution allocations of the partners?

7. What limited recourse liability does each project sponsor have? construction cost overrun? others? Does each have the creditworthiness to perform their obligations?

8. What rights does each project sponsor have to sell its interest in the project company?

9. What restrictions do the laws of the host country place on equity ownership of the project?

The Project Site – Physical and Geographical

1. Where is the project site located geographically?

2. What is the terrain on which the site will be developed?

3. What is the terrain of access roads, fuel storage areas, and other important elements of the project?

4. Consider the implications of mountains, valleys, deserts, wetlands, rain forests, jungles, swamps, rivers, lakes, flood areas, and other geographic and topological characteristics.

The Infrastructure – Existing and Needed

1. What is the existing and needed infrastructure necessary to access the site?

2. What is the condition and weight tolerance of roads, road shoulders, intersections, and bridges?

3. What is the condition and gauge of railways?

4. What is the depth of waterways? Are there seasonal variations in the depth restricting navigability?

5. What is the condition of harbors and ports?

6. What is the quantity and quality of water at the project site for construction and operation? Are water treatment facilities needed?

7. What is the quantity and quality of sewage facilities?

8. What is the available access to telephone service?

9. What is the available access to electricity and natural gas?

Political Considerations

1. What tax laws and regulations affect the project?

2. How are profits and capital repatriated?

3. What currency and exchange controls apply?

4. What is the regulatory framework under which the project must operate?

5. How will privatization programs affect the project?

6. What is the host country's ability to provide guarantees for a project financing?

7. Are implementation agreements necessary to provide a stable environment for a project financing?

Economic Considerations

1. What is the country's foreign trade and balance of payments?

2. How do trade alliances and relationships of the host country affect the project?

3. What are the general relationships between labor and management?

4. How do the public and private sectors interact in the economy?

Legal and Regulatory Considerations

1. What are the specific laws and regulations applicable to the project?

2. What laws and regulations affect investment in the project? Are there investment limitations applicable to foreign investors?

3. What is the privatization program of the host country? If not yet applied to the industry in which the project operates, how could future privatization affect the project, including project contracts?

4. What type of business organization is required for the project company (corporation, partnership, limited liability company, other)?

5. What governmental approvals, permits, licenses, concessions, filings, and other governmental actions are required for the project and each of the project participants?

Overall Financial and Sensitivity Analysis

1. Does the project construction budget include the costs of development, infrastructure development, site, construction, equipment installation, interest during construction, start-up, financing, legal, consultant, and working capital?

2. Are all assumptions used in preparation of the construction budget and financial projections reasonable, including interest rates, foreign exchange, inflation, fuel price escalation, raw material price escalation, construction schedule, and maintenance schedule?

3. Do the financial projections include the terms and sources of all debt financing and equity, with the respective interest rates and equity returns?

4. Do the construction budget and projections reflect sufficient equity and standby equity?

5. Does the creditworthiness of any major project participant require additional credit support?

Construction-Period Support by Project Sponsors

1. What are the funding commitments of each of the project sponsors during the project development period?

2. What are the funding commitments of each of the project sponsors during the project construction period?

3. If there is more than one project sponsor, is the funding liability joint and several?

4. What are the conditions to these funding commitments?

5. What events trigger the funding obligations? Are the events consistently defined in the financing documents?

6. If a construction cost overrun occurs, what are the funding obligations of the project sponsors?

Other Construction-Period Support

1. Is there a construction period cost overrun credit facility, available to fund construction cost overruns?

2. If so, what are the conditions to use of the proceeds of the construction period cost overrun facility?

3. Is the construction cost overrun facility available to be used before, after, or simultaneously with additional equity contributions?

4. Has the contractor agreed to a retainage of 5 percent to 10 percent of construction contract price payments? Can this be converted to subordinated debt if the project is in need of additional money due to cost overruns?

Construction Contingencies

1. Is the amount of the construction contingency in the project's construction budget adequate in comparison with similarly situated projects?

2. What conditions exist to the allocation of contingency budget amounts to cost overruns?

3. What are the potential cost overruns not addressed in firm price contracts, contingency funding obligations, or other support mechanisms?

Potential Sources of Construction Cost Overruns

1. Have the construction costs been verified by an independent consultant? How reliable is the cost estimation?

2. What assumptions have been made in determining the construction-period budget (interest rates, inflation, start-up and testing costs, delays)?

3. Are there any related facilities that must be constructed and in operation during the construction period, such as infrastructure, water processing facilities, docks)?

The Construction Contract

1. Has a firm price, fixed completion date construction contract with performance guarantees been executed?

2. What is excluded from the firm price?

3. Who is the contractor and what is its experience and resources with regard to similar projects in the host country?

4. Who are the subcontractors and vendors, and what are their experience and resources with regard to similar projects in the host country?

5. Is the construction contract for the entire facility? If not, how will the contractors be coordinated?

6. Does the scope of work adequately describe the project?

7. What is excluded from the scope of work and retained as a responsibility of the project company?

8. Is the construction schedule realistic?

9. Does sufficient local labor exist near the project site? If not, what housing developments are necessary?

10. Is the local labor collectively organized? What is the recent and historical experience with the relationship of labor to management?

11. In what currency are the price and damages denominated?

12. If export-import financing is a potential source of funds, do the contractor and its subcontractors and vendors satisfy the relevant source criteria?

13. Are the delay liquidated damages adequate to compensate the project company for a completion delay (debt service, contract penalties)?

14. Are the performance guarantees acceptable?

15. Are liquidated damages payable for the contractor's failure to perform at guaranteed levels sufficient to compensate the project company for reduced project capacity, increased operating costs, and the like?

16. Is credit enhancement necessary to support the creditworthiness of the contractor, such as a guarantee, bond, or letter of credit?

17. Is the force majeure provision integrated with the other project contracts?

Input Agreements

1. Is the input price firm? If not, is it reasonably predictable based on supply sources and historical and future expectations about pricing and supply?

2. What is excluded from the firm price?

3. Are price escalators, floors, and ceilings reasonable?

4. Are escalators based on indices that are market driven or politically driven?

5. If the input supply is owned or regulated by the host government, are there any conditions under which the price could change or the contract be cancelled?

6. Who is the input supplier, and what is its experience and resources with regard to similar projects in the host country?

7. Is the input contract for the entire input supply needed by the project? If not, how will the additional needs be provided?

8. Is the contract term sufficient to provide input price predictability to the project?

9. Does the description of input quality and characteristics adequately describe the project needs, particularly so that neither the contractor nor the operator are excused from performance guarantees due to poor input quality or characteristics?

10. Is the delivery schedule realistic?

11. What alternative supply sources are there, and what is the availability and cost of these alternative supplies?

12. In what currency are the price and damages denominated?

13. Must deliveries begin on a specified date? If so, and the date is missed, is the contractor

obligated to pay contract damages to the input supplier?

14. If the input is not delivered, is the supplier obligated to pay liquidated damages or other damages to the project? If so, will these compensate the project for any increased input costs?

15. Is the force majeure provision integrated with the other project contracts?

16. Is credit enhancement necessary to support the creditworthiness of the supplier, such as a guarantee or letter of credit?

17. If the host government owns the input supply, is a host-government guarantee needed?

18. What on-site storage needs does the project have to guard against supply interruptions?

Off-Take Agreements

1. Is the off-take price firm? If not, is it reasonably predictable based on supply sources and historical and future expectations about pricing and demand?

2. Is the capacity component of the price sufficient for debt service and other fixed costs? Is the operation component sufficient to pay variable operating costs?

3. When do capacity payments begin?

4. Are price escalators, floors, and ceilings reasonable?

5. Are escalators based on indices that are market driven or politically driven?

6. If the off-take purchaser is owned or regulated by the host government, are there any conditions under which the price could change or the contract be cancelled?

7. Is the contract term sufficient to provide revenue predictability to the project for debt service payments and operating costs?

8. In what currency are the price and damages denominated?

9. Must deliveries begin on a specified date? If so, and the date is missed, is the contractor obligated to pay contract damages to the off-take purchaser?

10. If the off-take is not delivered, is the project company obligated to pay liquidated damages or other damages to the off-take purchaser?

11. Is the force majeure provision integrated with the other project contracts?

12. Is credit enhancement necessary to support the creditworthiness of the off-take purchaser, such as a guarantee or letter of credit?

13. If the host government owns the off-take purchaser, is a host-government guarantee needed?

Operation and Maintenance Agreement

1. Has an operating and maintenance agreement been executed?

2. How is the cost of service determined under the agreement?

3. Who is the operator and what is its experience and resources with regard to similar projects in the host country?

4. Who are the subcontractors and vendors, and what is their experience and resources with regard to similar projects in the host country?

5. Is the agreement for operation and maintenance of the entire facility? If not, how will the operators be coordinated?

6. Does the scope of services adequately describe the project?

7. What is excluded from the scope of work and retained as a responsibility of the project company?

8. Does sufficient local labor exist near the project site? If not, what housing developments are necessary?

9. Is the local labor collectively organized? What is the recent and historical experience with the relationship of labor to management?

10. In what currency are the price and damages denominated?

11. Are the performance guarantees acceptable?

12. What are the contractual incentives for performance at or under the operating budget established by the project company?

13. Is credit enhancement necessary to support the creditworthiness of the operator, such as a guarantee, bond, or letter of credit?

14. Is the force majeure provision integrated with the other project contracts?

Technology

1. Is the technology new or proven?

2. Are there any local characteristics that could cause historical technology performance to deteriorate in the local environment?

3. Is a guarantee of technology performance included in the construction contract?

General Contract Review

1. Is the law chosen to govern the project contract developed and predictable?

2. Will the dispute resolution process result in prompt resolution of disputes?

3. Will disputes be resolved outside of the host country?

4. Is the contract enforceable?

5. Does the contract permit collateral assignment to the project lender and subsequent assignment to a purchaser of the project in a foreclosure proceeding?

6. If one of the contracting parties is the host government, or an entity majority owned by the host government, is there a waiver of sovereign immunity?

Agreement With the Host Government

1. Has sovereign immunity been waived?

2. Is there a forum for dispute resolution outside of the host government?

3. What involvement by the host government is necessary to ensure project success? Are these elements included in the agreements with the host government?

Environmental Considerations

1. Does the technology satisfy local or World Bank environmental standards?

2. Is an environmental compliance program established?

Financing

1. What are the potential private-sector sources of financing?

2. What are the potential government-sector sources of financing?

3. What guarantees and insurance are needed from government-sector financing sources to obtain private-sector financing?

4. Are local capital markets available to provide funds for the project company?

UNCITRAL LEGISLATIVE GUIDE ON PRIVATELY FINANCED INFRASTRUCTURE PROJECTS

I. General legislative and institutional framework

Constitutional, Legislative and Institutional Framework

Recommendation 1. The constitutional, legislative and institutional framework for the implementation of privately financed infrastructure projects should ensure transparency, fairness, and the long-term sustainability of projects. Undesirable restrictions on private sector participation in infrastructure development and operation should be eliminated.

Scope of Authority to Award Concessions

Recommendation 2. The law should identify the public authorities of the host country (including, as appropriate, national, provincial and local authorities) that are empowered to award concessions and enter into agreements for the implementation of privately financed infrastructure projects.

Recommendation 3. Privately financed infrastructure projects may include concessions for the construction and operation of new infrastructure facilities and systems or the maintenance, modernization, expansion and operation of existing infrastructure facilities and systems.

Recommendation 4. The law should identify the sectors or types of infrastructure in respect of which concessions may be granted.

Recommendation 5. The law should specify the extent to which a concession might extend to the entire region under the jurisdiction of the respective contracting authority, to a geograph-ical subdivision thereof or to a discrete project, and whether it might be awarded with or without exclusivity, as appropriate, in accordance with rules and principles of law, statutory provisions, regulations and policies applying to the sector concerned. Contracting authorities might be jointly empowered to award concessions beyond a single jurisdiction.

Administrative Coordination

Recommendation 6. Institutional mechanisms should be established to coordinate the activities of the public authorities responsible for issuing approvals, licenses, permits or authorizations required for the implementation of privately financed infrastructure projects in accordance with statutory or regulatory provisions on the construction and operation of infrastructure facilities of the type concerned.

Authority to Regulate Infrastructure Services

Recommendation 7. The authority to regulate infrastructure services should not be entrusted to entities that directly or indirectly provide infrastructure services.

Recommendation 8. Regulatory competence should be entrusted to functionally independent bodies with a level of autonomy sufficient to ensure that their decisions are taken without political interference or inappropriate pressures from infrastructure operators and public service providers.

Recommendation 9. The rules governing regulatory procedures should be made public. Regulatory decisions should state the reasons on which they are based and should be accessible to interested parties through publication or other means.

Recommendation 10. The law should establish transparent procedures whereby the concessionaire may request a review of regulatory decisions by an independent and impartial body, which may include court review, and should set forth the grounds on which such a review may be based.

Recommendation 11. Where appropriate, special procedures should be established for handling disputes among public service providers concerning alleged violations of laws and regulations governing the relevant sector.

II. Project risks and government support

Project Risks and Risk Allocation

Recommendation 12. No unnecessary statutory or regulatory limitations should be placed upon the contracting authority's ability to agree on an allocation of risks that is suited to the needs of the project.

Government Support

Recommendation 13. The law should clearly state which public authorities of the host country may provide financial or economic support to the implementation of privately financed infrastructure projects and which types of support they are authorized to provide.

III. Selection of the concessionaire

General Considerations

Recommendation 14. The law should provide for the selection of the concessionaire through transparent and efficient competitive procedures adapted to the particular needs of privately financed infrastructure projects.

Pre-Selection of Bidders

Recommendation 15. The bidders should demonstrate that they meet the pre-selection criteria that the contracting authority considers appropriate for the particular project, including:

(a) Adequate professional and technical qualifications, human resources, equipment and other physical facilities as necessary to carry out all the phases of the project, namely, engineering, construction, operation and maintenance; (b) Sufficient ability to manage the financial aspects of the project and capability to sustain the financing requirements for the engineering, construction and operational phases of the project; (c) Appropriate managerial and organizational capability, reliability and experience, including previous experience in operating public infrastructure.

Recommendation 16. The bidders should be allowed to form consortia to submit proposals, provided that each member of a pre-selected consortium may participate, either directly or through subsidiary companies, in only one bidding consortium.

Recommendation 17. The contracting authority should draw up a short list of the pre-selected bidders that will subsequently be invited to submit proposals upon completion of the pre-selection phase.

Procedures for Requesting Proposals
Single Stage and Two Stage Procedures for Requesting Proposals

Recommendation 18. Upon completion of the pre-selection proceedings, the contracting authority should request the pre-selected bidders to submit final proposals.

Recommendation 19. Notwithstanding the above, the contracting authority may use a two-stage procedure to request proposals from pre-selected bidders when it is not feasible for it to formulate project specifications or performance indicators and contractual terms in a manner sufficiently detailed and precise to permit final proposals to be formulated. Where a two stage procedure is used, the following provisions should apply: (a) The contracting authority should first call upon the pre-selected bidders to submit proposals relating to output specifications and other characteristics of the project as well as to the proposed contractual terms;

(b) The contracting authority may convene a meeting of bidders to clarify questions concerning the initial request for proposals; (c) Following examination of the proposals received, the contracting authority may review and, as appropriate, revise the initial project specifications and contractual terms prior to issuing a final request for proposals.

Content of the Final Request for Proposals

Recommendation 20. The final request for proposals should include at least the following: (a) General information as may be required by the bidders in order to prepare and submit their proposals; (b) Project specifications and performance indicators, as appropriate, including the contracting authority's requirements regarding safety and security standards and environmental protection; (c) The contractual terms proposed by the contracting authority; (d) The criteria for evaluating the proposals, the relative weight to be accorded to each such criterion and the manner in which the criteria are to be applied in the evaluation of proposals.

Clarifications and Modifications

Recommendation 21. The contracting authority may, whether on its own initiative or as a result of a request for clarification by a bidder, modify the final request for proposals by issuing addenda at a reasonable time prior to the deadline for submission of proposals.

Evaluation Criteria

Recommendation 22. The criteria for the evaluation and comparison of the technical proposals should concern the effectiveness of the proposal submitted by the bidder in meeting the needs of the contracting authority, including the following: (a) Technical soundness; (b) Operational feasibility; (c) Quality of services and measures to ensure their continuity; (d) Social and economic development potential offered by the proposals.

Recommendation 23. The criteria for the evaluation and comparison of the financial and com-

mercial proposals may include, as appropriate: (a) The present value of the proposed tolls, fees, unit prices and other charges over the concession period; (b) The present value of the proposed direct payments by the contracting authority, if any; (c) The costs for design and construction activities, annual operation and maintenance costs, present value of capital costs and operating and maintenance costs; (d) The extent of financial support, if any, expected from the Government; (e) Soundness of the proposed financial arrangements; (f) The extent of acceptance of the proposed contractual terms.

Submission, Opening, Comparison and Evaluation of Proposals

Recommendation 24. The contracting authority may establish thresholds with respect to quality, technical, financial and commercial aspects to be reflected in the proposals in accordance with the criteria set out in the request for proposals. Proposals that fail to achieve the thresholds should be regarded as non-responsive.

Recommendation 25. Whether or not it has followed a pre-selection process, the contracting authority may retain the right to require the bidders to demonstrate their qualifications again in accordance with criteria and procedures set forth in the request for proposals or the pre-selection documents, as appropriate. Where a pre-selection process has been followed, the criteria should be the same as those used in the pre-selection proceedings.

Final Negotiations and Project Award

Recommendation 26. The contracting authority should rank all responsive proposals on the basis of the evaluation criteria set forth in the request for proposals and invite for final negotiation of the project agreement the bidder that has attained the best rating. Final negotiations may not concern those terms of the contract which were stated as non-negotiable in the final request for proposals.

Recommendation 27. If it becomes apparent to the contracting authority that the negotiations with the bidder invited will not result in a project agreement, the contracting authority should inform that bidder that it is terminating the negotiations and then invite for negotiations the other bidders on the basis of their ranking until it arrives at a project agreement or rejects all remaining proposals.

Concession Award without Competitive Procedures

Recommendation 28. The law should set forth the exceptional circumstances under which the contracting authority may be authorized to award a concession without using competitive procedures, such as: (a) When there is an urgent need for ensuring continuity in the provision of the service and engaging in a competitive selection procedure would therefore be impractical; (b) In case of projects of short duration and with an anticipated initial investment value not exceeding a specified low amount; (c) Reasons of national defense or national security; (d) Cases where there is only one source capable of providing the required service (for example, because it requires the use of patented technology or unique know-how); (e) In case of unsolicited proposals of the type referred to in legislative recommendations 34 and 35; (f) When an invitation to the pre-selection proceedings or a request for proposals has been issued but no applications or proposals were submitted or all proposals failed to meet the evaluation criteria set forth in the request for proposals, and if, in the judgment of the contracting authority, issuing a new request for proposals would be unlikely to result in a project award; (g) Other cases where the higher authority authorizes such an exception for compelling reasons of public interest.

Recommendation 29. The law may require that the following procedures be observed for the award of a concession without competitive procedures: (a) The contracting authority should publish a notice of its intention to award a concession for the implementation for the proposed project and should engage in negotiations with as many companies judged capable of carrying out the project as circumstances permit; (b) Offers should be evaluated and ranked according to the evaluation criteria established by the contracting

authority; (c) Except for the situation referred to in recommendation 28 (c), the contracting authority should cause a notice of the concession award to be published, disclosing the specific circumstances and reasons for the award of the concession without competitive procedures.

Unsolicited Proposals

Recommendation 30. By way of exception to the selection procedures described in legislative recommendations 14–27, the contracting authority may be authorized to handle unsolicited proposals pursuant to specific procedures established by the law for handling unsolicited proposals, provided that such proposals do not relate to a project for which selection procedures have been initiated or announced by the contracting authority.

Procedures for Determining the Admissibility of Unsolicited Proposals

Recommendation 31. Following receipt and preliminary examination of an unsolicited proposal, the contracting authority should inform the proponent, within a reasonably short period, whether or not there is a potential public interest in the project. If the project is found to be in the public interest, the contracting authority should invite the proponent to submit a formal proposal in sufficient detail to allow the contracting authority to make a proper evaluation of the concept or technology and determine whether the proposal meets the conditions set forth in the law and is likely to be successfully implemented at the scale of the proposed project.

Recommendation 32. The proponent should retain title to all documents submitted throughout the procedure and those documents should be returned to it in the event that the proposal is rejected.

Procedures for Handling Unsolicited Proposals that do not Involve Proprietary Concepts or Technology

Recommendation 33. The contracting authority should initiate competitive selection procedures under recommendations 14–27 above if it is found that the envisaged output of the project can be achieved without the use of a process, design, methodology or engineering concept for which the author of the unsolicited proposal possesses exclusive rights or if the proposed concept or technology is not truly unique or new. The author of the unsolicited proposal should be invited to participate in such proceedings and may be given a premium for submitting the proposal.

Procedures for Handling Unsolicited Proposals Involving Proprietary Concepts or Technology

Recommendation 34. If it appears that the envisaged output of the project cannot be achieved without using a process, design, methodology or engineering concept for which the author of the unsolicited proposal possesses exclusive rights, the contracting authority should seek to obtain elements of comparison for the unsolicited proposal. For that purpose, the contracting authority should publish a description of the essential output elements of the proposal with an invitation for other interested parties to submit alternative or comparable proposals within a certain reasonable period.

Recommendation 35. The contracting authority may engage in negotiations with the author of the unsolicited proposal if no alternative proposals are received, subject to approval by a higher authority. If alternative proposals are submitted, the contracting authority should invite all the proponents to negotiations in accordance with the provisions of legislative recommendation 29 (a)–(c).

Confidentiality

Recommendation 36. Negotiations between the contracting authority and bidders should be confidential and one party to the negotiations should not reveal to any other person any technical, price or other commercial information relating to the negotiations without the consent of the other party.

Notice of Project Award

Recommendation 37. The contracting authority should cause a notice of the award of the project to be published. The notice should identify the con-

cessionaire and include a summary of the essential terms of the project agreement.

Record of Selection and Award Proceedings

Recommendation 38. The contracting authority should keep an appropriate record of key information pertaining to the selection and award proceedings. The law should set forth the requirements for public access.

Review Procedures

Recommendation 39. Bidders who claim to have suffered, or who may suffer, loss or injury owing to a breach of a duty imposed on the contracting authority by the law may seek review of the contracting authority's acts in accordance with the laws of the host country.

IV. Construction and operation of infrastructure:

Legislative Framework and Project Agreement
General Provisions on the Project Agreement

Recommendation 40. The law might identify the core terms to be provided in the project agreement, which may include those terms referred to in recommendations 41–68 below.

Recommendation 41. Unless otherwise provided, the project agreement should be governed by the law of the host country.

Organization of the Concessionaire

Recommendation 42. The contracting authority should have the option to require that the selected bidders establish an independent legal entity with a seat in the country.

Recommendation 43. The project agreement should specify the minimum capital of the project company and the procedures for obtaining the approval by the contracting authority of the statutes and by-laws of the project company and fundamental changes therein.

The Project Site, Assets and Easements

Recommendation 44. The project agreement should specify, as appropriate, which assets will be public property and which assets will be the private property of the concessionaire. The project agreement should identify which assets the concessionaire is required to transfer to the contracting authority or to a new concessionaire upon expiry or termination of the project agreement; which assets the contracting authority, at its option, may purchase from the concessionaire; and which assets the concessionaire may freely remove or dispose of upon expiry or termination of the project agreement.

Recommendation 45. The contracting authority should assist the concessionaire in obtaining such rights related to the project site as necessary for the operation, construction and maintenance of the facility. The law might empower the concessionaire to enter upon, transit through, do work or fix installations upon property of third parties, as required for the construction, operation and maintenance of the facility.

Financial Arrangements

Recommendation 46. The law should enable the concessionaire to collect tariffs or user fees for the use of the facility or the services it provides. The project agreement should provide for methods and formulas for the adjustment of those tariffs or user fees.

Recommendation 47. Where the tariffs or fees charged by the concessionaire are subject to external control by a regulatory body, the law should set forth the mechanisms for periodic and extraordinary revisions of the tariff adjustment formulas.

Recommendation 48. The contracting authority should have the power, where appropriate, to agree to make direct payments to the concessionaire as a substitute for, or in addition to, service charges to be paid by the users or to enter into commitments for the purchase of fixed quantities of goods or services.

Security Interests

Recommendation 49. The concessionaire should be responsible for raising the funds required to construct and operate the infrastructure facility

and, for that purpose, should have the right to secure any financing required for the project with a security interest in any of its property, with a pledge of shares of the project company, with a pledge of the proceeds and receivables arising out of the concession, or with other suitable security, without prejudice to any rule of law that might prohibit the creation of security interests in public property.

Assignment of the Concession

Recommendation 50. The concession should not be assigned to third parties without the consent of the contracting authority. The project agreement should set forth the conditions under which the contracting authority might give its consent to an assignment of the concession, including the acceptance by the new concessionaire of all obligations under the project agreement and evidence of the new concessionaire's technical and financial capability as necessary for providing the service.

Transfer of Controlling Interest in the Project Company

Recommendation 51. The transfer of a controlling interest in a concessionaire company may require the consent of the contracting authority, unless otherwise provided.

Construction Works

Recommendation 52. The project agreement should set forth the procedures for the review and approval of construction plans and specifications by the contracting authority, the contracting authority's right to monitor the construction of, or improvements to, the infrastructure facility, the conditions under which the contracting authority may order variations in respect of construction specifications and the procedures for testing and final inspection, approval and acceptance of the facility, its equipment and appurtenances.

Operation of Infrastructure

Recommendation 53. The project agreement should set forth, as appropriate, the extent of the concessionaire's obligations to ensure: (a) The adaptation of the service so as to meet the actual demand for the service; (b) The continuity of the service; (c) The availability of the service under essentially the same conditions to all users; (d) The non-discriminatory access, as appropriate, of other service providers to any public infrastructure network operated by the concessionaire.

Recommendation 54. The project agreement should set forth: (a) The extent of the concessionaire's obligation to provide the contracting authority or a regulatory body, as appropriate, with reports and other information on its operations; (b) The procedures for monitoring the concessionaire's performance and for taking such reasonable actions as the contracting authority or a regulatory body may find appropriate, to ensure that the infrastructure facility is properly operated and the services are provided in accordance with the applicable legal and contractual requirements.

Recommendation 55. The concessionaire should have the right to issue and enforce rules governing the use of the facility, subject to the approval of the contracting authority or a regulatory body.

General Contractual Arrangements

Recommendation 56. The contracting authority may reserve the right to review and approve major contracts to be entered into by the concessionaire, in particular contracts with the concessionaire's own shareholders or related persons. The contracting authority's approval should not normally be withheld except where the contracts contain provisions inconsistent with the project agreement or manifestly contrary to the public interest or to mandatory rules of a public law nature.

Recommendation 57. The concessionaire and its lenders, insurers and other contracting partners should be free to choose the applicable law to govern their contractual relations, except where such a choice would violate the host country's public policy.

Recommendation 58. The project agreement should set forth: (a) The forms, duration and amounts of the guarantees of performance that the concessionaire may be required to provide in connection with the construction and the operation of the facility; (b) The insurance policies that the concessionaire may be required to maintain; (c) The compensation to which the concessionaire may be entitled following the occurrence of legislative changes or other changes in the economic or financial conditions that render the performance of the obligation substantially more onerous than originally foreseen. The project agreement should further provide mechanisms for revising the terms of the project agreement following the occurrence of any such changes; (d) The extent to which either party may be exempt from liability for failure or delay in complying with any obligation under the project agreement owing to circumstances beyond their reasonable control; (e) Remedies available to the contracting authority and the concessionaire in the event of default by the other party.

Recommendation 59. The project agreement should set forth the circumstances under which the contracting authority may temporarily take over the operation of the facility for the purpose of ensuring the effective and uninterrupted delivery of the service in the event of serious failure by the concessionaire to perform its obligations.

Recommendation 60. The contracting authority should be authorized to enter into agreements with the lenders providing for the appointment, with the consent of the contracting authority, of a new concessionaire to perform under the existing project agreement if the concessionaire seriously fails to deliver the service required or if other specified events occur that could justify the termination of the project agreement.

V. Duration, extension and termination of the project agreement

Duration and Extension of the Project Agreement

Recommendation 61. The duration of the concession should be specified in the project agreement.

Recommendation 62. The term of the concession should not be extended, except for those circumstances specified in the law, such as: (a) Completion delay or interruption of operation due to the occurrence of circumstances beyond either party's reasonable control; (b) Project suspension brought about by acts of the contracting authority or other public authorities; (c) To allow the concessionaire to recover additional costs arising from requirements of the contracting authority not originally foreseen in the project agreement that the concessionaire would not be able to recover during the normal term of the project agreement.

Termination of the Project Agreement
Termination by the Contracting Authority

Recommendation 63. The contracting authority should have the right to terminate the project agreement: (a) In the event that it can no longer be reasonably expected that the concessionaire will be able or willing to perform its obligations, owing to insolvency, serious breach or otherwise; (b) For reasons of public interest, subject to payment of compensation to the concessionaire.

Termination by the Concessionaire

Recommendation 64. The concessionaire should have the right to terminate the project agreement under exceptional circumstances specified in the law, such as: (a) In the event of serious breach by the contracting authority or other public authority of their obligations under the project agreement; (b) In the event that the concessionaire's performance is rendered substantially more onerous as a result of variation orders or other acts of the contracting authority, unforeseen changes in conditions or acts of other public authorities and that the parties have failed to agree on an appropriate revision of the project agreement.

Termination by Either Party

Recommendation 65. Either party should have the right to terminate the project agreement in the event that the performance of its obligations is rendered impossible by the occurrence of circumstances beyond either party's reasonable control. The parties should also have the right to

terminate the project agreement by mutual consent.

Consequences of Expiry or Termination of the Project Agreement
Transfer of Assets to the Contracting Authority or to a New Concessionaire

Recommendation 66. The project agreement should lay down the criteria for establishing, as appropriate, the compensation to which the concessionaire may be entitled in respect of assets transferred to the contracting authority or to a new concessionaire or purchased by the contracting authority upon expiry or termination of the project agreement.

Financial Arrangements upon Termination

Recommendation 67. The project agreement should stipulate how compensation due to either party in the event of termination of the project agreement is to be calculated, providing, where appropriate, for compensation for the fair value of works performed under the project agreement, and for losses, including lost profits.

Wind-up and Transitional Measures

Recommendation 68. The project agreement should set out, as appropriate, the rights and obligations of the parties with respect to: (a) The transfer of technology required for the operation of the facility; (b) The training of the contracting authority's personnel or of a successor concessionaire in the operation and maintenance of the facility; (c) The provision, by the concessionaire, of operation and maintenance services and the supply of spare parts, if required, for a reasonable period after the transfer of the facility to the contracting authority or to a successor concessionaire.

Settlement of disputes
Disputes Between the Contracting Authority and the Concessionaire

Recommendation 69. The contracting authority should be free to agree to dispute settlement mechanisms regarded by the parties as best suited to the needs of the project.

Disputes between Project Promoters and Between the Concessionaire and its Lenders, Contractors and Suppliers

Recommendation 70. The concessionaire and the project promoters should be free to choose the appropriate mechanisms for settling commercial disputes among the project promoters, or disputes between the concessionaire and its lenders, contractors, suppliers and other business partners.

Disputes Involving Customers or Users of the Infrastructure Facility

Recommendation 71. The concessionaire may be required to make available simplified and efficient mechanisms for handling claims submitted by its customers or users of the infrastructure facility.

PROJECT FINANCE TERMS, ABBREVIATIONS, AND ACRONYMS

ADB   Asian Development Bank

AfDB   African Development Bank

AfDF   African Development Fund

AIC   Agency for International Cooperation (*Spain*)

AusAID   Australian Agency for International Development

advance payment guarantee   a guarantee, in which a contractor is the guarantor and the project company is the guarantee, wherein the contractor agrees to return advance payments made under the construction contract if not earned within a specified time or the construction contract is not otherwise performed by the contractor

amortization   reduction of principal outstanding under a debt instrument, through repayment

assignment   transfer of title to an asset

BADC   Belgium Administration for Development Cooperation

BADEA   Arab Bank for Economic Development in Africa

BAWI   Federal Office of Foreign Economic Affairs (*Switzerland*)

BFCE   Banque Française du Commerce Extérieur (*France*)

BITS   Swedish Agency for International Technology and Economic Cooperation

BMZ   Bundesministerium für Wirtschaftliche Zusammenarbeit (*Germany*)

backup power   reserve power (steam or electricity) for special circumstances, such as an emergency or system failure of the main power plant

bankable   capable of being financed; capable of supporting a financing

bilateral agency   an institution established by one country to promote trade, such as an export-import agency

BOO   build-own-operate; as when a private owner builds, owns and operates an infrastructure facility

BOOT   build-own-operate-transfer; as when a private owner builds, owns, and operates an infrastructure facility and then transfers it to another entity after a specified period of operation

BLT   build-lease-transfer; as when a private owner builds an infrastructure facility, leases it for use and then transfers it to another entity after a specified period of use

BOT   build-operate-transfer; as when a private owner builds, operates, and transfers an infrastructure facility to another entity

BTO   build-transfer-operate; as when a private owner builds, and then transfers ownership of an infrastructure facility to another entity, and then operates it for that entity

business interruption   cessation of normal business operations

cash call   an event that requires the infusion of additional money into a project company's accounts by its owners, made in the form of a loan or capital contribution

cash deficiency agreement   an agreement between a parent corporation and creditors of its subsidiary, promising that it will invest additional cash in the subsidiary necessary to meet certain, negotiated obligations

CDC   Commonwealth Development Corporation (*United Kingdom*)

CESCE   Export Credit Insurance Company (*Spain*)

CFD   Caisse Française de Developpement (*France*)

CIDA Canadian International Development Agency

COFACE Compagnie Française d'Assurance pour le Commerce Extérieur (*France*)

collateral assignment transfer of certain ownership interests in an asset, such as contracts, contract rights, claims, and debt, to an entity solely as security for a debt or other obligation

commercial risk events, the occurrence or nonoccurrence of which have the potential to affect the technical or economic feasibility of a project and which are nonpolitical in nature

completion in a construction contract, the satisfaction by the contractor of agreed-upon performance requirements; the start of a project's operating period

completion guarantee a guarantee, in which a project sponsor is the guarantor and the project company is the guarantee, wherein the project sponsor agrees to complete the project if the project company fails to do so

concession or concession agreement an agreement between a project company (and the project sponsors, in some situations) and the host government, in which the project company is granted authority to develop, construct, and operate a project for a limited period of time until financing is paid and a negotiated equity return is earned; commonly used in BOT and BOOT projects

counter guarantee a third-party guarantee used as a credit enhancement device when a purchaser of goods or services is of such a creditworthiness level that its ability to make payments therefor is so far in question that the provider of the goods or services insists upon the guarantee to ensure that payments are made

creeping expropriation a series of acts which, over time, have an expropriatory effect

currency risk the difficulties encountered by a foreign borrower or foreign affiliate in making future payments due in a currency other than the currency in which revenues are earned; also called *currency devaluation risk*

debt service periodic payment of principal and interest on loans, bonds, notes and other debt instruments

devaluation a government action designed to reduce the purchasing power or value of its currency as against convertible currencies

developing country a non-industrialized country; currently, the World Bank classifies countries as "developing" if per capita gross national product (GNP) (1993 dollars) is at or less than US$4,900

double tax treaty an agreement between two countries that restricts or eliminates double taxation of income or capital gains that would otherwise occur as a result of operations in one country and residency in another

drawdown the act of borrowing a loan under a credit agreement

EBRD European Bank for Reconstruction and Development

ECGD Export Credit Guarantee Department (*United Kingdom*)

ECO expanded co-financing operations of the World Bank, which formerly administered a program to employ the bank's guarantee powers

EDU Export Development Corporation (*Canada*)

EFC Danish Export Finance Corporation

EFIC Export Finance and Insurance Corporation (*Australia*)

EID Export Insurance Division (*Japan*)

EIB European Investment Bank

EKN Swedish Export Credits Guarantee Board

EKR Eksportkreditraadet (*Denmark*)

enclave project a project financeable by the IBRD in a country otherwise ineligible for IBRD loans because the project can generate enough foreign exchange to service the debt; guarantees or other credit enhancement exist for the benefit of the IBRD; and project revenues are capable of segregation for servicing of the IBRD loan

EPC Contract engineering, procurement, and construction contract

exchange controls procedures established by a government to allow conversion of local currency to foreign, hard currency in an orderly manner that promotes policy goals

exchange rate the amount of currency that can be bought or sold for a specific amount of another currency

export country a country from which equipment, raw materials, fuel, or some other project input will be supplied to the project

export credits credit facilities or guarantee programs made available by a country for the benefit of exporters of goods or services in that country, in an effort to promote exports

Exportfinans export credit agency in Norway

expropriation a forced transfer of ownership from a private owner to a government

FAC Fonds d'Aide et de Cooperation (*France*)

FEC Finnish Export Credit Limited

feedstock the raw material or other inputs needed in an industrial process

finance lease a finance structure that provides the lessor lease payments equal to debt service payment plus a return on equity, and provides the lessee the long-term lease of the property, usually for the purpose of transferring tax benefits

financeable capable of being financed; capable of supporting a financing

financial closing the event in a project at which each of the conditions precedent to the initial drawdown of funds under the credit agreement are either satisfied by the project company, as borrower, or waived by the project lender

force majeure an event outside of the reasonable control of the effected party to a contract, which it could not have prevented by good industry practices or by the exercise of reasonable skill and judgment, which typically excuses certain negotiated portions of contract performance during its pendency

full recourse a finance structure that requires the borrower *and its owners* to repay all debt loaned to the borrower, usually through the use of guarantees

GEIK Guaranti-Instituttet for Eksportkreditt (*Norway*)

governing law the law to be applied to the interpretation of the terms and conditions of a contract, as set forth in the contract or as applied by a court

hard currency all major convertible currencies, such as the United States dollar, the British pound, the German mark, the Japanese yen, the Swiss franc, the Italian lira, and the Dutch guilder

hell-or-high-water a contractual obligation that requires a purchaser of goods produced by, or a user of a project's capacity, to pay for output or services even if a force majeure or other adverse event interferes with production or use

host country the country in which the infrastructure or other project is taking place

IBRD International Bank for Reconstruction and Development, also called the World Bank

IDA International Development Association

IDA-only country a country ineligible for IBRD loans because of its credit standing

IDB Inter-American Development Bank

IDC interest during construction

IEC Institute for Economic Cooperation (*Portugal*)

IFC International Finance Corporation, the private-sector lending arm of the World Bank

IMF International Monetary Fund

implementation agreement a project-specific agreement between the government and a developer that provides government assurances and guarantees to developers required for successful project development and allocation of risks that promotes equity investments and debt financing

indemnification agreement an agreement allocating liability to a party that is designed to protect another party against the consequences of agreed-upon actions in certain circumstances

investment grade the quality of a borrower to repay debt obligations, which, at a minimum, is rated BBB by Standard and Poor's

IPP independent power producer; the term has become a synonym for any power producer not owned by a government; in the United States, it is synonymous with a non-governmental, non-utility power generator

IRR internal rate of return

IsDB Islamic Development Bank

Kexim Export-Import Bank of Korea

letter of credit a financial instrument issued by a financial institution for the benefit of its customer (account party) under which a financial institution agrees to pay money to the beneficiary thereof upon demand or upon the occurrence of specified events

LIBOR   London Interbank Offer Rate, being the rate at which banks borrow money from other banks in the London interbank market

license   a governmental grant providing authority to undertake an activity or business

limited recourse   a lending arrangement under which repayment of the debt is recourse to the owners of the borrowing entity in the event of certain defaults, but in general the lenders rely on the project cash flow for debt repayment

liquidated damages   specific amounts, often with a cap, a contracting party is required to pay to another contracting party in the event an agreed-upon area of performance is not achieved

limited recourse   limitations on the project lender's ability to seek payment of debt and other obligations, and on the other project participant's ability to seek contract damages and other obligations, from the project sponsors

MIGA   Multilateral Investment Guarantee Association, a member of the World Bank Group

MITI   Ministry of International Trade and Industry (*Japan*)

MOEF   Ministry of Economy and Finance (*Spain*)

MOF   Ministry of Finance (*Japan*)

MW   megawatt (10^6 watts)

multilateral agency   an institution organized by a group of countries to promote development, throughout the world, as with the World Bank and the International Finance Corporation, or in a specific region, such as Inter-American Development Bank

negative pledge   an agreement by a borrower or guarantor not to create or permit creation of liens, security interests, or other encumbrances on its assets

NDF   Nordic Development Fund

NIB   Nordic Investment Bank

nonrecourse   a lending arrangement under which repayment of the debt is nonrecourse to the owners of the borrowing entity and the lenders rely on the project cash flow for debt repayment

O&M   operations and maintenance

OECD   Organisation for Economic Cooperation and Development

OEKB   Oesterreichische Kontrollbank (*Austria*)

off-balance-sheet financing   an obligation that does not appear as a liability of the balance sheet of an entity

off-take   the product of a project

off-taker (off-take purchaser)   the purchaser of a project's output

off-take agreement   an agreement to purchase all or a substantial part of the product produced by a project, which typically provides the revenue stream for a project financing

OPIC   Overseas Private Investment Corporation

participation   an arrangement between two banks, wherein one bank (the participant) participates in a loan made by the other bank, without direct privity to the borrower

performance bonds   surety obligations issued by commercial banks or insurance companies for an entity to guarantee the performance of a contract according to performance requirements

political risk   financial exposure to uncertainty as a result of politically or socially generated changes

project company   a special-purpose entity that develops, owns, and operates a project

project debt   funds borrowed by the project company from any of various debt sources, including commercial lenders

project equity   funds and other assets contributed to the capital of the project sponsor to provide the capital needed for the project

project financing   the arrangement of debt, equity, and credit enhancement for the construction or refinancing of a particular facility in a capital-intensive industry, in which lenders base credit appraisals on the projected revenues from the operation of the facility, rather than the general assets or the credit of the promoter of the facility, and rely on the assets of the facility, including the revenue-producing contracts and cash flow, as collateral for the debt

project sponsor   an entity that develops a project and owns, in whole or in part, a project company

PSEDF   Private Sector Energy Development Fund (*Pakistan*)

put-or-pay agreement (supply-or-pay)   an agreement that obligates a supplier to either provide materials to a project or, if it cannot, then to pay an amount necessary for the project to obtain the supply elsewhere

put option an agreement between the project sponsors and specified parties (such as passive equity investors and project lenders) whereby the project sponsors agree to purchase equity interests or debt obligations, as the case may be, if certain contingencies (equity returns or debt repayment, for example) are not satisfied

retention a percentage amount of payments otherwise due to the contractor under the construction contract, as security for completion of the work, which is usually released to the contractor upon project completion

retention money guarantee a guarantee, provided in lieu of retention, that gives the project company, as beneficiary, the right to receive from the contractor payments equal to the amount that would otherwise have been retained from construction contract payments, if the project is not completed or defects are discovered within an agreed upon period

ROL refurbish-operate-lease, as when a private owner refurbishes, operates, and leases an infrastructure facility from another entity

SACE Sezione Speciale per Assicurazione del Credito all'sportazione (*Italy*)

set-off a contract provision that provides one party the right to set-off any cash it holds for the account of such party and apply it against amounts due by that party

sovereign guarantee a government guarantee agreement

sovereign immunity the legal doctrine that prohibits a private entity from suing or seizing the assets of a government or government-controlled entity, subject to certain exceptions

sovereign risk the risk that the host-country government will default in its contractual undertaking with the project or another project participant, such as under guarantees, indemnity agreements or input and off-take contracts

standby letter of credit a letter of credit that provides the beneficiary the right to draw under it upon presentation of a certificate stating that an event has not occurred, such as payment or performance of some obligation

subordinated debt debt which is junior in right of payment, lien priority and otherwise to the rights of other lenders

supply-or-pay contract a contract in which the supplier agrees to provide goods or services to a project over a period of time for a negotiated compensation, and if it is unable to do so, it must either provide the goods or services from an alternate source at its expense or pay damages to the project for expenses incurred by the project in securing the goods or services itself

swap agreement the exchange of one interest rate for another; also used for currency

syndication prior to closing a credit facility, a credit made available by many lenders to a borrower, each with pre-defined amounts; after a credit facility is closed, an arrangement between two banks, wherein one bank purchases an interest in a credit facility made by the other bank, with direct privity to the borrower

take-and-pay contract a contract that requires the buyer to take and pay for the good or service *only if delivered*; confusion often exists with the meaning of the terms *take-or-pay contract* and *take-and-pay contract*, and they are often used, incorrectly, interchangeably (the foregoing definition is preferred)

take-or-pay contract a contract that creates an *unconditional obligation* on the part of the buyer (offtaker) to pay even if no good or service is provided or producible by the seller

tax holiday a benefit granted to a project that provides project owners an exemption from taxation for a negotiated or statutory time period

throughput contract a contract that requires the user of a project, such as a pipeline, to pay a negotiated amount (typically, an amount equal to the project's debt service obligations and operating expenses) whether or not the service or capacity is used

tolling agreement an agreement under which a project company imposes tolling charges on each project user as compensation for the raw material processed

transfer risk the difficulty encountered by foreign borrowers or foreign affiliates in converting local earnings into a foreign currency, as a result of exchange controls imposed by the local government

transit country   a country through which the output of the project must pass to ensure project success

transnational project finance   project financing in which two or more project participants are entities organized in or owned by entities organized in different countries, or in which the project is located in a country different from the project participants

turnkey contract   a construction contract that provides for the complete design, procurement, construction, and start-up of a facility, by a date certain, for a fixed sum, and at guaranteed performance levels

UNCTAD   United Nations Conference on Trade and Development

USAID   United States Agency for International Development

USExim   United States Export-Import Bank

working capital maintenance agreement   a guarantee or other undertaking in which a creditworthy entity, usually the project sponsor, undertakes to provide working capital for a project, usually the subsidiary of the project sponsor, in an amount necessary to satisfy its obligations under project and debt documents

SELECT BIBLIOGRAPHY

Amison, Martin, *Privatization and Project Finance in the Middle East*, 14 Int'l Fin. L. Rev. 14 (1995).

Augenblick, Mark, & B. Scott Custer Jr., *The Build, Operate and Transfer ("BOT") Approach to Infrastructure Projects in Developing Countries*, World Bank Working Paper No. 498 (1990).

Baragona, Katharine C., *Symposium: Markets in Transition: Reconstruction and Development: Part Two – Building up to a Drawdown: International Project Finance and Privatization – Expert Presentations on Lessons to Be Learned: Project Finance*, 18 Transnat'l Law. 139 (2004).

Barrett, Matthew, *Project Finance Develops New Risks*, Euromoney, Oct., 1986, at 73.

Barrett, Matthew, *Putting Your Equity on the Line*, Euromoney, Oct., 1987, at 119.

Barru, David, *How to Guarantee Contractor Performance on International Construction Projects: Comparing Surety Bonds With Bank Guarantees and Standby Letters Of Credit*, 37 Geo.Wash. L. Rev. 51 (2005).

Baughman, David, & Matthew Buresch, *Mobilizing Private Capital for the Power Sector: Experience in Asia and Latin America*, Joint World Bank–USAID Discussion Paper (1994).

Beenhakker, Henri L., Risk Management in Project Finance and Implementation (1997).

Benoit, Philippe, *Project Finance at the World Bank: An Overview of Policies and Instruments*, World Bank Technical Paper No. 312 (1996).

Bishop, R. Doak, Sashe D. Dimitroff, & Craig S. Miles, *Strategic Options Available When Catastrophe Strikes the Major International Energy Project*, 36 Tex. Int'l L. J. 635 (2001).

Bjerre, Carl S., *International Project Finance Transactions: Selected Issues Under Revised Article 9*, 73 Am. Bankr. L. J. 261 (1999).

Bjerre, Carl S., *Project Finance, Securitization and Consensuality*, 12 Duke J. Comp. & Int'l L. 411 (2002).

Blumenthal, David, *Sources of Funds and Risk Management for International Energy Projects*, 16 Berkley J. Int'l L. 267 (1998).

Bond, Gary, & Laurence Carter, *Financing Private Infrastructure Projects – Emerging Trends from IFC's Experience*, International Finance Corporation Discussion Paper No. 23 (1994).

Bonime-Blanc, Andrea, *Structuring Letter of Credit Backed Gold Loans*, Int'l Fin. L. Rev., Nov. 1988.

Brelsford, Gregg, *International Investment Insurance – The Convention Establishing the Multilateral Investment Guarantee Agency*, 27 Harv. Int'l L. J. 735 (1986).

Brooke, A. F., II, *Great Expectations: Assessing the Contract Damages of the Take-or-Pay Producer*, 70 Tex. L. Rev. 1469 (1992).

Broome, Lissa Lamkin, *Framing the Inquiry: The Social Impact of Project Finance*, 12 Duke J. Comp. & Int'l L. 439 (2002).

Buljevich, Esteban C., & Yoon S. Park, Project Financing and the International Financial Markets (1999).

Cahn, Jonathan, *Challenging the New Imperial Authority: The World Bank and the Democratization of Development*, 6 Harv. Hum. Rts. J. 159 (1993).

Carroll, J. Speed, *Legal Aspects of Project Finance: The Borrower's View, in* Sovereign Borrowers – Guidelines on Legal Negotiations With Commercial Lenders (Lars Kalderén & Qamar S. Siddiqi eds. 1985).

Castle, Grover R., *Project Financing – Guidelines for the Commercial Banker*, J. Com. Bank Lending, Apr. 1975, at 14.

Chance, Clifford, Project Finance (1991).

Chao, Daniel, & Michael Selvin, *Project Development and Finance: The Evolving Role of the Engineering/Construction Contractor, in* Project Finance Yearbook 1994/5 1 (Adrian Hornbook ed. 1994).

Choharis, Peter, *U.S. Courts and the International Law of Expropriation: Toward a New Model for Breach of Contract*, 80 S. CAL. L. REV. 1 (2006).

CLARK, BARKLEY, THE LAW OF SECURED TRANSACTIONS UNDER THE UNIFORM COMMERCIAL CODE ¶ 11.01[2] (2006).

Clarke, Pamela, & Sarah Martin, *The Big Swing to Project Finance*, EUROMONEY, Oct. 1980, at 233.

Comeaux, Paul, & N. Stephan Kinsella, *Reducing Political Risk in Developing Countries: Bilateral Investment Treaties, Stabilization Clauses, and MIGA & OPIC Investment Insurance*, 15 N. Y. L. SCH. J. INT'L & COMP. L. 1 (1994).

Comment, *Collateral in Eastern Europe: Problems & Solutions*, 28 INT'L LAW. 83 (1994).

Comment, *Modern Russian Secured Transaction Law and Foreign Investors' Rights Thereunder*, 4 IND. INT'L & COMP. L. REV. 371 (1994).

Cook, Jacques, *Infrastructure Project Finance in Latin America*, 24 INT'L BUS. LAW. 260 (1996).

Cremades, Bernardo, *International Financial and Secured Transactions*, 31 INT'L LAW. 301 (1997).

Crothers, John D., *Emerging Markets in Central and Eastern Europe: Project Finance in Central and Eastern Europe from a Lender's Perspective: Lessons Learned in Poland and Romania*, 41 McGILL L. J. 285 (1995).

CURLEY, MICHAEL, HANDBOOK OF PROJECT FINANCE FOR WATER AND WASTEWATER SYSTEMS (1993).

Daintith, Terence, & Ian Gault, *Pacta Sunt Servanda and the Licensing and Taxation of North Sea Oil Production*, 8 CAMBRIAN L. REV. 27 (1977).

Darrow, Peter V., Nicole V. F. Fong, & J. Paul Forrester, *Financing Infrastructure Projects in the International Capital Markets: The Tribasa Toll Road Trust*, THE FINANCIER, Aug. 1994, at 9.

DARROW, PETER V., BETH LOEB, & KATHLEEN KAPMICK, *Rating Agency Requirements*, in SECURITIZATION OF FINANCIAL ASSETS (J. Kravitt ed. 1991).

Delaume, Georges R., *Economic Development and Sovereign Immunity*, 79 AM. J. INT'L L. 319 (1995).

Delaume, Georges R., *The Foreign Sovereign Immunities Act and Public Debt Litigation: Some 15 Years Later*, 78 AM. J. INT'L L. 257 (1994).

Delaume, Georges R., *State Contracts and Transnational Arbitration*, 75 AM. J. INT'L L. 784 (1981).

DELMON, JEFFREY, PROJECT FINANCE, BOT PROJECTS AND RISK (2005).

Dickstein, Michael E., *Revitalizing the International Law Governing Concession Agreements*, 6 INT'L TAX & BUS. LAW. 54 (1988).

Dugue, Christopher, *Dispute Resolution in International Project Finance Transactions*, 24 FORDHAM INT'L L. J. 1064 (2001).

Dymond, Christopher M., & Richard A. Sturges, *Financing Merchant Power: USGen's Portfolio Approach* 5 J. PROJECT FINANCE 43 (Spring 1999).

ESTY, BENJAMIN C., *The Equate Project: An Introduction to Islamic Project Finance*, 5 J. PROJECT FIN., No. 4, pp. 7–20 (Winter 2000).

ESTY, BENJAMIN C., *Improved Techniques for Valuing Large-Scale Projects*, 5 J. PROJECT FIN. 9 (Spring 1999).

Esty, Benjamin C., MODERN PROJECT FINANCE: A CASEBOOK (2005).

Esty, Benjamin C., *Returns on Project-Financed Investments: Evolution and Managerial Implications*, 15 J. APPLIED CORP. FIN., No. 1, pp. 71–86 (Spring 2002).

Esty, Benjamin C., & William L. Megginson, *Creditor Rights, Enforcement, and Debt Ownership Structure: Evidence From the Global Syndicated Loan Market*, 38 J. FIN. QUANTITATIVE ANALYSIS, No. 1, pp. 37–59 (2003).

Feldman, Roger D., & Scott L. Hoffman, *Basic Concepts of Project Finance Documentation: Risk Allocation, Drafting, and Regulatory Considerations for Power Sales and Fuel Supply Contracts*, in PROJECT FINANCING, 1987, at 433–34 (PLI REAL EST. L. & PRACTICE COURSE HANDBOOK SERIES NO. 297, 1987).

FIGHT, ANDREW, INTRODUCTION TO PROJECT FINANCE (2006).

FINANCING THIRD WORLD DEVELOPMENT: A SURVEY OF OFFICIAL PROJECT FINANCE PROGRAMS IN OECD COUNTRIES (Fariborz Ghadar ed., 1987).

FINNERTY, JOHN D., PROJECT FINANCING – ASSET-BASED FINANCIAL ENGINEERING (1996).

Fitzgerald, Peter F., ed., PROJECT FINANCING 1996 (PLI COMM. L. & PRACTICE COURSE HANDBOOK SERIES No. A-734, 1996).

Fitzgerald, Peter F., & Barry N. Machlin, eds., PROJECT FINANCING UPDATE 2004: REWORKING & BUILDING NEW PROJECTS IN DEVELOPING MARKETS (PLI COMM. L. & PRACTICE COURSE HANDBOOK SERIES No. A-866, 2004).

Frilet, Marc, *Some Universal Issues in BOT Projects for Public Infrastructures*, 14 INT'L CONSTRUCTION L. REV. 499 (1997).

GOLDSWEIG, DONALD, & ROGER CUMMINGS, INTERNATIONAL JOINT VENTURES: A PRACTICAL APPROACH TO WORKING WITH FOREIGN INVESTORS IN THE U.S. AND ABROAD (1990).

Goodwin, Lee M., & Thomas R. Hoffmann, *Project Finance: Easy Going in Jamaica (International Financing of the Rockport Electric Power Project near Kingston, Jamaica)*, 133 Pub. Util. Fort. 38 (Jan. 1, 1995).

Gordon, Michael, *Of Aspirations and Operations: The Governance of Multinational Enterprises by Third World Nations*, 16 U. Miami Inter-Am. L. Rev. 301 (1984).

Guasch, J. Luis, Granting and Renegotiating Infrastructures Concessions – Getting It Right (World Bank Development Studies 2004).

Hagler Bailly Consulting, Inc., *The Financing Capability of Indian Institutions to Provide Alternatives to Sovereign Guarantees*, U.S. AID Report No. 96–01 (1995).

Han, Mei, & Jerry Shi Zhiyong, *How to Assess the Profitability of a Project Finance Deal – From the Lender's Perspective*, 3 J. Project Fin. 21 (1997).

Hansen, Joy E., *Legal and Operational Issues for the Borrower in Project Financing, in* Mineral Law Series: Rocky Mountain Mineral Law Foundation 18A-1 (1994).

Hardy, Charles, Risk and Risk-Bearing (1923).

Harris, Paul I., *Negative Pledge, in* Sovereign Borrowers – Guidelines on Legal Negotiations With Commercial Lenders (Lars Kalderén & Qamar S. Siddiqi eds. 1985).

Harvey, Charles, Analysis of Project Finance in Developing Countries (1983).

Hensley, Matthew L., & Edward P. White, *The Privatization Experience in Malaysia: Integrating Build-Operate-Own and Build-Operate-Transfer Techniques Within the National Privatization Strategy*, 28 Colum. J. World Bus. 70 (1993).

Hoffman, Scott L., *Cross Border Project Finance, in* International Mergers and Acquisitions (David BenDaniel and Arthur Rosenbloom eds. 1997).

Hoffman, Scott L., *A Practical Guide to Transactional Project Finance: Basic Concepts, Risk Identification, and Contractual Considerations*, 45 Bus. Law. 181 (1989).

Hoffman, Scott L., *Project Financing: Loans Based on Cash Flow and Contracts*, 4 Comm. Lending Rev. 18 (1989).

Hollis, Sheila, *International Energy and Natural Resources*, 31 Int'l Law. 287 (1997).

Hudes, Karen, *Protecting Against Inconvertibility and Transfer Risk: An Outline of Trade Financing Programs of the Export-Import Bank of the United States*, 9 Hastings Int'l & Comp. L. Rev. 461 (1986).

Hull, C. W., *Project Structure and Financing*, 12 J. Int'l Law & Econ. 199 (1978).

Hurlock, Matthew H., *New Approaches to Economic Development: The World Bank, the EBRD and the Negative Pledge Clause*, 35 Harv. Int'l L. J. 345 (1994).

Hurstel, Daniel, & Mary Ann Carpenter-Pecquet, *Privatization and the Public Interest*, 13 Int'l Fin. L. Rev. 34 (1994).

Inman, Jonathan, *Government Guarantees for Infrastructure Projects*, 68 Project Fin. Int'l 36 (Mar. 16, 1995).

John, Teresa A., & Kose John, *Optimality of Project Financing: Theory and Emprical Implications in Finance and Accounting*, 1 Rev. Quantitative Fin. & Acct. 51 (Jan. 1991).

John, William Tudor, *Sovereign Immunity, in* Sovereign Borrowers – Guidelines on Legal Negotiations With Commercial Lenders (Lars Kalderén & Qamar S. Siddiqi eds. 1985).

Kantor, Mark, *International Project Finance and Arbitration With Public Sector Entities: When Is Arbitrability a Fiction?*, 24 Fordham Int'l L. J. 1122 (2001).

Kemp, H. Hovey, & Frederick W. Damour, *Gold Mine Project Finance for the "Junior" Gold Company, in* Mineral Law Series: Rocky Mountain Mineral Law Foundation 4–1 (1988).

Kessler, Judd L., *A World of Risks (Investing in Foreign Projects)*, 131 Pub. Util. Fort. 11 (Aug. 1, 1993).

Kensinger, John, & John Martin, *Project Financing: Raising Money the Old-Fashioned Way*, 3 J. Applied Corp. Fin. 69 (Fall 1988).

Khan, M. F. K., & R. J. Parra, Financing Large Projects: Using Project Finance Techniques and Practices (2003).

Kirkland, Janis L., Nancy G. Simms, & Turner T. Smith Jr., *An International Perspective on Environmental Liability, in* 1 Environmental Dispute Handbook: Liability and Claims (David A. Carpenter et al., eds. 1991).

Kissam, Leo T., & Edmond K. Leach, *Sovereign Expropriation of Property and Abrogation of State Contracts*, 28 Fordham L. Rev. 177 (1959).

Lalive, Jean-Flavien, *Contracts Between a State or State Agency and a Foreign Company*, 13 Int'l & Comp. L. Q. 503 (1962).

Landsittel, David L., & John E. Stewart, *Off-Balance-Sheet Financing; Commitments and Contingencies in* Handbook of Modern Accounting 26–2 to 26–23 (Sidney Davidson & Roman L. Weil, 4th ed. 1980).

LANG, L. H. P., PROJECT FINANCE IN ASIA (1998).

Leeper, Rosamund, *Perspective on Project Financing*, 129 BANKER, August 1979, at 77.

Leeper, Rosamund, *Project Finance – A Term to Conjure With*, 128 BANKER, August 1978, at 67.

LEVY, S. M., BUILD, OPERATE, TRANSFER: PAVING THE WAY FOR TOMORROW'S INFRASTRUCTURE (1996).

Likosky, Michael B., *Mitigating Human Rights Risks Under State-Financed and Privatized Infrastructure Projects*, 10 IND. J. GLOBAL LEG. STUD. 65 (2003).

Letterman, G., LETTERMAN'S LAW OF PRIVATE INTERNATIONAL BUSINESS (1990 & Supp. 1991).

Macey, Jonathan R., *The Limited Liability Company: Lessons for Corporate Law*, 73 WASH. U. L. Q. 433, 448 (1995).

MACMAHON, THOMAS M., J. Andrew Schlickman, & Nicoline Van Riel, INTERNATIONAL ENVIRONMENTAL LAW AND REGULATION (1991).

Malinasky, Laura A., *Rebuilding With Broken Tools: Build-Operate-Transfer Law in Vietnam*, 14 BERK. J. INT'L L. 438 (1996).

Malloy, Michael P., *Symposium: Markets in Transition: Reconstruction and Development: Part Two – Building Up to a Drawdown: International Project Finance and Privatization – Expert Presentations on Lessons to Be Learned: International Project Finance: Risk Analysis and Regulatory Concerns*, 18 TRANSNAT'L LAW. 89 (2004).

Mann, Frederick A., *State Contracts and International Arbitration*, 42 BRIT. Y. B. INT'L L. 1 (1967).

Mann, Frederick A., *The State Immunity Act 1978*, 50 BRIT. Y. B. INT'L L. 43 (1979).

Manuel, John G., *Common Contractual Risk Allocations in International Power Projects*, 1996 COLUM. BUS. L. REV. 37 (1996).

Marcks, Eric, *Avoiding Liability for Human Rights Violations in Project Finance*, 22 ENERGY L. J. 301 (2001).

Marple, Allen C., *What Is Project Finance?*, THE BANKER, Dec. 1977, at 47.

Martin, Julie A., *Structuring Project Finance to Reduce Risks: What Risks Can OPIC Cover?*, 1995 PRIV. INV. ABROAD 13–1 (1995).

Martin, M. P., *Project Financing for Offshore and Onshore Gas Facilities – Alternative Methods of Financing from a Legal Viewpoint*, 28 OIL & GAS INST. 1997, at 273–291.

Mazzini, Danielle, *Stable International Contracts in Emerging Markets: An Endangered Species?*, 15 B. U. INT'L L. J. 343 (1997).

McCormick, Richard, *Legal Issues in Project Finance*, J. ENERGY & NAT. RESOURCES LAW 22 (1982).

McCutcheon, Edward D., *Think Globally, (En) Act Locally: Promoting Effective National Environmental Regulatory Infrastructures in Developing Nations*, 31 CORNELL INT'L L. J. 395 (1998).

McMillen, Michael J. T., *Islamic Shariah-Compliant Project Finance: Collateral Security and Financing Structure Case Studies*, 24 FORDHAM INT'L L. J. 1184 (2001).

McQuiston, Raymer, *Drafting an Enforceable Guaranty in an International Financing Transaction: A Lender's Perspective*, 10 INT'L TAX & BUS. LAW. 138 (1993).

Mettala, Kimmo, *Governing-Law Clauses of Loan Agreements in International Project Financing*, 20 INT'L LAW. 219 (1986).

Moore, Harold F., & Evelyn D. Giaccio, *International Project Finance (A Practitioner's Guide to International Banking and Trade Finance)*, 11 N. C. J. INT'L L. & COM. REG. 597 (1986).

Myers, James J., *Developing Methods for Resolving Disputes in World-Wide Infrastructure Projects*, 13 J. INT'L ARB. 101 (1996).

NASSAR, NAGLA, *Project Finance, Public Utilities, and Public Concerns: A Practitioner's Perspective*, 23 FORDHAM INT'L L. J. 60 (2000).

NASSAR, NAGLA, SANCTITY OF CONTRACTS REVISITED: A STUDY IN THE THEORY AND PRACTICE OF LONG-TERM INTERNATIONAL COMMERCIAL TRANSACTIONS 35 (1995).

NEVITT, PETER K., PROJECT FINANCING (7th ed. 2000).

Nolan, Robert B., Jr., *Take-or-Pay Contracts: Are They Necessary for Municipal Project Financing?*, 4 MUN. FIN. J. 111 (1983).

Note, *International Arbitration and Project Finance in Developing Countries: Blurring the Public/Private Distinction*, 26 B. C. INT'L & COMP. L. REV. 355 (2003).

Note, *Measuring Local Legal Risk Premium in Project Finance Bonds*, 40 VA. J. INT'L L. 1125 (2000).

Note, *Moving Towards a Competitive Electricity Market? The Dilemma of Project Finance in the Wake of the Asian Financial Crisis*, 9 MINN. J. GLOBAL TRADE 715 (2000).

Note, *Project Finance: Europe*, 11 B. U. INT'L L. J. 165 (1993).

Note, *The Equator Principles: The Private Financial Sector's Attempt at Environmental Responsibility*, 40 VAND. J. TRANSNAT'L L. 197 (2007).

Ogden, L. Patrick, *How to Evaluate Off-Balance Sheet Financing*, THE BOND BUYER, Aug. 30, 1982, at 9.

PCHEINKESTEL, NORA L., RETHINKING PROJECT FINANCE: ALLOCATING AND MITIGATING RISK IN AUSTRALASIAN PROJECTS (1998).

Pedamon, Catherine, *Essay: How Is Convergence Best Achieved in International Project Finance?*, 24 FORDHAM INT'L L. J. 1272 (2001).

Penrose, James F., *Special-Purpose Entities in Project Finance Transactions*, 2 J. PROJECT FIN. 59 (1996).

Philpott, Julia, *Keeping It Private, Going Public: Assessing, Monitoring, and Disclosing the Global Warming Performance of Project Finance*, 5 SUSTAINABLE DEV. L. & POL'Y 45 (2005).

PROJECT FINANCE IN EUROPE (Haydn Shaughnessy ed., 1995).

Radez, Richard E., *Opportunities in Project Financing*, 128 BANKER, Aug. 1978, at 53.

Ramsey, Michael D., *Acts of State and Foreign Sovereign Obligations*, 39 HARV. INT'L L. J. 1 (1998).

Rauner, Stewart E., *Project Finance: A Risk Spreading Approach to the Commercial Financing of Economic Development*, 24 HARV. INT'L L. J. 145 (1983).

Raynaud, Alain-Pierre, & David Syed, *Take-or-Pay Financing in Manufacturing Projects*, INT'L FIN. L. REV. 25 (January 1990).

RAZAVI, HOSSEIN, FINANCING ENERGY PROJECTS IN EMERGING ECONOMIES (1996).

Riedy, Mark J., *Legal and Practical Considerations in Structuring Business Transactions in India for the Conference Entitled: India Power*, 3 CARDOZO J. INT'L & COMP. L. 313, 318 (1995).

Rigby, Peter N., *Merchant Power: Assessing Project Finance Risks*, 2 J. PROJECT FIN. 33 (1996).

Ryan, Joseph, & Lorin M. Fife, *Take-or-Pay Contracts: Alive and Well in California*, 19 URB. LAW. 233 (1987).

Sader, Frank, *Attracting Foreign Direct Investment Into Infrastructure – Why Is It So Difficult?*, Foreign Investment Advisory Service Occasional Paper No. 12 (IFC and World Bank, 2000).

Samy, Sharadchandra A., *Lessons From Dabhol – Dealing With Political Risk in Indian Power Projects*, 79 PROJECT FIN. INT'L 39 (Apr. 31, 1995).

Sandrock, Otto, *Is International Arbitration Inept to Solve Disputes Arising out of International Loan Agreements?*, 11 J. INT'L ARB. 33 (1994).

Sarmet, Marcel, *International Project Financing – The European Approach*, 130 BANKER, Aug. 1980, at 89.

SCHODER, STEWART A., PROJECT FINANCE: THE CREDIT PERSPECTIVE (1984).

Seipp, Walter, *Project Financing Relies on Bank Prudence*, 129 AMERICAN BANKER, September 7, 1982, Supp. at 26.

Selacuse, Jeswald W., *Renegotiating International Project Agreements*, 24 FORDHAM INT'L L. J. 1319 (2001).

Semkow, Brian W., *Syndicating and Rescheduling International Financial Transactions: A Survey of Legal Issues Encountered by Commercial Banks*, 18 INT'L LAW. 869 (1984).

Shah, Salman, & Anjan V. Thakor, *Optimal Capital Structure and Project Financing*, 42 J. ECON. THEORY 209 (June 1987).

Shanks, Robert B., *Insuring Investment and Loans Against Currency Inconvertibility, Expropriation and Political Violence*, 9 HASTINGS INT'L & COMP. L. REV. 417 (1986).

Shalakany, Amr A., *Arbitration and the Third World: A Plea for Bargaining Bias Under the Specter of Neoliberalism*, 41 HARV. INT'L L. J. 419 (2000).

Shaw, Frank C., *Reconciling Two Legal Cultures in Privatizations and Large-Scale Capital Projects in Latin America*, 30 LAW & POL'Y INT'L BUS. 147 (1999).

Short, Rodney, *Export Credit Agencies, Project Finance, and Commercial Risk: Whose Risk Is It, Anyway?*, 24 FORDHAM INT'L L. J. 1371 (2001).

Sington, Anne, *Financing the Channel Tunnel*, EUROMONEY, Mar. 1986, at 13.

SKADDEN, ARPS, Slate, Meagher & FLOM, PROJECT FINANCE: SELECTED ISSUES IN CHOICE OF LAW (1996).

Slattery, P. D., *Project Finance – An Overview*, 6 CORP. & BUS. L. J. 61 (1993).

Smith, Robert Thornton, ed., PROJECT FINANCING 1993 (PLI COMM. L. & PRACTICE COURSE HANDBOOK SERIES No. A-672, 1993).

Smith, Robert Thornton, ed., PROJECT FINANCING 1992 (PLI COMM. L. & PRACTICE COURSE HANDBOOK SERIES No. 605, 1992).

Smith, Robert Thornton, ed., PROJECT FINANCING 1991 (PLI COMM. L. & PRACTICE COURSE HANDBOOK SERIES No. 568, 1991).

Smith, Robert Thornton, ed., PROJECT FINANCING 1990 (PLI REAL EST. L. & PRACTICE COURSE HANDBOOK SERIES No. 345, 1990).

Smith, Robert Thornton, ed., PROJECT FINANCING 1989 (PLI REAL EST. L. & PRACTICE COURSE HANDBOOK SERIES No. 326, 1989).

Smith, Robert Thornton, ed., PROJECT FINANCING 1987 (PLI REAL EST. L. & PRACTICE COURSE HANDBOOK SERIES No. 297, 1987).

Smith, Robert Thornton, ed., PROJECT FINANCING 1986 (PLI REAL EST. L. & PRACTICE COURSE HAND-BOOK SERIES NO. 284, 1986).

Smith, Robert Thornton, ed., PROJECT FINANCING 1985 (PLI REAL EST. L. & PRACTICE COURSE HAND-BOOK SERIES NO. 270, 1985).

Smith, Robert Thornton, ed., PROJECT FINANCING (PLI REAL EST. L. & PRACTICE COURSE HANDBOOK SERIES NO. 252, 1984).

Smith, Robert Thornton, & Peter F. Fitzgerald eds., PROJECT FINANCING FROM DOMESTIC TO INTERNA-TIONAL (PLI COMM. L. & PRACTICE COURSE HAND-BOOK SERIES NO. A-707, 1995).

Soloveytchik, Viktor, New Perspectives for Concessions Agreements: A Comparison of Hungarian Law and the Draft Laws of Belarus, Kazakhstan, and Russia, 16 HOUS. J. INT'L L. 261 (1993).

Soulard, Alain, The Role of Multilateral Financial Institutions in Bringing Developing Countries to U.S. Markets, 17 FORDHAM INT'L L. J. S145 (1994).

Sozzi, Christopher J., Comment, Project Finance and Facilitating Telecommunications Infrastructure Development in Newly-Industrialized Countries, 12 COMPUTER & HIGH TECH. L. J. 435 (1996).

Stansbury, Philip R., Trends in International Project Contracting and Financing, 1977 PRIV. INV. ABROAD – PROBLEMS AND SOLUTIONS IN INTERNA-TIONAL BUSINESS 127 (1977).

Stebbins, R. B., Perspective on Project Financing, 161 BANKER'S MAG., May–June 1981, at 53.

Stebbins, R. B., Project Financing: A Banker's Perspective, 62 J. COM. BANK LENDING, Oct. 1979, at 36.

Stelwagon, William M., Financing Private Energy Projects in the Third World, 37 CATH. LAW. 45 (1996).

SULLIVAN, RONALD F., FINANCING TRANSNATIONAL PROJECTS (1988 & Supp. 1993).

Taylor, John L., & E. Waide Warner, eds., PRO-JECT FINANCING 1998 – BUILDING INFRASTRUCTURE PROJECTS IN DEVELOPING MARKETS (PLI COMM. L. & PRACTICE COURSE HANDBOOK SERIES NO. A-763, 1998).

Taylor, John L., & E. Waide Warner, eds., PROJECT FINANCING IN EMERGING MARKETS 1997 – SUCCESS-FUL DEVELOPMENT OF MINING, POWER, OIL AND GAS, TRANSPORTATION AND TELECOMMUNICATIONS PROJECTS (PLI COMM. L. & PRACTICE COURSE HAND-BOOK SERIES NO. A-757, 1997).

TINSLEY, RICHARD, ADVANCED PROJECT FINANCE: STRUCTURING RISKS (2000).

Torrado, Paola Morales, Political Risk Insurance and Breach of Contract Coverage: How the Interven-tion Of Domestic Courts May Prevent Investors From Claiming Insurance, 17 PACE INT'L L. REV. 301 (2005).

Trevino, L., Access to U.S. Capital Markets for Foreign Issuers: Rule 144A Private Placements, 16 HOUS. J. INT'L L. 159 (1993).

U.S. Agency for Int'l Development, Minimum Debt Financing Requirements for Private Power Projects in India, U.S. AID Report No. 95–01 (1995).

Vandevelde, K., U.S. Bilateral Investment Treaties: The Second Wave, 14 MICH. J. INT'L L. 621 (1993).

VINTER, GRAHAM D., & GARETH PRICE, PRACTICAL PROJECT FINANCE (3rd ed. 2005).

Waelde, Thomas W., & George Ndi, Stabilizing Inter-national Investment Commitments: International Law Versus Contract Interpretation, 31 TEX. INT'L L. J. 216 (1996).

Wallace, Don, Jr., Host Country Legislation: A Neces-sary Condition?, 24 FORDHAM INT'L L. J. 1396 (2001).

Wallace, Don, Jr., UNCITRAL Draft Legislation Guide on Privately Financed Infrastructure Projects: Achievements and Prospects, 8 TUL. J. INT'L & COMP. L. 283 (2000).

Wallenstein, Stephen, Situating Project Finance and Securitization in Context: A Comment on Bjerre, 12 DUKE J. COMP. & INT'L L. 449 (2002).

Walsh, Richard, Pacific Rim Collateral Security Laws: What Happens When the Project Goes Wrong, 4 STAN. J. L. BUS. & FIN. 115 (1999).

Weissman, H. Ronald, General Guidelines Under Present Accounting Rules, in Project Financing, at 23 (REAL EST. L. & PRACTICE COURSE HANDBOOK SERIES NO. 252, 1984).

Wells, Louis, & Eric Gleason, Is Foreign Infrastructure Investment Still Risky?, HARV. BUS. REV., Sept.–Oct. 1995, at 44.

West, Gerald T., Managing Project Political Risk: The Role of Investment Insurance, 2 J. OF PROJECT FINANCE 5 (1996).

Williams, S., Political and Other Risk Insurance: OPIC, MIGA, EXIMBANK and Other Providers, 5 PACE INT'L L. REV. 59 (1993).

Wiwen-Nilsson, Tore, Underlying Conditions for Suc-cessful Infrastructure BOT Projects, 14 INT'L CON-STRUCTION L. REV. 513 (1997).

WOOD, PHILIP, LAW AND PRACTICE OF INTERNATIONAL FINANCE (1990).

WOOD, PHILIP, PROJECT FINANCE, SUBORDINATED DEBT AND STATE LOANS (1995).

World Bank, *Submission and Evaluation of Proposal for Private Power Generation Projects in Developing Countries*, World Bank Industry and Energy Department Occasional Paper No. 2 (1994).

Wynant, Larry, *Essential Elements of Project Financing*, HARV. BUS. REV., May–June 1980, at 165.

Wynant, Larry, *Project Financing: Coping With the Capital Demands for Resource Projects*, 45 BUSINESS QUARTERLY, Summer 1980, at 59.

YESCOME, EDWARD, PRINCIPLES OF PROJECT FINANCE (2002).

UNITED NATIONS, UNCITRAL LEGAL GUIDE TO DRAWING UP INTERNATIONAL CONTRACTS FOR CONSTRUCTION OF INDUSTRIAL WORKS, United Nations Publication A/CN/9/SER.B/2 (1988).

INDEX

Made in the USA
Lexington, KY
27 June 2014